THE BURGER COURT

THE BURGER COURT

Political and Judicial Profiles

Edited by
Charles M. Lamb
and Stephen C. Halpern

UNIVERSITY OF ILLINOIS PRESS

Urbana and Chicago

Publication of this work was made possible in part by a grant from the
Research Foundation of the State University of New York at Buffalo.

All photographs are from the collection of
the Supreme Court of the United States.

This book is printed on acid-free paper.

Library of Congress Cataloging-in-Publication Data

The Burger Court : political and judicial profiles / edited by Charles
M. Lamb and Stephen C. Halpern.
    p.   cm.
    Includes bibliographical references.
    ISBN 0-252-01733-1 (cloth : alk. paper). — ISBN 0-252-06135-7 (paper :
alk. paper).
    1. United States. Supreme Court—History. 2. Judges—United
States—History. 3. Burger, Warren E., 1907–   .   I. Lamb, Charles
M. II. Halpern, Stephen C.
KF8742.B76 1991
347.73'26—dc20
[347.30735]   90-10851
                                          CIP

To S. Sidney Ulmer

CONTENTS

Acknowledgments   ix

1. The Political and Historical Context of the Burger Court
   CHARLES M. LAMB AND STEPHEN C. HALPERN   1

2. Justice Hugo L. Black: The Enduring Effort to Realize
   Law over Judicial Discretion
   HOWARD BALL   35

3. Justice Harry A. Blackmun: Transformation from
   "Minnesota Twin" to Independent Voice
   STEPHEN L. WASBY   63

4. Justice William J. Brennan, Jr.: Policy-Making
   in the Judicial Thicket
   STANLEY H. FRIEDELBAUM   100

5. Chief Justice Warren E. Burger: A Conservative
   Chief for Conservative Times
   CHARLES M. LAMB   129

6. Justice William O. Douglas: Conscience of the Court
   PHILLIP J. COOPER   163

7. Justice John Marshall Harlan: *Non sub Homine* . . .
   WALLACE MENDELSON   193

8. Justice Thurgood Marshall: The Race for Equal Justice
   WILLIAM J. DANIELS   212

9. Justice Sandra Day O'Connor: Transition to a
   Republican Court Agenda
   BEVERLY B. COOK   238

10. Justice Lewis F. Powell, Jr.: Balance Wheel of the Court
    JACOB W. LANDYNSKI   276

11. Justice William H. Rehnquist: Right-Wing Ideologue or
    Majoritarian Democrat?
    SUE DAVIS   315

12. Justice John Paul Stevens: The Lone Ranger in a
    Black Robe
    BRADLEY C. CANON   343

13. Justice Potter Stewart: Decisional Patterns in Search of
    Doctrinal Moorings
    TINSLEY E. YARBROUGH   375

14. Justice Byron R. White: Good Friend to Polity and Solon
    DANIEL C. KRAMER   407

15. The Burger Court and Beyond
    CHARLES M. LAMB AND STEPHEN C. HALPERN   433

    Select Bibliography   463

    Notes on Contributors   475

    Case Index   479

    General Index   499

ACKNOWLEDGMENTS

We have accumulated many debts during this project. Our contributors, to whom we are most indebted, are leading political scientists with expertise in constitutional law and judicial politics. They had to read extensively from their justices' opinions in order to write their chapters, and, since few of them had previously specialized in judicial biography, we wish to thank them for venturing away from the genre of research to which they were most accustomed. In addition, they were willing to shorten their chapters during revision. We deeply appreciate their cooperation in that process and their patience for the duration of the project.

Others helped in important ways to make this book possible. We were most fortunate to have Sheldon Goldman of the University of Massachusetts–Amherst, Joel B. Grossman of the University of Wisconsin–Madison, Harold J. Spaeth of Michigan State University, and Robert J. Steamer of the University of Massachusetts—Boston as readers of an early version of the manuscript. They made numerous suggestions for improvements in the volume, and we are greatly indebted to them. Special thanks go to Shelly Goldman, who not only stimulated our thinking about the Burger Court and its justices but graciously permitted us to reprint his data in three tables in Chapter 1. Richard A. Brisbin, Jr., of West Virginia University also allowed us to use his data, which appears in Chapter 8. J. Woodford Howard, Jr., of The Johns Hopkins University, William Lasser of Clemson University, and Robert H. Stern of the State University of New York at Buffalo furnished constructive comments on Chapters 1 and 15. We sincerely thank them all.

Early versions of these studies of the Burger Court justices were presented at convention panels at the American, Midwest, Northeastern, and New York State Political Science Association meetings over the past several years. We wish to thank those organizations for providing public forums for presentation. Thanks also go to Kathleen Vullo, Amilcar Barreto, and especially Joanna Drzewieniecki, who gave valuable assistance to Charles Lamb in preparing the indexes. Judy Torrico and Lisa Hummer assisted in proofreading. The energy that they brought to that job was sorely needed. Earlier in the project, other graduate students—particularly Andrea Ebrahimpour and Michael Spense—helped in organizational and planning tasks. Joyce Farrell and Margaret Kasprzyk typed various parts of the manuscript. Lawrence Malley, formerly of the University of Illinois Press, provided early support for the project and stimulated its completion. Beth Bower, assistant editor at the press, copyedited the manuscript, making indispensable editorial suggestions that added to the book's coherence and readability. Finally, the Research Foundation of the State University of New York provided financial assistance to aid in the publication of this volume. Without all of this help, it would never have been completed.

1

THE POLITICAL AND HISTORICAL CONTEXT OF THE BURGER COURT

CHARLES M. LAMB
AND STEPHEN C. HALPERN

This book consists of a collection of original essays on the thirteen justices who served on the United States Supreme Court during the chief justiceship of Warren E. Burger. By focusing on these justices' philosophies and contributions during the Burger Court years, we hope to better understand leading developments in constitutional law from 1969 through 1986 and the role of the Court during that era of American politics.

Neither the justices nor the Court itself can be fully understood without appreciating the broader political and historical context within which the Burger Court functioned. Therefore, as a preface to the chapters on the individual justices, a survey of that context follows. It highlights significant developments relating to the presidency, Congress, political parties, and changes in Supreme Court personnel during the Burger Court era.[1] A chronology of key Supreme Court decisions during these years is also provided at the end of this introduction (see Table 1.4, pp. 21–24), along with data on the Court's productivity and the justices' opinion writing and voting behavior (Tables 1.5–1.10, pp. 25–34).

A Brief Political Overview

Prior to Chief Justice Burger's ascendancy to the Supreme Court's center chair, liberal Democrats had dominated national politics for nearly two generations, and a sizable percentage of voters identified with the Democratic party.[2] From 1932 to 1968, Democrats controlled the White House for all but eight years—the Eisenhower

1

interregnum—and controlled both houses of Congress for all but three sessions. Moreover, Eisenhower's success was not so much that of the Republican party. Rather, his was the success of a popular military commander, with limited prior affiliations with either party, who adroitly projected himself as being above partisan politics. Indeed, in choosing Ike in 1952, the Republicans passed over Senator Robert Taft of Ohio—"Mr. Republican," the longtime leader of the party's conservative wing.

During the Kennedy-Johnson years of the 1960s, Democrats continued their control of both houses of Congress and undertook a variety of new domestic and international initiatives. The Democratic party still basked in the afterglow of Franklin D. Roosevelt's Democratic liberalism and the transformation of national politics that Roosevelt's coalition had wrought. In the early 1960s, America embraced federal programs assisting the needy at home and abroad. These programs swelled the federal budget as well as the bureaucracy.

In the 1964 presidential election, the conservative wing of the Republican party tried to alter this liberal political course. It nominated Arizona's Barry Goldwater, Taft's successor as the ideological leader of the Republican right.[3] Goldwater railed against what he viewed as the excesses of the liberals and the end product of their excesses—a bloated, intrusive federal government. Ridiculing Goldwater and exploiting the electorate's fear of him and his ideas, liberal Democrats portrayed Goldwater's conservatism as an anathema to domestic social progress and as a threat to American international security. Lyndon Johnson promised to out–New Deal the New Deal, offering Americans nothing less than a Great Society produced, directed, and financed by Washington. He trounced Goldwater in the general election. Meanwhile, during these years the Warren Court continued to leave its liberal imprimatur on American society through its decisions supporting civil rights and liberties.[4] From the Capitol to the White House to the courthouse, liberalism reigned triumphant.

Although Goldwater was soundly defeated in 1964, the political tide turned relatively quickly as severe domestic and foreign problems staggered Democratic liberals. On the domestic front, discontent with the Vietnam War escalated, the black civil rights movement went about as far as white America would permit after passage of the Civil Rights Acts of 1964 and 1968, and the War on Poverty ran out of political support and funding. Crime emerged as a leading problem in the mind of the American public. The assassinations of Martin Luther King, Jr., and Robert F. Kennedy in 1968, the urban riots of that year, and the nationally televised melee at the Democratic National Convention in Chicago all gave impetus to the "law and order" concerns of Americans.

On the foreign front, the Vietnam War continued to sour, growing increasingly unpopular during the late Johnson presidency. It looked as if America would "lose" its first war. Many Republicans attributed the nation's poor showing in Vietnam to the unwillingness of the Democrats to use the United States' military might effectively and identified racial and campus unrest with permissive liberalism. Defeat abroad and disorder at home were both laid at the doorstep of the Democratic party. Democratic liberalism, which no longer seemed anchored in the middle class and middle-class values, was on the defensive politically and philosophically.

The debacle in Vietnam and the "law and order" issue facilitated the political comeback of that hard-line, anti-Communist, Democratic nemesis — Richard M. Nixon.[5] Like Eisenhower before him, Nixon promised a better way to prosecute a war and to end it. An outspoken critic of the Warren Court, Nixon pledged to clamp down on the "law and order" problem. He insisted that the Warren Court had become too solicitous of the rights of criminals and had gone too far in mandating school desegregation. He promised, if elected, to appoint "strict constructionists" to the Supreme Court.[6]

The 1968 presidential election was the first one in the modern era in which the Democratic party's message and image was out of sync with its traditional core of working-class white support. The Democrats were in a state of disorder: weakened, divided, lacking confidence. After Johnson declined to run for re-election, Nixon narrowly defeated Hubert Humphrey, Johnson's perhaps too loyal vice president. Just as Taft was the exemplar of conservative Republicans of his era, Humphrey — the Happy Warrior preaching the politics of joy — was Mr. Liberal Democrat of his generation. Humphrey became the first of a series of liberal Democratic presidential standard bearers (followed by McGovern in 1972, Mondale in 1984, and Dukakis in 1988) who were to be rejected by the American electorate, but in 1968 the Democrats retained control of both houses of Congress.

Obviously, 1968 was a watershed year. If one year, more than any other, marked the beginning of the decline of Democratic liberalism in American politics, 1968 was it. Liberals alienated working-class whites by what that group perceived as Democratic indecisiveness in combating communism in Vietnam and by their all-too-eager decisiveness in support of blacks, disaffected college students, feminists, and even homosexuals. Many blue-collar Democrats found George Wallace's political themes very appealing. The Democrats were deeply divided, and the fruits of their divisiveness were played out before a national television audience during the historic 1968 Democratic National Convention. Just four years after the Democrats had so effectively ridiculed Goldwater, it was the Republicans' turn to do the mocking.

All this was prelude to the Burger Court. Some analysts maintain that roughly about the time of the Burger Court's inception, and without a critical election, the American party system experienced a realignment.[7] Burger's appointment, therefore, generally coincided with the end of liberalism's dominant hold on American politics. Beginning in 1968, sixteen years of Republican presidencies would follow. The first eight years, under Nixon and Gerald Ford, and especially the second eight, under Ronald Reagan, marked a different period in national politics.

During his first administration, Nixon succeeded in withdrawing the nation's troops from Vietnam. But the Watergate scandal ended Nixon's elective political career as it became increasingly apparent between 1972 and 1974 that he had been directly involved in an illegal cover-up of the break-in at the Democratic National Committee headquarters. Nixon's Watergate role was not fully revealed, however, until after his landslide re-election victory in 1972 against George McGovern, the eloquent spokesman of the Democratic left wing. McGovern was the Democrats' Barry Goldwater—less politician than spokesman for a cause, a vision of what was, to the faithful, a set of compelling and principled values. Like Goldwater, McGovern and his small army of zealous supporters held to a system of rights and wrongs demarcated by bright lines. McGovern symbolized the excesses and extremes of a liberalism no longer linked to the American workingman but rather to congeries of alienated and disaffected minorities, many of whom mainstream Americans disliked, distrusted, and feared. As a consequence, like Goldwater in 1964 and Humphrey in 1968, McGovern lost the vote of significant ideological segments of his own party.[8]

After Nixon's resignation, Ford ascended to the presidency, but the Democratic majorities in both congressional chambers were substantially strengthened in the November 1974 elections. Two years later Jimmy Carter narrowly defeated Ford. Encountering serious problems with high inflation and unemployment, the energy crisis, and the Iran hostage crisis, Carter was often perceived as lacking strong leadership skills and a sense of personal and national direction.[9] Even in retrospect, it is difficult to know what to make of Carter's election and one-term presidency. He clearly was not cut out of the McGovern mold. An engineer by training, a successful farmer and governor of a southern state, he ran as a Washington outsider and anti-politician. Projecting a strong sense of personal decency and honesty, Carter was able to capitalize on his image in the aftermath of the Johnson and Nixon years and the presidential deception related to Vietnam and Watergate. Yet once in office, Carter seemed unable to govern effectively. The Democrats, having won their first presidential election in twelve years, seemed uncertain, without an internal compass to set them, and the nation, straight.

Carter's rudderless liberalism set the stage for the conservative coup de grace offered up with aplomb and a perfect television style by Ronald Reagan.[10] Reagan, who had placed Goldwater's name in nomination in 1964, had inherited the mantle of leader of the conservative wing of the Republican party. In many ways Reagan offered in 1980 what the electorate had categorically rejected sixteen years earlier. This time the message sold, and the one-time actor and former governor of California was swept into office in the most resounding electoral college defeat of an incumbent president since the defeat of Herbert Hoover in 1932. In sharp contrast to Carter, who had been perceived as an uncertain chief executive, Reagan was viewed by much of the public as a confident leader who would pull the nation out of its domestic economic woes and international timidity. The American people had elected their most conservative president since the 1920s, but the 1980 election was more a rejection of Carter than a broad mandate for conservative policy.[11]

Reagan's victory in 1980 brought with it Republican control of the Senate for the first time since the Eisenhower administration. Nonetheless, while Republicans controlled the Senate for six of the Reagan years, Democrats retained their long-standing majority in the House of Representatives. The Reagan administration slashed expenditures for many domestic welfare programs, significantly accelerated defense spending, and cut taxes to stimulate the economy. Although inflation and interest rates dropped, the nation experienced a grim recession in the early 1980s. Still, as measured by most economic indicators, by 1984 the economy was back to good health, notwithstanding a growing national deficit and a significant world trade imbalance.

In some ways 1984 was a replay of 1964: a presidential contest pitting the uncompromising spokesman of the Republican right— Mr. Reagan—against a symbol of conventional Democratic liberalism—Minnesota's Walter Mondale. What a difference twenty years can make! The contrast between 1964 and 1984 was striking. Whereas Goldwater stirred feelings of fear and anxiety and resoundingly lost, Reagan stirred feelings of optimism and pride and resoundingly defeated his opponent. Despite a huge national debt, worsening problems for the poor, and the Iran-Contra scandal, those feelings seemingly carried over in 1988 with the election of a more moderate-sounding Republican, George Bush, over yet another liberal Democrat, Michael Dukakis. No critical election had occurred during the 1970s and 1980s, but the ideological flavor of national politics at the presidential level had taken a profound turn to the right. In all, although *liberal* Democratic candidates were unable to win the White House between 1968 and 1988, the Democratic party maintained considerable power in Congress and the statehouses.

Supreme Court Personnel Changes and National Political Trends

The Burger Court was a product of personnel changes that began with the retirement of Earl Warren in 1969 and the selection of the new chief justice by President Nixon. Table 1.1 (p. 18) shows Supreme Court personnel changes during the Burger era and identifies the Warren Court holdovers. The Burger Court grew out of Republican presidential domination during this period. Controlling the Oval Office for sixteen of the twenty years between 1969 and 1988, Republicans made all six Supreme Court appointments during that time.

Most important, Nixon had the rare opportunity to make four appointments within four years. Warren E. Burger, a native Minnesotan with an active but moderate Republican past, was appointed chief justice in 1969 from his post on the U.S. Court of Appeals for the District of Columbia Circuit, where he had served for thirteen years. Nixon's next successful nomination went to Harry A. Blackmun, another Republican from Minnesota, with eleven years of experience on the U.S. Court of Appeals for the Eighth Circuit. Blackmun, replacing Justice Abe Fortas, was confirmed only after an unusually politicized debate in which the

Members of the United States Supreme Court as of June 1969 through June 1970. *Seated, from left to right:* Justice John Marshall Harlan, Justice Hugo L. Black, Chief Justice Warren E. Burger, Justice William O. Douglas, and Justice William J. Brennan, Jr. *Standing, from left to right:* Justice Thurgood Marshall, Justice Potter Stewart, and Justice Byron R. White. This photograph and the ones following appear courtesy of the collection of the United States Supreme Court.

Senate refused to confirm Nixon's nominations of Clement F. Haynsworth and G. Harrold Carswell to fill Fortas's seat.

Nixon's third and fourth choices for the Supreme Court came in 1972 with the retirement of Justices Hugo L. Black and John Marshall Harlan. As a replacement for Black, Nixon chose Lewis F. Powell, Jr., a Virginia Democrat in private practice and former president of the American Bar Association. To replace Harlan, Nixon nominated William H. Rehnquist, a brilliant young Arizona Republican then serving as assistant attorney general in the Office of Legal Counsel of the Department of Justice. All four Nixon appointees were generally viewed as conservatives at the time of their nominations. With the appointees in place, some Court watchers anticipated the possibility of a "constitutional counterrevolution."

The next vacancy on the Court arose with the retirement of Justice William O. Douglas in 1975. To fill it, President Ford chose John Paul Stevens, an Illinois Republican who for five years had been a member of the U.S. Court of Appeals for the Seventh Circuit. The final Republican addition to the Burger Court came in 1981, when Justice Potter Stewart retired and President Reagan selected Sandra Day O'Connor to fill Stewart's seat. O'Connor, the first woman to be nominated to the Supreme Court and another Sun Belt Republican like Rehnquist, had served for several years in the Arizona state senate and for three years on the Arizona Court of Appeals. Like the four Nixon appointees, she was thought to be a conservative by most observers. Justices William J. Brennan, Byron R. White, and Thurgood Marshall were the three Warren Court holdovers on the Burger Court. Of the thirteen justices who served on the Burger Court from 1969 through 1986, only White and Marshall had been appointed by a Democratic president.

These personnel changes on the Court stand out as one of the most enduring legacies of the Republican domination of the White House from 1969 through 1988. Imagine how the composition of the Court and the direction of American constitutional law might have differed had the Democrats prevailed in one or more of the contests they lost. For example, what if Hubert Humphrey, a champion of liberal Democratic social welfare and civil rights policies, had been elected in 1968 and had filled the four vacancies for which Nixon chose Burger, Powell, Blackmun, and Rehnquist? Consider the probable differences if McGovern rather than Ford had selected a successor for Justice Douglas, or if Carter rather than Reagan had selected a successor for Justice Stewart.

Although Republican presidents made six consecutive appointments to the Court, the rate at which vacancies occurred during this period was well below the rate that has prevailed over the Court's history. Table 1.2 (p. 18) provides data on the number of vacancies on the Court by decade from 1790 to 1989. On average, throughout the Court's history, slightly over five changes in the Court's composition occurred per decade—roughly one every two years. In the twentieth century, before the advent of the Burger Court, an average of about six openings occurred per decade, or about one every twenty months. During the seventeen-year Burger Court period, though, only six vacancies arose, or approximately one every thirty-four months. Only one change took place in the decade between 1976 and Burger's retirement. That 1981 vacancy was filled by O'Connor. The remaining personnel changes between 1980 and 1989 came after Burger's retirement when Reagan promoted Rehnquist to chief justice, appointed Antonin Scalia to take Rehnquist's old seat, and, one year after Burger's departure, appointed Anthony Kennedy to replace Justice Powell.

One would think that the fewer-than-average number of opportunities that Republican presidents had to make nominations to the Court during Burger's tenure might explain in part why no constitutional counterrevolution developed during the Burger Court era.[12] Certainly a counterrevolution would have been more likely had Presidents Nixon, Ford, and Reagan been able to fill the seats occupied by Justices Brennan and Marshall. Yet this explanation is not highly persuasive. Nixon and Ford had appointed a majority of the Court's members by 1975, and that majority grew by one after Reagan's selection of Justice O'Connor in 1981. Even with these six appointees and ample time to overturn some leading Warren Court precedents, no constitutional counterrevolution was forthcoming.

On the other hand, Republicans used their appointments rather effectively to select basically conservative justices. In contrast to President Eisenhower's "mistake" of appointing Chief Justice Warren and Justice Brennan, no "liberal surprises" turned up in the appointments made during the Burger years. Yet while Burger, Rehnquist, O'Connor, and, to a lesser extent, Powell were usually quite consistent in their conservatism, Stevens and Blackmun proved to be independent and moderate.[13] Here, then, lies a more convincing reason why no counterrevolution occurred. As Chapter 15 suggests, over the years neither Blackmun nor Stevens could necessarily be counted on to join the more conservative members of the Court. At times even Burger and Powell deviated from the rightward drift of the Court. Without at least five solid votes consistently in the conservative column, no new era of constitutional jurisprudence could be expected.

To further place the Burger Court in historical perspective, it is useful to examine personnel changes on the Supreme Court over the nation's entire history, as summarized in Table 1.3 (pp. 19–21). This table documents historical waves of party control over the Supreme Court nominating process. When a party had regular control of the White House over an extended period, it also enjoyed a number of consecutive opportunities to fill Supreme Court vacancies.[14]

What is striking about these earlier periods of party hegemony is that the prevailing party regularly controlled not only the presidency but also both houses of Congress. The periods during which one party controlled numerous consecutive Court appointments were also the periods during which that party was able to put in place a "law-making majority."[15] These majorities existed because of enduring national political coalitions that yielded party control over the White House, Congress, and the Court, that is, control over the entire national policy-making process.

For example, during the period of Republican hegemony from 1861 through 1893, Republican presidents made all but two of twenty appointments to the Court, and Republicans controlled both houses of Congress the vast majority of the time. Interrupted briefly by President Grover Cleveland's second term, Republican hegemony reasserted itself from 1897 through 1932. In that era, Republican presidents made seventeen of twenty appointments to the Supreme Court, while Republicans usually held the majority in both the House and the Senate. Then, during the Democrats' hegemony over the national political process from 1932 to 1968, Democratic presidents made sixteen of twenty-one appointments to the Court, with the Democratic party almost always maintaining a majority in both houses of Congress.

The pattern during the Burger years contrasts markedly with that of previous eras.[16] Indeed, there has been nothing quite like it in American political history. While a Republican sat in the Oval Office 80 percent of the time between 1969 and 1988, the Republicans never once controlled both houses of Congress. The best they did was to control the Senate during the first six years of the Reagan administration. Hence, for all their successes, and notwithstanding all the foibles and disappointments of their Democratic opponents, during the Burger years Republicans failed to establish the political hegemony over the national political process that they had historically enjoyed. Thus they lacked the political wherewithal to enact national policies reflecting their party's positions and priorities.

The Court proved to be an important political issue for Republicans during the Burger era. Many of the political themes advanced by Nixon and Reagan were prompted by Court decisions. Nixon's cry for law and order and his "Southern strategy" in 1968 were both linked to Supreme Court civil liberties decisions protecting criminal defendants and racial minorities. Similarly, Reagan's social agenda regarding such provocative issues as school prayer, affirmative action, school desegregation, and abortion was also a response to Supreme Court policies. Hence, the Court was a foil for Republican presidents and presidential candidates during this period, who defined their candidacies and presidencies at least partially in terms of their opposition to Supreme Court policies.[17]

The stasis in American national politics during the Burger years also may have contributed to the politicization of the nomination process for federal judgeships. The Republicans' inability to control Congress in addition to the presidency as they had in earlier historical periods heightened the value of Court vacancies to them. It is not surprising that both Nixon and Reagan strongly desired to have nominees to the federal bench reflect their political views. The importance of Court vacancies, and of the opportunity to influence the direction of American constitutional law through judicial nominations, was greater for both parties precisely because neither one dominated the national political process. Accordingly, for the Republicans, the possibility of leaving their imprint on the policies of the Court may have been a larger concern than in the past.

To be sure, presidents have always tried to nominate individuals to the Court who possessed political views similar to their own. However, during the contemporary Republican era the judicial selection process became notably politicized.[18] Partly, Republicans were reacting to what they perceived as the "liberal excesses" of the Warren Court, but the reason they sought control of the Court with a vengeance and made it a priority in their political agenda was because the federal judiciary had become a more critical outlet through which to realize Republican priorities. Republicans grew especially concerned about the Court in part because they sensed their own political weaknesses. These weaknesses were reflected in the low proportion of the American electorate that identified with the Republican party (see Figure 1).

During the era of Democratic dominance from 1937 through 1968, not only did Democrats typically control the presidency and Congress, but significantly more Americans identified with the Democratic party than with the Republican party. The Republicans made some progress during the late New Deal and the Reagan years in increasing the percentage of Americans who identified with them, but they were unable to achieve the kind of popularity they enjoyed in the late nineteenth and early twentieth centuries (or that the Democrats enjoyed from 1932 through 1968). In only one year, 1946, was public identification greater with the Republican party than with the Democratic party. Little wonder that the Republican party remained weak in Congress during the Burger era despite notable accomplishments in presidential politics.

Because no governing political coalition emerged during the Burger years, no overarching, prevailing public philosophy developed to shape the broad contours of American national policy. The following chapters suggest how the Court stepped into this vacuum and how far it stepped.

The Focus on the Individual Justice

There is something seemingly anomalous about a book on the Supreme Court being organized around the philosophy and contributions of individual justices rather than the Court as an institution or substantive areas of law. Yet this focus illuminates the Court and its work in special ways. Indeed, a long and rich tradition of scholarship already exists that analyzes the Court, its decisions, and the evolution of constitutional doctrine from the perspective of the work of individual justices.[19] Studies oriented toward particuiar justices continue to appear on a regular basis.[20]

Certain traits of the Supreme Court make it appropriate to focus on the individual justice. The size of the Court as a decision-making group—nine members in all—increases the significance of its individual members and the role that each plays in influencing colleagues, the Court's ultimate vote, and the direction and development of constitutional law. The Court has remained a small, even intimate institution. Although the staffs of the White House, Congress, and government agencies have swollen in size in recent decades, each justice typically only works with three or four law clerks recently graduated from law school, two secretaries, and a

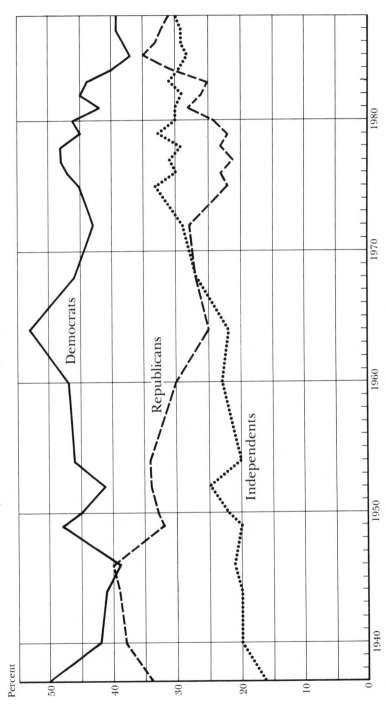

FIGURE 1

Party Identification Percentages in the United States, 1937–88

Note: People who said they had no party preference or who named other parties (3 to 4 percent in the latest surveys) are excluded. *Source:* Derived from data presented in Robert L. Lineberry, *Government in America: People, Politics, and Policy,* 4th ed. (Boston: Little, Brown, 1989), p. 251.

messenger. The chief justice has four clerks, an administrative assistant, four secretaries, and a messenger.[21]

Given the Court's size, the philosophy, ideology, and attitudes of the individual justices are often central to their nomination to the Court. Presidents recognize that their Supreme Court appointments may constitute a vital part of their legacy. Hence, both presidents and senators, in evaluating nominees, traditionally scrutinize their writings and philosophies out of respect for the impact that even a single justice's jurisprudence may have. The Senate's scrutiny, for example, is typically much closer for Supreme Court nominees than for nominees to the president's cabinet because of the justices' life tenure and the close link between their jurisprudence and the policies of the Court. Rarely do the philosophies of cabinet secretaries fundamentally change bureaucracies, but the philosophies of individual justices may have an enduring impact on Supreme Court policy and the nation.

No less than its size, the manner in which the Court conducts its work makes it a highly personal institution suitable for study from the perspective of the individual justice. Unlike congressional representatives, who interact with changing groups of colleagues on various committees or with myriad bureaucrats or lobbyists in different policy areas, the members of the Court continually function within the context of the same group. The degree of personal contact among them is generally greater than that among political elites in the House, Senate, or federal bureaucracies. The justices have no constituents, and no ongoing personal or professional relations with organized interest groups or other government officials outside the Court, save perhaps the Office of the Solicitor General. Most litigants before the Court are "one-shotters" who appear before the Court once and only once.[22] The justices' personal contact with them is limited to interaction with their attorneys at oral argument. The justices do not expect the litigants or their attorneys to be back again.

The Court's size, the way it goes about its work, and its insulation from the electorate, from interest groups, and from other governing institutions combine to magnify the importance of the individual justice. The character of the Court's work also means that a justice's life, like that of an academic, is inner-directed, even cloistered. The inner-directedness comes from job security, the intellectual character of the work, and the crucial place of writing in that work. The touchstone of the justices' performance is the quality of their thinking and writing and the coherence, complexity, and even elegance of the judicial philosophy advanced in their written opinions. As any academic can attest, organizing thoughts on complex matters and presenting them in print for review and criticism by colleagues and other professionals can be a wrenching experience. That experience is heightened on the Court by a tradition—which some would say has been much abused in recent years—that permits colleagues to take pen in hand to write concurrences, or worse, dissents, dissecting the weaknesses in a colleague's analysis. On the other hand, once in office justices enjoy an enormous degree of professional freedom, political independence, and insulation from those outside the Court. This detachment encourages them to develop and articulate a system of constitutional jurisprudence, apply that system to cases before the Court, and work to see that their constitutional philosophies emerge as national public policy.

The Court's internal deliberations remain beyond the public gaze, shielded from outside scrutiny. Given that they are prominent national policymakers, the justices are able to lead remarkably private lives. Discussion, debate, and decision making do not occur on the Court as they do in Congress—in a forum to which scores of colleagues and members of the public may have access or input. Rather, the Court's decision making is marked by closed, secret conferences in which only the justices participate, and by the private reactions of colleagues or clerks to drafts of opinions. In this closed environment, the justices' law clerks may also affect Supreme Court policy by influencing the cases selected for decision and by writing drafts of opinions.[23]

During an era in which governmental institutions at all levels have become highly bureaucratized and impersonal from the vantage point of the public and the public servant alike, the Supreme Court is something of an anachronism. There is a quaintness and intimacy in its operations. Not uncommonly, justices and their clerks remain in contact with one another many years after the clerks have left the Court. A strong human and even intimate dimension prevails on the Court. In addition, the Court's membership tends to be more stable and fixed than that of other political institutions.

All of the above considerations suggest that the Court is an institution in which a single individual may play a crucial role in formulating many decisions of great consequence. Witness the extraordinary public controversy triggered in 1987 by the nomination of Judge Robert Bork for the Supreme Court; protagonists on both sides of the battle recognized that this single addition to the Court could well result in dramatic new directions in American constitutional law.[24] Because the Court makes national policy by majority vote in a "vital national seminar," the thinking and writing of a proposed new participant in that seminar merits especially close attention. We therefore believe that the individual unit of analysis on which this book is based is a valuable and useful perspective from which to seek to understand the Court and its decisions. The special value of this perspective to understanding the Court helps to explain why the long scholarly tradition of the judicial biography is unmatched by a similarly impressive body of biographical studies focusing on the bureaucratic or legislative process.

NOTES

1. See also Sheldon Goldman, *Constitutional Law: Cases and Essays* (New York: Harper and Row, 1987), chap. 3.

2. See Leon D. Epstein, *Political Parties in the American Mold* (Madison: University of Wisconsin Press, 1986), chap. 8.

3. See Theodore H. White, *The Making of the President, 1964* (New York: Atheneum, 1965).

4. See, for example, *Heart of Atlanta Motel v. United States* (1964) and *South Carolina v. Katzenbach* (1966) (civil rights); *Griswold v. Connecticut* (1965) (privacy); *New York Times Co. v. Sullivan* (1964) (freedom of press); *Engel v. Vitale* (1962) and *Abington School District v. Schempp* (1963) (establishment of religion); *Baker v. Carr* (1962) and *Reynolds v. Sims* (1964) (reapportionment); *Mapp v. Ohio* (1961), *Gideon v. Wainwright* (1963), and *Miranda v. Arizona* (1966) (criminal procedure).

5. See Theodore H. White, *The Making of the President, 1968* (New York: Atheneum, 1969).

6. See Henry J. Abraham, *Justices and Presidents: A Political History of Appointments to the Supreme Court,* 2d ed. (New York: Oxford University Press, 1985), chap. 11.

7. John R. Petrocik, *Party Coalitions: Realignments and the Decline of the New Deal Party System* (Chicago: University of Chicago Press, 1981).

8. Arthur H. Miller et al., "A Majority Party in Disarray: Policy Polarization in the 1972 Election," *American Political Science Review* 70 (1976): 753–78.

9. See Theodore H. White, *America in Search of Itself: The Making of the President, 1956–1980* (New York: Warner, 1982), chap. 7.

10. See ibid., chaps. 8–13.

11. Herbert B. Asher, *Presidential Elections and American Politics,* 4th ed. (Chicago: Dorsey, 1988), pp. 186–87.

12. See Vincent Blasi, ed., *The Burger Court: The Counter-Revolution That Wasn't* (New Haven, Conn.: Yale University Press, 1983).

13. See Tables 1.8, 1.9, and 1.10, pp. 31–34. Note, however, that in selected cases and fields of law, Burger and Powell were sometimes less than predictable. See Chapter 15 of this volume.

14. See also Robert G. McCloskey, *The American Supreme Court* (Chicago: University of Chicago Press, 1960).

15. Robert A. Dahl, "Decision-Making in a Democracy: The Supreme Court as a National Policy-Maker," *Journal of Public Law* 6 (1957): 279–95.

16. For theoretical implications, see James L. Sundquist, "Needed: A Political Theory for the New Era of Coalition Government in the United States," *Political Science Quarterly* 103 (1988): 613–35.

17. See generally William Lasser, *The Limits of Judicial Power: The Supreme Court in American Politics* (Chapel Hill: University of North Carolina Press, 1988), chap. 5.

18. See, for example, Sheldon Goldman, "Reagan's Judicial Legacy: Completing the Puzzle and Summing Up," *Judicature* 72 (1989): 318–30.

19. For prominent examples, see the literature surveyed in J. Woodford Howard, Jr., "Judicial Biography and the Behavioral Persuasion," *American Political Science Review* 65 (1971): 704–15.

20. See, for example, Bernard Schwartz, *Super Chief: Earl Warren and His Supreme Court—A Judicial Biography* (New York: New York University Press, 1983); Bruce Allen Murphy, *Fortas: The Rise and Ruin of a Supreme Court Justice* (New York: Morrow, 1988); Tinsley E. Yarbrough, *Mr. Justice Black and His Critics* (Durham, N.C.: Duke University Press, 1988); Sue Davis, *Justice Rehnquist and the Constitution* (Princeton, N.J.: Princeton University Press, 1989).

21. David M. O'Brien, *Storm Center: The Supreme Court in American Politics* (New York: Norton, 1986), pp. 122, 124.

22. Marc Galanter, "Afterword: Explaining Litigation," *Law and Society Review* 9 (1975): 347–57.

23. On the role of the Court's law clerks, see William H. Rehnquist, *The Supreme Court: How It Was, How It Is* (New York: Morrow, 1987), chaps. 1–3.

24. See, for example, the articles in the *Harvard Law Review* 101 (1988): 1165–1229.

TABLE 1.1
Members of the Burger Court

Personnel Changes	Year of Change	Appointing President
Burger for Warren	1969	Nixon
Blackmun for Fortas	1970	Nixon
Powell for Black	1972	Nixon
Rehnquist for Harlan	1972	Nixon
Stevens for Douglas	1975	Ford
O'Connor for Stewart	1981	Reagan
Warren Court Holdovers	Year Appointed	Appointing President
Brennan	1956	Eisenhower
White	1962	Kennedy
Marshall	1967	Johnson

TABLE 1.2
Number of Personnel Changes on the Supreme Court by Decade

Decade	Number	Decade	Number
1790–99	8	1890–99	6
1800–1809	4	1900–1909	4
1810–19	2	1910–19	8
1820–29	3	1920–29	5
1830–39	6	1930–39	7
1840–49	4	1940–49	9
1850–59	3	1950–59	5
1860–69	5	1960–69	5
1870–79	5	1970–79	4
1880–89	7	1980–89	4

Sources: Henry J. Abraham, *Justices and Presidents: A Political History of Appointments to the Supreme Court,* 2d ed. (New York: Oxford University Press, 1985), pp. 384–91; Sheldon Goldman, *Constitutional Law: Cases and Essays* (New York: Harper and Row, 1987), pp. 75–77, 84–85, 96–97, 108–9, 121, 136–37, 155.

TABLE 1.3
A History of Supreme Court Personnel Changes

Year	Personnel Change	Appointing President	President's Political Party	Control of Congress Senate/House
1791	T. Johnson for J. Rutledge	Washington	Fed.	Fed.
1793	W. Paterson for T. Johnson	Washington	Fed.	Fed. Dem./ Rep.
1795	J. Rutledge for J. Jay	Washington	Fed.	Fed.
1796	O. Ellsworth for J. Rutledge	Washington	Fed.	Fed.
	Samuel Chase for J. Blair	Washington	Fed.	Fed.
1798	B. Washington for J. Wilson	J. Adams	Fed.	Fed.
1799	A. Moore for J. Iredell	J. Adams	Fed.	Fed.
1801	J. Marshall for O. Ellsworth	J. Adams	Fed.	Fed.
1804	W. Johnson for A. Moore	Jefferson	Dem./Rep.	Dem./Rep.
1806	H. Livingston for W. Paterson	Jefferson	Dem./Rep.	Dem./Rep.
1807	T. Todd (added by Act of 1807)	Jefferson	Dem./Rep.	Dem./Rep.
1811	J. Story for W. Cushing	Madison	Dem./Rep.	Dem./Rep.
	G. Duval for Samuel Chase	Madison	Dem./Rep.	Dem./Rep.
1823	S. Thompson for H. Livingston	Monroe	Dem./Rep.	Dem./Rep.
1826	R. Trimble for T. Todd	J. Q. Adams	Dem./Rep.	Coalition
1829	J. McLean for R. Trimble	Jackson	Dem.	Dem.
1830	H. Baldwin for B. Washington	Jackson	Dem.	Dem.
1835	J. Wayne for W. Johnson	Jackson	Dem.	Dem.
1836	R. Taney for J. Marshall	Jackson	Dem.	Dem.
	P. Barbour for G. Duval	Jackson	Dem.	Dem.
1837	J. Catron & J. McKinley (added by Act of 1837)	Van Buren	Dem.	Dem.
1841	P. Daniel for P. Barbour	Van Buren	Dem.	Dem.
1845	S. Nelson for S. Thompson	Tyler	Whig	Whig/Dem.
1846	L. Woodbury for J. Story	Polk	Dem.	Dem.
	R. Grier for H. Baldwin	Polk	Dem.	Dem.
1851	B. Curtis for L. Woodbury	Fillmore	Whig	Dem.
1853	J. Campbell for J. McKinley	Pierce	Dem.	Dem.
1858	N. Clifford for B. Curtis	Buchanan	Dem.	Dem.
1862	S. Miller for P. Daniel	Lincoln	Rep.	Rep.
	N. Swayne for J. McLean	Lincoln	Rep.	Rep.
	D. Davis for J. Campbell	Lincoln	Rep.	Rep.
1863	S. Field (added by Act of 1863)	Lincoln	Rep.	Rep.
1864	Salmon Chase for R. Taney	Lincoln	Rep.	Rep.
1870	W. Strong for R. Grier	Grant	Rep.	Rep.
	J. Bradley (added by Act of 1869)	Grant	Rep.	Rep.
1872	W. Hunt for S. Nelson	Grant	Rep.	Rep.
1874	M. Waite for Salmon Chase	Grant	Rep.	Rep.
1877	J. Harlan for D. Davis	Hayes	Rep.	Rep./Dem.
1880	W. Woods for W. Strong	Hayes	Rep.	Rep./Dem.
1881	S. Matthews for N. Swayne	Garfield	Rep.	Rep.
	H. Gray for N. Clifford	Arthur	Rep.	Rep.
1882	S. Blatchford for W. Hunt	Arthur	Rep.	Rep.

TABLE 1.3 (Continued)

Year	Personnel Change	Appointing President	President's Political Party	Control of Congress Senate/House
1888	M. Fuller for M. Waite	Cleveland	Dem.	Rep./Dem.
	L. Lamar for W. Woods	Cleveland	Dem.	Rep./Dem.
1889	D. Brewer for S. Matthews	Harrison	Rep.	Rep.
1890	H. Brown for S. Miller	Harrison	Rep.	Rep.
1892	G. Shiras for J. Bradley	Harrison	Rep.	Rep./Dem.
1893	H. Jackson for L. Lamar	Harrison	Rep.	Rep./Dem.
1894	E. White for S. Blatchford	Cleveland	Dem.	Dem.
1895	R. Peckham for H. Jackson	Cleveland	Dem.	Rep.
1898	J. McKenna for S. Field	McKinley	Rep.	Rep.
1902	O. Holmes for H. Gray	T. Roosevelt	Rep.	Rep.
1903	W. Day for G. Shiras	T. Roosevelt	Rep.	Rep.
1906	W. Moody for H. Brown	T. Roosevelt	Rep.	Rep.
1909	H. Lurton for R. Peckham	Taft	Rep.	Rep.
1910	C. Hughes for D. Brewer	Taft	Rep.	Rep.
	W. Van Devanter for E. White	Taft	Rep.	Rep.
	J. Lamar for W. Moody	Taft	Rep.	Rep.
1912	M. Pitney for J. Harlan	Taft	Rep.	Rep./Dem.
1914	J. McReynolds for H. Lurton	Wilson	Dem.	Dem.
1916	L. Brandeis for J. Lamar	Wilson	Dem.	Dem.
	J. Clarke for C. Hughes	Wilson	Dem.	Dem.
1921	W. Taft for E. White	Harding	Rep.	Rep.
1922	G. Sutherland for J. Clarke	Harding	Rep.	Rep.
	P. Butler for W. Day	Harding	Rep.	Rep.
1923	E. Sanford for M. Pitney	Harding	Rep.	Rep.
1925	H. Stone for J. McKenna	Coolidge	Rep.	Rep.
1930	C. Hughes for W. Taft	Hoover	Rep.	Rep.
	O. Roberts for E. Sanford	Hoover	Rep.	Rep.
1932	B. Cardozo for O. Holmes	Hoover	Rep.	Rep./Dem.
1937	H. Black for W. Van Devanter	F. Roosevelt	Dem.	Dem.
1938	S. Reed for G. Sutherland	F. Roosevelt	Dem.	Dem.
1939	F. Frankfurter for B. Cardozo	F. Roosevelt	Dem.	Dem.
	W. Douglas for L. Brandeis	F. Roosevelt	Dem.	Dem.
1940	F. Murphy for P. Butler	F. Roosevelt	Dem.	Dem.
1941	J. Byrnes for J. McReynolds	F. Roosevelt	Dem.	Dem.
	R. Jackson for H. Stone	F. Roosevelt	Dem.	Dem.
1943	W. Rutledge for J. Byrnes	F. Roosevelt	Dem.	Dem.
1945	H. Burton for O. Roberts	Truman	Dem.	Dem.
1946	F. Vinson for H. Stone	Truman	Dem.	Dem.
1949	T. Clark for F. Murphy	Truman	Dem.	Dem.
	S. Minton for W. Rutledge	Truman	Dem.	Dem.
1953	E. Warren for F. Vinson	Eisenhower	Rep.	Rep.
1955	J. Harlan for R. Jackson	Eisenhower	Rep.	Dem.
1956	W. Brennan for S. Minton	Eisenhower	Rep.	Dem.
1957	C. Whittaker for S. Reed	Eisenhower	Rep.	Dem.

TABLE 1.3 (Continued)

Year	Personnel Change	Appointing President	President's Political Party	Control of Congress Senate/House
1958	P. Stewart for H. Burton	Eisenhower	Rep.	Dem.
1962	B. White for C. Whittaker	Kennedy	Dem.	Dem.
	A. Goldberg for F. Frankfurter	Kennedy	Dem.	Dem.
1965	A. Fortas for A. Goldberg	Johnson	Dem.	Dem.
1967	T. Marshall for T. Clark	Johnson	Dem.	Dem.
1969	W. Burger for E. Warren	Nixon	Rep.	Dem.
1970	H. Blackmun for A. Fortas	Nixon	Rep.	Dem.
1972	L. Powell for H. Black	Nixon	Rep.	Dem.
	W. Rehnquist for J. Harlan	Nixon	Rep.	Dem.
1975	J. Stevens for W. Douglas	Ford	Rep.	Dem.
1981	S. O'Connor for P. Stewart	Reagan	Rep.	Rep./Dem.
1986	A. Scalia for W. Rehnquist	Reagan	Rep.	Rep./Dem.
1988	A. Kennedy for L. Powell	Reagan	Rep.	Dem.
1990	D. Souter for W. Brennan	Bush	Rep.	Dem.

Note: On three occasions a new chief justice was promoted from associate justice: in 1910 when White was promoted by Taft to succeed Fuller, in 1941 when Stone was promoted by Roosevelt to succeed Hughes, and in 1986 when Rehnquist was promoted by Reagan to succeed Burger. These promotions are not shown as personnel changes on the Court.

Sources: For columns 1–4, Abraham, *Justices and Presidents*, pp. 384–91. For column 5, *Members of Congress since 1789*, 3d ed. (Washington, D.C.: Congressional Quarterly, 1985), pp. 182–83.

TABLE 1.4
Leading Burger Court Decisions

Harris v. New York (1971)	Incriminating statements obtained in violation of *Miranda v. Arizona* (1966) may be admitted at trial to impeach the credibility of a criminal defendant who takes the witness stand and testifies contrary to earlier statements.
Swann v. Charlotte-Mecklenburg Board of Education (1971)	Mathematical ratios are a useful starting point in fashioning remedies for unconstitutional segregation in education, and busing may be relied on as one means to combat dual school systems.
Lemon v. Kurtzman (1971)	Violations of the establishment clause are to be determined by a three-pronged test: a law cannot have a religious purpose, promote or inhibit religion, or foster excessive government entanglement with religion.

TABLE 1.4 (Continued)

New York Times Co. v. United States (1971)	The federal government failed to meet the heavy burden of proof required to justify prior restraint of the publication of the Pentagon Papers.
Reed v. Reed (1971)	A state law that prefers men over women as administrators of decedents' estates contravenes the equal protection clause.
Argersinger v. Hamlin (1972)	The Sixth Amendment requires a right to counsel in misdemeanor trials that could result in imprisonment.
Furman v. Georgia (1972)	Death penalty laws are repugnant to the Eighth Amendment if they permit too much discretion to juries.
Roe v. Wade (1973)	Laws violate the constitutional right to privacy if they outlaw abortions before the third trimester of pregnancy.
Frontiero v. Richardson (1973)	Basing the award of benefits to military personnel on gender violates the due process clause of the Fifth Amendment.
Miller v. California (1973)	To determine if material is obscene, "[t]he basic guidelines for the trier of fact must be: (a) whether 'the average person, applying contemporary community standards,' would find that the work, taken as a whole, appeals to the prurient interest; (b) whether the work depicts or describes, in a patently offensive way, sexual conduct specifically defined by the applicable state law; and (c) whether the work, taken as a whole, lacks serious literary, artistic, political, or scientific value."
Keyes v. School District No. 1, Denver (1973)	Racial discrimination by school boards and other governmental bodies that leads to school segregation will be treated like de jure segregation and may be remedied through busing.
United States v. Nixon (1974)	Executive privilege exists to promote confidentiality and candor in the presidential decision-making process, but executive privilege is not absolute and must yield in a criminal prosecution where nondisclosure would interfere with the responsibility of the courts to do justice.

TABLE 1.4 (Continued)

Milliken v. Bradley (1974)	Busing cannot be used across district lines unless both school districts involved acted unconstitutionally or unless illegal segregation in one district had a significant segregative effect on the other district.
Bigelow v. Virginia (1975)	By ruling that a state cannot prohibit the advertisement of a legal activity, the Court suggested that commercial speech is protected by the First Amendment.
Washington v. Davis (1976)	For an employment law or practice to be ruled unconstitutional, intent to discriminate must be proven.
National League of Cities v. Usery (1976)	Under its commerce clause powers, Congress cannot impose minimum wage and maximum hour requirements upon the states as employers. (Overruled in 1985 in *Garcia v. San Antonio Metropolitan Transit Authority.*)
Gregg v. Georgia (1976)	The death sentence for murder is not repugnant to the Eighth Amendment.
Craig v. Boren (1976)	Basing differences in the state drinking age on gender violates the equal protection clause.
Regents of the University of California v. Bakke (1978)	Institutions of higher education may rely on admissions procedures designed to promote affirmative action as long as racial quotas are not used.
United Steelworkers v. Weber (1979)	Title VII of the 1964 Civil Rights Act does not forbid private employers and unions from agreeing voluntarily on a bona fide affirmative action plan involving racial quotas intended to eliminate a conspicuous racial imbalance in segregated job categories.
Payton v. New York (1980)	The Fourth Amendment requires police to obtain a warrant to enter a home to make a routine felony arrest.
Rostker v. Goldberg (1981)	A federal law providing for male-only draft registration does not violate the Constitution.

TABLE 1.4 (Continued)

Michael M. v. Superior Court of Sonoma County (1981)	The equal protection clause is not violated by a state law that makes it a crime for a male to engage in intercourse with an underage female without making it a crime for a female to engage in intercourse with an underage male.
INS v. Chadha (1983)	The legislative veto provision of the Immigration and Nationality Act is unconstitutional.
Lynch v. Donnelly (1984)	The First Amendment does not prohibit the inclusion of a nativity scene in a city-sponsored Christmas display.
Nix v. Williams (1984)	Although obtained unconstitutionally, evidence need not be excluded at trial if it would have been inevitably discovered in the normal course of a police investigation.
Firefighters Local Union No. 1784 v. Stotts (1984)	Although an employer has violated Title VII of the 1964 Civil Rights Act, a federal court cannot order retroactive seniority for employees who were not victims of that discrimination.
Hudson v. Palmer (1984)	The Fourth Amendment does not protect a prisoner from unannounced searches by guards because prisoners do not have a reasonable expectation of privacy.
United States v. Leon (1984)	Evidence gained with a defective warrant is admissible if the police, in good faith, believed the warrant was valid.
Wallace v. Jaffree (1985)	A state law that authorizes one minute of silence for meditation or voluntary prayer in public schools is unconstitutional under the First Amendment.
Bowers v. Hardwick (1986)	Sexual activity between consenting homosexual adults is not protected under the constitutional right to privacy.
Bowsher v. Synar (1986)	The Balanced Budget and Emergency Deficit Control Act of 1985 violates the doctrine of separation of powers.

TABLE 1.5
Number of Cases Decided by the Burger Court, 1969–85 Terms

	1969	1970	1971	1972	1973	1974	1975	1976	1977
Full Opinions									
Unanimous	27 (28.7%)	23 (18.9%)	34 (22.5%)	35 (21.3%)	33 (21.0%)	34 (24.8%)	36 (23.1)	48 (33.8%)	37 (27.4%)
Nonunanimous	67 (71.3%)	99 (81.1%)	117 (77.5%)	129 (78.7%)	124 (79.0%)	103 (75.2%)	120 (76.9%)	94 (66.2%)	98 (72.6%)
Total	94	122	151	164	157	137	156	142	135
Memorandum Orders									
Unanimous	50 (58.8%)	86 (43.9%)	93 (61.2%)	126 (49.4%)	91 (55.5%)	126 (83.4%)	132 (75.4%)	153 (75.4%)	101 (82.1%)
Nonunanimous	35 (41.2%)	110 (56.1%)	59 (38.8%)	129 (50.6%)	73 (44.5%)	25 (16.6%)	43 (24.6%)	50 (24.6%)	22 (17.9%)
Total	85	196	152	255	164	151	175	203	123

	1978	1979	1980	1981	1982	1983	1984	1985
Full Opinions								
Unanimous	50 (36.2%)	37 (24.8%)	43 (31.2%)	54 (32.3%)	57 (35.2%)	65 (39.9%)	61 (40.4%)	46 (29.0%)
Nonunanimous	88 (63.8%)	112 (75.2%)	95 (68.8%)	113 (67.7%)	105 (64.8%)	98 (60.1%)	90 (59.6%)	113 (71.0%)
Total	138	149	138	167	162	163	151	159
Memorandum Orders								
Unanimous	72 (75.0%)	80 (75.5%)	83 (71.6%)	99 (84.6%)	91 (84.3%)	61 (75.3%)	59 (73.7%)	98 (94.2%)
Nonunanimous	24 (25.0%)	26 (24.5%)	33 (28.4%)	18 (15.4%)	17 (15.7%)	20 (24.7%)	21 (26.3%)	6 (5.8%)
Total	96	106	116	117	108	81	80	104

Note: Cases are classified as unanimous if there was no dissent, regardless of concurrences.
Source: See the statistics section of the *Harvard Law Review* 84–100 (Nov. 1970–86).

TABLE 1.6

Opinion Writing on the Burger Court, 1969–85 Terms

	1969	1970	1971	1972	1973	1974	1975	1976	1977	1978	1979	1980	1981	1982	1983	1984	1985
Black																	
Opinions of Court	10	14	—	—	—	—	—	—	—	—	—	—	—	—	—	—	—
Concurrences	9	10	—	—	—	—	—	—	—	—	—	—	—	—	—	—	—
Dissents	17	14	—	—	—	—	—	—	—	—	—	—	—	—	—	—	—
Total	36	38	—	—	—	—	—	—	—	—	—	—	—	—	—	—	—
Blackmun																	
Opinions of Court	0	9	12	14	15	13	16	14	12	13	14	12	14	15	16	16	14
Concurrences	0	8	10	11	7	5	8	14	14	18	16	18	18	12	6	3	10
Dissents	0	9	12	7	9	5	8	9	13	10	21	11	12	17	9	4	16
Total	0	26	34	32	31	23	32	37	39	41	51	41	44	44	31	23	40
Brennan																	
Opinions of Court	10	11	18	13	15	15	15	13	13	13	14	13	16	15	16	13	13
Concurrences	8	13	3	6	6	1	9	13	7	7	7	8	11	13	10	14	7
Dissents	8	16	14	29	17	18	26	24	13	21	20	17	17	18	29	25	28
Total	26	40	35	48	38	34	50	50	33	41	41	38	44	46	55	52	48
Burger																	
Opinions of Court	10	13	12	19	14	14	16	15	16	17	15	13	16	16	16	17	14
Concurrences	3	3	16	6	0	8	10	11	6	6	5	7	6	3	2	7	15
Dissents	8	4	13	9	6	6	4	14	7	1	8	6	12	5	0	4	5
Total	21	20	41	34	20	28	30	40	29	24	28	26	34	24	18	28	34
Douglas																	
Opinions of Court	12	14	13	16	14	6	0	—	—	—	—	—	—	—	—	—	—
Concurrences	6	7	14	9	8	8	1	—	—	—	—	—	—	—	—	—	—
Dissents	17	26	43	53	47	26	1	—	—	—	—	—	—	—	—	—	—
Total	35	47	70	78	69	40	2	—	—	—	—	—	—	—	—	—	—

TABLE 1.6 (Continued)

	1969	1970	1971	1972	1973	1974	1975	1976	1977	1978	1979	1980	1981	1982	1983	1984	1985
Harlan																	
Opinions of Court	8	8	—	—	—	—	—	—	—	—	—	—	—	—	—	—	—
Concurrences	15	19	—	—	—	—	—	—	—	—	—	—	—	—	—	—	—
Dissents	7	18	—	—	—	—	—	—	—	—	—	—	—	—	—	—	—
Total	30	45	—	—	—	—	—	—	—	—	—	—	—	—	—	—	—
Marshall																	
Opinions of Court	9	9	15	12	13	11	17	12	15	13	14	13	15	17	15	13	15
Concurrences	1	4	3	8	4	4	7	6	4	4	7	1	5	3	2	6	6
Dissents	2	10	20	21	19	8	16	21	20	15	21	12	4	27	16	13	31
Total	12	23	38	41	36	23	40	39	39	32	42	26	24	47	33	32	52
O'Connor																	
Opinions of Court	—	—	—	—	—	—	—	—	—	—	—	—	13	16	17	16	17
Concurrences	—	—	—	—	—	—	—	—	—	—	—	—	12	7	10	11	12
Dissents	—	—	—	—	—	—	—	—	—	—	—	—	10	11	9	9	7
Total	—	—	—	—	—	—	—	—	—	—	—	—	35	34	36	36	36
Powell																	
Opinions of Court	—	—	12	17	16	17	14	15	15	12	16	15	16	18	18	13	18
Concurrences	—	—	5	7	12	6	19	13	18	11	15	14	13	9	11	5	10
Dissents	—	—	5	8	7	8	5	10	15	17	17	10	22	8	7	6	11
Total	—	—	22	32	35	31	38	38	48	40	48	39	51	35	36	24	39
Rehnquist																	
Opinions of Court	—	—	11	16	17	15	17	15	14	16	15	15	17	20	19	17	19
Concurrences	—	—	0	2	4	6	0	3	7	12	3	10	7	5	3	1	3
Dissents	—	—	9	21	15	12	13	15	24	12	26	15	15	16	14	15	15
Total	—	—	20	39	36	33	30	33	45	40	44	40	39	41	36	33	37

TABLE 1.6 (Continued)

	1969	1970	1971	1972	1973	1974	1975	1976	1977	1978	1979	1980	1981	1982	1983	1984	1985
Stevens																	
Opinions of Court	—	—	—	—	—	—	9	13	14	15	14	11	15	15	16	16	17
Concurrences	—	—	—	—	—	—	8	17	10	7	12	17	15	12	18	9	15
Dissents	—	—	—	—	—	—	17	27	21	13	21	25	26	27	34	33	36
Total	—	—	—	—	—	—	34	57	45	35	47	53	56	54	68	58	68
Stewart																	
Opinions of Court	11	15	18	16	17	16	16	14	15	15	15	15	—	—	—	—	—
Concurrences	5	9	6	10	8	6	9	7	10	10	4	8	—	—	—	—	—
Dissents	7	8	8	16	9	11	16	9	13	20	13	15	—	—	—	—	—
Total	23	32	32	42	34	33	41	30	38	45	32	38	—	—	—	—	—
White																	
Opinions of Court	13	13	18	17	19	16	15	15	15	16	15	15	19	19	18	18	19
Concurrences	5	9	12	8	8	7	15	7	5	3	10	8	8	6	6	6	11
Dissents	4	10	6	14	13	7	11	11	17	13	9	8	17	11	9	8	12
Total	22	32	36	39	40	30	41	33	37	32	34	31	44	36	33	32	42
Per Curiam																	
Opinions of Court	11	16	22	24	17	14	21	16	6	8	17	16	26	11	12	12	13
Total																	
Opinions of Court	94	122	151	164	157	137	156	142	135	138	149	138	167	162	163	151	159
Concurrences	52	82	69	67	57	51	86	91	81	78	79	91	95	70	68	62	89
Dissents	70	115	130	178	142	101	117	140	143	122	156	119	135	140	127	117	161
Total	216	319	350	409	356	289	359	373	359	338	384	348	397	372	358	330	409

Note: Data include all full opinions, unanimous and nonunanimous.

Source: See the statistics section of the *Harvard Law Review* 84–100 (Nov. 1970–86).

TABLE 1.7
Dissent Voting on the Burger Court, 1969–85 Terms

	1969	1970	1971	1972	1973	1974	1975	1976	1977	1978	1979	1980	1981	1982	1983	1984	1985
Black																	
Opinion[a]	25	26	—	—	—	—	—	—	—	—	—	—	—	—	—	—	—
Memorandum[b]	13	47	—	—	—	—	—	—	—	—	—	—	—	—	—	—	—
Total	38	73	—	—	—	—	—	—	—	—	—	—	—	—	—	—	—
Blackmun																	
Opinion	0	18	24	16	16	10	17	16	23	14	29	23	28	34	25	15	46
Memorandum	2	6	14	5	10	3	2	12	0	5	5	10	3	2	3	4	1
Total	2	24	38	21	26	13	19	28	23	19	34	33	31	36	28	19	47
Brennan																	
Opinion	13	33	39	50	56	34	56	51	38	47	48	42	49	45	59	50	57
Memorandum	1	4	5	72	26	7	11	21	10	4	10	10	3	5	4	4	2
Total	14	37	44	122	82	41	67	72	48	51	58	52	52	50	63	54	59
Burger																	
Opinion	24	19	29	20	20	17	15	23	30	21	21	20	37	15	10	18	22
Memorandum	16	9	19	5	7	5	6	13	2	4	4	5	2	1	1	0	2
Total	40	28	48	25	27	22	21	36	32	25	25	25	39	16	11	18	24
Douglas																	
Opinion	21	40	59	75	70	52	2	—	—	—	—	—	—	—	—	—	—
Memorandum	11	44	32	98	50	8	1	—	—	—	—	—	—	—	—	—	—
Total	32	84	91	173	120	60	3	—	—	—	—	—	—	—	—	—	—
Harlan																	
Opinion	12	24	—	—	—	—	—	—	—	—	—	—	—	—	—	—	—
Memorandum	12	16	—	—	—	—	—	—	—	—	—	—	—	—	—	—	—
Total	24	40	—	—	—	—	—	—	—	—	—	—	—	—	—	—	—
Marshall																	
Opinion	4	30	34	48	53	31	50	48	41	48	47	48	47	59	56	48	62
Memorandum	1	3	2	71	22	6	12	19	10	3	4	11	6	4	6	1	2
Total	5	33	36	119	75	37	62	67	51	51	59	59	53	63	62	49	64

TABLE 1.7 (Continued)

	1969	1970	1971	1972	1973	1974	1975	1976	1977	1978	1979	1980	1981	1982	1983	1984	1985
O'Connor																	
Opinion	—	—	—	—	—	—	—	—	—	—	—	—	27	28	18	17	14
Memorandum	—	—	—	—	—	—	—	—	—	—	—	—	4	2	5	2	2
Total	—	—	—	—	—	—	—	—	—	—	—	—	31	30	23	19	16
Powell																	
Opinion	—	—	13	14	13	13	7	13	21	19	24	16	28	20	14	8	15
Memorandum	—	—	4	2	3	2	8	7	3	3	0	5	1	0	3	0	0
Total	—	—	17	16	16	15	15	20	24	22	24	21	29	20	17	8	15
Rehnquist																	
Opinion	—	—	14	37	26	23	28	26	41	29	50	25	43	32	26	26	31
Memorandum	—	—	9	8	13	6	9	18	5	14	10	11	6	4	6	5	3
Total	—	—	23	45	39	29	37	44	46	43	60	36	49	36	32	31	34
Stevens																	
Opinion	—	—	—	—	—	—	18	29	30	27	33	32	32	47	53	41	54
Memorandum	—	—	—	—	—	—	6	21	6	5	13	10	8	8	5	5	2
Total	—	—	—	—	—	—	24	50	36	32	46	42	40	55	58	46	56
Stewart																	
Opinion	16	17	16	40	18	22	24	24	20	35	26	25	—	—	—	—	—
Memorandum	7	6	4	74	19	4	3	6	2	7	8	8	—	—	—	—	—
Total	23	23	20	114	37	26	27	30	22	42	34	33	—	—	—	—	—
White																	
Opinion	10	20	13	17	22	14	19	19	28	19	23	14	28	18	12	16	23
Memorandum	4	6	9	9	8	9	1	7	6	5	7	7	2	4	1	4	0
Total	14	26	22	26	30	23	20	26	34	24	30	21	30	22	13	20	23
Total																	
Opinion	125	227	241	317	294	216	236	249	272	259	301	245	319	298	273	239	324
Memorandum	67	141	98	344	158	50	59	124	44	50	61	77	35	30	34	25	14
Total	192	368	339	661	452	266	295	373	316	309	362	322	354	328	307	264	338

[a] Number of dissenting votes in cases with full opinions.
[b] Number of dissenting votes in cases with memorandum orders.

TABLE 1.8

Voting Blocs on the Burger Court in Nonunanimous Civil Liberties Decisions, 1969–85 Terms

Term	Bloc Membership	Average Agreement of Justices in Bloc	Type of Bloc
1969	Douglas, Brennan, Marshall	79%	Liberal
	White, Harlan	86	Conservative
	Stewart, Burger, Black	62	Conservative
1970	Douglas, Brennan, Marshall	83	Liberal
	Burger, Blackmun, Harlan, Stewart, White, Black	68	Conservative
1971	Douglas, Brennan, Marshall, Stewart	74	Liberal
	Burger, Blackmun, Rehnquist, Powell, White	81	Conservative
1972	Douglas, Brennan, Marshall	86	Liberal
	Burger, Blackmun, Rehnquist, Powell, White, Stewart	73	Conservative
1973	Douglas, Brennan, Marshall	85	Liberal
	Stewart, Powell, White	77	Conservative
	Burger, Blackmun, Rehnquist	83	Conservative
1974	Douglas, Brennan, Marshall	79	Liberal
	Burger, Blackmun, Rehnquist, Powell, White, Stewart	74	Conservative
1975	Marshall, Brennan	97	Liberal
	Burger, Blackmun, Rehnquist, Powell, White, Stewart, Stevens	72	Conservative
1976	Brennan, Marshall, Stevens	75	Liberal
	Burger, Rehnquist, White, Blackmun, Powell, Stewart	73	Conservative
1977	Brennan, Marshall	90	Liberal
	Powell, Blackmun	75	Conservative
	White, Burger, Stewart, Rehnquist, Stevens	61	Conservative

TABLE 1.8 (Continued)

Term	Bloc Membership	Average Agreement of Justices in Bloc	Type of Bloc
1978	Brennan, Marshall, Stevens	75	Liberal
	White, Blackmun	80	Conservative
	Burger, Stewart, Rehnquist, Powell	76	Conservative
1979	Brennan, Marshall, Stevens	82	Liberal
	Powell, Stewart	78	Conservative
	Burger, White, Blackmun, Rehnquist	64	Conservative
1980	Brennan, Marshall	89	Liberal
	Burger, White, Blackmun, Rehnquist, Powell, Stewart, Stevens	65	Conservative
1981	Brennan, Marshall	91	Liberal
	Stevens, Blackmun	67	Moderate
	Burger, Rehnquist, Powell, White, O'Connor	75	Conservative
1982	Brennan, Marshall, Stevens, Blackmun	70	Liberal
	Burger, Powell, White, Rehnquist, O'Connor	79	Conservative
1983	Brennan, Marshall, Stevens	72	Liberal
	Burger, Powell, White, Rehnquist, O'Connor, Blackmun	78	Conservative
1984	Brennan, Marshall, Stevens	77	Liberal
	Burger, White, Rehnquist, Powell, O'Connor, Blackmun	75	Conservative
1985	Brennan, Marshall, Stevens, Blackmun	70	Liberal
	Burger, Rehnquist, O'Connor, White, Powell	79	Conservative

Source: Sheldon Goldman, Constitutional Law: Cases and Essays (New York: Harper and Row, 1987), Table 5.12, p. 159. Reprinted with the permission of the author.

TABLE 1.9

Pro-Civil Liberties Voting Percentages on the Burger Court, 1969–85 Terms

	1969	1970	1971	1972	1973	1974	1975	1976	1977	1978	1979	1980	1981	1982	1983	1984	1985
Black	58	51	—	—	—	—	—	—	—	—	—	—	—	—	—	—	—
Blackmun	—	35	42	36	34	39	27	30	46	42	49	40	56	58	40	49	66
Brennan	79	77	84	86	87	76	85	70	77	83	87	74	81	76	81	84	78
Burger	37	35	36	28	28	32	18	16	38	25	28	23	15	26	22	29	21
Douglas	86	90	96	91	92	92	—	—	—	—	—	—	—	—	—	—	—
Harlan	53	43	—	—	—	—	—	—	—	—	—	—	—	—	—	—	—
Marshall	70	80	88	89	85	75	83	72	80	80	89	78	84	85	79	81	86
O'Connor	—	—	—	—	—	—	—	—	—	—	—	—	29	25	24	34	30
Powell	—	—	36	37	42	40	28	30	46	34	43	31	28	28	28	40	33
Rehnquist	—	—	27	16	21	26	13	8	18	18	9	14	16	15	19	22	14
Stevens	—	—	—	—	—	—	44	55	55	59	66	51	53	68	58	63	62
Stewart	45	47	72	58	50	54	41	34	51	40	49	33	—	—	—	—	—
White	57	46	58	33	42	42	31	33	50	47	39	42	37	33	29	34	32
Court Total	63	50	56	41	44	44	31	33	49	40	48	34	40	36	30	45	37

Note: Percentages are rounded. Data based on all decisions with full opinions, both unanimous and nonunanimous.
Source: Derived from data presented in Goldman, Constitutional Law, Table 5.13, p. 160, with the permission of the author.

TABLE 1.10

Pro-Economic Liberalism Voting Percentages on the Burger Court, 1969–85 Terms

	1969	1970	1971	1972	1973	1974	1975	1976	1977	1978	1979	1980	1981	1982	1983	1984	1985
Black	55	—	—	—	—	—	—	—	—	—	—	—	—	—	—	—	—
Blackmun	—	27	29	27	14	58	67	45	44	47	69	67	87	67	69	70	85
Brennan	82	75	79	82	82	92	89	91	95	73	75	93	100	73	100	90	69
Burger	10	20	0	30	14	24	44	27	26	33	19	47	19	47	46	10	39
Douglas	73	81	93	70	81	75	—	—	—	—	—	—	—	—	—	—	—
Harlan	27	33	—	—	—	—	—	—	—	—	—	—	—	—	—	—	—
Marshall	88	47	64	73	77	73	78	82	91	87	81	87	100	100	85	90	77
O'Connor	—	—	—	—	—	—	—	—	—	—	—	—	29	7	39	30	54
Powell	—	—	0	55	15	23	38	40	43	54	25	36	33	36	23	38	39
Rehnquist	—	—	20	30	0	31	22	13	35	20	0	21	13	20	39	10	39
Stevens	—	—	—	—	—	—	50	55	52	64	13	47	63	27	77	40	54
Stewart	55	19	46	52	24	39	11	40	50	47	25	39	—	—	—	—	—
White	90	53	43	48	55	62	78	45	74	73	50	60	80	73	55	50	54
Court Total	64	44	50	48	27	46	56	36	57	53	25	60	88	53	54	40	54

Note: Percentages are rounded. Data based on nonunanimous decisions with full opinions.

Source: Derived from data presented in Goldman, *Constitutional Law*, Table 5.14, p. 162, with the permission of the author.

2

JUSTICE HUGO L. BLACK:
The Enduring Effort to Realize Law
over Judicial Discretion

HOWARD BALL

Black's Southern Heritage

Hugo Black was born on February 27, 1886, in a log cabin in rural Clay County, Alabama. Named after two well-known Frenchmen, Victor Hugo and the fabled Marquis de Lafayette, Black was the eighth and last child of Martha and William Black. Fifty-one years later, in 1937, Black was appointed to the Supreme Court, where he served for thirty-four years. In September 1971 at the age of eighty-five, he was hospitalized after suffering an incapacitating stroke, and sadly he resigned his seat. A few days later, on September 25, 1971, this gentle, steely southerner was dead, and an elemental force in American jurisprudence was gone from the high bench.

When his name was sent to the Senate by President Roosevelt in 1937, Klan leadership in Alabama gave information about Black's past Klan membership to a conservative newspaper, the *Pittsburgh Post-Gazette*. When the story broke, Justice Black had already been confirmed by the Senate and was on a European vacation with his wife prior to taking his seat on the Court. The story exploded across the nation. The *American Mercury* called him "a vulgar dog"; *Time* magazine uttered that "Hugo won't have to buy a robe, he can dye his white one black."[1] When Black returned from Europe, he went on national radio for about eleven minutes and said: "I did join the Klan. I never rejoined."[2]

President Roosevelt, on September 14, 1937, told his press conference "that he had not known of any Klan link when he appointed

Black to the Court. 'I only know what I have read in the news-paper.' "[3] Justice Black, however, had a different memory. In 1968 in a private note (later found in his files, appended to a letter he had sent to one of his biographers about the Klan issue), Black wrote that "President Roosevelt, when I went up to lunch with him, told me that there was no reason for my worrying about my having been a member of the Ku Klux Klan. He said that some of his best friends and supporters he had in the state of Georgia were strong members of that organization. He never, in any way, by word or attitude, indicated any doubt about my having been in the Klan nor did he indicate any criticism of me for having been a member of that organization. The rumors and the state-ments to the contrary are wrong."[4]

Certainly, Black's activity on the high bench, beginning with civil rights cases such as *Chambers v. Florida*, quickly indicated to his critics that he was not a Klansman in a black robe. By the time the watershed school integration decision *Brown v. Board of Edu-cation* (1954) was handed down by a unanimous Court, Black was having difficulty with his Birmingham crowd. After *Brown* he found it increasingly painful to return to the South. Eventually, his oldest son, Hugo L. Black, Jr., was forced to relinquish his law practice in Birmingham and move to Miami because of the adverse impact of his father's civil rights activities on the high bench.

This ostracism, directed at both Black and his family, was ex-tremely difficult for the southern jurist. Toward the end of his life, Black's greatest happiness was being invited back to the South, a place that had strongly influenced him. He loved the South and, as a lawyer, legislator, and jurist, he "tried to help free it from the obsession [racism] which has stunted its development."[5] Black was an optimist: he saw a new South slowly emerging from the ashes of Jim Crowism.

Black's Personality

Justice Black's actions on the high bench "combined the wisdom and breadth of vision of a learned student of history with the disingenuous certitude of a backwoods politician."[6] A combination of "the steel hard and the soft,"[7] gracious and unpretentious, Black was an indomitable jurist when he made up his mind on an issue of law. However, he was not "a 'court politician,' and did not seek to impose or push his views in any face-to-face kind of way."[8] Although constantly engaged in conversations with his brethren,

Justice Hugo L. Black

Black was "willing to discuss points but did not seek to impose them."[9] Nevertheless, his determination often led him to engage in actions that were labeled "blackmail" by some of his brethren.

During conference sessions Black communicated with his colleagues by way of written memos and oral arguments. If suggestions flew, he was a tough negotiator, and one of his memos would usually find its way into the Court opinion; if one did not, then he would use it as the basis of a statement of concurrence or dissent. One of Black's basic tendencies was to resist what he believed were the incorrect constitutional positions of his colleagues. "He is concerned only with his work," wrote a law clerk. "Indeed, there is no Justice more committed to the business of the court than he."[10] During his thirty-four-year tenure as associate justice, Black repeatedly bombarded his colleagues with legal memos about points of law they might have overlooked in reviewing litigation. In fact, the correspondence between the brethren reveals that the other justices often responded to these memos by changing their minds and voting differently. In one example, Justice Tom Clark wrote Black: "I'm sorry about the FHA case—I never studied the claim frankly—From what I've read of the brief since you called my attention to it, I believe you are right—I may change my vote tomorrow."[11]

Clarity and simplicity of expression were hallmarks of the many statements Black produced during his years as Supreme Court justice. He was extremely critical of his brethren when they misused legal language—whether it involved constitutional roaming in search of the meaning of due process or a seemingly simple letter to a colleague who had retired. At times his criticism left a bad taste in the mouths of some of his colleagues. Nevertheless, although Black was forceful and cunning in fighting for his ideas, he was also compassionate. Many people sought his advice, on and off the federal bench. Over time, justices came to Black in the hope that he would handle personal and legal problems involving them and the Court. For example, in August 1965, Douglas wrote to Black asking him to speak with the wife of a new justice to the Supreme Court. "Abe Fortas's wife is very upset over Abe's appointment. It is apparently a very serious crisis. I thought maybe you could think of something to do."[12] In spite of his occasional anger over Black's actions, Justice Murphy wrote memos to Black asking him to listen to his personal "troubles."[13] Earl Warren, a few years before his retirement as chief justice, also thanked Black for his help, writing that "nothing in the past thirteen years has given me more pleasure and satisfaction than my association with you. That association has really made them rewarding years for me."[14]

Other men came to Black so that he might counsel them in their efforts to gain a seat on the federal bench. While Sherman Minton was serving on the Seventh Circuit Court of Appeals in Chicago, he wrote Black about that "god awful town [Chicago]," and how he "missed you all in Washington."[15] In January 1943, Wiley Rutledge wrote Black to thank him for his help while Rutledge was in Washington, D.C., testifying before the Senate Judiciary Committee prior to his elevation to the Court. "Without making any assumption whatever as to what action the Senate may take, I want you to know how very much I treasure your kindness. Believe me, it means a great deal to me. I am sorry that you went to so much trouble to get the message through."[16]

Black strongly supported people whom he believed were ideologically in line with Roosevelt and the New Deal. This "political" tactic of his annoyed a number of his colleagues but their consternation did not faze the Alabaman. As Justice Reed said to Frankfurter: "You can't change people. Black always was a politician and he didn't and can't cease to be one by becoming a judge."[17]

As an ideologue, a fervent New Dealer, and a lover of Jefferson's democracy, Justice Black was committed to the supremacy of the actions of elected representatives. By October 1969, when Warren Burger began his tenure as chief justice, Black had already developed a fairly comprehensive political theory of government in a representative democracy. Having written almost eleven hundred opinions over the preceding thirty-two years, he had a well-developed set of beliefs about the nature of governmental power, the relationship between the states and the federal government, the role and functions of the federal judges, and the fundamental constraints upon governmental and judicial powers in a democracy.

Black was committed to a dream of an ongoing and vigorous democracy.[18] In his effort to realize this dream, he overlooked the fallibility of his fragile colleagues. He was a classic true believer, unshakable in his beliefs about governmental powers and the limits on those powers. While the "overriding personal impression of the Judge was one of great humanity, love, warmth, and youth,"[19] Black had an unremitting, "intense moral commitment, concentrated through the focus of an unwavering vision, and brought to bear with an immense prowess."[20] He would not compromise his principles, even if it meant classification as judicial blackmailer and flapdoodler.

Black's Political Jurisprudence in 1969

In 1969, when Chief Justice Burger took over the Court's leadership, Hugo Black had served for thirty-two years as an associate justice and had crafted a complete political jurisprudence. Before examining Black's activities as a member of the Burger Court, it is important to examine Black's judicial philosophy as it had developed by 1969. In a letter to a Mississippi citizen who had complained to his fellow southerner about the Supreme Court's school desegregation policy, Black wrote: "[Y]ou worry about citizens being denied their 'freedom of choice.' Government is bound to deny citizens freedom of choice at some time, to some extent, and on certain subjects. That is one of the great objects of government; so that we have a country of law and order instead of one of anarchy and riot, and I believe in having the former kind of country as I always did back in the days when you were in my Sunday School class in Birmingham."[21] This response captured the essence of Black's political jurisprudence: the need for a government strong enough to provide for orderliness and security but not so strong as to deprive persons of their inalienable rights as free citizens in a representative democracy.

While Black has been labeled with many, often contradictory, titles—liberal, activist, nationalist, states' righter, literalist, conservative, and so on—Black's political jurisprudence, as it unfolded, consisted of legal positivism. He was, first and foremost, a twentieth-century Jeremy Bentham with the "zeal to reform the laws, to cleanse away its excrescences, to look upon law as a clear instrument of the popular will, not as the patina of the judges' gloss."[22]

Justice Black's philosophies on governmental powers and the federal judges' role in our constitutional system clearly revealed his positivism. He was an eighteenth-century thinker functioning in the twentieth century. His political jurisprudence rejected the idea of natural law and the view that judges ought to be social engineers. Black believed that the "only relevant law is the positive law, the commands made and enforced by the sovereign."[23] Lawmaking in a democracy was a legislative, not a judicial, function. Legislators, freely elected by the people in a democracy, had the

constitutional responsibility for legislating for the common good—
as determined by the legislature.

Judges are responsible for interpreting the "law" (i.e., the Constitution or statutes) by going to the intent of the founders or the
legislators and, if necessary, going to the literal meaning of the
words themselves. Furthermore, a law may be unwise or ridiculous,
but unless it runs afoul of a specific prohibition of another "positive
law of superior status" (i.e., the clear prohibitions of the Bill of
Rights and, to a lesser extent, the generalities in the Fourteenth
Amendment), it is a valid law. Judges must not put their gloss on
the law of the legislature nor substitute their values for those of
the legislators.

This view of the role and responsibility of the representatives
elected by the people (who are themselves the key to a functioning
democracy) was the bedrock of Black's legal positivism. The 1787
Constitution established a pattern of representative government
that had, at its heart, the concept of elected public officials, empowered and restricted by the document and its Bill of Rights.
The "human evils" addressed in the Bill of Rights were perennial
ones. Black did not consider it to be an outmoded, eighteenth-
century "straitjacket"[24] but believed that the problems of 1787
still existed, and that free speech and a free press, freedom of
religion, the right to a jury trial, and the rest are necessary for
the continuation of democracy.

The constitutional system gave federal judges the primary role
of ensuring that these freedoms of expression and thought, vital
to a democracy, were rigorously enforced. They were also to monitor the legislative efforts of elected political leaders, who occasionally tried to restrict these rights. But these federal judges had
to restrain themselves from interfering with governmental activities
not specifically prohibited by the supreme positive law of the system: the Constitution.

Governmental Powers

Quoting Justice Holmes, Black clearly stated his position on
governmental powers: " 'A legislature can do whatever it sees fit
to do unless it is restrained by some express prohibition in the
constitution. . . . Courts should be careful not to extend such prohibitions beyond their obvious meaning by reading into them conceptions of public policy that the particular court may happen to
entertain.' "[25] The fundamental responsibility of political leaders
in a democracy is to "develop definite and precise laws under the

authority of a written constitution."[26] Furthermore, Black believed, the Constitution enables a legislature "to do virtually anything [it] wishes in controlling the economy,"[27] and he indicated in a letter to one of his students that government at all levels is "fully clothed with the power to govern and to maintain order."[28]

The Japanese Exclusion Cases, 1942–44, exemplify Black's commitment to the principle of legislative-executive supremacy in the conduct of war and foreign affairs and those agencies' basic responsibility to provide for law and orderliness in time of national emergency. During World War II, both the Roosevelt administration and Congress accepted the necessity of a policy that excluded Japanese aliens and citizens of Japanese descent from the United States' West Coast.[29] By 1943, over 120,000 such persons, including over 70,000 U.S. citizens, were incarcerated in almost a dozen relocation centers scattered across the western states and Arkansas.

In 1944 in *Korematsu v. United States,* Black wrote that "military orders called for the exercise of military, not judicial judgment. . . . [I]t is unnecessary for us to appraise the possible reasons which might have prompted the [relocation] order to be used in the form it was" (323 U.S. at 214). Justice Black and the Court majority deferred to the judgment of the president and Congress. He believed that the loss of freedom was a small cost to pay for the maintenance of the democratic system. He never recanted from his position in *Korematsu:* "Pressing public necessity may sometimes justify the existence of some restrictions [on liberty]" (214). Throughout his career as a justice, Black felt compelled to support strong law-and-order actions on the part of public officials, subject only to the constraints of the words of the Constitution.

Restricting Governmental Powers

Legislators and executives were given fairly wide latitude under the Constitution to make economic and social policy without federal judicial intervention. But the Constitution prohibits legislation that would deprive persons of their basic civil liberties. Justice Black believed that a historical pattern lay behind the relative ease with which America's deviant groups lost their liberties. Black concluded through his readings of historical events that a democracy could only survive through the maintenance of the basic freedoms of speech, press, assembly, and religion, as well as the right to an open and fair public trial. Therefore, federal judges were responsible for protecting these fundamental freedoms. "The most prominent feature [of his jurisprudence] was this: In the absolutism of the First Amendment lies the only security for the maintenance of a democratic society under law."[30]

The "Firstness" of the First Amendment. The Bill of Rights (especially the First Amendment), the Civil War amendments, and the federal civil rights statutes formed the basis of the fundamental positive law that restricted legislators from infringing upon the inalienable rights of individuals. Black "took the Declaration of Independence seriously when it referred to inalienable rights; the Bill of Rights was the corollary to those inalienable rights."[31]

For Black, "the right to think, speak, and write freely without governmental censorship or interference is the most precious privilege of citizens vested with power to select policies and public officials."[32] He believed that absolute freedom from governmental control over speech and thought provided hope for an open and just society. Throughout his career he was an ardent advocate of the unfettered right of free speech, free press, freedom of assembly, and freedom of religion. He rejected all of the Court's judicially created tests for resolving First Amendment litigation (such as clear and present danger, bad tendency, and especially the balancing formula employed by Frankfurter and Harlan).

Black never deviated from his commitment to the "firstness" of the First Amendment. In 1947 in *Adamson v. California,* he expressed his belief that the First Amendment was "the supreme law of the land." He continued, declaring that he "put these freedoms of speech and press wholly beyond the reach of federal power to abridge. No other provision of the Constitution purports to dilute the scope of these *unequivocal commands* of the First Amendment. Consequently, I do not believe that any federal agencies, including Congress and this Court, have power or authority to subordinate speech and press to what they think are more 'important interests' " (332 U.S. at 73) (emphasis added).

It was fitting that Black's last opinion on the Court also dealt with a First Amendment controversy—the Pentagon Papers litigation. In *New York Times Co. v. United States* (1971), he again maintained his absolutist position, writing that "the First Amendment was offered to *curtail* and *restrict* the general powers granted to the Executive, Legislative, and Judicial branches" (403 U.S. at 713) (emphasis added). Black consistently defended the basic constitutional freedoms, even when they arose in cases involving controversial issues such as obscenity, loyalty oaths, anti-subversive legislation, and congressional investigations. For the Alabaman, the First Amendment freedoms were "the lifeblood of any representative democracy" (713).

While Justice Black was certain about the absoluteness of the First Amendment, he always distinguished between cases involving speech from those involving conduct as well as speech, such as picketing. "I draw the line between speech and conduct," wrote Black in 1968. "I am vigorously opposed to efforts to extend the First Amendment's freedoms of speech beyond speech. . . . [The Constitution] does not immunize other conduct in addition to these particularized freedoms."[33] Black felt that a vast difference existed between conduct, especially the actions of street protestors, and speech, for example, the printing and distribution of a pamphlet by a radical organization. "Reading history, Black believed that tramping, singing, marching, demonstrating people with the most worthy of motives but acting outside the boundary of the law to achieve their goals would lead to counter-demonstrations, marches, tramping by their opponents."[34] These passionate actions carried the possibility of a breakdown of law and order and the rejection of reasoned, rational discussion on public issues.

For the justice, the loss of societal orderliness had to be prevented in order to maintain the fragile fabric of a representative democracy. "The crowds that press in the streets for noble goals today can be supplanted tomorrow by street mobs pressing the courts for precisely opposite ends," Black wrote in a partial dissent in 1965 in *Cox v. Louisiana* (379 U.S. at 584-85). Congress and the states, in Black's view, were responsible for the prevention of lawlessness.

Civil Rights in the Fourteenth Amendment. The First Amendment was absolutely clear for Black, but the due process and equal protection clauses in the Fifth and Fourteenth Amendments were less clear. For Black, the language of the due process clause was troublesome. "No one," he said, "has ever marked its boundaries," and consequently, he believed, due process (along with equal protection) is "as elastic as rubber."[35] This elasticity led some of the Supreme Court justices on a subjective search for the meaning of due process.

Black went to the Constitution's historical antecedent, the Magna Carta, for his conception of the essential meaning of due process. "Due process of law," according to Black, meant that persons were to be tried in accordance with the procedural guarantees in the Bill of Rights (Fourth, Fifth, Sixth, and Eighth Amendments) and in accordance with "laws passed pursuant to constitutional power, guaranteeing to all alike a trial under the general law of the land."[36] All criminal defendants must be given equal treatment according to "the law of the land that already existed at the time the alleged offense was committed."[37] Black's understanding of history and his concern about substantive judicial interpretations of due process (such as Frankfurter's "shock the conscience" standard) led him to develop an interpretation of procedural due process that emphasized equal treatment in the legal process for all persons, regardless of wealth, age, or race. Justice Black hoped his interpretation would be adopted ultimately by the Supreme Court majority.

Black translated the Fourth Amendment in very restrictive terms, emphasizing the language of the amendment rather than its historical roots. It is evident from a review of his Fourth Amendment cases—from *Wolf v. Colorado* (1949) through *Mapp v. Ohio (1961)*, and from *Berger v. New York* (1967) and *Katz v. United States* (1967) to *Coolidge v. New Hampshire* (1971) (the last case was heard during the last term he served on the Court)—that Black was reluctant to extend the meaning of the search and seizure language. He had misgivings about the exclusionary rule the Court created in *Mapp,* and he argued against its use in light of the protection against self-incrimination already present in the Fifth Amendment.[38] Some have speculated that Black, as a southern police court judge, and later, as a crusading prosecuting attorney in Birmingham, strongly believed that "how you catch a thief is not important provided he got a fair trial afterwards."[39] As the Fourth Amendment most directly affected police work in the investigatory and accusatory stages of criminal prosecution, he may have empathized with law enforcement agents and consequently restricted his perception of unreasonable searches and seizures.

As seen in the Warren Court majority's opinions in *Berger, Katz,* and *Griswold v. Connecticut* (1965), the Court was moving specifically toward a new definition of the concept of privacy. The Court majority found this concept, not in the Constitution itself, but in its "penumbras" (*Griswold*). Black vehemently dissented from the majority's substantive interpretation of due process in this line of cases. His overriding concern was that the majority was using the clauses of the Bill of Rights, including the Fourth and Fourteenth Amendments, to broadly paint new judicially created rights.

The "Equal Protection of the Laws" language in the Fourteenth Amendment presented Black with an even more problematic constitutional expression than due process of law.[40] In order to compensate for the vagueness of the Equal Protection clause, Black returned to the clause's historical context for some sense of its drafters' original intent. In time he came to believe that the clause was the constitutional prohibition of all state actions that invidiously discriminated on the basis of race. For Black, race was the only major "suspect" category in equal protection cases. The Supreme Court, as well as other federal courts, was obligated to strictly scrutinize all cases, such as school segregation cases, that involved official state discrimination based on race.

Except in the case of civil rights violations involving state action and racial discrimination, fundamental limits governed the use of the equal protection clause. Black did not believe in a broad, substantive interpretation of the clause. Instead, in his view, most state action litigation that came to the federal courts for review merely required analysis under the "reasonableness" test.

Justice Douglas's majority opinion in *Harper v. Virginia State Board of Elections* (1966), in which the Court majority struck down a Virginia poll tax law as constituting invidious discrimination, was an example of substantive interpretation. Black, dissenting, criticized the majority for giving "equal protection a new meaning. . . . I have heretofore had many occasions to express my strong belief that there is no constitutional support whatever for this Court to use the Due Process Clause as though it provided a blank check to alter the meaning of the Constitution as written so as to add to it substantive constitutional changes which a majority of the Court, at any given time, believes are needed to meet present-day problems. Nor is there, in my opinion, any more constitutional support for this Court to use the Equal Protection Clause, as it has today, to write into the Constitution its notions of what it thinks is good governmental policy" (383 U.S. at 663). Congress, rather than the Supreme Court, has the constitutional power to change the meaning of the equal protection clause through constitutional amendment. Short of a massive display of arbitrary and repugnant racial discrimination, ill-advised or distasteful state laws cannot be overturned by federal judges simply because they find them unwise.

The Role of Federal Judges

Hugo Black insisted throughout his career in politics, and while on the Court, that judges must be tethered to the words of the Constitution. Black had been taught that legislators made the laws, and he witnessed the ability of federal judges and the Supreme Court to block legitimate social engineering by Congress and President Roosevelt throughout most of the 1930s. Consequently, Black utterly rejected the concept of a federal judiciary that would leave the federal judges "completely free to decide constitutional questions on the basis of their own policy judgment" and decided that judges had no constitutional right to tell a community what social policy was good or bad for them.[41]

Justice Black criticized judicial forays into the "natural law" wonderland of "substantive" due process or equal protection accompanied by subjective judicial standards such as "fundamental fairness" or "shock the conscience." He insisted that federal judges go along with the plain meaning of the laws rather than substitute their views for those of elected representatives. Engaged in a lifelong effort to constrain the legislative proclivities of federal judges, Black believed, according to one of his law clerks, that due process of law "encompassed all of the specific prohibitions of the Bill of Rights and the Constitution. It did not encompass anything else."[42]

The *Adamson v. California* dissent of Justice Black in 1947 reflected his strong feelings about judicial meddling. In an interview given shortly before his death in 1971, Black declared that this 1947 opinion was "his most significant opinion written."[43] In *Adamson*, the Court split five to four over the constitutionality of a California trial practice that permitted the trial judge and lawyers to comment on, and juries to consider, as evidence of guilt a defendant's refusal to testify on his behalf during the trial. The majority opinion, written by Justice Stanley Reed, upheld the defendant's conviction, stating, "The Due Process Clause of the Fourteenth Amendment does not draw all the rights of the federal Bill of Rights under its protection." While most states do not allow the California practice, the opinion continued, "we see no reason why comment should not be made upon his silence. It seems quite natural" (332 U.S. at 54).

Justice Black dissented because, in his opinion, the Reed opinion, and especially Frankfurter's concurrence, "reasserted a constitutional theory . . . that this Court is endowed by the Constitution with boundless power under 'natural law' periodically to expand and contract constitutional standards to conform to the Court's conception of what at a particular time constitutes 'civilized decency' and 'fundamental principles of liberty and justice' " (332 U.S. at 69–70). Reviewing the legislative history of the Fourteenth Amendment led Black to conclude that "one of the chief objects [of the amendment] was to make the Bill of Rights applicable to the states. . . . And I further contend that the 'natural law' formula which the Court used to reach its conclusion in this case should be abandoned as an *incongruous excrescence* on our Constitution. I believe that formula to be itself a violation of our Constitution, in that it subtly conveys to courts, at the expense of legislatures, ultimate power over public policies in fields where no specific provision of the Constitution limits legislative power" (75) (emphasis added). For Black, the Bill of Rights was a set of relevant protections against governmental mischief.

> I cannot consider the Bill of Rights to be an outworn 18th Century 'straightjacket.'. . . Its provisions may be thought outdated abstractions by some. And it is true that they were designed to meet ancient evils. But they are the same kind of human evils that have emerged from century to century wherever excessive power is sought by the few at the expense of the many. . . . I would follow what I believe was the original purpose of the Fourteenth Amendment—to extend to all the people of the nation the complete protection of the Bill of Rights. To hold that this Court can determine, what, if any, provisions of the Bill of Rights will be enforced, and if so, to what degree, is to frustrate the great design of a written constitution. (89)

Legislatures, said Black, have the fundamental "right to invade my privacy unless prohibited by some specific constitutional prohibition."[44] Judges must be prevented, he believed, from using their powers to review cases in order "to substitute their wisdom for that of the people's representatives."[45] In his thirty-four-year tenure as a Supreme Court justice, Black was steadfast in this general concern about federal judges having the freedom to rewrite the fundamental law and how that freedom would negatively affect a democracy.

Black on the Burger Court, 1969 and 1970 Terms

In 1969, "still driven by a burning evangelical need to persuade his colleagues of his views, Black worked intensely at the job."[46] This year marked Warren Burger's initial term on the Supreme Court as the new chief justice. Justice Hugo Black served with Chief Justice Burger for two terms, 1969 and 1970. A review of the major opinions of the Court during this time reveals Black as a tough jurist who continued to joust with his brethren on the perennial questions of governmental power and the restraints on that power.[47] During these two terms, he wrote a total of 24 majority opinions, 19 concurring opinions, and 31 dissenting opinions (see Table 1.6).

The specific policy disputes during the 1969–70 period differed somewhat from past ones. They concerned domestic and foreign crises involving everything from black activism, urban rioting, civil rights disturbances, and the executive branch's war powers, to protests against the Vietnam War, public school and university campus unrest, and sensational public trials such as the "Chicago Eight" trial, not to mention political assassinations, the impact of reapportionment, and so on. For Justice Black, these crises illuminated anew the perennial dilemmas involving governmental power, the liberties of the people, and the role of the federal judges in these constitutional controversies.

For the octogenarian jurist, the issues (sit-ins, busing, antiwar protests, disrespect in the courtroom), as well as the expansive "natural law" interpretations given to the due process and equal protection clauses by his brethren, forced Black to dissent and to vote with different cliques than usual during his last two years on the Court (see Tables 1.7–1.10). Because of the issues, Black tended to vote more often with Stewart and Burger (62 percent of the time during the 1969 term) than he did with his longtime colleague and friend Bill Douglas. Given Black's personality traits, tough-mindedness, and steel will, even in his last two terms on the Court, Black was a formidable opponent in the minority. And, on occasion, he was able to develop a majority on some very critical federalism/civil rights issues because of his strength of purpose and because of the new personnel on the Court, Burger and Blackmun. His role on the Court during these last two terms was not to be negligible: Black was the critical element in a 1970-term coalition that included Burger, Blackmun, Harlan, Stewart, and White, which voted as a bloc in civil liberties issues 68 percent of the time (see Table 1.8).

It was the substance of the civil rights cases that began to reach the Court in the late 1960s that led to Black's movement away from Douglas, Brennan, and Marshall. For example, in *Swann v. Charlotte-Mecklenburg Board of Education* (1971), a unanimous Court decision, Black consistently opposed Douglas's view that a federal district court could develop student ratios and, among other things, order the busing of schoolchildren from their neighborhood schools to others across town in order to desegregate public schools. For Black, who had vigorously fought for an end to segregated schools and who had single-handedly pushed the Court to end the era of "all deliberate speed" in *Alexander v. Holmes County Board of Education* (1969), massive judicially mandated across-town busing was too much of a judicial intrusion. As he said in the conference session on *Swann,* the Constitution did not contain the word "bus." (He would have been very happy had the president or Congress dealt with policy initiatives such as busing.) In the end, however, although he had written a dissent in *Swann,* he pulled it and joined the unanimous Court opinion that validated the district court's busing order. Ironically, the concerns he raised about busing involved values associated with the local community — the same kinds of values that Burger and President Nixon were openly supporting.

Governmental Powers

In the many opinions Black wrote over the course of his last two terms on the Court, he strongly argued that local and state government officials were free to establish or to revoke public policies, unless the officials were specifically prohibited by a clear constitutionally imposed constraint. In *Evans v. Abney* (1970) and *Palmer v. Thompson* (1971), two controversial cases involving state action with racially discriminatory overtones, Black's narrow majority opinions concluded that the challenged "state action" in Georgia (involving the return of public lands to private parties) and in Mississippi (involving the closing of public municipal swimming pools) did not run afoul of the equal protection clause of the Fourteenth Amendment. Local governments, in the absence of a clear and unambiguous showing of discriminatory purpose, were not in violation of the Constitution simply because some people thought these local governmental actions were discriminatory.

In *Evans,* Black's opinion let stand a Georgia court decision that validated city officials' actions involving a piece of land that had been given to the city by a nineteenth-century benefactor. Under the terms of the will, the public park had to be operated on a racially exclusive basis: for whites only. Rather than integrate the park (and violate the terms of the racially restrictive but private trust), the local officials returned the property to the heirs because the city could not carry out the terms of the trust. Black, for the majority, wrote: "Any harshness that may have resulted from the state court's decision can be attributed solely to its intention to effectuate as nearly as possible the explicit terms of the . . . will. . . . The effect of the Georgia decision eliminated all discrimination against Negroes in the park by eliminating the park itself, and the termination of the park was a loss shared equally by the white and Negro citizens of Macon, Georgia" (396 U.S. at 444–45). In *Palmer*, Black upheld a decision of the local government in Jackson, Mississippi, to close all public swimming pools rather than integrate them. No court has ruled that a "legislative act may violate equal protection solely because of the motivations of the men who voted for it. . . . Furthermore, there is an element of futility in a judicial attempt to invalidate a law because of the bad motives of its supporters." In Black's opinion, the record showed "no state action affecting blacks differently from whites" (403 U.S. at 224–25).

Chief Justice Burger, who considered himself a moderate in racial matters, felt uncomfortable with the *Evans* opinion. He believed that the Court could rectify the matter even though the local officials had not acted in violation of the Fourteenth Amendment. "We are the Supreme Court and we can do what we want," he reportedly told a perplexed Justice Harlan. Finally, Burger wrote Black a letter: "Dear Hugo: This is a difficult case with a result I do not relish, but the question is one for the states (states, unlike federal agencies and this Court, are not infallible). Seeing it as a state question, I join your opinion."[48]

In dissenting opinions, Black supported state determinations of the nature of juvenile statutes. In *In re Winship* (1970), for example, he maintained that the state could use the "preponderance of evidence" standard in juvenile proceedings. "Nowhere in [the Constitution] is there any statement that conviction of crime requires proof beyond a reasonable doubt" (397 U.S. at 383). Contrary to the Court majority, Black argued that the Constitution did not require this type of proof and that the majority's "natural law–due process notion" violated the principle of a government of limited power (384). *Winship* was the last occasion Black had to debate this position with his philosophical opponent, Justice Harlan. Black considered the Court majority's response yet another example of tampering with the words of the Constitution, a judicial practice Black fought against throughout his tenure on the Court.

In a number of other opinions decided during the 1969 and 1970 terms—in cases regarding comity, illegitimate children, probable cause for police searches and seizures, public school regulations on hair length, and state referendums—the senior justice strongly supported the states' right to develop and implement social policy without federal judicial meddling.[49] The case of *Illinois v. Allen* (1970), which arose during the 1969 term, concerned the action of a trial judge who had expelled a noisy defendant from the courtroom during trial. Given the domestic turbulence of the times, *Allen* took on special importance for Justice Black. He believed in the primacy of order and respect for law and was grievously troubled to see the spectacles taking place in U.S. courtrooms toward the end of the 1960s. Thus, when *Allen* came to the Court, Black pushed it through quickly in an attempt to respond to the courtroom travesties he had been reading about in the press.

Chief Justice Burger asked Black to write the opinion for the majority. Black enthusiastically attacked the case because it provided him the opportunity "to tell trial judges how they could deal with disorderly courtroom behavior without violating the rights of the accused" (397 U.S. at 337). In his opinion, Black extolled courtrooms as "palladiums of liberty" and "citadels of justice" and concluded that in order to maintain decorum a trial judge could constitutionally bind and gag defendants, cite them for contempt, or expel them from the courtroom until their behavior improved. (Although the *Allen* case did not involve a political defendant or an antiwar protestor, Douglas dissented because he felt the precedent set in *Allen* was a harsh one when applied in political trials.)

In one of his last opinions, *Boys Markets, Inc. v. Retail Clerks Union Local 770* (1970), which focused on the powers of Congress in the area of labor relations, in dissent Black reaffirmed his commitment to the supremacy of the legislative power and to the limited role of the federal courts, including the Supreme Court. The Court majority had overturned an interpretation of the Norris-LaGuardia Act of 1932 whereby courts had been barred from enjoining a strike in breach of a no-strike clause in a collective bargaining agreement. In *Boys,* the Court held that the grievance was subject to arbitration and that an injunction could be issued while the matter was being arbitrated.

Black maintained that the Court majority had not practiced self-restraint by deferring "to the primary responsibility of the legislature in the making of laws. . . . The Court undertakes the task of interpretation not because the Court has any special ability to fathom the intent of Congress, but rather because interpretation is unavoidable in the decision of the case before it" (398 U.S. at 257). Sharply, Black told his brethren that "altering the important provisions of a statute is a legislative function. . . . It is the Congress, not this Court, that responds to the pressures of political groups, pressures entirely proper in a free society. . . . This Court should . . . interject itself as little as possible into the law-making and law-changing process" (258).

It is evident from a review of Black's opinions on the general question of local, state, and national governmental power that Black maintained his original jurisprudential position during his service with Chief Justice Burger. Implementing social and economic policy rested with elected officials. In 1965 in *Griswold v. Connecticut*, Black wrote, "[M]any good and able men have eloquently spoken and written, sometimes in rhapsodical strains, about the duty of this Court to keep the Constitution in tune with the time. . . . I must with all deference reject that philosophy" (381 U.S. at 539). Judges must not use their "subjective considerations" to invalidate legislation that they dislike. In his last two terms on the Court, Black continued to urge judicial self-restraint—with the same mixed results he had realized in his previous thirty-two years on the high bench.

Restricting Governmental Powers

A number of highly controversial issues confronted the Burger Court during Black's two terms: selective service and conscientious objectors, obscenity, national security, the Vietnam War and freedom of the press, voting rights, and cruel and unusual punishment, among others. Black's responses to these issues and the underlying principles they involved were characteristic of his general response over the decades to litigation involving fundamental freedoms and governmental intrusions. In litigation involving government censorship of the press, press libel and slander of public officials, the right of association and admission to the bar, obscenity, and freedom of expression, Black was unwavering in his insistence that First Amendment freedoms provide persons with an unfettered freedom to speak, write, associate, and express themselves in traditional ways.[50]

New York Times Co. v. United States (1971), the most controversial of these First Amendment cases, came to the Court at the very end of Black's tenure as associate justice. On June 13, 1971, the *New York Times* began publishing a top secret government report documenting the history of American involvement in the Vietnam War. On Tuesday, June 15, 1971, when U.S. Attorney General John Mitchell obtained an order from a federal district court judge enjoining future publication of the report by the *Times*, "Black was stunned. 'They're actually stopping it,' he said to his clerks."[51]

This serious attempt by the national government to prevent the press from publishing an important story was, in Black's opinion, an egregious form of prior restraint. But the fact that the judiciary was being used as the instrument to suppress First Amendment liberties was even worse.

The Court granted the case certiorari on June 25, 1971, and in a brief per curiam note set aside the injunctions. The national government, it held, "carries a heavy burden of showing justification for the enforcement of such a restraint. [Lower federal courts] held that the Government had not met that burden. We agree. . . . So ordered" (403 U.S. at 713). All of the justices wrote or joined in concurring or dissenting opinions. Justice Black's concurrence was his last written opinion, and it contained a strong statement on behalf of the absoluteness of the First Amendment's freedom of the press: "The press was protected so that it could bare the secrets of government and inform the people. Only a free and unrestrained press can effectively expose deception in government. And paramount among the responsibilities of a free press is the duty to prevent any part of the government from deceiving the people and sending them off to distant lands to die of foreign fevers and foreign shot and shell. In my opinion, far from deserving condemnation for their courageous reporting, [the newspapers] should be commended for serving the purpose that the Founding Fathers saw so clearly" (826–27).

The justices were involved in a difficult set of negotiations in order to resolve the dilemma the case posed. While there were four justices (Black, Douglas, Brennan, and Marshall) in favor of granting certiorari on June 25, one additional vote was needed to hear the case as an emergency appeal from the court of appeals. Four other justices—Burger, Harlan, White, and Blackmun—wanted to hear oral arguments in October and continue the injunctions until then. The critical, deciding vote belonged to Justice Potter Stewart, a jurist whom many thought Nixon would name as Warren's replacement in 1969. Stewart finally, reluctantly, decided to vote for certiorari.

After hearing oral arguments on June 26, 1971, the justices attempted to resolve the case by reviewing the secret documents. Only Black, Douglas, and Brennan believed that the press had an absolute right to publish. For the others, the contents of the documents were to play a major role in their deliberations on the case.[52] The justices met again in disagreement: Burger wanted more argument, while only Black, Douglas, and Brennan were clearly on the side of the press. Stewart, the key vote, concluded that the government had not shown that there was a danger to national security, and he voted to lift the injunctions. The logjam was broken with a final vote of six to three, with Burger, Blackmun, and Harlan in the minority.

Black also asserted First Amendment freedoms in the various selective service cases that came to the Court during this time.[53] In *Astrup v. INS* (1971), he sided with a young man who had been intentionally mistreated by the government, and he was able to get a unanimous Court to rule that the government had committed a wrong. (Chief Justice Burger, in a note to Black, felt that the young person had simply worked out a bad bargain but felt compelled by Black's argument to join in the majority opinion.)

While Black generally defended the rights of young persons to hold unorthodox views, he nevertheless felt compelled to dissent in *Cohen v. California* (1971). In *Cohen* a young man had been convicted of "offensive conduct" for wearing a jacket in a Los Angeles courthouse with the words "Fuck the Draft" emblazoned on its back. At first Black voted to summarily dismiss the conviction, but, as the case dragged on and he heard oral arguments, he had a change of heart. "What if Elizabeth [his wife] were in that corridor. . . . Why should she have to see that word?" he reportedly asked his clerks.[54] In the end, he decided to join the dissenting opinion written by Justice Blackmun (joined, also, by Burger). For Blackmun and Black, "Cohen's absurd and immature antic . . . was mainly conduct and little speech" (403 U.S. at 195).

Many controversial criminal procedure cases came to the Court during the last terms of Black's service. Black's judgments continued to reflect his long-held views on both due process and the role of federal judges in that area of constitutional law.[55] Three cases, *Coolidge, Coleman,* and *Ashe,* reflected Black's continuity of jurisprudence in due process litigation before the Court.

In *Coleman v. Alabama* (1970), a case that concerned the Sixth Amendment, Black concurred with the majority, in an example of a Court turnaround in deciding an important constitutional issue. In conference the justices had voted seven-to-one that a person charged with a crime had no right to an attorney at a preliminary hearing before a magistrate to determine whether there was sufficient evidence to go to trial. The justices' initial reaction was that assistance of counsel did not extend to pretrial proceedings. The sole dissenter, Harlan, thought preliminary hearings to be part of the prosecutorial process.

Brennan wrote the opinion for the majority. Then Black, after reading the Brennan draft, decided to join Harlan's dissent.[56] This behavior, evidently, was not unusual. In a letter to the author, Black wrote that "my votes at conference are never final. They are tentative and I am always ready to change the vote if I reach the conclusion that my vote was wrong. . . . Nor is there anything altogether extraordinary in the fact that a Justice to whom an opinion is assigned to write one way may write it another way."[57] Burger wrote to Black asking the senior justice to explain his turnabout. Black responded tartly: "Dear Chief, Amendment VI." He went on to say, "Although the Sixth Amendment doesn't go into detail on when [a person's right to the assistance of counsel begins], . . . it would disregard reality to say that a preliminary trial is not an important part of a prosecution under which a state is preparing to punish a man. . . . Where is there anything in the Constitution that says although a man had the right at the time of prosecution, he cannot claim that help the first time he needs counsel?"[58]

The next occurrence illuminated Black's words on turnabouts on the Court. After Harlan circulated his *Coleman* dissent, supported by Black, Brennan began to worry that he would lose his majority and changed his position. He revised his opinion so as to defend Coleman's right to have an attorney at a preliminary hearing. With that change accomplished, most of the other justices stayed with Brennan, much to Burger's chagrin. In this surprising development the chief found himself on the losing side of the controversy. When Black's concurring opinion was announced in *Coleman*, it emphasized that "the explicit commands of the Constitution provide a full description of the kind of 'fair trial' the Constitution guarantees, and in my judgment that document leaves no room for judges either to add or *detract* from these commands" (399 U.S. at 12–13, emphasis added).

Ashe v. Swenson (1970) involved a man charged with robbing six men at a poker game. The state found Ashe not guilty to the charge of robbing one of the six and then tried him for robbing another poker player. This time the jury found him guilty. With the exception of the chief justice, all the justices believed the defendant should be set free. Black assigned Stewart to write the opinion for the majority. Stewart's opinion focused on the meaning of double jeopardy and collateral estoppel. Black, still concerned about judicial creativity, wrote a separate concurring opinion that focused on his now familiar theme of judicial self-restraint. "In my view, it is a wholly fallacious idea that a judge's sense of what is fundamentally 'fair' or 'unfair' should ever serve as a substitute for the explicitly written provisions of our Bill of Rights" (397 U.S. at 477).

Coolidge v. New Hampshire (1971) involved the scope of the Fourth Amendment's search and seizure protections. Edward Coolidge was arrested for and convicted of murdering a fourteen-year-old girl, primarily on the basis of evidence seized by the police through the cooperation of his wife. Coolidge had spoken with the police about the crime and had voluntarily shown the officers three guns. A few days later, police officers — without a warrant — visited his home and spoke with his wife, who showed them four guns and allowed the police to take them, along with some of her husband's clothing. On the basis of that new evidence, Coolidge was arrested and his car searched (on the basis of a signed warrant) and towed to the police station. Over the course of the next year, the car was searched two times for incriminating evidence. That evidence, along with the gun and clothing given to the police earlier by his wife, led to Coolidge's conviction. He appealed on the ground that the searches were unreasonable ones because they were not based on a search warrant issued by a detached and neutral magistrate and that therefore the evidence uncovered was inadmissible in light of *Mapp* and the exclusionary rule.

Black believed that all the evidence seized was admissible and that the conviction should stand — although he evidently did not want to overturn *Mapp*. The Court was again evenly divided. Harlan appeared to be the swing justice and tentatively opted for excluding the evidence in the light of *Mapp*. After heated discussions among the justices and their clerks, Harlan agreed to join the Stewart opinion, which reversed and remanded, while all the justices agreed to hold off a full-blown discussion of the continued viability of *Mapp* for a better, cleaner case.[59]

The five-man majority opinion had reversed and remanded because the search warrant that had enabled the police to search Coolidge's automobile had been issued by the state's attorney general (who had been actively in charge of the investigation and later had served as the key prosecutor at the trial) instead of a neutral and detached magistrate. Black's dissent in *Coolidge* was a bitter one. Laying into the majority's judicial creativity, Black argued that the exclusionary rule had been "judicially created" and that the Fourth Amendment, "properly construed, contains no such exclusionary rule. The Fourth Amendment prohibits unreasonable searches and seizures. The Amendment says nothing about consequences. It certainly nowhere provides for the exclusion of evidence as the remedy for violation" (403 U.S. at 496). The Court majority, Black concluded, believed it had a Fourth Amendment "rulemaking capacity" to modify the words of the Constitution, when in fact it did not have this power. For Black the search of the automobile had been a reasonable one, the warrant had been issued properly, and the conviction should have been upheld by the Court. "It is difficult for me to believe the Framers of the Bill of Rights intended that the police be required to prove a defendant's guilt in a 'little trial' before the issuance of a search warrant" (499). Black continued to dissent in other criminal justice cases because he felt that the majority was unconstitutionally tampering with the words of the Constitution.

The Role of Federal Judges

Justice Black sharply dissented thirty-one times during his last two terms because, for the most part, the Court majority placed an arbitrary gloss on the words of the Constitution and on the plain meaning of legislation. (See, for example, his dissents in *Winship, Coleman, Carter v. Kentucky* [1981], and *Boys Market.*) In *Mills v. Electric Auto-Lite Co.* (1970), Black dissented from the Court's opinion, which vacated a federal court of appeals ruling involving the Securities and Exchange Act of 1934 that would have allowed the plaintiffs to collect attorney's fees in the absence of statutory provisions for such fees. "The courts are interpreters, not creators, of legal rights to recover," Black wrote, "and if there is a need for recovery of attorney's fees to effectuate the policies of the Act here involved, that need should in my judgment be met by Congress, not by this Court" (396 U.S. at 397).

Black dissented in *Bivens v. Six Unknown Named Agents of the Federal Bureau of Narcotics* (1971), in which the Court majority created a federal cause of action for damages for an unreasonable search by federal agents. This was the task of the Congress, not the courts, Black maintained. In *Boddie v. Connecticut* (1971), another dissent, Black criticized the Court majority for reversing a lower federal court decision against a party who had claimed that the Connecticut divorce statute (requiring nominal fees) was unconstitutional. The Supreme Court held that, absent specific constitutional or statutory provision, marriage and divorce are controlled by state policy. Also, because this was a civil action, the Bill of Rights safeguards against obtrusive and illegal governmental action did not apply, since those safeguards protect criminal defendants only. Restating strands of his philosophy, Black explained that, in civil suits, government is neutral. Natural law concepts lack any constitutional precision. They "mark no constitutional boundaries and cannot possibly depend on anything but the belief of particular judges, at particular times, concerning particular interests which those judges have divined to be of 'basic importance.'. . . I believe that the only way to steer this country toward its great destiny is to follow what our Constitution says, not what judges think it should have said" (401 U.S. at 393, 394). Justice Black also dissented in a number of cases involving civil rights, the breadth of the equal protection clause, and the power of Congress to remedy voting rights discrimination.

To summarize Justice Black's tenure on the Burger Court, Black was insistent that ours is a government of laws. Federal judges are obligated to validate these laws when controversial litigation comes to the Court. The Black refrain was a clear one: when judging the constitutionality of legislation, federal judges must go to the literal words and the historical chronicles of the Constitution and its framers. If changes are needed in these fundamental, positive laws, they have to be made by the people's representatives in constitutionally prescribed ways. "This approach can easily be seen as naive, but is in fact extremely complex, with deep philosophical and jurisprudential roots."[60] And, for Black, "government at all levels was fully clothed with the power to govern and to maintain order."[61]

Conclusion

Because he had witnessed mischievous acts by federal judges, Justice Black was fully and deeply committed to a political jurisprudence of judicial self-restraint in the making and unmaking of social and economic public policies. At the same time, he was equally committed to an aggressive federal judiciary that would protect the people's fundamental freedoms to participate as free men and women in the civic culture and the polity. A determined, gritty yet gracious jurist, Black was continually working, from 1937 until his final days on the Court in July 1971, to educate his brethren about these solemn judicial responsibilities and obligations. For Black, divining the line between restraint and activism would be easier if federal judges would disabuse themselves of subjective values such as "shock the conscience," "fundamental sense of civilized justice," "offend the community," "sporting sense of fair play," and other such "natural law" standards. In his correspondence with Frankfurter, Black often spoke of their mutual differences. But these differences related to the means that were most likely to achieve the end both justices envisioned.

Hugo Black's ultimate goal, only partially achieved while he sat on the bench, was to minimize judicial discretion and "leave basic policy changes to the democratic processes."[62] This democratic ideal was Black's intimate nexus to the political thought of another great southerner, Thomas Jefferson. Black and Jefferson believed that only an enlightened citizenry could maintain the very fragile fabric of democratic processes in a free society. His striving for this principle of representative democracy has become the enduring legacy of Justice Hugo L. Black.

NOTES

1. Quoted in Daniel M. Berman, "Hugo L. Black: The Early Years," *Catholic University Law Review* 8 (1989): 103.

2. Quoted in Virginia Van der Veer Hamilton, *Hugo Black: The Alabama Years* (University: University of Alabama Press, 1982).

3. Berman, "Hugo L. Black: The Early Years," p. 104.

4. Note in Van der Veer file, Hugo L. Black Papers, Box 31, Library of Congress, Manuscript Division, Washington, D.C. (hereafter referred to as the Black Papers).

5. Daniel M. Berman, "Hugo Black and the Negro," *American University Law Review* 10 (1961): 35,42.

6. Vincent Blasi, ed., *The Burger Court: The Counter-Revolution That Wasn't* (New Haven, Conn.: Yale University Press, 1983), p. 240.

7. Daniel J. Meador, "Mr. Justice Black: A Tribute," *Virginia Law Review* 57 (1971): 1113.

8. Correspondence with Black's law clerk, 1961 term, who said at one point that Black did not "lobby."

9. Ibid.

10. Daniel J. Meador, "Justice Black and His Law Clerks," *Alabama Law Review* 8 (1963): 1161.

11. Black Papers, Box 58.

12. Ibid., Box 59.

13. Ibid., Box 61.

14. Ibid., Box 64.

15. Ibid., Box 62.

16. Ibid., Box 28.

17. Quoted in Joseph P. Lash, ed., *From the Diaries of Felix Frankfurter* (New York: W. W. Norton, 1975), p. 64.

18. See Howard Ball, *The Vision and the Dream of Justice Hugo L. Black: An*

Examination of a Judicial Philosophy (University: University of Alabama Press, 1975), chap. 1.

19. Correspondence with Black's law clerk, 1969 term.

20. Anthony Lewis, "Hugo Black—An Elemental Force," *New York Times,* Sept. 26, 1971.

21. Black Papers, Box 53.

22. Paul Freund, "Mr. Justice Black and the Judicial Function," *UCLA Law Review* 14 (1967): 473. See also Tinsley E. Yarbrough, "Mr. Justice Black and Legal Positivism," *Virginia Law Review* 57 (1971): 376.

23. Yarbrough, "Mr. Justice Black and Legal Positivism," p. 377.

24. See Black's dissent in *Adamson v. California* (1947).

25. Hugo L. Black, *A Constitutional Faith* (New York: Knopf, 1968), p. 68.

26. Hugo L. Black, foreword in Lenore Cahn, ed., *Confronting Injustice: The Edmond Cahn Reader* (Boston: Little, Brown, 1966), p. xi.

27. Daniel M. Berman, "Hugo Black at Seventy-five," *American University Law Review* 10 (1965): 50.

28. Black Papers, Box 28.

29. See, generally, Roger Daniels, Sandra C. Taylor, and Harry H. L. Kittano, eds., *Japanese Americans: From Relocation to Redress* (Salt Lake City: University of Utah Press, 1986).

30. Meador, "Mr. Justice Black: A Tribute," p. 1109.

31. John P. Frank, "Hugo L. Black: Free Speech and the Declaration of Independence," *University of Illinois Law Forum* 1977: 582.

32. Black, *A Constitutional Faith*, p. 43.

33. Ibid., pp. 44–45, 53.

34. Ball, *The Vision and the Dream of Justice Hugo L. Black*, p. 197.

35. Quoted in Tinsley E. Yarbrough, "Justice Black, the Fourteenth Amendment, and Incorporation," *University of Miami Law Review* 30 (1976): 233.

36. Black, *A Constitutional Faith*, p. 34.

37. Ibid., p. 33.

38. See Jacob W. Landynski, "In Search of Justice Black's Fourth Amendment," *Fordham Law Review* 45 (1976): 453.

39. Ibid., p. 495.

40. See Tinsley E. Yarbrough, "Justice Black and Equal Protection," *Southwestern University Law Review* 9 (1977): 899.

41. Black, *A Constitutional Faith*, p. 43.

42. Correspondence with Black's law clerk, 1961 term.

43. Yarbrough, "Justice Black, the Fourteenth Amendment, and Incorporation," p. 231.

44. Black, *A Constitutional Faith*, p. 9.

45. Quoted in Yarbrough, "Mr. Justice Black and Legal Positivism," p. 935.

46. Bob Woodward and Scott Armstrong, *The Brethren: Inside the Supreme Court* (New York: Simon and Schuster, 1979), p. 62.

47. See *Citizens to Preserve Overton Park v. Volpe* (1971) (DOT), concurring;

Wyman v. Rothstein (1970), dissent; *Lewis v. Martin* (1970) (HEW), dissent; *Dandridge v. Williams* (1970) (DOT), concurring; *Rosado v. Wyman* (1970) (HEW), dissent; *Wheeler v. Montgomery* (1970), dissent; *Goldberg v. Kelly* (1970), dissent; *Zuber v. Allen* (1969) (USDA), dissent.

48. *Evans v. Abney* (1970). Quoted in Woodward and Armstrong, *The Brethren,* p. 187.

49. *James v. Valtierra* (1971); *Karr v. Schmidt* (1971); *Labine v. Vincent* (1971); *Wisconsin v. Constantineau* (1971); *Vale v. Louisiana* (1970), dissenting; *Colonnade Catering Corp. v. United States* (1970), dissenting.

50. *New York Times Co. v. United States* (1971); *Rosenbloom v. Metromedia, Inc.* (1971), concurring; *United States v. Thirty-Seven Photographs* (1971), dissenting; *United States v. Reidel* (1971), dissenting; *Ocala Star-Banner Co. v. Damron* (1971), concurring; *Time, Inc. v. Pape* (1971), concurring; *Patriot Co. v. Roy* (1971), concurring; *Law Students Civil Rights Research Council v. Wadmond* (1971), concurring; *In re Stolar* (1971); *Baird v. State Bar of Arizona* (1971); *Ginzburg v. Goldwater* (1970), dissenting.

51. Woodward and Armstrong, *The Brethren,* p. 139.

52. Ibid., pp. 139ff.

53. *Welsh v. United States* (1970); *Toussie v. United States* (1970); *Breen v. Selective Service Local Board No. 16* (1970).

54. Woodward and Armstrong, *The Brethren,* p. 131.

55. *Coolidge v. New Hampshire* (1971); *United States v. White* (1971), concurring; *Williams v. United States* (1971), dissenting; *Mayberry v. Pennsylvania* (1971), concurring; *Baldwin v. New York* (1970), concurring; *Coleman v. Alabama* (1970), concurring; *Ashe v. Swenson* (1970), concurring; *Turner v. United States* (1970), dissenting.

56. Woodward and Armstrong, *The Brethren,* p. 69.

57. Black to Ball, Jan. 21, 1969.

58. Woodward and Armstrong, *The Brethren,* p. 70.

59. Ibid., pp. 116ff.

60. Correspondence with Black's law clerk, 1961 term.

61. Meador, "Mr. Justice Black: A Tribute," p. 1110.

62. Wallace Mendelson, *Justices Black and Frankfurter: Conflict on the Court,* 2d ed. (Chicago: University of Chicago Press, 1961), pp. 73–75.

3

JUSTICE HARRY A. BLACKMUN:
Transformation from "Minnesota Twin"
to Independent Voice

STEPHEN L. WASBY

Introduction

Harry A. Blackmun, sixty-one years old when he took his seat on the Supreme Court, had already been a federal appellate judge for eleven years. Born in southern Illinois in 1908, he had been raised in Minnesota, like Chief Justice Burger, whom he had known since both of them were five years old; later he was best man at Burger's wedding. Blackmun went to Harvard for both college ('29) and law school ('32). He had a scholarship from the Harvard Club of Minnesota and raised money for his expenses by working at a variety of jobs. His undergraduate major was mathematics—a fact, some have suggested, that may help explain his willingness, not shared by most of his colleagues, to discuss statistics (see *Castaneda v. Partida,* 1977) or to draw on statistically based social science studies (see *Ballew v. Georgia,* 1978).[1] Although he was later to say, "I probably would have been a poor physician,"[2] he considered going to medical school.

Blackmun obtained his first exposure to the federal judiciary by serving as a clerk for Eighth Circuit Judge John H. Sanborn, to whose seat he would be appointed slightly over twenty-five years later. Then followed sixteen years of private practice in Minneapolis, and then, in 1950, fulfilling his early medical interest, nine years as resident counsel for the Mayo Clinic. He considers that a very happy time. In his own words, "I was able to have a foot in both camps—law and medicine."[3] This experience definitely affected his later work, particularly his approach in the famous

63

abortion rulings—indeed, he retreated to the Mayo Clinic library to work on that opinion—and other cases that had medical aspects or that affected doctors. Indeed, on the basis of his use of medical information and his support for medical concerns in his opinions, one might call him "the doctor's friend in Court," and he has spoken openly of his "profound confidence in the American physician."[4]

In 1959, he became Judge Blackmun, appointed by President Eisenhower, some say with the help of Warren Burger, then a member of the D.C. Circuit. His service over the years on the Eighth Circuit did not place him among leading appellate jurists. However, his opinions did reflect strains of thought that made him attractive to President Nixon, who was looking for someone to share his views on defendants' rights and related issues and his negative views about the permissive nature of society. Characterized as a civil rights moderate and as a conservative on defendants' rights and civil liberties issues, Judge Blackmun is said to have exhibited judicial restraint. "From an ideological standpoint, he seemed to be exactly what Nixon was looking for: a judge who believed in judicial restraint, was strong on law and order, and weak on civil liberties."[5]

He was to be the solution when Richard Nixon's "southern strategy" failed and the Senate consecutively rejected the nominations of Judges Clement Haynsworth and G. Harrold Carswell. Apparently not bothered by the fact he was not the first nominated for the Fortas vacancy, Blackmun referred to himself as "Old No. 3," an instance of his penchant for self-effacement and an indication of his humility. Nominated on April 15, 1970, Blackmun was confirmed unanimously less than a month later.

Commissioned on May 14, 1970, Blackmun took his Supreme Court seat on June 9, 1970. His first opinion for the Court came the next term in *Wyman v. James* (1971), but his first separate statement came less than three weeks after he joined the Court—a dissent to the per curiam opinion in *Hoyt v. Minnesota* (1970) overturning an obscenity conviction from his home state of Minnesota. The opinion perhaps telegraphed some general themes that would be present in his later doctrinal output. While not showing explicit distaste for obscene materials, Blackmun exhibited deference to the states and particularly to state courts. He argued against a "national and uniform measure" for state regulation of obscenity, instead preferring "one capable of some flexibility and resting on concepts of reasonableness." He also acknowledged his

Justice Harry A. Blackmun

debt to Justice Harlan, who was also to influence his views on the retroactivity of criminal procedure rulings.

After reaching the Supreme Court, Justice Blackmun underwent considerable resocialization. Not only did he move toward increased concern for civil liberties and civil rights claims outside criminal procedure, but he also thought more about the process of judging. He learned to look at the broader picture and to understand the need to consider the Court's internal politics. His comments about the Court's alignment and his movement to counter other justices' moves suggest he came to work toward specific self-defined goals.

Although perhaps surprising for someone of sixty-one years of age, Blackmun was unsure of himself when he came on the Supreme Court. Competence in one position does not necessarily transfer to competence in others, and his long service on an unexceptional lower appellate court had produced long-ingrained habits. For example, courts of appeals judges are accustomed to reviewing the trial record for error, and Blackmun's Eighth Circuit experience may help explain his proclivity for the "harmless error" rule in criminal cases, based as it is on examination of the trial record. Blackmun's circuit court service, much longer than that of other recent justices who had come from federal appellate courts—it was nearly twice as long as Stevens's and more than twice Stewart's—perhaps made it more difficult for him to shift his focus to the larger constitutional and statutory questions with which the Supreme Court more frequently deals.

Blackmun's early writing style on the Court, with considerable use of numbered paragraphs, was labored; only after some time did his opinions flow more easily. He has admitted agonizing over important decisions such as the abortion ruling and letting that agonizing show, thus violating Justice Black's advice,[6] but once a decision is made, he is able to put the matter aside. Instead of talking with his clerks about pending cases or "debating" with them, or assigning them to draft briefs, he takes the lead in reading all necessary materials. In 1975 he observed that although he "had labored to the limits of my ability in private practice" at the Mayo Clinic and on the Eighth Circuit, "I have never worked harder and more concentratedly than since I came to Washington."[7] In the last few years, Blackmun has shown considerable candor, both in his written opinions and his public statements. Perhaps, like that other midwesterner, Harry Truman, Blackmun has been aware of his limitations and, although more slowly than Truman, has grown in the job, in part by learning to work to his strengths and by not letting his limitations immobilize him.[8]

Blackmun's change in position is quite evident. He had initially shown insensitivity to the poor, as in his comment in *United States v. Kras* (1973) that the bankruptcy filing fee was "less than the price of a movie and little more than the cost of a pack or two of cigarettes" (409 U.S. at 449), and he had adopted quite conventional positions with respect to obscenity or unpopular views. Over a decade later, he spoke positively and protectively on behalf of interests he thought not adequately recognized by his colleagues, particularly in his 1986 *Bowers v. Hardwick* dissent.

Nor was the 1986 dissent atypical. Blackmun had for some time been calling for the Court to heed the "real world" concerns of individuals subject to hurtful action either by government or private business, not only those needing government funding for abortions, but also injured workers seeking compensation and working women discharged because of discrimination. In empassioned language, he criticized the horrendous jail conditions from which prisoners had escaped (*United States v. Bailey*, 1980) and spoke on behalf of uneducated and disadvantaged parents who, without an attorney or other resources, would be at the mercy of a government well prepared for hearings on termination of parental rights (*Lassiter v. Department of Social Services of Durham County, North Carolina*, 1981; *Santosky v. Kramer*, 1982). Suffice it here to say that the change was not in so much Blackmun the individual, long thought to be concerned about fairness and justice, as in Blackmun the judge, with convergence occurring between the individual and his judicial role.

Blackmun's numerous public statements have included an extended 1982 interview with Daniel Schorr for CNN, an interview for the *New York Times Magazine* in 1983, and many speeches. He has given us not platitudes about the judicial process or general discussion of constitutional doctrine, but detailed views on the Court's workings, on the justices' health, and even on their nicknames. In comments among the most forthright from any sitting Supreme Court justice, he spoke particularly of the Court's alignments and on judicial strategy for responding to them, as when he said he voted with Justices Brennan and Marshall "to maintain a centrist balance" and "to correct the imbalance [Justice O'Connor's] presence creates," or when he spoke of his "trying to hold the center," which had "bled a lot. And it needs more troops."[9]

Influence

In his early Court years, Harry Blackmun appears to have been influenced by others rather than to have exerted influence, perhaps as other justices, attempting to influence him and to win him away from the chief justice, tried to take advantage of the possibility that a judge new to the Court might, in close or doubtful cases, take his "lead" from others, like a base runner looking to the third-base coach as to whether to stay or go. His plodding working style may have allowed Blackmun to be influenced by his colleagues, as their more rapid pace allowed them to have more effect on coalition building.

The earlier friendship of Burger and Blackmun, coupled with speculation that Burger played a role in Blackmun's appointment, led to the perception that the two would vote together. During Blackmun's confirmation hearings, Senator Edward Kennedy (D-Mass.) inquired whether, given their past close personal ties, Blackmun would have difficulty working with Burger. Their conjoint voting soon led to the "Minnesota Twins" label and the appellation "Hip Pocket Harry," suggesting that their voting was perhaps a repetition of Justice Stephen Field's having a second vote in his nephew Justice David Brewer. That Burger expected Blackmun to vote with him was apparent to Blackmun himself, who said, once he had moved away from Burger, "I am fairly positive that he feels I have not been the supportive arm he would have liked me to be."[10]

Voting Patterns

Blackmun's shift of position within the Court is reflected in his voting pattern.[11] In the 1970 term, Blackmun's first full term, he voted with the chief justice in 69 of 72 nonunanimous cases (95.8 percent), including all criminal procedure cases but one, *United States v. Jorn* (1971), in which Blackmun took the more conservative position. That agreement decreased in the next term, if only temporarily, to 83.9 percent; one of their disagreements was about standing (*Sierra Club v. Morton*, 1972), on which Blackmun was regularly to be more supportive of access to the courts. Once Powell and Rehnquist joined the Court, Burger and Blackmun voted together in over four-fifths of the nonunanimous cases, but during the 1974 term, Blackmun was the Nixon appointee most likely to defect, moving into the majority in civil liberties cases.

The 1975 term demonstrated the beginning of a change, with agreement between Burger and Blackmun decreasing, falling to just over half in the 1977 term. Burger's agreement with Rehnquist exceeded his agreement with Blackmun, a situation that continued throughout the Burger Court. Although Blackmun had initially cast relatively few dissenting votes, and several times had the lowest number of dissents on the Court, his increasing independence from his fellow Nixon appointees can be seen in the high level of his dissents, particularly in the 1982 term.

Justice O'Connor's 1981 appearance on the Court marked another change in Blackmun's interaction patterns. His agreement with the chief justice in nonunanimous cases fell sharply to 40.9 percent and his defection from his erstwhile conservative colleagues grew. In 5-4 decisions, he was more likely to be found with Brennan and Marshall than with Burger, Rehnquist, and O'Connor, and his level of agreement with Brennan and Marshall rose significantly to over 70 percent, where it stayed thereafter. Indeed, in the 1981 term, he voted with Brennan more than twice as often as he did with Rehnquist. Now most of the time when he opposed Burger, Powell, and Rehnquist, he was in dissent, and he even appeared on the liberal side of some close criminal procedure cases.

Blackmun's relation to his colleagues is also seen in his voting record in civil liberties and civil rights cases, defined to include those involving access to the courts. During his first term, Blackmun's support of civil liberties claims was almost identical to Burger's; in close cases (those decided by 5-4 and 5-3 votes), when a justice's vote is more crucial, each supported civil liberties claims only 9.5 percent of the time, the lowest support in the Court. Thereafter Blackmun's record was more liberal (support for his claim that he had always been more liberal than Burger),[12] and he was generally the most liberal of the Nixon appointees. In 1974 and 1975, when Burger supported no civil liberties claims in close cases, Blackmun did so roughly one-third of the time. By the 1977 term, his support of civil liberties claims was almost double Burger's. The 1981 term, already noted as a turning point, and the 1982 term saw Blackmun's support of civil liberties rise dramatically. Indicating the nature of his transformation, in Burger's last term Blackmun supported a full two-thirds of all civil liberties claims, placing him behind only Marshall and Brennan, and during several terms his support in close cases exceeded 80 percent.

Blackmun also wrote quite critically about his conservative colleagues' opinions, using fairly blunt language. He particularly criticized Rehnquist and O'Connor, calling the former's analysis in *Toll v. Moreno* (1982) "wholly irrational" and his "exegesis of the

Court's reasons . . . simplistic to the point of caricature" (458 U.S. at 20). In *Federal Energy Regulatory Commission v. Mississippi* (1982), writing for a sharply divided Court, he complained that O'Connor's "rhetorical devices make for absorbing reading" but "unfortunately are substituted for useful constitutional analysis" and embody a view "that is almost mystical" (456 U.S. at 762 n. 27, 767 n. 30).

Reasons for Change

Although it did not start immediately, since the "early Blackmun" lasted at least several terms, Blackmun's change, if not completely linear, has been clear over time. Perhaps Blackmun's ruling in *Roe v. Wade* (1973) started the process, with greater attention being paid to him, but no across-the-board elevated change took place immediately after that ruling. Justice O'Connor's coming to the Court marked a step-increase in change. We must be careful, however, not to confuse Blackmun's greater public outspokenness and the greater visibility it brought him with separately identifiable change in doctrine or in voting.

Why did Blackmun change? One reason may be that the chief justice may have taken him for granted. Certainly Burger appears not to have been sensitive to his colleague's feelings about the derogatory "Minnesota Twins" label and (particularly) the "Hip Pocket Harry" label, and public perception of Burger's dominance offended Blackmun: "I have a little anger underneath it all. . . . Anger from being categorized over the 12 years I've been here in a way I think never fit."[13] We cannot know how Blackmun would have supported Burger over the longer term if Burger, instead of showing an inability to shepherd a potentially useful resource, had respected Blackmun's autonomy, but Blackmun might not have moved as far away and Burger might have retained an ally.

Burger's assignment of opinions may well have played a role in Blackmun's response to the chief. The small number of cases assigned to Blackmun—the proportion of times he was chosen when available to the chief justice was the smallest for any justice during the 1970–74 and 1977 terms—might have been a function of Blackmun's work habits, but the lack of assignments did help alienate him.[14] Certainly, after he had moved away from Burger, he would have been less likely to have been rewarded with opinions in important or close cases, but it was in the early years that Burger gave Blackmun a large proportion of his opinions in unanimous or wide-margin (8-1 and 7-2) cases. He also received more than his share of tax cases and Indian cases even before he had "left the reservation," although the tax assignments could have resulted from his experience as a tax lawyer and his Eighth Circuit authorship of many opinions in that field.[15]

Blackmun's change of position was more a matter of moving outside the chief justice's range of influence than of influencing others. Blackmun neither influenced nor was influenced by any one other justice on concurrences and dissents.[16] He generally did quite well in getting more than the minimum four others to join his opinions for the Court. However, there were several terms (1973, 1976, 1978, and 1981) when he could muster only four justices to join him in a significant portion of his opinions, and most of his concurring opinions, often written to take a narrower ground to state reasons for a narrow reading of the Court's opinions, were not joined by others—true of all such opinions in the 1975, 1983, and 1984 terms. Yet in all but the 1982 term he had at least one "joiner" in far more than half his dissenting opinions, and there were very few instances in which he was the only dissenter, a position he found uncomfortable.[17]

Judicial Philosophy

When appointed to the Court, Harry Blackmun was a somewhat unspectacular representative of moderate midwestern Republicanism. His judicial ideology encompassed President Nixon's views on criminal procedure, on which he was to change least, and certain traditional values. These were coupled with a somewhat idealistic and conventional social vision and a trust in the propriety and effectiveness of social and governmental institutions, toward which he took a self-restrained stance involving deference to the legislature, the executive, and the bureaucracy. Over the years, he developed a measured, thoughtful approach and, moving away from his early criticism of the unconventional and lauding of the traditional, came to "protect and safeguard apparently vulnerable individuals"[18] other than criminal defendants and to exhibit greater skepticism about the government's willingness to act appropriately. He moved from a seemingly unreflective centrism to a more responsive, intentional centrism along with his growing appreciation of his own position and the Court's direction. When ideology threatened to move the Court too far to the right, he was stimulated to try to maintain a centrist philosophy for the Court.

Blackmun came to seek a centrist approach at least as much as moderate results. This can be seen in his criticism of the Court's reaching too far to decide issues when, for example, it ruled there was no case or controversy but nonetheless engaged in discussion of a major issue. It could also be seen in his comment that "complex constitutional issues cannot be decided by resort to inflexible rules or predetermined categories,"[19] and in his "reluctance to commit himself to any doctrinaire position."[20]

There are dissenters to the proposition that Justice Blackmun underwent "a remarkable transformation."[21] Dorsen, for example, argues that Blackmun's change has been "more apparent than real," with his more recent opinions reflective of values seen years ago in his Eighth Circuit opinions.[22] Yet a reading of Justice Blackmun's opinions provides support for the notion that he did change, a change perhaps reinforced by those with whom he voted. Just as Chief Justice Burger may have earlier contributed ideas to his "Minnesota Twin," the liberals may well have contributed more to his opinions as he moved toward them, thus helping to explain an increasingly liberal tone beyond any shift in values.

Not chosen because of specific issue positions, Justice Blackmun may have joined the Court with somewhat open-ended conceptions, at least in areas other than criminal procedure. His openness provided the possibility for change, but some stimulus was probably also necessary. Blackmun may have responded to external political change directly (political change leading to Blackmun's change), with conservatives' harsh positions moving him in a liberal direction as he realized he had responded insufficiently to societal problems. This explanation is supported by his liberal movement after election of a president who was far more conservative than the one who appointed him and who was committed to cutting back on efforts to achieve the equality, particularly racial equality, that Blackmun sought, and to pushing a social agenda that would undo Blackmun's 1973 abortion ruling.

Blackmun's response may, however, have been mediated by intra-Court relations (political change to Supreme Court's change to Blackmun's change). This possibility is supported by the somewhat gradual nature of Blackmun's change, which began before the 1980 election. As an increasingly self-assured Burger Court majority developed certain doctrines to which Blackmun had earlier adhered, he may have seen the implications of the doctrines more clearly. The effect of changes within the Court is also shown by the fact that his increasingly liberal statements, voting with Justices Brennan and Marshall, harsher criticism of conservative positions, and remarks about conscious efforts to keep the Court in the center came after centrist Justice Stewart's replacement by more conservative Justice O'Connor.

Separation of Powers

Access

Judicial deference to the other branches of government is exhibited by judicial rulings making it difficult for plaintiffs to get into court. Blackmun showed greater flexibility than his conservative colleagues in interpreting "cases and controversies" and evinced a greater willingness to make access to the courts available. At first, in *Gilligan v. Morgan* (1973), Blackmun exhibited a narrow view of access. Deferring to institutional authority, he denied Kent State University students' challenge to National Guard procedures as seeking "judicial surveillance of highly subjective and technical matters involving military training and command" (413 U.S. at 14). Later, using a traditional view of mootness in opposition to, not in support of, a conservative result, he argued that the side payment in *Nixon v. Fitzgerald* (1982) prior to the Supreme Court ruling made the case inappropriate for decision.

The earliest example of Blackmun's flexible approach to what constituted a "case or controversy" was the expansive and hardly strict constructionist language of his dissent in *Sierra Club* (1972): "Must our law be so rigid and our procedural concepts so inflexible that we render ourselves helpless when the existing methods and the traditional concepts do not quite fit and do not prove to be entirely adequate for new issues?" (405 U.S. at 755–56). Blackmun also expanded access in the abortion area, both by allowing the doctors to assert the third-party rights of women seeking abortions in *Singleton v. Wulff* (1976) and by asserting in *Roe v. Wade* (1973) that abortion challenges were justiciable as "capable of repetition, yet evading review" (410 U.S. at 125), an idea Blackmun applied to other cases.

Deference to Legislature and Executive

Deference to the legislature can be seen in the distinction Blackmun made between a legislator's exercise of values and a judge's more limited implementation of those values, for example, his comment in *Johnson v. Louisiana* (1972), "Were I a legislator, I would disfavor [the split-verdict system] as a matter of policy. Our task here, however, is not to pursue and strike down what happens to impress us as undesirable legislative policy" (406 U.S. at 356).

This view of his role was most evident in his anguished statement in *Furman v. Georgia* (1972) about the conflict between the death penalty and his personal values (408 U.S. at 405–6, 410–11). It can also be seen in his general reluctance to overturn legislative judgments, which he felt need not be perfect nor complete to be sustained. Courts, he felt, should accept the legislature's "necessary 'balancing' and 'accommodation' of . . . goals" (*Bowsher v. Merck & Co., Inc.,* 1983, 460 U.S. at 861), particularly where the legislature acted carefully, and when judges found it necessary to invalidate a law, they should do so "with the least disruption of congressional objectives" (*Bowsher v. Synar,* 1986, 478 U.S. at 780).

Although "in the absence of a congressional solution, courts cannot avoid difficult problems by refusing to apply the law," Congress was the preferred policymaker, with the "adjustment of interests" in commerce clause matters "a task better suited for Congress than this Court."[23] Congress could also correct the Court's errors, as we see in *Flood v. Kuhn* (1972), where Blackmun said that "any inconsistency or illogic" in the Court's long-standing position that baseball was not subject to antitrust laws was "to be remedied by the Congress and not by this Court" (407 U.S. at 284). At times he even seemed to invite such correction.[24]

Blackmun also showed deference to the executive, particularly to its discretion to limit travel for internal security reasons. He strongly supported the executive exercise of congressionally delegated power—first, in *Kleindienst v. Mandel* (1972), to exclude, even in the face of First Amendment claims, those who would come to this country to speak, as long as the executive provided "a facially legitimate and bona fide reason" (408 U.S. at 770) and then, in *Haig v. Agee* (1981), to withdraw a U.S. citizen's passport. Three years later, however, Blackmun argued in his *Regan v. Wald* (1984) dissent that the president's discretionary authority over foreign affairs had been curtailed, making restrictions on travel to Cuba improper. This deference is on a par with his deference to other institutional authority such as that of military commanders to conduct courts-martial or that of academic officials to admit students or dismiss them for academic reasons.[25] However, he warned against "careless invocations of 'deference' " that would lead to a return to the "hands-off" approach to prison concerns.[26]

Administrative Law: Deference to Bureaucracy

If Justice Blackmun was expected to defer to governmental authority, he did not fully meet that expectation in the case of ad-support for administrators' authority with instances in which agency discretion was not upheld. In general, Blackmun supported government regulation at a time when deregulation was developing. Perhaps largely as a result of his strong support for underlying substantive programs, Blackmun strongly supported administrative authority in taxation and securities regulation and gave investors standing to provide additional enforcement.

Evidence of his deference appears in a variety of situations. He upheld limitations on judicial review of agency action. In Freedom of Information Act (FOIA) cases, he supported the government in not releasing or in delaying release of information. He also did not require agencies to administer massive doses of "due process." Blackmun was not a strong supporter of due process in the context of traditional economic regulation.[27] Where the "new property" was concerned, he argued for flexibility in defining interests before determining necessary procedures. Although in *Bishop v. Wood* (1976), he distanced himself from the *Arnett v. Kennedy* (1974) plurality's view of due process as limited to that granted by statute, *O'Bannon v. Town Court Nursing Center* (1980) shows he also thought that property rights in public benefits could be terminated by the government's removing "the underlying source of those benefits" as long as "prescribed procedures" were used (447 U.S. at 796). Blackmun's due process views were signaled by his statement in *Richardson v. Perales* (1971), a case that tapped his deference to doctors and his lack of enthusiasm for welfare programs, that doctors' written reports were "substantial evidence" to support disability rulings. Showing the inverse relationship between due process requirements and agency deference, he stressed the increased agency work that would result from mandating more extensive procedures, and he showed a disinclination to require pre-termination hearings.

Blackmun also upheld administrative exercise of discretion under delegated authority. For example, in the tax area he often deferred to the commissioner of internal revenue's interpretations and supported enforcement flexibility for the Internal Revenue Service. In *Alexander v. "Americans United," Inc.* (1974), however, Blackmun, "disturbingly aware of the overwhelming power of the Internal Revenue Service," expressed his concern about the commissioner's "virtual plenipotentiary power" to revoke tax-exempt status when "the means to challenge that power are unfavorable and unsatisfactory at best" (416 U.S. at 763; see also *Commissioner of Internal Revenue v. Shapiro*, 1976). Blackmun's opinions also show lessened deference to other agencies in some situations. For example, in the labor area, Blackmun placed a high value on non-interference with collective bargaining and on associations' rights to establish their own rules for membership, as demonstrated in *Pattern Makers' League of North America v. NLRB* (1985).

Federalism

Justice Blackmun's major contribution on federalism can be found in the series of cases on Congress's commerce clause authority to regulate state and local activities, extending from his brief concurrence in *National League of Cities v. Usery* (1976) through his opinion for the Court in *Garcia v. San Antonio Metropolitan Transit Authority* (1985).[28] However, his views on federalism are also apparent elsewhere. One might expect a Nixon appointee to give great heed to "states' rights," but, on the whole, Justice Blackmun often showed support for the national government. On the other hand, although he opposed state actions discriminating against interstate commerce, he supported state taxation of businesses in interstate commerce and supported flexibility of state regulation against challenges brought under the privileges and immunities clause. Throughout, he was careful and thoughtful, not doctrinaire, as can be seen in his comment that "we must avoid the temptation to let 'federalism' become the Natural Law of the 1980's, a brooding omnipresence to which duly enacted statutes are made to pay homage."[29]

Federalism and the Courts

Perhaps of greatest significance among Justice Blackmun's statements on federal-state court relations was his opinion for the Court in *Oregon v. Hass* (1975). Here he told the states that, whatever they did "as a matter of [their] own law" (420 U.S. at 719), they could not interpret the federal Constitution to give protections the Supreme Court had refused to provide. This position, argues Laurence Tribe, makes a state court's "heresy" on federal constitutional law error only if "the Constitution is only and always what the Supreme Court says it is."[30] Quite different was Blackmun's later refusal, in *Michigan v. Long* (1983), to join the Court's "presumption of jurisdiction over cases coming here from state courts" (463 U.S. at 1054).

Blackmun early made clear his feeling that the Court had taken habeas corpus far beyond "traditional notions."[31] Nonetheless, his opposition to racial discrimination led him to insist that federal habeas remain available to state prisoners raising claims of such discrimination in the criminal justice system; he also wished to make it available for parents challenging a state's obtaining custody of their children and terminating their parental rights.[32] Blackmun was respectful of the state on other aspects of federal-state judicial relations. He joined the *Younger v. Harris* (1971) set of cases ordering federal court noninvolvement in pending state criminal proceedings as well as the rule's extension to civil proceedings, but he felt that a federal court suit could proceed when people had been threatened with prosecution but not yet prosecuted (*Ellis v. Dyson*, 1975).

Other values, however, appeared to affect the comity he would require in federal-state court relations. Particularly important was Justice Blackmun's desire to keep federal courts open for civil rights actions. His position on the Eleventh Amendment, contrary to what he viewed as the Court's "long-standing constitutional mistake" in *Atascadero State Hospital v. Scanlon* (1985) (473 U.S. at 303), was that it did not immunize states from damage suits for violation of federal statutory rights. He also strongly supported "1983 actions" both on and off the bench. In *Rizzo v. Goode* (1976), he would have allowed a lower federal court remedy involving "federal-court intervention in the daily operation of a large city's police department" (423 U.S. at 381), and, in *Allen v. McCurry* (1980), contrary to his usual position on Fourth Amendment search issues and particularly on the exclusionary rule (see pp. 90–91 below), he objected that the majority had "disregard[ed] the important federal policies that underlie . . . enforcement" of §1983" (449 U.S. at 105-6). He also criticized the holdings that public defenders were not acting "under color of law" for §1983 purposes (*Polk County v. Dodson*, 1981) and that there was no basis in §1983 for challenging police officers' perjured trial testimony (*Briscoe v. LaHue*, 1983). Blackmun did, however, wish to protect municipalities from punitive damages in §1983 suits and ruled in their favor in *City of Newport v. Fact Concerts, Inc.* (1981). And in *Migra v. Warren City School District Board of Education* (1984), he showed little sympathy with a §1983 claimant who could have gone to federal court first but chose instead to bring some but not all of her claims in state court.

Blackmun also strongly supported §1983 and the federal court's role in upholding federal rights in his 1984 James Madison Lecture. He criticized his colleagues for being "inclined to cut back §1983

in any way it can, short of ignoring the language of the statute or
existing rulings," and he warned against schemes to restrict the
scope of the law, saying any such plan "comes with a heavy burden
of justification—a burden that is both constitutional and historical." He rejected the argument that §1983 cases were "burdening
the federal courts" and said they created only "illusory" federalism
problems. Calling for renewed support for §1983, he pointed to
its symbolism "for the commitment of our society to be governed
by law and to protect the rights of those without power against
oppression at the hands of the powerful."[33]

The Tenth Amendment

Justice Blackmun joined the opinion in *National League of Cities
v. Usery* (1976), in which some saw the Tenth Amendment's revival.
He had reservations about "certain possible implications" but made
peace with the ruling by viewing it as having adopted a "balancing
approach" under which federal power in areas like the environment would not be eliminated (426 U.S. at 856). His reservations
led to continuing discomfiture, which was evident when he wrote
for a five-justice majority in *Federal Energy Regulatory Commission
v. Mississippi* (1982) to uphold federal statutory directions that the
states *consider* rate-making standards and *follow* certain procedural
requirements, a position that simply extended the Court's ruling
upholding the Surface Mining Control and Reclamation Act but
clearly limited the reach of *National League of Cities*.

With this groundwork laid, with little hesitation and none of his
earlier incrementalism, came his opinion for a five-justice majority
in *Garcia* (1985) overruling *National League of Cities*, whose approach, he felt, had been tried and found wanting; efforts to draw
lines between traditional and nontraditional governmental functions had been and would be unsuccessful. Using judicial self-
restraint to achieve a result allowing a far more active national
government, Blackmun said there were no standards to distinguish
protected from unprotected governmental functions that could be
"faithful to the role of federalism in a democratic society" (469
U.S. at 546) because all forced the judiciary to decide what was
appropriate. The core of his position—that states were to be
protected not by "discrete limitations on the objects of federal
authority" but by their place in our governmental structure, with
"the fundamental limitation . . . one of process rather than one of
result" (at 552, 554)—was said to overestimate the states' ability
to protect their interests. If *National League of Cities* came at the

end of eight years of a Republican administration that made some efforts to return matters to the states, *Garcia* came during a subsequent Republican administration far more committed to not merely limiting but reducing national government power. By sustaining national authority, Blackmun helped take the Court's majority on a path counter to the thrust of contemporary political developments.

Preemption

Blackmun generally supported national over state interests in other settings. He felt that congressional policy should have precedence over state policy unless Congress clearly intended otherwise, and thus he found state law preempted in several regulatory areas. For example, in the worker safety case (*Silkwood v. Kerr-McGee Corp.*, 1984), he felt the Court-sustained, state-allowed punitive damages award, much higher than Nuclear Regulatory Commission (NRC) penalties, "wreak[ed] havoc with the regulatory structure that Congress carefully created" (464 U.S. at 259). He felt decisions on how to construct and operate nuclear power plants were for the NRC, not the states, to decide, but found the Atomic Energy Act did not preempt state decisions to ban nuclear power plants because of safety concerns.[34] Despite the states' primary role in developing marriage and divorce law, he found that state divorce courts that treated federal retirement benefits as divisible community property or altered the disposition of federal insurance interfered with congressional policy.[35] In the labor field Blackmun generally presumed preemption.[36]

Blackmun also reached some nonpreemption outcomes. For example, his highly negative view of highway carnage led him to uphold a state law in *Perez v. Campbell* (1971), against a preemption claim based on federal bankruptcy law, that allowed a court to suspend the license of a driver at fault in an automobile accident. In *Wheeler v. Barrera* (1974), feeling Congress had a "pronounced aversion" (417 U.S. at 416) to providing uniform federal law on programs of assistance to nonpublic schools, he found against preemption of state laws limiting education. His civil rights values led him, in *Shaw v. Delta Airlines* (1983), to find state laws—on pregnancy disability coverage—only partly preempted, because full preemption would impair enforcement of the 1964 Civil Rights Act's Title VII, which relied on state human rights provisions. Here, Blackmun used deference to Congress to slough off problems the ruling might cause the states. And when Congress did rewrite

Supreme Court rulings, he was quite willing to find an absence of preemption. Throughout, he carefully examined congressional intent and used a measured approach. Thus in *Cantor v. Detroit Edison Co.* (1976), while finding that the Sherman Act generally preempted inconsistent state law, he opposed a flat rule and argued instead for a "rule of reason" in which no one factor would be determinative.

The States and Commerce

Justice Blackmun became a major voice on state taxation of businesses engaged in commerce.[37] In *Colonial Pipeline v. Traigle* (1975) he stated that, because states and the federal government were now in a mature state of coexistence, states could impose nondiscriminatory and properly apportioned franchise taxes as long as Congress did not prohibit it. This statement foreshadowed his opinion in *Complete Auto Transit, Inc. v. Brady* (1977) upholding a state sales tax on the privilege of doing business in the state and specifically overruling *Spector Motor Service v. O'Connor* (1951). Although Blackmun upheld state taxes that made interstate commerce pay a fair share of government costs, he also held that a state could not force interstate commerce to pay more than its own way by shifting burdens to out-of-state consumers.[38] Any tax on a foreign company's property, however, was a constitutional violation because there was a need to avoid conflict from potential multiple taxation and "asymmetry in the international tax structure" (*Japan Line, Ltd. v. County of Los Angeles*, 1979, 441 U.S. at 450).

In instances where states potentially discriminated against interstate commerce, Justice Blackmun supported flexibility in state economic policy but opposed economic parochialism. Thus in *Exxon Corp. v. Governor of Maryland* (1978) he held that a law that "effectively and perhaps intentionally" protected locally owned businesses from competition from out-of-state businesses was invalid (437 U.S. at 137, 140). Likewise, in *Lewis v. BT Investment Managers* (1980), he thought that although states retained significant police power over banking, "overtly prevent[ing] foreign enterprises from competing in local markets" was improper (447 U.S. at 39). Nor could states penalize companies doing proportionately more of their export shipping from other states (*Westinghouse Electric Corp. v. Tully*, 1984).

Blackmun could, however, support state policy-making. In *Maine v. Taylor* (1986), referring to the snail darter controversy in saying

"Once again, a little fish has caused a commotion," he found no commerce clause violation when Maine banned the importation of live baitfish because of their parasites (447 U.S. at 132). And in *Reeves, Inc. v. State* (1980) he said that during a shortage, a state could legitimately restrict the sale of cement from its own cement plant to state residents because, as a "market participant," the state should be free from commerce clause limitations to the same extent as private market participants. Blackmun did not, however, accept the "market participant" rationale when at least half the work force on city-funded construction projects had to be city residents: in that case the city was telling private firms with whom *they* must deal. On the other hand, he did not believe such "beggar thy neighbor" policies violated the privileges and immunities clause. He took the view that the use of distinctions based on state citizenship or residency had never been fully barred by that clause.[39] Thus states did not have absolute authority over wildlife, yet they could charge nonresidents higher fees for recreational sport hunting. As Blackmun put it in *Baldwin v. Fish and Game Commission of Montana* (1978), "[E]quality in access to Montana elk is not basic to the maintenance or well-being of the Union" (436 U.S. at 388).

Civil Liberties and Civil Rights

The First Amendment: Free Speech

The early Justice Blackmun ranked deference to the legislative and executive branches over free speech values and let the content of speech affect his opinions. During his first Court years, in *Cohen v. California* (1971), Blackmun called the famous "Fuck the Draft" jacket (worn in a courthouse) an "absurd and immature antic" (403 U.S. at 27) and found it well within the ban on "fighting words." He applied the label of immaturity to a flag worn on the seat of someone's pants (*Smith v. Goguen*, 1974) and also accepted a ban on "opprobrious" and "abusive" language (*Gooding v. Wilson*, 1972). Only one year later, however, perhaps because abortion advertising rather than citizen abuse of the police was at issue, he strongly supported First Amendment overbreadth challenges (*Bigelow v. Virginia*, 1975). Blackmun's strongest early statement was his concurrence in *Parker v. Levy* (1974), in which the Court upheld the court-martial of an officer for criticism of the Vietnam War. There he espoused "an orderly and dutiful fighting force" and, focusing on "concepts of 'right' and 'wrong,' " argued that "times have not changed in the area of moral precepts" and that "situation ethics" and the "relativistic notions of right and wrong," which had attained "a disturbingly high level of prominence in this country," were wrong (417 U.S. at 762–65).

In the few early Burger Court internal security cases, Blackmun exhibited a Cold War view of communism, saying in *Baird v. State Bar of Arizona* (1971), for example, that prospective attorneys' refusal to answer political association questions was "reminiscent of the obstructionist tactics" the Court had earlier condemned (401 U.S. at 17). *In re Stolar* (1971) demonstrated his traditional view of lawyering: admission to law practice was a privilege, not a right; would-be lawyers could not seek to come to the bar on their own terms; and the state could demand "what fundamentally is character" before it vested people with a lawyer's "great professional and fiduciary power" (401 U.S. at 34). Internal security concerns also colored Blackmun's "Pentagon Papers" dissent in *New York Times Co. v. United States* (1971), where he asserted that the First Amendment was "only one part of an entire Constitution," which also "vests in the Executive Branch primary power over the conduct of foreign affairs and . . . the responsibility for the Nation's safety" (403 U.S. at 761).

Later, Blackmun made strong statements favoring First Amendment free speech claims, such as his *Island Trees* concurrence, in which he found limits to school boards' leeway when officials denied access to ideas found in books in school libraries because they disapproved of them for political reasons (*Board of Education, Island Trees Union Free School Dist. No. 26 v. Pico*, 1982). In the early stages of *Nebraska Press Association v. Stuart* (1975), Blackmun, as circuit justice, stayed state court "gag orders." In so doing, he stressed that "each passing day [of a direct prior restraint] may constitute a separate and cognizable infringement of the First Amendment" that would be "irreparable" (423 U.S. at 1329). Emphasizing that there is a heavier presumption against use of prior restraints than against use of criminal penalties for speech, he also struck down a city's refusal to allow use of its municipal auditorium for the performance of "Hair" (*Southeastern Promotions, Ltd. v. Conrad*, 1975). He also refused to support zoning measures to control adult movies, largely because the vagueness of the statute in question gave movie theater operators no guidance, leading to self-censorship (*Young v. American Mini Theatres, Inc.* 1976), and partly because city officials' discretion to grant waivers was virtually without control. Likewise, in *Arcara v. Cloud Books, Inc.* (1986), he opposed a mandatory one-year closing of a bookstore as a nuisance because solicitation of prostitution had occurred there. There were less restrictive ways to control the problem.

Commercial Speech. Blackmun made his most significant First Amendment contribution, on "commercial speech," in three major opinions for the Court spanning three consecutive years and several separate opinions. He first stressed that First Amendment concerns were not negated by an advertisement's commercial aspects, but this holding, made in *Bigelow v. Virginia* (1975), may have been limited by a "public interest" in abortion ads, which were thus more than a merely commercial matter. Then, confronting Virginia's ban on advertising of prescription drugs in *Virginia State Board of Pharmacy v. Virginia Citizens Consumer Council* (1976), Blackmun extended the holding: speech on a commercial subject retained First Amendment protections; listeners' and society's rights were engaged (he observed aptly that consumers might well be more interested in drug advertising than political matters); and the state did not protect citizens by keeping them ignorant. His next opinion, *Bates v. State Bar of Arizona* (1977), was his most important on the subject. He carefully limited his holding to fees for routine legal services, but the implications of his rejecting the idea that lawyers' advertising was per se misleading were far broader. He continued to support other forms of commercial speech, including the practice of optometry under trade names and a utilities' promotional advertising of electricity, although he felt a state's ability to regulate monopoly power overrode First Amendment concerns in the case of a state-created monopoly (a utility) that mailed inserts with its bills discussing controversial public policy issues, thus coercing customers to subsidize the utility's speech.[40]

Church and State

Justice Blackmun adopted a position of moderate separation not consonant with the Court's recent accommodationist posture. He also expressed concern that government support could injure religion, seen in his complaint in *Lynch v. Donnelly* (1984) that making the crèche "a neutral harbinger of the holiday season, useful for commercial purposes," had undercut its religious meaning (465 U.S. at 727). He also showed greater sensitivity than his colleagues to the position of minority religions in *Goldman v. Weinberger* (1986), where he discarded his oft-deferential posture toward the military and rejected the air force's refusal to allow a psychologist to wear a yarmulke while on duty (475 U.S. at 525).

Blackmun supported some state assistance to parochial schools while rejecting other aid. His opinions might suggest liberal movement, but perhaps Justice O'Connor's arrival and the movement of other justices, not Blackmun's, explain the change.[41] Although he approved of state-supported diagnostic services in nonpublic schools and therapeutic guidance and remedial services on neutral sites, textbook loans and testing and scoring programs were another matter. In *Wolman v. Walter* (1977) he disapproved the loan of instructional materials and equipment to nonpublic schools because of "the impossibility of separating the secular education function from the sectarian" (433 U.S. at 250), and he felt the Court took "a long step backward" in *Committee for Public Education and Religious Liberty v. Regan* (1980) in allowing reimbursement to parochial schools for state-mandated testing and reporting services (444 U.S. at 662). His concern here that the Court follow precedent provides support for the argument that his "increasing tendency to vote against his former compatriots on establishment questions was promoted more by a lawyerly concern with consistent application of precedent than any change in attitude on his part."[42]

Civil Rights

Justice Blackmun's most notable civil rights contributions were his defense of aliens' rights to hold most types of public jobs and of a woman's right to obtain an abortion, although his support of women's rights was otherwise only lukewarm. Not only did he support a woman's right to make fundamental decisions affecting her own body, but in *Bowers v. Hardwick* (1986) he also strongly supported the right of individuals to make their own decisions "whether to engage in particular forms of private, consensual sexual activity," going so far as to say that an Eighth Amendment issue might exist if someone were to be imprisoned for acting on the basis of homosexual orientation, which "may well form part of the very fiber of an individual's personality" (478 U.S. at 199, 202 n. 2).

His opinion in *North Haven Board of Education v. Bell* (1982) that Title IX covers employment discrimination certainly benefited women, but its emphasis on the statute's "program-specific" aspects foreshadowed the Court's ruling in *Grove City College v. Bell* (1984). His other cases containing rulings supporting sex discrimination claims, *Stanton v. Stanton* (1975) and *Califano v. Westcott* (1979), were easy cases. He joined in striking down laws requiring husbands but not wives to pay alimony, but he still felt *Kahn v. Shevin* (1974), which upheld benefits for women but not men in some circumstances, to be good law (*Orr v. Orr*, 1979). He was clearly uncomfortable with equating women's and men's contributions to pension plans in *City of Los Angeles v. Manhart* (1978), and in *Mississippi University for Women v. Hogan* (1982), sounding like the "old" Blackmun, he was clearly hostile to the gender discrimination claim at issue and protective of single-sex education.

His record on the rights of newer minorities other than homosexuals was at best mixed. He was not supportive of illegitimates' rights, ruling that only a "rational means" test need be met by statutory presumptions turning on legitimacy (*Mathews v. Lucas*, 1976). Although he wrote for the Court in *Jackson v. Indiana* (1972) against the indefinite commitment of a mentally defective deaf mute for incompetence to stand trial, his statements in *Youngberg v. Romero* (1982) and *Board of Education v. Rowley* (1982) about mentally ill or retarded persons and disabled individuals were only moderately rights-reinforcing.

Aliens' Rights. Aliens' rights was an area to which Blackmun made an important contribution and strongly advocated a consistent position.[43] His first opinion in this area, *Graham v. Richardson* (1971), struck down long durational welfare residence requirements for aliens as interfering with exclusive federal power to control aliens' entry into the United States—the same basis he used to invalidate other types of restrictions, including exclusion of resident aliens from state financial aid for higher education.[44] He joined the majority in *Plyler v. Doe* (1982) in overturning state laws denying public education to the children of undocumented aliens. Even though the right to education is not specifically mentioned in the Constitution, he found particularly serious the fact that the state placed barred children "at a permanent and insurmountable competitive disadvantage," making them "a discrete underclass" (457 U.S. at 237).

His key opinion on states' inability to exclude aliens from public employment came in *Sugarman v. Dougall* (1973). Perhaps this was an easy case because the state government barred all aliens from the classified civil service. However, Blackmun's opinion was nonetheless important in demanding that states be precise when differentiating aliens from citizens and particularly important in indicating (in later dictum) that states could exclude aliens from elected and high policy-making positions. Excluding aliens from the practice of civil engineering was also not difficult to invalidate

(*Examining Board of Engineers, Architects and Surveyors v. Flores de Otero*, 1976). More difficult, however, were cases involving exclusion from the state police, the only bar Blackmun thought valid because the state was limiting its political community (*Foley v. Connelie*, 1978); deputy probation officer positions, where he dissected California's "peace officer" statute for its erratic reservation of criminal justice system positions for citizens (*Cabell v. Chavez-Salido*, 1982); and public school teaching (*Ambach v. Norwick*, 1979). The last exclusion case, *Ambach*, drove him to note the law's origin "in the frantic and overreactive days of the First World War when attitudes of parochialism and fear of the foreigner were the order of the day" (442 U.S. at 82) and to criticize the illogic and absurdity of excluding qualified aliens from teaching subjects with which they were far more familiar than American citizens.

Racial Discrimination. In *Palmer v. Thompson* (1971), in an early narrow and unperceptive view, Justice Blackmun said that a city's closing its swimming pools after a court desegregation order was not an "official expression of inferiority toward black citizens" (403 U.S. at 229). However, in *Tillman v. Wheaton-Haven Recreation Association, Inc.* (1973) he did uphold the use of 42 U.S.C. §1982 to invalidate the denial to blacks of community swimming pool membership where they had purchased property. Looking closely at how the recreation arrangements affected school desegregation obligations instead of ignoring the relation as he had in the *Palmer* case, he also spoke for the Court in striking down the allocation of city park facilities to segregated private schools (*Gilmore v. City of Montgomery*, 1974).

After seldom speaking out on race relations during the 1970s, Blackmun "moved to a broader appreciation of the wrong at issue" and moved toward Justices Brennan, Marshall, and White, particularly in the Dayton and Columbus school segregation cases.[45] As the nation's commitment to school desegregation diminished, Blackmun's increased. This was particularly clear in *Washington v. Seattle School District No. 1* (1982), where for a 5-4 Court he stressed local school boards' ability to remedy desegregation and, applying earlier housing discrimination cases, said that decision-making structures could not be altered to make it more difficult to resolve only racial matters. However, in *Crawford v. Board of Education of City of Los Angeles* (1982), a companion case, he agreed that state voters did not act improperly in repealing a state constitutional provision requiring more school desegregation than the federal constitution required, even if the result was greater difficulty in accomplishing school desegregation.

Jobs and Affirmative Action. Justice Blackmun read Title VII procedures to effectuate the act's broad reach on such matters as time periods for filing complaints (*Mohasco Corp. v. Silver,* 1980), and he allowed the use of 42 U.S.C. §1981 without prior use of Title VII's administrative procedures. Particularly significant was his ruling in *Logan v. Zimmerman Brush Co.* (1982) that, because due process protected the right to use state-established procedures, a state's failure to hold a mandated hearing in timely fashion did not allow dismissal of an individual's fair employment practices complaint. He also gave attorney fee provisions considerable scope. Particularly striking and controversial was Blackmun's ruling in *Pulliam v. Allen* (1984) that despite a judge's immunity from damage awards, attorney's fees could be recovered under the Civil Rights Attorneys Fees Act from a judge whose acts—requiring bail for nonjailable offenses and jailing those who could not post it—had been (properly) enjoined.

We see additional evidence of Justice Blackmun's support for civil rights in his views on the litmus test of "affirmative action." Perhaps foreshadowing his position on job discrimination remedies for blacks and women, in *Morton v. Mancari* (1974) he upheld statutory employment preferences for native Americans in the Bureau of Indian Affairs as a legitimate way to aid Indian self-governance and meet the government's "solemn commitment" to native Americans. He then joined the Brennan bloc in *Regents of the University of California v. Bakke* (1978) while writing separately to say that, under the Fourteenth Amendment, affirmative action remedies were permissible "until complete equality is achieved in the area" (438 U.S. at 405), although he spoke realistically about the length of time this might take. His support for affirmative action continued in *Weber v. Aetna Casualty & Surety Co.* (1972) where he found voluntary efforts going beyond Title VII to deal with employment discrimination supported by "considerations, practical and equitable, only partially perceived, if perceived at all" by Congress (406 U.S. at 209). When the Court's retreat in *Firefighters Local Union No. 1784 v. Stotts* (1984) fed the fuel of the Reagan administration's attack on quotas, Blackmun stood his ground.

Abortion. The legal contribution for which Justice Blackmun is best known is, of course, the establishment of a woman's right to obtain an abortion. Here his medical background gave him a firm footing in responding positively to the growing voice of feminism, and whatever agonizing Blackmun experienced in writing his 1973 opinions paid off in his extensive examination of abortion as a common law and statutory crime, exploration of whether a fetus is a person, and development of a tripartite division of pregnancy. As he recently observed, states' continued efforts to limit abortions have produced four votes to grant review in such cases, leading the "other five of us [to] heave a deep sigh and wish we didn't have to go through this traumatic experience again."[46]

Throughout his opinions, we find an emphasis on doctors, including their integrity. His particular focus on individual doctors' discretion led him to strike down laws requiring reviewing committees and the presence of two M.D.'s at an abortion[47] and to rule that legislatures could not make medical judgments about the point of viability, preferred abortion methods, or the conduct of pathology exams.[48] He was, however, willing to uphold laws requiring written informed consent (although not ones mandating that particular statements be used) and certain (but only certain) types of record keeping.[49] His emphasis on abortion as a joint decision by a woman and her doctor led him to invalidate spousal consent requirements and, at least where an absolute veto had been created, parental consent laws.[50]

The strength of Blackmun's commitment to *any* woman's right to obtain an abortion within the *Roe v. Wade* guidelines was nowhere clearer than in his 1977 dissent in *Beal v. Doe*, in which the Court upheld limits on government financing of abortions. In language he quoted when the federal Hyde Amendment was upheld (*Harris v. McRae*, 1980), he went beyond medical concerns to exhibit earlier-unseen compassion for poor women dependent on government financing for effectuation of their rights. He chastised the majority for a "punitive and tragic" ruling embodying "condescension" and a position "almost reminiscent of 'Let them eat cake' " and criticized the people of St. Louis for punishing a needy minority "with a touch of the devil-take-the-hindmost" (432 U.S. at 462–63).

Justice Blackmun's involvement with the abortion issue has brought him voluminous hate mail and even death threats,[51] as well as strident opposition from the right-to-life movement, which *Roe v. Wade* certainly helped stimulate. However, the strength of his commitment did not diminish, and was likely even strengthened, perhaps as Blackmun reacted to the opposition's shrillness and the harshness of efforts to undercut his landmark ruling, and in the 1986 *Thornburgh* case he spoke of being "sworn to uphold the law even when its content is in dispute" (*Thornburgh v. American College of Obstetricians and Gynecologists*, 476 U.S. at 771).

Criminal Justice

Criminal justice is the area in which Justice Blackmun voted most frequently with the other Nixon appointees and where his independence and change of position were least evident; however, he was not irredeemably conservative, and his tone on some matters did change somewhat over time. His conservatism was most evident on Fourth Amendment issues, about which he wrote the most, and Fifth Amendment issues, but less so on Sixth Amendment ones. Justice Blackmun consistently upheld the death penalty, but its application caused him increasing uneasiness. In general he adopted a flexible approach stressing case-by-case development of the law based on "totality of the circumstances," which gave officials more freedom than per se rules, but he could be critical of per se rules adopted in support of law enforcement. Of a piece with this approach was Blackmun's use of the "harmless error" rule; although the rule usually is used to excuse many trial errors, Blackmun used it even when his conservative colleagues abandoned it. As he told lower court judges in *Wright v. Florida* (1986), the rule "was meant to be more than merely a formula to incant before affirming the results of constitutionally infirm prosecutions" (474 U.S. at 1097).

Justice Blackmun exhibited deference to criminal justice officials in several ways. He gave a broad reading to substantive criminal statutes—particularly those on felons' gun possession, because Congress wanted to ban any such possession and no statutory ambiguity was present to trigger the Rule of Lenity.[52] At times, however, he read criminal statutes narrowly. For example, in *United States v. Enmons* (1973), despite his "visceral reaction to immaturely conceived acts of violence of the kind charged" (410 U.S. at 412), he agreed that the Hobbs Act did not reach the use of violence to achieve legitimate union objectives.

Blackmun supported prosecutors in several ways—by rejecting defendants' demands for material arguably subject to *Brady v. Maryland* (1963), by limiting defendants' ability to appeal before trial, and by allowing prosecutors to file certain appeals. However, his position on prosecutorial vindictiveness was mixed. He agreed on a relatively narrow ground in *Goodwin v. United States* (1980) that the addition of a felony indictment after the defendant had failed to plead guilty to a misdemeanor was not vindictive, but in *Bordenkircher v. Hayes* (1978) he argued that prosecutors should present proper charges at the beginning of the plea-bargaining process instead of engaging in deliberate overcharging. That his deference to prosecutors had clear limits was seen in *Darden v. Wainwright* (1986), in which he spoke out strongly against a prosecutor's improper closing argument.

Blackmun also deferred to prison administrators, sustaining the between-prison transfer of prisoners without a hearing. He was, however, concerned lest the Court return to a "hands-off" position, and in *Cleavinger v. Saxner* (1985) he was willing to grant members of a prison's Institution Discipline Committee only qualified, rather than absolute, immunity from suit. He supported prisoners in some §1983 suits against prison officials. Although he joined the *Parratt v. Taylor* (1981) majority in denying a prisoner's claim for only negligent loss of property, he dissented strongly when the Court refused to allow §1983 suits for attacks by another prisoner in *Davidson v. Cannon* (1986). His significant concern over prison conditions was also exhibited when duress and necessity were raised as defenses to the crime of escape in *United States v. Bailey* (1980).

Fourth Amendment

Blackmun's major statement about the exclusionary rule came in *United States v. Janis* (1976), in which the Court refused to extend the rule to a federal civil tax proceeding. Here he adopted his conservative colleagues' basic positions that the exclusionary rule was a "comparatively late judicial creation" rather than a basic part of the Fourth Amendment, that its purpose was deterrence, and that the high costs of excluding evidence would not justify extending the rule (428 U.S. at 443). He felt the Court had to rely on "common sense" in judging the exclusionary rule's deterrent effect because empirical studies provided no clear picture or else were "flawed." Yet eight years later, concurring in *United States v. Leon* (1984), Blackmun underscored "the unavoidably provisional nature" of the Court's decision to adopt the partial good-faith exception to the exclusionary rule—provisional because based on "an empirical judgment" about the rule's effect (468 U.S. at 927). Thus, were evidence to appear that the exception was weakening police compliance with the exclusionary rule, the time would have come for rethinking it.

Blackmun did not join the chief justice's 1971 *Bivens* attack on the exclusionary rule (*Bivens v. Six Unknown Named Agents of the Federal Bureau of Narcotics*). Instead, sounding like Gilbert and Sullivan's "the policeman's lot is not a happy one," he asserted that the Court's ruling would "tend to stultify proper law enforcement and to make the day's labor for the honest and conscientious officer even more onerous and more critical" (403 U.S. at 430). Although he there opined that "other quite adequate remedies have always been available" for Fourth Amendment violations, in *Franks v. Delaware* (1978), he appeared to change his mind, saying that *Mapp v. Ohio* had "implicitly rejected the adequacy" of the exclusionary rule's various alternatives such as perjury prosecutions, administrative discipline, contempt orders, and civil suits (438 U.S. at 169). Blackmun actually supported the rule's use "where a Fourth Amendment violation has been substantial and deliberate" (171). That the rule "served interests and policies" under the Fourth Amendment different from those under the Fifth Amendment led him to hold that *Miranda* warnings, although a factor in a totality-of-circumstances approach to determine the voluntariness of a post-arrest confession, alone were insufficient to eliminate the taint of an improper arrest (*Brown v. Illinois*, 1975). Likewise at the intersection of Fourth and Fifth Amendment concerns was a case involving the seizure of business records, *Andresen v. Maryland* (1976), in which Blackmun ruled for the Court that a person whose records were sought was not being compelled to help find, produce, or authenticate them, despite the dissenters' objection that the Court was overturning *Boyd v. United States* (1886).

Blackmun's first search case, also his first opinion for the Court, was *Wyman v. James* (1971), on "home visits" at an Aid to Families with Dependent Children (AFDC) recipient's home. There his conventional views of welfare—bordering on seeing it as charity, not a right—and his view of welfare recipients, who seemed to him to want benefits on their own terms, overcame privacy interests. Blackmun concluded that the search was not in violation of the Fourth Amendment and certainly was not an unreasonable one. In an opinion not likely written by the "later" Blackmun, the benevolent caseworker was called "not a sleuth but rather, we trust, . . . a friend in need" (400 U.S. at 322–23). Nine years later, and without welfare's blurring effect, in *Payton v. New York* (1980) Blackmun held that a "suspect's interest in the sanctity of his home . . . outweighs the governmental interests" so as to require a warrant (445 U.S. at 603).

Payton led Blackmun to set forth a serious reassessment of the

Court's retroactivity doctrine, in which he gave particular attention to concerns stated by Justice Harlan. Earlier, in dealing with the retroactivity of a ruling restricting courts-martial, he had deferred to military reliance on the old rule and stressed the highly negative effects of favoring retroactivity (*Gosa v. Mayden*, 1973). In *United States v. Johnson* (1982), ruling that the *Payton* rule should apply to all convictions not yet final when *Payton* was decided, he adopted a very different stance: *Payton* had not announced "an entirely new and unanticipated principle of law" and the "constitutional protection traditionally accorded to the privacy of the home" should have led police to "resolve any doubts regarding the validity of a home arrest in favor of obtaining a warrant" (457 U.S. at 552, 561). Later, in *Shea v. Louisiana* (1985), and for the same 5-4 Court, Blackmun found that Justice Harlan's concerns applied "with equal force" to the retroactivity of Fifth Amendment concerns (470 U.S. at 59).

Justice Blackmun supported law enforcement officers' search efforts outside the home, strongly advocating significant leeway for warrantless car searches. He also supported searches that, in his view, did not invade privacy, such as the installation and use of pen registers and company employees' opening of missent packages of obscene films.[53] Blackmun gave privacy interests lip service in car search cases and then set them aside. He first found no Fourth Amendment violation in a warrantless external search of a car or a seizure, also in a public place, of cars to satisfy tax obligations.[54] His principal car search pronouncements then came in the line of cases from *United States v. Chadwick* (1977) to *United States v. Ross* (1982), where he argued for a "clear-cut" rule to aid prosecutors and law enforcement officers. Joining Rehnquist in *Chadwick*, Blackmun took a more conservative position than Burger by advocating a rule that warrants were "not required to seize and search any movable property in the possession of a person properly arrested in a public place" (433 U.S. at 19) and, in *Arkansas v. Sanders* (1979), "that a warrant should not be required to seize and search any personal property found in an automobile that may in turn be seized and searched without a warrant pursuant to *Carroll* and *Chambers*" (442 U.S. at 772).

In two contexts—detentions of travelers at airports and searches of students' school lockers—Blackmun did, however, exhibit qualms over his colleagues' support of law enforcement authorities. His concern about drugs in schools led him to agree to warrantless locker searches, and he agreed that only "reasonable suspicion" was required for temporary detention of certain travelers, but he feared the Court went too far toward eliminating "probable cause."[55] This fear was part of his criticism of less-than-narrow rulings, whether by liberals or conservatives.

Other Criminal Procedure

Blackmun's unhappiness with *Miranda* was clear in his unwillingness to extend it in *Fare v. Michael C.* (1979): because of the "burdens" it would place on "the juvenile justice system and the police," its "rigid rule" should not be extended to allow a juvenile to invoke his rights by calling for a probation officer (442 U.S. at 723). And, in *United States v. Henry* (1980), which dealt with the Fifth Amendment's intersection with the right to counsel, Blackmun quoted the chief justice as to the "high price society pays" for the "drastic remedy" of excluding voluntary statements and added that he would have restricted the rule in *Massiah v. United States* (1964) to situations in which federal agents deliberately sought information from defendants in the absence of counsel (377 U.S. at 280).

Justice Blackmun supported indigent defendants' right to counsel at trial and in trial-like proceedings. Indeed, in *Scott v. Illinois* (1979) he went further than the majority to argue for providing counsel at trial in the case of all prosecutions for an offense punishable by more than six months' imprisonment, not merely in cases actually resulting in imprisonment. However, he was reluctant to extend the right to counsel to pretrial events such as a witness's examination of photographs.[56] Blackmun's strongest support for the right to counsel came in the 1981 *Lassiter* case, where his acceptance of the conventional value of "family" led him to insist on increased due process in the context of termination of parental rights (*Lassiter v. Department of Social Services of Durham County, North Carolina*). Uncharacteristically he argued against a totality-of-circumstances approach and instead insisted that indigent parents had the right to counsel at all such proceedings because of their punitive nature and the very serious imbalance of power between the state and the parents. In *Faretta v. California* (1975), however, he complained about granting the right of self-representation in criminal proceedings, tartly observing that, given the "old proverb that 'one who is his own lawyer has a fool for a client,' " the Court was "bestow[ing] a *constitutional* right on one to make a fool of oneself" (422 U.S. at 852).

Justice Blackmun was disinclined to extend situations in which juries were required. Thus in *McKeiver v. Pennsylvania* (1971) he rejected the claim that juries were required in juvenile court, whose informal and rehabilitative model and unique way of functioning he supported. In the adult system, he thought juries unnecessary at the first tier of a state's two-tier trial system because they were available at a de novo trial at the second level, and unnecessary for extended publishments for contempt because having a different judge impose sentence gave sufficient protection.[57] However, Blackmun rejected the reduction of the jury's size beyond six. His 1978 *Ballew v. Georgia* plurality opinion rejecting the use of five-person juries was joined only by Justice Stevens, and, because it relied heavily on post–*Williams v. Florida* social science research, was attacked by Justice Powell for its "numerology" (435 U.S. at 246).[58] His concern voiced there about the negative affect of jury size on representation of minority groups on juries was also fully evident in his opinion invalidating systematic exclusion of Mexican-Americans from grand juries (*Castaneda v. Partida*, 1977). He supported the use of federal habeas corpus for such exclusion claims in *Rose v. Mitchell* (1979), where he wrote passionately about the "pernicious" quality of racial discrimination in the administration of justice.

The Death Penalty

Starting with his Eighth Circuit rulings, Harry Blackmun, as a judge, upheld states' adoption of the death penalty, but, as a person, he expressed considerable personal conflict over it in *Furman v. Georgia* (1972), stating his "distaste, antipathy, and . . . abhorrence" for capital punishment, reinforced by his view that it "serves no useful purpose that can be demonstrated" (408 U.S. at 405–6). He expressed concern that the *Furman* ruling might result in statutes, "regressive and of an antique mold," making the death penalty mandatory for certain offenses "without any alternative for the imposition of a lesser punishment in the discretion of the judge or jury" (413). Despite that dissent, and citing only it, he disagreed when the Court did invalidate mandatory death penalty statutes. After first writing in *Roberts v. Louisiana* (1977) that "mitigating factors need not be considered in every case" (431 U.S. at 641), he joined the Court in *Lockett v. Ohio* (1978) in requiring individualized consideration of mitigating circumstances, but only because one could not execute someone who had only aided and abetted a murder without considering the degree of involvement or mens rea. Giving the states considerable leeway, he allowed judges to impose the death sentence over jury recommendations of life imprisonment.[59]

The last few years of the Burger Court demonstrated Blackmun's unhappiness with some death penalty procedures and discomfort with the haste with which the penalty was being applied. He was the deciding vote in *Bullington v. Missouri* (1981), which held that a sentencing jury's vote for life over death was an implied acquittal of the death penalty, preventing its imposition after the defendant's reconviction. Two years later, in *California v. Ramos* (1983), he attacked the majority's "intellectual sleight of hand" (463 U.S. at 1029) in approving a required jury instruction calling attention to the governor's ability to commute a life sentence but not including a similar statement about commutation of the death sentence. He repeated his view that such rulings disserved the "rule of law" in *Barclay v. Florida* (1983) when he objected to the Court's failure to find a federal constitutional violation when a state court considered an aggravating circumstance that was improperly considered under state law: "The end does not justify the means even in what may be deemed to be a 'deserving' capital punishment situation" (463 U.S. at 991).

Blackmun's strongest statement of opposition to capital punishment sentencing procedures came when the majority upheld in *Barefoot v. Estelle* (1983) the testimony of psychiatrists who routinely predicted that defendants would commit future crimes. Not only, Blackmun said, could one not square the use of such testimony with the requirement that capital sentencing had to be reliable because it "is wrong two times out of three." The testimony itself, he continued, drawing on the scientific literature to blast the alleged experts' testimony, is "so unreliable and unprofessional that it violates the canons of medical ethics" (463 U.S. at 923).

A Concluding Comment

Whatever the wishes of the president who named him to the Court or the chief justice who once was his friend, Justice Harry A. Blackmun has not been an ideologue but a centrist with a balanced, thoughtful approach. His centrism has not, however, meant that he has driven down the center line in all areas, or from the beginning. Instead he demonstrated variations between areas of the law and over time. He has generally supported national power in federalism cases, exhibiting considerable deference, particularly to the executive and bureaucracy, for most of his time on the bench, although that deference has diminished. Although he has shown considerable conservatism in the criminal justice area except for prison cases, he has demonstrated growing liberalism on civil liberties issues outside the criminal justice area and on civil rights. He started his Supreme Court service with a rather conventional outlook toward the disadvantaged, such as welfare recipients. However, as he realized that the system he had assumed would function benignly was not doing so, he came to side more with the individual against the government, demanding that his colleagues pay heed to problems of the "real world" that he himself had not closely examined in his early opinions, and calling for greater judicial protection of those individuals, even if doing so was in aid of conventional values. His opinions have been thoughtful, particularly so when, in separate concurrences, he has spelled out alternative routes to the majority's result. For the most part, he has abjured hard rules, preferring a totality-of-circumstances approach. Through his deference and measured approach, he can be said to have given "judicial self-restraint" a good name.

NOTES

I would like to acknowledge the comments of Professors Phillip J. Cooper, Sue Davis, and Joseph F. Zimmerman, and Dr. Susan S. Daly, who read an earlier version of this chapter. A longer version of this chapter appeared as Stephen L. Wasby, "Justice Harry A. Blackmun in the Burger Court," *Hamline Law Review* 11 (1988): 183–245.

1. See Steven R. Schlesinger and Janet Nesse, "Justice Harry Blackmun and Empirical Jurisprudence," *American University Law Review* 29 (1980): 405–37.

2. John A. Jenkins, "A Candid Talk with Justice Blackmun," *New York Times Magazine*, Feb. 20, 1983, p. 24.

3. Ibid.

4. "Managing Our Miracles: Health Care in America," Columbia University Seminars on Media and Society, 1986.

5. Jeffrey M. Shaman, "Justice Harry A. Blackmun: The Evolution of a Realist," *American Bar Association Journal* 72 (1986): 39.

6. Daniel Schorr, interview with Justice Blackmun, Sept. 25, 1982, broadcast on CNN, May 4, 1983; Jenkins, "A Candid Talk with Justice Blackmun," p. 25.

7. Commission on Revision of the Federal Court Appellate System, *Structure and Internal Procedures: Recommendations for Change* (Washington, D.C., 1975), pp. A-237–38 (Justice Harry A. Blackmun to Senator Roman Hruska, May 30, 1975).

8. See Jenkins, "A Candid Talk with Justice Blackmun," p. 23, for Yale Kamisar's suggestion of similarity to Truman.

9. Ibid., p. 57. Neil A. Lewis, "Blackmun on Search for the Center," *New York Times*, Mar. 8, 1986, p. 7; Stuart Taylor, Jr., "The Morning Line on the Bench, as Revised," *New York Times*, Sept. 25, 1986.

10. Jenkins, "A Candid Talk with Justice Blackmun," p. 22.

11. The data presented here were collected by the author (data table available on request from author). See also Russell W. Galloway, Jr., "The First Decade of the Burger Court: Conservative Dominance (1969–1979)," *Santa Clara Law Review* 21 (1981): 891.

12. Jenkins, "A Candid Talk with Justice Blackmun," p. 25.

13. Ibid., p. 23.

14. See Stephen Wermiel, "High Court Cuts Back Some, Overturns Few, Rulings on Warren Era," *Wall Street Journal*, June 14, 1984, p. 25.

15. See Donald Lay, "The Cases of Blackmun, J., on the United States Court of Appeals for the Eighth Circuit 1959–1970," *Hamline Law Review* 8 (1985): 3.

16. Harold J. Spaeth and Michael Altfeld, "Influence Relationships within the Supreme Court: A Comparison of the Warren and Burger Courts," *Western Political Quarterly* 38 (1985): 78.

17. *Alexander v. "Americans United, Inc."* (1974), 416 U.S. at 763; *Polk County v. Dodson* (1981), 454 U.S. at 328.

18. Note, "The Changing Social Vision of Justice Blackmun," *Harvard Law Review* 96 (1983): 719, also 731.

19. Shaman, "Justice Harry A. Blackmun," p. 40.

20. Richard S. Arnold, "Mr. Justice Blackmun: An Appreciation," *Hamline Law Review* 8 (1985): 22. See also Shaman, p. 40, speaking of Blackmun's "pragmatist's distrust of ideology."

21. Note, "The Changing Social Vision," p. 717.

22. Norman Dorsen, "A Change in Judicial Philosophy?" *National Law Journal*, Feb. 18, 1985, p. 13.

23. *SONY Corp. of America v. Universal City Studios* (1984), 464 U.S. at 819; *Reeves, Inc. v. State* (1980), 447 U.S. at 439.

24. See *United States v. Enmons* (1973) and *McCarty v. McCarty* (1981).

25. *Relford v. Commandant* (1971), 401 U.S. at 368–69; *Board of Curators of the University of Missouri v. Horowitz* (1978); *Bakke* (1978), 438 U.S. at 404.

26. *Rhodes v. Chapman* (1981), 452 U.S. at 369; *Block v. Rutherford* (1984), 468 U.S. at 594.

27. See *New Motor Vehicle Board of California v. Orrin W. Fox Co.* (1978), 439 U.S. at 114.

28. See Joseph F. Kobylka, "Justice Harry A. Blackmun and Federalism: A Subtle Movement with Potentially Greater Ramifications," *Creighton Law Review* 19 (1985–86): 9.

29. Harry A. Blackmun, "Section 1983 and the Federal Protection of Individual Rights—Will the Statute Remain Alive or Fade Away?" *New York University Law Review* 60 (1985): 23.

30. Laurence H. Tribe, *American Constitutional Law* (Mineola, N.Y.: Foundation Press, 1978), pp. 31–32.

31. *Hensley v. Municipal Court* (1973), 411 U.S. at 353; *Braden v. 30th Judicial Circuit Court of Kentucky* (1973), 410 U.S. at 501.

32. *Rose v. Mitchell* (1979); *Lehman v. Lycoming County Children's Services Agency* (1982).

33. Blackmun, "Section 1983," pp. 21, 23–24, 28.

34. *Pacific Gas & Electric Co. v. State Energy Resources Conservation and Development Commission* (1983).

35. *Hisquierdo v. Hisquierdo* (1979); *McCarty v. McCarty* (1981); *Ridgway v. Ridgway* (1981).

36. See *Wisconsin Department of Industry, Labor and Human Relations v. Gould, Inc.* (1986), 475 U.S. at 288; *Golden State Transit Corp. v. City of Los Angeles* (1986); and *Allis-Chalmers Corp. v. Lueck* (1985).

37. Karen Nelson Moore, "Justice Blackmun's Contribution on the Court: The Commercial Speech and State Taxation Examples," *Hamline Law Review* 8 (1985): 29.

38. *Department of Revenue of State of Washington v. Association of Washington Stevedoring Companies* (1978), 435 U.S. at 748; and *Commonwealth Edison Co. v. Montana* (1981), 453 U.S. at 648.

39. *White v. Massachusetts Council of Construction Employers* (1983); and *United Building and Construction Trades Council of Camden County and Vicinity v. Mayor and Council of City of Camden* (1984), 465 U.S. at 234–35.

40. *Friedman v. Rogers* (1979); *Central Hudson Gas and Electric Corp. v. Public Service Commission of New York* (1980); *Consolidated Edison Co. of New York v. Public Service Commission of New York* (1980), 447 U.S. at 550–51.

41. Joseph F. Kobylka, "Justice Harry A. Blackmun and Church-State Questions: A 'Born Again' Separationist?" (Paper presented at a meeting of the Law and Society Association, San Diego, 1985), p. 37.

42. Ibid., p. 46.

43. See Harold Hongju Koh, "Equality with a Human Face: Justice Blackmun and the Equal Protection of Aliens," *Hamline Law Review* 8 (1985): 52–53.

44. *Nyquist v. Mauclet* (1977), 432 U.S. at 10, and *Toll v. Moreno* (1982).

45. Paul Dimond, *Beyond Busing: Inside the Challenge to Urban Segregation* (Ann Arbor: University of Michigan Press, 1985), p. 398.

46. David Lauter, "Race Dominates Court's Docket," *National Law Journal*, Oct. 7, 1975, p. 1. After this chapter was written, Bernard Schwartz's *The Unpublished Opinions of the Burger Court* (New York: Oxford University Press, 1988) was released. Schwartz shows that Justice Blackmun's initial circulation to the Court "did not go nearly as far as the final opinion" (p. 83) but instead stressed vagueness as the basis for invalidating state antiabortion laws. It also gave more weight to the states' interest than did his ultimate opinion in *Roe v. Wade*.

47. *Doe v. Bolton* (1973), 410 U.S. at 196–97 (integrity of doctors), 199 (presence of two M.D.'s); *Planned Parenthood Association of Kansas City, Missouri,*

Inc. v. Ashcroft (1983), 462 U.S. at 499–503; *Thornburgh v. American College of Obstetricians and Gynecologists* (1986), 476 U.S. at 769–71.

48. *Planned Parenthood of Central Missouri v. Danforth* (1976), 428 U.S. at 77–79 (methods); *Colautti v. Franklin* (1979), 439 U.S. at 398–99 (viability); *Planned Parenthood Association of Kansas City,* at 494–98 (pathology).

49. *Planned Parenthood v. Danforth,* at 66–67, and *Thornburgh,* at 759–64 (informed consent); *Planned Parenthood v. Danforth,* at 79–81, and *Thornburgh,* at 765–68 (record keeping).

50. *Planned Parenthood v. Danforth,* at 69–71 (spousal consent), at 74–75 (parental consent); see also *Bellotti v. Baird* (1976).

51. The Army of God, characterized as a radical antiabortion group, threatened Justice Blackmun's life in October 1984, and he has received other death threats at other times as well. A shot came through the window of his apartment on February 28, 1985, but the police thought it was a random shot or a wandering shot at a distant target.

52. *United States v. Bass* (1971), 404 U.S. at 353; *Barrett v. United States* (1976).

53. *Smith v. Maryland* (1979), 442 U.S. at 743–44; *Walter v. United States* (1980).

54. *Cardwell v. Lewis* (1974); *GM Leasing Corporation v. United States* (1977).

55. *New Jersey v. T. L. O.* (1985) (school lockers); *Florida v. Royer* (1983) and *United States v. Place* (1983) (airport searches).

56. *United States v. Ash* (1973); *Manson v. Brathwaite* (1977), 432 U.S. at 99, 112.

57. *Ludwig v. Massachusetts* (1976); *Codispoti v. Pennsylvania* (1974).

58. During oral argument in a subsequent case, Blackmun interrupted the lawyer to call attention to that criticism: "Blackmun made this announcement almost apologetically," wrote an observer, "as though fully conceding that he alone favored this approach." Letter from Louise Korns, Assistant District Attorney, New Orleans, to Bernard Grofman, Feb. 26, 1979.

59. *Spaziano v. Florida* (1984); *Baldwin v. Alabama* (1985).

4

Justice William J. Brennan, Jr.:
Policy-Making in the Judicial Thicket

STANLEY H. FRIEDELBAUM

Introduction

Of the Supreme Court Justices whose service predates the Burger Court era, none shaped the Court's contemporary role more compellingly than William Joseph Brennan, Jr. It is remarkable that a Democrat, appointed by a Republican president during the McCarthy years, came to exert such leadership. It is no less exceptional that Brennan's persuasiveness and direction succeeded so well, not only during the Warren Court, when his views were compatible with the majority outlook, but later as well. Until his retirement in July 1990 his influence continued, albeit more often in dissent, in a Court less receptive to his emphatic activism.

That a chief justice, by reason of temperament, ability, or interests, may not always place his distinctive imprint on the products of the Court over which he presides is accepted lore. Hugo Black, more than Earl Warren, influenced judicial developments during the Warren years. Yet because of Black's intransigence and insistence on an "absolutist" construction of constitutional language, it often fell to Justice Brennan to serve as an intermediary between opposing blocs. Brennan, the proponent of pragmatic liberalism, proved capable of attracting broad-based support from his colleagues.

What factors and events molded this adept master of coalition building? What elements in Brennan's background gave rise to his unusual skill in the art of decision making? How did he come upon a strategy, however makeshift or randomly planned, that projected an image of flexibility and reasonableness but that sometimes yielded little in terms of specific policy objectives and the means for their attainment? Wherein lay the clues to three decades of achievement in the implementation of goals that, in many ways, transformed the United States more significantly and dramatically than the acts of better-known politicians? When final judgments are made, will Brennan be regarded less as an ideologue and staunch advocate of social change than as an adroit jurist whose philosophy happened to coincide with the nation's avant-garde mood at a historically opportune time?

The Early Years: A Brief Retrospective

William Brennan was born in 1906 in Newark, New Jersey. He was the second of eight children of Irish immigrant parents. His father, who served as business agent for several labor unions after having previously protested the lack of democratic control in these unions,[1] subsequently became Newark's director of public safety. Justice Brennan attended parochial schools during his early years but later transferred to the public school system. Thereafter he graduated from the Wharton School of the University of Pennsylvania with a degree in economics. After attending Harvard Law School on a scholarship, he was awarded a law degree in 1931. A clerkship, dating from his law-school days, led to a post in one of New Jersey's leading law firms, where the young practitioner specialized in the labor relations field. During World War II, Brennan served as an officer in charge of military procurement operations, and his responsibilities again included labor relations work.[2] Yet the precise course that he was to pursue remained unclear despite these promising beginnings.

A reform climate in postwar New Jersey prompted efforts to revise an antiquated state constitution, especially its outmoded and cumbersome judicial article.[3] Brennan appeared before the judiciary committee of the constitutional convention of 1947 in his capacity as an associate editor of the *New Jersey Law Journal.*[4] Indeed, Brennan's participation in the campaign to adopt a new constitution, approved by the electorate the same year and establishing one of the most acclaimed court systems in the nation, led to his first appointment to judicial office. Having secured a seat on the superior court, a statewide tribunal of original jurisdiction, Brennan was subsequently assigned to the appellate division, the state's intermediate court. In 1952, he became an associate justice of the Supreme Court of New Jersey. Brennan's interest in pretrial procedures, designed to expedite the course of litigation, brought him to the attention of Chief Justice Arthur T. Vanderbilt, nationally renowned as a judicial administrator. It was Vanderbilt who recommended Brennan's successive nominations, first to the superior court and then to the state supreme court, by New Jersey's Republican governor, Alfred E. Driscoll.

When Associate Justice Sherman Minton resigned in 1956, President Dwight D. Eisenhower selected Brennan as Minton's replacement on the United States Supreme Court. In part, the nomination may have resulted from Eisenhower's misplaced reliance on the contents of a "conservative" speech that Brennan had not written but had merely agreed to deliver for an ailing Vanderbilt. All the same, the candidate met other conditions that the president and his attorney general, Herbert Brownell, reportedly had set forth. Brennan was relatively young (fifty years old at the time) with seven years' experience at various levels in the revitalized New Jersey court system. Reports on the candidate by the American Bar Association and local bar groups were reassuringly favorable. Probably not lost on the president, then in the midst of a reelection campaign, were the political gains to be realized by restoring the Roman Catholic seat on the Court and appointing a Democrat attractive to the Eastern Establishment.[5]

Eisenhower's misgivings over the possible consequences of a judicial stalemate because of an evenly divided Court caused him to ask Brennan to serve immediately on an interim basis. That decision proved to be a source of embarrassment for both Brennan and the Senate since questions raised at Brennan's confirmation hearings touched upon issues in pending cases. As a result, Brennan's responses before the Senate Judiciary Committee in February 1957 were notably vague. In addition, Senator Joseph McCarthy of Wisconsin, whose stridently anticommunist crusade was in decline by this time, harassed the candidate by introducing segments of his earlier speeches out of context and by making unfounded charges based on innuendo.[6] Neither the committee nor the Senate itself was impressed by McCarthy's diatribe; in the final Senate tally, McCarthy cast the only vote opposing Brennan.

How did Brennan's prior experiences affect his judicial outlook and affect his move to the Supreme Court? New Jersey's state supreme court had developed practices that closely paralleled those of the nation's highest court, and it was a collegial tribunal without panels, whose members, to a great extent, determined its limited docket. More important, the New Jersey Supreme Court, under the leadership of Chief Justice Vanderbilt, early developed an activist tradition and a penchant for public policy-making. The court's

Justice William J. Brennan, Jr.

dedication to a result orientation was, if anything, more overt than that usually reflected in the United States Supreme Court's decisions, even those produced during the Warren years. In advance of Justice Brennan's pathbreaking opinion in *Baker v. Carr* (1962), for example, the New Jersey Supreme Court had entered reapportionment politics, in effect ordering the state legislature to reallocate congressional seats on the basis of current census data. Brennan's effortless transition to his new post also may have had its roots in his close personal association with Vanderbilt and his interactions with colleagues on the state court. Surely the conduct of judicial conferences and the search for consensus in the drafting of opinions were not alien to Brennan,[7] as, indeed, they have been to some appointees.

While Justice Brennan's influence reached its zenith in the last years of the Warren Court,[8] it predictably declined as the Nixon appointees (including the new chief justice) began to exercise more effective control over the Court's agenda. Yet it ought not to be assumed that most of the controversial precedents of the Warren era were abruptly swept aside or that innovative decisions no longer could be expected. To the surprise of Court watchers, Justice Harry Blackmun slowly but unmistakably moved toward the center and, at times, to the liberal wing of the Court. Justice Lewis Powell, though not a replica of the second Justice John M. Harlan, maintained a steady course slightly to the right of the centrist position. Justice John Paul Stevens, the sole Ford appointee, revealed that he could be a maverick, and, on more occasions than anticipated, he joined the liberal justices.

It is always difficult to mark the exact location of a justice on the Court's political scale. Yet, by any measure, Brennan emerged as the leader of the liberal faction during the Burger era. In fact, Brennan's dedication to "progressive" causes became more pronounced, perhaps by comparison with the attitudes of the Nixon appointees or because of a maturing and deepening of his own predilections.

Brennan's brief but eventful tenure on the New Jersey courts helped to mold his philosophy. If, in fact, the New Jersey Supreme Court's record may be described as one of the most progressive in the nation, it is equally apparent that its instances of activism have been selective. The court's major impact has been in the area of social reform, particularly with its much-heralded initiatives regarding exclusionary zoning and school finance.[9] During the past three decades, the range of Justice Brennan's work on the United

States Supreme Court was far broader, though his contributions reflected in spirit, if not in substance, those of his tenure on the New Jersey courts.

Egalitarian Activism and the Court

The most pervasive theme extending through Justice Brennan's opinions during the Burger years is egalitarianism. This persistent quest for social reform derives from the same tradition that gave rise to such New Jersey Supreme Court cases as *Robinson v. Cahill*[10] and *Mt. Laurel*.[11] The former struck down the state's system of financing public education. Before the issue of adequate funding was resolved, the court had enjoined any expenditures for the support of the schools—a draconian step that forced passage of the state's first viable income tax law. Yet the impact of *Mt. Laurel* has been even more dramatic and long-lived and without parallel in any other state or federal court. Essentially, the New Jersey ruling (and its progeny) requires municipalities to provide for a variety of housing needs for low- and moderate-income persons to ensure that each community meets its "fair share" of the regional housing obligation. In these and related cases, the state court has entered upon a quest for far-reaching and expansive social reform.

As a justice, Brennan revealed a like commitment to the positive state and to an affirmative role for government in meeting the needs of the deprived and oppressed in American society. He condemned prejudice and poverty and pledged to eradicate both of them and their myriad causes.[12] In an effort to translate these goals into a workable design, Brennan took advantage of the changing political currents of the 1960s, a decade that witnessed a civil rights reawakening unparalleled in the nation's history. New approaches to the protection of civil rights became evident in an imposing array of cases including, but not limited to, *Brown v. Board of Education* (1954) and its progeny. For the first time since Reconstruction, Congress was prompted to pass civil rights legislation, including the Civil Rights Act of 1964, one of the most significant and remarkable statutes of the twentieth century. It was within the context of this reawakening, complemented by the additional passage of civil rights legislation during the 1970s and the proposal of the Equal Rights Amendment, that Brennan acted on his long-held dedication to equality.

Like his colleagues, Brennan initially embraced a color-blind conception of constitutional equal protection. This objective was superseded by affirmative action programs that recognized color-conscious alternatives, at least on an interim basis. For Brennan a posture of neutrality no longer sufficed; as he envisioned it, nothing short of extraordinary measures could reverse decades of indifference, if not open resistance, to an elusive equality.

Justice Brennan first advanced this view of affirmative action (apart from school integration precedents) in *United Steelworkers v. Weber* (1979). The case arose from a white production worker's challenge to a plan for selecting black employees for a craft training program over white employees with greater seniority. A federal district court granted injunctive relief to the white worker, finding that applicable provisions of the Civil Rights Act of 1964 prohibited racial discrimination in employment. A divided panel of the court of appeals affirmed. The terms of the statute were unusually clear; it barred any preferential apprenticeship or training program as "an unlawful practice." Though Justice Brennan's opinion for the Supreme Court sustained the validity of the plan, he conceded at the outset that Weber's argument was "not without force" (443 U.S. at 201). The core of his assertions rested on what he acknowledged was a "narrow statutory issue"—not with what Title VII of the Civil Rights Act of 1964 required but whether it forbade voluntary agreements in the private sector that provided for racial preferences (200).

How was it possible for Brennan to construe what two lower courts had found to be unambiguous language into an opposite meaning? Brennan's opinion represents an adroit exercise in managing words and their meaning—an exercise designed to uncover, by way of statutory construction, purposes that Congress had not overtly evinced. Brennan assumed a congressional intent to permit affirmative action if the employer could establish a palpable imbalance in "traditionally segregated job categories" (443 U.S. at 197). There was a rejection of "literal interpretation"; a superficial review of legislative history; a refusal to "define in detail the line of demarcation between permissible and impermissible affirmative action plans" though the plan in question was said to fall "on the permissible side of the line"; a claim that the "purposes of the plan mirror those of the statute"; and vague references to the plan as a "temporary measure" that did not unnecessarily "trammel" the interests of white employees nor create an "absolute bar" to their advancement (201–9).

Result orientation emerges as the dominant principle that led to these conclusions. It was difficult to refute the charge of Chief

Justice Burger, in dissent, that Brennan had effectively amended the law to bring about a desirable result (443 U.S. at 216). Justice William Rehnquist, even more pointedly, referred to the majority opinion as a tour de force reminiscent of "escape artists such as Houdini," in which the court set aside "clear statutory language, 'uncontradicted' legislative history, and uniform precedent" to reach a predetermined conclusion (222).

Justice Brennan's performance lies within a tradition more closely associated with constitutional interpretation than with statutory construction. For some, notions of social progress permissibly may influence the interpretation of a constitution but do not readily lend themselves to the exposition of statutes. The search for the legislative intent underlying statutes may not be dismissed so cavalierly. Admittedly, judicial discretion in determining the purposes of a congressional scheme is broad. Yet it is difficult to accept Justice Blackmun's observation, in a concurring opinion, that additional considerations, "practical and equitable," support the Court's conclusions because the problems presented by *Weber* had been only partially perceived, if at all, by the enacting Congress (443 U.S. at 209). It is less disconcerting to acquiesce in Blackmun's closing comment that, if the Court has "misperceived the political will," Congress was free to correct the error (216). No matter how laudable the majority's motivations may have been, the methods resorted to were controversial and questionable.

Interestingly enough, subsequent efforts to overrule *Weber* have been unavailing. Three of the dissenting justices in the 1987 gender-related promotion case, *Johnson v. Transportation Agency*, sought to abandon *Weber.* Yet the Court, speaking through Justice Brennan, extended its affirmative action standards to encompass women in public employment. Justice Sandra Day O'Connor, concurring in the judgment, made much of the need to adhere to the principle of stare decisis in applying the guidelines in *Weber.* Whether a commitment to precedent should control in such cases is problematic. Justice Brennan's prevailing opinion noted that Congress had not amended the statute after *Weber* to signal disapproval of the Court's position. In a lengthy footnote, the Court concluded that legislative inaction indicated that the majority's interpretation was correct. On occasion, Brennan observed, "an invitation declined is as significant as one accepted" (94 L. Ed.2d at 629 n. 7). Justice Antonin Scalia, in dissent, responded that a presumed vindication premised on inaction was a "canard" (657).

The Court remains steadfast in its adherence to strong affirmative action guidelines. Justice Brennan continued to lead in this area, where a reservoir of support appears to have been virtually unaffected by personnel changes in the Burger Court and even in the Rehnquist Court. The prevailing majority seems determined to sustain statutory indicators, whether derived from the Civil Rights Act of 1964 or from more tenuous sources dating from Reconstruction. In any event, Brennan was often able to garner majority support in favor of affirmative action. But it is not clear whether his unorthodox approaches to statutory construction in general, and to legislative intent in particular, reflected the views of all members of the controlling coalition.

Justice Brennan's inclination to expand newfound standards of egalitarianism achieved considerable success in the legislative apportionment cases that followed *Baker v. Carr* (1962). Yet it was not always a stringently applied equal protection clause that served as the catalyst in the decision-making process. Brennan conceded a degree of flexibility to legislative judgments tied to factors other than population equality. He acknowledged, however grudgingly, that a threshold, permitting a 10-percent maximum deviation from equality, was tolerable. But all such deviations, even those considered *de minimis,* had to be justified by a rational state policy.[13]

Justice Brennan came closest to his ideal of equality in the congressional districting cases that, ironically, found no doctrinal support in the Fourteenth Amendment. In *Karcher v. Daggett,* a 1983 New Jersey case, he carried a narrowly divided Court (largely because of an unexpected vote by Justice O'Connor), using a contrived "equal representation" principle derived from Article I, Section 2 of the Constitution. The provision in question called for representatives to be apportioned among the states "according to their respective Numbers." It was this nondescript language that led Brennan to urge perfect population equality as a constitutional imperative. The New Jersey legislature's redistricting plan was set aside as unacceptable despite a maximum population variance of less than 1 percent—trifling when compared with the undercount generally expected in the compilation of census figures.

In an opinion marked by its literal attachment to a numerical standard and which provided little substantiation for that standard in Article I, Justice Brennan referred to the "aspirations" of the clause that "absolute population equality be the paramount objective" in congressional districting (462 U.S. at 732–33). Even minimal deviations were not acceptable without justification. Thus, as Brennan perceived it, the onus of responsibility lay with the state in sustaining any differences "with particularity" (739). Justice Byron White's dissent was critical of the majority for its "unreasonable insistence on an unattainable perfection" in the equalization of districts (766). The application of the one person–one vote principle, he concluded, was "sterile" and "mechanistic" (774). Nowhere was any effort made to address the problem of deliberate partisan gerrymandering (776). Justice Powell echoed the views expressed in White's dissent, as did Justice John Paul Stevens in a concurring opinion (787, 750).

Though Justice Brennan had nimbly applied a rigorous definition of equality in cases affecting congressional representation, he encountered a far more serious challenge when, the following year, he sought to harmonize a fundamental clash of values: promoting civil rights necessitates affirmative state intervention, yet traditional conceptions of personal liberties require that judges confine the reach of government. It was the preservation of fundamental liberties, in this instance freedom of association, that seemed threatened in *Roberts v. United States Jaycees* (1984). Regular membership in the Jaycees was limited to young men; women and older males could join but only on an associate basis that precluded them from voting or holding office. When a state human rights law was used to end the exclusion of women from full membership, the national Jaycees, invoking the First Amendment, alleged that the state was infringing upon "highly personal relationships" previously secured in a number of decisions (468 U.S. at 618).

This dilemma posed a conflict between the protection of First Amendment freedoms and the elimination of discriminatory behavior based on gender. How might a balance be struck when valued liberties, traditionally accorded high priority in the constitutional scale, needed to be weighed? In the opinion for the Court, Brennan declined to underwrite sexual stereotyping, though he conceded that the act would cause some "incidental abridgment" of protected speech. This abridgment, he noted, was no greater than that necessary to achieve the state's legitimate purposes in combating acts of invidious discrimination (468 U.S. at 628–29). A compelling interest in assuring women equal access justified any impact that the law might have on the Jaycee members' freedom of expressive association. So long as infringements on First Amendment rights, tied to objectives "of the highest order," were not overtly related to the suppression of ideas, the regulations could be accepted as tolerable. Justice Brennan noted that associational freedoms were not absolute and that significantly less restrictive means of ensuring equality were not available.

Brennan's choice was an unusually perplexing one—the product of a clash of values that could not readily be reconciled. The quest for egalitarianism, it seems, no longer may be treated by reference to unilateral objectives. At times, the effects upon cherished liberties must be taken into account. Whether Justice Brennan was willing to admit it or not, compromises had to be made if an accommodation of interests was to be reached.

Traditional Liberties and Rights

Freedom of Expression

The extent of Justice Brennan's espousal of First Amendment rights has been difficult to gauge. Has he, for example, demonstrated a sufficient dedication to free speech guarantees as to place him among such absolutists as Black and Douglas? During his early years on the Court, Brennan was not convinced that obscene materials ought to enjoy the protection of the First Amendment. When, in *Roth v. United States* (1957), the question was presented directly for the first time, he found that obscenity lay beyond the bounds of constitutional safeguards. However, he noted that "sex and obscenity are not synonymous" (354 U.S. at 487). The tests that Brennan set forth subsequently opened an era of unusual permissiveness. No longer were there unshakable impediments to prevent the distribution of materials which, in an earlier time, would have been banned.[14]

The Burger Court fashioned a new obscenity policy, substantially modifying *Roth* by substituting local standards to judge sexual representations.[15] Brennan, now writing in dissent in *Paris Adult Theatre I v. Slaton* (1973), acknowledged that his *Roth* tests had failed, that they had created disharmony, and that they did not yield "stable and manageable standards" (413 U.S. at 73). He proposed abandonment of a case-by-case approach to obscenity. In its place, Brennan concluded, "at least in the absence of distribution to juveniles or obtrusive exposure to unconsenting ădults," the state and national governments should be precluded from suppressing "sexually oriented materials" (113). This solution, he argued, though hardly a "complete and infallible answer," would reduce pressures on the courts and ensure freedom of expression while protecting legitimate governmental interests (114).

Among the First Amendment issues that continue to confound

the Court are those raising questions of free speech by public employees. Justice Brennan, writing for the Court in *Keyishian v. Board of Regents* (1967), declared that a state might not condition public employment upon a "surrender" of constitutional rights that could not be abrogated directly.[16] The following year, Justice Thurgood Marshall, submitting an opinion in *Pickering v. Board of Education* (1968), which Brennan joined, noted the need to strike a balance between the employee's interests in commenting on "matters of public concern" and the state's interest as employer in promoting the efficacy of the services it provides. The test was diluted fifteen years later when the Court, speaking through Justice White in *Connick v. Myers* (1983), sustained the dismissal of an employee by stressing the need to maintain discipline and morale in the workplace. Justice Brennan dissented, charging that the Court had deferred excessively to the state's claims of possible disruption in the workplace (461 U.S. at 163, 168). Yet Brennan barely touched upon the permissible range of First Amendment rights apart from the attenuated public concern test devised in *Pickering*.

A latter-day variant of the ruling in *Connick* assessing free expression in the workplace emerged from *Rowland v. Mad River Local School District* (1985), which was denied plenary review by the Supreme Court. In a dissent from a denial of certiorari, Justice Brennan, joined by Justice Marshall, considered the plight of a public high school guidance counselor who, by revealing to fellow employees that she was bisexual, set in motion events that led to her dismissal. Brennan, after noting that discrimination based upon sexual preference violated equal protection, went on to examine the conduct in question. A casual remark to a fellow employee concerning unconventional sexual behavior, without any effort to proselytize, was protected by the First Amendment, especially in view of the nondisruptive nature of the speech. Justice Brennan urged the Court to address "this issue of national importance, an issue that cannot any longer be ignored." Apparently the Court's aversion to considering questions of homosexual behavior, coupled with fears of interfering in public school operations, led to rejection of the employee's plea.

Justice Brennan's views of free expression by public employees, clearly not shared by a majority, carried over into other contexts as well. In *Board of Education, Island Trees Union Free School Dist. No. 26 v. Pico* (1982), a controversy arose over a school board's order to remove books from school libraries. The volumes in question were said to be "anti-American, anti-Christian, anti-Semitic, and just plain filthy." In a suit for declaratory and injunctive relief, student readers challenged the board's action. Justice Brennan, who wrote the plurality opinion, sustained the students' plea, holding that the board's discretion had to be exercised in a way that conformed to the "transcendent imperatives" of the First Amendment (457 U.S. at 864). He acknowledged that although control of a school's curriculum and educational program was generally beyond the purview of courts, the school library occupied a unique position. There, Brennan averred, a "regime of voluntary inquiry . . . holds sway," and the broad discretion that the board exercises in the "compulsory environment" of the classroom does not prevail (869).

The dissenters took issue with the special status that Brennan had accorded to school libraries. Chief Justice Burger denied that decisions about retaining books were subject to federal judicial review. Nor was the Court privileged to constitute itself a "super censor" of school board determinations (457 U.S. at 885). In an even sharper rejoinder, Justice William Rehnquist differentiated the role of government as educator from that of the state in its sovereign capacity. School board members, in their role as educational managers, proceed on the basis of their own "personal or moral" convictions or mirror those of the community. Their decisions arise from performance of the board's assigned functions in administering the operations of a school district (909–10). The board's actions do not proscribe books or other materials for citizens generally (or for students), who, if they elect to do so, may secure them elsewhere. Thus board members are not confined by the same First Amendment precepts that apply when the government acts as sovereign (915).

In a kindred setting, by the terms of a collective bargaining agreement negotiated for teachers, a teachers' union had gained the exclusive right to use the internal mail system of a school. A rival union charged that the preference violated the First Amendment and the equal protection clause. In *Perry Education Association v. Perry Local Educators' Association* (1983), the Supreme Court found exclusive access consistent with the school district's interest in allocating its property to the use for which it was "lawfully dedicated" and also found it to be a permissible public sector labor practice. Justice White, for the Court, noted that since an exclusive bargaining agent had special responsibilities, the mail policy furthered a legitimate state purpose.

Justice Brennan, joined by Justices Marshall, Powell, and Stevens,

dissented, arguing that First Amendment interests had been infringed. The district could not overcome that objection by justifying the policy as an effort to preserve labor peace in the schools.
The state's interest in assuring labor stability was substantial, Brennan conceded, but it did not justify exclusive access (460 U.S. at
65–71) and the resulting chilling impact on the exercise of First
Amendment rights in the school.

Few questions so persistently engaged Justice Brennan as those
affecting the First Amendment and the law of defamation. His
opinion in *New York Times Co. v. Sullivan* (1964) extended to critics
of public officials immunity from suits for damages unless proof
existed of "actual malice," defined as knowing falsehood or reckless
disregard of the truth. Thus libel was held to an exacting First
Amendment test that went beyond previous conceptions of freedom of expression.[17]

In *Gertz v. Robert Welch, Inc.* (1974), the vigorous requirements
established in the *New York Times* case were relaxed. The Court
accorded greater recognition to the reputational interests of private
individuals, who were said to be more vulnerable to injury than
public officials and public figures and more justified in recovering
against offending publishers or broadcasters (418 U.S. at 344, 345).
The states were afforded greater discretion in defining an appropriate standard so long as liability was not imposed "without fault,"
or at least a showing of negligence, and any award of compensation
was limited to actual injury (347, 349). Justice Brennan, dissenting,
criticized the new guidelines for denying free expression the
"breathing space" it requires (361).

An even less demanding test was applied most recently to information supplied by a credit reporting agency in *Dun & Bradstreet, Inc. v. Greenmoss Builders, Inc.* (1985). In effect, a divided
Court placed reduced constitutional emphasis on speech related
to issues of *private* concern (472 U.S. at 759–60). Justice Brennan,
once again in dissent, would now have applied the *Gertz* rule regardless of the public/private dichotomy. Yet he expressed satisfaction that a lack of consensus in treating "idiosyncratic facts"
did not obscure the Court's "solid allegiance" to the *New York Times*
principles (776). Whether the Court's case-by-case determinations
reflect the degree of fidelity to which Brennan referred remains
problematic.

Reassessing the Death Penalty

Apart from First Amendment issues, the abolition of capital
punishment came to occupy a central position in Justice Brennan's

list of unfulfilled accomplishments. A Warren Court majority was never persuaded to find the death penalty invalid as "cruel and unusual punishment" prohibited by the Eighth and Fourteenth Amendments.[18] What emerged were guidelines that linked the Eighth Amendment to "evolving standards of decency that mark the progress of a maturing society"; but these vague criteria, suggested by Chief Justice Warren, referred to loss of citizenship, not to the excesses of a criminal sentence.[19]

A turning point occurred in 1972 when, in *Furman v. Georgia*, the Court, by way of a per curiam opinion, set aside death sentences in one murder case and in two rape cases. The vote was five to four, with each justice writing an individual opinion. Justice Brennan argued that the state did not have the power to inflict capital punishment (408 U.S. at 257). The deliberate infliction of death, he contended, does not comport with human dignity; the death sentence is often imposed arbitrarily and selectively; such drastic punishment has been largely rejected by contemporary society; and the practice has little deterrent effect. Death as a punishment for crime stands condemned, he insisted, as "fatally offensive to human dignity" (305).

In an effort to meet the objections of several justices in *Furman*, a number of states revised their capital punishment laws to make them fairer. Some of these procedural changes resulted in supportive rulings by the Supreme Court, and capital punishment itself was not held unconstitutional.[20] Brennan dissented in these cases. He joined the Court in cases where state laws, providing automatic sentences of death, were set aside.[21] To Brennan, it mattered little whether a bifurcated trial was required by the state, or whether state laws addressed the problem of a flagrant disproportion between the sentence and the crime.[22] Such marginal remedies did not affect the proposition that capital punishment was cruel and unusual punishment—a theme he set forth in *Furman* and to which he continued to adhere.

The depth of Justice Brennan's opposition to the death penalty (and his apparent lack of success in achieving its abolition by judicial fiat) led him to select the topic for one of the lectures celebrating Harvard University's 350th anniversary.[23] He took exception to the argument that the framers of the Constitution did not consider the death penalty to be "cruel and unusual." He refused to tie the clause to a fixed meaning "frozen in time" and confined to the dogmas of the eighteenth century.[24] Instead, he argued for constitutional relativism, marked by flexible and enlightened standards of justice based upon reason and insight. The law, he advised, can be a "vital engine not merely of change but of other civilizing change."[25]

Preceding his impassioned plea at the Harvard convocation, Brennan filed an unusual dissent from a denial of certiorari in the late spring of 1985. He prepared a piercing essay denouncing the death penalty and describing the process and the results of electrocution in graphic terms.[26] In unsparing language, Brennan invited his colleagues to share with him the progression of violence, gruesome deeds, and pain and indignities that accompany capital punishment. He denied that electrocution, or indeed any other method such as lethal gas or barbiturates, was ever humane. He called for an end to state executions as incompatible with human dignity. Singling out electrocution as particularly odious, Justice Brennan characterized it as "nothing less than the contemporary technological equivalent of burning people at the stake."[27]

If perpetuating capital punishment was repulsive to Brennan, the Burger Court's decisions in the area of criminal law were almost equally repugnant. Brennan had difficulty accepting a narrowing of *Miranda* (1966) safeguards and other "police practices" decisions that had contributed much to the legacy of the Warren years. Nonetheless, the Burger Court displayed far greater moderation than most critics (including Brennan) had predicted. In fact, a student of selected aspects of criminal procedure during the Burger years found that the work of the Warren Court was never dismantled and that reports to that effect were "considerably exaggerated."[28]

The Several Images of Federalism

Regardless of the Burger Court's tempered performance in criminal law, Justice Brennan embarked on a venture in state constitutionalism intended to counteract what he foresaw as a retrenchment by the Court.[29] Doubtless the activism of the New Jersey Supreme Court set the pattern and persuaded him to look to judicial federalism, and even to an experiment in benevolent parochialism, as an antidote to Burger Court "backsliding." Interestingly, Brennan encountered little or no opposition from his colleagues, many of whom embraced the "new federalism" for a variety of reasons unrelated to the Court's "illiberal" holdings.[30]

One of Justice Brennan's early references to state alternatives lay in a case that many believed diluted *Miranda* requirements concerning custodial interrogation. In a 5-4 decision in *Michigan v. Mosley* (1975), the Court sustained a second police interrogation of a suspect after he had invoked his right to remain silent. Apparently the second interrogation involved charges not related to those that had been the subject of the first inquiry. Justice Brennan, in dissent, noted that the *Miranda* guidelines were being eroded and that the ultimate overruling of *Miranda* was likely (423 U.S. at 112). Brennan advised state courts to impose higher standards than those required by the Constitution—standards premised upon independent and adequate state grounds. He urged such action because, he claimed, protections once provided by federal law had been "increasingly depreciated" by decisions of the Burger Court (120–21).[31] Justice Brennan cited provisions in state constitutions that could be developed by obliging state judges.

To like effect, Justice Brennan cautioned counsel not to ignore state-law questions where they might be applicable. During the Warren years, he averred, a dependence on federal constitutional issues might have sufficed; in fact, the nationalization of the Bill of Rights had just reached fruition. By contrast, an exclusive reliance on the federal Constitution in subsequent proceedings was said to open advocates to risks that were "increasingly substantial."[32] Justice Brennan's fears of diminished constitutional protections also extended to the Fourth Amendment's right of privacy. Bank patrons, the Court declared in *United States v. Miller* (1976), had no "legitimate expectation of privacy" in their transactions (425 U.S. at 442). In what can only be described as a candor bordering upon disparagement, Justice Marshall, joining Brennan in dissent, referred to the majority's performance in sharp language: "I wash my hands of today's extended redundancy by the Court."[33]

Justice Brennan took pains to assure that state rights, once having been asserted, would not be overlooked, especially when the state privilege was derived from or rested upon independent and adequate state grounds.[34] It is ironic that Brennan, a staunch nationalist despite his state judicial roots, became so strong an advocate of state court protections. But a changing Court offered few other viable alternatives.

If a selective revival of state constitutional safeguards appealed to Justice Brennan as a means of counteracting the conservative initiatives and general tenor of the Burger Court, he never faltered in espousing Rooseveltian principles in economic and social programs. Having experienced near-poverty and the Great Depression of the 1930s, he was not attracted to the notion that major public services could be returned to the states. Brennan believed that the centripetal forces in the economy had to prevail in an age of national, if not of international, commercial and industrial systems. Centralized planning had been the order of the day for many decades, and political slogans and dogmas about a "new" federalism had changed little except nomenclature and peripheral minutiae. Brennan was equally convinced that any effort to restrict Congress's powers under the commerce or taxation clauses was ill-advised.

Unlike Justices Douglas and Black, Brennan was not so unalterably opposed to review of regulatory programs, state or federal, as to favor a policy of judicial nonintervention. Brennan embraced "procedural" guidelines that came surprisingly close to crossing the boundary that set apart the old substantive areas of conflict. For example, he substituted a property right of "welfare entitlement" for a promise of charity.[35] Justice Brennan was also among the Court's pacesetters in equal protection formulations when, in his dissent in a federal railroad retirement benefits case, he undertook an inquiry into the legislative record, the objectives of the statute, and the extent to which the challenged classification had achieved these aims.[36] No longer would a perfunctory rational basis test be the sole criterion of review.

Yet, in the areas that had proved so contentious for the New Deal Court, Brennan's views were clear. He opposed any effort to resuscitate the Tenth Amendment in order to diminish, however minimally, the commerce powers of Congress, or to reinvigorate the Constitution's contract clause as a negative restraint on state powers. His dissenting opinions sometimes conveyed such outrage as to recall Justice Black's antagonism to any suggestion of a return to the "mischief" of pre-1937 judicial decision making.

Few constitutional clauses have exhibited the versatility and adaptability of the commerce clause. Since the judicial debacle of 1937–38, the clause has served as the single most important source of federal police power. Instances of legislative reliance on the commerce power (often not mentioned explicitly) have been legion, ranging from the Civil Rights Act of 1964 to agricultural controls affecting so trivial an event as the wheat produced by a farmer for home use.[37] Like the commerce clause's range, its durability has been extraordinary; before *National League of Cities v. Usery*, for almost four decades, no federal statute tied to the clause had been held unconstitutional. It was noteworthy, if not wholly unexpected, when, in 1976 in *National League of Cities*, the Court invalidated a series of amendments to the Fair Labor Standards Act involving wage and overtime requirements for state and local employees. A narrow majority, led by Justice Rehnquist, held that the requirements invaded state sovereignty preserved by the Tenth Amendment, which, in turn, limited the breadth of Congress's commerce powers. The Court rejected Congress's attempts to displace state powers "to structure integral operations in areas of traditional governmental functions" (426 U.S. at 849, 852).

The language in Brennan's dissent in *National League of Cities* reflected an acerbic style reserved for particularly distasteful occasions. The case was, Brennan reported, a "catastrophic judicial body blow" to Congress's power, a "patent usurpation" of the role of the political process, an "ill-conceived abstraction" with "profoundly pernicious consequences" revealing a "roughshod" disregard of precedents, "an ominous portent of disruption of our constitutional structure," and a "mischievous decision" (426 U.S. at 858–59, 875–78). Yet the Court's findings were neither sweeping nor particularly novel when judged by long-term cyclical developments. And, Justice Brennan admitted, Congress could readily have restored its minimum wage and overtime standards by conditioning grants upon compliance by state and local employers. Brennan was particularly disturbed that the ambiguous political safeguards of federalism were being replaced by more demanding constitutional standards.

A transitional case, *EEOC v. Wyoming* (1983), provided an opportunity for the dissenters to regroup. A state fish and game supervisor had been forced to retire at age fifty-five contrary to the provisions of the federal age discrimination act, which Congress had extended to include employees of state and local governments. How was it possible for the Court to sustain the federal age discrimination provisions in this case when the federal wage and hour requirements in *National League of Cities* had been struck down under authority of the commerce clause? Might the two laws be distinguished regardless of striking parallels? Did the cases lack comparability because the statutes sought to remedy disparate problems?

Justice Brennan prepared an adroit, if not always a convincing, revision of *National League of Cities'* teachings in *Wyoming*. Perhaps the timing for a direct overruling was inappropriate, or perhaps more was required to convince Justice Blackmun of his errant conduct seven years earlier. In any event, Brennan claimed that a lesser degree of federal intrusion existed in *Wyoming*. He accepted the need to ensure the continuing existence of states as distinct entities by protecting against federal interference in "core" state functions. At the same time, Brennan asserted, the principle of immunity was not intended to create a "sacred province of state autonomy" (460 U.S. at 236). Even if the federal law regulated the states as states and treated matters conventionally left to the states, there still was no impairment of the state's ability to "structure integral operations," that is, to function effectively in traditional areas (239). Contrary to the minimum wage and overtime rate requirements set aside in *National League of Cities*, Justice Brennan argued, the age act had neither a direct nor an obvious negative impact on state finances (243).

Wyoming proved to be only a deferring action. *National League of Cities* was overruled in *Garcia v. San Antonio Metropolitan Transit Authority* (1985). For the same majority that had prevailed in *Wyoming*, Justice Blackmun reaffirmed the plenary nature of the commerce clause and returned the Tenth Amendment to its previously moribund state. The preservation of state sovereignty was recommitted to the political process (469 U.S. at 552–57). Justice Blackmun's opinion in *Garcia* incorporated the principles that Justice Brennan had articulated in his *National League of Cities* dissent.

By comparison with the dramatic turnabout in relation to the Tenth Amendment and the commerce power, Justice Brennan's efforts to prevent a revival of negativism by way of the contract clause were notably less successful. In *United States Trust Co. of New York v. New Jersey* (1977), the Court, speaking through Justice Blackmun, held that the state legislature's repeal of a bondholder covenant constituted state impairment. Such an action could only be justified if it were "reasonable and necessary" to serve an important public purpose (431 U.S. at 29). Justice Brennan responded with much of the same fervor and bluntness that characterized his dissent in *National League of Cities*. He branded the majority's view of the contract clause as "wooden" and the reasonableness test as "schizophrenic" (54 n. 17). But this reproof did not result in a reversal of the *United States Trust* case; instead, the Court merely moderated its decisions. Within a few years the Court began to adopt a more deferential attitude[38] as the threat of direct impairment and disavowals of the state's own contractual obligations started to recede. Admittedly, the clause had not returned to a semi-dormant state. Nonetheless, Justice Brennan's strong objections to the strict standard of *United States Trust Co.* no longer

obtained as the Court moved to modify the reach of the controversial reasonableness and necessity test.[39]

The Review Process, Interpretivism,
and the Constitution

Over the years, critics and scholars have examined the right of
the "least accountable" branch of government to review legislative
decisions in a variety of settings. The opening decades of the
twentieth century bore witness to the Court's espousal of Social
Darwinism and the consequent role of the majority sitting as a
"superlegislature." Searching inquiries ensued concerning the legitimacy of judicial review. Some were convinced that the Court
had usurped power.[40] During the McCarthy era of the 1950s,
broadside attacks upon the Court were countered by "academic"
critics who, while generally approving the results of the adjudicatory process, took exception to the means by which they had
been achieved. There were calls for "neutral principles,"[41] for a
return to the "passive virtues,"[42] and for an end to blatant result
orientation. More recently, a renewed emphasis on constitutional
theory has posed elusive issues of original intent, interpretivism,
and the appropriate province of the courts.[43] The current focus
is on constitutional policy-making and the permissible discretion
of judges to move beyond the "intent" of the framers in articulating the Constitution's provisions.

It is the emphasis on interpretive versus noninterpretive scrutiny
that occasioned controversial exchanges between former Attorney
General Edwin Meese and Justice Brennan, although neither ever
mentioned the other by name. Such contention is most uncommon;
even the Court-packing episode of New Deal days never gave rise
to anything comparable to it. The initial salvo was issued by Meese
when, in an address before the American Bar Association in July
1985, he castigated "too many" of the Court's opinions as "more
policy choices than articulations of constitutional principle," revealing a greater fidelity to judicial conceptions of public policy
than a "deference to what the Constitution—its text and intention—may demand." He extolled a "Jurisprudence of Original
Intention," charging that any other standard risked "pouring new
meaning into old words."[44] The attorney general went on to describe the "administration's approach" to constitutional interpretation as one tied to "first principles"; he assailed judicial activism
as a "chameleon jurisprudence, changing color and form in each

era."[45] The object of Meese's diatribes was to prevent any return to the "radical egalitarianism and expansive civil libertarianism" of the Warren Court.[46]

Justice Brennan decided to reply to Meese's accusations with vigor and in a manner intended to discredit the "administration's approach" to the adjudicatory process. Brennan referred to the "majestic generalities," the "ennobling pronouncements," and the ambiguity of a Constitution that has served as the "lodestar for our aspirations."[47] He noted the propensity of Americans to cast significant political, economic, social, and philosophical questions in the form of lawsuits. In blunt terms, Justice Brennan portrayed Meese's intentionalism as one that "feigns self-effacing deference" to the framers but, in reality, "is little more than arrogance cloaked as humility."[48] Brennan reminded critics that the justices read the Constitution as twentieth-century Americans; that the Court is required to play a "unique interpretive role"; that stare decisis ought to be a flexible device; and that constitutional explication must not fall captive to the "anachronistic views of long-gone generations."[49] In sum, for him the evolutionary process emerged as the "true interpretive genius" of the text.[50]

Little more than a week following Justice Brennan's presentation, Justice Stevens joined the debate. He limited his inquiries to the Bill of Rights and its extension to the states. What troubled Justice Stevens was the attorney general's references to a "founding generation," his concentration on original intentions, and his apparent rejection of the theory of incorporation or absorption. Stevens characterized Meese's arguments as "somewhat incomplete" and unmindful of the effects of the Reconstruction amendments.[51] Most strikingly Stevens alluded to the attorney general's failure to recognize that "no Justice who has sat on the Supreme Court during the past sixty years" has ever questioned the First Amendment's applicability to the states.[52] Justice Stevens reminded Meese that any effort to discover original intent necessitated an assessment of the views of a varied group—one that Stevens described as a "rather broad and diverse class."[53]

What emerges from these unprecedented exchanges? Judicial review, often referred to as one of America's major contributions to statecraft, is as controversial today as it has been during the past two centuries. In the clash over intentionalism, interpretivism, and noninterpretivism, a resort to historicism as a serious tool of construction may be little more than an exercise in semantics, of questionable value to the members of the Court who seek to apply the Constitution to present-day events.[54] Constitutional relativism remains essential in the development of a vibrant charter, but it is difficult to set aside criticisms of an "imperial judiciary"—one that reflects a fundamental distrust of the American democratic process and of popularly elected legislators. As the debate over judicial review continues, neither the exaggerated activism of Justice Brennan nor Attorney General Meese's excessive reliance on the past seems likely to endure. The nation has long been committed to a pragmatic, centrist philosophy and to a jurisprudence that reflects it. A centrist Court need not be a passive tribunal; it may and should demonstrate respect for principle and history as well as for contemporary currents and trends.

Conclusion: A Summing Up and Appraisal

William Brennan, long the senior associate justice on the Court, participated actively and effectively in the decision-making process, often from a position of leadership, for more than three decades. On the occasion of his thirtieth year on the Court, and in the course of an interview with a former law clerk, he provided a provocative self-description of his service. Brennan made it clear that he did not consider himself "on the extreme left" of the Court or a majority of Americans, and he revealed his own impression that one day he would be known as "Brennan the right-winger."[55] He claimed that Justices Black and Douglas were far more intense and doctrinaire in their absolutist approaches to such First Amendment issues as obscenity, libel law, and the religion clauses.

In a departure from charges often made in his dissenting opinions, Brennan characterized the Burger Court as one that had not "unraveled the work of the Warren Court" but one that had, in fact, produced the decision that legalized abortion, the first case to strike down the death penalty in a number of states, and affirmative action rulings. If change had been inevitable with the advent of the Burger era, there was, as he phrased it, still "room for the old dog."[56] Justice Brennan apparently never lost faith that, in an ordered society, problems are "redressable somehow by law."[57]

Despite his remarkable record of consensus building in a disparate succession of cases and in a Court beset by a plethora of personnel shifts, Brennan did not look upon his role as that of "play-maker."[58] But, engrossing though this observation and other self-styled appraisals may be, evaluations ought not to be left solely to Brennan.

Justice Brennan became the foremost social reformer and critic on the Court, an astute and avid advocate who was responsible for an unusual progression of precedents in a moderate, sometimes conservative, tribunal. If any section of the Constitution served as his guide in spirit as well as in substance, it was the Fourteenth Amendment's equal protection clause. Brennan's attempts to advance the cause of the underprivileged, of those who seek representational equality, of proponents of affirmative action, and of victims of discrimination were prolific. His unrelenting opposition to capital punishment was a part of the same social agenda, designed to ameliorate the effects of poverty and injustice. In a commencement address, Brennan expressed his views with exceptional candor as he challenged the "establishment" to make sacrifices to eliminate the "legal inequities" in society—to demonstrate real efforts rather than "meaningless tinkerings which do little more than salve our own consciences." To do otherwise, he warned, might cause the disadvantaged to be tempted by the "apostles of violence and revolution."[59]

Justice Brennan was a strong supporter of traditional rights and liberties. However, at times he was prone to make concessions and seek out temperate positions,[60] as he was wont to do in the libel law cases. He was never a literalist or as impervious to persuasion as were Justices Black and Douglas in their defenses of the First Amendment. Brennan was inclined to negotiate and, wherever possible, to join in opinions acceptable to a majority of his colleagues.

Since the early years of the Burger Court, Justice Brennan advocated an increasingly significant role for state judges proceeding under their own state constitutions. But his most recent displays of activism were limited to specific aspects of judicial federalism, notably those extending state bills of rights beyond the scope of the national Bill of Rights. Brennan's motivations were never difficult to discern, tied, as they were, to the Supreme Court's conservative turn. Brennan was a leading exponent of the nationalization of the Bill of Rights throughout the Warren years. Brennan's espousal of an "enlightened" provincialism in the Burger era arose out of necessity, not merely by choice—the product of altered and far less receptive conditions for the promotion of human rights on the Supreme Court.

Apart from a recent emphasis on the virtues of state judicial initiatives, Brennan was firmly committed to vigorous central control, especially in the exercise of the federal regulatory power. He opposed attempts to restore the Tenth Amendment as a viable constitutional restraint on national power. Brennan also sought to preclude any negative results that might flow from a revival, even in limited form, of the contract clause or of any diminution of Congress's commerce power. He was unwilling to approve a return to a regimen of broad judicial discretion to invalidate congressional economic policy.

A thirty-year veteran of judicial maneuvering and conflict, Justice Brennan developed an expansive view of the positive state that served as his lodestar. He never wavered in his vision of a just society and in his willingness, indeed his zeal, to resort to the courts as instruments in converting that vision into reality. Striving for reform within the framework of a remarkably adaptive charter, Brennan regarded attention to social conditions as obligatory in the interpretation of its ambiguous and, at times, arcane phraseology.

The genius of the Constitution, as Brennan perceived it, lies in the accommodation and application of its great principles to current needs and problems. Since his appointment to the Court, Brennan never recoiled from pursuing a myriad of doctrinal routes toward the achievement of imposing, and sometimes eminent, goals. That he so often succeeded in advancing these goals, in a Court not always responsive to an assertive egalitarianism, is a tribute to his personal qualities—his cogency and persuasiveness, his collegiality, his buoyant spirit, and, perhaps most important, his political acumen. Perhaps Judge Abner J. Mikva of the Court of Appeals for the District of Columbia Circuit best captures the spirit, as well as the cumulative impact, of Justice Brennan's long years of service: "His footprints are everywhere."[61]

NOTES

I gratefully acknowledge the support of the Rutgers University Research Council, especially in the early phases of this study.

1. Charles W. Dorman, "Justice Brennan: The Individual and Labor Law," *Chicago-Kent Law Review* 58 (1982): 1004.

2. A brief review of Brennan's early years may be found in Elizabeth F. De Peis, "Justice William Brennan: An Appraisal," in Elizabeth Ferrer, ed., *New Jersey and the Constitution* (New Brunswick: New Jersey Committee for the Humanities, 1986), p. 12.

3. Stanley H. Friedelbaum, "Constitutional Law and Judicial Policy-Making," in Richard Lehne and Alan Rosenthal, eds., *Politics in New Jersey* (New

Brunswick, N.J.: Eagleton Institute of Politics, Rutgers University, 1979), pp. 199–200.

4. State of New Jersey, *Constitutional Convention of 1947*, IV: 201–4.

5. A brief but revealing account of Brennan's candidacy may be found in Henry J. Abraham, *Justices and Presidents: A Political History of Appointments to the Supreme Court* (New York: Oxford University Press, 1985), pp. 262–65.

6. See U.S. Senate, *Hearings before the Committee on the Judiciary on the Nomination of William Brennan, Jr.*, 85th Cong., 1st sess. (Washington, D.C.: U.S. Government Printing Office, 1957).

7. Frederic W. Hall, "Mr. Justice Brennan—The Earlier Years," *Harvard Civil Rights–Civil Liberties Law Review* 15 (1980): 288–89. For a thoughtful assessment, see Edward V. Heck, "The Socialization of a Freshman Justice: The Early Years of Justice Brennan," *Pacific Law Journal* 10 (1979): 707. Interestingly enough, Brennan himself has rejected the notion that service on a state supreme court offers useful preparation for the nation's highest court. In 1973 he wrote, "I say categorically that no prior experience, including prior judicial experience, prepares one for the work of the Supreme Court." William J. Brennan, Jr., "The National Court of Appeals: Another Dissent," *University of Chicago Law Review* 40 (1973): 473, 484.

8. See Edward V. Heck, "Justice Brennan and the Heyday of Warren Court Liberalism," *Santa Clara Law Review* 20 (1980): 841.

9. See Friedelbaum, "Constitutional Law and Judicial Policy Making," pp. 197–228.

10. 62 N.J. 473, 303 A.2d 273 (1973).

11. *Southern Burlington County NAACP v. Township of Mt. Laurel*, 67 N.J. 151, 336 A.2d 713 (1975).

12. Justice Brennan once referred to the meaning of the equal protection clause as "equal protection today." William J. Brennan, Jr., "Constitutional Adjudication," *Notre Dame Lawyer* 40 (1965): 559, 567.

13. See, for example, Justice Brennan's dissenting opinion in *Brown v. Thompson*, 462 U.S. at 850 (1983).

14. Brennan's criteria were applied to strike down a state court's holding of obscenity in *Memoirs v. Massachusetts* (1966). The book in question had been condemned as pornographic for two centuries.

15. *Miller v. California* (1973); *Paris Adult Theatre I v. Slaton* (1973).

16. *Keyishian v. Board of Regents*, 385 U.S. at 605–6 (1967).

17. See *Rosenbloom v. Metromedia, Inc.* (1971), seeking to apply the test to matters of public interest without a political affairs component.

18. The Eighth Amendment was made applicable to the states in *Robinson v. California* (1962).

19. *Trop v. Dulles*, 356 U.S. at 101 (1958).

20. *Gregg v. Georgia* (1976); *Proffitt v. Florida* (1976); *Jurek v. Texas* (1976).

21. *Woodson v. North Carolina* (1976); *Roberts v. Louisiana* (1976).

22. *Enmund v. Florida* (1982). But see *Pulley v. Harris* (1984), rejecting

any invariable rule that comparative proportionality review is required in capital cases.

23. William J. Brennan, Jr., "Constitutional Adjudication and the Death Penalty: A View from the Court," *Harvard Law Review* 100 (1986): 313.

24. Ibid., 327.

25. Ibid., 331.

26. *Glass v. Louisiana* (1985).

27. Ibid. at 1094.

28. Yale Kamisar, "The Warren Court (Was It Really So Defense-Minded?), the Burger Court (Is It Really So Prosecution-Oriented?), and Police Investigatory Practices," in Vincent Blasi, ed., *The Burger Court: The Counter-Revolution That Wasn't* (New Haven, Conn.: Yale University Press, 1983), p. 68.

29. See William J. Brennan, Jr., "State Constitutions and the Protection of Individual Rights," *Harvard Law Review* 90 (1977): 489.

30. A series of case studies emphasizing the cooperative and creative aspects of judicial federalism may be found in Stanley H. Friedelbaum, "Reactive Responses: The Complementary Role of Federal and State Courts," *Publius* 17 (1987): 33.

31. With respect to the double jeopardy clause, see also Justice Brennan's concurring opinion in *Oregon v. Kennedy*, 456 U.S. at 680 (1982). While Brennan often reiterated his support of state-derived rights and liberties, he also stressed the need for a "double source" of security. He warned that the "revitalization of state constitutional law is no excuse for the weakening of federal protections and prohibitions." William J. Brennan, Jr., "The Bill of Rights and the States: The Revival of State Constitutions as Guardians of Individual Rights," *New York University Law Review* 61 (1986): 552.

32. *United States v. Miller*, 425 U.S. at 454–55 n. 4 (1976).

33. Ibid., 456.

34. *New Jersey v. Portash*, 440 U.S. at 461 (1979).

35. *Goldberg v. Kelly*, 397 U.S. at 262 n. 8 (1970).

36. *United States Railroad Retirement Board v. Fritz*, 449 U.S. at 187 (1980).

37. See *Heart of Atlanta Motel v. United States* (1964); *Katzenbach v. McClung* (1964); and *Wickard v. Filburn* (1942).

38. See *Energy Reserves Group, Inc. v. Kansas Power & Light Co.*, 459 U.S. 400 (1983) and *Exxon Corp. v. Eagerton*, 462 U.S. 176 (1983).

39. *Energy Reserves Group, Inc. v. Kansas Power & Light Co.*, 459 U.S. at 412–13 n. 14.

40. See, for example, Louis B. Boudin, *Government by Judiciary* (New York: William Godwin, 1932) and Morris R. Cohen, "Is Judicial Review Necessary?" *New Leader* 19 (1936): 5. As the Magna Carta had been revived during the Puritan Revolution of the 1640s, so an obscure state case, *Eakin v. Raub* (Pa., 1825) (and the dissenting opinion in particular), was cited in the 1920s and 1930s for the proposition that John Marshall's logic in *Marbury v. Madison* (1803) was fatally flawed.

41. Herbert Wechsler, "Toward Neutral Principles of Constitutional Law," *Harvard Law Review* 73 (1959): 1.

42. Alexander M. Bickel, "The Passive Virtues," *Harvard Law Review* 75 (1961): 40.

43. See, for example, Raoul Berger, *Government by Judiciary: The Transformation of the Fourteenth Amendment* (Cambridge, Mass.: Harvard University Press, 1977); Robert H. Bork, "Neutral Principles and Some First Amendment Problems," *Indiana Law Journal* 47 (1971): 1; Michael J. Perry, *The Constitution, the Courts, and Human Rights* (New Haven, Conn.: Yale University Press, 1982); Mark V. Tushnet, "Following the Rules Laid Down: A Critique of Interpretivism and Neutral Principles," *Harvard Law Review* 96 (1983): 781.

44. *The Great Debate: Interpreting Our Written Constitution* (Washington, D.C.: The Federalist Society, 1986), pp. 9–10. Judge Robert H. Bork of the United States Court of Appeals for the District of Columbia, in an address at the University of San Diego Law School, put Meese's argument within a different framework: "[O]nly by limiting themselves to the historic intentions underlying each clause of the Constitution can judges avoid becoming legislators, avoid enforcing their own moral predilections, and ensure that the Constitution is law." Ibid., p. 52.

45. Ibid., p. 40.

46. Ibid., p. 9.

47. William J. Brennan, Jr., "The Constitution of the United States: Contemporary Ratification" (Paper delivered at Text and Teaching Symposium, Georgetown University, Washington, D.C., Oct. 12, 1985), p. 1.

48. Ibid., p. 4.

49. Ibid., p. 15.

50. Ibid., p. 16.

51. John Paul Stevens, Address to a Luncheon Meeting of the Federal Bar Association, Chicago, Illinois, Oct. 23, 1985, pp. 7–9.

52. Ibid., p. 9.

53. Ibid., p. 10.

54. See Alfred H. Kelly, "Clio and the Court: An Illicit Love Affair," *Supreme Court Review* 1965: 119; Charles A. Miller, *The Supreme Court and the Uses of History* (Cambridge, Mass.: The Belknap Press of Harvard University Press, 1969).

55. Jeffrey T. Leeds, "A Life on the Court: A Conversation with Justice Brennan," *New York Times Magazine*, Oct. 5, 1986, 26.

56. Ibid., p. 77.

57. Ibid., p. 79.

58. Ibid., pp. 74–75.

59. Stuart Taylor, Jr., "Brennan Asks the Wealthy to Help the Poor," *New York Times*, May 18, 1987, p. B6, cols. 1–3.

60. Justice Brennan's opinions in such religion clause cases as *Grand Rapids School District v. Ball* (1985) and *Aguilar v. Felton* (1985) have not been treated in this essay. They do not provide striking departures from existing norms,

and their value as precedents is unsettled. If Brennan's usual espousal of personal autonomy was more innovative than that displayed in the religion cases, it never progressed to the point of an explicit adherence to substantive due process. Such a predicate would have permitted a major expansion of judicial discretion in the area of personal autonomy, but Brennan elected not to pursue this course. Indeed, Brennan has been accused of "tiptoeing around" the "central issue" of liberty in *Smith v. Organization of Foster Families,* 431 U.S. at 857–58 (1977) (Stewart, J., concurring).

   61. As quoted in Leeds, "A Life on the Court," p. 26.

5

CHIEF JUSTICE WARREN E. BURGER: A Conservative Chief for Conservative Times

CHARLES M. LAMB

Introduction

Richard Nixon signaled the end of the Warren era and the beginning of the Burger Court by announcing on May 21, 1969, the unexpected nomination of Warren Earl Burger as the fifteenth chief justice. Born in 1907 in St. Paul, Minnesota, Burger was a distinguished-looking, sometimes charming sixty-one-year-old at the time of his nomination. His presence was marked by a rich baritone voice and an impressive head of white hair. A graduate of the St. Paul College of Law (now the William Mitchell College of Law), Burger had diligently worked his way from a modest Swiss-German working-class background to one of the great pinnacles of American political and legal power—the center seat of the United States Supreme Court.[1]

Burger's active political and professional background is key to understanding his selection by two presidents for judgeships on the nation's most important federal courts. A lifelong Republican, Burger identified with the more moderate elements of the party. While practicing law for a living, he worked closely with Harold Stassen in Minnesota politics from the late 1930s until the early 1950s, managing Stassen's unsuccessful bids for the presidential nomination at the Republican National Conventions of 1948 and 1952. He was an acquaintance of several other leading Republican politicians, including Herbert Brownell and Thomas Dewey. (He had first met Nixon in 1948.) Burger's support for Dwight Eisenhower, rather than for the more conservative Robert Taft, during the 1952 Republican convention influenced his appointment in 1953 as assistant attorney general to head the Justice Department's Civil Division. After moving from St. Paul to Washington, D.C., Burger gained a reputation for handling maritime and labor law litigation for the government and one well-publicized McCarthy-era case involving the dismissal of a government consultant on loyalty grounds.

With over two decades of experience in private law practice in Minnesota and two years at the Justice Department, Burger was nominated by Eisenhower in 1955 for a seat on the U.S. Court of Appeals for the District of Columbia Circuit. There he became known as a hardworking, outspoken jurist. A critic of Warren Court criminal procedure jurisprudence during the 1960s, he was frequently at odds with his more liberal lower court colleagues, especially Judge David Bazelon. An ambitious man, who was said to have possessed a particularly intense desire to sit on the Supreme Court, Burger ultimately served as chief justice for seventeen years. Only three persons served longer in that capacity—John Marshall, Roger Taney, and Melville Fuller.

The politics of the late 1960s, Nixon's election in 1968, and the new president's views on criminal procedure all contributed to Burger's elevation to chief justice. He assumed these reins of power at the end of a stormy, unique decade highlighted by Democratic liberalism, civil rights breakthroughs, and the Vietnam War; however, national developments in criminal justice most directly affected his selection for the high court.[2] Given rising crime rates and several landmark Warren Court decisions expanding the rights of persons accused of crime, "law and order" grew into a widely debated political issue. The emphasis on criminal justice during the 1968 election year reflected the concerns of a large percentage of Americans and leading political figures. Opinion polls in 1968 indicated that Nixon was perceived as the presidential candidate who would most effectively deal with the country's criminal justice problems. During the 1968 campaign, Nixon openly criticized Warren Court policy, stressing that a principal way to resolve the law and order problem was to appoint Supreme Court justices who were "strict constructionists" in criminal procedure.

Keenly aware of the significance of his selection of a new chief justice, Nixon carefully made his choice and took pains to explain it publicly. The president viewed Burger as a so-called strict constructionist who would "apply" the law, not broadly "legislate" social policy. He told reporters that Burger had authored opinions,

Chief Justice Warren E. Burger

speeches, and articles on criminal procedure that expressed "the minority view of the Supreme Court. It happens to be my view," Nixon observed.[3] He expected Burger to interpret constitutional rights narrowly, particularly those designed to protect persons accused of crime. Thus the president must have grown increasingly disappointed over the years, as Burger and his three other appointees—Blackmun, Powell, and Rehnquist—never brought about a "constitutional counter-revolution."[4] So much for best-laid schemes, just as Eisenhower had learned after choosing Warren and Brennan for the Court. In most respects Burger lived up to his law and order billing. But *Miranda v. Arizona* (1966) and other watershed criminal procedure decisions from the Warren era, though whittled back, survived Burger's tenure.

From the announcement of Burger's nomination through his Senate confirmation, his selection was eagerly scrutinized. The press characterized the nominee as a conservative, strict constructionist judge. During the Judiciary Committee hearings, the questioning was friendly, consuming less than two hours. The American Bar Association (ABA) gave Burger a "highly acceptable" rating, and correspondence to the committee on the nomination was overwhelmingly positive. The hearings focused on Burger's views on constitutional interpretation by Supreme Court justices. Several senators referred to his strict constructionist tendencies; others spoke of his "judicial restraint." Very quickly, the committee unanimously approved Burger's nomination, although a few liberals expressed a lack of enthusiasm for it. Six days later the Senate completed deliberations with a 74-to-3 vote on the floor. So, when compared to Rehnquist's confirmation as chief justice in 1986, or the ill-fated Bork nomination in 1987, Burger experienced virtually no political opposition from within or outside the Senate.

What the nation would get was a conservative chief for conservative times—a man who deferred to executive rather than legislative or judicial power and who decided overwhelmingly against civil liberties claims during a political era dominated by Richard Nixon and Ronald Reagan.[5] For seventeen years Burger labored long hours carrying out the responsibilities of chief justice, regularly being distracted from opinion writing by his ceremonial roles and his intense interest in the legal profession and judicial administration.[6] Yet, despite diligence and energy, he never displayed the intellectual or leadership qualities of his extraordinarily gifted predecessor, Earl Warren. Nor was Burger a productive opinion writer. Table 1.6 indicates that he authored about fifteen majority opinions per term, roughly the Court average for 1969 through 1985, and that he wrote comparatively few concurring and dissenting opinions. Although one would expect a chief justice to dissent less frequently than most of his colleagues in order to control opinion assignments, Burger authored fewer dissenting opinions than any other justice, on the average, when all seventeen years are combined. Hence, when the average total number of opinions (majority, concurring, and dissenting) for each justice is calculated from Table 1.6, the figures show that he ranked as the least productive opinion writer during his years on the Court.

Although not a highly productive justice, Burger was highly conservative, as Tables 1.8, 1.9, and 1.10 document. A member of the Court's conservative voting bloc in civil liberties issues from start to finish, he voted against civil liberties claims 62 to 85 percent of the time between the 1969 and 1985 terms. During these years he also voted against the economic liberal position in 53 to 100 percent of all nonunanimous economic decisions handed down with full opinion. His overall voting agreement was highest over time with Rehnquist, the Court's most conservative member, followed by Justices O'Connor, Powell, White, and Stewart. The chief and Justice Blackmun, who were lifelong friends, saw eye-to-eye for several years, but their alliance grew uneasy as Blackmun became more liberal after the 1976 term. Burger never consistently agreed with liberal Justices Brennan, Marshall, and Douglas.[7] At retirement he remained the second most conservative Burger Court justice.

Given Burger's role as a conservative chief justice during the Nixon-Reagan era, these were probably not only rewarding years professionally for him but also years in which he was comfortable with major political trends. And his retirement on June 17, 1986, was a politically important event. Its timing afforded a very conservative lame-duck Republican president ample time to replace Burger with a younger, brighter, more conservative conservative. Reagan's promotion of Rehnquist to chief justice, combined with his selection of Antonin Scalia as associate justice, set the stage for a more conservative Court than that inherited by Burger. Powell's retirement in 1987, and Reagan's eventual choice of Anthony Kennedy to fill his shoes, may have ensured the nation its most conservative Supreme Court in four decades or more.

Powers of Government

The allocation of constitutional power among the three branches of government has always been a most fundamental aspect of

American politics and law. Probably reflecting a personal need to lead the Court and to leave his mark on constitutional jurisprudence, Burger self-assigned several historic decisions on the individual branches and separation of powers. It becomes apparent from reading these cases that no one coherent, overarching philosophy of governmental power consistently guided his decision making. It is equally apparent that the chief deferred more to the exercise of executive rather than legislative power, and more to the exercise of legislative rather than judicial power. This was in contrast to the Warren Court liberals and may be consonant with Burger's image as an advocate of restraint. Yet, although strands of a restraint outlook periodically emerged from his decisions, in many cases they did not, and, in any event, those strands certainly never fit together into a philosophy for Burger as they did for Frankfurter or Holmes.

Legislative Power

Burger will be remembered for a handful of decisions on separation of powers and, secondarily, for decisions on legislative immunity. In the former area he wrote for the Court in *Bowsher v. Synar* (1986), striking down a major provision of the Balanced Budget and Emergency Deficit Control Act of 1985 (the Gramm-Rudman-Hollings Act), which sought to control the growth of the federal budget deficit. Burger found that the provision violated the doctrine of separation of powers because it assigned to the comptroller general, an agent of Congress, functions that properly belonged to the executive branch. Burger's most memorable decision on congressional power, though, occurred in *INS v. Chadha* (1983).

A cardinal trait of twentieth-century American politics has been the enormous growth in the power of the executive branch since the Great Depression. After 1932, to offset this trend, some form of legislative veto provision was included in over two hundred federal statutes. Typically these provisions permitted Congress to reject an administrative agency's rules or regulations within a specified time, thereby bypassing a presidential check on congressional action. Understandably, the legislative veto emerged as a source of substantial friction between the executive and legislative branches; presidents normally took the position that the legislative veto was an unconstitutional restriction on executive power.

The Court confronted the constitutionality of the legislative veto in *Chadha*, where Burger's majority opinion announced that the veto provision of the Immigration and Nationality Act was un-constitutional. In his typically straightforward manner, the chief explained that Article I establishes a bicameral legislature, that a majority of each house must approve of all laws passed, and that the president must be presented with, and have an opportunity to approve or disapprove, all legislation before it becomes law. That process was imperative to the framers of the Constitution and is fundamental to the concept of separation of powers. Bicameralism and the presidential veto were adopted by the framers, Burger argued, to ensure that statutes were not enacted without full and careful consideration by nationally elected officials.

Yet a one-house veto was involved in *Chadha*, and the president was afforded no opportunity to overrule Congress's action. Be-lieving that Congress's veto in *Chadha* was in effect legislation, Burger declared that any future congressional veto must be ap-proved by both the Senate and the House and then be forwarded to the president for approval or disapproval. Although the legis-lative veto might be "a convenient shortcut," the framers never intended or foresaw this shortcut. "There is no support in the Constitution or decisions of this Court," wrote Burger, "for the proposition that the cumbersomeness and delays often encountered in complying with explicit Constitutional standards may be avoided, either by the Congress or by the President. . . . With all the obvious flaws of delay, untidiness, and potential for abuse, we have not yet found a better way to preserve freedom than by making the ex-ercise of power subject to the carefully crafted restraints spelled out in the Constitution" (462 U.S. at 958–59).

Ultimately, Burger's opinion in *Chadha* is significant because it ostensibly weakened congressional oversight and potentially al-tered the relationship between the president and Congress in an era when many observers called for greater legislative power and more checks on the executive establishment. Beyond that, it must be viewed as an activist decision since, by implication, it invalidated provisions in numerous federal statutes. This led Justice White to emphasize in dissent "the destructive scope of the Court's holding," noting that "[t]oday's decision strikes down in one fell swoop pro-visions in more laws enacted by Congress than the Court has cumulatively invalidated in its history" (462 U.S. at 1002).

Receiving far less public attention than *Chadha* were Burger's opinions in a group of divided cases that turned on the meaning of the speech or debate clause of Article I, Section 6. That clause, which guarantees that members of Congress are immune from

lawsuits for statements made in an official capacity, concerns sep-
aration-of-powers protections for Congress rather than separation-
of-powers limitations. It was designed to help ensure legislative
independence in a system of separation of powers.[8] Legislative
immunity was intended to protect members of Congress from
executive branch intimidation or from being held accountable
before a hostile judiciary. Burger's writings on the speech or debate
clause indicate his penchant for construing congressional immunity
narrowly, unlike his more liberal colleagues. During an era of
American politics when many observers were seriously troubled
about the growth of executive power relative to that of the legislature, these opinions symbolized the chief justice's greater concern with political abuses by members of Congress than with legislative independence and power. In light of the legal doctrine he
advanced for the Court majority in these cases, and the fact that
the Court has handed down relatively few speech or debate clause
decisions throughout its history, Burger carved out a niche for
himself in this area of American constitutional law. Though none
of these decisions, when taken individually, is nearly as historic as
Chadha, taken collectively they tell of Burger's conceptions of legislative immunity and separation of powers.

United States v. Brewster (1972) illustrates the chief justice's interpretation of the speech or debate clause. In *Brewster,* the Court
ruled that the clause did not protect a member of Congress from
prosecution for accepting a bribe to behave a particular way on
legislation. To Burger, the clause was designed not "simply for the
personal or private benefit of Members of Congress, but to protect
the integrity of the legislative process by insuring the independence
of individual legislators" (408 U.S. at 507). After presenting a
lengthy examination of the historical interpretation of the speech
or debate clause, he concluded that the government may prosecute
a member of Congress under a criminal statute if a case does not
rest on legislative acts or a congressman's motives in performing
those acts.

So ruling, Burger drew a sharp distinction between legislative
and political acts by members of Congress—a distinction important
to the evolving interpretation of the speech or debate clause. A
legislative act, he emphasized, is one that relates to business before
Congress and is constitutionally protected, but political acts include
a broad variety of activities not legislative in nature and not protected. Although members of Congress cannot be prosecuted for
their legislative acts, they are not immune from prosecution for

political or nonlegislative acts, even if these are unquestionably related to the legislative process, including "a wide range of legitimate 'errands' performed for constituents, the making of appointments with Government agencies, assistance in securing Government contracts, preparing so-called 'news letters' to constituents, news releases, and speeches delivered outside the Congress" (408 U.S. at 512). Bribery is a political act, falling outside the immunity afforded by the Constitution, and the chief justice did "not think it sound or wise, simply out of an abundance of caution to doubly insure legislative independence, to extend the privilege beyond its intended scope, its literal language, and its history, to include all things in any way related to the legislative process" (500).

Having advanced this legislative/political distinction, Burger had laid the constitutional foundation for *Hutchinson v. Proxmire* (1979), in which the Court ruled that the protections of the speech or debate clause do not extend to a United States Senator being sued for libel because of statements made in a congressional press release or newsletter. Narrowly construing the clause again, Burger's majority opinion argued that the clause was never meant to create complete immunity from lawsuits in the case of defamatory comments by members of Congress made outside actual congressional chambers; the only speech protected is that which occurs within a legislative proceeding. The chief reasoned that "[a] speech by Proxmire in the Senate would be wholly immune and would be available to other members of Congress and the public in the Congressional Record. But neither the newsletters nor the press release was 'essential to the deliberations of the Senate' and neither was part of the deliberative process" (443 U.S. at 130). Even though newsletters and press releases help to inform constituents and members of Congress, Burger insisted that they are "not a part of the legislative function or the deliberations that make up the legislative process" (133). Thus, he once more confidently advanced the notion that activities outside the halls of Congress are not an essential part of the legislative process. Critics quickly pointed out that Burger's decision negatively affected the public's right to know and reflected a further retrenchment of the scope of the speech or debate privilege—a narrowing trend that had become evident earlier in *Gravel v. United States* (1972), *Doe v. McMillan* (1973), and *Brewster.*[9]

Although holding that the speech or debate clause prohibits evidence of legislative acts from being introduced in the prosecution of a member of Congress for bribery, *United States v. Helstoski*

(1979) further suggests the chief's propensity to interpret the protections of the clause narrowly. His majority opinion acknowledged that the clause prohibits references in such a prosecution to a congressman's past legislative acts and inquiries into the motivation for those acts. Because Helstoski had not explicitly and unequivocally waived his privilege, the government could not introduce evidence pertaining to his legislative acts. However, extending the distinction between legislative and political acts, Burger stated that "it is clear from the language of the Clause that protection extends only to an act that has already been performed. A promise to deliver a speech, to vote, or to solicit other votes at some future date is not 'speech or debate.' Likewise, a *promise* to introduce a bill is not a legislative act" (442 U.S. at 490). While Helstoski was successful on appeal, the chief justice's opinion may not bode well for members of Congress who seek protection in future cases under Article I, Section 6.

These speech or debate clause opinions collectively paint the portrait of a judge narrowly reading the Constitution and one with a greater concern for political abuse than legislative independence. Burger's majority opinion in *Eastland v. United States Servicemen's Fund* (1975), by contrast, shows his willingness to reconsider the clause's traditional meaning when an internal security investigation is involved. In *Eastland*, the Senate Subcommittee on Internal Security, chaired by James Eastland, had subpoenaed the bank records of the U.S. Servicemen's Fund, which was being investigated for providing forums of dissent for American military personnel during the Vietnam War. The Servicemen's Fund filed suit to enjoin enforcement of the subpoena. Burger never reached the claim that the subpoena had a chilling effect on First Amendment rights but instead ruled that complete immunity extended to subcommittee members and their aides because congressional investigations fall within the "legitimate legislative sphere." Specifically, the power to investigate through a compulsory process and to issue subpoenas is essential to Congress's power to investigate, and an inquiry into the sources of money used for activities that might undermine military morale is a legitimate congressional task.

Burger's potential contribution to constitutional law in *Eastland* rests mainly in his suggestion that judicial review is not available in cases where actions taken by Congress or its committees are "essential to legislating" and where review by the courts delays or disrupts the legislative process. As emphasized by commentators, this novel idea plainly departed from past constitutional interpretation; no decision had previously held that the personal immunity provided congressmen under the clause also protected the exercise of congressional power from judicial review.[10] Only time will tell whether the chief's unique views will find life in future jurisprudence.

Executive Power

During a typical term of the Supreme Court, a fairly small proportion of the Court's decisions directly address the subject of executive power. Still, an examination of the Burger Court's decisions in this area indicates that the chief justice was prone to defer to the presidency and the executive branch. In *Schick v. Reed* (1974), Burger announced that the only limits on the president's power to pardon are those stated in the Constitution. In *Nixon v. Fitzgerald* (1982), where the Court held that the president has absolute immunity from damages in civil cases for his official acts, Burger concurred to point out that "the needs of a system of government sometimes must outweigh the rights of individuals to collect damages" (457 U.S. at 759). The chief justice deferred to the president in matters of foreign affairs as well. When President Nixon alleged that the publication of the Pentagon Papers would be detrimental to the national interest, Burger's dissent in *New York Times Co. v. United States* (1971) emphasized that the majority was acting too hastily in permitting publication and joined Justice Harlan's dissent, which broadly construed the president's inherent powers in foreign affairs and narrowly construed the judicial branch's function in cases challenging presidential foreign policy. Additionally, Burger wrote the majority opinion in *Haig v. Agee* (1981), ruling that the secretary of state may revoke a citizen's passport under statutory law to protect national security, and he joined the majority in *Regan v. Wald* (1984), upholding an executive-branch prohibition on travel to Cuba.

While some of these decisions may have staying power in the field of constitutional law, undoubtedly Burger will be better remembered for his first major opinion on the presidency: the much-heralded case of *United States v. Nixon* (1974). Although this case was a resounding defeat for Nixon personally, emphatically demonstrating that "law and order" can cut more than one way, it nevertheless deferred in part to the presidency by recognizing an executive privilege—a president's right to withhold certain information—for the first time in Supreme Court jurisprudence. It is important to recount briefly the politics permeating the case; the chief justice's opinion hardly underscores them.

During the Watergate scandal, Richard Nixon faced the imminent threat of impeachment because of the illegal cover-up of the Watergate break-in. On June 17, 1972, workers for the Committee to Re-elect the President were caught breaking into the headquarters of the Democratic National Committee, located in the Watergate apartment complex in Washington, D.C., in an effort to steal information that might assist Nixon's re-election campaign. Senate hearings into the break-in suggested that the president might have known of these illegal activities and revealed the existence of taped Oval Office conversations that might shed light on the ongoing criminal investigations. The problem, of course, was obtaining the tapes, and the president claimed executive privilege in an attempt to conceal his own involvement. After various political and legal developments, Special Watergate Prosecutor Archibald Cox subpoenaed some of the tapes for use in grand jury proceedings and was fired as an executive branch subordinate when he refused to accept summaries of the tapes instead of the originals.

Support for Nixon's impeachment gained substantial momentum across the political spectrum as a result of Cox's firing. The new special prosecutor, Leon Jaworski, complicated Nixon's troubled life even further in 1974 by securing a subpoena for other tapes and documents necessary for the trial of the Watergate conspirators. Some two years after the break-in, after being named by a grand jury as an unindicted coconspirator, Nixon once more refused to release the actual tapes, providing edited transcripts instead. His attorney insisted that the case was nonjusticiable because it was an intra-executive branch dispute between Nixon and the special prosecutor and, more importantly, that the judiciary could not review a chief executive's assertion of executive privilege. The district court ruled against Nixon, and the controversy was appealed to the Supreme Court to force the release of the original tapes and documents.[11]

According to some reports, Chief Justice Burger initially defended Nixon in private, opposed the Court taking the dispute, and experienced problems in exercising leadership in the case.[12] Yet he ultimately self-assigned the 8-0 opinion, Rehnquist not participating. In ruling against the president who appointed him, Burger's opinion reflected little of the excitement and drama swirling so forcefully around the entire controversy. After addressing whether the Supreme Court could in fact hear the case (procedural issues relating to the appeal and requirements for a subpoena *duces tecum*), Burger concluded that the attorney general had delegated to the special prosecutor unique authority to conduct a criminal investigation. Indeed, the special prosecutor was given "explicit power to contest the invocation of executive privilege in the process of seeking evidence deemed relevant to the performance of these specially delegated duties. . . . So long as this regulation is extant it has the force of law" (418 U.S. at 695). Under these circumstances, the special prosecutor possessed the legal authority to contest Nixon's claims of executive privilege; the special prosecutor could only be removed by the attorney general with the consent of Congress; and the Supreme Court could properly resolve a dispute that was part of a federal criminal prosecution in which the special prosecutor sought relevant evidence that the president refused to provide.

More crucial constitutional issues revolved around Nixon's assertions that the doctrine of separation of powers precluded the courts from reviewing his claim of executive privilege and that the privilege was absolute. The chief justice rejected both arguments. On the first, Burger observed that although each branch may initially interpret the Constitution in carrying out its responsibilities, the courts must ultimately determine what the Constitution means. The judiciary's role of having the final say-so in constitutional interpretation, he wrote, "can no more be shared with the Executive Branch than the Chief Executive, for example, can share with the Judiciary the veto power, or the Congress share with the Judiciary the power to override a Presidential veto. Any other conclusion would be contrary to the basic concept of separation of powers and the checks and balances that flow from the scheme of a tripartite government" (418 U.S. at 704).

Significantly, in deference to the executive, Burger's opinion for the first time bestowed Supreme Court recognition of a "presumptive privilege" against disclosure. Such a privilege, according to Burger, derives from the enumerated powers in Article II and is necessary to promote confidentiality and candor in the presidential decision-making process. Equally significant, however, he rejected Nixon's contention that executive privilege is absolute. An absolute privilege in a criminal prosecution would interfere with the judiciary's responsibility to do justice. The president's claim of executive privilege in this case, therefore, had to give way to the obvious need for evidence in a criminal proceeding. This was especially true since the unqualified privilege asserted by Nixon was based "on no more than a generalized claim of the public interest in confidentiality of nonmilitary and nondiplomatic discussions" (418 U.S. at 707). Had military and diplomatic secrets been involved, greater deference would have been given to the president's claim of privilege.

All in all, Burger's decision in *United States v. Nixon* was important in two ways. Politically, it resolved the constitutional crisis generated by Nixon's refusal to comply with the subpoena and the likely impeachment that would have been forthcoming, and it led to the president's resignation seventeen days after the Court's proclamation. Legally, it recognized a qualified conception of executive privilege and addressed key constitutional issues involving separation of powers, especially the power of the judiciary to produce evidence and to define the boundaries of executive privilege. Although the result of the opinion was widely acclaimed, various sources contend that it was the work product of several justices and, in large measure, simply bears Burger's name.[13]

Judicial Power

Although the *Nixon* case strengthened the power of judicial review, many of Burger's decisions indicate a strong penchant for restricting access to the courts. They also voice the view that courts are improper forums for bringing about certain types of social and political reforms—even if major constitutional violations are asserted. If this is judicial restraint, then it certainly characterized Burger's decision making on questions involving access to the courts. As Justice Douglas once described the Burger philosophy, the "Court would sedulously avoid meeting contentious issues and would sit in resplendent dignity aloof from the issues of the day."[14]

Consider a few illustrations. The Court dealt with military surveillance of civilian political activities in *Laird v. Tatum* (1972). Burger's majority opinion ruled that since no direct injury had occurred, the plaintiffs could not challenge in court the constitutionality of the surveillance. His inclination to limit access was similarly evident in *United States v. Richardson* (1974), declaring that a taxpayer lacked standing to challenge the secrecy of the Central Intelligence Agency's budget because the litigants had not suffered a specific injury distinguishable from that experienced by the public generally. In *Schlesinger v. Reservists Committee to Stop the War* (1974), Burger decided that a citizens' group lacked standing to challenge whether members of Congress could also serve in the military reserves under the separation of powers doctrine. The chief's

opinions in these and other cases established a hard-nosed reputation that distinguished him from the Warren Court majority.
They also opened the floodgates for criticism by those who wanted
the judiciary to resolve the issues presented in these cases. During
the remainder of the 1970s, he voted to deny standing to litigants
in sensitive claims regarding the environment, civil rights damages,
and Medicaid coverage for abortions.[15] Discontent in liberal circles
did little to dissuade Burger from continuing along the basic path
charted during his early years on the Court.

Restraints on Government

No one has ever seriously asserted that Warren Burger was an
egalitarian. That was not the nature of this midwestern Republican,
a judge who was more concerned with the rights of society writ
large and who only occasionally came to the defense of political
dissidents, small religious groups, racial minorities, or women. This
was even more true in the case of those accused of crimes. Selected
by Nixon largely because of his "strict constructionist" orientation
on criminal procedure, Burger maintained a law-and-order profile
throughout his seventeen terms on the Supreme Court. When his
overall civil liberties voting record is examined, one finds that
Burger consistently ranked among the two most conservative justices (see Tables 1.8 and 1.9). The following survey of his opinions
nonetheless suggests some variation in conservatism across issues,
with moderate to liberal views emerging in several prominent free
press and civil rights cases.

First Amendment Freedoms

Claimed violations of freedom of speech were rarely viewed
sympathetically by Chief Justice Burger. In a few instances he wrote
for an antilibertarian majority, but, with most of the brethren often
not sharing his views, he frequently found himself in dissent. In
two cases that arose in the wake of the Vietnam War, he objected
to overturning state convictions for showing contempt toward, or
improper use of, the American flag.[16] In another case he parted
ways with the majority when it overturned a city ordinance prohibiting the use of obscene language toward an on-duty police
officer.[17] On the other hand, Burger spoke for the Court in overruling a state court order that had prevented a group from peace-
fully handing out leaflets in the neighborhood of a broker allegedly
responsible for blockbusting.[18] He also wrote for the Court in a

case striking down, as unconstitutionally vague, an ordinance stip-
ulating that advance written notice be given to the police before
the solicitation of funds for a political campaign or charitable cause,
and in a case deciding that a lawyer could not be suspended from
practicing law in a federal court because he had criticized a federal
judge.[19] Yet Burger reverted to his more characteristic mode of
thinking in *Bethel School District No. 403 v. Fraser* (1986) when he
agreed that high school authorities did not infringe First Amendment rights by suspending a student for a lewd speech made during
a school assembly.

None of these free speech opinions approach the status of land-
marks, but the chief justice did write in several heralded free press
cases, from time to time sounding quite moderate. Speaking for
a unanimous Court in *Miami Herald Publishing Company v. Tornillo*
(1974), Burger nullified a Florida statutory provision requiring
newspapers to print, without cost, a political candidate's response
to critical editorials. In *Nebraska Press Association v. Stuart* (1976),
he again wrote for all the justices in striking down a gag order
prohibiting the press from reporting on a sensational murder case
for eleven weeks. Although Justice Brennan insisted that all gag
orders violated the First Amendment, the chief seemed to believe
that they might be permissible in extreme situations. Rejecting a
strict construction of the First Amendment in *Richmond Newspapers,
Inc. v. Virginia* (1980), and apparently seeking to erase confusion
caused by *Gannett Co. v. DePasquale* (1979), Burger's majority opinion took the view that the public and the press have an implicit
First Amendment right to attend trials.[20]

Contrasted to these liberal-leaning majority statements were other
ones in free press cases in which the chief struck a more conservative note. In *New York Times Co. v. United States* (1971), he would
not have permitted publication of the Pentagon Papers without
more time and greater judicial scrutiny, thus effectively deciding
against the free press claim. In *Houchins v. KQED, Inc.* (1978), he
argued for the majority that the media could not be given greater
access to a county jail than that allowed to the general public. And
his concurring opinion in *First National Bank of Boston v. Bellotti*
(1978) reflected unsympathetic views toward the press. There the
Court ruled that a state could not prohibit corporations from
spending money to voice their views on referenda questions (in
this case, a graduated personal income tax) that did not materially
affect their business or property. Burger believed that all corporations, not simply those in the media, have a First Amendment

right to express their preferences on issues not affecting their economic interests. "Media conglomerates," such as the *New York Times,* have no "institutional privileges," according to Burger (435 U.S. at 796).

Some have observed that the chief justice possessed an intense personal dislike for pornography and felt the public should be protected from it.[21] Perhaps because of this, Burger departed from Warren Court policy and was attuned to the more conservative viewpoint that localities should be allowed to define what constituted obscenity. His most famous opinion in this area came in *Miller v. California* (1973), a ruling that rethought past definitions of obscenity advanced by the Supreme Court. Burger announced in *Miller* that "[t]he basic guidelines for the trier of fact must be: (a) whether 'the average person, applying contemporary community standards' would find that the work, taken as a whole, appeals to the prurient interest . . . ; (b) whether the work depicts or describes, in a patently offensive way, sexual conduct specifically defined by the applicable state law; and (c) whether the work, taken as a whole, lacks serious literary, artistic, political, or scientific value" (413 U.S. at 24). Revising some of the Court's previous definitions of obscenity, the chief justice emphasized that local community standards could be adopted to determine what was obscene in a particular community and that, understandably, those standards would vary throughout the nation. Further, he rejected in *Miller* the Warren Court's "utterly without redeeming social value" test. The effect of the decision was to enlarge the scope of material considered obscene, and thus not protected by the Constitution, and to make the prosecution of distributors of obscene material easier.

On the same day that *Miller* was handed down, Burger announced the Court's judgments in *Paris Adult Theatre I v. Slaton* (1973) and *United States v. Orito* (1973). In *Paris Adult Theatre,* his majority opinion ruled that adult theaters may be regulated by the state if they exhibit obscene materials, even though children and unconsenting adults are warned that such materials might be considered obscene. In *Orito,* his majority opinion held that Congress may prohibit the transportation of obscene materials in interstate commerce, even though those materials were intended exclusively for the personal use of their owners. Burger's conservative contribution to the law of obscenity tapered off markedly after the summer of 1973, however. As the Court became more unified in obscenity cases, the chief typically either assigned opinions to his colleagues or voted in dissent. Nonetheless, obscenity was one of the few civil liberties areas in which the Burger Court made significant conservative alterations in Warren Court policy, and the chief justice influenced that movement to the right.

Although responsible for some freedom of religion opinions such as *Wisconsin v. Yoder* (1972), holding that Amish children were exempt from state compulsory school attendance laws, Chief Justice Burger was far better known for his establishment clause decisions. Indeed, his opinions in this field constitute perhaps his strongest First Amendment legacy. The first came in *Walz v. Tax Commission of the City of New York* (1970), where he announced for the majority that the First Amendment allows property tax exemptions for church-owned land used solely for religious purposes. Here he emphasized that the Court would not permit government interference with or establishment of religion, but that "[s]hort of those expressly proscribed governmental acts there is room for play in the joints productive of a benevolent neutrality which will permit religious exercise to exist without sponsorship and without interference" (397 U.S. at 669). Historically, property tax exemptions had recognized the charitable functions performed by churches, and the chief believed that they should continue to be viewed as constitutional since their purpose was not to aid religion.

More important, speaking for a unanimous Court in *Lemon v. Kurtzman* (1971), Burger established the basic standard to be applied by the judiciary in guaranteeing separation of church and state. In that case he declared that a law permitting state subsidies to nonpublic schools to help pay teachers' salaries in secular courses violated the Constitution. The chief indicated, furthermore, that the Court's cumulative decisions provided a three-pronged test for determining whether a statute violated the establishment clause: "First, the statute must have a secular legislative purpose; second, its principal or primary effect must be one that neither advances nor inhibits religion . . . ; finally, the statute must not foster 'an excessive entanglement with religion' " (403 U.S. at 612–13). Armed with the *Lemon* decision, the Court subsequently applied that test in a number of cases, such as *Tilton v. Richardson* (1971), in which Burger upheld a federal statute that provided aid to church-related colleges for the construction of buildings used for secular educational purposes.

Often divorcing himself from the Court's decisional path during the remainder of the 1970s, the chief justice authored only two additional majority opinions on the establishment clause.[22] Then in 1982 he returned as spokesman for his colleagues in several noteworthy cases. His opinion in *Larkin v. Grendel's Den, Inc.* (1982) declared unconstitutional a state law that allowed churches to veto applications for the issuance of liquor licenses to any establishment within five hundred feet of a church. Nevertheless, Burger typically sounded more conservative on establishment issues in the 1980s than he had in *Lemon.* He upheld the constitutionality of the state legislative practice of beginning daily sessions with a prayer given by a minister paid by the state in *Marsh v. Chambers* (1983). Likewise, Burger's opinion in *Lynch v. Donnelly* (1984) upheld the inclusion of a nativity scene in a city-sponsored Christmas display and suggested that the *Lemon* test should not be automatically applied to establishment questions. He dissented in two other prominent cases: one struck down a state law that authorized public schools to adopt one minute of silence for meditation or voluntary prayer; the other struck down state-sponsored programs for remedial education and counseling services for private and parochial school children.[23]

Civil Rights

It seems fair to say that Warren Burger was neither as conservative on civil rights as many had anticipated at the time of his appointment nor as conservative on civil rights as he was in some other areas of constitutional law. To be sure, the views that emerged troubled liberals, but Burger did not always assume the posture of an uncompromising conservative, especially during his early years on the Court. His political and judicial background partly suggested that he might be reasonably flexible on some civil rights questions. He had, after all, served responsibly on the Governor's Interracial Commission in Minnesota from 1948 through 1953 and as the first president of the St. Paul Council on Human Relations, and his civil rights reputation on the D.C. Court of Appeals had not been that of a pure conservative ideologue.

Burger's civil rights outlook was mixed, depending on the issue—for example, equal educational opportunity. The racial desegregation of American elementary and secondary public schools, initiated by the Warren Court in *Brown v. Board of Education* (1954), was largely implemented during the Burger Court years. To facilitate desegregation, the Court found itself confronted with a new explosive issue: court-ordered busing. The nation's leading political figures tirelessly debated this issue, but it was Chief Justice

Burger who first wrote for a unanimous Supreme Court in upholding busing as one means for desegregating schools.

A long history of intentional segregation existed in North Carolina's Charlotte-Mecklenburg school system, and by the late 1960s approximately two-thirds of its black students still attended essentially all-black schools. After the school board repeatedly failed to correct this situation, a federal district court judge ordered busing to bring about a racial balance in individual schools. The legal challenge to that busing order came to the Burger Court as the milestone case of *Swann v. Charlotte-Mecklenburg Board of Education* (1971).

Burger's opinion in *Swann* frowned upon the use of racial quotas for education but accepted the notion that mathematical ratios could serve as "a useful starting point in shaping a remedy to correct past constitutional violations" (402 U.S. at 25). One-race schools could only be permitted temporarily, and busing could be relied upon to combat dual school systems. Admitting the difficulty of precisely defining the extent to which busing was permissible to remedy intentional segregation, Burger observed that bus transportation had a long history in public educational systems. Indeed, nearly two-fifths of all public schoolchildren had recently relied on buses to be taken to and from school. Because bus transportation was a "normal and accepted tool of educational policy," and because desegregation would not be achieved if students were assigned to the schools closest to their homes, it was within the district court's power to provide equitable relief by ordering busing in this case (29–30). Sticking closely to the facts in *Swann* to justify his decision, Burger acknowledged that busing was objectionable if it presented a risk to a child's health or significantly impinged upon the educational process and implied that these considerations should be taken into account in future cases before the district courts.

Swann was the chief's first landmark opinion. Some suggest that he self-assigned that case to assert his leadership on the Court and to "measure up" to Earl Warren's early performance in *Brown*.[24] Whether true or not, it is clear that Burger had reservations about busing. He later emphasized to lower federal court judges that *Swann* did not require racial quotas or fixed racial balances.[25] Nonetheless, he concurred in the result in *Keyes v. School District No. 1, Denver* (1973), the famous northern school busing decision, while Rehnquist dissented and Powell dissented in part.

During the next fourteen years Burger self-assigned only two other prominent opinions that turned on the meaning of equal educational opportunity. In *Milliken v. Bradley* (1974), he wrote for a highly fragmented majority that restricted *Swann* by announcing that busing could not be used across district lines to desegregate public schools unless illegal segregation in one school district had a significant segregative effect on segregation in the other district. "Boundary lines may be bridged where there has been a constitutional violation calling for interdistrict relief," he concluded, "but the notion that school district lines may be casually ignored or treated as mere administrative convenience is contrary to the history of public education in our country" (418 U.S. at 741). By contrast, in *Bob Jones University v. United States* (1983), upholding an Internal Revenue Service decision denying tax-exempt status to private schools that practiced racial discrimination in admissions, Burger reaffirmed the nation's commitment to equal educational opportunity. "[T]here can no longer be any doubt that racial discrimination in education violates deeply and widely accepted views of elementary justice," he observed. "Over the past quarter of a century, every pronouncement of this Court and myriad Acts of Congress and Executive Orders attest a firm national policy to prohibit racial segregation and discrimination in public education" (461 U.S. at 592–93).

Unlike the Warren Court, the Burger Court defined many of the parameters of equal employment opportunity law. The chief justice penned two of these key decisions. One, *Griggs v. Duke Power Co.* (1971), upheld the power of Congress to prohibit job discrimination on grounds of race; concluded that Title VII of the Civil Rights Act of 1964 did not permit employers to require a high school diploma or a minimum intelligence test score as a prerequisite for employment if unrelated to required job skills; and, surprisingly, said that discriminatory intent need not be proven to establish a violation of Title VII. The other, *Fullilove v. Klutznick* (1980), upheld a federal statute requiring recipients of federal grant funds for local public works projects to spend a minimum of 10 percent of the funds to purchase services and supplies from minority-owned businesses.

Despite these two liberal decisions, Burger took exception with the majority in other leading job discrimination cases. One case held that back pay cannot be denied, when Title VII has been violated, if the employer's discriminatory actions conflicted with the statute's basic goals of deterring racial discrimination and remedying injuries resulting from past discrimination. Another stated that retroactive seniority could be awarded to racial minorities who had been discriminated against under Title VII. The last case, the famous *Weber* decision, upheld a voluntary agreement between a company and union to set aside half the slots in a training program for black employees, who traditionally had been discriminated against, until the percentage of black craft workers approximated the percentage of blacks in the local labor force.[26]

As was true of the Republican presidents and much of the general public during these years, Burger harbored some serious reservations about affirmative action. Nor does his record suggest that he was an advocate of sexual equality, even though the Burger Court broke new ground in several leading gender discrimination cases. In *Reed v. Reed* (1971), the Court for the first time declared a state law unconstitutional because it discriminated against women. Burger, writing for a unanimous majority, announced that the equal protection clause does not permit a state to prefer a father automatically over a mother as executor of a child's estate. But *Reed* was an exception to the chief's normal decisional direction. For example, he objected to the Court's declaring that due process was violated by a requirement that female teachers take maternity leave five months before giving birth, and he rejected the notion that classifications based on sex are inherently suspect, thereby requiring strict scrutiny.[27]

Burger also did not trumpet the rights to privacy, abortion, or birth control. Indeed, he dissented in some of the leading decisions in those areas. In *Eisenstadt v. Baird* (1972), the majority ruled that a state violated the equal protection clause by banning distribution of contraceptives to unmarried persons, but Burger's dissent complained that "these opinions seriously invade the constitutional prerogatives of the States and regrettably hark back to the heyday of substantive due process" (405 U.S. at 467). He also dissented in *Planned Parenthood of Central Missouri v. Danforth* (1976), which declared unconstitutional a state requirement that a woman must obtain her husband's consent before having an abortion, and in *Thornburgh v. American College of Obstetricians and Gynecologists* (1986), which reaffirmed *Roe v. Wade* (1973). In *Doe v. Bolton* (1973), Burger emphasized in concurrence that the Constitution does not require "abortions on demand" (410 U.S. at 208). In *Thornburgh* he again stressed that "abortion on demand" was rejected by each justice in *Roe* and that "[t]he Court's opinion today . . . plainly undermines that important principle" (476 U.S. at 782–83). When the majority concluded in *Bowers v. Hardwick* (1986) that sexual activity between consenting homosexual adults was not protected under the Court's privacy doctrine, Burger concurred "to underscore my view that in constitutional terms there is no such thing as a fundamental right to commit homosexual sodomy" (478 U.S. at 196). In some ways *Bowers* was Burger's swan song—a hard-hitting statement at the end of his chief justiceship that clearly reflected his basic conservative nature.

Frequently the chief justice assumed the dissenting role on election and voting rights questions as well. Illustrative were his votes in cases holding that Congress lacked the power to lower the voting age for state and local elections to eighteen; that a state electoral law's residency requirements of at least one year for state elections, or at least three months for county elections, were unconstitutional; and that racial criteria could be used to reapportion state legislative districts to comply with the Voting Rights Act of 1965 even though the reapportionment diluted the voting power of Hasidic Jews.[28] Burger's majority opinions on voting rights and elections principally came during his first five terms and were written for cases experiencing little or no disagreement on the Court.

Criminal Procedure

The popular perception of Warren Burger as a steadfast, hard-line constitutional conservative is most accurate in light of his record in criminal procedure cases. The chief's penchant for favoring the prosecution is well known.[29] Although President Nixon was undoubtedly disappointed by Burger's decisions on some constitutional issues, surely he was proud of the chief's general performance in the area of criminal procedure, even though a "constitutional counter-revolution" was not forthcoming. The chief's sympathetic views toward the prosecution were especially obvious in his criminal procedure dissents, which were typically his most forceful and eloquent opinions.

The Burger Court moved to the right of the Warren Court on the law of search and seizure, and Burger played a leading role in that movement. His first plurality opinion for the Court came in *United States v. Harris* (1971), which held that probable cause for a search warrant could be based on a tip from an anonymous informant who was not proven to be reliable. This effectively undermined the Warren Court's position in *Spinelli v. United States* (1969), in which the Court had ruled that police officers must demonstrate to a magistrate that an anonymous informant is credible before a warrant can issue. By the mid-1970s, the chief's intense views on search and seizure led to increasing outspokenness.

He concurred in *United States v. Ortiz* (1975), where the Court held that border patrol officials could not search a private vehicle at a checkpoint over sixty miles away from the Mexican border unless they had probable cause or consent. In this case the chief justice, obviously troubled deeply by the Immigration and Naturalization Service's lack of power to stop the flow of illegal aliens across the border, prophesied that "[p]erhaps these decisions will be seen in perspective as but another example of a society seemingly impotent to deal with massive lawlessness. In that sense history may view us as prisoners of our own traditional and appropriate concern for individual rights, unable—or unwilling—to apply the concept of reasonableness explicit in the Fourth Amendment in order to develop a rational accommodation between those rights and the literal safety of the country" (422 U.S. at 899). In subsequent years he spoke his mind in majority opinions holding that the Fourth Amendment does not forbid the police from conducting a warrantless search as part of a standard inventory of a car that has been legally impounded, and that the training and experience of border patrol officials justifies their stopping a suspicious vehicle near the border and asking questions.[30]

This pronounced pattern continued in the 1980s: Burger's opinions for the prosecution in search and seizure cases were predictable as he continued to write with his own brand of personal conviction. Many of these opinions arose when the Court was seriously divided. One 6-3 opinion in 1982 upheld the constitutionality of a warrantless search under the "plain view" doctrine in the case of a policeman who had discovered and seized illegal drugs when accompanying the defendant's arrested roommate to the defendant's room.[31] In one important 5-4 case in 1984, Burger's majority opinion declared that the Fourth Amendment does not protect a prisoner from unannounced searches by guards because prisoners do not have a reasonable expectation of privacy.[32] Speaking for the Court in a 6-3 case in 1985, he ruled that a movable motor home may be searched without a warrant.[33] In a 7-2 decision extending the amount of time that a suspect may be held by the police without probable cause, another 1985 opinion by the chief held that detention for twenty minutes while officers confirmed their suspicions of a possible crime was not a violation of the Fourth Amendment.[34] During his final term, his majority opinions in two 5-4 cases upheld the reasonableness of aerial surveillance, without a warrant, over a fenced-in backyard and aerial surveillance over a heavily secured industrial plant.[35]

Rarely do Supreme Court justices decide invariably in one direction, no matter how intense their views. This was true of Burger on search and seizure. During his seventeen years on the Court he wrote relatively few pro-defendant decisions, but occasionally he struck a different note, especially in the late 1970s. These exceptions included a 1977 holding that a footlocker seized at the time of arrest could not be opened without a search warrant; a 1979 case deciding that it was unconstitutional for the police to confiscate a variety of evidence when the search warrant mentioned only two items to be seized; and a 1979 ruling that police officers must have a reasonable suspicion to think that an individual is breaking a law before they may stop the suspect, demand identification, and require the reason for the suspect's presence.[36]

Throughout much of his career as a federal judge, Warren Burger remained a staunch, outspoken, occasionally eloquent foe of the exclusionary rule.[37] While the chief was unable to convince his colleagues to abandon the rule, over time he influenced them to trim its scope. His long-standing unhappiness with the exclusionary rule was voiced early in his Supreme Court service, the best illustration being *Bivens v. Six Unknown Named Agents of the Federal Bureau of Narcotics* (1971).[38] The majority in *Bivens* announced that federal agents could be sued for damages for violating the Fourth Amendment. Dissenting, Burger used the occasion to assert that the theory underlying the exclusionary rule (that the police would be deterred from violating the Constitution if they knew that evidence gained illegally would be suppressed) was "hardly more than a wistful dream." The rule should be abandoned as soon as a "meaningful substitute" was developed, he wrote, and Congress—not the courts—should undertake that task (403 U.S. at 415). The chief's spirited, vigorous opposition continued. Concurring in *Stone v. Powell* (1976), he asserted that it was "an abdication of judicial responsibility to exact such exorbitant costs from society purely on the basis of speculative and unsubstantiated assumptions" that the suppression of evidence had a deterrent effect on illegal police conduct (428 U.S. at 500).

The *Stone* opinion nevertheless indicated that Burger was softening; he was willing to settle for something less than the total abolition of the exclusionary rule. This change was subsequently confirmed in several cases as he seemingly toned down his rhetoric.[39] Then in 1979 he spoke for the majority when the Court created its first "good-faith" exception to the rule. The chief justice announced in *Michigan v. DeFillippo* that the exclusionary rule did not apply to seized evidence that had resulted from a good-faith arrest of an arrestee who had refused to reveal his identity to police officers. A better-known illustration of Burger's influence on the exclusionary rule appeared several years later in *Nix v. Williams* (1984). Establishing the "inevitable discovery" exception in right-to-counsel cases, there Burger announced that "[i]f the prosecution can establish by a preponderance of the evidence that the information ultimately or inevitably would have been discovered by lawful means . . . then the deterrence rationale has so little basis that the evidence should be received. Anything less would reject logic, evidence, and common sense" (467 U.S. at 444).

On Fifth Amendment self-incrimination questions, Chief Justice Burger's tendency to decide for the prosecution was also pronounced. Although he did not actively seek to directly overrule *Miranda v. Arizona* (1966), some of these cases demonstrate his predilection to whittle away at it or to construe it narrowly. Over a bitter dissent by Brennan, Douglas, and Marshall, Burger trimmed the arguable scope of *Miranda* in *Harris v. New York* (1971) by ruling that even though the *Miranda* warnings were not properly given, incriminating statements made to the police could nevertheless be introduced at trial to at least impeach the credibility of a suspect's statements made on the witness stand. The chief insisted, "The shield provided by *Miranda* cannot be perverted into a license to use perjury by way of a defense, free from the risk of confrontation with prior inconsistent utterances" (401 U.S. at 226). In other cases Burger ruled that a taxpayer, not under arrest in his own home, need not be given the complete *Miranda* warnings before being questioned by IRS officials, and he refused to extend *Miranda* to grand jury witnesses suspected of committing crimes.[40] Although these decisions were typical of Burger, in a few he assumed a position more supportive of *Miranda* and its spirit. Thus, in *Estelle v. Smith* (1981) the chief surprisingly found a Fifth Amendment violation: the defendant had not been warned of his right to counsel before agreeing to a psychiatric interview that led to his conviction and death sentence.

Compared to other criminal procedure issues, Burger produced fewer right-to-counsel opinions, dissented less frequently in them, and even authored several pro-defendant majority opinions. One ruled that the right to counsel was violated when a defendant was not allowed to speak to his lawyer during an evening recess at the point in the trial when he was being questioned on the witness stand; another held that three defendants were denied effective assistance to counsel when a trial judge appointed the same lawyer to represent all three; yet another decided that the Sixth Amendment was violated when the prosecution used incriminating statements at trial made by a paid informant who had been incarcerated with the suspect before trial.[41] Despite the liberal direction apparent in these opinions, the chief demonstrated his more conservative side in another case, in which he found no constitutional violation when, a few days before trial, a judge assigned a new lawyer for the defendant instead of granting a delay when his own attorney was unable to go to trial due to illness. In yet another case Burger held that all nonfrivolous issues suggested by a defendant to a court-appointed lawyer need not be raised by the attorney on appeal.[42]

The chief justice's first fair trial opinion came in *In re Winship* (1970), in which he objected to the majority's position that juvenile defendants must be found guilty beyond a reasonable doubt, like adult defendants.[43] Burger charged that due process dictated no such standard and that the decision was "a manipulation of progress to transform juvenile courts into criminal courts," which would "turn the clock back to the pre–juvenile court era" (397 U.S. at 376). Also divorcing himself from the Court in *Coleman v. Alabama* (1970), which held that the right to counsel applies to the "critical stage" of the preliminary hearing, he asserted that "by inventing its own verbal formula the prevailing opinion seeks to reshape the Constitution in accordance with predilections of what is deemed desirable" (399 U.S. at 23). After primarily playing a dissenting role for several years, Burger spoke for the Court majority in 1976, announcing that trials conducted by judges who lack legal training do not violate due process as long as a legally trained judge is available on appeal, and again in 1978, declaring that no infringement of due process occurred when a judge increased a defendant's sentence because he was convinced the defendant had committed perjury during trial.[44] More important, the chief's majority opinion in *Chandler v. Florida* (1981) held that the televising of a state criminal trial does not inherently abridge the rights to fair trial and due process. Placing a high premium on the role of the states as governmental laboratories, and advancing a questionable assumption concerning state courts in criminal cases, he argued: "We are not empowered by the Constitution to oversee or harness state procedural experimentation; only when the state action infringes fundamental guarantees are we authorized to intervene. We must assume state courts will be alert to any factors that impair the fundamental rights of the accused" (449 U.S. at 582). Subsequent fair trial opinions by Burger often spoke for a Court majority and usually were decided against claims of constitutional violations.[45]

On the Eighth Amendment's prohibition against cruel and unusual punishment, Burger does not appear to have played a highly influential role on the Court. *Furman v. Georgia* (1972) cast doubt on the constitutionality of death penalty statutes in the United States, and the chief dissented, suggesting that the majority had injected its personal values in disposing of the issue. However, when the Court swerved from *Furman* in *Gregg v. Georgia* (1976), holding that the death sentence for murder was not repugnant to the Eighth Amendment, his concurring statement reflected no concern over the injection of judicial values. Burger again dissented in *Coker v. Georgia* (1977), in which the Court found that the death penalty was excessive for the crime of rape. In this case he complained, somewhat as in *Furman,* that the Court had gone beyond its proper role. The chief justice's most important capital punishment opinion came in *Lockett v. Ohio* (1978), in which the Court decided that Ohio's death penalty law was unconstitutional because it narrowly limited the mitigating factors a judge could weigh in determining whether to impose the death penalty. In this case Burger concluded that the Constitution demands "that the sentencer, in all but the rarest kind of capital case, not be precluded from considering, *as a mitigating factor,* any aspect of a defendant's character or record and any of the circumstances of the offense that the defendant proffers as a basis for a sentence less than death" (438 U.S. at 604). Thus, as in *United States v. Henry* (1980) and *Estelle v. Smith* (1981), Burger was not always restrictive in his interpretation of criminal procedure protections.

Conclusion and Appraisal

When contrasted to the 1960s, with its political liberalism, the 1970s and 1980s were conservative years in American politics. Gone were the New Frontier and the Great Society, if not the New Deal coalition itself. Democratic liberalism was significantly weakened and had been put on the defensive both politically and philosophically. In place of the 1960s was a political era dominated by two conservative Republican presidents, Richard Nixon and Ronald Reagan. As always, new political tides would ultimately be reflected in new Supreme Court appointments.

A conservative shift on the Supreme Court was initiated with Nixon's appointment of Warren Burger as chief justice. Burger, a devoted Republican, had been active in Minnesota politics for over a decade, had played a role in Dwight Eisenhower's nomination at the Republican convention of 1952 and served as assistant attorney general during the first Eisenhower administration, and then had earned a reputation as a law-and-order judge on the D.C. Court of Appeals. Nixon selected Burger as the fifteenth chief justice mainly because of his so-called strict constructionist views, especially on criminal procedure. Yet, although those views arguably emerged in many of the chief justice's opinions during his seventeen terms on the Supreme Court, the Warren Court's foremost liberal activist decisions survived all those years, despite five other additions to the Burger Court by Republican presidents. At the time of his unexpected retirement in the summer of 1986, Burger had been more than an acceptable chief justice in the eyes of his admirers; a good administrator and an innovative reformer, he had played his ceremonial roles with dignity and style. To critics, he had been unacceptable—too conservative on most constitutional issues, too lacking in the skills needed to lead the Court, he was said to use his position as chief in questionable ways to influence the Court's decision making.

To understand the man, one might underscore that Burger was a tireless, dedicated jurist with impeccable Republican credentials. No doubt these characteristics opened doors and permitted opportunities throughout his long career. In fact, they probably helped Burger overcome various obstacles, for in some ways he was an atypical Supreme Court justice. Although about nine of ten justices throughout the Court's history have come from well-to-do families and have attended the best law schools,[46] not so Warren Burger, the son of a railroad cargo inspector and traveling salesman, a law student who received his training at a largely unknown night law school. With his modest economic background, Burger was a Horatio Alger figure who had assisted with family finances as a child and had worked his way through law school by selling insurance. Despite hardship, he became a successful jurist and one of only three millionaires on the Court during the mid-1980s.[47]

Chief Justice Burger's constitutional outlook has been characterized in various ways by other observers, but this analysis of his Supreme Court career indicates that his opinions articulated no one overarching, well-developed constitutional philosophy. (By "philosophy" I mean a consistently held, interrelated set of well-developed, fundamental theoretical premises and principles that lead to consistent substantive legal conclusions.) Being neither a philosopher nor a deep thinker, Burger's opinions tended to be short on constitutional theory and long on fine points required to dispose of cases. They were characteristically straightforward and matter-of-fact, workmanlike, reasonably well written but less than eloquent, and well grounded in precedent. When he delved into the theory underlying the Constitution, it was virtually always through the words of other justices at other times. To be sure, one finds the rhetoric of restraint in his writings—references to the framers' intent, mention of the responsibility of judges to eschew political questions or to avoid reading their own personal preferences into the Constitution, the idea that many societal ills should not be redressed through the courts, and warnings that judges should avoid constitutional issues where possible and not discard the concept of stare decisis. Yet these elements of restraint emerge without the elaboration, consistency, persuasiveness, force, or visceral quality that one easily detects from reading a justice like Frankfurter, for instance. Moreover, a number of Burger's opinions reflect potent activist traits. The Supreme Court and the American political system seemed somewhat rudderless during the period of Burger's chief justiceship, without the apparent sense of purpose and direction that characterized the 1960s. If this is true, perhaps it should come as no surprise that the chief justice himself possessed no overall philosophy to shape and guide the broad contours of his own decision making.

While the chief justice failed to exhibit a clear-cut, coherent, mature constitutional philosophy, his conservative decisional preferences were abundantly clear. In terms of the powers of government, he typically deferred to presidential power, the Watergate case being an exception. He was not a justice to defer generally to the powers of Congress or the courts, striking down the legislative veto and congressional efforts to control the budget deficit, narrowly construing the speech or debate clause, and restricting access to the federal judiciary in myriad cases. On civil liberties, Burger's views emerged in various nonegalitarian shades. Most conservative and outspoken on criminal procedure, he was conservative on free speech and establishment issues as well. At times his freedom of press opinions were more moderate, while his civil rights decisions contained a mixture of liberal and conservative positions. Because of his desire to lead the Court and to control opinion assignments, perhaps many of his more liberal majority opinions were influenced substantially by his brethren. If this is true, then his general conservative voting patterns were probably the most valid overall indicator of his civil liberties attitudes, rather than individual opinions. His contributions to American constitutional law were case specific, spotty, and scattered across a number of issues. His opinions reflect some degree of doctrinal consistency, but substantially less than that in Rehnquist's, the Court's arch-conservative intellectual, who wrote with more persuasion, elegance, and creativity. With little doubt, history will prove Rehnquist to be a better choice as a Nixon-Reagan type chief justice: brighter, more conservative, with a more coherent judicial philosophy and a greater ability to lead the Supreme Court.[48]

In the final analysis, political historians and students of the judiciary will find Warren Burger plainly distinguishable from his Supreme Court colleagues. Unlike Justice Douglas, he was not a social reformer. In contrast to Justice Black, he was not deeply committed to the protection of individual rights. He did not display the strong leadership qualities that Justice Brennan did, and his position and vote, unlike those of Justice Powell, were not crucial in a number of controversial issues. Unlike Justice Stevens, he was not an independent voice on the Court. Unlike Justice Rehnquist, he was not an intellectual force among his colleagues. Compared with some of his brethren, he did not exhibit a broad or coherent jurisprudence that led to wide-ranging contributions to American constitutional law beyond particular cases and issues. And unlike his predecessor, Earl Warren, he will never be known as a great chief justice, save perhaps in the realm of judicial administration. To put it most simply, Warren Burger was a hard-working, conservative justice of average to below-average abilities by Supreme Court standards, a product of midwestern Republicanism whose legacy will rest in a number of landmark Supreme Court decisions (which would have been historic almost regardless of who wrote for the majority) and several innovative administrative reforms (which were distinctively Burger's). Ultimately he proved to be a conservative chief for conservative times—although probably not as conservative as Presidents Nixon or Reagan would have preferred.

NOTES

1. For a fairly detailed biographical sketch, see "Warren E. Burger," *Current Biography* (New York: H. W. Wilson Co., 1969), pp. 62–64, which is

relied on occasionally throughout this chapter. Insights into Burger's personal and judicial traits are also provided by William Rehnquist and others in "A Tribute to Chief Justice Warren E. Burger," *Harvard Law Review* 100 (1987): 969–1001, and by Bernard Schwartz in *The Ascent of Pragmatism: The Burger Court in Action* (Reading, Mass.: Addison-Wesley, 1990).

2. See Leonard W. Levy, *Against the Law: The Nixon Court and Criminal Justice* (New York: Harper and Row, 1974), pp. 12–25.

3. *Public Papers of the Presidents of the United States: Richard M. Nixon* (Washington, D.C.: U.S. Government Printing Office, 1971), p. 396.

4. Vincent Blasi, ed., *The Burger Court: The Counter-Revolution That Wasn't* (New Haven, Conn.: Yale University Press, 1983), esp. chap. 4. But the conservative direction of the Court during these years is nonetheless obvious. For a liberal critique, see Herman Schwartz, ed., *The Burger Years: Rights and Wrongs in the Supreme Court, 1969–1986* (New York: Viking, 1987).

5. This essay regularly refers to the concepts of liberalism, conservatism, activism, and restraint as defined in the political science literature on the courts. For liberalism and conservatism, see Sheldon Goldman and Thomas P. Jahnige, *The Federal Courts as a Political System*, 3d ed. (New York: Harper and Row, 1985), chap. 5, esp. pp. 137–46. For activism and restraint, see Stephen C. Halpern and Charles M. Lamb, eds., *Supreme Court Activism and Restraint* (Lexington, Mass.: Lexington Books, 1982), esp. chaps. 1–2.

6. This study addresses Burger's constitutional decision making, not his administrative role as chief justice. For that highly touted dimension of his performance, see Edward A. Tamm and Paul C. Reardon, "Warren E. Burger and the Administration of Justice," *Brigham Young University Law Review* 1981: 447–521.

7. See Sheldon Goldman, *Constitutional Law: Cases and Essays* (New York: Harper and Row, 1987), pp. 158–61, and the voting agreement data among individual justices in the statistics section of the *Harvard Law Review* 84–100 (Nov. 1970–86).

8. Laurence H. Tribe, *American Constitutional Law*, 2d ed. (Mineola, N.Y.: Foundation Press, 1988), p. 370.

9. See, for example, "The Supreme Court, 1978 Term," *Harvard Law Review* 93 (1979): 161–71.

10. "The Supreme Court, 1974 Term," *Harvard Law Review* 89 (1975): 134–39.

11. For a good account of political and legal events leading up to the *Nixon* decision, see Archibald Cox, *The Court and the Constitution* (Boston: Houghton Mifflin, 1987), pp. 2–25.

12. On these points respectively, see Bob Woodward and Scott Armstrong, *The Brethren: Inside the Supreme Court* (New York: Simon and Schuster, 1979), p. 287; William O. Douglas, *The Court Years, 1939–1975: The Autobiography of William O. Douglas* (New York: Random House, 1980), p. 139; Goldman, *Constitutional Law*, pp. 163–64.

13. Woodward and Armstrong, *The Brethren*, pp. 315–47 passim. See also David M. O'Brien, *Storm Center: The Supreme Court in American Politics* (New

York: Norton, 1986), pp. 220–22; Bernard Schwartz, *The Unpublished Opinions of the Burger Court* (New York: Oxford University Press, 1988), pp. 160–62, 276–82.

14. Douglas, *The Court Years*, p. 55.

15. See, for example, *United States v. Students Challenging Regulatory Agency Procedures (SCRAP)* (1973); *Wood v. Strickland* (1975); *Singleton v. Wulff* (1976).

16. *Smith v. Goguen* (1974); *Spence v. Washington* (1974).

17. *Lewis v. City of New Orleans* (1972).

18. *Organization for a Better Austin v. Keefe* (1971).

19. *Hynes v. Mayor of Oradell* (1976); *In re Snyder* (1985).

20. On Burger's lack of task leadership in these cases, see Goldman, *Constitutional Law*, p. 164. On other aspects of his leadership, see Robert J. Steamer, *Chief Justice: Leadership and the Supreme Court* (Columbia: University of South Carolina Press, 1986), chap. 4, and Joseph F. Kobylka, "Leadership on the Supreme Court of the United States: Chief Justice Burger and the Establishment Clause," *Western Political Quarterly* 42 (1989): 545–68.

21. Woodward and Armstrong, *The Brethren*, pp. 193–204, 245–53.

22. *Levitt v. Committee for Public Education and Religious Liberty* (1973); *NLRB v. Catholic Bishop of Chicago* (1979).

23. *Wallace v. Jaffree* (1985); *Aguilar v. Felton* (1985).

24. Woodward and Armstrong, *The Brethren*, p. 95.

25. William Lasser, *The Limits of Judicial Power: The Supreme Court in American Politics* (Chapel Hill: University of North Carolina Press, 1988), p. 201.

26. *Albemarle Paper Co. v. Moody* (1975); *Franks v. Bowman Transportation Co.* (1976); *United Steelworkers of America v. Weber* (1979).

27. *Cleveland Board of Education v. LaFleur* (1974); *Frontiero v. Richardson* (1973).

28. *Oregon v. Mitchell* (1970); *Dunn v. Blumstein* (1972); *United Jewish Organizations of Williamsburgh, Inc. v. Carey* (1977).

29. Burger's pro-prosecution outlook carried over from his years on the D.C. Court of Appeals. See Charles M. Lamb, "The Making of a Chief Justice: Warren Burger on Criminal Procedure, 1956–1969," *Cornell Law Review* 60 (1975): 743–88.

30. *South Dakota v. Opperman* (1976); *United States v. Cortez* (1981).

31. *Washington v. Chrisman* (1982).

32. *Hudson v. Palmer* (1984).

33. *California v. Carney* (1985).

34. *United States v. Sharpe* (1985).

35. *California v. Ciraolo* (1986); *Dow Chemical Co. v. United States* (1986).

36. *United States v. Chadwick* (1977); *Lo-Ji Sales, Inc. v. New York* (1979); *Brown v. Texas* (1979).

37. See Mark K. Braswell and John M. Scheb II, "Conservative Pragmatism versus Liberal Principles: Warren E. Burger on the Suppression of Evidence, 1956–86," *Creighton Law Review* 20 (1987): 789–831.

38. From the early 1970s, see also *Williams v. United States* (1971) and *Harris v. New York* (1971).

39. See, for example, *Brewer v. Williams* (1977); *United States v. Chadwick* (1977).

40. *Beckwith v. United States* (1976); *United States v. Mandujano* (1976); *United States v. Washington* (1977).

41. *Geders v. United States* (1976); *Holloway v. Arkansas* (1978); *United States v. Henry* (1980).

42. *Morris v. Slappy* (1983); *Jones v. Barnes* (1983).

43. To supplement this discussion, see Burger's free press–fair trial opinions referred to earlier under First Amendment freedoms.

44. *North v. Russell* (1976); *United States v. Grayson* (1978).

45. See, for example, *United States v. MacDonald* (1982); *United States v. Young* (1985).

46. Goldman, *Constitutional Law*, pp. 70–71. Burger was also one of only four justices in Supreme Court history who came from humble economic backgrounds but were not Democrats. Ibid., p. 71.

47. The others were Powell and O'Connor. O'Brien, *Storm Center*, p. 97.

48. See David M. O'Brien, "The Supreme Court: From Warren to Burger to Rehnquist," *PS* 20 (1987): 14–15.

6

Justice William O. Douglas: Conscience of the Court

PHILLIP J. COOPER

Introduction

It is common to think of the Burger Court as a group of justices who came to the high bench during and after the presidency of Richard Nixon. Of course, as with any period of Supreme Court development, there was no quick shift to a new body of judges. And although Nixon named four men to the Court, these appointees joined a group of seasoned and quite different justices. William O. Douglas was one of those long-time residents of the marble temple. Indeed, Douglas had seen several Courts, having served longer than any other member of the high bench, some thirty-six years. The contemporary picture of Douglas as a contentious dissenter who represented the far left of those who remained from the Warren Court does not appreciate the complexity of the man or his situation in the Court during the later years of his tenure.

The son of a Presbyterian minister, William Orville Douglas was born in Maine, Minnesota, in 1898.[1] Three years later, the Douglas family moved west, finally settling in Yakima, Washington. The next few years were extremely difficult for the Douglases. William was stricken with infantile paralysis to such an extent that the family physician predicted he would never regain the use of his legs and that he would not likely survive beyond his fortieth birthday. With his mother's care and his rigorous regimen of outdoor exercise, he improved so much that he eventually became known as a prominent hiker and outdoorsman. Then in 1904 William's father died unexpectedly. His untimely death ultimately meant that the future justice would experience firsthand what it meant to be poor. During those years William worked at all manner of odd jobs, including annual stints as a farm worker. He felt the sting of social discrimination based upon class and wealth, a fact that helps to explain so many of his later opinions.

Douglas concentrated on his studies, attempting to excel in academics in a way that he could not in athletics. He graduated as valedictorian from Yakima High, received a scholarship to attend Whitman College, and headed east in 1922 to attend Columbia Law School, arriving in New York City with six cents. The future justice excelled in law school as he had in his earlier studies, becoming an editor of the law review and graduating second in his class.

After graduation in 1925, Douglas joined a prestigious New York firm, but it was not his idea of a long-term career. He returned to Yakima but soon accepted an offer to join the Columbia law faculty. Less than two years later, though, he resigned from Columbia and took an associate professorship at the Yale Law School. The years Douglas spent at Columbia and Yale were extremely important to the development of his expertise in corporate law and finance and to the shaping of his jurisprudence. These were the centers of the neorealist movement in American jurisprudence. The neorealists insisted that judges are important participants in government and the society it serves. The law is, and must be, influenced by a range of factors including the economy, politics, and social reform. Douglas carried this sense of the nature and character of law with him throughout his career.

Soon Douglas was called to Washington by the Hoover administration as a consultant on bankruptcy to the secretary of commerce. Then, in 1936, he began his service as a member of the Securities and Exchange Commission, where he was elevated to chair in 1937. His rhetoric and behavior was that of a free market capitalist. Indeed, he was lauded for his service by *Babson's 95% Republican Reports.*[2] One of the few criticisms raised during his later confirmation proceedings in the Senate was an allegation that he was too close to corporate management.

Before Burger

In March 1939, President Roosevelt offered Douglas the seat on the Supreme Court formerly occupied by Louis Brandeis, an appointment that brought much praise and drew few adversaries. The Brotherhood of Railroad Trainmen offered token opposition on the grounds that the union "consider[ed] Douglas too close to

Justice William O. Douglas

Wall St. to be fit for such a high Judicial Post."[3] At forty, Douglas was one of the youngest nominees to be elevated to the nation's highest tribunal. He settled into life in the marble temple relatively quickly. The only truly stressful problem emerged when Roosevelt asked him to head defense production in 1941. Douglas's confidant on this, and many other occasions, was Hugo Black, to whom he wrote: "I do not want to leave the Court. I desire to stay just where I am. I hate even to consider the prospect of leaving. I am very happy right there and I want nothing but the opportunity to slug away along side of you for the next 30 years."[4]

The environment grew even more pleasant as New Dealers quickly took over the Court. Justices Douglas, Black, Murphy, and Rutledge often joined together to form the nucleus of Roosevelt Court majorities. While tensions developed around Justices Frankfurter and Jackson and their relationships with the other members of the Court, Douglas gave every indication that he was just where he wanted to be. It was no surprise when he turned down Truman's offer of a cabinet post in 1946. He also refused Truman's request to be his running mate in 1948.

Douglas was determined to be an active citizen willing to speak his mind even though a member of the Court. His significant off-the-bench activity included an amazingly productive career as a writer. Beyond his many popular works, Douglas became probably the Court's most prolific writer of articles and monographs on law and politics, a number of which were important because they forthrightly insisted upon a commitment to constitutional rights and liberties at a time when it was not popular to defend those principles.[5] Douglas also dabbled in a limited amount of political activity while on the Court. During the New Deal and the Truman administration, he brought observations from his international travels back to the White House. His active involvement with presidents ended after his break with Truman over Douglas's suggestion that the United States should recognize the People's Republic of China. Although he would have a strong personal relationship with the Kennedy family and Lyndon Johnson, Douglas was never really an insider again. His inability to make progress with Johnson on his view of the United States' involvement in Vietnam was a source of severe disappointment for him that eventually destroyed their friendship.

Douglas was drawn into political controversy at a number of points in his career. The first call for his impeachment came at the time of the Julius and Ethel Rosenberg case, in which Douglas issued a stay of execution soon dissolved by the Court. His opposition to the Vietnam War also engendered criticism. Finally, he was deemed a vulnerable target by Warren Court critics after Justice Fortas was driven from the Court amid charges of impropriety. Efforts were made to see whether President Nixon could not be afforded yet another nomination. Republican Congressman Gerald Ford brought an unsuccessful impeachment proceeding against Douglas in April 1970, after two of Nixon's nominees to the Supreme Court had been rejected.[6]

Douglas at the Birth of the Burger Court

Because of health problems, domestic turmoil, and changing national politics, William O. Douglas's life was extraordinarily complex by the time the Warren Court passed from the scene. The year 1969 marked the end of his third decade at the Court, an event he celebrated at age seventy. Surprisingly for such a robust man, Douglas had undergone pacemaker surgery in 1968, and he suffered a major stroke in December 1974, which ultimately led to his retirement the next year. He was also living with widespread public criticism of his personal life after his fourth marriage. The public's image of him as a man who did not properly value the sanctity of marriage and family life is ironic in light of the fact that his first marriage lasted some 30 years, his second 10, and his last 14. Nor was the political climate pleasant for a continuing New Dealer. He broke with Johnson over Vietnam and had no use for Richard Nixon. The backlash against the civil rights movement and the attack on the Warren Court by the Nixon administration were hard to bear.

Changes on the Court added to the complications in Douglas's life. The departure of Frankfurter and Goldberg changed the Court's dynamics. Fortas, a close friend of forty years, was driven from the Court in a way that absolutely infuriated Douglas. Most important, Black left the Court and died soon after. Even before his departure, Black and Douglas had begun to part company on important issues, but Douglas felt Black's loss deeply. Beyond all that, the advent of the Burger Court newcomers meant challenges to hard-fought doctrines produced during the Warren years. By 1971 it was clear that Douglas would increasingly play the role of dissenter, not merely on constitutional and statutory issues but also in decisions about what cases to take and what role the Court should play in American society. On the other hand, the role of dissenter and challenger was one that Douglas was more than willing to accept.

Constitutional Powers and Limits

Douglas mistrusted those possessing power, political or economic. During the Burger Court years he worried that executive power was on the rise, and that legislative power was used less to challenge the executive than to interfere with individual liberties. He also concluded that judicial power was not sufficiently available to the citizens who needed to have it exercised on their behalf when their liberties were threatened.

Executive Power

Douglas saw at least two major types of executive power problems. The first stemmed from abuses by the president, and the second concerned his view of the growing power of administrative agencies. Over time, he underwent a change in attitude toward presidential power. Though always suspicious of people with power, in the 1940s he was willing to grant considerable deference to the executive branch in foreign policy and in the prosecution of declared war.[7] But things changed. He concurred with the Court's *Youngstown Sheet & Tube v. Sawyer* (1952) ruling against Truman's seizure of the nation's steel mills during the Korean War, arguing that the separation of powers was not intended to produce efficiency but to protect liberties. "Today a kindly President uses the seizure power to effect a wage increase and to keep the steel furnaces in production," he warned. "Yet tomorrow another President might use the same power to prevent a wage increase, to curb trade-unionists, to regiment labor as oppressively as industry thinks it has been regimented by this seizure" (343 U.S. at 634). He also asserted that because the exercise of certain governmental powers is contingent upon legislative or judicial involvement, the president could not seize property if the legislature had not authorized funds to provide just compensation for the former owners as required by the Fifth Amendment.

The principal presidential power issues arising during the Burger Court years centered on the Vietnam War, national security policy, and Watergate. Although a number of troubling issues came to the Court that touched upon aspects of the Vietnam War, Douglas found the draft questions particularly troublesome. They were more than First Amendment or due process problems; they raised issues of executive power. In his view, Vietnam was a "presidential war" not authorized by Congress, and that made all the difference.[8]

The draft challenges divide into several categories. First, there were the cases Douglas hoped would cause the Court to address the legitimacy of the Vietnam War directly. His opinions on this subject frequently appeared as dissents or dissents from denials of certiorari. Second, there were cases that dealt with the meaning and boundaries of conscientious objector (CO) status. Third, there was the problem of abuse of conscientious objectors by harassment before induction or their abuse while in the service as they attempted to process their CO claims. Fourth, there were issues of arbitrary and capricious administration of the draft laws by local draft boards and the selective service system officials. Finally, there were procedural questions associated with ensuring the availability of adequate legal oversight of the selective service system's operation.

The cases presenting challenges to the validity of the war in Vietnam came in many forms, often in litigation concerning the draft, but most of them also contained a foundation assertion that the legitimacy of the war itself was in question. Recalling this period, Douglas asserted: "I wrote numerous opinions stating why we should take these cases and decide them. Once or twice Potter Stewart and Bill Brennan joined me. But there was never a fourth vote. I thought then — and still do think — that treating the question as a 'political' one was an abdication of duty and a self-inflicted wound on the Court."[9] While it is certainly true that Douglas had strong views on Vietnam, it would be an oversimplification to attribute his behavior in all of the draft cases to that fact. For example, he had been concerned about the interpretation and administration of CO status under the selective service laws since at least World War II.[10]

During the Vietnam War, Douglas joined the Court in its rulings expanding CO standards to cover more than association with a particular recognized religious group that required pacifist behavior and more than religious belief narrowly defined.[11] But Douglas was prepared to go beyond that. He dissented from the Court's opinion in *Gilette v. United States* (1971). This case presented claims to CO status by men who were not opposed to all war but only to those they considered unjust or immoral. In *Gilette*, Douglas rejected the idea that CO status could be limited to those who objected to all wars. He was even more concerned that CO status had to be related to a religious belief, however broadly defined.

He would have anchored conscientious objection in what he called freedom of conscience (401 U.S. at 465–66). If CO status is limited to persons asserting a religious base for their objection, then, in Douglas's view, plain discrimination on the basis of religious belief is at the core of these cases.

Douglas was also concerned that those who claimed CO status were subject to the not-so-tender mercies of military justice and were often harassed by local draft boards or members of the military. Thus he rejected the idea that men who had received notice of induction should honor it and then process their claims while in uniform.[12] Since Douglas thought that one could be opposed to a particular war, his concern extended to members of the military who faced abuse or punishment for merely expressing their views on Vietnam.[13]

Among the more common draft cases were suits alleging that the administration of the selective service laws was patently arbitrary and capricious. One of the most troublesome aspects of draft board behavior for Douglas was the use of the board's authority to label a particular registrant as a delinquent and then hasten his induction. For example, Douglas wrote for the majority in *Gutknecht v. United States* (1970), which concerned a man who had already been classified 1A (first draft priority) and was appealing that classification. The registrant participated in a protest against the war and returned his draft card. As a consequence, his pending appeal was denied and he was placed at the top of the induction list. Douglas complained that the draft board had acted with "a broad, roving authority, a type of administrative absolutism not congenial to our law-making traditions" (396 U.S. at 306–7). Indeed, on other occasions he labeled the behavior of local draft boards "lawless."[14]

Finally, Douglas contended that the gravity of induction into the military, with its attendant loss of liberty and possible assignment to a war zone, argued in favor of affording opportunities for full judicial evaluation of CO cases at the earliest possible time.[15] He objected to technical defenses against appeal in these cases, and he was fully prepared to issue whatever stays or preliminary injunctions were necessary to freeze the cases until they could be fully considered by the Court. His position engendered a campaign against him by House Armed Services Committee member F. Edward Hebert. After Douglas issued a stay precluding shipment of a group of reservists to Vietnam,[16] Hebert wrote Chief Justice Warren in protest. When Chief Justice Burger replaced Warren, he promptly received a similar missive from the congressman. In fact, Hebert insisted that "Justice Douglas has disqualified himself to pass judgment on any cases involving Vietnam, the draft, or the military in general as far as that goes."[17] That letter concerned *Parker v. Levy* (1974), a case that was still very much alive. Levy's lawyer got word of Hebert's action and quickly protested to Senator Ervin, chairman of the Subcommittee on Separation of Powers of the Senate Judiciary Committee.[18]

Beyond his concerns with Vietnam, Douglas was troubled by the domestic activities of the Nixon administration undertaken in the name of national security. He was upset, first, by the fact that a number of them were unsupported by any statutory authorization and were simply claimed to be implied by Article II. He was frustrated as well because several of the activities posed very direct threats to First Amendment freedoms. The fact that the abuses were justified on grounds of national security and covered up by a classification stamp bothered him even more. Douglas repeatedly complained about what he called the abuse of the secret stamp— the unnecessary and inappropriate use of security classifications. And all the abuses were exacerbated, in his view, by an unwillingness within the Court to take some of the national security cases and resolve them quickly and on the merits.

The abuses in *New York Times Co. v. United States* (1971) led the list. In this case Douglas attacked the government's effort to enjoin publication of the Pentagon Papers. To begin with, no statute authorized the action the government sought. He rejected the executive's claim of inherent powers to move against the publishers on the grounds that the executive's war power could not be asserted in this situation since "the war power stems from a declaration of war. . . . Nowhere are presidential wars authorized" (403 U.S. at 722). He was further frustrated in this case by what he saw as a clear abuse of the secret stamp to cover mistakes rather than to protect vital information.

In *United States v. United States District Court* (1972), the Court was faced with another case in which the government alleged an implied power on the part of the president; this time it was an asserted power to use warrantless wiretaps to prevent threats to the nation by subversives. The Court rejected the idea that such a power was to be inferred from the Omnibus Crime Control and Safe Streets Act or from the Constitution; Douglas concurred. He saw this case as part of a much larger problem: "As illustrated by a flood of cases before us this Term, . . . we are currently in the throes of another national seizure of paranoia, resembling the hysteria which surrounded the Alien and Sedition Acts, the Palmer Raids, and the McCarthy era. Those who register dissent or who petition the government for redress are subjected to scrutiny by grand juries, by the FBI, or even by the military. Their associates are investigated. Their homes are bugged and their telephones are wiretapped. They are befriended by secret government informers. Their patriotism and loyalty are questioned. . . . More than our privacy is implicated. Also at stake is the reach of the Government's power to intimidate its critics" (407 U.S. at 329–33).

The government's attempt to abuse power did not surprise Douglas, but he did have great difficulty accepting the Court's reluctance to meet the challenge to rights and liberties that he saw as so obvious and so serious. As indicated in his dissent in *Laird v. Tatum* (1972), he saw the domestic surveillance program conducted by the military as resting on "brute power" and nothing more, an act that "must be repudiated as a usurpation dangerous to the civil liberties on which free men are dependent" (408 U.S. at 24). He termed it "a cancer on the body politic . . . a measure of the disease which afflicts us," and, given that the "Constitution was designed to keep government off the backs of the people," he found it difficult to believe that the Court would stand by and allow this sort of thing to happen (28). Douglas could not take seriously the Court's conclusion that no injury had in fact occurred to citizens whose lives had been the subject of government intelligence gathering.

According to Douglas's view of the general pattern of behavior in the White House, and given his disdain for Richard Nixon, Douglas was not surprised by the Watergate debacle. In fact, in his dissent in *Gravel v. United States* (1972), Douglas suggested that the problem presented by the use of the secret stamp and of executive privilege to prevent congressional inquiry into the government's practices "looms large as one of separation of powers" (408 U.S. at 638–39) and was bound to lead to abuses. Douglas joined the Court's unanimous opinion in *United States v. Nixon* (1974) and, in fact, played a role in the collective effort of the justices to arrive at an opinion all could join.

The other kind of executive power that Douglas addressed with some regularity was the authority vested in administrative agencies. He had headed one of the nation's leading regulatory commissions and had been one of the Court's experts on administrative law since his earliest days on the bench. He understood the necessity of substantial delegations of authority to administrative bodies and the usefulness of the expertise they could bring to bear on the day-to-day problems of governance.[19] At the same time, Douglas knew just as well the potential danger those same agencies posed to the citizens they were designed to serve. Thus he once declared, "Law has reached its finest moment when it has freed man from the unlimited discretion of some ruler, some civil or military official, some bureaucrat."[20] Above all, he was not prepared to allow a claim to expertise to justify a violation of law or to let administrative action go unreviewed merely because an administrator asserted expertise as the basis for action. He wrote, "Unless we make the requirements for administrative action strict and demanding, expertise, the strength of modern government, can become a monster which rules with no practical limits on its discretion."[21]

By the arrival of the Burger Court years, Douglas had seemed to focus upon four categories of administrative law problems. The first category challenged the Court with fine-tuning the relationship between the need for administrative discretion and the importance of control over administrative power. In such cases Douglas was willing to be flexible and weigh the competing concerns.[22] The second class of cases important to him concerned the Freedom of Information Act. Douglas was not prepared to see agencies hide behind exemptions to the act when a possible need for knowledge about government performance was at issue.[23] The third set of cases concerned the availability of judicial review, whether the issue was reviewability or standing. In these cases Douglas was uncompromising. The idea of unreviewable administrative power was simply unacceptable under all but the most unusual circumstances,[24] and in cases in which agencies threatened critical constitutional freedoms such as privacy or freedom of the press, he was equally adamant.[25] In all of this, Douglas was very much aware that the needs of the people, expressed through the legislature, could only be met with an ongoing development of administrative law.

Legislative Power

As a New Deal liberal, Douglas was supportive of an energetic legislature. He even saw himself as something of a Jeffersonian democrat. Upon entering the Court, Douglas joined with the other Roosevelt Court justices in reversing doctrines remaining from an earlier era in which the judiciary used freedom of contract and loosely interpreted standards of rationality to assess the acceptability of legislation. Indeed, Douglas authored two of the most frequently cited opinions for the Court, insisting that it does "not sit as a super-legislature to weigh the wisdom of legislation."[26]

Unless he saw a violation of constitutional rights and liberties, Douglas was prepared to grant the legislature the lead role in policy-making. He joined the series of cases decided during his time on the Court extending congressional authority under the commerce clause and taxing and spending powers. In fact, Douglas was willing to move beyond those rulings to suggest that more attention be given to the enforcement powers granted to Congress under the Fourteenth and Fifteenth Amendments. He concurred in *Heart of Atlanta Motel v. United States* (1964) and *Katzenbach v. McClung* (1964), in which the Court upheld the Civil Rights Act of 1964, but Douglas argued that the Court and Congress should avoid tortured readings of the commerce power in favor of a more direct application of the enforcement clause of the Fourteenth Amendment. If that meant overturning the infamous *Civil Rights Cases* (1883), then so be it.

Notwithstanding his fear that the Burger Court was too often ready to hide behind the political question doctrine rather than face important issues, Douglas was willing to use that doctrine to maintain the institutional integrity of Congress. He concurred in one of the last Warren Court rulings in this area, *Powell v. McCormack* (1969), and dissented in *Roudebush v. Hartke* (1972), one of the Burger Court's first assessments. If Congress had taken a vote to expel Adam Clayton Powell after he had been seated, rather than refusing to seat him after he had been duly elected, Douglas said, this case would have been a nonjusticiable political question. In a slightly different context three years later, Douglas dissented from the *Hartke* decision on the grounds that determining which of two candidates had won a Senate race was the exclusive province of the Senate and not the judiciary. "What the Senate should do in the merits is not a justiciable controversy. The role of the courts is to protect the Senate's exclusive jurisdiction over the subject matter" (405 U.S. at 33).

Douglas considered the speech or debate clause of Article I an important mechanism, not because it protected members of Congress but because it ensured a free and open debate. The public, in turn, could draw information from the congressional exchanges and use it to support discussions outside government. Largely for this reason, he dissented from the Court's decision in *Gravel v.*

United States (1972), which rejected Senator Gravel's claim that he and his aide were completely protected by the clause for their actions in disclosing the Pentagon Papers to publishers.

Judicial Power

For Douglas the power of the judiciary entailed judicial responsibility. The abdication of the judicial duty to decide cases and controversies arising under the Constitution and under federal laws was just as dangerous as the abuse of judicial power. As Douglas observed in *Flast v. Cohen* (1968): "There has been a school of thought that the less the judiciary does, the better. . . . The late Edmund Cahn, who opposed that view, stated my philosophy. He emphasized the importance of the role that the federal judiciary was designed to play in guarding basic rights against majoritarian control. He chided the view expressed by my Brother Harlan: 'we are entitled to reproach the majoritarian justices of the Supreme Court . . . with straining to be reasonable when they ought to be adamant' " (392 U.S. at 110). A responsible judiciary must be made up of courageous independent judges. It was critical, in his view, that citizens could believe that a potent forum for obtaining justice would be available to them.

Douglas's great fear was that the Burger Court was developing precisely the wrong image. The Court was, in his view, using various procedural devices to avoid important questions presented in the form of properly developed cases and controversies. Furthermore, the Court seemed unwilling to make the kind of substantive decisions needed to ensure checks on abuse of power by other units of government and to guarantee constitutional rights and liberties.

From 1970 until 1974 Douglas produced a variety of opinions on standing to sue, including a number of majority opinions written for the Court, in which he advocated a flexible and open policy.[27] But during 1974 and 1975 the Court's rulings suggested an intention to stop the expansion of the standing doctrine and, in fact, to read standing much more narrowly than it had been interpreted for some time.[28] Douglas responded angrily.[29] In one of his last opinions, *Warth v. Seldin* (1975), he expressed his frustration with the Court's changing view. In *Warth* the Court denied standing to a wide variety of plaintiffs seeking to prosecute an open housing case concerning a zoning decision in an upstate New York community. Douglas wrote in dissent: "Standing has become a barrier to access to the federal courts, just as 'the political question' was in earlier decades. The mounting caseload of federal courts is well known. But cases such as this one reflect festering sores in our society; and the American dream teaches that if one reaches high enough and persists there is a forum where justice is dispensed. I would lower the technical barriers and let the courts serve that ancient need. They can in time be curbed by legislative or constitutional restraints if an emergency arises" (422 U.S. at 519).

The trend toward tighter readings of procedural rules governing access to the court system was not limited to the question of standing. Douglas saw it in the Court's rulings on abstention and mootness and in its more guarded approach to the use of class-action suits.[30] He viewed these cases as "monuments to the present Court's abdication of its constitutional responsibility to decide cases properly within its jurisdiction."[31]

Constitutional Rights and Liberties

While Douglas understood power and had been willing to use it himself over the years, he was more concerned with liberty. The only way to maintain the kind of nation envisioned by the Constitution, as Douglas said so often, was to "keep government off the backs of the people." The Constitution, and the Court as the institution created by it for the protection of liberties, must ensure that citizens enjoy individual freedom, freedom from discrimination, and protection against invasion of privacy, which all citizens need to maintain their individuality in a large and complex society. The constitutional amendments ensuring these essential conditions were not simply individual protections, but elements of a larger body of constitutional principles for the preservation of necessary rights and liberties.

The First Amendment

Douglas found the First Amendment and the freedoms it protects at the core of this structure of liberty. Though his approach to the First Amendment was clearly and heavily influenced by Hugo Black, it was distinct. It was in his later years on the Court that Douglas fully developed his First Amendment position.

Douglas's approach to First Amendment freedoms undoubtedly began with Hugo Black's position that this amendment prohibited any interference with freedom of speech or press. Like Black, Douglas contended that the clear and present danger test, or any standard that drew a line short of action, was an unacceptable basis for assessing the outer boundaries of free speech. With Black,

Douglas insisted that the clear and present danger idea, which had filtered down through various rulings with changing interpretations from the time it was announced in *Schenck v. United States* (1919), had too often provided little real protection in times of stress.[32]

Yet Douglas was prepared to go even further than Black. He did not accept the idea that a hard and fast line could be drawn between speech and action. One of the strongest disagreements between the two emerged over the question of "speech plus" versus symbolic speech.[33] During the Burger Court years, Douglas joined those Court opinions that supported demonstrations and various types of symbolic expression like the burning of draft cards. He joined dissenters in decisions that tended to define expression narrowly, as in the shopping center case *Lloyd Corporation v. Tanner* (1972).[34]

On the other hand, even Douglas had his limits. So long as no content-based discrimination was involved, he was content with time, place, and manner regulations for marches and demonstrations. He was prepared to accept a ban on speech in the form of violent conduct. For example, he concurred in *Samuels v. Mackell* (1971), in which he found that some of the "overt acts relate to the acquisition of weapons, gunpowder, and the like, and the storing of gasoline to start fires. Persuasion by such means plainly has no First Amendment protection" (401 U.S. at 75).[35]

Though he was a strong defender of the First Amendment rights of college students during the period of campus unrest in the late 1960s and early 1970s, Douglas warned, "This does not mean that free speech can be used with impunity as an excuse to break up classrooms, to destroy the quiet and decorum of convocations, or to bar the constitutional privileges of others to meet together in matters of common concern."[36] Convinced that the political climate of that time posed serious threats to academic freedom, Douglas thought that some of the cases coming to the Court concerning dismissals of college instructors did not involve issues of due process so much as matters of academic freedom protected by the First Amendment. Dissenting in *Board of Regents v. Roth* in 1972, Douglas warned, "No more direct assault on academic freedom can be imagined than for the school authorities to be allowed to discharge a teacher because of his or her philosophical, political, or ideological beliefs" (408 U.S. at 581). The other key academic freedom issue Douglas saw emerging during this period was the state's attempts to limit access to controversial speakers. He dissented vigorously when, in *Kleindienst v. Mandel* (1972), the Court upheld a State Department decision withholding a visa from a Marxist speaker who had been invited to address a number of university audiences in the United States. Douglas contended, "The First Amendment involves not only the right to speak and publish but also the right to hear, to learn, to know" (408 U.S. at 771).

His broad view of freedom of expression, association, and political action was not limited to the college campus. Douglas found Burger Court decisions upholding the Hatch Act's restrictions on public employees' freedom of expression and political association extremely troublesome. He had first addressed the Hatch Act in 1947, dissenting from the Court's ruling upholding the statute.[37] The cases that reached the Court in the 1970s challenged the act and also state statutes modeled on it on grounds of vagueness and overbreadth.[38] While Douglas maintained his earlier argument that the act's restrictions violated the First Amendment, he was particularly concerned that the Court was willing to allow the statute and its regulations to stand in light of a history of uncertainty as to the kinds of behavior that were permissible. The regulations provided little help for a civil servant who wanted to play even a minimal role as a citizen in the electoral process. Douglas saw risks not merely for the individuals employed by the government, but also risks for the bureaucracy. As he observed in *Broadrick v. Oklahoma* (1973): "A bureaucracy that is alert, vigilant, and alive is more efficient than one that is quiet and submissive. It is the First Amendment that makes it alert, vigilant, and alive. It is suppression of First Amendment rights that creates faceless, nameless bureaucrats who are inert in their localities and submissive to some master's voice" (413 U.S. at 621).

The 1970s were also a time for new discussions about freedom of the press. Douglas found nothing particularly complicated in this field. The First Amendment freedoms were absolute, and they covered the ability to acquire, edit, and disseminate news. The claim by reporters that freedom of the press included the acquisition and editing of news as well as unfettered publication pressed the Court into new areas. Douglas dissented from the Court's decisions that rejected a number of such claims even though the Court accepted, in principle, the idea that the acquisition of news is protected. He dissented from *Branzburg v. Hayes* (1972), which required reporters testifying before grand juries to reveal confidential sources. He objected to the Court's rulings upholding the authority of state and federal officials to limit reporters' access to prisons to interview inmates.[39] Douglas also dissented from the Court's decision in *Dyson v. Stein* (1971), which vacated and remanded, on abstention grounds, a decision concerning a pending Texas prosecution of a publication known as *Dallas Notes*. In his view a dramatic violation of the First Amendment had occurred when Texas authorities staged a massive search and seizure of the publication's offices. And his position on dissemination was clear: Douglas saw no authority for any governmental restraint on the press. He had joined Black's position in *New York Times v. Sullivan* (1971), in which Black rejected the idea that libel applied to public matters or public officials.[40]

One problem the Court has struggled with since the mid-1960s is the status of broadcasters under the First Amendment. While the First Amendment clearly applies to broadcasters, the Court has pointed to differences between print and broadcast media that require different treatment under free press guarantees. Douglas rejected this distinction, arguing that "TV and radio stand in the same protected position under the First Amendment as do newspapers and magazines."[41]

Commercial speech was another area in which Douglas thought the Court had drawn excessively narrow boundaries of First Amendment coverage. Though he had previously joined the Court in its conclusion that commercial speech was not to be accorded full First Amendment protection, Douglas changed his mind in 1973.[42] The Court would later come to a similar conclusion.[43]

One of the most difficult First Amendment problems for many members of the Court during the 1970s was obscenity. Douglas, like Black, had no difficulty with it. The Court faced a string of obscenity cases in 1973 and 1974 that led to significant doctrinal changes and modifications of voting alignments on the Court. Brennan made clear his intention to switch position—from one of the Court's leading authors in obscenity decisions to one who would oppose obscenity convictions except in cases where the material had been thrust upon unwilling recipients or had been made available to children.[44] The doctrinal change came in *Miller v. California* (1973), which permitted the use of a local community standard in obscenity cases. Douglas rejected the Court's approach and insisted that under the new standard it would be impossible for authors to know whether their works would be protected by the First Amendment.[45] Beyond that, he found it utterly ridiculous that the Court would decide in *Stanley v. Georgia* (1969) that willing adults could have obscene literature in their own homes but could be prohibited from purchasing it or be prosecuted for transporting it.[46]

The final area of First Amendment debate in which Douglas was heavily involved was the free exercise and establishment of religion, a field in which he underwent a substantial change over the years. He had joined Justice Black's opinion in *Everson v. Board of Education* (1947), upholding a New Jersey program that allowed public funds to be used to reimburse students' transportation expenses for secular and sectarian schools. He had authored the opinion for the Court in *Zorach v. Clauson* (1952), allowing New York City to operate a released-time program in which children left public schools to attend religious instruction in church facilities. In *Zorach*, he chastised those demanding a complete separation of church and state with the assertion, "We are a religious people whose institutions presuppose a Supreme Being" (343 U.S. at 313).

On the other hand, this is the same Douglas who would later attack definitions of religion applied to conscientious objector classification cases that required belief in a supreme being before CO status would be granted. Indeed, he repudiated his vote in *Everson* in his dissent from *Walz v. Tax Commission of the City of New York* (1970), which challenged a New York tax exemption for church property. He wrote that "the Everson decision was five to four and, though one of the five, I have since had grave doubts about it, because I have become convinced that grants to institutions teaching a sectarian creed violate the Establishment Clause" (397 U.S. at 703). As if to underscore his realignment, Douglas appended a copy of Madison's "Memorial and Remonstrance" to his *Walz* dissent. Justice Rutledge had done the same in his *Everson* dissent. In addition to the other factors that may have prompted his change in approach, Douglas had determined that the United States had "gradually edged into a situation where vast amounts of public funds are supplied each year to sectarian schools."[47]

Douglas was not impressed by arguments that the programs at issue were secular textbook loans or construction or operating funds going for nonsectarian educational purposes. It was impossible in any realistic sense to separate the secular and sectarian elements of education in a religious school without producing the kind of excessive entanglement between church and state that would surely result in the hostility that the establishment clause was designed to prevent.[48] Further, while textbooks may not be fungible, funds are—meaning that government assistance freed dollars from one part of the church schools' budgets that could be spent elsewhere. Thus the government was underwriting baseline financing of religious education, albeit quite apart from any particular program or activity. It was for this reason that Douglas could not accept Chief Justice Burger's attempt to define a line between acceptable and unacceptable forms of financial assistance in *Lemon v. Kurtzman* (1971) and *Tilton v. Richardson* (1971). For Douglas, any assistance was too much. Despite his hard line on establishment issues, however, he remained sensitive to the complexity of some of the more difficult free exercise issues, as was most evident in his effort to resolve the difficult questions presented by the Amish school attendance case, *Wisconsin v. Yoder* (1972).

The Fourteenth Amendment

Douglas was keenly aware of the central role played by the Fourteenth Amendment in providing protections not only for First Amendment-related freedoms but for the other liberties protected by the Bill of Rights. He had been involved in most of the important cases in which the Bill of Rights guarantees were applied to the states through the incorporation doctrine. He was fond of quoting Hugo Black's opinions on that subject and painfully aware that not all of his colleagues shared the view that the Fourteenth Amendment due process clause had totally incorporated the Bill of Rights.

But Douglas was also concerned about due process in its more common form—procedural due process in civil and criminal matters. For him, procedural due process was an end to a means, the assurance of fair treatment at the hands of an increasingly powerful government. His concern with fundamental fairness in adjudications was heightened by his view of the threat to liberty posed by administrative agencies. He was particularly troubled when it seemed that those at risk were the poor, the weak, or the unpopular. He joined a number of the Court's decisions requiring due process protections for minors, families receiving government aid, and social security claimants.[49] He was also concerned that the courts were apparently being used to coerce the weak or the poor to benefit financial institutions or large firms, as in cases of wage garnishment or repossession of property.[50] Finally, he was alert for situations in which government action held up an individual to public scorn or ridicule, as in *Wisconsin v. Constantineau* (1971). Douglas warned, "Where a person's good name, reputation, honor, or integrity is at stake because of what the government is doing to him, notice and an opportunity to be heard are essential" (400 U.S. at 437).

A great deal of equal protection language emerges in Douglas's opinions on due process. For him, due process required fairness, which, at a minimum, necessitated protection of those least able to obtain fair treatment in a sophisticated legal system. He was, for example, always on guard against government procedures that seemed to block due process because of the wealth or age of the citizen involved.

The cases brought during the early Burger Court years raising claims under the equal protection clause of the Fourteenth Amendment and the due process clause of the Fifth Amendment presented Douglas with a variety of difficulties. Most of the cases that had arisen in his previous experience had been racial discrimination suits emanating from jurisdictions that had mandated segregation by statute. But two things changed in the Burger Court period.

The most obvious change was a new cast of characters on the Court with a rather different orientation to equal protection questions. Gone were the days when strings of unanimous rulings on school desegregation issued from the Supreme Court. The second change was the increasing variety of discrimination suits and the contemporary contexts in which they developed. By now, the segregation statutes had been eliminated, and few officials openly declared any intention to engage in discrimination. Of course, conduct did not always match the change in rhetoric. These less obvious cases required the Court to wrestle with two critical issues: What standards of proof and evaluation would the Court employ in the absence of an obvious mandate for segregation—the de jure versus de facto problem? Beyond that, how would the Court now deal with the question whether state action could be found that supported obvious acts of discrimination committed by private individuals? Further, the types of equal protection claims had expanded well beyond the racial issues that Douglas had seen most often before. Assertions of discrimination on the basis of gender, legitimacy, alienage, and wealth came to the Court for resolution. Would they be treated like race or handled on some other grounds? Another type of new equal protection claim was the "benign discrimination suit" involving programs intended to benefit previously victimized classes. Examples included special programs to benefit widows and affirmative action options for minorities seeking equal employment and educational opportunities.

The state action question presented some difficulty for Douglas precisely because he did not want to interpret the Court's state action doctrine so as to undermine the freedom of association and the right to privacy that he valued so highly.[51] Yet he did not want communities to get away with indirect discrimination and accomplish by subterfuge that which they could not have done directly. In general, Douglas interpreted the state action doctrine broadly and was bothered by his colleagues' increasing tendency to read it more narrowly.[52]

Douglas's answer to the de jure versus de facto distinction was to eliminate it. Interestingly, his position was joined by Justice Powell. Both wrote separate opinions in *Keyes v. School District No. 1* (1973) that argued against the distinction. In this case and others, Douglas found it ironic and clearly unacceptable that segregation was treated as accidental when it had resulted from years of governmental participation. The means of government involvement were many and varied, ranging from the encouragement of racially restrictive covenants, discriminatory zoning decisions, discriminatory administration of school districts, assignment of personnel on the basis of race, and administration of grant programs so as to perpetuate segregation within a community. Dissenting in *Milliken v. Bradley* (1974), Douglas warned: "The issue is not whether there should be racial balance but whether the state's use of various devices that end up with black schools and white schools brought the Equal Protection Clause into effect. . . . It is conceivable that ghettos develop on their own without any hint of state action. But since Michigan by one device or another has over the years created black school districts and white school districts, the task of equity is to provide a unitary system for the affected area where, as here, the state washes its hands of its own creations" (418 U.S. at 761–62).

Another source of debate within the Court as it left the 1960s and entered the 1970s was whether to handle the various new equal protection claims in the same manner as the old claims based on race. Douglas joined the Court's rulings that sought to add gender and alienage to the list of categories the Court would consider inherently suspect under the equal protection clause, like race, thus triggering strict judicial scrutiny.[53] Douglas was particularly responsive to claims of discrimination on the basis of legitimacy.[54] On the other hand, he tended not to speak of suspect classes in such cases. In some instances, as when state law treated illegitimate children differently, it was unnecessary for him to reach the question of strict scrutiny since, like Brennan, he thought that classifications such as legitimacy could not withstand even the minimal rational relationship test. Indeed, Douglas thought that classifications involving gender and legitimacy were often based on nothing more than administrative convenience.

When he found a case that involved more than mere convenience or concerned efforts to meet the effects of past discrimination, Douglas was prepared to be flexible. Writing for the Court in *Kahn v. Shevin* (1974), he upheld a Florida tax exemption that applied to widows but not to widowers. He found that this distinction was not based merely on administrative convenience but rested "upon some ground of difference having a fair and substantial relationship to the object of the legislation" (416 U.S. at 355). Noting the historic discrimination against women in the workplace, Douglas found the situation that often confronted widows forced back into the marketplace quite different from that of the widower.

In the other major case of affirmative action that he faced, *DeFunis v. Odegaard* (1974), Douglas sought to be flexible in response to historic patterns of racial discrimination, but he was not willing to allow the use of programs that relied solely on race as the criterion for government action. Race alone was no justification for action. Anticipating the position the Court would eventually take in *Regents of the University of California v. Bakke* (1978), Douglas argued that race could be one factor among many that universities might take into consideration in admission decisions, but rejected the idea of a minority-only admission program.

The Right to Privacy

Justice Douglas wrote in many rights and liberties cases in addition to those already considered. Probably none of the others was more important to Douglas or caused more controversy than the right to privacy cases. For him, the need to keep government off the backs of the people and protect their right to be let alone was crucial. He did not come to his position on privacy in the late 1960s or reach it because he wanted to justify birth control or abortion; he borrowed the rudiments of his theory and some of its language from Brandeis, and developed the rest through his experience as a lawyer and as a justice.

Douglas was hardly writing on a clean slate when he authored *Griswold v. Connecticut* (1965), in which the Court anounced the constitutional right to privacy for the first time. Even though the Court had decided *Pierce v. Society of Sisters* (1925) and *Meyer v. Nebraska* (1923) on due process grounds, those cases had been argued largely in terms of the right of families to make basic decisions about the rearing of children without governmental interference. Justice Brandeis's ringing dissent in *Olmstead v. United States* (1928) had referred to "the right to be let alone—the most comprehensive of rights and the right most valued by civilized men" (227 U.S. at 478). Other earlier Fourth and Fifth Amendment cases had also referred to the constitutional importance of privacy.[55] Douglas himself had spoken of decisions concerning marriage and procreation as implicating fundamental civil rights as early as 1942, in *Skinner v. Oklahoma*.

The *Griswold* decision was but one step in the development of a much longer and larger debate on the Court, which was highlighted during the Burger Court years. The first part of that ongoing debate was a continuation of the birth control controversy, this time concerning unmarried persons. In *Eisenstadt v. Baird* (1972), the Court overturned, on equal protection grounds, the conviction of a person charged under a Massachusetts law with advising single persons about birth control and distributing contraceptives to them. Douglas concurred, but he saw the case as presenting more of a First Amendment issue since Baird was not operating a clinic or purporting to prescribe for individual persons but only making the information and materials available in connection with his lecture. Nevertheless, Douglas also joined the Court's equal protection argument.

Of course, it was the 1973 *Roe v. Wade* decision recognizing the right of a woman, in consultation with her physician, to terminate a pregnancy that produced the most recent round of controversy. But *Roe* was not the first abortion case to come to the Burger Court. In *United States v. Vuitch* (1971), a badly fragmented Court upheld the District of Columbia's ban on abortions unless they were required for the life or health of the woman. Douglas dissented, finding that the terms *health* and *life* were so broad that juries considering criminal prosecutions in such a volatile field might very well depart substantially from what physicians might decide was necessary for the health or life of their patients. He would not permit such vagueness in an area so directly affecting fundamental privacy rights. In fact, Justice Blackmun's first draft of the *Roe* opinion relied on a vagueness argument and deliberately avoided "the more complex Ninth Amendment issue."[56] Brennan and Douglas pressed Blackmun to respond to the discussion in conference and reach the core issue.[57] Douglas was already at work on a draft opinion for the Court in the Georgia companion case to *Roe, Doe v. Bolton* (1973), that reached the merits. Portions of that draft later appeared in Douglas's concurrence in *Roe.* The cases were carried over into the 1972 term, when Blackmun produced the final opinions in both.

The fact that Douglas played an important role in the development of the modern right to privacy does not mean he was willing to sacrifice all other interests to the privacy claim. In his opinion for the Court in *Village of Belle Terre v. Boraas* (1974), Justice Douglas upheld a zoning ordinance limiting the number of unrelated persons who might live together in a single family dwelling in the face of a variety of constitutional claims, including privacy and associational freedoms. He saw neither a right to privacy problem nor a freedom of association issue in the case, and, as he had done since his earliest days on the Court, Douglas accorded substantial authority to local governments to make zoning decisions that might have an incidental effect on lifestyle.

Criminal Process

Douglas demonstrated little enthusiasm for constitutional criminal law with two exceptions: (1) those cases in which it seemed to him that the defendant was being treated badly because of poverty, weakness, political views, or membership in a disadvantaged group, and (2) cases in which he saw the likelihood of broad applications of the principle at issue to the wider society, such as wiretaps and other uses of technology to invade individual privacy. For the most part, Douglas joined, rather than led, Warren Court criminal due process innovations.

The field that he saw as being most threatening to privacy during the Burger Court years was search and seizure, particularly the use of surveillance or wiretaps. His position on wiretaps and search and seizure, developed in the late 1940s, intensified over his years on the Court. In *United States v. White* (1971), he wrote: "Electronic surveillance is the greatest leveler of human privacy ever known. To be sure, the Constitution and Bill of Rights are not to be read as covering only the technology known in the 18th century. . . . [T]he concepts of privacy which the Founders enshrined in the Fourth Amendment vanish completely when we slavishly allow an all-powerful government, proclaiming law and order, efficiency, and other benign purposes, to penetrate all the walls and doors which men need to shield them from the pressures of a turbulent life around them and give them the health and strength to carry on" (401 U.S. at 756).[58]

Douglas saw a strong relationship between Fourth Amendment search and seizure issues and Fifth Amendment self-incrimination questions. Illustrative was Douglas's dissent from *Couch v. United States* (1973), a case involving the use of a summons by the Internal Revenue Service to an accountant ordering him to produce a client's books. He thought that the decision upholding that tactic provided "yet another tool of the ever-widening government invasion and oversight of our private lives" (409 U.S. at 338).

One can see in Douglas's opinions on Sixth and Eighth Amendment issues his concern with protecting the underdog, particularly the poor and minorities. He argued that the right to counsel should be interpreted as broadly as possible, and he supported the Warren Court rulings extending Sixth Amendment protections. During the Burger years, he joined the Court in its further development of the right to counsel. For example, he wrote for the Court in *Argersinger v. Hamlin* (1972), holding that a defendant is entitled to be represented by counsel at the public expense even in misdemeanor cases as long as jail is a possible punishment.

Douglas's defense of the underdog was apparent as well in a number of the fair jury cases decided in the Burger Court period. While he concurred with the Court's decision upholding state laws allowing juries of less than twelve, he drew the line at laws permitting criminal convictions to be based on less than unanimous jury verdicts.[59] The risk of easy prosecutions was just too great. In *McKeiver v. Pennsylvania* (1971), he also advocated the extension of the right to a jury trial to juveniles facing delinquency charges and sentences to custody if the charges against the juvenile were the equivalent of felonies under state law.

Douglas's opinions on death penalty questions indicated that he saw Eighth Amendment cases in a similar light. His principal objection was the arbitrary administration of the death penalty and the history of discrimination in its administration. Concurring in *Furman v. Georgia* (1972), in which the Court struck down the arbitrary and capricious use of the death penalty, Douglas argued: "In a Nation committed to equal protection of the laws there is no permissible 'caste' aspect of law enforcement. Yet we know that the discretion of judges and juries in imposing the death penalty enables the penalty to be selectively applied, feeding prejudices against the accused if he is poor and despised, lacking political clout, or if he is a member of a suspect or unpopular minority, and saving those who by social position may be in a more protected position" (408 U.S. at 255). Indeed, his evaluation of the states' use of the death penalty suggested that it was "pregnant with discrimination and discrimination is an ingredient not compatible with the idea of equal protection of the laws that is implicitly in the ban on 'cruel and unusual punishments' " (256–57).

Conclusion

William O. Douglas was, in many respects, the conscience of the Supreme Court, though his influence is difficult to assess because of the length of his career and his quite different position relative to his colleagues over time. Douglas was always ready to sound the alarm whenever he saw the Court constraining the rights of the citizenry. He was aware that his dissents in later years were unlikely to prevent the Burger Court from moving in directions he thought erroneous, but that did not hinder him. He inherited the lead dissenter role from Hugo Black and used it with vigor. This vigor was maddening to some of his opponents and even some of his friends, but he persisted. In Lyndon Johnson's final break with Douglas, the president remarked, " 'Liberty and Justice . . . that's all you apparently think of. And when you pass over the last hill, I suppose you will be shouting 'Liberty and justice!' " Douglas replied, " 'You're goddamn right, Mr. President.' "[60]

Douglas's opinions as the conscience of the Court, however, were often about justice in the particular rather than in the abstract. And in the particular he was concerned with justice for the poor, the weak, and the politically isolated. In case after case he warned against interpretations of the law that undermined "Equal Justice Under Law," the words carved in stone above the entrance to the court.[61] He was willing, on occasion, to yield to the suggestions of his colleagues, especially Black and Brennan. More often he was a loner, perfectly prepared to issue lone opinions. He was also ready to blow the whistle, as it were, if he thought that the Court's handling of a case had been inadequate. By inadequate Douglas meant not merely erroneous action but also judicial abdication through refusal to address critical legal questions because of an unwarranted timidity. And Douglas was not as dogmatic on a number of issues as it may first appear. Indeed, it was his willingness to admit in his opinions that he had made mistakes in the past that caused some of his colleagues considerable consternation.

On a personal level, Douglas could be extremely caustic and

harsh in his exchanges. By the same token, he retained cordial relations with a number of colleagues with whom he often disagreed. There is little doubt that his intensely held views; his intellectual gifts, which many classify as that of a genius or near-genius; and a very shy aspect to his character combined to produce a stirring but occasionally enigmatic figure. Though he did not lead the Burger Court, he certainly played an important role in shaping the law in the cases that met the Burger group as it came to the Court.

Once the transition had begun, he played an important role in the discussion of a wide range of critical and controversial issues. He left the Court with the legacy of a courageous justice committed to liberty and equality—a person willing to stand for the poor as well as the rich, the political outcast as well as the pillar of the establishment.

NOTES

Portions of this chapter appeared as Chapter 13 in Phillip J. Cooper and Howard Ball, *Of Power and Right: Justices Black and Douglas and America's Tumultuous Years, 1937–1975* (New York: Oxford University Press, 1991).

1. The general biographical information given here is based on several autobiographies by Douglas, including *Of Men and Mountains* (New York: Harper, 1950); *Go East, Young Man: The Early Years* (New York: Dell, 1974); and *The Court Years, 1939–1975* (New York: Random House, 1980). I also draw upon interviews of Douglas's contemporaries and colleagues and research analyzing the presidential and judicial papers of his contemporaries.

2. Douglas was so amused by this that he sent a copy to the White House. Memorandum, Douglas to Marvin McIntyre, Dec. 3, 1937, Official Files 34–3, FDR Papers, Franklin Delano Roosevelt Library, Hyde Park, New York.

3. A. F. Whitney to Franklin D. Roosevelt, Mar. 7, 1939, Personal Papers File 6389, FDR Papers.

4. Douglas to Hugo Black, July 23, 1941, Box 308, William O. Douglas Papers, Library of Congress.

5. See, for example, *An Almanac of Liberty* (Garden City, N.Y.: Doubleday, 1954); *The Rights of the People* (Garden City, N.Y.: Doubleday, 1954); *America Challenged* (Princeton, N.J.: Princeton University Press, 1958); *The Anatomy of Liberty* (New York: Trident Press, 1963).

6. U.S. House of Representatives, Final Report of the Special Subcommittee on H.Res. 920 of the Committee on the Judiciary, *Associate Justice William O. Douglas*, 91st Cong., 2d Sess., 1970.

7. See, for example, *United States v. Pink* (1942); *Korematsu v. United States* (1944).

8. Douglas, *The Court Years*, p. 55.

9. Ibid. See also Douglas's opinions in *Massachusetts v. Laird* (1970); *Mora v. McNamara* (1967); *Mitchell v. United States* (1967).

10. See, for example, *Estep v. United States* (1946).

11. *Welsh v. United States* (1970), dissenting; *United States v. Seeger* (1965), concurring.

12. *Ehlert v. United States* (1971), dissenting.

13. *Parker v. Levy* (1974), dissenting.

14. *McKart v. United States* (1969), 395 U.S. at 203–4.

15. See, for example, *United States v. Weller* (1971), dissenting; *Parisi v. Davidson* (1972), concurring; *Fein v. Selective Service System* (1972), dissenting.

16. *Morse v. Boswell* (1969).

17. F. Edward Hebert to Warren E. Burger, Aug. 8, 1969, Box 59, Hugo Black Papers, Library of Congress.

18. Charles Morgan, Jr., to Sam J. Ervin, September 30, 1969, Box 59, Black Papers.

19. William O. Douglas, *We the Judges* (Garden City, N.Y.: Doubleday, 1956), p. 179.

20. *United States v. Wunderlich* (1951), 342 U.S. at 101.

21. *New York v. United States* (1951), 342 U.S. at 884.

22. See, for example, *American Farm Lines v. Black Ball Freight* (1970); *Weinberger v. Hynson, Wescott & Dunning* (1973).

23. See, for example, *Environmental Protection Agency v. Mink* (1973), dissenting.

24. See, for example, *Association of Data Processing Service Organizations, Inc. v. Camp* (1970); *Barlow v. Collins* (1970); *Sierra Club v. Morton* (1972), dissenting.

25. See, for example, *CBS, Inc. v. Democratic National Committee* (1973), concurring; *United States v. Midwest Video* (1972), dissenting; *National Cable Television Association, Inc. v. United States* (1974).

26. *Day-Brite Lighting Co. v. Missouri* (1952); *Williamson v. Lee Optical Co.* (1955).

27. See, for example, *Association of Data Processing Service Organizations*.

28. See, for example, *Warth v. Seldin* (1975); *O'Shea v. Littleton* (1974).

29. See *National R.R. Passenger Corp. v. National Assn. of R.R. Passengers* (1974), dissenting; *O'Shea*, dissenting; *United States v. Richardson* (1974), dissenting; *Schlesinger v. Reservists Committee to Stop the War* (1974).

30. See, for example, *Eisen v. Carlisle & Jacquelin* (1974), dissenting.

31. *SEC v. Medical Committee for Human Rights* (1972), 404 U.S. at 411.

32. *Brandenburg v. Ohio* (1969), concurring.

33. *Adderley v. Florida* (1966).

34. For Douglas's positions on these cases, see *Amalgamated Food Employees v. Logan Valley Plaza, Inc.* (1968), concurring.

35. His position here was not new. Indeed, he had said almost exactly the same thing in his dissent in *Dennis v. United States* (1951).

36. *Jones v. Board of Education* (1970), 397 U.S. at 33–34.

37. *United Public Workers v. Mitchell* (1947), dissenting.

38. *Civil Service Commission v. National Association of Letter Carriers* (1973), dissenting; *Broadrick v. Oklahoma* (1973), dissenting.

39. *Pell v. Procunier* (1974), dissenting; *Saxbe v. Washington Post Co.* (1974).

40. See also *Rosenblatt v. Baer* (1966), concurring; *Time v. Hill* (1967), concurring.

41. *Columbia Broadcasting v. Democratic National Committee* (1973), 412 U.S. at 148.

42. *Pittsburgh Press Co. v. Pittsburgh Commission on Human Relations* (1973), dissenting.

43. *Virginia State Board of Pharmacy v. Virginia Citizens Consumer Council* (1976).

44. *Paris Adult Theatre I v. Slaton* (1973), dissenting.

45. *Miller v. California* (1973), dissenting; *Paris Adult Theatre*, dissenting; *Kaplan v. California* (1973), separate opinion; *Hamling v. United States* (1974), dissenting.

46. *United States v. 12,200-Ft. Reels of Super 8MM. Film* (1973), 413 U.S. at 137. See also *United States v. Orito* (1973), 413 U.S. at 146.

47. *Lemon v. Kurtzman* (1971), 403 U.S. at 630.

48. *Board of Education v. Allen* (1968), dissenting.

49. See, for example, *Goldberg v. Kelly* (1970); *Richardson v. Perales* (1971), dissenting.

50. *Sniadach v. Family Finance Corp.* (1969).

51. *Moose Lodge No. 107 v. Irvis* (1972), 407 U.S. at 179–80.

52. *Evans v. Abney* (1970), dissenting; *Palmer v. Thompson* (1971), dissenting; *Moose Lodge v. Irvis* (1972).

53. See, for example, *Frontiero v. Richardson* (1973), 411 U.S. at 682; *Graham v. Richardson* (1971), 403 U.S. at 371–72.

54. See, for example, *Levy v. Louisiana* (1968); *Boddie v. Connecticut* (1971), concurring; *United States v. Kras* (197), dissenting.

55. See, for example, *Mapp v. Ohio* (1961).

56. Harry A. Blackmun to Conference, May 18, 1972, Box 282, William J. Brennan Papers, Library of Congress.

57. William J. Brennan to Blackmun, May 18, 1972, Box 282, Brennan Papers; Douglas to Blackmun, May 19, 1972, Box 281, Brennan Papers.

58. See also *On Lee v. United States* (1952), dissenting; *Berger v. New York* (1967), concurring; *Katz v. United States* (1967), concurring; *Terry v. Ohio* (1968), dissenting.

59. *Apodaca v. Oregon* (1972), dissenting; *Johnson v. Louisiana* (1972), dissenting.

60. Douglas, *The Court Years*, pp. 329–30. This incident was confirmed in an interview with Cathleen Douglas-Stone, November 14, 1986, Boston, Massachusetts.

61. See, for example, *Sniadach; Goldberg; Rosado v. Wyman* (1970); *Dandridge v. Williams* (1970); *Wyman v. James* (1971); *Richardson v. Perales* (1971); *Lindsey v. Normet* (1972); *Papachristou v. City of Jacksonville* (1972); *Ortwein v. Schwab* (1973).

7

JUSTICE JOHN MARSHALL HARLAN:
Non sub Homine . . .

WALLACE MENDELSON

Justice Harlan was active on the Burger Court for only two terms—
after having served with Chief Justice Warren some fourteen years.
Plainly, the lines of his jurisprudence were developed in the earlier
period. Discussion of his efforts on the Burger Court, then, necessarily
entails reference to what went before, and a comparison with Warren
is revealing.

John Harlan, like Earl Warren, was a Republican; like Warren he
was appointed to the Supreme Court by President Eisenhower (the one
in 1953, the other in 1955). Here the similarity ends. Harlan had been
a consummate lawyer and leader of the bar—matters not unrelated
to his elevation to the bench. Warren had been a consummate politician—his handling of the California delegation at the Republican
National Convention in 1952 was hardly unrelated to his court appointment.

Harlan came from a distinguished, old, upper-class family. He was
a Rhodes scholar, studied jurisprudence at Oxford, and won a "First"—
the highest student honor obtainable. Warren came from a laboring-
class family in which poverty was not unknown. He was, at best, an
average college and law school student.

When the young Harlan returned from England, he joined Root,
Clark in New York—one of the nation's most prestigious law firms.
He soon became a partner, and eventually a leader of the American
bar. Following a family tradition of some three hundred years, however,
he devoted a major part of his time and energy to public service—
first as a reforming assistant U.S. district attorney; then as an aide to
Emory Buckner in a major New York cleanup effort; then via military
service during World War II; and later as chief counsel of the New

York Crime Commission. So, too, he served as director of the Legal Aid Society and as chairman of the Professional Ethics and Judiciary Committees of the New York bar. Warren, on the other hand, had some difficulty in finding a job after graduating from law school. Eventually he got one in a county prosecutor's office. Making a career of prosecution, he rose with remarkable political skill to the office of attorney general of California. This led, in due course, to the governorship.

On the bench, Warren—true to his political career—was essentially a politician (in the best sense); that is, a judge whose chief concern was policy-making. Neither admirers nor critics of the Warren Court have spent much time insisting it was deeply concerned for the rule of law. Its forte, rather—like that of its chief—was policy fabrication with a special bent in favor of those to whom fate had been less than kind. Its values, in sum, sprang from the heart. For a decade at least—especially in the 1960s—the Warren Court played a leading role in the ordering of American domestic affairs. Yet, over vigorous dissent, it showed remarkable self-restraint in the Vietnam cases, involving, as they did, foreign policy. While the chief justice generally wrote the more crucial opinions of our highest court, little of his effort was addressed to those learned in the law. It is said his touchstone for decision was simply "Is it fair?" *Per contra* Harlan was a superb legal craftsman. Highly cerebral, he was devoted to the rule of law and the basic American principle of diffused governmental power. His jurisprudence was as complex as the cases that came before him. He simply could not accept the Warrenite view that the Court's function was to solve, as a matter of policy, all deficiencies (real or imagined) in American society, and to solve them compatibly with the sentiments of the Court's liberal constituency.

Professor Paul Freund reported that his students at the Harvard Law School were quite aware of the difference between cardiac and cerebral decision making: "[T]he very students who more often than not regret [Justice Harlan's] position freely acknowledge that when he has written a concurring or a dissenting opinion they turn to it first, for a full and candid exposition of the case and an intellectually rewarding analysis of the issues. They sometimes regret that their heart's desire has not been supported with equal cogency in the Court's prevailing opinion, sharing as they do an aversion to what a certain English judge called well-meaning sloppiness of thought."[1] No doubt both Harlan and Warren were devoted to democracy, but Harlan could not accept the Warren Court's effort to "bespeak the people's general will when the vote comes out wrong." Neither, according to Gallup polls, could the

Justice John Marshall Harlan

American people. However admirable Warren Court policy-making had seemed on our campuses, by 1969 when Warren left the bench, the Supreme Court had reached its nadir in public esteem.[2]

Unable to accept the role of guardian of Rousseau's "general will," Harlan was the chief dissenter in Warren's era—just as Holmes had been a chief dissenter in the old activist era. Holmes dissented, not because he was a liberal among conservatives—far from it—but because he could not accept wholesale judicial legislation. Similarly, Harlan did not dissent because he was a mossback on a liberal court. After all, it was Harlan who, in *Poe v. Ullman* (1961), planted the seed that became the *Griswold v. Connecticut* (1965) right to privacy. It was he who, concurring in *Garner v. Louisiana* (1961), laid the groundwork for the modern doctrine of symbolic speech. It was he who, writing for the Court in *Cohen v. California* (1971), stretched freedom of expression to the breaking point (even the redoubtable Black could not go so far). It was Harlan also who, on behalf of the Court, put new bite into freedom of association in *NAACP v. Alabama* (1958). So, too, for the Court in *Marchetti v. United States* (1968), he added a crucial new dimension to the privilege against self-incrimination. He concurred, of course, in *Griswold* and *Gideon v. Wainwright* (1963). And he spoke out against what an admirer of the Warren Court called its "vigilante justice" in *Ginzburg v. United States* (1966). One of Harlan's associates at Root, Clark said that the only time he ever saw the future justice angry was when he failed to win reversal of a decision that prevented the allegedly subversive Bertrand Russell from teaching at City College.[3] The point is simply this: the many differences between Warrenite and Harlan opinions are not explicable in liberal versus conservative terms; they spring, rather, from differing conceptions of the role of judges in a democracy predicated on the dual diffusion of authority that we call federalism and the separation of powers.

Freedom of Expression

Harlan wrote several of the Warren Court's most important free speech opinions. Apart possibly from the obscenity cases in which the justices were hopelessly divided, Harlan went as far as the Warren Court would go in protecting freedom of expression. On at least two occasions he went much farther: he dissented in *Ginzburg*, in which the Court upheld an obscenity conviction based on an ex post facto application of judge-made law, and it was he alone in *Garner* who saw the sit-in demonstrations in the early 1960s as exercises in free speech. In a long series of cases, the Warren Court decided in favor of the sit-ins, but always on sterile, happenstance grounds that evaded the crucial issues. Harlan cut the Gordian knot in *Garner* with what Harry Kalven called "imaginative daring."

The most important free speech decision in the early Burger regime came in 1971 in *New York Times Co. v. United States* and *United States v. Washington Post* (the *Pentagon Papers Cases*). They were resolved in a one-paragraph, per curiam opinion that said in essence: any system of prior restraint carries a heavy presumption of unconstitutionality, which in these cases the government has not overcome. But did it have a fair opportunity to do so?

The trial court heard and decided the *Post* case between 8:00 A.M. and 5:00 P.M. on a single day. Another trial court heard the *Times* case in one day and issued its decision the next day. Both courts held against the government—not without dissent. A federal appellate court in each case held a hearing in one day and gave decision the following day. The *Times* decision favored the government; the *Post* decision favored the *Post*. Obviously no judge at any level, nor counsel, could have read the forty-seven volumes that constituted the papers in question. As the chief justice put it: "We do not know the facts of the cases. . . . The precipitate action of this Court aborting trials not yet completed is not [appropriate] judicial conduct. . . . It is interesting to note that counsel on both sides . . . were frequently unable to respond to questions [from the bench] on factual points. Not surprisingly they pointed out that they had been working literally 'around the clock' and simply were unable to review the documents that give rise to these cases and were not familiar with them" (403 U.S. at 748, 749, 751–52). No wonder, then, that the Supreme Court made no effort whatsoever to explain in what respect the plaintiff had failed to meet its "heavy burden" of proof, a task that, in each case, it had less than a day to accomplish.

Another difficulty concerns the prior restraint rule itself. Prior restraints (that is, administrative licensing) had rightly earned a bad name in English history, and the term itself came to us—and remains with us—as a buzz term of evil connotation. But in a series of cases, the Warren Court had made clear that prior restraints—however evil in the context of long-gone English administrative censorship—were not inherently bad in the context of adversarial judicial proceedings.[4] Of course, the *Pentagon Papers Cases* were, in form, adversarial judicial proceedings. The majority judges—all Warren Court holdovers—paid no attention to what the Warren Court had wrought. Instead their per curiam rested on the old, outmoded buzz-term approach. Who will argue that obscurantism is necessarily at odds with statesmanship? Yet the majority justices were not willing to leave it at that. Six concurring opinions demonstrate that they were far from agreement on the rationale of their joint decision—and unwilling to spend enough time to make, or discover, a congenial governing principle of law. They disposed of the two cases in about ninety-six hours. All told, the entire litigation was pushed through three tiers of judges in sixteen days. It would have gone much faster, if four members of the final majority had had their way. Justices Black, Douglas, Brennan, and Marshall had voted to discontinue the restraining orders and deny certiorari. For them no hearing was necessary—their decision had already been made (shades of the kangaroo).

Harlan, joined by Burger and Blackmun, dissented primarily on the ground of undue haste. In his view the cases should have been remanded for further hearings, but, forced by a majority to face the merits, he turned his decision on separation of powers grounds. All save one of the majority justices had rested on the First Amendment, though in express terms it applies only to Congress. Yet no act of Congress was at issue in the *Pentagon Papers Cases*. How strange especially that Justice Black, who had long claimed to be a literalist with respect to the Constitution, nevertheless wrote in pure First Amendment terms. Only Justice Marshall on the majority side found separation of powers decisive.

In Harlan's view, the Court should not get caught up in the conduct of American foreign affairs. Yet "in performance of its duty to protect the values of the First Amendment . . . the judiciary must review the initial Executive determination to the point of satisfying itself that the subject matter . . . does lie within the proper compass of the President's foreign relations power. . . . Moreover, the judiciary may properly insist that the determination [of irreparable injury] be made [personally] by the head of the Executive Department concerned" (403 U.S. at 757). Beyond these two inquiries, Harlan thought, judges respectful of separated powers should not go. It was not, in his view, the function of a court to "redetermine for itself the probable impact of disclosure on the national security" (757). As Paul Freund put it in a related context, it is not for judges to "speculate in historical futures."

In disposing of the cases with such race-course speed, surely the Supreme Court stooped to conquer. No doubt some good resulted, yet the operative meaning of the *Pentagon Papers Cases* seems to be this: government secrets are permissible, but, if the press can discover them by hook or by crook, publication is protected. This approach does not seem an effective way to promote either freedom of the press or national security. Which of them might prevail in a given context would depend upon happenstance, including the luck, guile, or integrity of this or that reporter. Surely Harlan's was a more rational way to balance such critical constitutional interests—news and safety—when they run into one another. How easy the judge's job would be, if, in each case, only one great constitutional principle were at stake.

A thought in passing: the First Amendment outlaws only congressional interference with freedom of speech and press. The founders' exclusion of the president from the First Amendment ban could hardly have been inadvertent. Was it perhaps a recognition of his authority to block harmful publication in the context of his special functions, particularly in foreign affairs?

Finally, a word on *Cohen v. California.* Young Mr. Cohen, it seems, felt deeply about the draft. As though unable to contain his feelings, he appeared in public places with three provocative words displayed on his jacket, obviously for their shock value. In sum, he chose what he must have felt was the only way available to him to get and move an audience. His was not an effort to debate rationally, but rather to air his emotional distaste for conscription, and to do it in a way bound to outrage the "bourgeoisie" upon whom he inflicted himself. He was convicted for disturbing the peace, which no doubt is precisely what he had intended to do, if only in a small way. Harlan, writing one of his last opinions for the Burger Court, masterfully reviewed the traditional limitations upon the right of free speech and found none of them applicable. Then, as in *Garder,* he gave another flashing insight that added a new dimension to "freedom of speech": "[W]e cannot overlook the fact, because it is well illustrated by the episode involved here, that much linguistic expression serves a dual communicative function: it conveys not only ideas capable of relatively precise, detached explication, but otherwise inexpressible emotions as well. In fact, words are often chosen as much for their emotive as their cognitive force. We cannot sanction the view that the Constitution, while solicitous of the cognitive content of individual speech, has little or no regard for that emotive function which, practically speaking, may often be the more important element of the overall message sought to be communicated" (403 U.S. at 25–26).

Civil Rights: State Action

Just as Harlan joined Warren in the great *Brown* (1955) desegregation case (part two), so he joined Burger in *Swann* (1971)—the Supreme Court's first critical step on the road from desegregation to integration. Over and over he indicated by word and deed that, whatever else the

Fourteenth Amendment might mean, for him its chief concern (as for his grandfather in *Plessy*) was racism. Even so, he was not unaware of its explicit limitations. Like the First Amendment, and indeed all other provisions of the Constitution, it is aimed in express terms at governmental, as distinct from private, conduct. This is the state-action problem that the Warren Court so studiously avoided in the sit-in cases. (Recall Harlan's view in *Garner* above that sit-in demonstrations were an exercise in the "free trade in ideas" protected by the First and Fourteenth Amendments.)

In the Warren-era cases, the sit-in demonstrators had been the defendants, typically in trespass actions. Conversely, in *Adickes v. S. H. Kress* (1970) in the Burger era, the demonstrator was the plaintiff. A white woman, she had been denied service at a Kress lunch counter because she was in the company of blacks. She sued under a law (derived from the Civil Rights Act of 1871) that prohibits, inter alia, racism based on the "custom, or usage, of any State."[5] Behind this measure stands the state-action problem. The Court per Harlan held that to trigger the statute there must be "state involvement" via, for example, an arresting policeman; "long-standing social habit" does not suffice.[6] Justice Marshall did not participate. Brennan argued in dissent that the statutory term "custom" means "custom of the people of a state," or a "widespread and long-standing practice," not necessarily "backed by the force of the State."[7] This view no doubt would bring *Adickes* within the statute, but Brennan did not explain how the statute, so construed, could be brought within the Fourteenth Amendment. Douglas, dissenting, avoided the state-action issue by resting on the Thirteenth Amendment. Thus in *Adickes,* Harlan, like the Warren Court in its sit-in cases, honored the state-action limitation; but whereas he did so forthrightly, the Warren Court did so by evasion—by what some see as embarrassing ad hoc improvisation. It is noteworthy that just as the justice read the word "State" in the Fourteenth Amendment to mean "state," so in the *Pentagon Papers Cases* he read the term "Congress" in the First Amendment to mean "congress."

The special significance of *Adickes* is that it marks a return to the written limitation in Amendment Fourteen—specifically, its "no state" provision. For in Warren's day the state-action requirement had undergone a lingering death. Its renaissance—foreshadowed in *Adickes*— came in *Moose Lodge No. 107 v. Irvis* (1972) a few months after Harlan's departure. There in dissent, Douglas, joined by Marshall, paid this—no doubt unintended—tribute to Harlan and the state-action requirement: "The associational rights which our system honors permits all white, all black, all brown, and all yellow clubs to be formed. They also permit all Catholic, all Jewish, or all agnostic clubs to be established. Government may not tell a man or woman who his or her associates must be. The individual can be as selective as he desires. . . . [Moose Lodge race selectivity] is constitutionally irrelevant, as is the decision of Black Muslims to admit to their services only members of their race" (407 U.S. at 179–80). This "zone of privacy" is, of course, what the no-state provision of the Fourteenth Amendment is all about. Douglas being Douglas, however, sought to derive it rather from "the First Amendment and the related guarantees of the Bill of Rights." Thus, a private bar's refusal to serve an outsider would somehow be justified by the Bill of Rights. How far afield Douglas and Marshall were willing to go to avoid honoring the "no state" provision of the Fourteenth Amendment!

Substantive Equal Protection

Initially the Supreme Court found that state law "which discriminated . . . against [Negroes] as a class, was the evil to be remedied" by the equal protection clause.[8] Later, activist judges stretched the clause to cover nonracial classifications. That raised problems. If judges were to go beyond its historic purpose, where would they find guides for determining what conditions would, and what would not, justify unequal treatment of some human beings? Classification, after all, is close to the heart of the legislative function: some must pay higher taxes than others; the needy may deserve welfare benefits, others may not. Thus "equal protection" in nonracial cases came to mean merely that legislative classifications must be reasonable; that only people in similar circumstances must be treated similarly. This, the orthodox rule, was settled long ago. The Warren Court, however, went far to make the equal protection clause a substantive limitation in support of its values, just as the old laissez-faire judicial activists had devised substantive due process to support their values. Harlan opposed substantive equal protection on the same grounds that Holmes and Brandeis had opposed substantive due process. The Warren Court did not repudiate the orthodox reasonableness test; rather, it devised a supplementary "strict scrutiny" test for use in cases involving what it deemed "fundamental" rights. Laws trenching upon the latter were ipso facto invalid unless the state could prove them justified by a "compelling state interest." The true meaning of this innovation is revealed in its history: the Warren Court never found a state measure sufficiently compelling to override anything it deemed "fundamental."

In its last days, the Warren Court went too far even for its chief justice. In *Shapiro v. Thompson* (1969), the Court found a violation of equal protection in a state law denying welfare aid to persons who had not resided in the state for at least one year. Like Warren, Harlan dissented, but on different grounds.

> [T]o extend the "compelling interest" rule to all cases in which such rights [as these] are affected would go far toward making this Court a "super-legislature." This branch of the doctrine is also unnecessary. When the right affected is one assured by the Federal Constitution, any infringement can be dealt with under the Due Process Clause. But when a statute affects only matters not mentioned in the Federal Constitution and is not arbitrary or irrational, I must reiterate that I know of nothing which entitles this Court to pick out particular human activities, characterize them as "fundamental," and give them added protection under an unusually stringent equal protection test. (394 U.S. at 661–62)

A few months later, in *Dandridge v. Williams* (1970), the Burger Court picked up one of Harlan's thoughts in *Shapiro*. Though it accepted the new dual standard, it dropped freewheeling interpretation at the top level: only rights recognized by the Constitution were to have the benefit of upper-level protection. Some have found that this decision was to Warren Court equal-protection activism what *West Coast Hotel v. Parrish* (1937) was to the old Court's due-process activism; namely, the end of the road. Harlan was not so sanguine. Concurring in the result, he said: "Except with respect to racial classifications, to which unique historical considerations apply, . . . I believe the constitutional provisions assuring equal protection of the laws impose a standard of rationality of classification, long applied in the decisions of this Court, that does not depend upon the nature of the . . . interest involved" (397 U.S. 489).

In extended and carefully wrought opinions, Harlan dissented in *Baker v. Carr* (1962) and *Reynolds v. Sims* (1964). In his view, they not only departed from the Constitution and from precedent, but undertook to resolve political problems beyond the competence of the judiciary. *Whitcomb v. Chavis* (1971), decided early in the Burger era, goes far to prove the latter point. The trial court had found an illicit gerrymander at the expense of a black ghetto in a multimember voting district. The Supreme Court disagreed. Justice Douglas, the father of *Baker v. Carr*[9] — joined by Justices Brennan and Marshall — dissented. In their view, the "gerrymander is the other half of *Reynolds v. Sims*."[10] After all, the principle of one person, one vote by itself means merely that all gerrymandered and other districts in a given polity must be equal in population. That kind of equality permits, indeed invites, what the Warren Court called diluted votes. Recognizing this, Douglas faced the majority's crucial problem, which he posed and "resolved" in these terms: "It is said that if we prevent racial gerrymandering today, we must prevent gerrymandering of any special interest group tomorrow, whether it be social, economic, or ideological. I do not agree. Our Constitution has a special thrust when it comes to voting; the Fifteenth Amendment says the right . . . to vote shall not be 'abridged' on account of 'race' " (403 U.S. at 180). This solution permits all gerrymander voting inequalities except those based on race. Gerrymandering against laborers or a college community, for example, would be permissible — the dissenters having pegged their stand, not on generalized equal protection, but on the race-oriented Fifteenth Amendment.

Permitting any but racial votes to be "diluted" by gerrymander, while forbidding dilution caused by unequal numbers, is hardly a stand one would have expected from such stalwart Warrenites as Douglas, Brennan, and Marshall. The explanation seems obvious. Fair political representation is a function of many factors, not numbers alone. One person, one vote might prevent diluted votes if all interests were uniform in strength and spread evenly throughout the polity. In the real world they are not thus homogenized. Some interest groups are large, some small; some are geographically compact, some widespread, and some spotty; some have advantages of prestige, some of organization, and some of dedication — others are correspondingly handicapped. The result is layered, crazy-quilt patterns of changing interests. Equal-sized voting districts imposed on such an uneven base are bound to produce uneven results, that is, diluted votes, or what might be called inadvertent gerrymandering. Consider, for example, a polity divided into equal-sized districts first by north-south boundary lines, and then alternatively by east-west lines. Because of the uneven interest base, the former almost certainly will favor one set of voters; the latter another. Yet both satisfy the *Reynolds v. Sims* test of size equality.

Against this background, Douglas in *Whitcomb* made three crucial points in what may be the most candid and illuminating opinion by an activist judge in a reapportionment case. First he recognized that one person, one vote is not an adequate solution to the problem of vote fairness — it leaves unsolved "the other half of *Reynolds*." (Worse yet, he might have added, it exudes a false impression of equality and fairness.) Then he recognized that the inadvertent gerrymander is nonetheless a gerrymander. Such, in fact, was the situation in *Whitcomb* itself, the plaintiff having admitted that the district in question had been innocently designed. Finally Douglas recognized that, except with respect to race, the gerrymander problem is too complex for the judicial process. Briefly then, in the real world of nonhomogenized interests, we cannot have "undiluted" votes without facing the gerrymander, and most gerrymandering is beyond the competence of courts. Surely this, inter alia, is why, for years prior to *Baker,* the Supreme Court treated districting as a political question.

Both the Warren and the Burger courts persistently avoided the gerrymander problem.[11] And so we are left with one person, one vote, which, by itself, Douglas et al. recognized, is about as functional as a bicycle with only one wheel. The young Douglas of *Colegrove v. Green* (1946) had not anticipated his dilemma in *Whitcomb.* In short, Harlan was right in the first place. He put it more modestly: "This case is nothing short of a complete vindication of Mr. Justice Frankfurter's warning nine years ago [in *Baker v. Carr*] 'of the mathematical quagmire (apart from diverse judicially inappropriate and elusive determinants), into which this Court today catapults the lower courts' " (403 U.S. at 170).

The upshot is that, though we have the comforting catchphrase, we are far from "one person, one equal vote." For example, after years of reapportionment, the Democrats in 1978 won 64 percent of the seats in the national House of Representatives with only 54 percent of the total vote. In 1980 the figures were 56 versus 50; in 1982, 62 versus 55; in 1984, and 1986, 59 versus 55; and in 1988, almost 60 versus 53. The reapportioning, as it happens, had been done largely by, or on behalf of, Democrat-dominated state legislatures. For a gross example of gerrymandering by a Republican legislature, see *Davis v. Bandemer* (1986), wherein the Supreme Court denied relief though the Democrats won 52 percent of the votes but only 43 percent of the seats in the lower house of the Indiana legislature.

Some justices of Warren vintage and many admirers of *Reynolds v. Sims* have sought to justify the *Reynolds* test on the ground that it was a much-needed reform that only the judiciary could provide. The argument was that those who benefit from malapportionment will not vote away their advantage. This reasoning entails a strange rationale of separation (and federal diffusion) of power, for its premise is that, if the voters and their legislatures do not do—now—what a few activists want them to do, then this legislative function becomes a judicial function. One wonders whether those who accept this view, accept its converse as well.

Over and over again Harlan insisted it was not the federal courts' role to make good the supposed failures of other organs of government; he could not accept such a concentration of power—least of all in the nonelected branch. Behind his rejection of judicial legislation lay an abiding commitment to the democratic process. He knew that an aroused public is not helpless in the face of malapportionment. He knew that, again and again, those with excessive representation had been forced by political pressure to give up their advantage: that, after all, is how England got rid of its rotten boroughs; that is how, in state after state, we eliminated property qualifications on suffrage; that is how, in state after state, we got rid of religious qualifications on suffrage; that is how the poll tax was abolished in state after state until the Court intervened; that is how women and eighteen-year-olds got the vote; and that is how we abolished the old system of selecting federal senators and took from the electoral college its power to choose presidents.

"We the people" did not much try to kill malapportionment in the pre-*Reynolds* era presumably because we did not find it much of a problem[12] — just as we do not now consider gross malapportionment vis-à-vis the federal senate much of a problem. Yet at the time of *Reynolds,* the platonic Dauer-Kelsay Index of Representativeness (so dear to academic idealists) revealed that 16 percent of the voters could elect a majority of our senators. Only six state senates and three state houses of representatives were more severely malapportioned.[13]

Obviously, the constitutional scheme for electing senators and presidents is at odds with the one-person-one-vote ideal. Those, then, who gave us the Constitution could hardly have objected in principle to "malapportionment." As the Warren Court recognized in the state senate case, *Lucas v. Colorado General Assembly* (1964), no matter how pure the representation in the house, the legislature will be impure if the senate is impure. As Justices Frankfurter and Harlan observed in *Baker v. Carr,* one person, one vote "was not the English system, it was not the colonial system, it was not the system chosen for the national government by the Constitution, it was not the system exclusively or even predominantly practiced by the States at the time of adoption of the Fourteenth Amendment, it is not predominantly practiced by the States today" (369 U.S. at 301). Out of many diverse theories of representation, the Supreme Court selected one and imposed it (except vis-à-vis the Senate) upon a supposedly sovereign people. If the goal was equally weighted votes for all voters, surely proportional representation would have been a better choice.

Procedural Equal Protection

Writing for the Burger Court in *Boddie v. Connecticut* (1971), Harlan held that indigents could not be denied access to divorce solely because of inability to pay court costs (which averaged sixty dollars). Such an impediment violated due process, "given the basic position of the marriage relationship in this society's . . . values, and the concomitant state monopolization of [divorce proceedings]" (401 U.S. at 374). This decision, resting solely on due process, marks a victory for Harlan in his long battle against the Warren Court's use of the equal protection clause in court-access, and related poverty, cases—a battle that began in *Griffin v. Illinois* in 1956. The crux of Harlan's position is best expressed in this language from *Douglas v. California* (1963), which concerned state limitations on the assignment of counsel to indigent criminal defendants:

> To approach the present problem in terms of the Equal Protection Clause is, I submit, but to substitute resounding phrases for analysis. I dissented from this approach in *Griffin v. Illinois* [which relied on a blend of the equal protection and due process clauses], and I am constrained to dissent from the implicit extension of the equal protection approach here. . . .
> . . . The Equal Protection Clause does not impose on the States "an affirmative duty to lift the handicaps flowing from differences in economic circumstances." To so construe it would be to read into the Constitution a philosophy of leveling that would be foreign to many of our basic concepts of the proper relations between government and society. The State may have a moral obligation to eliminate the evils of poverty, but it is not required by the Equal Protection Clause to give to some whatever others can afford. . . .
> The real question in this case, I submit, and the only one that permits of satisfactory analysis, is whether or not the state rule, as applied in this case, is consistent with the requirements of fair procedure guaranteed by the Due Process Clause. (372 U.S. at 361–63)

In sum, *Boddie* and *Dandridge* (discussed above) mark the end of the Warren Court's equal protection explosion—an explosion calculated to expand a constitutional ban on de jure discrimination into an affirmative duty of the state to eliminate economic hardships. The equal protection clause looks to equality against a background of slavery. The poverty problem is quite another matter. We do not expect government to make us all economically equal to the wealthiest person in America. Our aim, rather, is to provide a floor of "minimum protection" for indigents.[14] Talk of equality is utterly confusing when our purpose is merely to alleviate "severe deprivation." The preindustrial Fourteenth Amendment simply does not address this problem. At best, courts can deal with it only peripherally. To lighten the misfortune of the poor is, as Harlan saw it, a legislative, and also a private, function— unless, of course, traditional due process interests are at stake. In this context, it is not to be forgotten that Harlan had been a vigorous and imaginative director of the New York bar's Legal Aid Society.

Incorporation

When Harlan joined the Court, *Palko v. Connecticut* (1937) was the law of the land. In his view it should have remained so, for he could find no language in the Fourteenth Amendment that incorporates the Bill of Rights. Nor could he find evidence that refuted Fairman.[15] He did find Supreme Court cases (decided soon after adoption of the amendment) in which incorporation might have played an important role but in fact had played no role at all—indeed, had not even been mentioned by counsel or by any judge. In one such case, the incorporation doctrine, had it been known to counsel or the Court, might have saved a man's life.[16] All those involved in that litigation—parties, lawyers, trial and appellate judges—had known Reconstruction first-hand and had lived amid the strenuous debates that attended the adoption of the Fourteenth Amendment. How could all of them have been oblivious to incorporation, if it in fact had been a prime goal of the amenders?

For Harlan, incorporation was a post hoc invention—a poor one, indeed, because it neglected some vital interests, yet covered others that were relatively unimportant. This difficulty was demonstrated in two cases early in Burger's day. In one, *In re Winship* (1970), the Court reversed a state criminal conviction because it was based only on a preponderance of evidence (as distinct from proof beyond a reasonable doubt). Justice Black—father of modern incorporation—pointed out in dissent that there is no reasonable-doubt rule in the Bill of Rights or anywhere else in the Constitution.[17] On the other hand, in *Williams v. Florida* (1970) the Court upheld the use of a six-person jury in criminal trials. Yet for centuries the Bill of Rights' guarantee of a jury trial had meant a jury of twelve—as the Supreme Court had recognized over and over again.

Harlan concurred in both decisions on *Palko* grounds. In his view, crucial interests were jeopardized in *Winship* but not in *Williams*. Proof beyond reasonable doubt, after all, is the heart of an old Anglo-American effort to ensure against conviction of the innocent. On the other hand, trial by precisely twelve jurors is merely historical accident (there is no magic in the number twelve). Without acknowledging it, the Burger Court (with seven Warren-era holdovers) had, in effect, gone back to *Palko*. Indeed, there was only one alien vote (Justice Blackmun was not involved in either decision). In reality, Harlan did not concur with the Court; rather, the Court concurred with him. Of the sixteen judicial votes in these two cases, only Black's dissent in *Winship* and Marshall's dissent in *Williams* were true to both incorporation and the historic meaning of the Bill of Rights.

In Harlan's view, the Court in *Williams* had watered down the constitutional right of trial by jury in federal courts to escape the "straitjacket" of incorporation: "The decision evinces a recognition that the 'incorporationist' view . . . must be tempered to allow the States more elbow room. . . . With that much I agree. But to accomplish this by diluting [a Bill of Rights provision] is something to which I cannot possibly subscribe. . . . Can it be doubted that a unanimous jury of 12 provides a greater safeguard than a majority vote of six?" (399 U.S. at 118–19). A few months later, in *Apodaca v. Oregon* (1972), the Court backed down on the dilution process. The justices were divided four to four on jury unanimity in state trials. Harlan's successor, Justice Powell, provided the decisive ninth vote. In his view, presumably as in Harlan's, Fourteenth Amendment due process does not require unanimity, but the Sixth Amendment does. That is, unanimous jury verdicts are a long-settled Bill of Rights tradition, but a state conviction by at least ten out of twelve jurors (as in *Apodaca*) is not fundamentally unfair on Fourteenth Amendment due process grounds. Another blow to incorporation in favor of *Palko*—this time without compromising the Bill of Rights.

Conclusion

Judicial activism is so alien to our principles of government that no Supreme Court justice has ever proclaimed or admitted in public that he was an activist.[18] On the contrary, judicial activists trumpet their innocence. In *Miranda,* for example, the chief justice announced, "We start . . . with the premise that our holding is not an innovation."[19] In *Gideon,* Justice Black pretended that *Powell v. Alabama* (1932) had long before established a general right to appointed counsel. In *Griswold,* Douglas claimed that the use of contraceptives was sanctioned by "penumbras" and "emanations"[20] from the eighteenth-century Bill of Rights somehow made applicable to the states by a fair trial (due process) provision in a Reconstruction Amendment. Yet, as we have seen, when it suited his purpose, Douglas had said incorporation would tame due process by tying it down to the "clearly marked . . . boundaries" and the "specific" and "particular standards enumerated" in the Bill of Rights. Earlier, in *United States v. Butler* (1936), Justice Roberts explained, "This Court neither approves nor condemns any legislative policy." It simply lays the Constitution beside the challenged law and decides "whether the latter squares with the former."[21] All this, one suggests, is what Plato called "noble fiction"—calculated to hide from the governed the naked power of their magistrates. Harlan, rejecting government by judges, had no need for pretense.

Even those who can stomach judicial make-believe and wholesale lawmaking by judges must find litigation a less-than-adequate vehicle for major shifts in public policy. Consider, for example, three Warren Court cases decided within an eight-day period in 1966: *Schmerber v. California, Miranda,* and *Johnson v. State of New Jersey.* Only Brennan was on the majority side in both *Schmerber* and *Miranda.* Thus he alone on the bench found them compatible—the one case permitting forceful extraction of a person's blood for evidentiary purposes; the other rejecting unwarned custodial confessions, no matter how voluntary in fact. *Johnson* teaches that *Miranda* "rights" are "futuristic" only. They do not help others who, prior to *Miranda,* had confessed their way to jail. Surely constitutional rights must apply equally to all people; if so, *Miranda* entails not a constitutional right, but merely a judge-made remedy. Thus the Court in *Johnson,* a few days after *Miranda,* plainly reaffirmed the traditional view that there is nothing inherently wrong with convictions based on voluntary confessions (as in the pre-*Miranda* era). If such convictions were all constitutionally amiss, Mr. Johnson and a host of others would have to be released. Thus *Miranda* and *Johnson* are fundamentally incompatible.

Indeed, only three justices—Warren, Brennan, and Fortas—supported both decisions. Their six colleagues found nothing in the Constitution that would justify deciding the one case differently from the other: four thought both convictions should be upheld; two thought both should be reversed. Only one justice was on the majority side in all three cases. This raises a problem in activist ethics: Was it proper to protect Miranda—a confessed rapist[22]—whose conviction was based on a long-settled, and still valid, rule of constitutional law, when the Court was so splintered, contradictory, and confused as to the new meaning of self-incrimination? For Harlan the answer was no.

Plato's ancient question still haunts us: Is it better to be ruled by men or by law?[23] Rejecting the platonic answer, we have long since chosen the rule of law. Yet platonism prevails from time to time, as in the heyday of Lyndon Johnson, Richard Nixon, and Earl Warren.[24] In that much-troubled era, Justice Harlan kept the faith. His opinions are classics in the enduring struggle to keep government within the law—and law within control of the democratic processes.

NOTES

1. See Freund's foreword to David L. Shapiro, ed., *The Evolution of a Judicial Philosophy: Selected Opinions and Papers of Justice John M. Harlan* (Cambridge, Mass.: Harvard University Press, 1969), p. xiv.

2. See *New York Times,* June 15, 1969, sec. 1, p. 43.

3. Freund in Shapiro, *The Evolution of a Judicial Philosophy,* p. xxi.

4. *Freedman v. Maryland* (1965); *A Quantity of Copies of Books v. Kansas* (1964); *Marcus v. Search Warrant* (1961); *Kingsley Books, Inc. v. Brown* (1957).

5. 42 *U.S.C.A.* §1983.

6. *Adickes v. S. H. Kress & Co.,* 398 U.S. at 166.

7. Ibid., at 231, 224, 225.

8. *Slaughter House Cases* (1873).

9. When the "original" reapportionment case—*Colegrove v. Green* (1946)— was first considered in conference, Chief Justice Stone (who was to die before a decision could be handed down) "made a long statement on why the courts should stay out" (letter to the author from Alpheus Thomas Mason, Nov. 17, 1964). Only Justice Douglas was in opposition. Later he won two converts, and eventually, in *Baker,* a majority.

10. *Whitcomb v. Chavis,* 403 U.S. at 176.

11. *Gaffney v. Cummings* (1973) seems to foreclose any "hope" of judicial involvement in nonracial gerrymandering. See also *Davis v. Bandemer* (1986).

12. Have we so soon forgotten that the purpose of the pre-*Baker* reapportionment "drive" was to free urban America from "rural domination"? Malapportioned state legislatures, we were told, were responsible for the growing ills of city life. See Anthony Lewis, "Legislative Apportionment and the Federal Courts," *Harvard Law Review* 71 (1958): 1057, 1063; Gordon E. Baker, *Rural v. Urban Political Power* (Garden City, N.Y.: Doubleday, 1955), 4: 27–39; John F. Kennedy, "The Shame of the States," *New York Times Magazine,* May 18, 1958, 12; *One Man-One Vote* (New York: Twentieth Century Fund, 1962). Yet we have long since reapportioned without a hint of the promised renaissance of the cities. The persistence of urban difficulties suggests that the problem has little to do with legislative apportionment. Unlike numerous academicians, "we the people"—free of blinding ideology and the never-never-land Dauer-Kelsay Index of Representativeness—seem to have been correct in discounting the alleged rural sabotage of urban America.

13. Council of State Governments, *The Book of the States* (Lexington, Ky.: Council of State Governments, 1969), 17: 66–67.

14. See Frank I. Michelman, "Foreword: On Protecting the Poor through the Fourteenth Amendment," *Harvard Law Review* 83 (1969): 7–59.

15. Charles Fairman, "Does the Fourteenth Amendment Incorporate the Bill of Rights? The Original Understanding," *Stanford Law Review* 2 (1949): 5–139.

16. *Twitchell v. Pennsylvania* (1869).

17. Unlike some others, Black—here and in *Griswold*—remembered the much-stressed rationale for incorporation, namely, avoidance of personal preference in due process cases in favor of the "clearly marked . . . boundaries," the "specific"

and "particular standards enumerated" in the Bill of Rights. See *Federal Power Commission v. Natural Gas Pipeline Co.*, 315 U.S. at 601, and *Adamson v. California*, 332 U.S. at 82, 83, 91, 92. Douglas had joined in this language.

18. See, however, Justice Brennan, "The Constitution of the United States: Contemporary Ratification" (Speech delivered at a symposium at Georgetown University, Washington, D.C., Oct. 12, 1985).

19. *Miranda v. Arizona*, 384 U.S. at 442.

20. *Griswold v. Connecticut*, 381 U.S. at 484.

21. *United States v. Butler*, 297 U.S. at 63, 62.

22. With the retroactive help of the Supreme Court, Miranda had committed a perfect crime. Then he made a mistake; he confessed again, this time in a manner that put him in jail for rape.

23. As Lord Coke said, *"Non sub homine, sed sub Deo et lege"* ("Not under the rule of man, but under God and the law").

24. It is due Plato to say that our guardians had not been trained in the prescribed manner befitting "philosopher kings." Perhaps that explains the result as described by Professor Philip Kurland: "At the close of Warren's tenure, both the Supreme Court and the law were at low tide so far as public reaction was concerned. The Court's lack of prestige was reflected in data published by the Gallup Poll. The disdain for the law was demonstrated not only by the FBI's crime statistics but by the behavior of all levels of American society. It is revealed no less in the actions of three presidents and five Congresses who have indulged a war not sanctioned by constitutional procedures and in those of organizations and individuals who set themselves above the law." Philip B. Kurland, *Politics, the Constitution and the Warren Court* (Chicago: University of Chicago Press, 1970), p. xxiii.

8

JUSTICE THURGOOD MARSHALL:
The Race for Equal Justice

WILLIAM J. DANIELS

Introduction

Justice Thurgood Marshall was born on July 2, 1908, on the Lower Side of Baltimore, Maryland. He had served the law for thirty-four years before his confirmation on October 2, 1967, as the first black justice to sit on the United States Supreme Court. For an institution that is inherently the most conservative one in American government, Marshall certainly was not an ordinary appointee. Not only had the previous ninety-six justices been white, but most had come from prominent, wealthy, and powerful families. "Usually they attended elite segregated schools, . . . represented powerful economic interests as lawyers, were well connected politically, and held high government office."[1]

Marshall's great-grandfather was a slave; the seat he assumed on the Court was vacated by Justice Tom Clark, whose grandfather fought as a member of the Confederate Army to preserve slavery. Thurgood was the younger brother of William (Aubrey) who was three years his senior; both were born to Norma Arica and William (Will) Canfield Marshall. Thurgood was named after his paternal grandfather, who took the first name Thoroughgood when he enlisted in the Union Navy during the Civil War in order to satisfy regulations that volunteers provide a first and last name for the records. By the time Marshall had reached the second grade, he had changed it to "Thurgood" because his given name was too burdensome to spell.[2]

Thurgood's father was well known and respected in the black community where the family resided. Druid Hill Avenue, where the Marshalls lived, had previously been all white, and the neighborhood was considered to be an elite one. Baltimore had been the first city to pass an ordinance that restricted the areas where blacks could live.[3] Socially, some class stratification existed among blacks at the time, based largely on the lightness of one's skin color. Both of Thurgood's parents were thought to be half white and were considered mulattoes.[4] According to Clarence Mitchell, director of the NAACP Washington, D.C., office, the Marshalls were not snobs, even though they were considered to be upper class in this stratified society.[5]

Thurgood had ample opportunity to learn the United States Constitution by heart at an early age. He tended to be unruly in elementary school, and for punishment on numerous occasions the principal sent him to the basement to memorize a section of the document.[6] Thus young Thurgood was in a position to compare the practices of Jim Crow segregation and racial injustices in Baltimore with the principles in the Constitution, and he asked his father about them. Will explained that the Constitution represented the way things should be. "Things will change son. It's all written there, just waiting for some smart young whippersnapper to come along and make it real."[7]

The Frederick Douglass High School was the only secondary school in Baltimore for blacks, and Thurgood was one of its most popular students. He organized the debating team and won most of his arguments.[8] Upon graduation, Thurgood joined Aubrey at Lincoln University, not far from Philadelphia, the oldest American educational institution for blacks. Lincoln was regarded as an elite institution; many of its faculty were graduates of Ivy League schools. They were well trained and dedicated, and they thought of themselves as having a mission.[9] Thurgood Marshall demonstrated a carefree attitude toward his studies at Lincoln, but he graduated cum laude in 1930.

Shortly after graduating, Marshall decided to attend law school, but his application to the University of Maryland was rejected because of his race. He quickly decided on Howard University Law School in Washington, D.C., because he had heard that the university and the law school were being upgraded by a new president, Mordecai Johnson, who had arrived in 1926. Johnson had been influenced by Louis Brandeis, then a justice of the United States Supreme Court.[10] Mordecai Johnson recruited several dynamic and gifted teachers for the Howard University Law School who influenced young Marshall: William Hastie, who came from Harvard to become the first black dean at Howard and taught

Marshall the value of meticulously preparing briefs; A. Mercer Daniel, the head law librarian, to whom Marshall expressed indebtedness for teaching him the proper use of law texts in research; and Charles Hamilton Houston, who arrived in 1929 to serve as vice-dean of the law school and had a profound influence on Marshall and other Howard Law School students during his fifteen-year tenure.[11] The curriculum at Howard emphasized Houston's "result-oriented" or "rights-oriented" approach to the law.[12] Howard became a laboratory where civil rights law was invented, where students and faculty developed the legal arguments that would propel the courts and the nation toward change. Marshall, who later had a long association with the NAACP, graduated magna cum laude in 1933 at the top of his class.

Marshall was admitted to the Maryland bar and had an active but unprofitable private practice in Baltimore. Given his inclination, training, and mindset, he became associated with the Baltimore Branch of the NAACP and consequently became involved in litigation dealing with issues of racial inequality. Marshall moved into the association gradually, first as a volunteer and then, about a year later, as counsel for the local branch.

The first major case Marshall handled involved a young man denied admission to the same school that he had been denied admission to, the University of Maryland School of Law. The year was 1935, and, working with the law firm of Warner T. McGuinn and Charles Houston, Marshall collaborated with Houston to convince the Maryland Court of Appeals to order the university to admit its first black. The court noted that the meager scholarship fund established by the state for blacks fell short of providing facilities for blacks substantially equal to those provided for whites.

In 1936, Charlie Houston asked Marshall to join him temporarily in New York as special assistant legal counsel to the NAACP. Marshall accepted the appointment and commuted from Baltimore for two years. When Houston became ill and resigned in 1938, Marshall was appointed in his place as special counsel in charge of litigation. He moved to New York City to assume his new responsibilities. Marshall's final position with the NAACP was director-counsel of the Legal Defense and Educational Fund, Inc., from 1950 through 1961.

The most celebrated case for Marshall and the NAACP was *Brown v. Board of Education of Topeka* (1954), in which the Supreme Court held "that in the field of public education the doctrine of 'separate but equal' has no place" (347 U.S. at 495). In *Brown*,

Justice Thurgood Marshall

Marshall achieved a milestone for which so many before him at the NAACP had worked for so long. During his tenure with the NAACP, Marshall argued thirty-two cases before the Supreme Court, winning twenty-nine. He was widely respected and admired as a brilliant advocate.

Marshall's appointment by President John F. Kennedy in 1961 to the U.S. Court of Appeals for the Second Circuit began a period of governmental service that closed out his legal career. The Second Circuit was considered a prestigious appointment because of the high quality of the judges who have served there in the past, including Learned Hand, Jerome Frank, and Harold Medina. Marshall's nomination ran into trouble in the Senate; he was subjected to intensive questioning on his civil rights activities before the Senate approved his appointment a year later by a vote of 54 to 16. During his four years on the court of appeals, Marshall participated on panels that decided approximately four hundred cases per term. He wrote 118 opinions—98 majority opinions, 8 concurrences, and 12 dissents. None of his opinions was reversed by the Supreme Court. President Lyndon B. Johnson appointed Marshall to two positions—as solicitor general in 1965 and as a justice of the Supreme Court two years later. Marshall was the first black solicitor general, and Johnson was not unmindful of that fact. During his two years in that office, Marshall argued nineteen cases before the Supreme Court; and the government prevailed in fourteen—an impressive record.

Marshall and the Burger Court

Justice Marshall came to the Burger Court having worked two terms under the leadership of Chief Justice Earl Warren. Given the change in the Court's orientation, Marshall felt compelled to speak his mind on the Burger Court, primarily through dissenting opinions. Strikingly, Marshall authored more dissenting opinions (276) than opinions for the Court (228) (see Table 1.6). On the average he authored sixteen dissents each term while writing only thirteen majority opinions, and he authored few concurring opinions during the Burger years.

In his role as a dissenter during the Burger Court years, Marshall cast 754 dissents in opinions and 183 dissents in memoranda decisions, for a total of 937 dissenting votes (Table 1.7). Marshall most often agreed with Justice Brennan, and he frequently disagreed with the Burger Court's conservatives (Table 1.8). In fact, data published in the *Harvard Law Review* for the 1969 through 1985 terms indicate that Marshall and Brennan agreed in 89 percent of their joint participations, while Marshall and Rehnquist agreed in only 40.2 percent. Justice Blackmun's pattern of agreement with Marshall continuously and significantly increased over the years. Marshall's agreement rate with Blackmun changed from around 50 percent during the early Burger Court years to over 70 percent during the 1981–85 terms.[13] Marshall's voting record shows increasing support for the disadvantaged in civil liberties cases and economic cases (Tables 1.9 and 1.10).

The strong philosophical differences between Marshall and Rehnquist can be traced as far back as the 1950s, when Rehnquist, as Justice Robert Jackson's law clerk, wrote to Jackson: "I realize that it is an unpopular and unhumanitarian position, for which I have been excoriated by 'liberal' colleagues, but I think *Plessy v. Ferguson* was right and should be re-affirmed."[14] President Nixon, in his search for a "strict constructionist," appointed Rehnquist to the Court because he was considered to be an intellectual with a deep abiding conservative philosophy. Few were surprised when Rehnquist immediately began to live up to his advance billing, "siding invariably with the prosecution in criminal cases, with business in antitrust cases, with employers in labor cases and with the government in speech cases."[15] Predictably, Marshall and Rehnquist were frequently at odds. As Stephen L. Wasby noted, during the six terms preceding the 1983 term, an average of 121 dissenting opinions had been written by the justices at the ideological extremes of the Court. Marshall and Brennan at one extreme, and Rehnquist on the other, had split equally the three years, each having written the most dissents during one of the three years.[16]

In the twenty cases in which Rehnquist wrote the opinion for the Court and Marshall wrote the sole dissenting opinion, Marshall advanced the notion that the legal system has an obligation to protect the powerless against the powerful. In these cases, Marshall supported the claims of litigants who might be considered the underdog—underprivileged or less politically powerful.[17] Racial issues, while often present in these cases, were incidental and not the key factor. In all of them, Marshall's concern for equal justice surfaced as a prevailing value, and they will be discussed later.

Two cases decided under Title VII of the 1964 Civil Rights Act illustrate Rehnquist's majority opinion views. *Furnco Construction Corp. v. Waters* (1979) addressed the criteria to be used in determining violations of Title VII. Although agreeing with the result—

a remand—Marshall disagreed with the idea that it was necessary to prove an intent to discriminate before a remedy could be imposed. Marshall argued that individuals may allege that they have been subject to "disparate treatment" or have suffered a "disparate impact" because of their race, even though the employer's practice in question is facially neutral (438 U.S. at 582). When this prima facie case is made, according to Marshall, the burden is then on the employer to prove that its rejection of a job candidate was legitimate and nondiscriminatory and that the alleged discriminatory practice had a "manifest relationship to the employment in question." Marshall believed that one need not show that the employer had a "discriminatory intent," but only that the particular practice operates to exclude blacks (583).

In the second case, *Meritor Savings Bank v. Vinson* (1986), Rehnquist held that Title VII requires a work environment where employees are free from sexual harassment and added that an employer may be held responsible for sexual harassment by a supervisor, but he limited the conditions under which an employer assumes liability under Title VII. While agreeing with the thrust of the majority opinion, Marshall insisted that there was "no justification for a special rule, to be applied *only* in 'hostile environment' cases, that sexual harassment does not create employer liability until the employee suffering the discrimination notifies other supervisors. No such requirement appears in the statute, and no such requirement can coherently be drawn from the law of agency" (477 U.S. at 77).

Due process of law—as it relates to an academic environment and to state correctional officials—was the stimulus for two other concurring opinions by Marshall that contrast his positions with those of Rehnquist. *Board of Curators of the University of Missouri v. Horowitz* (1978), a case dealing with a student dismissed from medical school, produced a Rehnquist opinion for the Court holding that dismissals for academic, as opposed to disciplinary, reasons do not require a hearing before the school's decision-making body. Marshall, although concurring, was concerned about the procedural due process issue in the case: "[C]haracterization of the reasons for a student's dismissal adds nothing to the effort to find procedures that are fair to the student and the school, and that promote the elusive goal of determining the truth in a manner consistent with both individual dignity and society's limited resources" (435 U.S. at 97–98).

In *Parratt v. Taylor* (1981), Justice Marshall concurred in part and dissented in part from Justice Rehnquist's majority opinion. Rehnquist decided that, because state law provided an adequate remedy for the loss, a prison inmate's due process rights were not infringed when prison officials negligently lost hobby materials the prisoner had ordered through the mail. Marshall reponded: "I join the opinion of the Court insofar as it holds that negligent conduct by persons acting under color of state law may be actionable. . . . I part company . . . over its conclusion that there was an adequate state-law remedy available to respondent in this case" (451 U.S. at 554–56). In a case like this, Marshall emphasized, "prison officials have an affirmative obligation to inform [an aggrieved] . . . prisoner about the remedies available under state law. If they fail to do so, then they should not be permitted to rely on the existence of such remedies as adequate alternatives to [an] . . . action for wrongful deprivation of property" (556).

Criminal Defendants' Rights

The transformation in criminal justice during the Warren Court was revolutionary. "More than that," Bernard Schwartz observed, "it was the rarest of all political animals: a judicially inspired and led revolution."[18] And, as Richard Funston noted, "no area of Burger Court decision-making suggested a greater disjunction with its predecessor than [criminal defendants' rights]."[19] Funston also captured the thrust of Burger Court criminal procedure policy.

> [The] right to counsel was limited to post-indictment lineups. The warrantless use of "bugged" informers was upheld. The emerging doctrines of the right to confrontation were stunted. Full-scale arrest searches of persons stopped for mere traffic violations were approved. The end of the road in extending the procedural safeguards of criminal trials to juvenile proceedings was apparently reached. Statements obtained in violation of *Miranda* were admitted for purposes of impeaching the credibility of the defendant who had testified in his own behalf. Even acknowledged violations of constitutional rights were dismissed as harmless errors, having no significance on the outcome of the trial and not worthy of appellate notice.
> In particular, the Burger majority was hostile to the exclusionary rule of the Fourth Amendment.[20]

To each of these Burger Court developments, Justice Marshall dissented.[21] Consider his views on confrontation in *Dutton v. Evans* (1970), *Nelson v. O'Neil* (1971), and *Mancusi v. Stubbs* (1972). In *Dutton*, the Court concluded that an extrajudicial statement, attributed to an alleged partner in crime and admitted at trial, did not deny the respondent's right to confront the witness against him. The Court ruled in *Nelson* that a cautionary instruction to the jury satisfied the full and effective cross-examination requirement in a trial in which a codefendant took the stand in his own defense and denied making an alleged out-of-court statement that implicated the defendant. Of course, the jury heard the statement anyway. The defendant did not take the stand in his own behalf. In *Mancusi*, the Court held that it was not constitutional error to permit a witness's prior recorded testimony to be read to the jury at trial when the witness was unavailable.

Disagreeing with these rulings, Marshall declared in *Dutton* that "the majority reaches a result completely inconsistent with recent opinions of this Court" (400 U.S. at 100). Furthermore, he would avoid the Court's standard of whether the evidence admitted was crucial or devastating and "confine the inquiry to traditional questions" (109). In *Nelson*, Marshall made a plea to the Court to adopt new rules regulating the use of joint trials as set forth in the American Bar Association's 1968 Project on Standards for Criminal Justice. He agued that saving time, money, and energy through the use of joint trials was no justification for violating constitutional rights (402 U.S. at 635–36). Nor did Marshall accept the assertion that the witness was unavailable in *Mancusi*. Even if neither state nor federal authorities had the power to compel the witness to appear, the state was still obliged "to make a good-faith effort to secure the witness's presence" (408 U.S. at 223).

In *United States v. Ross* (1982), the Court allowed police officers, acting on information that gave them probable cause to believe that contraband was concealed in the trunk of a car, to conduct a warrantless search of the car after they had stopped the automobile, seized the driver, and taken the car to police headquarters. Marshall believed that a search warrant should have and could have been obtained. The car, the driver, and all packages had been secured; a review by a neutral magistrate at this point is essential. However, given the conduct of the police and the decision by the majority, Marshall argued that the majority had created a new probable cause exception to the warrant requirement for automobiles. "The practical mobility problem—deciding what to do with both the car and the occupants if an immediate search is not conducted— is simply not present in the case of movable containers, which can easily be seized and brought to the magistrate" (456 U.S. at 832). Further, he suggested that the majority had ignored the "obvious difference between the function served by a magistrate in making a determination of probable cause and the function of the automobile exception" and that the new rule masked "the startling assumption that a policeman's determination of probable cause is the functional equivalent of the determination of a neutral and detached magistrate" (833).

Nearly twenty years after *Miranda v. Arizona* (1966), Justice Marshall wrote a dissenting opinion in a decision that he felt seriously undermined the protection provided by the *Miranda* warnings. The occasion was *Oregon v. Elstad* (1985), in which the Court held that a prior unlawful interrogation that resulted in a confession did not invalidate a subsequent confession made after the police gave the *Miranda* warnings. Marshall's dissenting opinion focused on two points: the practical realities of the custodial interrogation process were ignored, and the Court's implementation of its new rule appeared to be a part of its agenda. "The Court rejects as nothing more than 'speculative' the long-recognized presumption that an illegally extracted confession causes the accused to confess again out of the mistaken belief that he has already sealed his fate, and it condemns as extravagant the requirement that the prosecution affirmatively rebut the presumption before the subsequent confession may be admitted" (470 U.S. at 319).

Richard Funston has observed that the Burger Court's opinions on the exclusionary rule eroded the rule's foundation.[22] Marshall's dissent in *United States v. Leon* (1984) describes his perception of this erosion problem. The Court held in *Leon* that evidence obtained by officers acting with reasonable reliance on a search warrant issued by a detached and neutral magistrate, but ultimately found to be unsupported by probable cause, would not be barred by the exclusionary rule. Suggesting that the Court's gradual strangulation of the rule may have been complete now, much of Marshall's dissent dealt with the majority's rationale, which he found to be a "cost-benefit" analysis offering an illusion of technical precision. The broad purposes that the exclusionary rule seeks to serve are weightier than "the shifting sands of the Court's deterrence rationale," which was based on uncertain statistics and robbed the exclusionary rule of its legitimacy (468 U.S. at 897). He further maintained that applying the rule, even to evidence obtained on the mistaken belief that police conduct had been authorized, would compel police departments to instruct their officers to devote greater attention to providing sufficient information to establish probable cause when applying for a warrant. Not to apply the rule would permit the police to assume that any document signed by the magistrate automatically comports with the requirements of the Fourth Amendment. Acceptance of a "reasonable mistake" exception would "tend to put a premium on police ignorance of the law." As greater demands are placed on governmental officials to increase their efforts to combat crime, it becomes easier for them to seek "expedient solutions" (897).

Marshall's deeply felt precepts about the administration of criminal justice were reflected in his many dissenting opinions on the Burger Court. His view was that a judge has a crucial role to play in cases that involve a person's life and liberty and a responsibility to safeguard constitutional liberties. Executing this function may require the judge to question the logic or legislative intent, to advance the interests of the individual against the convenience of the government, and to apply constitutional prohibitions vigilantly. For Marshall, to do less to preserve individual liberty was to abdicate judicial responsibility.

Capital Punishment

Michael Perry has observed that every judge, like every policymaker, is a member of some moral community, but the judge represents a "morally pluralistic political community." When a judge interprets the Constitution, the community's interpretation should serve as the standard. Perry then asks, "On what moral beliefs ought a person to rely, in her capacity as a judge, in deciding whether public policy regarding some matter is constitutionally valid?"[23]

When confronting capital punishment cases, Justice Marshall provided an interesting response to that question. Until 1972, the Supreme Court had never squarely confronted the fundamental claim that the death penalty was a cruel and unusual punishment contrary to the Constitution. When the confrontation came— twice in four years—the Court handed down landmark decisions. The first, *Furman v. Georgia* (1972), was a 5 to 4 decision with nine separate opinions. A per curiam opinion held that the imposition and implementation of the death sentence was, in effect, cruel and unusual punishment contrary to the Eighth and Fourteenth amendments because the statutes under consideration permitted juries untrammeled discretion to impose or withhold the death penalty.

In a concurring opinion in *Furman*, Marshall pleaded for the abolition of capital punishment. Two years later, in *Gregg v. Georgia* (1976), two justices from the *Furman* majority, Stewart and White, formed a new majority and sustained a Georgia statute that specified that a jury had to find one of ten aggravating circumstances to impose capital punishment. The state supreme court was required to review and agree with the sentence. Marshall and Brennan filed dissenting opinions.

In his *Gregg* dissent, Marshall referred to his concurring opinion in *Furman* and indicated that his views had not changed. Responding to several developments since *Furman*, he acknowledged that, in the intervening two-year period, thirty-five state legislatures and Congress had enacted new statutes authorizing the death penalty for certain crimes. Presumably the people had spoken, albeit indirectly through their representatives, and had not found capital punishment morally unacceptable or inconsistent with their self-respect. Yet the new statutes could not be viewed as conclusive, he argued, because the constitutionality of the death penalty turned on the opinion of an informed citizenry, and nothing suggested that the legislative actions were predicated on the judgments of informed citizens.

Marshall's conclusion was based on the analysis of four interrelated ideas: what citizens know about capital punishment, how citizens would assess pertinent information, how judges find out what citizens know, and what judges might properly decide based on their assessment of citizen opinion.[24] He reasoned that citizens know almost nothing about capital punishment and that, if presented with the basic facts, the great mass of citizens would conclude that the death penalty was immoral, shocking to their conscience and their sense of justice, and therefore unconstitutional. He acknowledged that this conclusion was speculative because one can seldom learn accurately what the community actually feels, but he noted that the recognition of its truth does not undercut its validity.

Judges are not free to strike down penalties they find personally offensive, but they may properly ask whether a specific punishment is morally acceptable to the American people. The question then is: How does a judge move beyond his personal values to gain knowledge of the views of the community? In *Furman*, Marshall responded by pointing to the diversity of judges' human experience. "They have come into contact with many people, many ways of life, and many philosophies," he stressed. "If, after drawing on this experience . . . , judges conclude that these people would not knowingly tolerate a specific penalty in light of its costs, then this conclusion is entitled to weight" (408 U.S. at 369–70 n. 163).

Marshall brought his thinking together in *Gregg*, concluding that even enactment of post-*Furman* statutes authorizing the death penalty, on behalf of a presumedly informed citizenry, cannot serve as a substitute for a court deciding that the death penalty is unconstitutional because it is excessive (428 U.S. at 232–33). That is, an excessive penalty is unconstitutional whether or not the public supports it. A penalty is also excessive if it is not necessary to accomplish a legitimate legislative purpose. For Marshall, it is proper for the judiciary to make these determinations.

In 1983, after an execution, Marshall was asked if he had given up. He responded, "I'll never give up. On something like that, you can't give up and you can't compromise. It's so morally correct, I wouldn't think of giving it up." When asked if he thought things would turn in his favor, Marshall replied, "That's what I'm banking on. Tell me, do you know who is deciding who gets executed? Do you know what yardstick is being used? If you find out, let me know."[25] A subsequent Gallup poll found public support for the death penalty to be at its highest point in half a century, with seven out of ten Americans supporting it for murder. The poll also found, however, that their support declined from 72 to 56 percent if, in the alternative, convicted murderers were required to serve life imprisonment without any possibility of parole. Moreover, if it could be shown conclusively that the death penalty did not serve as a deterrent to murder, support would decline from 72 to 51 percent.[26]

Civil Rights and Equal Protection

The Supreme Court entered a new era with the *Brown* decision and subsequently began to expand equal protection doctrine as it related to race. The concepts "strict scrutiny" and "suspect classification" were woven into a standard of "fundamental rights." This approach aided the Court in developing tests to review the constitutionality of statutes challenged on equal protection grounds.

As noted, Justice Marshall had made a prominent mark on the development of civil rights law prior to entering governmental service in 1961. Later, in deciding equal protection cases on the Burger Court, he found that the Court's emphasis had shifted and the nature of the issues had changed. When the Court's opinion did not favor claimed violations of equal protection, Marshall typically dissented.[27] Whereas his life's work and the jurisprudence of the Warren Court had been devoted to advancing civil rights, the Burger Court was less sympathetic—that set the stage for his personal struggle on the Burger Court.

Marshall's concurring opinion in *Regents of the University of California v. Bakke* (1978) presented his thinking on why special consideration of minorities who have been legally disadvantaged is permissible under the equal protection clause in support of affirmative action plans.

> The experience of Negroes in America has been different in kind, not just in degree, from that of other ethnic groups. It is not merely the history of slavery alone but also that a whole people were marked as inferior by the law. And that mark has endured. . . . It is because of [this] legacy of unequal treatment that we must now permit the institutions of this society to give consideration to race in making decisions about who will hold the positions of influence, affluence, and prestige in America. If we are ever to become a fully integrated society, one in which the color of a person's skin will not determine the opportunities available to him or her, we must be willing to open those doors. I do not believe that anyone can truly look into America's past and still find that a remedy for the effects of that past is impermissible. (438 U.S. at 400–401)

The "rational basis," "mere rationality," or "rationality" test was the very least that should be applied in equal protection cases. According to Marshall, a lower level of scrutiny in the review of claims of reverse discrimination would allow the Court to sustain affirmative action plans designed to correct the legacy of past discrimination. To satisfy this test, one has merely to show that the interest of the state is legitimate, the classification is reasonable, and the relationship between the two is rational. "Strict scrutiny" is a more exacting standard for review. Here the presumption is that the legislation is invalid unless it is necessary to promote a compelling and legitimate state interest. Further, the state must show the unavailability of less intrusive or alternative means of achieving its interest.

In *San Antonio Independent School District v. Rodriguez* (1973), poor minority schoolchildren unsuccessfully attacked the Texas system of financing public education. The majority opinion found "neither the suspect classification nor the fundamental-interest analysis persuasive" (411 U.S. at 40). It rested its decision on other grounds, too: "A century of Supreme Court adjudication under the Equal Protection Clause affirmatively supports the application of the traditional standard of review, which requires only that the State's system be shown to bear some rational relationship to legitimate state purposes" (40). By contrast, Marshall's dissent advanced a sliding-scale analysis for equal protection claims, noting that, historically, the Court had applied "a spectrum of standards in reviewing discrimination allegedly violative of the Equal Protection Clause . . . [that] clearly comprehends variations in the degree of care with which the Court will scrutinize particular classifications, depending . . . on the constitutional and societal importance of the interest adversely affected and the recognized invidiousness of the basis upon which the particular classification is drawn." In fact, many of the Court's recent decisions had applied Marshall's approach, "that is, an approach in which 'concentration [is] placed upon the character of the classification in question, the relative importance to the individuals in the class discriminated against of the governmental benefits that they do not receive, and the asserted state interests in support of the classification' " (411 U.S. at 98–99, quoting *Dandridge v. Williams,* 397 U.S. at 520–21).

The Burger Court faced a new series of challenges to statutes that, while neutral on their face, resulted in disproportionate impacts on the poor and blacks. Marshall argued that the Court had a heightened responsibility to review such claims and that the government had a greater burden than it normally does to justify the challenged legislation. The Burger Court was not especially receptive to these claims, preferring to focus on whether the statutes could be shown to have a discriminatory intent. An example of Justice Marshall's thoughts on the intent/effect controversy arose in his dissent in *Mobile v. Bolden* (1980), which dealt with a challenge to an at-large election system and whether that system was intended to discriminate against blacks. Marshall protested "judicial deference to official decision-making" in this Fifteenth Amendment case. Marshall argued that because the Fifteenth Amendment was less sweeping than the Fourteenth Amendment and "explicitly [recognized the] right to vote free of hindrances related to race," a "disproportionate impact test" should apply. "Furthermore, a disproportionate impact test under the Fifteenth Amendment would not lead to constant judicial intrusion into the process of official decision making. Rather, the standard would reach only those decisions having a discriminatory effect upon the minority's vote" (446 U.S. at 134).

Ronald Kahn has noted that Marshall's sliding-scale approach was normally associated with the "rights-oriented" segment of the "process-oriented/rights-oriented" debate because it reflected a "consequentialist decision-making process."[28] Rights-oriented scholars and jurists believe that the creation of rights is supported by the open texture of the Constitution, and they favor their creation.[29] Process-oriented scholars and jurists tend to emphasize the political process and deemphasize rights as important values guiding the process of making constitutional law; primacy is given to values such as electoral politics, separation of powers, and a limited role for courts.[30] The problem with this dichotomy, according to Kahn, is that it oversimplifies the nature of constitutional values and the choices that the Supreme Court must make when it grapples with new issues and problems. A case may be made that Marshall "projected his own consequentialist, ends-oriented thinking process on his colleagues," but he also had "principles about rights and process that are not case specific. . . . We have seen in Marshall's opinions a consistency of rights and process values, not merely ends-oriented thinking."[31]

A glimpse at Marshall's dissents in three cases indicates how process values and rights values intersected from his perspective. In *Dandridge v. Williams* (1970), the Burger Court upheld, as constitutional, a limitation of $250 per month on an Aid to Families with Dependent Children (AFDC) grant, regardless of actual need or family size. In *Jefferson v. Hackney* (1972), the Court allowed states to separate AFDC from other categorical assistance programs and to support a lesser percentage of the need of these recipients than for recipients of aid for the aged and infirm. The system violated the equal protection clause, it was claimed, because AFDC recipients as a group had a much higher percentage of black and Hispanics than did the other groups of recipients. In the third case, *Rodriguez*, the Court permitted a Texas school financing system to stand even though its decision allowed, in effect, a statutory limit on school financing, since funding was based on the value of land in school districts, and taxes derived from that base served as the essential funding source for school districts.

In these cases, there was a consistent character to the rights values and process values articulated by Marshall. The rights values were that any and all rights created by statute must be enforced equally; that all children serving as the focus of welfare policy must be treated equally; that all persons suffering equally should be treated equally; that the right to a quality education ought to be considered a fundamental right; and that children as individuals are the most important units of equality in school districts. The process values enunciated by Marshall in these cases were that state statutory requirements are governed by the equal protection clause;

that state budgetary constraints cannot prevail over constitutional requirements; that the wealth of a state as a whole, not a school district's taxable property, should govern the allocation of school finances; and that the role of the courts is to monitor the political process and safeguard individual constitutional rights and fundamental interests. As for how fundamental interests are to be determined, Marshall suggested that, "[a]s the nexus between the specific constitutional guarantee and the nonconstitutional interest draw closer, the nonconstitutional interest becomes more fundamental and the degree of judicial scrutiny applied when the interest is infringed on a discriminatory basis must be adjusted accordingly."[32]

Executive Power

Justice Marshall was not a strong advocate of executive power and often voted against executive-branch claims.[33] Richard A. Brisbin's examination of Supreme Court decisions dealing with executive power is instructive.[34] As part of his study, Brisbin analyzed the justices' voting behavior in cases dealing with cabinet-level departments and independent agencies, the so-called extended executive (see Table 8.1). Marshall provided the lowest support of the three justices for federal agencies involved in disputes before the Supreme Court, with an average support score of 59 percent. This figure placed him below the average for a majority of justices, beginning with the Warren Court, who supported the agency position nearly 70 percent of the time.[35] The agencies that received the greatest support from Marshall were the Department of Interior, the Food and Drug Administration, the Federal Trade Commission, the Equal Employment Opportunity Commission, and the Federal Power Commission. By contrast, Marshall usually resisted agency claims in cases involving the Civil Service Commission, the Departments of Agriculture and Transportation, the Comptroller of the Currency, and the Immigration and Naturalization Service. Brennan's agency support scores tend to differ from Marshall's only in degree, while Rehnquist's differ both in the direction and magnitude of support.

The Bureaucracy

Marshall's dissenting opinions in cases involving the executive bureaucracy reflect his views on the rights of individuals confronting agencies and their often-imperfect rules. Early in his career, Marshall dissented in *Wyman v. James* (1971), in which the Court

TABLE 8.1
Percentage Support for Federal Agency Actions, 1967–85

Federal Agencies	Selected Justices		
	Marshall	Rehnquist	Brennan
Interior	94.1% (17)	75.0% (16)	81.8% (22)
FDA	87.5 (8)	85.7 (7)	71.4 (7)
FTC	87.5 (8)	66.7 (6)	93.8 (32)
EEOC	82.4 (17)	29.4 (17)	88.2 (17)
FPC/FERC	81.8 (22)	60.0 (20)	79.6 (49)
ICC	78.6 (28)	90.0 (20)	73.2 (71)
FRS/FRB	77.8 (9)	42.9 (7)	70.0 (10)
Labor	75.0 (24)	52.3 (21)	73.0 (37)
NLRB	74.3 (74)	58.6 (58)	77.5 (142)
FEC	71.4 (7)	71.4 (7)	71.4 (7)
IRS	71.3 (80)	69.2 (65)	71.6 (141)
EPA	68.2 (22)	57.9 (19)	77.3 (22)
SEC	66.7 (15)	46.2 (13)	73.9 (23)
OSHA	60.0 (5)	60.0 (5)	60.0 (5)
FCC	58.8 (17)	60.0 (15)	57.9 (19)
Other	57.4 (54)	76.9 (52)	55.3 (85)
AEC/NRC	50.0 (8)	83.3 (6)	50.0 (10)
FMC	33.3 (3)	50.0 (2)	50.0 (8)
HEW/HHS	33.3 (36)	77.4 (31)	36.8 (38)
INS	27.8 (18)	93.3 (15)	41.9 (31)
Comptroller	25.0 (4)	100.0 (1)	50.0 (4)
Transportation	25.0 (4)	100.0 (3)	50.0 (4)
Agriculture	16.7 (6)	100.0 (5)	33.9 (9)
Civil Service	11.1 (9)	90.0 (10)	23.1 (13)
CAB	(0)	100.0 (1)	100.0 (2)
Average Support	59.0%	71.8%	64.5%

Note: The total number of cases decided by each justice is shown in parentheses. For Marshall, $N = 495$; for Rehnquist, $N = 422$; and for Brennan, $N = 808$.

Source: Richard A. Brisbin, Jr., "The Supreme Court and Executive Authority: The Warren, Burger, and Rehnquist Courts" (Paper delivered at the Annual Meeting of the American Political Science Association, Sept. 3–6, 1987, Chicago, Ill.). Table reprinted with the permission of the author.

upheld home visitation by agents of the New York Department of Social Services as a condition for AFDC assistance. The Court majority announced that the visitation was a reasonable administrative tool and did not constitute an unlawful search and seizure or violate due process rights, but Marshall questioned the beneficent purposes advanced by the government in *Wyman*. He noted that the Fourth Amendment "governs all intrusions by agents of the public upon personal security" (400 U.S. at 338). Even if it does not obtain for every entry into the home, Marshall observed, "the welfare visit is not some sort of benevolent inspection" (339), and the analogy that the appellee was "no different from . . . a taxpayer who is required to document his right to a tax reduction" was seriously flawed (343). In Marshall's view, the majority's opinion suggested that, even if the intrusion had been unreasonable, the appellee had waived her constitutional right. He was unwilling to yield personal constitutional rights so easily nor to dismiss them because of the political pressure to reduce public expenditures. If the Court had dealt with the "question of whether the State can condition welfare payments on the waiver of clear constitutional rights," Marshall maintained, "the answer would be plain" (344).

A claimed violation of the Sixth Amendment's right to a speedy trial was addressed by the Burger Court in *United States v. Mac-Donald* (1982). The majority held that no speedy trial violation had occurred between the 1970 dismissal of military charges against MacDonald and his 1975 indictment on civilian criminal charges for the same offense because criminal charges were not pending against him during the entire period from his arrest on military charges and the later civilian indictment. The Court found that the dismissal of the military charges placed MacDonald in the same posture, legally and constitutionally, as if no charges had been made.

Responding to the majority in *MacDonald*, Marshall argued in dissent that suspending application of the right to a speedy trial in the period between successive prosecutions for the same crime by the same sovereign served no governmental interest. The majority's argument—that, if a charge was not technically pending, the speedy trial clause offered no protection to a criminal defendant during successive prosecutions—was too simple and without merit. In Marshall's words: "The majority's insistence that the dismissal of an indictment eliminates speedy trial protections is not only inconsistent with the language and policies of the Speedy Trial Clause and with this Court's decisions. It is also senseless. Any legitimate government reason for delay during the period between prosecutions can, indeed must, be weighed when the court determines whether the defendant's speedy trial right has been violated" (456 U.S. at 19).

In *Clark v. Community for Creative Non-Violence* (1984), the Burger Court sustained the constitutionality of a National Park Service anti-camping regulation. The measure disallowed symbolic over-night sleeping in tents for the purpose of calling attention to the homeless in Lafayette Park and on the Mall in the heart of Wash-ington, D.C. The Court held that the regulation was narrowly tailored to serve a significant governmental interest, noted that other communication channels remained open, and declared that the First Amendment had not been abridged because the regu-lation was justifiable without reference to the content of the reg-ulated speech.

In dissent, Marshall agreed that the government must explain what interest served as a foundation for its regulation and sustain the importance of that interest against charges that civil liberties were being abridged. In his critical examination of the interests advanced by the government in *Clark*, however, he found that the "majority failed to subject the alleged interests of the government to the degree of scrutiny required to assure that expressive activity protected by the First Amendment remains free of unnecessary limitations" (468 U.S. at 301). He concluded that the First Amend-ment requires the government to justify *every* instance of abridg-ment" (309).

According to Marshall, sleeping in the winter in a public place for the purpose of protesting homelessness clearly was symbolic speech protected by the First Amendment. Some of the most robust political demonstrations in the history of the republic have oc-curred in Lafayette Park; in these circumstances, sleeping in the park was most assuredly a political act. As for the interests advanced by the government, these were neither sufficient nor adequate to offset the civil liberties interests at stake. The administrative bur-den of issuing permits to others who might request to sleep in the park was only speculative, and the argument that the regulation served to deter around-the-clock demonstrations lasting for days on end and curtailed "wear and tear" on park properties was also flawed (468 U.S. at 309). To Marshall, the crux of this case was that the people must at all times be protected from the government because "government agencies by their very nature are driven to overregulate public forums to the detriment of First Amendment rights." According to Marshall, "public officials have strong in-centives to overregulate even in the absence of an intent to censor particular views" (315). Marshall stressed the inherent power im-balance in this case between those in the minority, who sought a forum in which to protest, and those of the majority, whose com-mand the public official serves.

Marshall's Path of Dissent

Justice Marshall's role on the Burger Court was largely that of a dissenting justice. Fulfilling that role was the primary way in which he contributed to constitutional law during the Burger era, and it involved various possible strategies. Once a justice has written a dissenting opinion and new cases arise that significantly relate to that dissent, the justice is confronted with several options, according to Maurice Kelman.[36] First, with due regard to stare decisis, an earlier dissent may be abandoned in order to join the majority in new cases, as though a concurrence had been written in the first place rather than a dissent. A second option is to adhere to the earlier dissent and mention it in some form. The justice could merely note "I dissent," as Marshall frequently did, or take the case at point and work through its weaknesses to underscore the majority's shortcomings. Another option represents a variation on the first: instead of departing from the earlier position, the justice could put it in "cold storage" and "accept the original decision as a predicate for . . . judicial reasoning in the next cases."[37] Marshall's dissenting postures may be viewed as variations on Kelman's themes.

In cases involving statutory construction, Marshall abandoned his *Buffalo Forge Company Inc. v. Steelworkers* (1976) dissent in *Jacksonville Bulk Terminals v. International Longshoreman's Association* (1982).[38] In *Buffalo*, Marshall and three other justices dissented from the majority, which had held that federal judges were not authorized under the Norris-LaGuardia Act to enjoin sympathy strikes by labor unions not directly involved in a dispute. The issue in *Jacksonville*, which dealt with cargo bound for the Soviet Union, was whether federal judges could enjoin longshoremen who refused to handle the cargo for political reasons. The petitioner, Jacksonville, asked for a reconsideration of *Buffalo Forge*, and both Marshall and Brennan abandoned their earlier dissent largely to adhere to precedent.

Marshall's contribution to constitutional law via dissent was perhaps strongest in the area of capital punishment. Marshall believed that the death penalty was contrary to the Eighth Amendment, and in spite of numerous rulings to the contrary, he augmented his position when occasion permitted. In *California v. Ramos* (1983), he emphasized, "Even if I accepted the prevailing view that the death penalty may constitutionally be imposed under certain circumstances, I could not agree that the State may tip the balance in favor of death by informing the jury that the defendant may eventually be released if he is not executed" (463 U.S. at 1015).

Kelman noted that "damage control" is a viable option for a dissenting justice—that is, to give temporary acquiescence to a view previously dissented against with a view "toward the gradual reshaping of a bad decision into good, or at least less noxious, law."[39] Damage control works when the dissenter may serve as the fifth vote with other justices who are interested in limiting the foundation decision. Marshall was able to use his *Ramos* dissent to form the majority and write the opinion in *Caldwell v. Mississippi* (1985), in which the Court invalidated under the Eighth Amendment a death penalty imposed by a jury that had been led by the prosecutor to believe that the responsibility for determining the appropriateness of the death penalty would rest with an appellate court rather than with the jury itself.

In *Caldwell*, Justice Marshall engaged in "spurious acceptance" of precedent. That is, he remained an unreconciled dissenter and reached results consistent with his own dissenting theories. Another variation on this strategy was represented by his concurrence in the unanimous decision of *Hills v. Gautreaux* (1976). The Court ruled that a metropolitan-area remedy for desegregating public housing was not impermissible as a matter of law and could be ordered by a district court in the exercise of its discretion. Marshall concurred in *Gautreaux* insofar as the opinion permitted a metropolitan remedy and appeared to reaffirm *Milliken v. Bradley* (1974), in which he had written a spirited dissent.

Keeping an issue alive and appealing to the "intelligence of a future day" are important objectives for a determined dissenter, who may then seek to create new opportunities for an issue to be reconsidered. In that vein, Marshall proposed solutions in his dissents that would have kept certain matters from reaching federal court and directed them to state courts instead. For example, dissenting in *Oregon v. Haas* (1975), Marshall argued that some matters should remain at the state level. In *Haas*, he provided "the most persuasive remedy that has been offered" to problems created when individual substantive and procedural rights are created by state supreme courts based on state constitutions that go beyond federal constitutional doctrine.[40] In *Haas* the Oregon Supreme Court ruled that statements a defendant made after he asserted his *Miranda* rights could not be used to impeach his testimony, and the U.S. Supreme Court reversed. Marshall believed, however, that the Court had a tendency to correct state courts when they had ruled on federal constitutional questions without giving sufficient consideration to the possibility that its ruling might only amount to an advisory opinion. Rather than proposing the extreme of letting the respective states strike a balance between police practices and individual rights, Marshall urged that at least "the Court should not review a state court decision . . . unless it is quite clear that the state court has resolved all applicable state law questions" (420 U.S. at 729).

Conclusion

Thurgood Marshall's judicial philosophy is linked to the larger social context that permeated his personal and professional life. What Marshall witnessed in this context included racism, oppression, segregation, discrimination, and the denial of equal protection of the laws. He struggled against these injustices by seeking to understand how the law functions as an instrument of social control and by developing the skills that would enable him to use the law to correct social injustices. Basic ideas in jurisprudence are related to dominant ideologies prevalent in society. An understanding of Marshall's judicial philosophy, therefore, should address the relationship between social conditions and the dominant political thought of twentieth-century America.

At the turn of the century, shortly before Marshall's birth in 1908, the classical mode of jurisprudence reflected the values inherent in laissez-faire economic policy, unregulated industrial capitalism, and vested property rights. At the conclusion of the Burger Court, these values had returned, albeit in modified form. The Burger Court era was characterized by the conservative political, economic, and social thought collectively known as "Reaganism." Major values that gained primacy during this time were conservative notions of individuality, equality of opportunity and access to the system, and limited government. Key political events at the national level included the election of Republican presidents from 1968 forward (save 1976), huge budget cuts for social programs, and a continuous stream of conservative "moralistic" rhetoric that set the tone for the period.

Justice Marshall's philosophy must be cast against this background. His approach to justice was Warren Court–style legal realism, with its social background of the civil rights movement and Great Society efforts. A major role of the courts during the Warren era was to accept and address civil rights and civil liberties claims and provide relief under the Constitution. Understandably, Marshall struggled against the dominant values of the Burger Court period. In his dissenting opinions he emphasized individual rights, fundamental fairness, equal opportunity and protection under the law, the supremacy of the Constitution as the embodiment of rights and privileges, and the Supreme Court's responsibility to play a significant role in giving meaning to the notion of constitutional rights.

As a member of the Burger Court, Marshall was foremost a dissenter. In his dissents, he put forth views that were traceable to legal traditions such as the Brandeis brief or the use of sociological data in framing responses to legal questions raising important social issues, and the acceptance of "living law" as well as logical and philosophical justice. Marshall never abandoned the themes emphasized in his legal training at Howard University Law School. It was there that he fully subscribed to becoming a social engineer and a partisan for individual and social justice. Upon becoming an "objective" judge, Marshall resolved the challenging problem of intellectual integrity by transferring his lawyer's partiality from persons to principles of law. He was keenly aware that jurisprudential concepts have real consequences and that court decisions can affect people's lives in powerful ways—his dissents reflect that awareness. As to Marshall's impact on the Court, the evidence suggests that Justice Blackmun was affected by his presence.[41] Federal appellate judge Arlin Adams believed that Marshall's mere presence in the conference room of the Supreme Court had a measure of significance beyond quantification.[42]

The first phase of Justice Marshall's contribution to the development of constitutional law was as a lawyer for the NAACP, where he and his associates worked successfully to give meaning to the equal protection clause. His tenure on the Supreme Court may be viewed as the second phase, during which he attempted to keep that meaning alive. Some have claimed that Marshall's opinions tended not to be formalistic treatises, symmetrical in form and substance, and that the intellectual elegance for his positions came primarily from Justice Brennan. These are, at best, arguable points. It is clear, however, that Marshall's opinions were candid statements that addressed the real-life situations of society's disadvantaged. His social perception was that life represents a never-ending struggle between the advantaged and disadvantaged. Justice Thurgood Marshall's concomitant political ideal was that legal activism is both a valued and imperative tool in helping the disadvantaged in that struggle. His decisions reflect the belief that the behavior of government officials must be given the greatest scrutiny when violations of constitutional rights are asserted.

NOTES

1. Ramsey Clark, "Thurgood Marshall," in Leon Friedman, ed., *The Justices of the United States Supreme Court: Their Lives and Major Opinions* (New York: Chelsea House, 1978), 5: 385.

2. Cynthia Kenney, "The Early Life of Thurgood Marshall" (Seminar paper presented at Cornell University, 1975), p. 12.

3. Richard Kluger, *Simple Justice: The History of Brown v. Board of Education and Black America's Struggle for Equality* (New York: Vintage Books, 1977), p. 88.

4. Randall W. Bland, *Private Pressure on Public Law: The Legal Career of Justice Thurgood Marshall* (Port Washington, N.Y.: Kennikat Press, 1973), p. 3.

5. Interview with Clarence Mitchell, reported in Kenney, "The Early Life of Thurgood Marshall," p. 25.

6. *Time*, Sept. 19, 1955, p. 24.

7. Lewis H. Fenderson, *Thurgood Marshall: Fighter for Justice* (New York: McGraw-Hill, 1969), p. 29.

8. Kenney, "The Early Life of Thurgood Marshall," p. 33.

9. Interview with Clarence Mitchell, reported in Kenney, p. 25.

10. Kluger, *Simple Justice*, p. 125.

11. Kenny, "The Early Life of Thurgood Marshall," p. 63.

12. For a discussion of the two themes, see Ronald Kahn, "The Burger Court and Equal Protection of the Law: The Changing Intersection of Process and Rights Values" (Paper delivered at the Annual Meeting of the American Political Science Association, Aug. 28–31, 1986, Washington, D.C.).

13. These data were tabulated from the statistics section of each November issue of the *Harvard Law Review* 84–100 (1970–86).

14. Quoted in Kluger, *Simple Justice*, p. 606.

15. Bob Woodward and Scott Armstrong, *The Brethren: Inside the Supreme Court* (New York: Simon and Schuster, 1979), p. 221.

16. Stephen L. Wasby, *The Supreme Court in the Federal Judicial System*, 2d ed. (New York: Holt, Rinehart, and Winston, 1984), p. 187.

17. The substantive issues of several of these cases are discussed in other sections of this chapter.

18. Bernard Schwartz, "The Warren Court and Era," in Robert J. Janosik, ed., *Encyclopedia of the American Judicial System* (New York: Charles Scribner's Sons, 1987), 1: 168.

19. Richard Funston, "The Burger Court and Era," in Janosik, ed., *Encyclopedia of the American Judicial System*, 1: 180.

20. Ibid.

21. See, for example, *Harris v. New York* (1971); *Kirby v. Illinois* (1972); *United States v. Leon* (1984).

22. Funston, "The Burger Court and Era," pp. 180–81.

23. Michael J. Perry, *Morality, Politics, and Law: A Bicentennial Essay* (New York: Oxford University Press, 1988), p. 121.

24. See generally Marshall's concurring opinion in *Furman v. Georgia*, 408 U.S. at 314–74.

25. Fred Barbash, "Two Old Men v. the Executioners: Why Brennan and Marshall Won't Give Up," *Washington Post* Weekly Edition, Dec. 19, 1983.

26. *The Gallup Report* No. 243, Dec. 1985, pp. 25–27.

27. See, for example, *James v. Valtierra* (1971); *Milliken v. Bradley* (1974).

28. Kahn, "The Burger Court and Equal Protection of the Law," p. 45.

29. See, for example, Laurence H. Tribe, *Constitutional Choices* (Cambridge, Mass.: Harvard University Press, 1985).

30. See, for example, John Hart Ely, *Democracy and Distrust: A Theory of Judicial Review* (Cambridge, Mass.: Harvard University Press, 1980).

31. Kahn, "The Burger Court and Equal Protection of the Law," pp. 3, 44–45.

32. Ibid., p. 41.

33. See, for example, *United States v. Nixon* (1974); *Nixon v. Fitzgerald* (1982); *Regan v. Wald* (1984).

34. Richard A. Brisbin, Jr., "The Supreme Court and Executive Authority: The Warren, Burger, and Rehnquist Courts" (Paper delivered at the Annual Meeting of the American Political Science Association, Sept. 3–6, 1987, Chicago, Ill.).

35. Ibid., p. 16.

36. Maurice Kelman, "The Forked Path of Dissent," *Supreme Court Review* 1985: 230.

37. Ibid., pp. 230-31.

38. Ibid., p. 237.

39. Ibid.

40. Peter J. Galie and Lawrence P. Galie, "State Constitutional Guarantees and Supreme Court Review: Justice Marshall's Proposal in *Oregon v. Haas*," *Dickinson Law Review* 28 (1978): 373.

41. See John A. Jenkins, "A Candid Talk with Justice Blackmun," *New York Times*, Feb. 20, 1983, p. 24.

42. Interview by author with Judge Arlin Adams, May 5, 1983.

9

Justice Sandra Day O'Connor: Transition to a Republican Court Agenda

BEVERLY B. COOK

Attention to the appointment of Sandra Day O'Connor to the U.S. Supreme Court in 1981 focused on her gender. The fact that she was the first woman justice had considerable symbolic significance for women's status in national politics. O'Connor, however, eschewed the role of woman justice. Although she took a strong stand for gender equality in her first term, she intended to build her reputation as a justice upon her resolution of issues important to the Republican party.

The two concerns on her personal judicial agenda before she reached the Court, federalism and judicial restraint, did not concern gender. Her avowed purpose as a justice was not to make substantive social policies, including those that would benefit women, but to rehabilitate traditional perspectives on state and judicial power. Ironically, her gender identity had confined O'Connor to a career pattern that had shaped her commitment to these two structural principles, and her gender roles as daughter and wife in a comfortable and traditional family had hidden from her the barriers to gender equality faced by women with fewer intellectual and financial resources.

Introduction

The limits placed by the American legal culture upon a woman lawyer became apparent immediately after O'Connor completed her professional degree at Stanford University in 1952, where she also obtained her undergraduate degree.[1] Her friend and classmate, William Rehnquist, moved directly onto the fast professional track, serving as a law clerk to a Supreme Court justice and becoming a partner in a Phoenix law firm before accepting a high political appointment in the U.S. Justice Department. Despite O'Connor's Order of the Coif and law review honors, the Los Angeles law firm of Ronald Reagan's attorney general rejected her application for an associate position on the basis of her gender. She took the slow-track, government law jobs available to women, first as an assistant county attorney and later with the U.S. Army abroad while her lawyer husband did his military service. Since she could rely on her husband's income and on her own property interest in her family's Arizona ranch, she was under no necessity to compete with male lawyers for a salary adequate to support her family. Thus she did part-time work while her three children were small. Her full-time job with the Arizona attorney general's office, beginning in 1965, was another of those public-sector positions with low pay and high turnover that were available to women applicants. She never held the kind of prestigious private and public law jobs that have prepared male lawyers for federal appellate judgeships, but she learned to appreciate the law work done at the state and local level.

O'Connor's activity in Arizona Republican politics led to her appointment to fill a vacancy in the Arizona state senate in 1969, and she won election to that office in 1970 and 1972. She ran successfully for Superior Court for Maricopa County in 1974. Five years later she was appointed to the Arizona Court of Appeals. Her political and judicial offices did not compare to those expected of a viable male candidate for the Supreme Court, namely, governor, U.S. senator, attorney general, solicitor general, and U.S. appellate court judge. As an overqualified woman who found her opportunities only in minor public offices below the national level, she developed a commitment to state and local government, legislative responsibility, and judicial modesty.[2]

During the 1980 presidential campaign, candidate Reagan promised to place a woman on the Supreme Court at one of his earliest opportunities. When Justice Stewart informed the Department of Justice in spring 1981 of his retirement plans, Reagan's advisers saw political advantage in fulfilling the promise immediately. Their consideration was the gender identity of the candidate, not the candidate's views on gender equality. The 1980 Republican party platform had abandoned the Equal Rights Amendment (ERA) and added a "family" plank, which was worded such that it could be construed as antithetical to women's autonomy. The gender of Reagan's nominee only provided a symbol of party recognition of an important electoral constituency.

The pool of Republican women judges qualified for a seat on the highest court proved to be extremely small. Eliminating those who were too old (and therefore could not perpetuate Reagan's agenda much beyond his own presidential term) and those who were too young or too low in the judicial hierarchy (and therefore would not have the experience and status required to win American Bar Association approval) left no more than six eligible Republican women judges.[3] Two survived screening by the White House and the Justice Department and appeared on the short list presented to the president. He chose to interview Sandra Day O'Connor and discovered a compatible and energetic personality who had learned to work comfortably as a peer with male colleagues. He was satisfied that her party activities evidenced loyalty to Republican principles and that her views promised the fulfillment of his administration's agenda for the Court.[4]

Three agendas provide a useful framework for evaluating Justice O'Connor's contribution to the work of the Burger Court: her own judicial agenda, Reagan's agenda for the Court, and the persisting Court agenda.[5] The political nature of the justices' role and of the conflicts they choose to review is reflected in their agenda issues and votes. These, in turn, are manifestations of values and structural principles that differentiate the Republican party of the 1980s from the Democratic party of the 1930s–1960s. O'Connor's personal agenda was revealed during her confirmation experience, and after she joined the Court she translated her values and principles into votes and opinions. In her opinions she offered some unique reasoning and new rules to support her voting choices favoring or rejecting values associated with the major parties. Her voice was muted, however, since she spoke in significant cases only in separate opinions. Like Marshall, O'Connor was not assigned to write the Court opinion by the chief justice in a single significant case between 1981 and 1986.[6] Therefore, her impact as a member of the Court can be reported more accurately by describing her voting pattern (see the next section) than in analyzing her opinions (see subsequent sections).

Setting the Agenda

In the judiciary, setting the agenda is a critical stage of policy-making, as it is in other branches of government. The Supreme Court agenda is in continuous incremental flux as the administration, interest group lawyers, and justices bring pressure to bear in its formulation. But core policy issues persist for long periods until they have been settled or have lost salience in a new political environment. Restructuring of the Court agenda occurs as a political party with a different philosophy moves toward majority status and gains control of national political and social institutions. Reagan proposed to the Burger Court an agenda that continued and expanded Nixon's Republican agenda, and in his first year as president he provided a new justice to implement it.

Justice Sandra Day O'Connor

The extent to which a justice reaches the Court with a well-developed personal agenda and proceeds to elaborate on it has been largely ignored, perhaps because the norms and practices that give the third branch considerable independence from the "political" branches require the nominee to deny having an agenda or a constituency. The events of the nomination process contradict these norms, bringing to light, more or less accurately, the predispositions of the nominee. Participants in the process try to uncover the nominee's personal agenda in order to inform their decisions and impose their own agendas.

O'Connor's Agenda

At Senate confirmation hearings, O'Connor denied the relevance of an agenda to her mode of judicial decision making, which she described as treating each court case as a unique event with a certain set of facts and some applicable law. Nevertheless, from her legislative experience O'Connor appreciated the importance of agenda setting. In her first term in *Federal Energy Regulatory Commission v. Mississippi* (1982), she wrote that policy-making includes "the power to decide which proposals are most worthy of consideration, the order in which they should be taken up, and the precise form in which they should be debated" (456 U.S. at 779). O'Connor's intent was to select and decide cases that would restore the significance of federalism in constitutional adjudication.

The focus of O'Connor's agenda was structural (where the decision was to be made) and not substantive (who will win what). State sovereignty is a term that captures her purpose better than federalism. Her great confidence in the wisdom of policies developed by subnational political officeholders meshed with the New Federalism plank in Reagan's platform. Their shared concept of federalism required a shift in the balance of power by reducing the size, cost, and complexity of the central government and restoring to state and local governments their direct responsibility for public safety, morality, and welfare.

At the time of her nomination, O'Connor's first law review article, on federal-state court relationships, appeared. She favored deference to state judges on grounds that their competence was equal to that of federal judges, and she recommended giving finality to state court judgments on federal rights questions in cases in which the complaint had received full and fair treatment. She questioned the "confusing and obtuse" standards applied in federal habeas review of state treatment of criminal offenders. On the new issues of counsel competence and waiver, she proposed deference to state practices.[7]

On the civil side, O'Connor foresaw serious confrontations between federal and state courts over school busing, electoral districts, prison conditions, and creditor's rights. She understood exhaustion of state remedies to be a prerequisite for filing Section 1983 suits and predicted that limitation or disallowance of attorney fees in federal courts would keep civil rights suits in state courts. In effect, she proposed federalism as the core value for resolution of disputes that had been conceptualized in the past as civil rights cases.[8] In her elevation of Court doctrines of comity and of deference to other public officials to the status of constitutional doctrine, her strategy was similar to that of Rehnquist, with whom she had shared experiences as a student at Stanford Law School, a Republican activist in Phoenix, and a protégé of Senator Goldwater.

Reagan's Republican Agenda

Reagan expected his appointee to transfer his Republican agenda to the Court's agenda. He explicitly promised in the 1980 party platform to select judges who respected "traditional family values" and opposed abortion ("who respect . . . the sanctity of innocent human life"), who viewed crime as a serious problem related to judge-made rules, and who believed in decentralization and deregulation. Reagan then used his solicitor general to press the Court to participate in his administration's initiatives in terms of their agenda choices and substantive votes.[9]

What was O'Connor's position on Reagan's agenda items? On public television she demonstrated her commitment to family values before the Judiciary Committee and to any of Reagan's constituents who were watching. She stated that without her husband's support she would not have accepted the president's offer, and she introduced each of her three sons with brief biographies that attested to her success as a mother. She quoted from the marriage ceremony she prepared as a trial judge: "Marriage is . . . the foundation of the family, mankind's basic unit of society, the hope of the world and the strength of our country."[10] This scene was effective at the symbolic level without binding O'Connor to any particular family policy.

O'Connor's domestic drama did not deflect questions on abortion, though. Reagan's nomination implied to his right-wing constituency that O'Connor was committed to reverse *Roe v. Wade* (1973), but abortion had not been a particularly salient issue during her legislative career. Against heavy pressure, O'Connor turned aside every effort to win her public commitment to overturn *Roe*. She offered instead her personal view that abortion was offensive and repugnant. She made her nomination marginally palatable to liberals by admitting a few exceptions; to the radical right, by reiterating that she would assign to legislative bodies the task of drawing lines on abortion. Her skillful balance between reticence and candor was an extraordinary political performance, and no less was required between the tigers and the lions to gain confirmation.

O'Connor's reputation on the state trial bench (1975–79) and on the intermediate appellate court (1979–81) went to her competence as a prepared, organized, demanding, and articulate judge—not to the substance of her decisions.[11] Although President Reagan chose to describe her as a tough sentencer, her record and self-description revealed a thoughtful fashioning of the penalty to fit facts properly on the record. While serving in the state senate, she had voted to restore, but not to mandate, the death penalty. Her purpose—to demonstrate respect for state officials and to make economical use of both state and federal judicial resources—had the effect of favoring the value order over the value due process.

The ability of organized religious groups to produce votes for Republican candidates made religion an important focus of Reagan's domestic agenda. The president accused the Court of failing to appreciate the religious inspiration behind the nation's founding; he promised to restore voluntary prayer to classrooms and to provide material support to parochial schools and parents of parochial schoolchildren. O'Connor reported no life experiences or memberships that suggested that her ideas on church/state relations were congruent with Reagan's. Only her avowed preference for policies made at the state level reassured her Republican sponsors.

The Court's Continuing Agenda

The principal contours of the Supreme Court's agenda had been shaped by Democratic presidents and their appointees between 1937 and 1968. During the New Deal period, governmental power to regulate the economy replaced property as the dominant Court value, and in the 1950s civil rights emerged as a new and central Court concern. By adopting the role of protector of minorities, the Court attracted controversies that tested the limits of the values of freedom and equality. Democratic presidents took the lead in fashioning economic, social welfare, and civil rights programs, which were tested before the Court.

No evidence suggests that O'Connor went through a consciousness-raising period like many women in her age cohort did in the 1960s. At the nomination hearings O'Connor admitted that job and pay inequities concerned her but explained the discrepancy between men's and women's wages by women's acceptance of lower-paying jobs. When asked to explain her "commitment to equal justice" on the Senate committee's questionnaire, O'Connor reported her success while a senator in reforming the Arizona code by equalizing spousal control over community property and child custody and eliminating sexist language and Progressive-era restrictions on women's working hours.

She had endorsed the ERA before its passage by Congress, but she took no action to encourage Arizona to ratify it after the state Republican party opposed the amendment. She rationalized her position on the ERA by claiming that the Constitution's equal protection clause was adequate to the purpose. On the issue of sex-segregated clubs, O'Connor distinguished between professional associations and the kind of women's service club in which she intended to retain her membership. During her service on the Defense Advisory Committee on Women in the Services, she revealed her appreciation of the need of military women for more opportunities by recommending changes in the definition of combat. She did not, however, personally approve of women participating in battlefield combat.[12] Her positions were unsatisfactory to both liberals and conservatives.

O'Connor opposed compulsory school busing to achieve racial balance. In the Arizona legislature she had voted for a memorial asking the federal government to ban the remedy in desegregation cases. At her confirmation hearings she recounted to the senators how a seventy-five mile bus trip from her ranch home to school, leaving home before daylight and returning after dark, had been "very disturbing to me as a child." She suggested that the educational benefits of a racially balanced classroom might be outweighed by the personal costs of busing to children.[13]

Values and Principles in O'Connor's Voting Record

The political nature of the judicial selection process provides grounds for expecting a relationship between party platforms and Supreme Court decisions. The values espoused by the two major parties, which stimulate many of the justices' voting choices, are the conflicting values of popular American political thought. Rohde and Spaeth have provided a useful framework for comparing justices by conceptualizing their political philosophies as different combinations of three basic values identified, through scalogram analysis of case votes, as the attitudinal stimuli for voting choices.[14] I have modified and expanded their design to place O'Connor within a matrix that includes the values and structural principles openly proselytized at her confirmation hearings by Republican party leaders (see Table 9.1).[15]

Two individual values—freedom and equality—and one social value—

TABLE 9.1

Values and Principles Supported by the Justices, 1981–86

Justices	Individual Values				Factor Loadings for Social Values			Structural Principles		
	FREE	EQUAL	(Gen)	PROP	WELF	(Aff)	ORDER	FED	SEP	JUD
Burger	−	−	(−)	+	−	(−)	+	+	−	+
Brennan	+	+	(+)	−	+	(+)	−	−	+	−
White	−[a]	−	(0)	−	−	(−)	+[a]	+	--	+
Marshall	+	+	(+)	−	+	(+)	−	−	+	−
Blackmun	0	+	(−)	0	+	(+)	0	−	+	−
Powell	−	−	(−)	0	−	(−)	+	+	0	+
Rehnquist	−	−	(−)	+	−	(−)	+	+	−	+
Stevens	+[a]	+	(+)	−[a]	+	(0)	−[a]	−	+	−[a]
O'Connor	−	−	(−)	+	−	(−)	+	+	−	+
Case N =	76	108	(25)	59	105	(28)	185	136	15	61
Eigenvalue =	4.7	4.9	5.0	4.6	5.0	4.9	4.0	4.9	4.9	5.1

Code for factor loadings: + = .60–.99   0 = .50–.59
                          − = .00–.49   -- = −.01–.10
[a] = communality less than .50.
FREEdom: First Amendment and substantive due process cases.
EQUALity: equal protection cases. (GENder: gender equality.)
PROPerty: takings, zoning, taxes, patents, bankruptcy.
WELFare: government regulation and protection of economic and social interests.
      (AFFirmative action: enforcement of programs for equal effect, fee issues.)
ORDER: criminal appeals, substantive and procedural.
FEDeralism: Tenth and Eleventh amendments, preemption, commerce, supremacy,
      sovereign immunity, judicial comity.
SEParation of church and state: First Amendment.
JUDicialRestraint: jurisdiction, standing, mootness, exhaustion of remedies, judicial
      discretion, deference to decision-makers.

government regulation—are the three New Deal values that Rohde and Spaeth and other scholars have recognized as the values stimulating justices' votes since the 1930s. I have added a second social value—order—deconstructed from the freedom value; the order scores are generated from the votes in criminal due process cases.[16] Two minor values—gender equality and abortion choice—were important to the administration and to the pressure groups involved in O'Connor's nomination. The Burger Court selected very few abortion cases for its agenda after O'Connor arrived, but those cases had high visibility. The value implicit in abortion cases is described as a component of the global Democratic value of freedom because the Burger Court minority did not succeed in reshaping the issues under a Republican value label of family or morality (as Reagan's right-wing followers proposed) or in terms of federalism (as O'Connor preferred).

The social value "government regulation" has been renamed "welfare" to emphasize the new constituencies, especially women and minorities, that have joined labor, farmer, and business groups as beneficiaries of government regulation and distribution. With the addition of controversies over new forms of welfare, particularly affirmative action cases, which do not fit with cases of equal treatment, the social value of government regulatory power persists in a new context.

The emergence of a strong Republican party, making a serious claim to majority party status under Presidents Nixon and Reagan, has affected not only the issues brought into the courts, but the way new litigants have shaped their arguments and what political philosophies judges hold. The value "property" was conceptualized by the Supreme Court in the 1890s as an individual value. Until the New Deal, when the social value of economic control began to dominate the Court's thinking about case issues, the justices understood property as a basic aspect of freedom. During the O'Connor period litigants again presented the claims of property rights, but the context had changed from the individual level to the group level. The Court generally perceives parties in the judicial forum as individual versus individual, government versus government, or individual against government, and it has not found a satisfactory theoretical niche for group interests and rights.

In this analysis of O'Connor's voting, three structural principles—federalism, separation of church and state, and judicial restraint—are proposed as stimuli to the justices' voting choices. The religious separation principle is another necessary deconstruction of the freedom value used in earlier studies, since religious free expression and establishment cases have never fit logically on a unidimensional scale. Moreover, the right to free exercise of religion is an individual freedom, while the principle of separation concerns the institutions of government and church.

Federalism, O'Connor's first agenda item, has been identified as the value underlying a minor scale in previous research.[17] After O'Connor's arrival, federalism issues shaped many decisions that formerly would have been treated as presenting government regulation or criminal justice issues. In her opinion writing O'Connor has made a major contribution in changing the perspective on such cases from a focus on social values to one on structural principle. Jurisdictional questions have been defined as "pure" judicial power issues,[18] but for O'Connor, as well as Rehnquist, almost every claim of unconstitutionality raised the restraint question. Moreover, most justices cannot avoid thinking about the substantive consequences of their decisions to assert or deny their authority to resolve a dispute.

A picture of O'Connor's performance emerges from an examination of the valences, based upon factor loadings produced by factor analyses of ten sets of cases, reported in Table 9.1. The plus symbol indicates support for the values of freedom, equality, property, welfare, and order, and for the principles of state sovereignty, separation of church and state, and judicial restraint. O'Connor's pattern of support of Reagan Republican ideals is identical to Burger's and Rehnquist's. Many observers expected O'Connor to vote in tandem with Rehnquist; their factor loadings show matching values on federalism, restraint, order, equality, and property; minor differences on welfare and freedom; and a major difference on separation of church and state.

O'Connor's votes contributed to the movement of the Court in a new conservative direction. She clearly rejected the Democratic party values, and she did not serve the cause of women's liberation through her votes on abortion or affirmative action. Her loadings on gender equality show that she has not even taken a strong position on equal treatment of men and women. Stevens's apparent change on the freedom value from neutral to positive was balanced by O'Connor's replacement of Stewart. O'Connor had a strong negative valence on freedom, while her predecessor had a neutral valence.

The number of abortion cases between 1981 and 1986 is too small for factor analysis, but a mini-scale of abortion votes shows that Blackmun, Marshall, Brennan, and Stevens (in that order) had positive valences; Powell was neutral; and White, Rehnquist, O'Connor, and Burger (in that order) had negative valences. Burger moved steadily toward the right after he joined Blackmun's landmark opinion in *Roe*. No doubt O'Connor's presence made Burger's behavioral shift easier by allowing him to join a majority.

A significant change occurred in the justices' response to equality issues after O'Connor's arrival. O'Connor helped to create majorities against support for equality claims; her attitude toward equality was negative, whereas Stewart's had been neutral. White's neutral valence on equality became negative after 1981, and Blackmun moved in the opposite direction, from a negative to a positive response to equality claims.[19] Brennan, not O'Connor, clearly took the lead in support of gender equality. O'Connor's score was higher on gender than on other equal protection claims, but her ranking among the justices was sixth for both.

By replacing Stewart with O'Connor, the president did not affect the Court's response to welfare claims, since both justices held negative attitudes in that area. However, three other justices appear to have changed their stands on government protection and regulation. White moved from neutral in the 1975–81 period to negative, and Blackmun and Stevens from neutral to positive. O'Connor has the same third-place ranking against government intervention for affirmative action purposes. The order value did not dominate the justices' thinking in criminal cases, since the first factor explained only 44 percent of the variation. However, the justices decided against the defendant in a large majority of the 185 criminal cases analyzed, and six justices had positive valences on the first factor. It seems reasonable, then, to recognize order as the emerging value in this set of cases and fairness or due process as the declining value. O'Connor had the highest correlation with the first factor, followed by Burger and Rehnquist.

O'Connor took the strongest position in favor of state sovereignty, closely followed by Burger and Rehnquist. She provided the critical fifth voice in support of deference to state courts and state legislatures. She was not successful, however, in persuading her colleagues to treat state criminal cases as issues of "judicial federalism," as indicated by the failure of state criminal case votes in combination with other federalism cases to form a major factor. O'Connor and Rehnquist were somewhat more sympathetic to due process concerns in federal cases, while the other justices failed to distinguish between the two contexts.

O'Connor's position on religious accommodation was more moderate than the administration had hoped; the extreme position for accommodation was taken by White and Rehnquist. As for property rights, O'Connor was part of the minority, along with Burger and Rehnquist, that recognized them. In addition, O'Connor fulfilled her promise to exercise restraint, with factor loadings like Rehnquist's and Burger's, which were above .90. Her presence was critical to the formation of a majority during the 1981–86 period for a modest employment of judicial power. Spaeth's 1962 study provides the findings for a cross-time comparison of the attitudes of two of the justices toward judicial restraint.[20] Brennan favored the use of judicial power throughout the Warren and Burger eras, while White shifted from power to restraint.

During the Warren Court era, at the height of the domination of the Court's agenda, as well as the justices' thinking, by Democratic values, Schubert described voting patterns with two global dimensions: civil liberties and rights, which combined freedom and equality, and national regulation of the economy.[21] During the Burger Court we see the breakdown of that hegemony and the outlines of a new ideology emerge that may eventually channel the justices' voting along two different global dimensions: order, as the central social value, and federalism, as the structural principle. The only individual value that the new Republican ideology may accommodate is property, but in conflicts with order or government authority, and particularly with state and local policies protected by federalism, its future as a Court value remains uncertain.

Republican Values in O'Connor's Opinions

O'Connor contributed to the strengthening of Republican values in Supreme Court jurisprudence by writing opinions on issues involving federalism and order. The disproportion between the percentage of criminal cases on the Court's agenda from 1981 to 1986 (24%) and the percentage of criminal case opinions for the Court written by O'Connor (38% of all her assigned opinions) suggests that the chief justice may have taken into consideration her recent experience on the trial court—a career experience that, among her colleagues, only Brennan had shared, doing so more than thirty years before her arrival—and her open commitment to support the worth and dignity of the state criminal trial judge. O'Connor wrote more than an equitable share of the Court opinions in the non-routine cases—21% versus 11% (defined as an equitable share). Nevertheless, the chief justice selected White to author 35%, and O'Connor only 12%, of opinions explaining the Court's resolution of criminal disputes recognized as important by academic authorities on the Court.[22] O'Connor sustained her federalism value as well as the president's crime control value in her criminal case writing; she considered her reasoning for affirmance of a state trial judge's disposition to be an expression of "judicial" federalism.

O'Connor's Contribution to Federalism

O'Connor promised at her confirmation hearing to develop and apply a constitutional theory of federalism that would restore deference to state power. In her attempt to provide an attractive federalism jurisprudence, she was in competition with other justices. Rehnquist (writing for five justices) offered a short-lived theory in *National League of Cities v. Usery* (1976); Burger wrote for four dissenters in *EEOC v. Wyoming* (1983); and Powell wrote for four dissenters in *Garcia v. San Antonio Metropolitan Transit Authority* (1985).

O'Connor's conceptualization of federalism, like Powell's, was dynamic, while Rehnquist's and Burger's were static. She agreed with Powell in *Wyoming* that the federalism that fundamentally structures our system of government changed its contours over two centuries. She saw the need for a new reading of the Tenth Amendment to include a doctrine of state immunity suitable to an American environment changed by an amended constitutional structure, the growth of economic and social infrastructures, and the increasing complexity of the political processes. Her purpose was to enlarge the scope of state governmental power by narrowly reading congressional intent and by using judicial restraint.

The Court's decision in *Federal Energy Regulatory Commission (FERC) v. Mississippi* (1982), which held that Congress could preempt state control of private energy production, gave O'Connor her first opportunity as a justice to present her views of federalism in a civil context. She employed a practical definition, found in a Black opinion, that viewed federalism as a sensitive recognition of the legitimate interests and activities of both the national and state levels of government. She did not attempt to provide a test in her separate opinion but seemed to accept Rehnquist's doctrine in *National League of Cities* that ambiguous "traditional" functions belonged to state and local governments; her balancing approach did not provide any clear guidelines.

O'Connor charged in *FERC* that federal interference in state procedures turned state bodies into field offices of the national administration and kidnapped state officials into the national organization of regulation. In her dissent in *Southland Corp. v. Keating* (1984), she offered similar arguments for the competence of state legislatures to decide on arbitration rights and for the ability of state courts to devise their own proceedings. In *Garcia*, O'Connor wrote a dissent to develop her ideas separately from Powell, who provided the major argument against overruling *National League of Cities*. She defined the true essence of federalism as the respect the national government is constitutionally bound to give to the legitimate interests of states. As in her abortion analysis, O'Connor recognized technological change as the catalyst of tensions that had led to national economic regulation but argued that the Court's generosity toward the national government in separation of powers disputes, which had emerged during the Roosevelt administration, had reached its limit. She thought that the Tenth Amendment gave the Court a special mandate to protect the states, a weak and endangered species, just as substantive due process gave the Court a special responsibility to protect powerless minorities.

The constitutional basis for O'Connor's federalism was not restricted to the Tenth Amendment, as for Burger and Powell, but arose from the "spirit" of the amendment and the federal structure underlying the Constitution. O'Connor's thesis was that federalism was such a basic principle in the constitutional system that the founders felt no necessity to explicate its contours. Like Douglas, who discovered privacy in a penumbra of constitutional rights, she found the constitutional anchors of federalism in various clauses and doctrines. These anchors included the Tenth and Eleventh Amendments, the common law doctrine of sovereign immunity, the founders' ideas implicit in federal court decisions, and the judicial conventions of strict construction, comity, and deference. She did not work out her theory into test form and confessed to the difficulty of crafting bright-line tests.

O'Connor took her most extreme position on federalism in a lone dissent in *Block v. North Dakota* (1983). She applied a 1938 precedent to a nation-state conflict to defend North Dakota's interests, using the common law principle of sovereign immunity, which states that time does not bar the sovereign. She argued that the Court should read the doctrine of sovereign immunity into the lacunae of federal statutes. She was particularly adamant since North Dakota stood to lose the beds of navigable waters, a resource that the state held in trust for its citizens, and on an equal footing with other states, as an incident of sovereignty. The other eight justices did not find the imprecision in the congressional language that allowed O'Connor to introduce the sovereignty doctrine.

In preemption cases O'Connor's language revealed the strength of her feeling for state government rights. In her first preemption case, *Brown v. Hotel & Restaurant Employees & Bartenders International Union Local 54* (1984), she did not find any conflict between the state casino control law and federally protected union conduct, since she read congressional intent to welcome state help in eradicating criminal elements from unions. White complained in dissent that her exercise of restraint in order to save the state law was the result of activism in rewriting federal labor law. Her vote also supported her crime control value.

O'Connor approved state power to regulate and protect local business against equal protection challenges. Dissenting in *Metropolitan Life Ins. Co. v. Ward* (1985), she wrote that the Court's equal protection basis for voiding a state tax intended to improve the competitive position of the domestic insurance industry and attract capital investment to the state astonished her by its lack of support in precedent. She applied the weak scrutiny test and criticized the majority for their drastic departure from doctrine in their use of a balancing approach that revitalized economic substantive due process thinking and placed a federal straitjacket on the states. Two months later she joined the Court majority in *Northeast Bancorp, Inc. v. Board of Governors of Federal Reserve System* (1985) in refusing to void a state statute under the equal protection clause or commerce clause for giving special preference to out-of-state banks within a certain geographical region. In her concurrence she pointedly drew the other justices' attention to the lack of any meaningful distinction between regional discrimination in banking and state discrimination in insurance, since both financial enterprises were historically of state concern.

O'Connor also insisted on applying the doctrine of deference to state judges, developed for criminal cases, to civil matters. She argued that the Court should not use the due process clause to rewrite state tax law and should not read congressional intent loosely in order to regulate state government bodies.[23] In general O'Connor preferred diversity of state procedures, even at the cost of judicial efficiency and certainty, parting company with Burger and Rehnquist in her ordering of values.[24]

O'Connor's Contribution to Order

A few cases indicate that O'Connor's substantive law and order value had priority over her federalism value. In *McElroy v. United States* (1982), she affirmed the defendant's federal conviction for forgery of securities without any proof that they were forged before their movement in interstate commerce. Stevens, the sole dissenter, insisted that Congress had not intended to encroach upon state responsibility for controlling forgery committed in-state. O'Connor's statutory interpretation in this case expanded national jurisdiction over crime, a change with the potential to lead to federal-state conflict. She interpreted the congressional purpose benignly, saying that it was "to aid states in their detection and punishment of criminals who evade state authorities" (455 U.S. at 659).

Access to Federal Courts. O'Connor made a large contribution to the Burger Court's effort to close the door to federal collateral review of criminal convictions. In *Stone v. Powell* (1976), the Court had reversed the Warren Court's doctrine in *Brown v. Allen* (1953) that every federal constitutional claim of a defendant was cognizable on its merits regardless of the fairness and fullness of state court treatment. O'Connor made an important change in habeas corpus doctrine in *Rose v. Lundy* (1982) by adding a rule of total exhaustion, which required federal trial judges to dismiss an entire petition if it contained any unexhausted state claim. Only three justices, however, agreed with her forecast of future decisions that a prisoner might lose the opportunity under the abuse of writ rule to present unexhausted state claims that were earlier dropped from a federal petition. Exhaustion was such an important matter to O'Connor that she gave advice to the federal trial judge on collateral estoppel in *Tower v. Glover* (1984), even though (as

Brennan pointed out) the question had not been briefed or argued
(467 U.S. at 924).

In *Engle v. Isaacs* (1982), O'Connor reaffirmed and expanded an
earlier Burger Court decision. In *Engle* a prisoner challenged an Ohio
precedent that had placed the burden of proving self-defense on the
defendant. She found no cause for the defendant's failure to raise the
constitutional issue at trial and therefore barred his claim as a defaulted
collateral claim. Using an economic model, she concluded that costs
to the efficiency of judicial administration, such as the frustration of
certainty and finality and the use of court time, were higher than the
contribution of the case to the protection of due process. In the
companion case, *United States v. Frady* (1982), O'Connor extended
the cause and prejudice rule to federal prisoners seeking collateral
review. She used the prejudice prong and found no evidence that the
alleged jury instruction errors had resulted in actual prejudice to the
defendant, who had been convicted of first-degree murder. The impact
of her two Court opinions was to reduce the constitutional protection
given to federal offenders and to halt the long-term efforts of federal
judges to raise state standards to the federal minimum through generous
oversight.

The explicit reliance of state judges on federal law and reasoning
impeded O'Connor's federalist goal of liberating state judges from
federal court supervision. In her second term she took up the challenge
of demarcating which cases contained adequate and independent state
grounds for decision and which did not. The need to distinguish cases
was embarrassingly evident in *South Dakota v. Neville* (1983), in which
her majority opinion reversed a state supreme court decision that had
held that the admission into evidence of a defendant's refusal to take
a blood-alcohol test violated the federal guarantee against self-incrimination. The dissenters wanted to deny certiorari since the federal
ground was not the sole or compelling basis of the decision. O'Connor
expressed her crime control value in *Neville* through her reading of
the Fifth Amendment, but at the price of denying her "judicial" federalism.

In *Michigan v. Long* (1983), O'Connor's holding created a new Court
policy: an explicit state court statement asserting that the legal theory
of the case was not federal was necessary now to rebut a presumption
of Supreme Court jurisdiction. Thus she reversed the traditional presumption of a state law basis absent a clear indication of a federal
ground. Her new rule stopped two intrusive and expensive Court
practices—close analysis of state opinions in search of adequate and
independent state grounds and demands upon state courts for clari-

fication. By adopting her innovative rule, the bare majority revealed its preference for order over federalism. Blackmun (concurring only in the judgment) and Stevens (in dissent) feared that her rule would further swell their certiorari and argument dockets with petitions from state officials to reverse state judgments.

The utility of her *Long* rule for advancing crime control became evident in later cases. In *New York v. Class* (1986), O'Connor's majority opinion allowed the state prosecutor's introduction at trial of a gun the police had uncovered when they searched the defendant's car for a vehicle registration number. It reversed a decision by the New York Court of Appeals that had overturned the defendant's conviction on federal grounds. Although O'Connor had argued in *Engle* that federal intrusions "seriously undermine the morale of our state judges" and that, as a result, "the fervor of state judges to root out [federal] constitutional errors may diminish" (456 U.S. at 128 n. 33), ironically, in *Long, Class,* and *Moran v. Burbine* (1986), it was the state judges who did root out federal constitutional error who were in jeopardy of reversal. O'Connor's message, frankly communicated in *Schall v. Martin* (1984), was that comity protected state judges who chose to uphold law and order over due process.

The Miranda *Precedent.* Any weakening of the *Miranda v. Arizona* (1966) rule served Reagan's political interests, regardless of the preference of law enforcement officers to continue to use the Warren Court's formula warning. In *Nix v. Williams* (1984), O'Connor cooperated in the labor of limiting the scope of *Miranda.* She did not approve a blunt overrule, however, because she appreciated the utility of the *Miranda* routine to the police, and she accused Rehnquist of blurring the clear line of *Miranda* in *New York v. Quarles* (1984).

In *Oregon v. Elstad* (1985), O'Connor contributed to the incremental process of circumscribing the exclusionary rule by holding that a "voluntary" statement made before the proper warning did not necessarily taint a later confession. Her reasoning was that suppression of evidence in that context would not achieve the end of truth in the courtroom or deter illegal police behavior. In allowing the defendant to prevail only by proving that his "free will" had in fact been overborne by police, she shifted the burden of proof, exactly as the administration had hoped. She accepted the formulation of the Court's right wing that the warning was a mere prophylactic standard rather than a constitutional right.

On the other hand, O'Connor refused to presume the correctness of a state court's finding of voluntariness in *Miller v. Fenton* (1985).

Writing for the Court, she insisted that voluntariness was a legal question meriting independent consideration. Her opinion followed old precedents that required "unmistakable clarity," and it abruptly cut off Rehnquist's efforts to keep self-incrimination issues raised in habeas corpus petitions out of federal court. In *Crane v. Kentucky* (1986), she wrote for a unanimous Court that due process and the Sixth Amendment required that evidence going to the credibility of a confession could not be excluded from the jury's consideration. Despite her disclaimer that the Court had broken no new ground, the case was one of first impression, in which she validated a new avenue for moving state cases into federal court, a result at odds with her usual deference to state judges.

The Right to Counsel. Burger Court doctrine placed a heavy burden on every defense attorney to ensure the fairness of the criminal justice system and thus changed the litigation target of convicted defendants from police and judges to their own attorneys. In *Strickland v. Washington* (1984), O'Connor helped to lighten that burden by formulating a weak standard for actual ineffectiveness of counsel, which required a defendant to show the serious deficiency of counsel's performance and actual prejudice to the outcome of the case. She refused in *Murray v. Carrier* (1986) to allow the standards of legal assistance to be raised to the point of adding to the costs of habeas corpus review, delaying finality, or frustrating state authority. Although *Carrier* had called into question the reliability of the conviction, O'Connor did not read the facts to fit her one exception to the strict rule denying the excuse of counsel ignorance, that is, if an "actually innocent" person were convicted.

In the companion case, *Smith v. Murray* (1986), O'Connor stated that federal courts had no warrant to reverse state convictions for ineffectiveness of counsel if defense counsel had made a deliberate tactical decision not to pursue a claim. The defense counsel's winnowing of weaker arguments in *Smith* showed competency, not deficiency, under her *Strickland* test. Besides raising barriers to defendants' complaints against counsel in federal court, O'Connor refused to find a constitutional violation in the failure of police to inform a suspect that a lawyer was trying to reach him in *Moran v. Burbine*. She found no denial of Fifth or Sixth Amendment rights in this case, in which a suspect had purposefully been deprived of counsel and then waived his *Miranda* rights and confessed. To O'Connor the police's conduct, although unethical, was not offensive enough to constitute a denial of fundamental fairness since no formal charge had yet been made.

Double Jeopardy. The Burger Court had examined the contours of the double jeopardy clause in federal prosecutions before 1981, but had not yet worked out the extent to which this clause protected state defendants before O'Connor arrived. In her pursuit of crime control and comity, O'Connor sacrificed the distinction that had previously existed between the prosecutor's authority to retry after reversal on evidentiary grounds versus procedural grounds. In *Tibbs v. Florida* (1982) O'Connor developed for the Court an interpretation of double jeopardy that gave state prosecutors a second chance, which federal prosecutors did not have, to win a conviction after a case had been reversed based on "weight of evidence." The established rule was that reversals on the ground of "insufficient evidence" could not be retried, while reversals based on procedural error could be retried. O'Connor made an exception to the no-retrial rule where the state court system adopted a "weight of evidence" ground. The progress of *Tibbs* through the Florida courts provided an example of the contradictions in O'Connor's "judicial" federalism because, in upholding the state supreme court justices (who vowed never to repeat their reversal on "weight of evidence" grounds), she necessarily disciplined the trial judge who was following the federal double jeopardy standards.[25]

In *Heath v. Alabama* (1985), a case of first impression, O'Connor announced for the Court that two states could each prosecute a defendant for the same criminal offense without violating the double jeopardy clause. She used the standard notion of crime as an offense against government to argue that, under the doctrine of dual sovereignty, two offenses actually occurred in one act. She found a satisfying compatibility between her two key values as she traced a line of precedent indicating that the governmental function of law enforcement was inherent in state sovereignty and preserved by the Tenth Amendment. In *Arizona v. Rumsley* (1984), however, O'Connor found a double jeopardy bar to a second sentencing hearing, which had replaced a life term with the death penalty, since the hearing had been a trial-type proceeding.

Capital Punishment. The justices fit into four subgroups in terms of their positions on the death penalty: Marshall and Brennan, who found a constitutional barrier; Stevens and Blackmun, who did not, but at least found some constitutional impediment in half of the capital punishment cases in which they voted; Powell, White, and O'Connor, who occasionally recognized an impediment; and Burger and Rehnquist, who practically never recognized an impediment. O'Connor voted against the capital defendant in about three-fourths of the cases she heard orally argued.

O'Connor wrote the dissenting opinion for four justices in *Enmund v. Florida* (1982), finding the death penalty not disproportionate for aiding and abetting a murder, even when the defendant did not participate in or witness the killing. She deferred to the trial judge or jury as "best able to assess the defendant's blameworthiness" and deferred to the legislature as "uniquely suited to select goals and modes of punishment" (458 U.S. at 826 n. 42). Nevertheless, she assuaged her discomfort with the capital sentence for the driver of the getaway car, proposing a remand for a new sentencing hearing that would consider mitigating circumstances. O'Connor also gave deference in *California v. Ramos* (1983) to the trial judge and jury, by rejecting the defendant's objection to the jury instruction, mandated by statute, on the governor's power to commute. But in *Caldwell v. Mississippi* (1985) she took the due process position that a prosecutor could not inaccurately describe appellate review of a death sentence to the jury. She had to write separately in order to distinguish her *Ramos* precedent, on which Rehnquist relied in dissent. Unlike Rehnquist, she chose good policy over good logic.

O'Connor's Contribution to Court Policy on Church-State Separation

The Burger Court was clearly in disarray over the conceptual basis for its establishment decisions when O'Connor arrived. Unlike Reagan and Burger, O'Connor did not treat religion as a social value rooted in American traditions. In her view, separation of church and state was a structural principle that set limits even on state policies generally protected by federalism. In her initiative to revise the test in *Lemon v. Kurtzman* (1971), she failed to persuade the rest of the Court, although her concurrence in *Lynch v. Donnelly* (1984) was more promising doctrinally than Burger's rambling historical opinion for the Court. O'Connor would allow a statute to survive, even in the absence of an express secular purpose, unless its purpose was the legislative endorsement of religion, as in *Wallace v. Jaffree* (1985). To invoke the effect prong of *Lemon,* in her view, the statute must actually convey a message of endorsement that an objective observer would note.

This "objective observer" (O'Connor's nonsexist term for a close relative of the ubiquitous "rational man") was her construct to test the constitutionality of laws implicating religion. As she noted in *Witters v. Washington Dept. of Services for the Blind* (1986), the objective observer would recognize the point when government accommodation of religion in fact turned into symbolic or behavioral endorsement. The other justices did not follow her lead. In *Jaffree*, Stevens rejected any modification of the *Lemon* test and Powell implicitly criticized her revision. Rehnquist and White in separate dissents discounted her proposal, urging drastic reversal of precedents. O'Connor nevertheless applied her revised *Lemon* test to various cases, with mixed results. She rejected the Reagan position in *Jaffree, Thornton, Estate of v. Caldor* (1985) and *Grand Rapids School District v. Ball* (1985) (community education) but accepted the Reagan position in *Grand Rapids* (shared time), *Witters,* and *Aguilar v. Felton* (1985).

O'Connor focused on the factual details of the aid programs for parochial schools. In this respect she differed from justices who favored a high wall and old bright-line rules (that is, rules clear enough to be mechanically applied) and differed, as well, from justices who favored a low wall and mechanistic new rules. She did not accept Brennan's catch-22 formula in *Grand Rapids* and *Aguilar* that the presence of state-paid teachers in religious schools had the primary effect of advancing religion unless the teachers were compartmentalized, but that government supervision of compartmentalized teaching created excessive entanglement. She refused to define monitoring as entanglement or to require every teacher paid with public funds for teaching in religious schools to be affiliated with a public school. Her proposed test allowed the approval of some forms of state aid for pupils in religious schools, but, unlike the tests of her close colleagues, her test would have increased the Court's case load and disappointed the president.

In cases concerning schoolchildren, O'Connor used the distinction between mature and immature minds, which had appeared in early Burger Court precedents, to guide her voting.[26] She argued that impressionable children in a school environment needed protection against the socialization of religious ritual more than adults in noncoercive environments. Secularized icons in public parks and routine prayers in legislative assemblies could survive First Amendment attacks, but public school prayers could not. Making the same distinction in *Grand Rapids,* she argued that parochial teachers working in a state-subsidized program would confuse children as to their religious or secular authority. Her age-based analysis was not attractive to liberals, who preferred to keep the high wall for adults and to trust children with more choice in free expression cases.

Although O'Connor's establishment analyses began with presumptions of the good faith of legislators and teachers, she did not accept all legislative mandates, unlike the positivistic Rehnquist.[27] In *Thorton,* she found a Connecticut law that guaranteed employees their chosen Sabbath day as a non-working day unconstitutional on its face. Her central concern in the religion cases was the preservation of a pluralistic—not a religious—society, and (joined by Marshall) she did not fail to notice the similarity of legislative initiatives for affirmative action and for affirmative religious accommodation.

O'Connor's Contribution to Property Rights

O'Connor's attitude toward property was confounded by her larger commitments to federalism and judicial restraint. She received the assignment to write the Court opinion in only one important property case, *Hawaii Housing Authority v. Midkiff* (1984), when she preferred to uphold the state's drastic land reform act over the protests of landowners. She described the Court's role as extremely narrow when the state was exercising its sovereign police power to reduce the oligopoly of real property. In disputes in which state and property owners were on the same side, her decisional task was easier. In *Greene v. Lindsey* (1982) O'Connor protested the majority's voiding of a state notification procedure as contrary to due process. It was also easier for her to choose property over freedom. Writing for the majority in *Harper & Row Publishers, Inc. v. Nation Enterprises* (1985) O'Connor protected copyright interests in President Ford's memoirs against free press claims.

O'Connor's Contribution to Judicial Restraint

Just as O'Connor upheld the crime control value by keeping defendants' claims out of federal court, she developed formulas to block challenges to the authority of government agency decisions. Writing for the Court, O'Connor weakened the settled presumption in favor of standing to review administrative action in *Block v. Community Nutrition Institute* (1984). She argued that authority free from public interest complaints was required to deal with a complex technical undertaking for which only the secretary of agriculture had the competence. When she reached the merits of a challenge to an agency decision, she offered the same deference to scientific expertise (*Baltimore Gas & Electric Co. v. National Resources Defense Council*, 1983).

The basic issue in these cases was the antithesis of the New Deal issue: instead of questioning the power of the government to regulate, the complainants demanded that the administration implement the statutory mandate. O'Connor gave deference to agency decisions not to use their powers fully to provide disaster relief in *Lyng v. Payne* (1986) or to set formal tolerance levels for carcinogens in *Young v.*

Community Nutrition Institute (1986). Her Court opinion in *Lyng* supported the Nixon policy of refusing to spend money appropriated for congressionally favored programs, thus undercutting the precedent set by *Train v. City of New York* (1975).

Even when federalism was at issue, O'Connor gave priority to bureaucracy. In *Secretary of Interior v. California* (1984), she approved an agency decision not to check on consistency with the state's environmental management program before proceeding with the sale of oil and gas leases, as urged by the solicitor general in oral argument. Her acceptance of the bureaucratic authority of a Reagan cabinet officer thus denied her usual deference to the trial judge and to state interests.

When congressional intent was not involved, as with *Thomas v. Union Carbide Agr. Products Co.* (1985), O'Connor employed separation of powers doctrine to uphold agency action, again giving weight to professionalism and efficiency. She used her Court opinion in *Commodity Futures Trading Commission v. Schor* (1986) to define a broad scope for deference to agencies. Brennan warned, in dissent, of further erosion of the judicial power to protect individuals from decisionmakers susceptible to majoritarian pressures.

When the challenge to agency authority was in defense of property rights, O'Connor revealed the contemporary nature of her conservatism by denying the property claims, as in *United States v. $8,850* (1983) and *Hudson v. Palmer* (1984). In property takings disputes, however, she dragged her feet in concurrences in *United States v. 50 Acres of Land* (1984) and *Connelly v. Pension Benefit Guaranty Corporation* (1986) to indicate that she would support property interests given other factual circumstances. Her form of judicial restraint transcended traditional deference to other officials and implied a Court obligation to respect other public officials' power to govern.[28]

Democratic Values in O'Connor's Opinions

When Rehnquist and O'Connor disagreed, she almost always joined the Court and he dissented. As Tables 1.6 and 1.7 indicate, the number of her dissenting opinions and the percentage of her dissenting votes compared to the Court's total steadily declined from 1981 to 1986, as she tried to position herself in the center. Her rate of agreement with the future chief on equality issues in significant cases was lower than the average rate of agreement between them. The senior justices provided her with several opportunities to write for the Court in support of and in opposition to the individual value of free expression in important cases.

O'Connor's Contribution to Freedom

The Burger Court developed a confusing First Amendment jurisprudence that tilted the balance away from protected rights and toward
governmental interests by distributing rights according to categories of
content, form, forum, location, stage of proceeding, and the role of
the individual. O'Connor contributed to this compartmentalization,
which fit with her appreciation of bright-line rules. She resisted most
free speech claims but protected free press and free exercise of religion.[29]

Free Speech. O'Connor revised the public forum doctrine for the
Court in *Cornelius v. NAACP Legal Defense and Educational Fund,
Inc.* (1985) when political and legal advocacy groups protested their
exclusion from the annual charity drive among federal civil servants.
In this case she refused to define the government's Combined Federal
Campaign as a limited public forum — the new category established in
Perry Education Association v. Perry Local Educators' Association (1983).
By requiring proof of government intent to create a limited public
forum, she put in official hands the key to certain First Amendment
rights. The deference she gave to the bureaucracy in *Cornelius* directly
aided the Reagan administration's policy of discouraging the legal defense organizations, which bring novel rights to the Court's attention.
She certainly showed no awareness of the impact of her holding upon
the rights of women, defended by such groups as the Federally Employed Women Legal Defense and Educational Fund. Nevertheless, she
followed a moderate and politic course by remanding for an examination of motives.

The opinion that most clearly revealed O'Connor's strategy of changing the Court's approach from a Democratic framework to a Republican
one was *Minnesota State Board for Community Colleges v. Knight*
(1984). In this case O'Connor upheld a state law that gave a union an
effective monopoly on communication with state policymakers (college
administrators). O'Connor denied that the meeting of the administrators
and union representatives in *Knight* was a public forum. The potential
coverage of her precedent was sweeping since the academic environment was irrelevant to her denial of a public official's obligation to
listen to assertive citizens. To avoid the hypothetical danger that legislatures would grind to a halt when faced by talkative constituents,
she even proposed a new state interest in hearing a single voice for
the majority. Her conclusions flowed from a political analysis, grounded
upon federalism and separation of powers, that the right of individual
citizens to participate would interfere with the legislative resolution of

the interest group struggle. Like Rehnquist, she holds stronger sympathies for representative democracy than for mass-action democracy.

Since both feminists and right-wing women have identified pornography as a form of harassment and oppression of women, O'Connor could satisfy both camps with the same vote. In *Maryland v. Macon* (1985), while Brennan and Marshall found a state statute controlling the distribution of obscene materials facially invalid, O'Connor, writing for the Court, held that the magazines in question, which had been bought by undercover police in an adult bookstore, had not been searched or seized and thus were admissible at trial. In *New York v. Ferber* (1982), in which the Court unanimously upheld the constitutionality of a state law forbidding distribution of depictions of sexual activity by children, O'Connor concurred so that she could advise legislators and judges that social value would not save material from censorship if its production involved child abuse. In *Hudnut v. American Booksellers Association* (1986), while O'Connor voted to give plenary consideration to the innovative Indianapolis ordinance that provided civil suit recourse for women claiming damages related to the distribution of pornography, the majority summarily affirmed its holding that the law on its face violated the First Amendment.

Free Press. In her second term O'Connor wrote, for the majority, a global defense of free press against differential methods of state taxation, in a direct confrontation with Rehnquist. She described *Minneapolis Star & Tribune Co. v. Minnesota Commissioner of Revenue* (1983) as a case of first impression since, unlike *Grosjean v. American Press Co.* (1936), there was no evidence of legislative intent to punish certain newspapers for their political views. While acknowledging the constitutionality of general economic and social regulation of the media as "beyond dispute," she insisted that special taxation of the press could not stand without a compelling justification by the state government.

In *Philadelphia Newspapers, Inc. v. Hepps* (1986), O'Connor continued to follow the Court's new trend toward weakening the effectiveness of the libel suit by introducing a constitutional rule that to recover damages a private-figure plaintiff must show both falsity and fault when the media report covered a matter of public concern. She read the Constitution to require that the balance of values be tipped to protect "true speech," over personal autonomy, although admitting that this emphasis on truth could result in a plaintiff's losing damages for loss of reputation despite a meritorious suit.

The apparent contradiction between O'Connor's free speech and free press jurisprudence can be explained in terms of her commitment to clean government. On the facts of the *Hepps* case, the newspaper was engaged in the press's classic function of uncovering corruption in government. O'Connor saw the press as a useful, if not entirely reliable, partner in maintaining government accountability. Her dissent in *Federal Bureau of Investigation v. Abramson* (1982) to allow the press access to information passed from the FBI to the White House, against the arguments of the administration and her conservative colleagues, can be understood as instrumental to her ideal of government responsibility to an informed electorate.

Freedom of Religion. O'Connor revealed more sensitivity to non-Christian and nonreligious people in free expression cases than in establishment cases. In *Goldman v. Weinberger* (1986), a case with a military context, she gave the plaintiff's free exercise claim to an orthodox Jewish practice more weight than some justices to her left. Joined by Marshall, O'Connor pointed out in dissent that the military had offered no evidence that the plaintiff's practice of wearing the yarmulke indoors posed any health, safety, or morale problem but instead had simply asserted a preference for uniformity. The links between her apparently contradictory stands in *Goldman* and *Lynch v. Donnelly* (1984) were her attention to facts and her pluralistic political theory, which valued diverse religious practices, even in governmental contexts.

O'Connor's Contribution to Autonomy

The modern line of privacy (or autonomy) decisions supports individual choice in sexual and reproductive behavior. In contrast to the value freedom, autonomy involves issues that cover activities in the private, rather than the public, sphere. The nineteenth-century polygamy cases belong in this category, as does *Bowers v. Hardwick* (1986), the last significant autonomy case of the Burger era, in which O'Connor voted with a minimal majority to recognize the state's police power to protect public morality, thereby supporting the social value of order.

In her first articulation of her abortion views as a justice, O'Connor wrote a dissent in *City of Akron v. Akron Center for Reproductive Health, Inc.* (1983) undercutting the reasoning in *Roe* by rejecting "an analytical framework that varies according to the 'stages' of pregnancy, where those stages, and their concomitant standards of review, differ according to the level of medical technology available" (462 U.S. at 452). In a powerful critique of *Roe*'s reasoning, she argued that the trimester analysis was unworkable because the medical advances to save immature fetuses and to improve the woman's safety in late-term abortions were on a collision course. Less persuasive were her assertions that the viability concept was meaningless and that the state had an interest in the fetus from the moment of conception. She adopted the assumption that a right to terminate pregnancy existed in some situations, but she proposed a different standard for examining state regulations—whether they imposed an undue burden on the exercise of the right.

In *Thornburgh v. American College of Obstetricians and Gynecologists* (1986), O'Connor complained in dissent that the Court's opinion was based upon an inadequate record. She again assumed the basic right of women to choose abortion and refused to reconsider *Roe*. But in giving the state a compelling interest in both maternal health and potential human life throughout gestation, she spoiled the balance of interests that Blackmun had carefully constructed in *Roe*. She proposed a new understanding of fundamental rights jurisprudence: that judges should apply weak scrutiny unless a state law placed an undue burden on the constitutionally protected right. In the context of the abortion right, she defined undue burden as an absolute obstacle to, or a severe limitation on, access to abortion. She implied, however, that, depending on the facts, she would be able to cast her vote for state regulation of abortion even when using the strict scrutiny test. The debate reflected in O'Connor's footnotes and Rehnquist's dissent in *Minneapolis Star and Tribune* revealed that his preferred test for state regulation of the press was synonymous with her preferred test for state regulation of abortion.

O'Connor's test was as obviously mechanical as the Court's test, which had invalidated almost all abortion regulations. The difference between the tests lay in their consequences for federalism. The *Roe* Court adopted a national judicial standard for all abortion laws, while O'Connor's standard would leave the states almost entirely free of supervision, to interfere or not with abortion choice. The substantive policy that her test would protect would depend entirely upon public opinion and interest aggregation within each state. O'Connor integrated her own values into her new abortion doctrine: she supported both federalism and judicial restraint by allowing great leeway to state and local legislative bodies yet still retaining the *Roe* precedent.

O'Connor's Contribution to Equality

O'Connor's boldest statement on gender equality and integration appeared in *Mississippi University for Women v. Hogan* (1982), her only Court opinion in support of gender equality in five terms. Her success in *Hogan* in disestablishing sex segregation in public schools came at the price of subordinating her commitments to federalism and judical restraint. In *Hogan* a male nurse brought suit for admission to a women's state school of nursing, but O'Connor analyzed the problem from the perspective of female nurses. Unlike the four dissenters, she saw the unpleasant face of female-exclusive institutions in perpetuating gender-based distinctions and discrimination. She asserted that the school's gender-based admissions policy fostered the stereotyping of the nursing profession as exclusively female, with concomitant low pay. O'Connor could discover no important state purpose in maintaining a nursing school that offered degrees only to women. In fact, she held that the state's purported affirmative action purpose did not even meet the minimum rationality standard.

O'Connor rejected the traditional and paternalistic arguments of four justices, reminding them in a footnote (458 U.S. 725 n. 10) of the Court's complicity in excluding women from occupations in decisions from *Bradwell v. Illinois* (1873) through *Goesaert v. Cleary* (1948). She applied the intermediate level of scrutiny, a test of the constitutionality of classifications of persons for differential treatment, which the Court had adopted for gender discrimination issues in *Craig v. Boren* (1976). Strict scrutiny, the level of analysis used by the Court for suspect classes (e.g., race, ethnicity, and national origin) and for classes denied a fundamental right, almost inevitably produces a decision invalidating the law. Weak scrutiny, the level of analysis employed when suspect classes or basic rights are not involved, results in a decision upholding the law's constitutionality. Before 1971 the Court used the weak scrutiny or "rational relationship" test to examine gender classifications and found laws that arranged for the unequal distribution of political and economic goods to be constitutional. Other justices thought that Burger had created the new intermediate test in *Reed v. Reed* (1971), the first Court decision to invalidate a gender classification. The *Craig* decision clearly established intermediate or "heightened" scrutiny as the appropriate test for gender classifications, after Brennan failed by one vote in his initiative to declare sex a suspect classification like race, and in effect read the ERA into the Fourteenth Amendment's equal protection clause (*Frontiero v. Richardson,* 1973).

By her rigorous use of intermediate scrutiny O'Connor reinforced the *Craig* precedent and halted the retreat of the Court toward the weak test exemplified by the majority's acceptance of traditional cultural excuses for giving males more responsibility and females more protection in *Rostker v. Goldberg* (1981) and *Michael M. v. Superior Court of Sonoma County* (1981). What O'Connor failed to do was to take the leadership in establishing gender as a suspect class and thereby creating a very strong presumption against any gender classfication (except, as with race, for affirmative action purposes). She had the votes of Brennan, White, and Marshall from the *Frontiero* case, and Stevens was likely willing to follow the imperative of the first woman on the Court if she had used her strong *Hogan* opinion to support adoption of the strict test. Instead, women are in a semi-suspect class, and the degree to which they are paternalized or penalized depends on judicial discretion in applying the unpredictable "heightened" scrutiny. She did not perform on the implied contract she made at her confirmation hearings that the equal protection clause was equivalent to the ERA.

In *Roberts v. United States Jaycees* (1984), O'Connor found the controversy over the integration of women into the Junior Chamber of Commerce (Jaycees) easier to resolve, since her vote for equal treatment also upheld the state of Minnesota's human rights policy. She failed to win the assignment to write the opinion in the case and serve as a voice for women's equal status because Brennan, the opinion assigner, could not accept her sharp distinction between organizations with expressive purposes and those with commercial purposes. She joined a unanimous Court in *Hishon v. King & Spalding* (1984) to bring about the integration of law firm partnerships under the 1964 Civil Rights Act, but voted against requiring the integration of grand juries by sex in the context of a criminal appeal in *Hobby v. United States* (1984).

O'Connor was the marginal justice in *Arizona Governing Committee v. Norris* (1983). She voted with four liberal justices to apply the precedent of *Los Angeles Department of Water and Power v. Manhart* (1978) that a state retirement plan that had paid lower benefits to women than to men upon retirement was illegal. She created a different majority with the justices on the right by refusing to make the holding retroactive. Her vote with the left on substantive policy and with the right on retroactivity was a compromise natural to her legislative experience, combining in the same case her individual value of equal opportunity and her structural principles of restraint and federalism. The four justices in the majority on the validity of the plan were more consistent in their votes, although the Court has no settled policy on retroactivity. If O'Connor was inconsistent in failing to back her policy choice with her vote on retroactivity, she exercised restraint in respect to the *Manhart* precedent with one vote and offered comity to a state government faced by a financial problem with her other vote. In three important cases — *Hogan, Roberts,* and *Norris* — O'Connor worked out a compromise that was not appreciated by either wing of the Court.

O'Connor joined the majority in holding that Title IX prohibited gender discrimination directed at employees as well as students in *North Haven Board of Education v. Bell* (1982), that the Pregnancy Discrimination Act covered workers' wives as well as women workers in *Newport News Shipbuilding and Dry Dock Co. v. EEOC* (1983), and that Title VII's prohibition of sex discrimination covered sexual harassment of a subordinate by a supervisor in the workplace in *Meritor Savings Bank v. Vinson* (1986). In voting against equal procedural rights for unwed fathers in *Lehr v. Robertson* (1983), she showed more concern for unwed mothers—and practical government solutions to difficult domestic conflicts—than for gender equality.

O'Connor's Contribution to the Welfare State

The regulatory issues of the New Deal period concerned the power of government to improve or equalize the status of economic groups; those of the Burger era increasingly concerned social groups. Affirmative and remedial policies to bring historically oppressed racial groups into a condition that would allow them to compete on an equal basis in the future were important agenda items when O'Connor arrived. Controversies over the enforcement of women's statutory rights were newer, and the first affirmative action case involving gender did not reach the docket until the Rehnquist Court.

Enforcement of Gender Equality. O'Connor spoke for the Court in *Ford Motor Co. v. EEOC* (1982) in limiting remedial compensation to women denied work on the basis of gender. She held that under Title VII the accused employer could limit future liability by offering jobs without seniority to victims of discrimination. She claimed an advantage to the women workers in regaining employment immediately instead of waiting for an award at the end of a lawsuit. O'Connor's underlying goal was to set a uniform national standard for Title VII awards that would reduce the discretion of trial judges to fit awards to case facts. Blackmun characterized her holdings as unnecessary and unfair in authorizing employers to make "cheap offers" and accused her of "studied indifference to the real-life concerns" of victims of sex discrimination (458 U.S. at 249, 255).

She did not write another opinion of this nature, but she signed the majority opinion in *American Tobacco Co. v. Patterson* (1982), which held that seniority systems that locked in the effects of past discrimination were not unlawful under Title VII. She also signed the dissent in *Connecticut v. Teal* (1982), which would have allowed the bottom-line theory of appropriate group balance to serve as a defense against employment discrimination. The liberal majority insisted that tests for promotion provide a fair competitive situation for the individual employee; the four dissenters were satisfied that the terms of the Civil Rights Act of 1964 were met if the racial balance of the promoted *group* was "fair." She voted for a narrow reading of Title IX in *Grove City College v. Bell* (1984), showing no awareness of the implications of the decision for women's athletic programs.

Enforcement of Racial Equality. O'Connor approved of devices for keeping affirmative action cases off the Court's agenda and found countervailing values to undergird her rejection of affirmative action programs. Nonetheless, her opinions revealed moderate and flexible views. She erected barriers against court access by minority complainants who were not specific victims of discrimination, but she did not impose a per se rule to bar their use of the courts. Her willingness to examine the unique facts of each case made her voting behavior less predictable than that of justices on the extreme left and right. She resisted the pressure of administration lawyers to adopt rigid rules of interpretation that would have reduced her discretion.

After her frank criticism of busing before the Senate Judiciary Committee during her confirmation hearings, O'Connor did not write separate opinions in the two school busing cases. But she voted as the president expected—to approve voters' initiative and referendum decisions to limit or prohibit school assignment and busing remedies in *Washington v. Seattle School District No. 1* (1982) and *Crawford v. Board of Education of City of Los Angeles* (1982). Her votes also supported local majority rule, and, as in her abortion jurisprudence, she would predictably accept the voters' will in favor of busing as well as against it.

O'Connor wrote the Court opinion for a bare majority in *Allen v. Wright* (1984), which denied standing to parents of black schoolchildren who brought a class action suit to force the IRS to revise and enforce its guidelines denying tax-exempt status to discriminatory private schools. In *Allen* she created a complex standing doctrine with a constitutional component and a prudential component of judge-made limits to protect court efficiency. Her core constitutional component required plaintiffs to allege having suffered distinct and concrete personal injury that was fairly traceable to a defendant's unlawful conduct and also redressable. Admitting that raising barriers to integrated education was a serious and cognizable injury, she could find no causal connection between the injury to the schoolchildren and the IRS guidelines. Her failure to apply a simple economic model to her causation prong was peculiar for a justice who used market analysis in criminal cases. Stevens pointed to the elementary economics of the connection between subsidies that enhance the attractiveness of segregated private schools by reducing costs to parents and the resegregation of public schools.

Brennan complained that O'Connor had slammed the courthouse door and had showed "startling insensitivity to the historical role played by the federal courts in eradicating race discrimination from our Nation's schools" (468 U.S. at 767). To the contrary, O'Connor was cognizant of that role and determined to end the era of national intervention in local affairs. She invoked separation of powers doctrine and related arguments for limiting the judiciary's role, warning against judicial monitoring of the executive branch. The vigor of the dialogue in *Allen* reflected the justices' understanding that O'Connor was introducing a Republican viewpoint in place of the equality value of the Democratic framework.

During the Burger Court's waning years, it decided four affirmative action cases on the merits—a challenge by teachers to a voluntary layoff policy that was part of a collective bargaining agreement between a city and union in *Wygant v. Jackson Board of Education* (1986) and three challenges to judicial decrees in *Firefighters Local Union No. 1784 v. Stotts* (1984), *Local 28 of Sheet Metal Workers' Intern. Ass'n. v. EEOC* (1986), and *Local Number 93, Intern. Ass'n of Firefighters, AFL-CIO CLC v. City of Cleveland* (1986). In *Wygant*, O'Connor's and White's votes were critical to the formation of the minimal majority that voided a layoff plan for teachers under an equal-protection rationale. O'Connor's vote was fact-driven, since she stated in her opinion that she would permit local government to use racial classifications to remedy its own past discrimination against nonwhite teachers but would not admit the compelling need of black students for black adult role models to validate race-based layoffs of teachers. Her real concern with the "innocent victim" of remedial plans did not carry her to the point of agreeing with the four majority justices to her right that layoffs were an intrusive and disruptive burden that could never serve as means to a valid legislative end. O'Connor's effort to pull together a set of consensual principles in her *Wygant* concurrence was ignored by the other justices.

In her *Stotts* concurrence, O'Connor proposed a rule that was more rigid and conservative in its impact on black entry to the workplace than White's Court opinion. She would have disallowed motions for the revision of voluntary settlements, regardless of the significance of the change in circumstances, in order to narrow access to the courts, while the majority simply held that the federal judge's injunction against seniority-based layoffs was improper. In *Local 93, Firefighters* O'Connor ignored the strong plea of the solicitor general and joined the Court's holding that race-based promotions that are arranged in a consent decree settling an employment discrimination suit must meet Title VII strictures, but, as she often did (*General Building Contractors Association v. Pennsylvania*, 1982), she offered advice to the employees to help them win their claims on remand. In *Sheet Metal Workers' Ass'n.*, in which the Court upheld a court order setting a racial goal for union membership, she again showed her moderation by concurring in part and dissenting in part.

Conclusion

O'Connor never went through a freshman period, that is, a time of philosophical uncertainty and social unease.[30] She acted immediately on her own agenda by articulating her theories of federalism in relation to state regulatory and state criminal justice policies. By her second term she had achieved a radical change in rules of access to federal courts for defendants. Burger gave her the opportunity, through his opinion assignments, to serve Reagan's agenda on law and order, and she vigorously supported prosecution interests in her creation of new rules, if not always in her dispositions and use of precedent. She took the responsibility, imposed upon her during the confirmation process, to oppose the Court's abortion rule by developing a thorough critique of *Roe* and a new formula for balancing fundamental rights against legislative purposes.

O'Connor performed as the woman justice on the Court only in her extrajudicial activities as a speaker and writer.[31] After her first term, when she raised her voice vigorously for a strong constitutional guarantee of gender equality but for weak remedies for gender discrimination, she retired as a spokesperson on women's rights. She never challenged a Court opinion that denied gender equality. The one attitude that could be associated with her personal experience as a mother in American culture was her sensitivity to children, which appeared in criminal, free expression, and church-state cases.[32]

On religious accommodation, the Republican agenda issue that was not pressed upon O'Connor, she made moderate, factually based decisions and offered a revision of accepted Court doctrine. Although she responded negatively to the values of equality, freedom, and welfare, her opinions revealed a willingness to examine case facts carefully and to eschew blind ideological voting. Her moderation partly explains why

Burger assigned her no significant case opinions and why Reagan did not elevate her to chief justice in 1986.

O'Connor persistently worked to take the policy leadership role not filled by the chief, proposing compromises and new doctrines to other justices. Her doctrinal successes writing for a majority were in cases involving crime control. Both wings of the Court rejected or ignored the reasoning in her separate opinions on federalism, accommodation, and affirmative action when she introduced complicated "tests" to achieve compromises between values. She used her two structural principles, deference to state power and judicial restraint, to avoid or to settle substantive matters that the justices, except for Burger and Rehnquist, preferred to argue on the basis of values. Her freedom opinions hinted of a nascent political philosophy that would also incorporate her ideals of a federal political system and an orderly society. She never adopted Rehnquist's simple majoritarian democratic theory, and she took up the challenge of making hard choices without the guidance of a fully articulated, conservative political philosophy.

From her experience as a state legislator and trial judge, O'Connor brought styles, skills, and knowledge to her decision making that were not fully appreciated by the other justices. Yet she won their respect by proving her competence and through her high productivity. It is not surprising that in 1983 the *New York Times* forgot that there was a woman on the Court.[33] O'Connor's contributions to the Burger Court's jurisprudence were characterized by her political sensibility, driven by her structural principles, and unmarked by her gender.

NOTES

1. See Penina Migdal Glazer and Miriam Slater, *Unequal Colleagues: The Entrance of Women into the Professions, 1890–1940* (New Brunswick, N.J.: Rutgers University Press, 1987); Karen Berger Morello, *The Invisible Bar: The Woman Lawyer in America, 1638 to the Present* (New York: Random House, 1986); Cynthia Fuchs Epstein, *Women in Law* (New York: Basic Books, 1981); James White, "Women in the Law," *Michigan Law Review* 68 (1967): 1051–82.

2. On O'Connor's pre-Court experience, see Orma Linford, "Sandra Day O'Connor: Myra Bradwell's Revenge," in Frank P. Leveness and Jane P. Sweeney, eds., *Women Leaders in Contemporary U.S. Politics* (Boulder, Col.: Lynne Rienner, 1987), chap. 10; and Beverly B. Cook, "Women as Supreme Court Candidates: From Florence Allen to Sandra O'Connor," *Judicature* 65 (1981–82): 314–26.

3. See Beverly B. Cook, "Women as Judges," chap. 2 in Cook, Leslie F. Goldstein, Karen O'Connor, and Susette M. Talarico, *Women in the Judicial Process* (Washington, D.C.: American Political Science Association, 1988).

4. Lyle Denniston, "Sandra Day O'Connor: First-Term Review," *California Lawyer* 1983: 29–30.

5. Richard L. Pacelle, Jr., "The Supreme Court Agenda across Time: Toward a Theory of Agenda-Building" (Paper presented at the Annual Meeting of the Midwest Political Science Association, Chicago, April 16–19, 1986).

6. The measure of case significance was two standard deviations or more from the mean score based on factor analysis of the cases chosen by twenty authorities on the Burger Court period. The measure of fairness in assignment was one standard deviation from the number of significant cases available per justice if distributed equally.

7. Sandra Day O'Connor, "Trends in the Relationship between the Federal and State Courts from the Perspective of a State Court Judge," *William and Mary Law Review* 22 (1981): 805–6, 814–15.

8. Ibid., pp. 809–10.

9. Elder Witt, *A Different Justice: Reagan and the Supreme Court* (Washington, D.C.: Congressional Quarterly Press, 1986), pp. 7–10, 100–101.

10. U.S. Senate, Committee on the Judiciary, *Hearings on Nomination of Sandra Day O'Connor,* 97th Cong., 1st Sess., Sept. 9–11, 1981 (Washington, D.C.: U.S. Government Printing Office, 1981), p. 58.

11. Robert E. Riggs, "Justice O'Connor: A First Term Appraisal," *Brigham Young University Law Review* 1983: 1–46.

12. *Hearings,* pp. 102–3, 127, 142, 148.

13. Ibid., pp. 77, 119, 177.

14. David W. Rohde and Harold J. Spaeth, *Supreme Court Decision Making* (San Francisco: W. H. Freeman, 1976), pp. 140–44.

15. The method employed to identify the justices' valences on the values and principles is principal components analysis with varimax rotation. Flango and Ducat proposed this method in 1977 (Victor E. Flango and Craig R. Ducat, "Toward an Integration of Public Law and Judicial Behavior," *Journal of Politics* 39 [1977]: 46–47) and utilized the method to examine economic cases in 1987 (Ducat and Robert L. Dudley, "Dimensions Underlying Economic Policy-Making in the Early and Later Burger Courts," *Journal of Politics* 49 [1987]: 521–39). The theoretical basis for this methodological choice is that each justice takes into account more than a single value in deciding a series of cases in the same issue area.

The justices' perceptions of case issues are presumed to be multidimensional, not unidimensional as posited by Schubert (Glendon Schubert, *The Judicial Mind,* Evanston: Northwestern University Press, 1965), by Spaeth (Harold J. Spaeth, "Unidimensionality and Item Invariance in Judicial Scaling," *Behavioral Sciences* 10 [1965]: 290–304), and by Ulmer (S. Sidney Ulmer, "The Dimensionality of Judicial Voting Behavior," *Midwest Journal of Political Science* 13 [1969]: 471–83). If the justices perceive the same issues and values in a topical set of cases, then a major factor, defined as a factor which explains 50 percent or more of the variance in the voting pattern, will exist. Since some justices are likely to define the issue and relevant values in some cases differently, minor factors are expected to appear in the analysis. The existence of minor factors is not understood to reflect judicial inconsistency but rather this difference in perception and evaluation. Table 9.1 reports valences for the first factor only. All first factors, except for law and order cases, met the criterion of 50 percent.

No attempt is made here to identify the values in minor factors, as Ducat and Dudley (1987) did in their work. However, different loadings and rank orders on the second factor indicate that O'Connor (and Blackmun) made more subtle distinctions on gender equality than the other justices. Stevens's perspective on some of the federalism and property cases was unique, as was White's perspective on federalism, freedom, and church-state relations.

A second indicator for the uniqueness of a justice's attitudinal rank order is a communality percentage of less than .50. Communality, the squared multiple correlation coefficient between one variable and all other variables in the analysis, indicates the strength of the linear association of the variables (vote correlations). Stevens and White played the maverick role on the Court as indicated by their low communalities on four, and two, value factors respectively. No communalities less than .40 appeared in the ten factor analyses reported. (Table 9.1 with the factor loadings inserted in place of the plus and minus symbols is available from the author.)

16. Changes in the justices' attitudes and in the issues before the Court during the Burger era are described in Ducat and Dudley, "Dimensions Underlying Economic Policymaking"; Lettie M. Wenner, "State Regulation of Business in the Warren, Burger, and Rehnquist Courts," (Paper presented at the Annual Meeting of the American Political Science Association, Chicago, September 3–6, 1987); and Dudley and Ducat, "The Burger Court and Economic Liberalism," *Western Political Quarterly* 39 (1986): 236–49.

17. No attitude toward federalism was apparent from an analysis of the justices' voting patterns in cases decided between 1889 and 1959 in John D. Sprague, *Voting Patterns on the United States Supreme Court* (Indianapolis: Bobbs-Merrill, 1968). From analyses of overlapping Court periods, others have concluded that federalism could be subsumed with reasonable consistency within the major Democratic values. See Glendon Schubert, *The Judicial Mind Revisited* (New York: Oxford University Press, 1974); Harold J. Spaeth, *Supreme Court Policy-Making* (San Francisco: W. H. Freeman, 1979).

18. Spaeth, "Judicial Power as a Variable Motivating Supreme Court Behavior," *Midwest Journal of Political Science* 6 (1962): 54–82.

19. Spaeth, *Supreme Court Policy-Making*, Table 3, p. 135.

20. Spaeth, "Judicial Power as a Variable Motivating Supreme Court Behavior," Figure 1, pp. 59–60.

21. Schubert, *The Judicial Mind*, chap. 5.

22. The measure for importance of a case is one standard deviation or more from the mean score (see note 6 above).

23. See *Asarco Inc. v. Idaho State Tax Commission* (1982); *F. W. Woolworth Co. v. Taxation and Revenue Department of the State of New Mexico* (1982); *Jefferson County Pharmaceutical Association, Inc. v. Abbott Laboratories* (1983).

24. See *DelCostello v. International Brotherhood of Teamsters* (1983); *Wilson v. Garcia* (1985); *Marrese v. American Academy of Orthopedic Surgeons* (1985).

25. A discussion of the concept of "judicial federalism" can be found in "Ju-

dicial Federalism: Don't Make a Federal Case Out of It . . . Or Should You?" *Judicature* 73 (1989): 146–54, 170.

26. See *Tilton v. Richardson* (1971); *Hunt v. McNair* (1973); *Roemer v. Maryland Board of Public Works* (1976).

27. Sue Davis, "Federalism and Property Rights: An Examination of Justice Rehnquist's Legal Positivism," *Western Political Quarterly* 39 (1986): 250–64.

28. Richard A. Cordray and James T. Vradelis, "The Emerging Jurisprudence of Justice Sandra Day O'Connor," *University of Chicago Law Review* 52 (1985): 383.

29. See Edward V. Heck and Paula C. Arledge, "Justice Sandra Day O'Connor and the First Amendment, 1981–1984" (Paper presented at the Annual Meeting of the Midwest Political Science Association, Chicago, Apr. 17–20, 1985).

30. John M. Scheb II and Lee W. Ailshie, "Justice Sandra Day O'Connor and the 'Freshman Effect,' " *Judicature* 69 (1985): 9–12. For a critical analysis of her first-term opinions and votes, see Virginia Kerr, "Supreme Court Justice O'Connor: The Woman Whose Word Is Law," *Ms.*, Dec. 1982: 52, 80–84. For a two-term review see Laurence Bodine, "Sandra Day O'Connor," *American Bar Association Journal* 69 (1983): 1394–98.

31. Sandra Day O'Connor, "Introduction: Achievements of Women in the Legal Profession," *New York State Bar Journal* 57 (Oct. 1985): 8–10.

32. Margaret A. Miller, "Justice Sandra Day O'Connor: Token or Triumph from a Feminist Perspective," *Golden Gate University Law Review* 15 (1985): 493–525; Laurel Leff, "And Justice for Some," *Savvy*, Mar. 1985, 94–100; and David J. Danelski, "Sandra Day O'Connor: The First Term," *The Stanford Magazine*, 1983, 42–49.

33. The *New York Times* Topics: "In the Name of the Law," Sept. 29, 1983, p. A30, referred to the "nine men" on the Court.

10

JUSTICE LEWIS F. POWELL, JR.:
Balance Wheel of the Court

JACOB W. LANDYNSKI

Introduction

The early appointees to the Burger Court arrived in the shadow, and with the burden, of what had come before. The sixteen-year period that ended in 1969 with the retirement of Chief Justice Warren had been the most noteworthy in American constitutional law since the era of the Marshall Court. Treating the Constitution as an instrument of social reform, the Warren Court had restlessly pursued an agenda of innovation. The resulting sharp division on constitutional matters within both Court and country had not abated when Lewis F. Powell, Jr., was named to the Court on October 21, 1971. Destined to become known as the "conscience" of the Court,[1] Powell served until his retirement in 1987, a tenure nearly coterminous with that of the Burger Court itself.

Powell took his seat under the most auspicious circumstances. General acclaim greeted the nomination of the Virginian selected to fill the seat occupied so long and illustriously by his fellow southerner, Hugo L. Black. No one at the time could have expected Powell to attain Black's stature as a truly heroic figure of the Court. His age alone (at sixty-four he was one of the oldest appointees to the Court) seemed to preclude the tenure that is usually requisite to establish the kind of judicial record upon which history bestows its accolade of greatness. Indeed, Powell's advancing years might have jeopardized his selection or confirmation were it not for his reputation as a national spokesman for the legal profession and his honor-laden career, featuring years of public service. The appointment was not one he sought: he accepted it only on the

276

personal entreaties of President Nixon after first asking for a day to think it over.[2]

Graduated first from his law class at Washington and Lee and with a Master of Law degree from Harvard, the patrician Powell, scion of a leading Virginia family and descendant of one of the original Jamestown settlers, "had perhaps as extensive and high-placed experience in the American legal profession as any man ever appointed to the Supreme Court."[3] A partner in a leading Virginia law firm specializing in corporate law, his record of public service was striking: he had been president of the American Bar Association, the American College of Trial Lawyers, and the American Bar Foundation; chairman of the Richmond Public School Board and the State Board of Education; and a member of President Johnson's Commission on Law Enforcement and Administration of Justice and President Nixon's National Advisory Committee on Legal Services to the Poor. Moreover, as an educational leader he "led the opposition to, and ultimately defeated, the state's 'massive resistance policy' " toward desegregation.[4] In the foremost rank of legal practitioners, he tirelessly lobbied the bar in support of federally financed legal services for the poor.[5]

Enviable, too, were the personal qualities of the man. There was general agreement on his "consideration for others, his compassion, and his respect for the dignity of the human personality."[6] A black woman attorney who had worked with him on behalf of legal services for the poor praised him as "above all, humane," with "a sense of decency and fair play and common sense."[7] Esteemed by all who knew him, without an ideological or partisan political background but with a proven talent for mediation and compromise, Powell seemed ideally suited to exert a calming influence on a fractious Court that had just lost its two leading luminaries, Justices Black and John M. Harlan.

Little wonder, then, that Powell's nomination was so warmly applauded. He was promptly endorsed by the Virginia NAACP. Legislators vied in praise of the appointment—Hubert Humphrey, for example, garbed him in the mantle of Holmes, Frankfurter, and Harlan.[8] The Senate, on December 6, 1971, made him Virginia's first member of the Supreme Court since Reconstruction by a vote of 89 to 1.

In part, approval of Powell's selection stemmed from relief that President Nixon, determined to halt the liberal swing of the Court during the Warren era, had finally named a man of stature. Much opposition had been aroused when word leaked out that the president was considering several lightweights after the Senate had already vetoed two Nixon nominees, federal appellate Judges Clement F. Haynsworth, Jr., and G. Harrold Carswell. In part, too, Powell was the beneficiary of liberal hostility generated by the simultaneous nomination of William H. Rehnquist to succeed Harlan, another of the Court's great justices, who had died almost the same time as Black. Critics of the "strict constructionist" role Nixon envisioned for the Burger Court vented their spleen on Rehnquist, a former Nixon aide and confirmed conservative, whom they feared would become a forceful judicial activist in support of the president. By comparison, Powell, a Democrat with centrist or mild conservative leanings, might be expected to fill some of the void left by Harlan, whose "finely wrought opinions rested on painstaking analysis, relatively neutral principles of law, and a fair evaluation of opposing arguments."[9] Powell seems to have consciously attempted to emulate Harlan; no previous justice was cited so frequently in his opinions as Harlan, and none more reverently.

Despite the liberal praise for Powell, President Nixon could find much in Powell's record to justify his pronouncement that the new jurist would "strengthen the hands of the peace forces"[10] against criminal elements. As a private citizen Powell had repeatedly spoken out in the 1960s on the menace of crime and the dangers of antigovernment agitation. Though he welcomed the Court's newfound concern for defendants' rights, he suggested it was time to pause and "concentrate our attention more on the rights of society in general."[11] "The immediate problem is one of balance" (a favorite Powell term that would become his judicial yardstick), and the "pendulum may indeed have swung too far"[12] in favor of defendants. Powell denounced, as "a tempest in a teapot" and "standard leftist propaganda," criticism of government wiretapping, from which "[l]aw-abiding citizens have nothing to fear."[13] And he wrote with passion against civil disobedience, whether exercised for or against desegregation or in opposition to the Vietnam War. He feared that the nationwide trend "toward organized lawlessness and even rebellion" might be a "prelude to revolution."[14] Injustice must be redressed by legal means, not by sowing the seeds of discord.

Justice Lewis F. Powell, Jr.

Criminal Justice

Unreasonable Searches

Powell's independence was tested during his first term by a case that combined these various concerns. His opinion for a unanimous Court in *United States v. United States District Court* (1972) has been rhapsodized as "a pronouncement worthy of the Court at its best," one that rivals "historic pronouncements by Holmes, Brandeis, and Stone."[15] The opinion is all the more noteworthy in that the sentiments Powell now expressed ran counter to those he had previously espoused. At issue was the legality of an "internal security" wiretap authorized by the U.S. attorney general without a judicial warrant, which led to the apprehension of a left-wing activist charged with dynamiting a CIA office. The practice being challenged had been authorized by every administration since at least Truman's and possibly even Franklin D. Roosevelt's.

Powell rejected the position that the definition of what an "unreasonable" search is may be determined without reference to the Fourth Amendment's warrant clause.[16] Rather, the warrant requirement is the principal gauge of reasonableness because it interposes a neutral magistrate between the executive and the citizen. He refused to countenance yet another "exigency" exception to the warrant clause and sharply rejected the suggestion that judges lack the experience to make internal security decisions or that they cannot be trusted to preserve the secrecy of the proceedings.

Powell's argument is of special significance for its attention to the First Amendment interests implicated in electronic eavesdropping. He spoke of the "convergence of First and Fourth Amendment values not present in cases of 'ordinary' crime" and warned, "The price of lawful public dissent must not be a dread of subjection to an unchecked surveillance power" (407 U.S. at 313–14). But almost lost in the general approbation of the Court's 8-0 decision was Powell's strong intimation—part of his emergent "balancing" approach—that it would be permissible for Congress to allow judicial authorization of warrants for internal security surveillance with more flexible standards of probable cause and time than those required by the Omnibus Crime Control Act of 1968, in view of the "long-range" nature of this type of surveillance and the difficulty of identifying "exact targets" (322).

When Powell was appointed, some Fourth Amendment issues that had agitated the Court in preceding decades—for example, the scope of searches incident to arrest—had been largely resolved.

New issues such as aerial observation and border searches demanded the Court's attention. Powell was guided by two basic criteria. On the one hand, the primary determinant of a reasonable search is satisfaction of the warrant requirement. On the other hand, exceptions for warrantless searches ought to be governed by exigent circumstances or by the absence of a justifiable expectation of privacy.

Although warrantless border searches had the sanction of longstanding legislative and judicial authority as an incident of national sovereignty, in *Almeida-Sanchez v. United States* (1973) Powell agreed that a stop and search of an automobile twenty-five miles from the Mexican border could not be sustained despite large-scale border crossings by illegal aliens because the border was too far away. In *United States v. Brignoni-Ponce* (1975)—which involved not a search, but the stopping of a car to question the occupants about their citizenship and immigration status—Powell spoke for the Court, holding that the apparent Mexican descent of the passengers was insufficient justification for the stop. Mexican ancestry can be one factor in meeting the *Terry v. Ohio* (1968) standard of "reasonable suspicion" for a stop, but it cannot be the only one.

A later case, *California v. Ciraolo* (1986), involved a search for marijuana by aerial observation, in which a private fenced-in backyard was viewed from an altitude of one hundred feet. The Court reasoned that, while the curtilage of the home is, like the home itself, protected by the Fourth Amendment from ground-level intrusions, individuals can have no reasonable expectation of privacy from aerial surveillance. Powell, dissenting, thought it was illogical for the majority to compare law enforcement's purposeful visual observation with the slight invasion of privacy incurred from ordinary airplane flights. His opinion for the Court in *Oliver v. United States* (1984), however, reaffirmed the open fields doctrine allowing warrantless entry into private fields. Except for searches in the vicinity of the home, he believed, society had no interest in recognizing a right of privacy out of doors since open fields are accessible to the public regardless of "No Trespassing" signs.

Loud rumbles of discontent with the exclusionary rule in Fourth Amendment cases have been heard on the Court for a long time, but it was Powell's position that set in motion the train of events that left the rule badly wounded. In *Schneckloth v. Bustamonte* (1973) in a concurrence, Powell proposed drastic restrictions on the use of federal habeas corpus review of alleged Fourth Amendment violations by state officials. These were cases, he pointed out, in which the defendant's innocence usually was not even claimed; moreover, the exclusionary rule itself should not be seen as a right but, rather, as a judicial prophylactic designed to vindicate a constitutional right. When the claim is made months or years after the deviant police behavior has taken place, the deterrent effect of the rule is bound to be minimal. Powell, three years later in *Stone v. Powell* (1976), wrote his view into law: since the Fourth Amendment, unlike other Bill of Rights guarantees, is not vital to the trustworthiness of the fact-finding process, and since exclusion serves merely as a judicial remedy, the rule must be balanced against competing policies. It was most unlikely that an illegal search would be deterred by the possibility that it might at some future date be challenged in federal habeas corpus proceedings after state courts had upheld it.[17] Finally, in *United States v. Leon* (1984), Powell's view of the purpose and scope of the exclusionary rule came full circle. The Court, with Powell in the majority, upheld the introduction of evidence seized by police acting in "good faith" on a defective judicial warrant, in the face of vociferous dissents that the exclusionary rule was suffering piecemeal destruction.

Fair Trial

By the time Powell joined the Court, the battle that had raged for close to a century over "incorporation" of the Bill of Rights into the Fourteenth Amendment as a protection against its violation by the states was largely over. By the end of the 1960s, most of the Bill of Rights was being applied with the same stringency to the states as to the federal government. Like Frankfurter and Harlan before him, Powell opposed the transformation of due process into a synonym for the Bill of Rights, though he did not seek to reverse the selective incorporation decisions of the Warren Court. He clearly stated his position in a pair of cases early in his tenure, *Apodaca v. Oregon* (1972) and *Johnson v. Louisiana* (1972), in which he argued that procedural rights are not incorporated in toto but only to the extent they are fundamental to a fair trial.

The question in both cases was whether a state may allow a less than unanimous jury verdict. The other eight justices were evenly divided: four rejected the unanimity requirement across the board, for federal as well as state trials; four others voted to retain it for federal trials and to extend it to state trials. Powell, concurring, cast the deciding vote. Respect for precedent constrained him to vote for retaining unanimity as a constitutional requirement in federal trials, while respect for federalism led him to oppose its extension to the states. Despite federal courts' having adopted the common law's requirement of unanimity, Powell did not believe that the Constitution mandated unanimous juries. The Court must not deprive the states of power to innovate and experiment: obsession with a single set of procedural standards for federal and state courts would be detrimental to both, for the Court could wind up diluting federal rights in order to accommodate the states' inability to meet stringent procedural standards.

In *Kastigar v. United States* (1972), Powell wrote the majority opinion, which limited the scope of immunity from prosecution (the government must grant immunity under the Fifth Amendment before it can compel testimony). Earlier federal laws had established immunity to be "transactional," meaning "absolute immunity against future prosecution for the offense to which the question relates" (*Counselman v. Hitchcock*, 142 U.S. at 586, 1892). The statute at issue in *Kastigar,* passed by Congress in 1970, granted immunity from the use and derivative use of the compelled evidence, but did not grant immunity in the event the government developed independent sources of evidence. Powell's assertion that "use immunity" is "protection commensurate with that afforded by the privilege" (406 U.S. at 453) has been severely criticized on historical grounds.[18]

Access to counsel by indigents was a subject to which Powell as a private citizen had devoted much thought and energy. The Court, in *Argersinger v. Hamlin* (1972), extended the right to appointed counsel for indigents in state cases to include even minor offenses involving a jail sentence; if a defendant was denied counsel he could not be imprisoned, no matter how short the term. Powell, in concurrence, preferred a flexible solution. Instead of a strict rule, he would have allowed broad judicial discretion subject to the complexities of the case, the length of the probable sentence in the event of a conviction, and such factors as the defendant's competence to stand trial and the community's attitude toward the defendant.

Powell's *Argersinger* guidelines bore a strong resemblance to the *Betts v. Brady* (1942) special circumstances rule, which had proved so unsatisfactory it had been unanimously discarded in *Gideon v. Wainwright* (1963). He believed, however, that the failure of state courts in the past to "live up to their responsibilities in determining on a case-by-case basis whether counsel should be appointed" (407 U.S. at 65) was not likely to be repeated. Perplexingly, Powell did not state the basis for his optimism.

Another of Powell's balancing opinions, this time for a unanimous Court, came in *Barker v. Wingo* (1972), delineating the speedy trial provision of the Sixth Amendment. Failure to provide a speedy trial, unlike failure to protect other procedural rights, he pointed out, may actually work to a defendant's advantage, because of witnesses' fading memories or their unavailability. The proper solution is a test that requires courts to weigh four major factors: (1) the length of the delay; (2) the government's justification for the delay (for example, a missing witness); (3) whether the defendant asserted the right at trial; and (4) whether the delay impaired the defense of the case. In *Barker*, concluded Powell, there had been no prejudice to the defendant, despite a five-year delay, since the record made it clear that he had not wanted a speedy trial.

Powell's balance fell on the defendant's side in some notable instances. Although he regarded plea bargaining as a benefit to both defendants and society, in *Bordenkircher v. Hayes* (1978) he could not support it. In this case a prosecutor threatened to reindict a defendant under a recidivism statute and subject him to a life term of imprisonment for refusal to accept a proffered five-year sentence in return for a guilty plea on a forged check charge. Powell protested the Court's affirmance of the defendant's conviction. Threats to escalate the charge solely to discourage the defendant from exercising his constitutional right to plead innocent, in his view, violated due process. He also dissented in *Martin v. Ohio* (1982), in which the Court allowed a state to impose the burden of proving self-defense on a defendant charged with murder. This shift in the burden of proof, he maintained, was inconsistent with the presumption of innocence required by due process.

Cruel and Unusual Punishment

When one considers Powell's lack of previous experience in criminal justice, it is remarkable how many of his most important criminal law opinions—*District Court, Schneckloth, Argersinger, Apodaca, Barker, Kastigar*—were filed near the beginning of his tenure. But none was more influential than his first-term dissent in *Furman v. Georgia* (1972), in which the Court effectually struck down the death penalty, as applied, in thirty-nine states and the District of Columbia. The opinion illustrates basic themes in Powell's overall jurisprudence.

The per curiam decision was supported by five concurring opinions offering a host of rationales. Powell was critical of "the shattering effect this collection of views has on the root principles of stare decisis, federalism, judicial restraint and—more importantly—separation of powers." Seldom did he catalogue so many deficiencies in a decision. Indeed, "I can recall no case in which, in the name of deciding constitutional questions this Court has subordinated national and local democratic processes to such an extent" (408 U.S. at 417–18).

To be sure, Powell agreed that cruel and unusual punishments and due process of law were not "static concepts whose meaning and scope were sealed at the time of their writing. They were designed to be dynamic and to gain meaning through application to specific circumstances." But since the due process clauses sanctioned the taking of life, "the Court is not free to read into the Constitution a meaning that is plainly at variance with its language" (408 U.S. at 420). The Court's unbroken series of precedents sanctioning capital punishment dated to 1879 and included several Warren Court decisions and one by the Burger Court only the year before. Powell conceded only that capital punishment might be excessive for particular crimes.[19]

As for the argument that standards of decency had evolved to the point that the death penalty must be considered cruel, he replied that legislatures, chosen by the people, were the best index of society's conscience in a democracy. Powell rejected as mere speculation Justice Marshall's contention that the public would oppose the death penalty if better informed of the moral issues. And the argument that the death penalty fell disproportionately on the poor and on minority groups left Powell sympathetic but unimpressed. Taken to its logical conclusion, this contention would vitiate any criminal justice system; such problems were rooted in social and economic conditions, not constitutional law.

Four years after *Furman*, in *Gregg v. Georgia* (1976), Powell's views largely triumphed, in a joint opinion with Stewart and Stevens constituting the judgment of the Court. Given the long acceptance of capital punishment in the United States, the Court found it impossible to say that the death penalty per se was forbidden for murder. The "standards of decency" argument was undermined by the fact that, since *Furman*, thirty-five states had reenacted capital punishment statutes.

Retribution is permissible, maintained Powell, indeed "essential in an ordered society that asks its citizens to rely on legal processes rather than self-help to vindicate their wrongs"; the death penalty was therefore a proper "expression of society's moral outrage."

Society was entitled to believe "that certain crimes are themselves so grievous an affront to humanity that the only adequate response may be the penalty of death" (428 U.S. at 183–84). And while deterrence may play no role in murders of passion, with some crimes—such as murder for hire—the prospect of paying the supreme penalty unquestionably deters. In any event, legislatures were the proper forum for this evaluation.

Powell made one significant concession. In *Furman* he had approved giving jurors in capital cases unbridled discretion to impose the death penalty. Now he agreed that to "minimize the risk of wholly arbitrary and capricious action" by the jury, it should be "given guidance regarding the factors about the crime and the defendant . . . relevant to the sentencing decision" (428 U.S. at 189, 192). Jurors must be carefully instructed regarding aggravating and mitigating circumstances.

In two capital punishment cases decided in his final term, Powell wrote for 5-4 majorities. *McCleskey v. Kemp* (1987) upheld the conviction of a black Georgia man convicted of killing a white policeman. The appeal was based on a statistical study showing that, in Georgia, murderers of blacks were less likely to be sentenced to death than murderers of whites, and white murderers were less likely to receive a capital sentence than black murderers. The study was deemed insufficient to meet the high standard of proof required to demonstrate that juries, which must consider numerous factors in sentencing decisions, had abused their discretion. In *Booth v. Maryland* (1987), on the other hand, Powell disallowed the introduction of a victim-impact statement in the sentencing phase of a capital case because the emotional views of the victim's family members may prejudice the jury against the defendant.

Powell occasionally revealed a considerable capacity for measured indignation in cases touching the core of his values. For instance, his opinions in the 5-4 decisions of *Rummel v. Estelle* (1980) and *Solem v. Helm* (1983) evidenced the quality of mercy. He prevailed, in *Solem*, to write his *Rummel* dissent into law. In *Rummel*, the Court upheld a life sentence for a third property-related felony (the three crimes together netted only $230) under a state recidivism statute. Powell protested that the sentence was grossly disproportionate to the severity of the crime and was unjust. In *Solem*, Justice Blackmun switched sides to join Powell and the other dissenters from *Rummel*—Justices Brennan, Marshall, and Stevens—to form the new majority, which nullified a life sentence without possibility of parole for a seventh nonviolent felony, imposed under a South Dakota recidivism statute. Measured by objective standards—including the gravity of the offenses, the severity of the sentence, the way other jurisdictions punish identical crimes, and the sentences given other types of criminals in the same jurisdiction—Solem's life term violated the Eighth Amendment. The crimes involved were relatively trivial, and at least forty-eight states would not have permitted such a sentence for offenses of this kind. Despite Powell's feeble attempt to square the two decisions, *Solem* effectively overruled *Rummel.*

Powell's ever-present solicitude for school authority led him to rule in *Ingraham v. Wright* (1977) that corporal punishment in schools, specifically authorized by twenty-one states at the time and forbidden in only two, was not covered by the Eighth Amendment. Powell saw no basis for "wrenching the Eighth Amendment from its historical context and extending it to traditional disciplinary practices in the public schools" (430 U.S. at 699), which are open institutions supervised by the community. The possibility of abuse is minimized by the ease with which cases of mistreatment can be protested.

The First Amendment

Free Speech and the Press

Powell's free speech and press opinions show a high degree of pragmatism. He cautioned in *Saxbe v. Washington Post Co.* (1974) that "we must look behind the bright-line generalities . . . and seek the meaning of First Amendment guarantees in light of the underlying realities of a particular environment" (417 U.S. at 875). He usually canvassed the "underlying realities" with great care, at times striking a different balance from that of the Court.

In two far-reaching decisions, *Elrod v. Burns* (1976) and *Branti v. Finkel* (1980), the Court ruled that hirings and firings of political employees based on political patronage violated the First Amendment. Powell dissented both times. While the idea that public employment should not depend on political affiliation has merit as an "abstract proposition," the Court must deal "with a highly practical and fundamental element of our political system, not the theoretical abstractions of a political science seminar" (427 U.S. at 381–82). Patronage was "a practice as old as the republic" (376), frankly utilized even by such presidents as Washington, Jefferson, Jackson, and Lincoln. Far from being objectionable, it helped to democratize government by loosening the aristocratic elite's domination of political affairs; patronage also "strengthened parties and hence encouraged the development of institutional responsibility to the electorate on a permanent basis" (379) since, "as every politician knows, the hope of some reward generates a major portion of the local political activity supporting parties" (385).

Again emphasizing the need for local autonomy, Powell dissented in *Board of Education v. Pico* (1982), in which the Court struck down the action of a local school board that had ordered some books, which Powell described as "vulgar or racist," removed from school libraries. It was the duty of a school board in our democracy, he declared, "to instill in its students the ideas and values on which a democratic system depends" and to remove from student purview materials that "are indecent; extol violence, intolerance, and racism; or degrade the dignity of the individual" (457 U.S. at 896–97).

The line of permissible speech, for Powell, stopped short of vulgar language offensive to others. In *Rosenfeld v. New Jersey* (1972), he set forth his view that the Court's ruling in *Chaplinsky v. New Hampshire* (1942), which withheld First Amendment protection from "fighting words" "is not limited to words whose mere utterance entails a high probability of an outbreak of physical violence. It also extends to the willful use of scurrilous language calculated to offend the sensibilities of an unwilling audience." Words "grossly offensive and emotionally disturbing" to an audience consisting in good part of women and children are properly subject to prosecution (408 U.S. at 905–6). Where, however, abuse is poured on a police officer, as in *Lewis v. City of New Orleans* (1972), Powell asserted that the officer's training should lead him "to exercise a higher degree of restraint than the average citizen" (408 U.S. at 913).[20]

On the other hand, Powell argued in favor of broader First Amendment rights than the majority was willing to concede in *Saxbe*. In that case the Court upheld a regulation banning interviews between reporters and federal prison inmates. Powell disagreed, asserting that, since members of the public could not obtain "the information needed for the intelligent discharge of [their] political responsibilities," it was necessary for the press to act "as an agent of the public at large," enabling the citizenry "to assert meaningful control over the political process" (417 U.S. at 863).

Powell also played an important role in cases that secured the right of businesses to communicate with the public and to prevent others from commandeering business facilities for their own communications. He wrote opinions that, respectively, upheld the right of a corporation to make expenditures for political purposes because society's interest in the free flow of information is thereby furthered; supported a public utility's inclusion of inserts discussing public policy issues in its monthly billing envelopes; and struck down a requirement that a public utility that had inserted in its billing statements a newsletter discussing public issues had to allow a consumer organization to include its own message.[21] In *Lloyd Corporation v. Tanner* (1972), writing for the 5-4 majority that permitted a shopping complex to ban handbilling, Powell declared that property does not "lose its private character merely because the public is generally invited to use it for designated purposes" (407 U.S. at 569).

Powell's most significant contribution to the law of free speech came in the case of *Gertz v. Robert Welch, Inc.* (1974). In an earlier decision, *New York Times Co. v. Sullivan* (1964), the Court had required that "actual malice" be proven before a public official could recover damages for defamation relating to his official conduct. Later this rule was extended in *Curtis Pub. Co. v. Butts* (1967) to cover "public figures." Should the rule now be further extended to include defamation of private individuals if the matter was one of public interest? Powell answered in the negative for the 5-4 majority. Private persons generally lack access to the channels of communication enjoyed by public officials and public figures; they "are therefore more vulnerable to injury, and the state interest in protecting them is correspondingly greater." Moreover, unlike public officials and public figures, they have not "voluntarily exposed themselves to increased risk of injury from defamatory falsehood" (418 U.S. at 344–45). The states may therefore permit a lower standard of negligence for this type of defamation action, rather than the intentional "actual malice" standard—though Powell conceded that compensation for negligent libel must be limited to actual injury only, thus excluding punitive damages.

The Establishment Clause

On issues of religion and the First Amendment, little need be said since Powell's views and the Court's constitutional law were virtually synonymous. In no other sphere did the Court more consistently adhere to Powell's views: in the more than thirty religion cases decided by the Court during Powell's tenure, he was in the majority nearly every single time.[22] Generally speaking, he took a strict, though not an uncompromising, separationist view of the establishment clause, following the lead charted by his predecessor, Justice Black.[23] Powell accepted the *Lemon v. Kurtzman* (1971) test: in order to pass constitutional muster, aid related to religion (1) must have a secular purpose; (2) must have no primary effect of advancing or inhibiting religion; and (3) must avoid excessive entanglement between government and religion. It was usually not hard to satisfy Powell in regard to secular purpose; nor was entanglement an especially difficult hurdle. But he bore down heavily on primary effect. For Powell, summed up one scholar, "it matters little who gets the money directly [i.e., the school or parent]. Nor does it matter that there is some substantial benefit of a nonreligious sort accruing to the direct grantee. If there is a substantial benefit to a religious institution, albeit at some remove from government, this is still 'primary effect.' "[24] To parents of low or moderate income who took advantage of the free exercise provision to educate their children in sectarian schools, Powell offered "great . . . sympathy" but no tea, as state statutes designed to relieve their financial burden regularly fell under his axe.[25]

Powell's position was shaped by his fear of political strife along sectarian lines and by a superficial reading of the history behind the establishment clause. (It is, however, possible to read the history more judiciously and still arrive at the same result.) In his last opinion on the subject, *Edwards v. Aguillard* (1987), Powell briefly sketched the roles of Madison and Jefferson in securing for Virginia a guarantee of religious freedom and a ban on religious establishment, then concluded: "both the guarantees of free exercise and against the establishment of religion were then incorporated into the Federal Bill of Rights by its drafter, James Madison" (482 U.S. at 606). The Bill of Rights was, it seems, Madison's personal creation, and he had simply inserted, jot for jot, the Virginia law on the subject of religion into the First Amendment.

Fundamental Rights

Powell often departed from self-proclaimed principles of restraint in his "fundamental rights" opinions. Together with a majority of the Burger Court, he consistently embraced the new substantive due process inaugurated in *Griswold v. Connecticut* (1965). The *Roe v. Wade* (1973) abortion case was first argued before Powell's appointment, then reargued on his insistence that it was his duty to participate. Upon seeing the final draft of Blackmun's majority opinion, Powell congratulated him for "exceptional scholarship."[26] This most-criticized of contemporary constitutional law decisions was also one of the boldest in that it effectually overturned nearly all abortion statutes across the land. Powell never explained how he reconciled *Roe* and its progeny with his oft-stated preference for local autonomy in local matters. Assuming he regarded personal autonomy as taking precedence over local autonomy in certain matters "fundamental" to the individual, a philosophical discussion on the limits of law seems to have been in order— something Powell (and his colleagues) never attempted. Assertion did the work of reason.

In *Bellotti v. Baird* (1979) Powell wrote the judgment for the Court, which invalidated a Massachusetts law requiring parental consent for abortion for a minor under eighteen. Despite his tribute to the parental role of "teaching, guiding and inspiring by precept and example," which demands "a substantial measure of authority over one's children" (443 U.S. at 638), Powell concluded that the mere existence of a minor's legal right to go to court to challenge parental refusal was inadequate. Since "many parents hold strong views on the subject of abortion," the pregnant girl must have the option "to go directly to a court without first consulting or notifying her parents" (647). This was "a constitutional right of unique character," and the court must not withhold authorization of an abortion if it finds the minor to be "mature and fully competent to make this decision independently" (650–51). What seems clear is that even if she is found to be immature, the court may assume the role of surrogate parent, deciding irrespective of the wishes of her father and mother. *Griswold*'s fundamental right of marital privacy was now a right of sexual privacy for minors no less than for adults. The right, moreover, was finely calibrated: in *City of Akron v. Akron Center for Reproductive Health, Inc.* (1983), Powell struck down a requirement that second-trimester abortions be performed in a hospital, although he conceded that it would have originally been consistent with *Roe*. In the interim, however, a new procedure had been introduced that increased the safety of second-trimester abortions performed in outpatient facilities.

Powell also wrote the opinion for the Court in *Maher v. Roe* (1977), the only decision in his tenure to erect an obstacle to access to abortions. In *Maher* he held that a state is not required to fund nontherapeutic abortions even though it pays for childbirth under Medicaid, since the state had not created the indigency that makes it difficult for a poor woman to get an abortion. Legislatures are fully justified in promoting childbirth as an alternative to abortion.

The high-water mark of Powell's fundamental rights jurisprudence came in *Moore v. City of East Cleveland, Ohio* (1977), in which his plurality opinion invalidated a zoning ordinance that had limited occupancy of dwelling units to single families, but had recognized "as a 'family' only a few categories of related individuals" (431 U.S. at 496). The complainant in the case was a woman who had been ordered to remove two grandsons living with her from her home. In designating the categories of relatives who may and may not live together, the ordinance, according to Powell, undertook "intrusive regulation of the family" for which there was no substantial justification. The ordinance did not prevent overcrowding, for example, because larger nuclear families were permitted. The family, through which "we inculcate and pass down many of our most cherished values, moral and cultural" (503–4), includes also the extended family: "Out of choice, necessity, or a sense of family responsibility, it has been common for close relatives to draw together and participate in the duties and the satisfactions of a common home" (504–5). Powell acknowledged that substantive due process "has at times been a treacherous field for the Court. . . . That history counsels caution and restraint. But it does not counsel abandonment" (431 U.S. at 502). In his view, the limits of substantive due process, though not subject to easy line drawing, must be grounded in the lessons of history and the basic values of our society.[27]

Powell finally did draw a bright line, writing for a 5-4 Court in the landmark case of *San Antonio Independent School District v. Rodriguez* (1973), by refusing to fashion a new fundamental right—beyond the complex of family relations and sexual intimacy—untethered to the Constitution's text, history, or structure. *Rodriguez* is not Powell's most famous opinion—a distinction that belongs to *Regents of the University of California v. Bakke* (1978)—but it was possibly his most important in terms of its influence on the future development of constitutional law. Had the decision gone the other way, the Court might have set off another escalating round of judicial public policy-making.

In this case, the method used to finance most of American public education was challenged. The Texas scheme relied in part on local property taxes, an arrangement common to nearly all the states. The difference in money spent per pupil between the most and least affluent school districts in the San Antonio area, for example, resulted in the substantial discrepancy of $594 against $356 for the 1967–68 school year.

It was argued that the Texas scheme required "strict" judicial scrutiny because it handicapped a "suspect" class, the poor, and impinged on education, urged now as a fundamental right. Powell replied that extraordinary protection from the democratic process was unnecessary: the class of persons affected had suffered no history of purposeful unequal treatment, nor was it politically powerless. The high importance of education, repeatedly recognized by the Court in the desegregation cases, among others, did not in itself qualify education as a fundamental right. "It is not the province of this Court," he announced, "to create substantive constitutional rights in the name of guaranteeing equal protection of the laws" (411 U.S. at 33). The determination depended, rather, on whether the right is "explicitly or implicitly" guaranteed by the Constitution. The close relation education bears to such specified rights as freedom of speech and press and the exercise of the ballot, which require education for their intelligent exercise, is insufficient to designate it as fundamental.

Moreover, Powell argued, the Court had "never presumed to possess either the ability or the authority to guarantee to the citizenry the most *effective* speech or the most *informed* electoral choice" (36). Powell asked the obvious question why education was more important than food or shelter, which, he seemed to suggest, might become the next judicial targets if the Court recognized education as a fundamental right. Federalism demanded a hands-off posture for the judiciary, for "it would be difficult to imagine a case having a greater potential impact on our federal system than the one now before us" (44). To overturn the state's scheme would cause "an unprecedented upheaval in public education" (56). Powell did not wrestle with the knotty problem of why the "liberty" of due process and abortion have a closer nexus than the First Amendment and education.

Powell's high regard for education once did get the better of his solicitude for federalism, when a state's policy denied some children an education altogether. In *Plyler v. Doe* (1982), another 5-4 decision, Powell again provided a decisive vote, this time to strike down a Texas policy denying free public education to alien children not legally in the United States. Powell's *Plyler* concurrence uncharacteristically reads like a social tract rather than a legal document. He sharply criticized Congress's failure to provide leadership in controlling illegal immigration and sympathized with states like Texas, which bore the brunt of its attendant problems. The children, however, should not be punished for their parents' actions; he could find no sufficient state interest to justify the denial. Indeed, "it can hardly be argued rationally that anyone benefits from the creation . . . of a subclass of illiterate persons many of whom will remain in the state" (457 U.S. at 241).

Racial Justice

School Desegregation

The key decision implementing *Brown v. Board of Education I* and *II* (1954 and 1955) was *Swann v. Charlotte-Mecklenburg Board of Education*, decided with surprising unanimity in 1971. In *Swann*, the Burger Court, prior to Powell's arrival, mandated extensive busing to eliminate deliberate racial imbalance in school systems. Despite Powell's opposition as chairman of Richmond's school board to Virginia's policy of "massive resistance" to *Brown*, he had been a gradualist, if not a minimalist, on school desegregation.[28] His primary objective was to keep the schools open. Powell was convinced that a strong judicial role in pushing maximum integration might prove self-defeating, leaving profound social costs in its wake. In these beliefs he never wavered, helping to shatter the consensus the Court had previously achieved in desegregation cases.

Keyes v. School District No. 1, Denver (1973), the first important school desegregation case after Powell's appointment, was also the first to reach the Court from a large nonsouthern city. Powell's separate opinion was mainly a belated dissent from *Swann*, a criticism he essentially reiterated in succeeding cases: "To the extent that *Swann* may be thought to require large-scale or long-distance transportation of students in our metropolitan school districts, I record my profound misgivings. Nothing in our Constitution commands or encourages any such court-compelled disruption of public education" (413 U.S. at 238).

In Denver, as in other northern cities with substantial minority populations, no legal action had mandated segregation, but predominantly minority schools existed in areas of the city. "There is segregation in the schools of many of these cities fully as pervasive as that in southern cities prior to the desegregation decrees of the past decade and a half," Powell declared. In a retort to northern hypocrisy, he added that, while substantial progress toward desegregation had been achieved in the South, "[n]o comparable progress has been made in many nonsouthern cities with large minority populations primarily because of the *de facto / de jure* distinction nurtured by the courts and accepted complacently by many of the same voices which denounced the evils of segregated schools in the South." The Court must abandon this distinction "and formulate constitutional principles of national rather than merely regional application" (413 U.S. at 218–19).

As Powell saw it, the Court had placed itself in this bind by transforming *Brown*'s requirement of "state neutrality" (413 U.S. at 220) into an affirmative duty to desegregate school systems in *Green v. County Board of Education of New Kent County, Va.* (1968), a case that had involved a rural county with 1,300 pupils. In *Swann*, however, the affirmative duty doctrine was applied to a major city, Charlotte, North Carolina, which had large areas of residential segregation. The conditions in *Swann* duplicated those "in *all* the biracial metropolitan areas of our country. . . . [S]egregated residential and migratory patterns . . . [are] a national, not a southern, phenomenon. And it is largely unrelated to whether a particular State had or did not have segregative school laws" (222–23). Residential patterns are beyond the ability of school boards to change, determined as they are by economic factors and voluntary preferences.

Transportation, argued Powell, has but a limited use in the desegregation process: it may be required only to the extent necessary to redress segregation caused by deliberate official policy. The goal must be a desegregated school *system* — to be achieved through integrated faculties and administration; equality of facilities, curriculum and instruction; attendance zones drawn to promote desegregation; and the opening of new schools and the closing of old ones with desegregation in mind. But not *"every school* must in fact be an integrated unit"* (413 U.S. at 227). Moreover, preoccupation with busing may well result in costs that outweigh the benefits since busing not only imposes severe economic burdens on school systems but also destroys the sense of community fostered by the neighborhood school; the child's welfare suffers through "an impairment of his liberty and his privacy" (247–48).

In later cases Powell emphasized what he had touched on more briefly in *Keyes* — the danger of resegregation through an exodus to private schools and flight to the suburbs. In *Estes v. Dallas NAACP* (1980), he warned, "A desegregation plan without community support . . . accelerates the exodus to the suburbs of families able to move," and the children who remain "are denied the opportunity to be part of an ethnically diverse student body" (444 U.S. at 450). The public schools then become the preserve of those who cannot afford, or do not care for, better education. Resentment against judicial interference divides communities and exacerbates rather than soothes racial tensions.[29]

In one of his angriest statements, Powell accused the Court, as well as the lower judiciary, of playing fast and loose with the evidence in desegregation cases in order to achieve social ends. The Court, he charged in *Columbus Board of Education v. Penick* (1979), "indulge[d] the courts below in their stringing together a chain of 'presumptions,' not one of which is close enough to reality to be reasonable," in upholding a finding that the lack of integration in a high percentage of the schools in Columbus and Dayton, Ohio, was caused by local school boards. This conclusion was "tainted on its face," unsupported by evidence, and seemingly "incredible," yet was accepted by the Court—to lay the groundwork for a requirement of "racial balance in each and every school" (443 U.S. at 480).

Affirmative Action

That Powell's views on busing would allow him to play a central role in placing the Court's imprimatur on compensatory affirmative action might seem highly improbable. Yet Powell's centrist opinion in *Regents v. Bakke* (1978), a case in which he mediated between two polarized groups of justices, paved the way for judicial approval of rigorous forms of affirmative action.[30]

Bakke concerned a special admissions program at the Davis medical school of the University of California in which 16 out of 100 places were annually reserved for minority applicants, who were also able to apply for admission on the same basis as others through the regular program. Disadvantaged whites in the applicant pool were not allowed to participate in the special program. Four justices (Brennan, White, Marshall, and Blackmun) would have upheld the special program on both constitutional and statutory grounds. Four others (Burger, Stewart, Rehnquist, and Stevens) refused to reach the equal protection issue but voted to nullify the program as violating Title VI of the Civil Rights Act of 1964. Powell's judgment for the Court struck down the Davis program but left the way open for race to be considered a plus in admissions decisions.

Powell rejected the premise that strict judicial scrutiny was not triggered when whites claimed discrimination. "The guarantee of equal protection cannot mean one thing when applied to one individual and something else when applied to a person of another color. If both are not accorded the same protection, then it is not equal," regardless of the fact that white males like Bakke are not members of a "discrete and insular" minority (438 U.S. at 289–90).[31] He argued that in the years since the adoption of the Fourteenth Amendment an important demographic change had taken place. As a result of waves of immigration, the United States had come to contain a multitude of minorities, each of which had been discriminated against at some time in our history, and each of which was entitled to the full protection of the Constitution. This pluralism constituted the heart of Powell's rationale:

> The concepts of "majority" and "minority" necessarily reflect temporary arrangements and political judgments. . . . [T]he white "majority" itself is composed of various minority groups, most of which can lay claim to a history of prior discrimination. . . . Not all of these groups can receive preferential treatment . . . for then the only "majority" left would be a new minority of white Anglo-Saxon Protestants. There is no principled basis for deciding which groups would merit "heightened judicial solicitude" and which would not. . . . The kind of variable sociological and political analysis necessary to produce such rankings simply does not lie within the judicial competence. (438 U.S. at 295–97)

Powell did recognize a compelling state interest in encouraging a diverse student body, but he asserted that the remedy—a rigid quota—was not narrowly drawn. He went beyond the parameters of the case, though, to write what was in effect an advisory opinion, commending the affirmative action program at Harvard College, which considered race a positive, though not the exclusive, factor in admissions.

Just two years later, a congressional act mandating that at least 10 percent of federal funds appropriated for local work projects be set aside for minority businesses withstood the Court's strict scrutiny in *Fullilove v. Klutznick* (1980). Powell concurred because, by 1977, when Congress had enacted the law, it had known that "other remedies had failed to ameliorate the effects of racial discrimination in the construction industry" (448 U.S. at 511). The mandated percentage was not inappropriate since minorities constituted 17 percent of the national population, and the measure was designed to remain in effect no longer than the discrimination it was intended to remedy. The impact on innocent third parties would be marginal and widely dispersed. As Powell put it later in *Wygant v. Jackson Board of Education* (1986): "We have recognized . . . that in order to remedy the effects of prior discrimination, it may be necessary to take race into account. As part of this Nation's dedication to eradicating racial discrimination, innocent persons may be called upon to bear some of the burden of the remedy" (476 U.S. at 280–81).

Powell wrote the plurality opinion in *Wygant,* holding that retaining minority teachers with less seniority than nonminority teachers in order to preserve an affirmative action hiring policy violated equal protection. Layoffs, he explained, are different from hiring goals, for which "the burden to be borne by innocent individuals is diffused to a considerable extent among society generally. Though hiring goals may burden some innocent individuals, they simply do not impose the same kind of injury that layoffs impose" (476 U.S. at 282).

The New Equal Protection

Gender

Powell helped shape the Court's position on gender equality with his concurring opinion in *Frontiero v. Richardson* (1973), in which he refused to label gender classifications as "suspect" and subject to strict judicial scrutiny. He favored, instead, traditional "rational basis" review but with "a sharper focus" (*Craig v. Boren,* 1976, 429 U.S. at 210–11n). In *Caban v. Mohammed* (1979), he wrote for a narrowly divided Court to strike down a New York statute that permitted an unwed mother, but not an unwed father, to withhold consent to their child's adoption. Powell reasoned that while mothers are usually closer than fathers to their offspring, the relationship of father to child might become closer as the child grows older and thereby become comparable to that of the mother, as the facts in the case demonstrated.

Powell, invariably attentive to the problems of the educational system, filed his most interesting opinion on gender in a case involving a university. The Court struck down, as violating equal protection, a state nursing school's policy of excluding males from the student body in *Mississippi University for Women v. Hogan* (1982). Powell dissented, pointing out that the male respondent in this case had no lack of educational opportunities in nursing schools located elsewhere in the state. This was not a case of "sexual stereotyping" but of providing "an *additional* choice for women" (458 U.S. at 736). Studies showed that single-sex higher educational institutions offered clear benefits over coeducational institutions.[32]

Alienage

While alienage has been treated as a suspect classification subject to strict scrutiny since *Graham v. Richardson* (1971), an exception is made when aliens are excluded from government positions requiring undivided loyalty to the state. In those circumstances, the traditional rationality standard continues to apply. Speaking for the Court in *In re Griffiths* (1973), Powell ordered admission to the bar of an alien who qualified in all respects other than citizenship. The lawyer is not an official of government or "so close to the core of the political process as to make him a formulator of government policy" (413 U.S. at 729).

In *Ambach v. Norwick* (1979), however—another Court opinion on his favorite subject, education—Powell held that a state may forbid aliens from serving as public schoolteachers if they had no intention of becoming citizens. His rationale was that the public schools prepared students for the tasks of citizenship and the preservation of societal values. By serving as role models through their close daily contact with students, teachers played a central part in this process. In the same vein, he dissented from *Nyquist v. Mauclet* (1977), a decision holding that a state may not deny financial assistance to college students who are aliens and do not intend to apply for citizenship. It was perfectly proper, he believed, to encourage allegiance to the United States by offering the incentive of financial aid only to those who signified a desire to become citizens.

Reapportionment

In reapportionment cases, Powell was opposed to rules requiring perfect equality of population size in voting districts. "I would not have thought," wrote Powell in 1973 in *White v. Weiser,* "that the Constitution—a vital and living charter after nearly two centuries because of the wise flexibility of its key provisions—could be read to require a rule of mathematical exactitude in legislative reapportionment" (412 U.S. at 798). Thus in *Connor v. Finch* (1977), he alone dissented from the holding that a deviation of 16.5 percent in state senate districts was unconstitutional. And in *Karcher v. Daggett* (1983), he entered a sharp dissent from a decision overturning a New Jersey plan for congressional districts that would have a maximum population deviation of less than 1 percent between the most and least populous districts; alternative plans with smaller deviations were available, said the Court. However, Powell prevailed in *Brown v. Thomson* (1983), in which he ruled for a 5-4 majority that a state that had always followed a policy of ensuring at least one representative to each county, no matter how small its population, may continue to do so.

With respect to gerrymandering, though, Powell moved beyond the Court majority. In *Karcher* he warned that "an uncompromising emphasis on numerical equality would serve to encourage and legitimate even the most outrageously partisan gerrymandering" (462 U.S. at 785). Powell called attention to the irrational shape of congressional districts in New Jersey and announced that he was prepared to entertain a future constitutional challenge to gerrymandering.

The Court finally addressed gerrymandering as a constitutional issue in *Davis v. Bandemer* (1986). Powell was one of only two justices (Stevens joined him in dissent) to refuse to uphold a blatant gerrymander of Indiana state legislative districts by Republicans in 1981. Three justices (Burger, Rehnquist, and O'Connor) held that gerrymandering raised a nonjusticiable "political" question. The plurality opinion by Justice White, upholding the gerrymander, ruled that the Court should intervene only when there has been a finding that vote dilution is likely to bring disproportionately partisan results over a series of elections and not merely in one, and that the vote dilution might distort the strength of one party statewide as well as in the gerrymandered districts.

Powell's dissent, one of his most vigorous, hammered heavily on the facts. Redistricting in Indiana was carried out by Republicans, with no Democratic party representation, and in secret. Despite promises of public hearings, none were held. The plan was revealed only two days before the end of the legislative session and was quickly adopted on a party-line vote. "The information fed into the computer," continued Powell, "primarily concerned the political complexion of the State's precincts" (478 U.S. at 162) and was designed to assure maximum political advantage for Republicans. The results were predictable: despite a clear majority at the polls in 1982, the Democrats came out on the short end of the tally, electing only 43 members as against 57 Republicans. Democratic votes were "stacked" into districts where their strength was preponderant or else were fragmented among other districts to reduce Democratic voting strength.

Powell recalled that, in *Reynolds v. Sims* (1964), the Court had emphasized the need for compact districts to alleviate the problem of gerrymandering. At that time, equal voting had been regarded as a means to prevent gerrymanders; now computer technology had made it possible to draw districts that were of equal population, yet design them to deliberately discriminate against distinct groups of voters. The Court, according to Powell, should stop avoiding a clear-cut decision in this thickest of political thickets. It was feasible to formulate standards to frustrate gerrymandering, in his view. The shape of voting districts and maintenance of established boundaries should count most heavily, but relevant also were the procedures used in adopting the reapportionment law. Applying these standards, the Indiana reapportionment scheme should have been held unconstitutional.

Powell essentially argued that the Court, in its pursuit of population equality, had lost sight of the primary goal of reapportionment—achieving political equality. Of what value is mandating population equality of districts if the Court allows other practices that blatantly perpetuate political inequality? For Powell, an electoral system that, despite equality of population, is slanted in favor of one political party no more meets the standard of equal protection than one weighted toward that party by districts of unequal population.

Liberty and Property

As we have seen with regard to the First Amendment, Powell did not subordinate property rights to other rights. In fact, he was quite receptive to constitutional property claims. His dissenting opinions in two Fifth Amendment just compensation cases make the point. In the first, *United States v. Fuller* (1973), Powell argued that compensation to be paid the owner of condemned private land should include the land's value as enhanced by its proximity to government property. In the second case, *Dames & Moore v. Regan* (1981), in which the Court held that a presidential order suspending all claims against the Iranian government was authorized by act of Congress and that it did not constitute a "taking" under the just compensation clause. Powell entered a solo dissent on the labor point: the government should pay just compensation for takings of private property when it "furthers the Nation's foreign policy goals by using as 'bargaining chips' claims lawfully held by a relatively few persons" (453 U.S. at 691).

With regard to procedural rights arising from property and liberty interests, Powell took a flexible balancing position, retreating from *Goldberg v. Kelly*'s (1970) requirement of a hearing prior to termination of welfare benefits. *Arnett v. Kennedy* (1974) concerned a federal employee who was dismissed for charging his superior with attempted bribery. Balancing the government's interest in efficiency against the employee's interest in his continued employment, Powell, in concurrence, found the government's interest more substantial, making a pre-termination hearing unnecessary. If the employee prevailed in his post-termination proceedings, he would be reinstated with back pay. While even a temporary interruption of income can have serious consequences, the interruption in this type of case was likely to be less drastic than in *Goldberg* because the employee might have independent resources or might be able to obtain a position in the private sector.

Similarly, in *Mathews v. Eldridge* (1976), Powell, this time writing for the Court, held that recipients of social security disability benefits need not be given an evidentiary hearing prior to termination of their benefits. The review process prior to termination was thorough and, also, the need of a social security recipient was likely to be less than that of a welfare recipient. Powell's opinion in *Mathews*, besides displacing the *Goldberg v. Kelly* approach to government benefits, established a balancing approach to procedural due process that has become the established guide in this area of constitutional jurisprudence. Powell wrote that procedural due process decisions required the application of a three-factor cost-benefit analysis weighing (1) "the private interest"; (2) "the risk of an erroneous deprivation of such interest. . . , and the probable value, if any, of additional or substitute procedural safeguards"; and (3) "the government's interest" (424 U.S. at 334). Powell's balancing approach has since been applied to all procedural due process questions.

Powell's balance sometimes tilted in favor of the individual. *Memphis Light v. Craft* (1978) concerned a municipal utility that proposed to terminate gas and electric service for nonpayment in a billing dispute. No procedure was provided for the customer to contest the proposed termination in advance. Powell ruled that a post-termination procedure was not enough because "the cessation of essential services for any appreciable time works a uniquely final deprivation" (436 U.S. at 20).

If *Mathews* was Powell's most influential procedural due process opinion, his dissent in *Goss v. Lopez* (1975) was his most interesting. As in his other opinions relating to schools, *Goss* drew on Powell's experience in education and reflected his values. The 5-4 majority invalidated an Ohio statute permitting up to ten days' suspension for a student without notice or hearing. Powell argued, however, that, while Ohio had elected to provide a free education, it was not an unqualified right; the power to suspend students was part and parcel of the statutory scheme. In any event, brief suspensions were not a constitutional matter since they would not affect students' overall performance or harm their reputation.

Discipline, Powell maintained in *Goss,* is an integral part of the educational system. It provides the student with "an early understanding of the relevance to the social compact of respect for the rights of others." Indeed, it is "a disservice" to immature students not to discipline them. "One who does not comprehend the meaning and necessity of discipline is handicapped not merely in his education but throughout his subsequent life. In an age when the home and church play a diminishing role in shaping the character and value judgments of the young, a heavier responsibility falls upon the schools" (419 U.S. at 593). The Court misunderstood the teacher-pupil relationship; it is "one in which the teacher must occupy many roles—educator, advisor, friend, and, at times, parent-substitute." That relationship becomes adversarial only "with respect to the chronically disruptive or insubordinate pupil whom the teacher must be free to discipline without frustrating formalities" (594).

Commerce and Federalism

In general, Powell voted to invest the federal government with broad power over national and foreign commerce, but allowed for important exceptions when he believed that congressional action imperiled principles of federalism. For example, in *Kassel v. Consolidated Freightways Corp.* (1981), he wrote for the Court, striking down an Iowa limitation on truck length as a burden on interstate commerce. He rejected the state's justification of safety as an illusion. In *Armco v. Hardesty* (1984), his opinion voided a state tax on the sale of tangible property as burdening interstate commerce because it exempted local manufacturers. He also voted, dissenting in *Moorman Co. v. Bair* (1978), to nullify Iowa's tax on interstate business income, which was based on a single-factor sales formula, arguing that, since nearly all other states utilized a multi-factor formula, an out-of-state corporation selling in Iowa would have higher total tax bills than local corporations. Similarly, he dissented from the Court's ruling in *Container Corp. v. Franchise Tax Board* (1983), which upheld a California franchise tax on domestic companies with foreign subsidiaries based on worldwide income. In view of the declared preference of the federal government for the international formula, which taxes multinational corporations on only their domestic operations, and the danger of foreign retaliation, the law was an impermissible "intrusion on national policy in foreign affairs" (463 U.S. at 205).

Powell inveighed against tests of "direct" and "indirect" burdens, in whatever guise, as the proper means to determine the validity of state regulations challenged on commerce grounds; instead, he concentrated on what he called "economic-reality" analysis. Thus he voted to uphold a state business tax imposed on goods imported from abroad but destined for another state (*Department of Revenue of State of Washington v. Association of Washington Stevedoring Companies,* 1978). The tax was justified to compensate the taxing state for providing police and fire protection for the stevedoring companies.

Two of Powell's most forceful attempts to limit state authority over commerce, each time in dissent, came in *Silkwood v. Kerr-McGee Corp.* (1984) and *Reeves, Inc. v. State* (1980). In *Silkwood,* the Court upheld a state jury award of ten million dollars in punitive damages against a nuclear facility for injuries caused by the escape of plutonium, despite the federal Nuclear Regulatory Commission's having found no serious violation of its safety requirements. Powell did not challenge the award of compensation to the plaintiff but would have held that punitive damages—designed to punish and deter bad conduct—were regulatory in nature and therefore subject only to federal action in such a case. In *Reeves,* he viewed South Dakota's decision to restrict the sale of scarce, state-produced cement to its own residents as forbidden "economic protectionism." The state could, of course, withhold the interstate sale of any cement it needed for public projects, but it had no justification for favoring its private in-state customers in its sales. Though the cement plant was state-owned, it did not serve an integral governmental function; it was a commercial enterprise through which the state "may not evade the constitutional policy against economic Balkanization." A state commercial enterprise should not be treated like a private producer, free to decide where it will sell and to whom, because it "frequently will respond to market conditions on the basis of political rather than economic concerns" (447 U.S. at 450).

Powell staked out his position for exceptions to the congressional commerce power based on federalism in a trio of dissents filed over a three-year period during the latter part of his tenure. In *Federal Energy Regulatory Commission v. Mississippi* (1982), he dissented from a decision upholding an act of Congress that imposed federal procedures on state regulatory commissions monitoring gas and electric public utilities. The fact that a state's regulatory powers can be preempted by the federal government and exercised by it alone did not mean that Congress could dictate to the states how they were to exercise those powers when they had not been preempted.

The same line of reasoning is evident in Powell's dissent in *EEOC v. Wyoming* (1983). Taking issue with the Court's ruling that state and local government agencies are subject to a federal age discrimination law, Powell maintained that foremost among the framers' objectives was the creation of "a National government within a federal system." The power to regulate commerce was only one among many others in Article 1, Section 8, and "was given no place of particular prominence" (460 U.S. at 268). Powell thought it "incredible" that even a few years ago the Court would have considered a state's requirement that its game wardens retire at age 65 rather than 70 as affecting commerce.

The final case of the trio, *Garcia v. San Antonio Metropolitan Transit Authority* (1985), elicited one of Powell's most impassioned dissents. There the Court upheld federal minimum wage and overtime requirements for state and local government employees, overturning its decade-old decision to the contrary in *National League of Cities v. Usery* (1976). The Court, protested Powell, would erode respect for its authority by the swift overruling; what was worse, it was continually reducing the Tenth Amendment to "meaningless rhetoric" by upholding federal statutes whenever Congress justified its action by reference to the commerce clause.

Powell was particularly hostile to the majority's thesis that, because state interests were well represented in Congress, judicial review should not be applied to political decisions affecting them. He charged the Court—"an unelected majority of five Justices"— with rejecting "almost 200 years of the understanding of the constitutional status of federalism" (469 U.S. at 560). According to Powell, the idea that state influence within the structure of the federal government could be relied upon to protect state interests originated with Professor Herbert Wechsler, whose 1954 article on federalism was written at a time when Wechsler could assert, "National action has . . . always been regarded as exceptional in our polity."[33] Current reality, of course, as manifested in the proliferation of national legislation, has undermined Wechsler's thesis; moreover, the weakened condition of political parties locally and the growth of the national media have tended to make Congress responsive more to national interests than state interests.

The states' role in the electoral process is no guarantee of states' rights since members of Congress are, after all, members of the federal government. Nor can the president realistically be viewed as a guardian of state interests. Moreover, federal legislation, Powell pointed out, is drafted by congressional committees; even conscientious legislators cannot be fully familiar with the statutes they enact. Finally, the drafting of implementing regulations, which are often more important than statutory texts, is left to agencies whose administrators may have little or no knowledge of local concerns and are bound to be less responsive to them than state legislators.

Powell regarded the Tenth Amendment not as a truism, but as "an essential part of the Bill of Rights" (469 U.S. at 565), designed to ensure that state prerogatives would not be usurped by the national government. As a positive affirmation of state power, the amendment, at a minimum, erects a stop sign that should alert the Court to take necessary steps to preserve federalism against national aggrandizement while making due allowances for modern conditions. Congress must not be allowed to use the commerce clause as a subterfuge to nibble away at the periphery, if not the core, of state authority.[34]

The Role of the Court

Powell's concern with maintaining the role of state and local units of government as viable decision-makers in the American constitutional scheme was responsible for his continual and partially successful efforts to limit access to federal courts by containing or contracting the scope of standing, habeas corpus, and liability under 42 U.S.C. §1983. His 5-4 majority opinion in *Warth v. Seldin* (1975) is instructive. In this case, Powell rejected a claim that a suburban town's zoning ordinance violated the rights of low-income persons by effectively excluding them from living in the town. Powell maintained that no "causal relationship" between the zoning practices and the alleged injury had been proved. The low-income plaintiffs had not demonstrated that their inability to find housing in the town was related to the restrictive zoning since none had ever applied for a variance. Nor was there any indication that efforts to build low-cost apartments by those plaintiffs who were developers would have provided the poor with affordable housing. Justice Brennan, dissenting, commented acidly that the decision was motivated "by an indefensible hostility to the claim on the merits" (422 U.S. at 520). But, as Powell explained in *United States v. Richardson* (1974), relaxed requirements of standing "significantly alter the allocation of power at the national level, with a shift away from a democratic form of government." As it was, the Warren Court years had witnessed a substantial lowering of the standing barrier, but the requirement of a "particularized injury" had not yet been eroded, and "we should refuse to go the last mile" (418 U.S. at 188, 194–95).

Powell opposed the Court's eagerness to review state court criminal convictions under federal habeas corpus jurisdiction (28 U.S.C. §2254). The justices, he thought, writing in *Rose v. Mitchell* (1979), had "come to accept review by federal district courts of state-court judgments in criminal cases as the rule, rather than the exception that it should be," and they were moving "toward the creation of a dual system of review under which a defendant . . . having exhausted his remedies in the state system, repeats the process through the federal system. The extent to which this duplication already exists in this country is without parallel in any other system of justice in the world" (443 U.S. at 581). Habeas corpus review was freely granted "even in cases in which the issue presented has little or nothing to do with innocence of the accused," he complained in *Blackledge v. Allison* (1977). "The substantial societal interest in both innocence and finality of judgments is subordinated in many instances to formalisms" (431 U.S. at 84). Claims should be entertained "only with restraint," he asserted in *Rose v. Mitchell* (1979), since, "contrary to principles of federalism, a lower federal court is asked to review not only a state trial court's judgment, but almost invariably the judgment of the highest court of the State as well" (443 U.S. at 579).

These considerations were equally valid, Powell argued in *Maine v. Thiboutot* (1980), with regard to Section 1983, which created a right to recovery in tort by persons deprived of constitutional rights. Originally enacted as part of the Civil Rights Act of 1871, it was now construed as conferring "upon the courts unprecedented authority to oversee state actions that have little or nothing to do with the individual rights defined and enforced by the civil rights legislation of the Reconstruction Era" (488 U.S. at 25).

One important tool for limiting free-wheeling judicial decision making is adherence to precedent, on which Powell repeatedly insisted. When the Court was asked to overrule the *Roe* abortion decision in *City of Akron* (1983), Powell bristled, "[A]rguments continue to be made . . . that we erred in interpreting the Constitution. Nonetheless, the doctrine of *stare decisis*, while perhaps never entirely persuasive on a constitutional question, is a doctrine that demands respect in a society governed by the rule of law. We respect it today, and reaffirm *Roe v. Wade*" (462 U.S. at 419–20). It is curious that Powell should concede that the doctrine was "never entirely persuasive" and yet equate its observance with adherence to the rule of law, especially since *Roe* was of recent vintage — a decision repeatedly supported during the decade of its existence, but by essentially the same bench of justices.

When he felt compelled to overrule a precedent, Powell could be more flexible in both language and result. The 1961 holding in *Monroe v. Pape* that local governments are not subject to liability under Section 1983 was overruled in 1978 in *Monell v. New York City Department of Social Services*. Powell concurred because stare decisis is "a cautionary principle," which "must give way to countervailing considerations in appropriate circumstances" (436 U.S. at 708). *Monroe,* he pointed out, had inconsistently exempted municipalities from liability even as it allowed suits against their employees when they acted pursuant to express authorization. Moreover, the Court's thorough review of legislative history showed that the *Monroe* opinion had relied on weak historical evidence.

Judge and Court

Powell's elucidation of judicial restraint was, on the surface, quite conventional, in the mold of Frankfurter and Harlan, and not to be confused with Black's idea of constitutional interpretation rooted in literal language and original intent. Powell believed that an eighteenth-century document required a twentieth-century gloss to be serviceable in the contemporary world. In a 1979 interview, he described the Constitution "as a sort of living political organism," which the Court's interpretations have kept "abreast of the vast changes that occur in the life of our nation."[35] Even so, the judiciary should beware of wielding a "grand oversight" over the elected branches. The Court's experience during the New Deal, when its abuse of power generated efforts to curb its authority, should serve as a warning. By limiting its own role, Powell explained in *United States v. Richardson,* the judiciary maintains "public esteem" and permits "peaceful coexistence" between democratic rule and the "countermajoritarian implications of judicial review" (418 U.S. at 192).

But Powell's was only a restraint relative to the unabashed activism of such colleagues as Justice Brennan. It seemed ingenuous of Powell to claim that in *Roe* "the Court expressed no view as to the wisdom or morality of abortions. We simply made a constitutional judgment."[36] Is it reasonable to suppose that the Court carefully constructed a new, unstated constitutional right of almost unrestricted access to a procedure it may have considered immoral?[37] More candid was Powell's explanation that "the concept of liberty was the underlying principle of the abortion case—the liberty to make certain highly personal decisions that are terribly important to people."[38] His votes on issues of substantive due process were exceptionally activist by Frankfurter's standards.

In truth, Powell's jurisprudence cannot be easily categorized. His claim to be a practitioner of judicial restraint is confirmed by such landmark decisions as *Rodriguez* and *Gregg*, but belied by his votes in cases involving substantive due process, the establishment clause, and affirmative action. His colleague, Justice O'Connor, paying tribute to Powell upon his retirement in 1987, noted that "at times . . . he may have been willing to sacrifice a little consistency in legal theory in order to reach for justice in a particular case."[39]

Professor Blasi has persuasively suggested that for the "pivotal justices" of the Burger Court, such as Powell, judicial activism became "a centrist philosophy . . . essentially pragmatic in nature, lacking a central theme or agenda."[40] An agenda was certainly one thing Powell disdained. Branding as "nonsense" the charge that the Burger Court was "rudderless," that it lacked a principled thematic jurisprudence, Powell asserted that the national interest requires judges to be independent-minded rather than bloc-oriented and to avoid being "dominated by a willful chief justice."[41] For Powell, a careful balancing of competing constitutional interests that aimed to preserve as much of all of them with the least sacrifice of any, was, despite its ad hoc quality, preferable to a jurisprudence of grand design and consistent results.

In Powell's hands, balancing was elevated to a highly nuanced fine art, as though constitutional law were a branch of common law. The Constitution almost appeared secondary to the common-sense balance that was struck: the balance seemed to be imposed on, rather than by, the Constitution. His opinions did not embody the classic posture of restraint—that the polity has made a decision that we as judges are unable to disturb. Rather, his opinions personalized the judgment: all things considered, the people have made the right decision, the school board has struck the right balance; therefore we must leave it alone.

That Powell was a pivotal member of the Burger Court is beyond question. Statistically, indeed, he was its vital center, justifying Professor Schwartz's assessment of him as "probably the most powerful judge of his time."[42] During the 1971–85 terms, he uniformly ranked at the top of the scale for majority participation (usually around 90 percent) and at the bottom for dissenting votes (Table 1.7).[43] Only Chief Justice Burger wrote fewer dissents than Powell over the same period (100 to Powell's 156), but Burger cast far more dissenting votes. A comparison of Powell's rate of dissent (in cases decided with full opinion) with that of the five other justices who served during that period is illustrative (see Table 10.1).

The four justices who served during only part of this period also averaged considerably more dissents per term: O'Connor, 20.8; Stewart, 25.0; Stevens, 36.0; and Douglas, a stratospheric 64.0. (Powell did, however, write more concurrences than most justices, ranking at the head of the list during some of the Court's terms [see Table 1.6].)

The justices with whom Powell most often agreed were Burger, Rehnquist, White, Stewart, and O'Connor (not necessarily in that order). He agreed least often with Brennan, Marshall, Stevens, and Douglas. His rate of agreement with Blackmun, originally high, decreased sharply as the latter became steadily more activist.

Does Powell's performance indicate that he was a leader or a follower, as Professor Mason once asked?[44] Perhaps a better way of framing the question would be not to ask whether Powell was

TABLE 10.1
Dissent Voting in Cases with Full Opinion, 1971–85 Terms

	Total Dissenting Votes	Average per Term
Powell	238	15.9
White	285	19.0
Burger	318	21.2
Blackmun	336	22.4
Marshall	720	48.0
Brennan	721	48.1

Source: Derived from Table 1.7.

a leader—a well-nigh impossible role on a bench of nine strong-willed and capable individuals—but to ask whether he was a consensus builder. We do not know for sure,[45] but the data cited above are highly suggestive, together with the fact that he was the justice most often in the majority in close 5-4 decisions throughout the 1980s.[46]

By temperament and heritage, Powell was very much a traditionalist. State and local authority, far more than national power, epitomized for him the ideals of democracy and self-government. He deplored the weakening influence of home, religion, and school. Alexander Solzhenitsyn he considered "perhaps the wisest philosopher and social historian of this century," and he stressed Solzhenitsyn's "melancholy" view that material pursuits have undermined the national will and respect for institutions and that rights have displaced obligations.[47]

Powell brought to the bench neither the literary style and eloquence of Holmes or Cardozo, nor the intellectual brilliance and historical ability of Frankfurter or Harlan.[48] Despite his lack of judicial experience, he quickly shaped a position on the Constitution that, in its basic outlines, remained virtually unchanged over his tenure. The legion of his admirers grew substantially throughout his years of service. A poll of legal scholars and practitioners, conducted in 1978, voted him "the best justice."[49] Whether history will place him in the select class of judges that includes Learned Hand and the second Harlan, where Professor Gunther surprisingly believes Powell belongs,[50] or a rung or two below, is something upon which one can only speculate. This much seems clear: Powell will continue to be viewed as a dedicated, compassionate, and pragmatic justice who left a deep imprint on the constitutional law of the Burger Court.

NOTES

My colleagues Henry J. Abraham, Felicia Deyrup, Roger McDonald, Eric Orts, and Marvin Schick have earned my gratitude for their helpful suggestions on an earlier draft of this chapter. From inception to completion, editors Steve Halpern and Chuck Lamb supplied gentle encouragement and superb scholarly guidance. I have also benefited from the assistance of Carolyn Weinstock Bootin, Ginnie Daugherty, and Kim Geiger, graduate students at the New School for Social Research.

1. Henry J. Abraham, *Justices and Presidents: A Political History of Appoint-*

ments to the Supreme Court, 2d ed. (New York: Oxford University Press, 1985), p. 309.

2. Ibid., p. 307.

3. J. Harvie Wilkinson III, *Serving Justice: A Supreme Court Clerk's View* (New York: Charterhouse, 1974), p. 70.

4. Abraham, *Justices and Presidents,* p. 308.

5. See, for example, Powell, "President's Annual Address," *American Bar Association Journal* 51 (1965): 821.

6. Dallin H. Oaks, "Tribute to Lewis F. Powell, Jr.," *Virginia Law Review* 68 (1982): 161, 162.

7. James F. Simon, *In His Own Image: The Supreme Court in Richard Nixon's America* (New York: McKay, 1973), pp. 246–47.

8. *Congressional Record,* Dec. 4, 1971, p. 44,764.

9. Leonard W. Levy, *Against the Law: The Nixon Court and Criminal Justice* (New York: Harper and Row, 1974), p. 38.

10. Quoted in Liva Baker, *Miranda: Crime, Law and Politics* (New York: Atheneum, 1983), p. 320.

11. Powell, "Address," *Nebraska Law Review* 44 (1965): 355, 356.

12. Powell, "An Urgent Need: More Effective Criminal Justice," *American Bar Association Journal* 51 (1965): 437, 439.

13. Quoted in Wilkinson, *Serving Justice,* p. 100.

14. Powell, "Civil Disobedience: Prelude to Revolution?," *New York State Bar Journal* 40 (1968): 172.

15. Alpheus Thomas Mason, *The Supreme Court from Taft to Burger,* 3d ed. (Baton Rouge: Louisiana State University Press, 1979), pp. 315, 322.

16. This view was dominant in Court opinions between 1950 and 1969. See Jacob W. Landynski, "The Supreme Court's Search for Fourth Amendment Standards: The Warrantless Search," *Connecticut Bar Journal* 45 (1971): 1.

17. Powell's views on the exclusionary rule had prevailed even earlier, in *United States v. Calandra* (1974). Again writing for the Court, he refused to bar a grand jury from questioning a witness on the basis of unlawfully seized evidence, since exclusion at the grand jury level would deter only those rare searches for evidence intended for grand jury use.

18. See the acerbic comments of Levy, *Against the Law,* pp. 174–75, on Powell's use of history in this case. David Fellman, *The Defendant's Rights Today* (Madison: University of Wisconsin Press, 1976), pp. 326ff., presents a fine discussion of *Kastigar* in the context of immunity statutes in general.

19. In *Coker v. Georgia* (1977), Powell held in concurrence that "ordinarily death is disproportionate punishment for the crime of raping an adult woman," especially when there was no "excessive brutality" and the victim did not sustain "serious or lasting injury" (433 U.S. at 601).

20. Powell's opinions on this subject were not always consistent, however. In *Erznoznik v. Jacksonville* (1975), writing for the Court, he struck down an ordinance that prohibited drive-in movie theaters from exhibiting films containing nudity when the screen was visible from the street or other public

place. In contrast, in *Young v. American Mini Theatres, Inc.* (1976) he concurred in the Court's decision, which upheld an anti–skid row ordinance that directed the removal of "adult" movie theaters from their locations. The reconciliation of these opinions requires more than ordinary insight.

21. *First National Bank of Boston v. Bellotti* (1978); *Consolidated Edison Co. of New York v. Public Service Commission of New York* (1980); *Pacific Gas and Electric Co. v. Public Utilities Commission of California* (1986).

22. Powell dissented, in whole or in part, in some relatively insignificant cases: *Wolman v. Walter* (1977), *Jones v. Wolf* (1979), and *Bender v. Williamsport Area School District* (1986).

23. See, for example, *McCollum v. Board of Education* (1948).

24. Richard G. Morgan, "The Establishment Clause and Sectarian Schools," *Supreme Court Review* 1973: 57, 76.

25. See, for example, his majority opinions in two vitally important 1973 establishment cases, *Sloan v. Lemon* and *Committee for Public Education v. Nyquist.* The "great . . . sympathy" quotation is from *Nyquist,* 413 U.S. at 778.

26. David M. O'Brien, *Storm Center: The Supreme Court in American Politics* (New York: Norton, 1986), p. 35.

27. Powell's position on fundamental rights also matched that of the Court when it voted to deny constitutional protection to homosexual relationships in *Bowers v. Hardwick* (1986).

28. Powell, caught in political crossfire, had promised that "every proper effort will be made to minimize the extent of integration when it comes." Raymond Wolters, *The Burden of Brown: Thirty Years of School Desegregation* (Knoxville: University of Tennessee Press, 1984), p. 93.

29. Powell also took a strong stand against federal interference in local voting. Section 5 of the Voting Rights Act of 1965 requires federal preclearance of voting law changes in certain states. Powell, like Black and Harlan before him, condemned it as an "unprecedented requirement of advance review of state or local legislative acts by federal authorities, rendered the more noxious by its selective application to only a few States" (*Georgia v. United States,* 1973, 411 U.S. at 545n).

30. See, for example, *Johnson v. Transportation Agency* (1987).

31. The reference to "discrete and insular" minorities draws on the now-famous footnote 4 of *United States v. Carolene Products Co.* (1938).

32. See also Powell's interesting concurrence in *Grove City College v. Bell* (1984), in which he blasted the "overzealousness" of the federal bureaucracy in enforcing gender discrimination law.

33. Wechsler's article is titled "The Political Safeguards of Federalism: The Role of the States in the Composition and Selection of the National Government," *Columbia Law Review* 54 (1954): 543, 544.

34. The Eleventh Amendment also received a generous interpretation by Powell as a bedrock of federalism in several decisions. For example, in the seminal case of *Pennhurst State School and Hospital v. Halderman* (1984), he refused to sanction a federal suit against a state officer for an alleged violation

of *state* law. Powell, speaking for a 5-4 majority, declared that it would be "difficult to think of a greater intrusion on state authority than when a federal court instructs state officials to conform their conduct to state law" (465 U.S. at 106).

35. Harry M. Clor, "Constitutional Interpretation: An Interview with Justice Lewis Powell," *Kenyon College Alumni Bulletin* (Summer 1979): 14–15.

36. Ibid., p. 16.

37. The untenability of such a notion seems well demonstrated by the *Bowers* decision. See note 27 above.

38. Clor, "Constitutional Interpretation," p. 17.

39. Sandra Day O'Connor, "A Tribute to Lewis F. Powell, Jr.," *Harvard Law Review* 101 (1987): 395–96.

40. Vincent Blasi, "The Rootless Activism of the Burger Court," in Blasi, ed., *The Burger Court: The Counter-Revolution That Wasn't* (New Haven, Conn.: Yale University Press, 1983), pp. 210–11.

41. Powell, "What Really Goes On at the Supreme Court," *American Bar Association Journal* 66 (1980): 721–23.

42. Herman Schwartz, "The Supreme Court, 1988–89: Testing the Conservative Justices," *The Nation*, Oct. 17, 1988, 1.

43. The data in these paragraphs were gathered from the statistical tables in the *Harvard Law Review*'s annual November survey of the Supreme Court for the years comprising Powell's tenure (vols. 86–101, 1972–87), supplemented by the tables in Chapter 1 of this volume. The data were so consistent year after year, that to elaborate further is unnecessary.

44. Mason, *The Supreme Court from Taft to Burger*, p. 300.

45. I have not found the several studies of influence in the Supreme Court to be very helpful in determining Powell's role.

46. The 1981 term was the first for which *Harvard Law Review*'s annual survey of the Supreme Court published data on judicial participation in 5-4 decisions.

47. Powell, "Duty to Serve the Common Good," *Catholic Lawyer* 24 (1979): 295, 298.

48. The corpus of Powell's extrajudicial publications consists of some twenty articles, more than half of them written before his appointment. Most of these pieces appeared in bar journals and are essentially expressions of opinion on legal issues and matters of public concern, often the texts of delivered speeches. Among the more scholarly is "Jury Trial of Crimes," *Washington and Lee Law Review* 23 (1966): 1.

49. Mason, *The Supreme Court from Taft to Burger*, p. 300.

50. Gerald Gunther, "A Tribute to Lewis F. Powell, Jr.," *Harvard Law Review* 101 (1987): 409, 414.

11

JUSTICE WILLIAM H. REHNQUIST: Right-Wing Ideologue or Majoritarian Democrat?

SUE DAVIS

Introduction

Three of Richard Nixon's four appointees to the Supreme Court must surely have disappointed him. Chief Justice Warren Burger was unable to lead the Court effectively; Harry Blackmun's judicial philosophy evolved into a thoughtful, moderate liberalism; and Lewis F. Powell became a moderating force on the Court—the "swing man"—rather than a dependable source of a conservative vote. But William H. Rehnquist proved to be precisely the sort of jurist that Nixon had sought in his quest to reshape the Supreme Court. As an associate justice, Rehnquist wrote 243 opinions for the majority, 66 concurrences, and 237 dissenting opinions (see Table 1.6). He consistently voted with the conservative bloc on the Court (see Table 1.8), and he cast the lowest percentage of votes in favor of civil liberties than any other member of the Burger Court (see Table 1.9).

As a presidential candidate in 1968, Nixon promised that he would fill vacancies on the Court with "strict constructionists," who would strengthen the "peace forces" against the "criminal forces," who would not act as "super legislators," and would "not twist or bend the Constitution in order to perpetuate [their] personal, political, and social views."[1] William Rehnquist seemed to be the incarnation of Richard Nixon's ideal jurist, whom the president expected to construe the Bill of Rights and the due process clause of the Fourteenth Amendment "strictly" to reverse the Warren Court's expansion of protections for criminal defendants and, in general, to favor a more modest role for the Court. The president's expectations were based in part upon Rehnquist's record in the Justice Department, where he served as assistant attorney general for the Office of Legal Counsel from 1969 until 1971. In that position, he supported inherent executive authority to order wiretapping and surveillance without a court order, no-knock entry by the police, preventive detention, abolishing habeas corpus proceedings after trial, and abolishing the exclusionary rule. He also supported the procedures used by the Washington, D.C., police in the 1971 May Day demonstrations, during which the police arrested about 12,000 people and detained them until the demonstration ended.[2]

It was not only Rehnquist's political conservatism that attracted Nixon but also his impressive credentials, reputed integrity, and intellectual ability. Barely two years had passed since the Senate had rejected the nominations of Clement F. Haynsworth and G. Harrold Carswell to fill the vacancy left by Justice Abe Fortas's resignation in 1969. When Justices Hugo Black and John Marshall Harlan retired, Nixon sent a list of six possible nominees—all of whom possessed marginal qualifications—to the American Bar Association's Commitee on Judiciary.[3] By dropping "the Six" and nominating Rehnquist and Powell, Nixon avoided another potential embarrassment for his administration.

The Senate, it appeared, was unwilling to confirm conservative "strict constructionists" who were subject to various allegations of financial improprieties, racism, and mediocrity. But in 1971 the Senate was not ready to reject a nominee of Rehnquist's caliber because of his political views and his judicial philosophy. His nomination aroused serious opposition from civil rights and civil liberties groups, and four members of the Judiciary Committee opposed his confirmation. Nevertheless, the Senate confirmed his nomination by a vote of 68 to 26.

William Rehnquist was born in 1924, grew up in a suburb of Milwaukee, attended school in Ohio for a short time, and served for three years in the Army Air Corps during World War II. He used the GI bill to attend Stanford University, from which he graduated Phi Beta Kappa in political science in 1948 and received his M.A. degree in 1949. He received a second M.A. in government from Harvard University in 1950. In December 1951, after attending two summer sessions, he graduated first in his class from Stanford Law School. Supreme Court Justice Robert H. Jackson

Justice William H. Rehnquist

selected him to serve as his law clerk. Rehnquist served him from February 1952 until June 1953.

Rehnquist is straightforward and outspoken. His willingness, even eagerness, to take an unpopular position was clear as early as 1952 when, as the Court was preparing to hear *Brown v. Board of Education,* he prepared a memorandum for Justice Jackson arguing in favor of upholding *Plessy v. Ferguson.*[4] He continued to be forthright about his political views during the sixteen years that he practiced law in Phoenix, Arizona, a time during which he participated in various political activities and became involved in local controversies, always taking the conservative position. He was actively involved in Barry Goldwater's 1964 presidental campaign. He appeared as a witness before the Phoenix City Council in opposition to a public accommodations ordinance, later allegedly explaining, "I am opposed to all civil rights laws."[5] He publicly opposed efforts to end de facto segregation in Phoenix high schools.[6] As a lawyer for the Republican Party from 1958 through 1966, he participated in a program challenging voters at the polls; he was later accused of intimidating and harassing prospective voters.[7] During his early years as a member of the Burger Court, he established a reputation as a justice who was willing to dissent alone. The presence of a small Lone Ranger doll—a gift from his law clerks—on the mantel in his chambers[8] attests to his position as "a one-man strong right wing."[9] While Justice Powell voted with the majority more than any other member of the Court, Brennan and Marshall were the only justices who cast more dissenting votes than Rehnquist every year from the 1972 term of the Court through the concluding term of the Burger Court.[10]

Rehnquist also has an exceptional mind. A professor at Stanford Law School recalled, "He has remained in my mind as one of the most impressive students I have had in some twenty-two years of teaching."[11] Even those who vehemently disagree with him concede that his judicial opinions invariably are clearly and logically reasoned. Henry J. Abraham praised one of Rehnquist's opinions as "passionate, eminently a priori logical, dramatic, sarcastic, [and] powerful."[12] He has been described as "[h]aving the best mind on the Court"[13] and as the justice who "carries more constitutional law in his head" than any other member of the Court.[14]

Additionally, he has an extremely attractive personal manner; descriptions of Rehnquist typically include the word "charming." A liberal political scientist who interviewed Rehnquist described him as "the most charming man I have ever met," and a liberal

law professor quipped that Rehnquist "took charm pills."[15] A former law clerk to Justice White described Rehnquist as "the nicest
person at the Court."[16] He is said to be a justice who establishes
warm working relationships with his clerks.[17]

These three characteristics—outspokenness, intelligence, and
charm—operate to Rehnquist's advantage in his interactions with
the other justices. His influence on the Court rose during the later
years of the Burger Court, perhaps in part as a result of his ability
to get along with the other justices and because of his propensity
to impress even his critics with his sharp wit and intelligence.
Rehnquist's heightened influence may also be explained in part
by Sandra Day O'Connor's appointment in 1981, which had the
effect of bringing the Court more closely in line with the general
mood of the Reagan administration. At any rate, the "one-man
strong right wing" of the 1970s had emerged as a major force on
the Court by the mid-1980s.

In 1985 A. E. Dick Howard asserted, "He's the one with the
agenda. . . . He has claim to the leadership role on the court."[18]
Just as Rehnquist began to command the attention of the legal
community and the media, he also captured the interest of the
Reagan administration. When Chief Justice Burger announced his
retirement in June 1986, William Rehnquist was the president's
choice for the sixteenth chief justice of the United States.

Rehnquist's Opinions

The Distribution of Powers: Congress and the Presidency

In his testimony at Rehnquist's nomination hearings in 1971,
Gary Orfield contended, "While [his] writings suggest that he
would narrowly interpret some sections of the Bill of Rights and
the Fourteenth Amendment, he has often read the Constitutional
grants of power to the executive branch very broadly indeed. He
is loath, for example, to put any limits on the government's power
to spy on its own citizens. . . . [H]e expands and contracts the
Constitution like an accordion to accommodate his extremely conservative political views."[19] Citing Rehnquist's record as assistant
attorney general, Orfield suggested that, if confirmed, the nominee
would stretch the accordion wide for executive power.

In 1987 Rehnquist recalled that, when he was Justice Jackson's
clerk and the Court was preparing to hear the *Steel Seizure Case*
(*Youngstown Sheet & Tube Co. v. Sawyer,* 1952), "my instincts favored
the position of the steel companies, . . . [and] I had gotten the

impression that the balance of power within the federal establishment had shifted markedly away from Congress and toward the president during the preceding fifteen years, and that this trend was not a healthy one."[20] But the opinions he wrote and the votes he cast as a member of the Burger Court manifest a much more deferential attitude toward presidential power.

Although he did not participate in the "Watergate Tapes" case (*United States v. Nixon*, 1974), he inferred a constitutional right of executive privilege based upon the principle of separation of powers (*Nixon v. Administrator of General Services*, 1977). In 1981 he wrote the opinion for the Court when all the justices agreed to uphold executive orders issued by President Carter pursuant to the executive agreement with Iran that provided for the freeing of the American hostages.[21] He referred approvingly to Felix Frankfurter's assertion in the *Steel Seizure Case* that "a systematic, unbroken, executive practice, long pursued to the knowledge of the Congress and never before questioned . . . may be treated as a gloss on 'Executive Power' " (*Dames & Moore v. Regan*, 453 U.S. at 686).

In 1984 five members of the Court voted to uphold President Reagan's ban on economic transactions by American tourists and businesses in Cuba—a regulation that virtually prohibited travel there (*Regan v. Wald*). Rehnquist, who wrote the majority opinion, found statutory authority for the regulation in a law authorizing the president to impose trade embargoes during times of war and national emergency.

Rehnquist was a member of the majority when the Court held, by a vote of five to four, that the president has absolute immunity from civil damages liability for acts that are within his official responsibility (*Nixon v. Fitzgerald*, 1982). He also argued, albeit unsuccessfully, that absolute immunity should extend to the president's aides (*Harlow v. Fitzgerald*, 1982) and to cabinet officers (*Butz v. Economou*, 1978).

Faithful to a notion of strictly separated powers of the national government, Rehnquist joined the Court in striking down congressional involvement in appointing members of the Federal Election Commission (*Buckley v. Valeo*, 1976). He joined the majority in invalidating, as a violation of the separation of powers, the section of the Gramm-Rudman-Hollings Act that assigned executive powers to the comptroller general, who is removable only by Congress (*Bowsher v. Synar*, 1986).

He delineated his view of the distribution of powers between

Congress and the executive most clearly in his attempts to revitalize the nondelegation doctrine, according to which Congress may not delegate its legislative powers to the executive. Rehnquist has argued that the Court has a "duty to invalidate unconstitutional delegations of legislative authority . . ." (*Industrial Union Dept., AFL-CIO v. American Petroleum Institute*, 448 U.S. at 686). He has also contended that the Occupational Safety and Health Act of 1970 exceeds Congress's power to delegate legislative authority to nonelected officials (*American Petroleum*) and that important choices of social policy must be made by elected representatives rather than nonelected officials in the executive branch (*American Textile Manufacturers Institute v. Donovan*, 1981).[22]

Federalism

Rehnquist's decision making reflects, above all else, a concern for protecting the position of the states in the federal system. He became an associate justice of a Supreme Court that seemed to have concluded the debate regarding the extent of Congress's power vis-à-vis the states. His most important contribution to the Burger Court was the crucial role he played in reviving that debate.

The federalism that Rehnquist has embraced entails a vision of the relationship between the federal government and the states that is fundamentally at odds with the view that prevailed on the Court from the late 1930s until the mid-1970s. He is committed to shifting power away from the federal government toward more extensive and independent authority for the states. His conception of state sovereignty limits Congress's power under the commerce clause and constrains the power of the federal courts.[23]

Rehnquist's federalism is most apparent in his broad construal of the power of the states. When state legislation is challenged on the grounds that it conflicts with a federal law or that it interferes with interstate commerce, he invariably supports the state. Indeed, he has urged the Court to take an extremely deferential posture toward state regulations. For example, in 1978 the Court invalidated a New Jersey statute that prohibited the importation of waste from out of state. Seven members of the Court agreed that the law discriminated against articles of commerce coming from out of state and constituted an "illegitimate means of isolating the State from the national economy" (*Philadelphia v. New Jersey*, 437 U.S. at 617). Rehnquist disagreed; in dissent he argued that the state statute should have been treated as a quarantine law. New

Jersey should have been allowed to cope in its own way with health and safety problems posed by the importation of solid waste.

Similarly, in 1981 when the Court held that Iowa's limitation on truck lengths constituted an impermissible burden on interstate commerce, Rehnquist objected that the majority had "seriously intrude[d] upon the fundamental right of the States to pass laws to secure the safety of their citizens" (*Kassel v. Consolidated Freightways Corp.*, 450 U.S. at 687). In *White v. Massachusetts Council of Construction Employers* (1983), Rehnquist wrote an opinion for the Court holding that the commerce clause did not prohibit the mayor of Boston's executive order requiring all construction projects funded either by city money or by a combination of city and federal funds to be performed by a work force at least half of whom were city residents. Rehnquist has complained that "the jurisprudence of the 'negative side' of the commerce clause remains hopelessly confused" (*Kassel*, 706). His opinions reflect the theme that dominates his judicial decision making: deference to state and local governmental processes.

Rehnquist's opinions manifest his fundamental disagreement with the Court's broad construction of Congress's power under the commerce clause. He admonished the other justices to adopt a heightened standard of review when examining challenges under the commerce clause to federal legislation (*Hodel v. Virginia Surface Mining and Reclamation Association*, 1981), and he advanced a doctrine of state sovereignty positing that, when Congress acts under the authority of the commerce clause, its action may constitute a violation of the constitutional protection provided to the states by the principles of federalism (*Fry v. United States*, 1975; *National League of Cities v. Usery*, 1976). Rehnquist maintains that Congress is prohibited from regulating activities under the commerce power when its regulation interferes with a state's governmental functions. "We have repeatedly recognized," he wrote in *National League of Cities*, "that there are attributes of sovereignty attaching to every state government which may not be impaired by Congress" (426 U.S. at 845). One of the most important functions of the Supreme Court, as Rehnquist sees it, is to serve as guardian of the federal system by carefully scrutinizing and invalidating federal legislation that interferes with state autonomy.

In Rehnquist's view the tradition of expanding federal judicial power has brought a series of unwarranted federal intrusions into areas that properly belong to the states. The enthusiasm with which he sought to limit the power of the federal courts prompted Justice

Brennan to accuse him of using federalism as an excuse for stripping the federal courts of the jurisdiction conferred upon them by Congress (*Francis v. Henderson,* 1976). Rehnquist has voted to expand the scope of the Eleventh Amendment to protect states from being sued in federal court. In 1974 he wrote an opinion for a five-member majority holding that the Eleventh Amendment bars federal courts from ordering retroactive relief against state governments (*Edelman v. Jordan*), and he joined the majority in subsequent decisions that extended the reach of the Eleventh Amendment as a bar to federal adjudication (*Pennhurst v. Halderman,* 1981; *Atascadero State Hospital v. Scanlon,* 1985).

Rehnquist also tried to limit access to the federal courts under 42 U.S.C. §1983, which provides a cause of action for the deprivation, "under color of law," of rights secured by the Constitution (*Paul v. Davis,* 1976; *Baker v. McCollan,* 1979; *Parratt v. Taylor,* 1981). Moreover, he wrote important opinions for the majority that had the effect of limiting the availability of habeas corpus for state prisoners who claim that they are being detained in violation of the federal law or the Constitution (*Wainwright v. Sykes,* 1977; *Sumner v. Mata,* 1981). Finally, he led the effort to limit the power of federal courts to forbid or halt state judicial proceedings that are allegedly unconstitutional except in exceptional circumstances (*Hicks v. Miranda,* 1975; *Huffman v. Pursue, Ltd.,* 1975). He even managed to extend that rule to preclude federal judicial intervention in the actions of state and local executive officials (*Rizzo v. Goode,* 1975).

Individual Rights

The Fourteenth Amendment

Rehnquist's position regarding the relationship between the Bill of Rights and the due process clause of the Fourteenth Amendment exemplifies his deferential posture toward the power of the states and consequent lack of concern for individual rights. The due process clause, in Rehnquist's view, does not incorporate the Bill of Rights; neither does it create any substantive rights; rather, it merely guarantees that government must follow fair procedures before it takes life, liberty, or property (*Roe v. Wade,* 1973). He has expressed his disagreement with the Court's doctrine of incorporation, characterizing it as a "mysterious process of transmogrification" (*Carter v. Kentucky,* 1981).

Due process, in Rehnquist's view, is not simply a shorthand term for the provisions in the first eight amendments. Indeed, he has asserted that the "liberty" protected by due process "embraces more than the rights found in the Bill of Rights" (*Roe v. Wade*, 410 U.S. at 173). He posits that, although some provisions in the Bill of Rights might apply to the states, they do so only coincidentally rather than by virtue of their automatic applicability through the due process clause. Thus, like Felix Frankfurter, Robert H. Jackson, and John Marshall Harlan (the younger), he argued that states need not comply with all the provisions in the Bill of Rights but need only treat individuals with fundamental fairness. In such a system, a "healthy pluralism" could thrive (*Richmond Newspapers v. Virginia*, 1980).

As a member of the Burger Court, Rehnquist repeatedly objected to applying provisions in the Bill of Rights to state criminal proceedings. When the Court held that the First and Fourteenth Amendments require that state criminal trials must be open to the public except under extraordinary circumstances, he objected that the public trial guarantee of the Sixth Amendment should not apply to the states. He suggested that a state's reasons for denying public access to a trial should not be subject to Supreme Court review and objected that the Court was "smother[ing] a healthy pluralism which would ordinarily exist in a national government embracing fifty states" (*Richmond Newspapers*, 448 U.S. at 606). In another case he contended that, under Section 5 of the Fourteenth Amendment, Congress does not have the same power to enforce a constitutional provision that has been incorporated, such as the cruel and unusual punishment prohibition of the Eighth Amendment, "a provision which was placed in the [Fourteenth] Amendment by the drafters" (*Hutto v. Finney*, 437 U.S. at 717–18).

Rehnquist's opinions in cases involving the rights of those accused of crimes are notable for their consistent support for law enforcement. He fulfilled Richard Nixon's goal of a justice who would swing the pendulum away from the protection of the rights of the accused. For example, he wrote opinions for the majority narrowing the "expectation of privacy" and restricting defendants' ability to achieve standing to challenge searches and seizures (*Rakas v. Illinois*, 1978; *United States v. Salvucci*, 1980; and *Rawlings v. Kentucky*, 1980). He wrote an opinion formulating a "totality of circumstances" standard that made it easier for police to obtain a warrant on the basis of an informant's tip (*Illinois v. Gates*, 1983). He wrote for the majority endorsing a "public safety" exception to the *Miranda* rule (*New York v. Quarles*, 1984). Furthermore, Rehnquist was a member of the majority when the Court approved the "good faith" exception to the exclusionary rule (*United States v. Leon*, 1984).

Rehnquist's opinions in the area of equal protection also illustrate his preference for deciding civil liberties cases in favor of the state. In his view, the Fourteenth Amendment was designed only to prevent the states from treating black and white citizens differently. Therefore, it should not be stretched beyond that purpose to embody an affirmative guarantee of equality, nor should it be applied to other disadvantaged groups. Because the immediate purpose of the Fourteenth Amendment was to prohibit states from enacting legislation that treated blacks differently from whites, classifications based on race are suspect, and in fact are presumptively invalid. According to Rehnquist, the determining factor in decisions involving suspect classifications is the presence of purposeful discrimination through legislation or other public policy. For example, in 1985 he wrote an opinion for a unanimous Court invalidating an Alabama constitutional provision that disenfranchised people convicted of misdemeanors involving moral turpitude. He pointed to statements made by the drafters of the Alabama Constitution regarding the purpose of the provision that suggested a discriminatory intent such as, "[W]hat is it we want to do? . . . [I]t is within the limits imposed by the Federal Constitution to establish white supremacy" (as quoted in *Hunter v. Underwood*, 471 U.S. at 229).

In more typical cases, however, the intent to discriminate is not so blatant. Rehnquist took the position that, unless there was official involvement that established such an intent, there is no constitutional violation. Moreover, in cases in which the outcome turned largely on the question of whether the official or purposeful elements were proven, he applied his tools of analysis to resolve that question in the negative. For example, he wrote an opinion for the majority holding that the required state action was absent in a liquor licensing scheme of a private club that refused to admit blacks to its restaurant and cocktail lounge. The club's state liquor license, he held, did not sufficiently implicate the state in racial discrimination to invoke the equal protection clause (*Moose Lodge No. 107 v. Irvis*, 1972). In 1986 he dissented when seven justices concluded that the use of peremptory challenges by the prosecutor in a trial of a black defendant to exclude all blacks from the jury solely on the basis of race amounted to purposeful discrimination (*Batson v. Kentucky*). He objected that the use of peremptory challenges does not violate the equal protection clause "so long as such challenges are also used to exclude whites in cases involving white defendants, Hispanics in cases involving Hispanic defendants, [or] Asians in cases involving Asian defendants" (476 U.S. at 137).

Throughout the years of the Burger Court, Rehnquist persistently objected to the Court's decisions that he believed blurred the distinction between de jure and de facto segregation. In 1973, when the Court upheld a district-wide desegregation plan in Denver despite the fact that intentional discrimination had been found in only one part of the district, Rehnquist was the sole dissenter (*Keyes v. School District No. 1, Denver*). He emphasized the factual differences between the segregation existing in the Denver school district and in southern school systems. He went further to argue that the "affirmative duty" to desegregate, announced by the Court in *Green v. County Board of Education* in 1968, should be limited to southern school systems in which segregation had once been mandated by law.

In two cases decided in 1979 the Court held that school boards that intentionally maintained dual systems in 1954 and subsequently remained segregated must show why they had not taken necessary steps to desegregate (*Columbus Board of Education v. Penick* and *Dayton Board of Education v. Brinkman*). In *Columbus* the Court stated that "actions having foreseeable and anticipated disparate impact are relevant evidence to prove the ultimate fact, forbidden purpose" (443 U.S. at 464). In dissent Rehnquist suggested that schools that were not legally segregated in 1954 should not bear the responsibility for achieving a unitary system. He argued that the burden of showing a discriminatory purpose should lie with the plaintiffs, and if no evidence exists proving or disproving the justification offered by a school board for its actions, no constitutional violation can be found.

The position that Rehnquist took regarding affirmative action further illustrates his belief that, in order to justify a legal remedy, a plaintiff must make a showing of purposeful discrimination. In 1978 the Supreme Court held that the admissions program at the University of California, Davis, medical school, which reserved sixteen places for minority group members, was illegal. Rehnquist joined Justice Stevens's opinion asserting that the policy violated Title VI of the Civil Rights Act of 1964 prohibiting racial discrimination in activities or programs receiving federal assistance (*Regents of the University of California v. Bakke*).

A year later the Court held that Kaiser Aluminum's affirmative action policy—which reserved 50 percent of the openings in its craft training programs for black employees until the percentage of black craftworkers reached a level approximating that of the percentage of blacks in the local labor force—did not violate Title VII of the Civil Rights Act (*United Steelworkers v. Weber*). Justice Brennan, writing for the majority, reasoned that Title VII should not be construed literally to prohibit all affirmative action plans. Instead, the prohibition against racial discrimination in employment practices must be interpreted within the context of its legislative history. The purpose of the provisions, he found, was to ameliorate economic inequality by opening employment opportunities for blacks in areas traditionally closed to them. Additionally, he noted that if Congress had intended to prohibit voluntary affirmative action programs, it would have stated that such programs were neither required nor permitted; instead, the law said only that they were not required. Race-conscious affirmative action programs, instituted voluntarily by private employers, were, therefore, not inconsistent with the purpose of Title VII.

In an extensive and acrimonious dissent Rehnquist accused the majority of intellectual dishonesty. In his view, Kaiser's policy violated the plain language of the provisions and the legislative history, which revealed that Congress had intended to outlaw all discrimination and preferential treatment. The majority, Rehnquist protested, had called upon the "spirit" of the act to reach the desired result. If the provision had a "spirit," he said, it was one that was consistent with its language and intent.

In the Burger Court's subsequent decisions regarding affirmative action, Rehnquist invariably found that race-conscious preferential programs violate antidiscrimination provisions in the law; he found it unnecessary to address the constitutional question of whether such programs are consistent with the equal protection clause (*Firefighters Local Union No. 1784 v. Stotts,* 1984; *Local No. 93, International Association of Firefighters, AFL-CIO v. City of Cleveland,* 1986; *Local 28, Sheet Metal Workers' International Association v. EEOC,* 1986). In his view, the law condemns racial discrimination in employment and education. It matters not that racial distinctions disadvantage whites for the purpose of increasing economic opportunities for blacks.

With rare exception, Rehnquist disagreed with the majority when the Court invalidated sex-based classifications. Voicing his objections to the Court's decisions, he often reiterated his belief that the Court should interpret the Fourteenth Amendment based on the intent of the framers, which was to prohibit the states from treating blacks differently from whites. Thus it was inappropriate for the Court to extend heightened scrutiny of legislative classifications to classifications based on gender (*Craig v. Boren*, 1976; *Michael M. v. Superior Court of Sonoma County*, 1981). While racial classifications must be presumptively invalid, in all other areas the principle of equal protection requires only "that persons similarly situated should be treated similarly."[24] If the Court were to adopt Rehnquist's approach, it would treat challenges to classifications based on gender as it has treated challenges to economic regulations since the late 1930s—by paying maximum deference to legislative decisions. Any conceivable relationship between a classification and its stated purpose, no matter how tenuous, would vindicate the classification.

The First Amendment: Freedom of Expression

Rehnquist stood out as the member of the Burger Court who was least supportive of First Amendment claims. From the beginning of his tenure through the 1984–85 term he voted in favor of freedom of expression claims in 23.1 percent of the 169 free speech cases in which he participated.[25] Even in those few cases in which he voted in support of a claim, he often did so on narrower grounds than several of the other justices.[26] Moreover, he objected to the Court's innovations in First Amendment doctrine, such as the Court's extension of protection to commercial speech (*Bigelow v. Virginia*, 1975; *Virginia State Board of Pharmacy v. Virginia Citizens Consumer Council*, 1976; *Bates v. State Bar of Arizona*, 1977; *Central Hudson Gas and Electric Corp. v. Public Service Commission of New York*, 1980). When the Court invalidated New York's restrictions on the advertising of nonprescription contraceptives, he rebuked the majority: "If those responsible for [the Bill of Rights and the Civil War amendments] could have lived to know that their efforts had enshrined in the Constitution the right of commercial vendors of contraceptives to peddle them to unmarried minors through such means as window displays and vending machines located in the men's room of truck stops, . . . it is not difficult to imagine their reaction" (*Carey v. Population Services International*, 431 U.S. at 717).

The Burger Court's extension of First Amendment rights to corporations was closely related to its bestowal of constitutional status on commercial speech. Rehnquist's view was that when the source of expression is a corporation, speech should not be accorded protection under the First Amendment (*First National Bank of Boston v. Bellotti*, 1978; *Central Hudson and Pacific Gas and Electric Co. v. Public Utilities Commission of California*, 1986).

Rehnquist often expressed the view that the provisions of the First Amendment do not apply to the states (see, for example, *First National Bank of Boston*, 435 U.S. at 823). He asserted that "not all the strictures which the First Amendment imposes upon Congress are carried over against the States by the Fourteenth Amendment, but rather that it is only the 'general principle' of free speech, that the latter incorporates" (*Buckley v. Valeo*, 424 U.S. at 191). Further, he stated that "cases which deal with state restrictions on First Amendment freedoms are not fungible with those which deal with restrictions imposed by the Federal Government" (191). In short, in Rehnquist's view, state action that is challenged as an abridgement of free speech should be examined by the Court to determine only whether it is consistent with the "general principle" of free speech. This suggests that Rehnquist would not apply the stringent standard of review, which requires a compelling state interest, when restrictions on expression are challenged. Rather, he would find a challenged state policy to be constitutionally acceptable if it merely bore a rational relation to a valid state objective.

Broad construction of state power is particularly apparent in Rehnquist's opinions regarding freedom of expression. For example, he wrote for the majority, upholding California's prohibition on sexually explicit live entertainment in establishments licensed to sell liquor by the drink. He found the regulation not unreasonable or irrational and emphasized the states' authority under the Twenty-first Amendment to control the manner and circumstances under which liquor may be dispensed. Moreover, he noted that the state regulations that were challenged did not forbid the entertainment; rather, they merely proscribed such performances in establishments licensed to sell liquor (*California v. LaRue*, 1972).

Rehnquist also wrote for the majority when the Court held that California could require owners of private shopping centers to provide access to people exercising their state constitutional rights of free speech (*Pruneyard Shopping Center v. Robins*, 1980). The Supreme Court had ruled earlier that such rights were not protected by the federal constitution (*Lloyd Corporation v. Tanner*, 1972; *Hudgens v. NLRB*, 1976); Rehnquist held that, nonetheless, each state has the authority to exercise its police powers and has a sovereign right to adopt, in its own constitution, individual liberties more expansive than those conferred by the federal constitution. In numerous opinions Rehnquist maintained that it was within the proper scope of a state's power to resolve free speech issues. For example, he maintained that states have the power to regulate and prohibit commercial advertising (*Bigelow*), to restrict the activities of members of the bar (*In re Primus*, 1978), and to restrict the political activities of corporations (*First National Bank of Boston*). All such restrictions, in his view, should be treated as economic regulations subject only to the standard of rationality.

I have found it useful to examine Rehnquist's contextual approach to freedom of expression to shed further light upon his decision making. He set forth the dimensions of that approach most clearly in his opinion in *Buckley v. Valeo*. He stated that "the limits imposed by the First and Fourteenth Amendments on governmental action may vary in their stringency depending on the capacity in which the government is acting" (424 U.S. at 290). The government, as proprietor, is permitted to limit constitutionally protected interests in ways that it might not be allowed to if it were simply proscribing conduct across the board. Similarly, he explained, the government as employer may prescribe conditions of employment in ways that might be in violation of the Constitution if they were enacted into rules applicable to the entire citizenry. Thus the nature of the protections offered by the First Amendment depend upon whether the government is acting as sovereign or lawmaker, making criminal laws that apply to the general population, or whether it is acting in a proprietary capacity. When that distinction is combined with Rehnquist's federalism, the principle emerges that interests protected by the First Amendment are at their strongest when a federal law is challenged and when that law directly prohibits speech; they are at their weakest when a state law is challenged and when the government acts as property owner or employer to regulate speech.

Rehnquist applied his distinction in a variety of situations. For example, he discussed the powers of the government to regulate expression in its capacity as a property owner when the Court found that a municipal board's denial of the use of a city-leased theater for a showing of the musical *Hair* was a prior restraint that violated the First Amendment. In his dissent he contended that a public auditorium is not the same as public streets and parks in that a city should be able to control its own property (*Southeastern Promotions, Ltd. v. Conrad*, 1975).

When the government acts as school administrator, it performs a proprietary function; thus, for Rehnquist, the First Amendment carries less weight in such a context than when the government acts as sovereign. In 1972 the Court held that a state-supported school violated the constitutional rights of students when it denied recognition to Students for a Democratic Society. Rehnquist wrote a concurring opinion in which he referred to the distinction between government as college administrator and government acting as sovereign to enforce criminal laws: "The government as employer or school administrator may impose upon employees and students reasonable regulations that would be impermissible if imposed by the government upon all citizens" (*Healy v. James*, 408 U.S. at 203). He also referred to "a constitutional distinction" between criminal punishment and "milder" administrative or disciplinary sanctions (203).

Rehnquist dissented when the Court held that a university student could not be expelled for distributing campus newspapers containing a picture of police officers raping the Statue of Liberty and Goddess of Justice and an article entitled "Motherfucker Acquitted." He objected that although the student could not have been criminally prosecuted for her conduct, expelling her did not abridge her rights of free speech: "[A] wooden insistence on equating, for constitutional purposes, the authority of the State to criminally punish with its authority to exercise even a modicum of control over the university which it operates, serves neither the Constitution nor public education well" (*Papish v. Board of Curators*, 410 U.S. at 677, 1973).

Rehnquist also objected when the majority held that the First Amendment limits school board discretion to remove library books from high school and junior high school libraries. "[G]overnment may act in other capacities than as sovereign," he reminded, "and when it does the First Amendment may speak with a different voice" (*Board of Education v. Pico*, 457 U.S. at 908, 1982). In a similar fashion, he supported prison regulations against First Amendment challenges because the government functions in a proprietary capacity when it acts as prison administrator (*Jones v. North Carolina Prisoners Union*, 1977; *Bell v. Wolfish*, 1979). He also applied his distinction to regulations imposed by the military (*Flower v. United States*, 1972; *Parker v. Levy*, 1974). In sum, the capacity in which the government acts when it regulates and Rehnquist's deference toward the states appear to be two factors that are most useful in explaining his decision making in the area of freedom of expression.

Judicial Philosophy

Some scholars have argued that, as a member of the Burger Court, Rehnquist had a political agenda but no judicial philosophy. I argue to the contrary: Rehnquist's judicial philosophy contains three components: the democratic model, moral relativism, and a distinct approach to constitutional interpretation.

He subscribes to a democratic model of the American political system that stresses majority rule and the accountability of elected officials through the electoral process while deemphasizing the notion that the Constitution protects certain individual rights regardless of the will of the majority.[27] Rehnquist's commitment to the democratic model is particularly clear in his dissent from the majority's conclusion that the death penalty, as it was then imposed, was cruel and unusual punishment in violation of the Eighth Amendment (*Furman v. Georgia,* 1972). In that opinion he cautioned judges to defer to legislative decisions, warning that "overreaching by the Legislative and Executive Branches may result in the sacrifice of individual protections that the Constitution was designed to secure against the action of the State, [but] judicial overreaching may result in sacrifice of the equally important right of the people to govern themselves" (408 U.S. at 470). His attempts to revive the nondelegation doctrine and his warnings to legislators that they must not pass the responsibility for making difficult decisions of national policy to executive officials also attest to his commitment to the democratic model. Similarly, his support for extensive executive powers in matters of national domestic and foreign policy might be partially explained with reference to the democratic model.

Moral relativism, the second component of Rehnquist's judicial philosophy, is manifest in his assertion that no value can be demonstrated to be intrinsically superior to any other—a particular value is authoritative only when it can claim the support of the majority. "The laws that emerge after a typical political struggle in which various individual value judgments are debated likewise take on a form of moral goodness because they have been enacted into positive law. . . . Beyond the Constitution and the laws in our society, there simply is no basis other than the individual conscience of the citizen that may serve as a platform for the launching of moral judgments."[28]

Such statements underline Rehnquist's view that a law derives its validity from the process by which it is enacted and that the written law carries greater authority than the abstract theorizing of judges about competing values. Accordingly, Rehnquist has argued that property rights do not exist by virtue of any precepts of natural law but only as a result of their enactment into the positive law. He expressed disapproval of decisions that have extended judicial protection to personal rights not mentioned in the Constitution. For example, dissenting from the Court's decision in *Roe v. Wade*, he argued that there is no right to privacy that encompasses a woman's right to decide to have an abortion, either in the Fourth Amendment or in the due process clause of the Fourteenth Amendment.

The third component of Rehnquist's judicial philosophy is his approach to interpreting the Constitution, which includes the belief that the Constitution is limited to the text of the document, the idea that it has a fixed meaning, and the view that it constitutes a set of rules to be strictly followed.[29] His approach requires an interpreter to rely on the words and clauses in the document itself. Where the words do not suffice, however, one may search for the intent of the framers.

An alternative approach to constitutional interpretation posits that, rather than limit the meaning to the text or the intent of the framers, one should search for underlying values and principles in the overall design of the document. Such an approach accepts the notion of a changing Constitution and posits a view of the Constitution as an aspirational document rather than a set of rules. For Rehnquist such an approach is unacceptable because it invariably results in judges' superimposing their own values on the Constitution, thereby altering its true meaning. He has expressed his belief that judicial alteration of the Constitution to suit judges' notions of what is good for society controverts the principles of a democratic society.[30] In fact, Rehnquist's approach to constitutional interpretation and his democratic model coexist comfortably—it is only by remaining faithful to the text and the framers' intent that constitutional interpretation can be consistent with the democratic process. His approach to constitutional interpretation also coincides nicely with his moral relativism insofar as such an understanding of the Constitution precludes judges from substituting their personal values for the rules that have been properly enacted into the law.

A prescription for a minimal role for the judiciary would seem to follow logically from the combination of the three components of Rehnquist's judicial philosophy. Rehnquist has severely criticized the form that modern judicial review has taken. Judges no longer function as guardians of the Constitution. Rather than "keepers of the covenant . . . [they] are a small group of fortunately situated people . . . [who] second-guess Congress, state legislatures, and state and federal administrative officers concerning what is best for the country."[31]

Additional support is provided for a minimal role for the judiciary when moral relativism is joined with the democratic model. Indeed, the preferences of majorities enacted into the positive law (statutes or the Constitution) establish a society's rules and distinguish right from wrong. Unless explicit constitutional provisions are violated, judges have no legitimate basis to invalidate legislation.

Rehnquist has placed federalism in the highest position in his hierarchy of values, property rights second, and individual rights in the lowest position. The three components of his judicial philosophy—the democratic model, moral relativism, and his approach to constitutional interpretation—combined with his ordering of values form the basis of his decision making.

In cases where state authority conflicts with property rights, Rehnquist has supported the state's power to regulate such rights so long as the state does not violate any explicit constitutional provision. In an opinion he wrote in 1980 he stated, "It is, of course, well-established that a State in the exercise of its police power may adopt reasonable restrictions on private property so long as the restrictions do not amount to a taking without just compensation or contravene any other federal constitutional provision" (*Pruneyard*, 447 U.S. at 81). When he finds that the state has violated an express constitutional provision, however, Rehnquist, faithful to the written law, withdraws his support from the state. He has been even more willing to support a state's authority when it conflicts with individual rights, consistently voting in favor of the state and giving constitutional provisions protecting individual rights the narrowest possible construction.

The interaction between the democratic model and the high value Rehnquist places on federalism is suggested by the following statement: "[T]he people are the ultimate source of authority; they have parceled out the authority that originally resided entirely with them by adopting the original Constitution and by later amending it. They have granted some authority to the federal government and have reserved authority not granted it to the states or to the people individually."[32] Because the laws derive their authority from their enactment by legislative bodies representing the will of the majority, the laws that are most clearly the product of the majority are the most legitimate. Additionally, Rehnquist seems to assume that small units of government—those closest to the people—will be more likely to reflect the will of the majority. Thus state laws are to be highly valued. In short, he finds strong support for his federalism in his notion of democracy. Additionally, his conviction that federalism is central to the Constitution as intended by the framers enables him to ground his preference for state autonomy in constitutional theory.

Rehnquist's democratic model, his approach to interpreting the Constitution, and his moral relativism go far to explain the lesser values he assigns to property and individual rights. These rights are protected only insofar as they are provided for in explicit provisions of the Constitution and in statutory law. Furthermore, such rights derive their existence and legal authority not from moral principles but from their presence in the written law.

The reason that Rehnquist assigns individual rights a lower position than property rights in his hierarchy of values is more difficult to explain. His democratic model and moral relativism, which prescribe a minimal role for the judiciary, would seem to leave the protection of both property and individual rights to elected officials. Thus no preference would be given to either right over the other. Moreover, Rehnquist's approach to constitutional interpretation would seem to place the two sets of rights on the same level. The Constitution explicitly provides for the protection of property in the due process clauses of the Fifth and Fourteenth amendments, in the taking clause of the Fifth Amendment, and in the contract clause of Article I, Section 10, but other express provisions protect individual rights, primarily the Bill of Rights and the Fourteenth Amendment.

Rehnquist construes due process as a procedural protection. Thus, when the Fourteenth Amendment prohibits the states from depriving "any person of life, liberty, or property without due process of law," it means that a state may deprive a person of life, liberty, or property as long as due process of law is followed. That interpretation would seem to put property and individual rights (life and liberty) on an equal basis in that people could be deprived of either liberty or property so long as the government followed the proper procedures. Moreover, the most explicit protection offered by the Constitution concerns individual, rather than property, rights: the First Amendment commands that "Congress shall make no law . . . abridging the freedom of speech." Still, Rehnquist minimizes the protection offered by the First Amendment. Perhaps he believes that the framers intended the Constitution to protect property more than liberty, although that intention is not explicit in the text of the document. Another possible explanation for his ordering of the values of property and individual rights is that he simply prefers property rights to individual rights, perhaps out of a belief that the protection of property leads to a more stable democratic society.

The three components of Rehnquist's judicial philosophy prescribe a minimal role for the courts. Still, his opinions in cases that involve a conflict between state and federal laws demonstrate that when he has perceived that federal action encroached on the states' integrity and their ability to function as governmental units, he has been quite willing to use judicial review. When state interests are at stake, judicial review becomes essential to preserve federalism. The necessity of judicial review in the context of federalism is entirely consistent with the democratic model for Rehnquist so long as the states govern in accordance with majority rule. Thus the exercise of judicial review in the interest of state autonomy protects not only federalism but also the democratic process.

The value that Rehnquist assigns to federalism is so high that it abrogates the prescription, which follows from the three components of his judicial philosophy, that the judiciary play a minimal role. In his view, the courts have a crucial role to play to protect federalism. The maxim of "judicial restraint," in short, applies when property rights or individual rights are involved but not when state autonomy is at risk.

Furthermore, in the interest of protecting federalism, Rehnquist's approach to constitutional interpretation has wavered, and some inconsistency seems to have emerged. While his basic perception of the Constitution has seemed to be that the Court should protect only rights explicitly mentioned in the Constitution, his references to "notions of a constitutional plan" and the "implicit ordering of relationships within the federal system" (*Nevada v. Hall*, 440 U.S. at 443, 1979) suggest that when federalism is at issue he is willing to reach beyond the text. He even conceded that "it is not the Tenth Amendment by its terms that prohibits congressional action which sets a mandatory ceiling on the wages of all state employees. Both [the Tenth and the Eleventh] Amendments are simply examples of the understanding of those who drafted and ratified the Constitution that the States were sovereign in many respects, and that although their legislative authority could be superseded by Congress in many areas where Congress was competent to act, Congress was nonetheless not free to deal with a State as if it were just another individual or business enterprise subject to regulation" (*Fry v. United States*, 421 U.S. at 557).

Politics and the Burger Court

What is the relationship between Rehnquist's judicial philosophy and the political context within which the Burger Court functioned? Richard Nixon nominated Rehnquist largely because his political views were so compatible with the agenda the president had for the Supreme Court. As an associate justice, Rehnquist fulfilled Nixon's hopes, enthusiastically taking positions in favor of the "peace forces" against the "criminal forces" and against school desegregation in the north. Moreover, he was supportive of executive power in an era when Watergate had cast so much aspersion on the presidency.

Although the positions that Rehnquist took on the Burger Court coincided with Nixon's agenda, the justice was never the "judicial conservative" that the president described. For example, a judicial conservative would consistently argue against judicial invalidation of legislation unless it contravened an explicit provision in the Constitution. It is, of course, true that Rehnquist has repeatedly admonished judges to defer to the decisions of legislators on the grounds that in a democratic society policy should be made by elected officials who are accountable to the people rather than by unaccountable judges. Nevertheless, he conceives the judiciary's role to include protecting state autonomy from the federal government and thus has urged the Court to invalidate federal legislation that interferes with the position of the states in the federal system. In addition, a judicial conservative would follow previous decisions of the Supreme Court. Rehnquist, however, has often admonished the Court to overrule prior decisions with which he disagrees, such as *Mapp v. Ohio* (1963), *Miranda v. Arizona* (1966), and *Roe v. Wade* (1973) and the entire doctrine of the incorporation of the Bill of Rights.

Although judicial conservatism has no place in a description of Rehnquist's decision making, his political conservatism coincides with his judicial philosophy and his judicial values. His judicial philosophy requires the judiciary to play an active role to protect the autonomy of the states, and the states usually support the political values he favors. For example, if the Court overruled *Miranda* and held that the police are not required to warn suspects that any statement they made would be used in court, more criminals would confess, be convicted, and sent to prison. That would support the political value of "law and order" as well as the judicial value of federalism. Similarly, state courts have traditionally offered fewer procedural protections to defendants than federal courts; therefore, for the Supreme Court to limit access to the federal courts would not only support Rehnquist's judicial value of federalism but also his political value of "law and order." The intersection of his judicial philosophy and his political conservatism is also readily apparent. Rehnquist has been stubbornly unsympathetic to all judicial attempts to protect the rights of racial minorities, women, and aliens. His democratic model and moral relativism preclude judicial intervention in those areas and help to preserve the status quo by prescribing that problems of equality and social justice be left to the political process.

Conclusion: Back to the Future

In order to appreciate Rehnquist's major contributions to the Burger Court one might imagine what the results would have been if a majority had shared his views. The major developments in civil liberties, including the extension of protection under the First Amendment to commercial speech, the expansion of the equal protection clause to at least partially protect women, and the extension of the right to privacy to reproductive rights would not have come to pass. If Rehnquist had commanded a majority, not only would the Burger Court have thoroughly undermined much of the doctrine of the Warren Court, it also would have eroded doctrines developed by the Court since the latter half of the 1930s.

The distribution of power between the federal government and the states would be drastically altered, with profound implications for civil liberties and rights. The Bill of Rights would be "unincorporated" and would not apply to criminal defendants in state courts. Although state courts would still be required to comply with the general principles of due process as provided by the Fourteenth Amendment, the states would be free to work out the details of the administration of their criminal justice systems in their own ways. They would no longer be constitutionally required, for example, to provide all indigents with free counsel, to exclude evidence seized in violation of the prohibition against unreasonable searches and seizures, or to provide a person accused of a crime with the "right to remain silent." As a result, huge disparities between the states in the protection of rights of those accused of crimes would, most likely, have emerged. Some states would provide free counsel for an indigent accused of a crime, while others would not; some states would allow the admission of illegally seized evidence while others would require its exclusion.

Because the First Amendment would no longer apply to the states, the federal judiciary would require only that state action be reasonable, even if it interfered with freedom of expression or religious freedom or created an establishment of religion. Disparities between the states would undoubtedly appear in regulations directed at films, books, and magazines with sexual content. Some states might even prohibit the distribution of literature that contained extreme political views. Moreover, some states would reinstitute school prayer and Bible reading and require public school-teachers to impart the creationist theory of the origins of human life along with the theory of evolution to their students.

Severely restricted access to the federal courts would have been an additional consequence of the Court's redefinition, at the behest of Rehnquist, of the relationship between the federal government and the states. Disputes involving federal statutes or constitutional issues would be relegated to state courts. Additionally, civil liberties and civil rights advocates might choose, in view of the new decisions of the Supreme Court, to avoid the federal courts and devote their efforts to the development of protective doctrine based on state constitutional law. In short, the state courts would have become the "main event," without supervision from the federal judiciary.

Outside the area of federalism, the Supreme Court would have minimized the role of the judiciary relative to the other institutions of government. Executive power would be stronger in both domestic and foreign policy. Legislative power would also be stronger, so long as it did not infringe on the autonomy of the states. In short, the Supreme Court might well have "give[n] us a different country: one in which our freedoms were less secure, official power less restrained."[33]

NOTES

1. "Transcript of the President's Announcement on Two Nominees for Supreme Court," *New York Times*, Oct. 22, 1971, p. 24. Nixon described a "strict constructionist" as a judge who would "interpret the Constitution

strictly and fairly and objectively," unlike some "who have gone too far in assuming unto themselves a mandate which is not there, and that is, to put their social and economic ideas into their decisions." As quoted in James F. Simon, *In His Own Image: The Supreme Court in Richard Nixon's America* (New York: David McKay, Inc.: 1973), p. 8.

2. Only a handful of those arrested were found guilty of any charge. U.S. Senate, Committee on the Judiciary, *Nominations of William H. Rehnquist and Lewis F. Powell, Jr.: Hearings before the Committee on the Judiciary*, 92d Cong., 1st Sess., 1971, pp. 43–48, 139–40, 185, 313–15.

3. For a chronicle of President Nixon's nominations, see Henry J. Abraham, *Justices and Presidents*, 2d ed. (New York: Oxford University Press, 1985), chaps. 2, 11.

4. *Newsweek* published excerpts from the memorandum on Dec. 13, 1971 (pp. 32–33). This issue appeared on the newsstands on December 5, 1971. The *New York Times* published the memorandum on December 9, 1971 (p. 26). When the memorandum became public during the Senate's consideration of his nomination to the Court in 1971, the nominee steadfastly maintained that it was not a statement of his own views but a rough draft of Jackson's views for the latter to use at the conference. Rehnquist's story has been disputed. Richard Kluger noted that Elsie Douglas, Justice Jackson's secretary, told the *Washington Post* that Rehnquist had "smeared the reputation of a great justice" by attributing pro-segregationist views to Jackson. She told *Newsweek* that Rehnquist's explanation of the memo was "incredible on its face." Richard Kluger, *Simple Justice: The History of* Brown v. Board of Education *and Black America's Struggle for Equality* (New York: Vintage Books, 1975), pp. 606–9. Also, Dennis Hutchinson, who is writing a biography of Justice Jackson, called Rehnquist's explanation "absurd." "Reagan's Mr. Right," *Time*, June 30, 1986, p. 27.

5. An Arizona state senator submitted an affidavit to the Senate Judiciary Committee in which he stated that after the council meeting he had asked Rehnquist why he opposed the ordinance. Rehnquist replied, "I am opposed to all civil rights laws" (*Hearings*, 1971, p. 320). Rehnquist wrote a letter to the editor of *The Arizona Republic* in which he argued, "The ordinance summarily does away with the historic right of the owner by a wave of the legislative wand; hitherto private businesses are made public facilities, which are open to all persons regardless of the owner's wishes" (306–7).

6. It was in this context that Rehnquist wrote another letter to the editor of *The Arizona Republic*, in which he contended that "many . . . would feel that we are no more dedicated to an 'integrated' society than we are to a 'segregated' society" (*Hearings*, 1971, p. 309).

7. *Hearings*, 1971, pp. 71–72.

8. "Reagan's Mr. Right," p. 24.

9. Warren Weaver, "Mr. Justice Rehnquist Dissenting," *New York Times Magazine*, Oct. 13, 1974, p. 36.

10. Justice Stevens dissented more often than Rehnquist during the 1976, 1980, and 1982–84 terms of the Court. During the 1972–74 terms Douglas

dissented more often than any of the others. See the statistics compiled by the *Harvard Law Review* 86–100 (Nov. 1972–86).

11. Letter to Senator James O. Eastland from Phil C. Neal, Nov. 10, 1971, in *Hearings*, 1971, p. 11.

12. Abraham, *Justices and Presidents*, p. 318.

13. Weaver, "Mr. Justice Rehnquist Dissenting," 36.

14. As quoted in A. E. Dick Howard, "A Key Fighter in Major Battles," *American Bar Association Journal* 72 (1972): 47.

15. These descriptions are recalled from the author's own informal conversations.

16. As quoted in Howard, "A Key Fighter in Major Battles," 47.

17. David M. O'Brien, *Storm Center: The Supreme Court in American Politics* (New York: W. W. Norton, 1986), p. 127.

18. John A. Jenkins, "The Partisan: A Talk with Justice Rehnquist," *New York Times Magazine*, Mar. 3, 1985, p. 31.

19. *Hearings*, 1971, p. 445.

20. William H. Rehnquist, *The Supreme Court: How It Was, How It Is* (New York: Morrow, 1987), p. 63.

21. The agreement required that all legal proceedings involving claims of United States nationals against Iran be terminated. The executive orders abrogated all claims to Iranian funds, including those pending in courts, and required banks holding Iranian assets to transfer them to the Federal Reserve Bank of New York to be held or transferred as directed by the secretary of the treasury.

22. His dissenting opinion in *INS v. Chadha* (1983) also suggests his opposition to the delegation of legislative power to the executive.

23. Jeff Powell, in "The Compleat Jeffersonian: Justice Rehnquist and Federalism," *Yale Law Journal* 91 (1982): 1328, referred to Rehnquist's doctrine of state sovereignty as a specific elaboration of his theory of federalism.

24. The "similarly situated" language comes from *Royster Guano Co., F.S. v. Virginia* (1920): "The classification must be reasonable, not arbitrary, and must rest upon some ground of difference having a fair and substantial relation to the object of the legislation so that all persons similarly circumstanced shall be treated alike" (243 U.S. at 415).

25. This statistic comes from Edward Heck's data, which include the Burger Court years through the 1984–85 term of the Court. See Edward V. Heck and Albert C. Ringelstein, "The Burger Court and Primacy of Political Expression," *Western Political Quarterly* 40 (1987): 419.

26. My purpose in using the statistical analysis at this point is simply to suggest how low Rehnquist's support for freedom of expression has been. Still, the use of the statistic raises questions regarding the type of exceptional situation in which Rehnquist did support a freedom of expression claim— does any pattern emerge? In the hope that I might answer those questions, I obtained a list from Edward Heck of the cases that he considered Rehnquist to have cast a vote in support of a claim.

Upon examining the list, I found, first, opinions that I would describe as not really upholding a claim of freedom of expression. For example, in *Pinkus v. United States* (1978), he joined the majority, which held that children may not be included as part of the "community" in defining obscenity. But the Court also held that sensitive persons can be included and that members of deviant groups can be considered in determining whether material appeals to prurient interest in sex. In *Miami Herald Publishing Co. v. Tornillo* (1974), the Court invalidated Florida's right to reply law. Rehnquist joined Brennan's concurring opinion, which asserted that the decision did not apply to retraction statutes affording plaintiffs able to prove defamatory falsehoods a statutory action to require publication of a retraction. It is questionable whether the *Miami Herald* decision, which shields newspapers from a requirement that they provide space for disgruntled objects of news stories, actually protects freedom of expression.

Second, in a large number of cases on Heck's list, although Rehnquist did support a claim of freedom of expression, he did so on narrower grounds than those expressed in the majority opinion, for example, *Healy v. James* (1972), *Communist Party of Indiana v. Whitcomb* (1974), and *Steffel v. Thompson* (1974), all concurring opinions. In the rest of the cases, he either joined the majority or wrote the majority opinion while several members of the Court stated that they would have gone further. For example, in *Jenkins v. Georgia* (1974) the Court held that the film *Carnal Knowledge* was not obscene and that juries do not have unbridled discretion in determining what is patently offensive, yet it also affirmed that community standards are local. The case *Nebraska Press Association v. Stuart* (1976) was one in which Rehnquist joined the majority opinion that struck down a gag order on news media reporting on a murder case. Concurring opinions authored by White, Powell, Brennan, and Stevens would have gone further than the majority to protect freedom of the press.

27. See Walter F. Murphy, "An Ordering of Constitutional Values," *Southern California Law Review* 53 (1980): 708.

28. William H. Rehnquist, "The Notion of a Living Constitution," *Texas Law Review* 54 (1976): 704.

29. The literature on constitutional interpretation is too voluminous to list here. For the most helpful comprehensive treatment, see Walter F. Murphy, James E. Fleming, and William F. Harris II, *American Constitutional Interpretation* (Mineola, N.Y.: Foundation Press, 1986).

30. "The Notion of a Living Constitution," p. 699.

31. Ibid., p. 698.

32. Ibid., p. 696.

33. Anthony Lewis, "The Court: Rehnquist," *New York Times*, June 20, 1986, p. 23.

12

JUSTICE JOHN PAUL STEVENS:
The Lone Ranger in a Black Robe

BRADLEY C. CANON

Introduction

President Ford appointed Justice John Paul Stevens to the Supreme Court in November 1975, following Justice William O. Douglas's retirement. Stevens was fifty-five years old and in his fifth year as a judge on the Court of Appeals for the Seventh Circuit. A native of Chicago and a graduate of the University of Chicago and of Northwestern Law School, he had clerked for Supreme Court Justice Wiley Rutledge in 1947 and then had practiced law in Chicago until named to the federal bench in 1971. Much of his practice had involved antitrust law, and he had written a few law review articles in that area. He had also taught antitrust law part-time on the Chicago and Northwestern law faculties in the 1950s. He was a moderately active Republican and a friend of Edward Levi, president of the University of Chicago and later Ford's attorney general.

Only one major professional analysis of Stevens's jurisprudence has appeared.[1] Some observers have seen him as a loner on the Burger Court,[2] but his interactive role on the Court has not been closely studied. The parameters of his legal positions and interactive behavior, however, can be seen in his voting and opinion behavior (see Table 12.1).[3] Because Stevens voted in favor of the civil liberties claimant in 58.8 percent of the cases analyzed— almost 18 percent higher than the Court's level of support—he can be termed overall as a reasonably strong civil libertarian. Stevens's support for civil liberties claims was greatest in the areas of criminal defendants' rights and separation of church and state; he followed the Court majority most closely in equal protection cases;

TABLE 12.1
Support for Civil Liberties Claimants and Federal Power
by Justice Stevens and by Court Majority, 1975–85 Terms

Type of Case	For Civil Liberties Claimant		Against Civil Liberties Claimant	
	Stevens	Court	Stevens	Court
Criminal justice	209	129	168	248
(N = 377)	(55.9%)	(34.2%)	(44.8%)	(65.8%)
Equal protection	82	70	47	59
(N = 129)	(63.6%)	(54.3%)	(36.4%)	(43.7%)
Freedom of expression	57	43	33	47
(N = 90)	(63.3%)	(47.7%)	(36.7%)	(52.3%)
Religious cases	18	13	8	13
(N = 26)	(69.2%)	(50.0%)	(30.8%)	(50.0%)
Substantive due process	8	5	9	12
(N = 17)	(47.1%)	(29.4%)	(52.9%)	(70.6%)
Total	374	260	265	379
(N = 639)	(58.5%)	(40.7%)	(41.5%)	(59.3%)

	For Federal Power		Against Federal Power	
	Stevens	Court	Stevens	Court
Federal supremacy	24	25	17	16
and preemption	(58.5%)	(61.0%)	(41.5%)	(39.0%)
(N = 41)				

Source: National Science Foundation, Supreme Court Data Collection Project (see note 3 of this chapter.)

and his support level was slightly below that of the Court's in cases upholding federal power.

Although Stevens carried his share of majority opinion assignments on the Burger Court (see Table 1.6), he wrote a large number of concurring and dissenting opinions, authoring more of these than any of his colleagues in each of the Court's last six terms. It seems that Stevens did not join his colleagues' analyses very often but frequently developed his own position. A comparison of the number of times that he joined other justices' concurring or dissenting opinions (156) with the number of times they joined his (196) is revealing (see Tables 12.1, 12.2, and 12.3).[4] In civil liberties cases, the other justices were attracted to Stevens's opinions about 2.4 times more often than he was to theirs. Justices Brennan and Marshall contributed most greatly to this asymmetry. (Even when they are excluded, Stevens was joined 47 times and

TABLE 12.2
Number of Times Stevens Joined Other Justices' Opinions

	Stew	Mars	Bren	Whit	Burg	Blkm	Powl	Rehn	O'Co
Civil liberties cases ($N = 67$)	4	19	22	5	1	6	3	6	1
Other cases ($N = 89$)	7	11	16	11	2	12	9	15	6
Total ($N = 156$)	11	30	38	16	3	18	12	21	7

Source: National Science Foundation, Supreme Court Data Collection Project (see note 3).

TABLE 12.3
Number of Times Other Justices Joined Stevens's Opinions

	Stew	Mars	Bren	Whit	Burg	Blkm	Powl	Rehn	O'Co
Civil liberties cases ($N = 160$)	8	52	61	4	6	14	5	9	1
Other cases ($N = 36$)	1	7	5	5	2	3	2	5	2
Total ($N = 196$)	9	59	66	9	8	17	7	14	3

Source: National Science Foundation, Supreme Court Data Collection Project (see note 3).

joined others' opinions only 26 times.) In non–civil liberties cases, the ratio was the reverse, with Stevens joining 2.5 more times as often as he was joined. In these cases Stevens joined Brennan most often, made Rehnquist his second choice, and joined White and Marshall an equal number of times. Thus Stevens was much more likely to follow his own course in civil liberties cases than in other types of cases.

These data clearly lend support to the descriptions of Stevens as a moderate civil libertarian who was not always ideologically predictable and who was often a loner in civil liberties opinion writing. His votes in this area were more often cast with Brennan and Marshall than with the other justices. Yet he was not aligned with them in an ideological bloc, and, with some frequency, he was in the company of Rehnquist, who is least supportive of civil liberties claims.

His Relationships with Other Justices

Indications of Stevens's independence are buttressed by his willingness to "take on" many of his colleagues in his opinions. Burger,

Rehnquist, and White were his most frequent targets, but all the justices, save Brennan and Stewart, were subject to his sometimes caustic pen.[5] He could write with a biting sarcasm hardly calculated to win friends and influence people. For example, in *Fullilove v. Klutznick* (1980), authored by Chief Justice Burger, Stevens wrote, "If the National Government is to make a serious effort to define racial classes by criteria that can be administered objectively, it must study precedents such as the First Regulation to the Reichs Citizenship Law of November 14, 1935" (448 U.S. at 534 n. 5).

Another favorite Stevens tactic was to cite particular justices against themselves. For example, dissenting from the chief justice's majority opinion in *Hudson v. Palmer* (1984), which severely constrained prisoners' rights and remedies, he recalled Burger's opinion in *Houchins v. KQED, Inc.* (1978) that prisoners retained privacy rights and were not to be treated like animals in a zoo. Stevens also used hyperbole in his dissents to describe the motivation or impact of majority opinions. Assertions that the majority had no appreciation for individual liberty (*Walters v. National Association of Radiation Survivors,* 1985, 373 U.S. at 358) or that it condoned procedures more appropriate to the Soviet Union (*Allen v. Illinois,* 1986, 478 U.S. at 383 n. 19) and other such comments show up now and again in his dissents. It seems likely that such behavior would have impaired Stevens's relationships with his colleagues.

Another characteristic that probably did not endear Stevens to the other justices was his habit of citing himself frequently. Far more than his colleagues, he reprinted or noted his earlier opinions (sometimes even one from his Seventh Circuit days) as if to say that he had always known the right answer.

His Vision of the Court's Role

Stevens saw a clear role for the Court—one hearkening to the Court's traditional legal functions yet at the same time recognizing the Court as a major national policymaker. He joined most of his colleagues in asserting that the Court's docket was overloaded but blamed his colleagues for it: the Court heard far too many trivial cases due to his colleagues' aggressiveness in putting them on the docket. Stevens proposed solutions both on and off the bench. His most famous off-court suggestion was that the Rule of Four be abolished.[6] Certiorari petitions receiving only four votes, he argued, were usually the least important cases. On the bench he argued that per curiam opinions were a likely sign of a case's unimportance—since no justice thought the case worthy of attributable craftsmanship. More generally, he charged his conser-

Justice John Paul Stevens

vative colleagues with taking cases simply because they were offended by the result below. In *Board of Education of Rodgers v.
McCluskey* (1982), he wrote: "As Justice Rehnquist has reminded
us, in our zeal to provide equal justice under law, we must never
forget that this Court is not a forum for the correction of errors. . . . Today we exercise our majestic power to enforce a school
board's suspension of a tenth grade student who consumed too
much alcohol on October 21, 1980" (458 U.S. at 972–73). The
Court especially erred in this manner in criminal cases. For example, Stevens criticized the Court in *Patton v. Young* (1984) for
taking the case in order to make "sure that an apparently guilty
defendant was not given too much protection by the law" (467
U.S. at 1053 n. 8).

Reflecting Justice Brandeis's philosophy in *Ashwander v. Tennessee
Valley Authority* (1936), Stevens often chided his colleagues for deciding more broadly than necessary in settling a case. Too often,
he complained in *Berkemer v. McCarty* (1984), "the majority—its
appetite for deciding constitutional questions only whetted—is
driven to serve up a more delectable issue to satiate it" (468 U.S.
at 445–46). Opinions that surpass the *ratio decidendi* are merely
advisory, he asserted, and lower courts need not follow them. For
this reason Stevens refrained from substantive participation in several important Burger Court decisions such as *Firefighters Local No.
1784 v. Stotts* (1984).

Even when a dispute was legally ripe, Stevens opted for caution.
Because the Court makes far-reaching policy, it should understand
the broader implications of its decisions before proceeding. If the
record was poorly developed, the nature of the legal problem was
just emerging, or another agency was likely to act, Stevens believed
the best course was to avoid a decision, or at least avoid establishing
a major precedent (see, for example, his dissent in *California v.
Carney*, 1985).

Federalism and Separation of Powers

Stevens's votes and opinions on federalism questions manifested
a jurisprudence that favored a national government with broad
authority. In *National League of Cities v. Usery* (1976), which revitalized the long-dormant Tenth Amendment, Stevens, in dissent,
was unable to see any constitutional difference between Congress's
regulation of state employees' wages and its conceded power to
regulate state safety or environmental practices under the commerce clause. Concurring in *EEOC v. Wyoming* (1983), Stevens

argued that the commerce clause was "the Framers' response to the central problem that gave rise to the Constitution," and he urged the Court to continue a jurisprudence interpreting that intent in terms of today's economy, which included the public, as well as the private, sector (460 U.S. at 244). He wanted *National League of Cities* overruled, an event that occurred two years later in *Garcia v. San Antonio Metropolitan Transit Authority* (1985). Even in cases not involving the commerce clause, Stevens believed that Tenth Amendment arguments were useless. He alone dissented when the Court granted South Carolina leave to challenge Congress's 1982 revenue act subjecting state and municipal bond interest to the income tax in *South Carolina v. Regan* (1983).

Fueled by the expansion of federal constitutional and statutory rights, a similar debate took place on the Court over the scope of the Eleventh Amendment. Stevens favored a limited state immunity. In his view the amendment's purpose was to embody the ancient concept of sovereign immunity in the Constitution; it did not prohibit federal courts from enjoining conduct prohibited by federal law or the state's own laws or from requiring payment due, as he argued in his dissent in *Pennhurst State School and Hospital v. Halderman* (1984). At first, however, Stevens rejected Brennan's textual interpretation that the Eleventh Amendment did not forbid federal courts from hearing a suit against a state by a citizen of that state. But after *Pennhurst*, Stevens became convinced that the majority's expansion of states' immunity was so at odds with past precedents that a "fresh examination of the Court's Eleventh Amendment jurisprudence" (473 U.S. at 304) would produce more benefits than harm, as he put it in his dissent in *Atascadero State Hospital v. Scanlon* (1985).

Nor was Stevens any more sympathetic to other claims of state immunity. Speaking for a unanimous Court in *Hutto v. Finney* (1978), he held that the Eleventh Amendment did not immunize states against costly federal court orders that were ancillary to enforcing federal constitutional and statutory rights. "Federal courts," he wrote, "are not reduced to issuing injunctions against state officers and hoping that they will be enforced" (437 U.S. at 690). Although federal courts cannot award common law monetary damages, they can fine states for noncompliance with their orders. Nor are state officers immune from *in rem* actions, Stevens wrote for the majority (*Florida Department of State v. Treasure Salvors, Inc.*, 1982). While he recognized the irony of labeling state officers' illegal acts as private under the Eleventh Amendment but as "state action" under the Fourteenth Amendment, he noted that this inconsistency "is one of the cornerstones" of modern constitutional jurisprudence (458 U.S. at 685).

The Burger Court decided several important cases involving the powers of the three branches and the limits on those powers, but Stevens did not play a major role in them. Generally he voted silently with the majority, occasionally adding a concurrence. He filed a long and complex one in *Bowsher v. Synar* (1986), the case in which the Court struck down the automatic budget cuts provision of the Gramm-Rudman-Hollings Act. Stevens argued that Congress's power under the act to remove the comptroller general made an official performing an executive function subservient to Congress. He rejected the majority's formalism and argued instead that, while the comptroller general is a part of the legislative branch, his function could not be clearly categorized—reality was more important than labels. Also, "the notion that the removal power . . . automatically creates a 'here and now subservience' to Congress . . . is belied by history" and by statutory provisions (478 U.S. at 739). The Gramm-Rudman-Hollings Act was unconstitutional, however, because the comptroller general's job was not clerical but instead involved sophisticated policy-making, and the first sentence of Article I requires that Congress itself exercise all legislative power that is exercised by the legislative branch.

The Establishment Clause

The Burger Court decided 26 cases concerning religion during Stevens's tenure: 16 establishment clause cases and 10 free exercise ones. Throughout the Court's eleven terms, Justices Stevens, Brennan, Marshall, and Blackmun constituted a voting bloc in these cases, voting together in 22 of them. This was far and away the most cohesive civil liberties policy bloc with which Stevens was aligned. Apparently this degree of like-mindedness with three other justices, along with a 74 percent victory rate, led Stevens to write fewer opinions in this area than in other civil liberties areas.

Stevens's establishment clause jurisprudence was governed by a belief, perhaps too simply stated, that a bright line should demarcate governmental and religious activities. Concurring and dissenting in *Wolman v. Walter* (1977), he argued that this line "should not differentiate between direct and indirect subsidies" or between various types of instructional materials. "A state subsidy of sectarian schools is invalid regardless of the form it takes . . . for all [forms] give aid to the school's educational mission, which at heart is religious" (433 U.S. at 265). The line, Stevens lamented, had become "blurred, indistinct and variable" (266). Dissenting in *Committee for Public Education and Religious Liberty v. Regan* (1980), he said he would resurrect Justice Black's "high and impregnable wall" and have the Court cease its "Sisyphean task" of trying to justify fine distinctions (444 U.S. at 671). Stevens himself, however, illustrated some of the difficulties of drawing bright lines when, in *Wolman,* he noted that student therapeutic and diagnostic services "may fall" on the permissible side of the line, although he had "some misgivings on this point," and was "concerned about the amount of money appropriated" (433 U.S. at 266).

In his only establishment clause opinion for the Court, *Wallace v. Jaffree* (1985), Stevens took clear issue with the argument, vigorously renewed in the 1980s by the Reagan administration and the religious right, that the clause does not forbid state aid to religion or encouragement of religion in general, but is intended only to prohibit government preference among sects. This may have been the prevailing interpretation "at one time," Stevens conceded, but the Court had "unambiguously" rejected it when the clause was "examined in the crucible of litigation" (472 U.S. at 52–53). Stevens responded to Burger's dissenting argument that the Alabama "minute of silence" statute was a mere shadow threat to an establishment of religion and should not be voided due to unsophisticated draftsmanship by asserting that "the importance of the principle does not permit us to treat this as an inconsequential case" (60).

Freedom of Expression

In freedom of speech, press, and association cases, Stevens was not closely aligned with any bloc or group of justices. Neither the claimant nor the government could count on his vote. He had a unique doctrinal approach to some First Amendment issues such as obscenity, and otherwise he often wrote for himself or argued that an issue could be avoided. While he was more often in the Brennan/Marshall camp in split decisions, several cases found him aligned with Burger and Rehnquist, especially when a content-neutral law limiting the use of one narrow means of communication among many alternatives was at issue, as it was, for example, in *FCC v. League of Women Voters of California* (1984).

Stevens was sympathetic with Brennan's virtual absolutist approach to prior restraint when it was based on content. This is seen in his concurring opinion in *Nebraska Press Association v. Stuart* (1976) and reiterated at greater length in his dissent in *Posadas de*

Puerto Rico Associates v. Tourism Company of Puerto Rico (1986). Dissenting in *Snepp v. United States* (1980), he opposed the imposition of post-publication clearance contracts on government employees, which he thought was nothing more than a "new species of prior restraint" (444 U.S. at 524).

But unlike Brennan and Marshall, Stevens had little use for the overbreadth doctrine. This position was best demonstrated in his opinion for the Court in *City of Los Angeles v. Taxpayers for Vincent* (1984), in which he argued that courts should permit a vicarious assertion of First Amendment rights only when "it was apparent" (as opposed to a hypothetical possibility) that "to enforce such legislation would create an unacceptable risk of suppression of ideas" (466 U.S. at 797). Similarly, Stevens sometimes avoided considerations of overbreadth by holding that a reasonable interpretation of the law in question would mean that the complaining party did not violate it, as he did concurring in *United States v. Grace* (1983). Indeed, Stevens's belief that constitutional questions should be avoided where possible showed up most often in freedom of expression and association cases.

In a like vein, he objected vociferously to the Court's willingness to reach out to make unnecessary First Amendment law in *Snepp*. The Court's solution—a constructive trust for the Central Intelligence Agency from the royalties on a former agent's book—was grounded in neither constitutional, statutory, nor common law, Stevens asserted, and amounted to blatant judicial activism. The transgression was all the more galling as it occurred without oral argument or a signed opinion.

Commercial Speech

The Supreme Court began according constitutional protection to commercial speech just as Stevens joined the Court, and the new justice soon developed a philosophy, usually expressed in concurring or dissenting opinions, about what constituted such speech and how much protection it should have. Stevens did not put it at the top of what might be termed his "continuum of protection," and, in his concurrence in *Carey v. Population Services International* (1977), he argued that the degree of protection had to be considered in context. Aesthetic and other kinds of zoning considerations justified restrictions on advertising, he asserted, concurring in *Metromedia, Inc. v. City of San Diego* (1981), although the dubious value of the product alone (a gambling casino) did not justify forbidding advertising in some geographical areas while allowing it in others (*Posadas*).

Stevens asserted in *Central Hudson Gas and Electric Corp. v. Public Service Commission of New York* (1980) that, because commercial speech is afforded less protection, "it is important that the commercial speech concept not be defined too broadly lest speech deserving of greater constitutional protection be inadvertently suppressed" (447 U.S. at 579). The concept "should not include the entire range of communication that is embraced within the term 'promotional advertising' " (580). While states can regulate advertising to limit the offensiveness of the form of communication (in terms of loudness or ugliness, for example), they should not be able to regulate advertising deemed offensive because recipients may disagree with it or not want to think about the topic, he wrote, concurring in *Bolger v. Youngs Drug Products Corp.* (1983). In Stevens's opinion, advertising itself—absent deception, misrepresentation, or advocacy of unlawful conduct—constitutes pure speech and cannot be proscribed because of the regulators' "fear that the audience may find [it] persuasive" (447 U.S. at 581). His position in *Bolger* was that advertising that mixes commercial and noncommercial speech must be treated as having the full range of First Amendment protections in the face of an undiscriminating statute.

Sexually Oriented Material

Sexually oriented material was also low on Justice Stevens's continuum of protection. His position became apparent a few months after he joined the Court when he wrote the majority opinion in *Young v. American Mini Theaters, Inc.* (1976) and upheld restrictions on the location of adult theaters. According to Stevens, "society's interest in protecting this type of expression is of a wholly different and lesser magnitude than the interest in untrammeled political debate that inspired Voltaire's immortal comment. . . . Few of us would march our sons and daughters off to war to preserve the citizen's right to see 'Specified Sexual Activities' in the theater of our choice" (427 U.S. at 70).

Although Stevens spoke for four other justices here, he could not keep a majority behind the continuum approach. Only Burger and Rehnquist subscribed to this perspective when Stevens announced the judgment of the Court in *FCC v. Pacifica Foundation* (1978). He argued here that differing levels of protection were not new to First Amendment jurisprudence, citing some cases from other areas of law and quoting from Justice Holmes's classic opinion in *Schenck v. United States* (1919). Speaking for the Court in *New York v. Ferber* (1982), he came close to adopting Holmes's own words, saying that "the question of whether a specific act of communication is protected by the First Amendment always requires some consideration of both its content and its context" (458 U.S. at 778). Each medium of communication is unique, and societal interests, especially in protecting the young, can require lesser protection of sexually oriented material in some media than in others.

Stevens was not comfortable with the Court's landmark *Miller v. California* (1973) obscenity decision. He believed that, generally, the problem of regulating sexually oriented material should not be approached through criminal prosecution. He equated such material with common law nuisances such as junkyards. This material is not criminal per se, and perhaps some of it is even useful given the widespread demand for it, but society certainly has a right to limit it in time and place. He conceded that obscenity prosecutions will continue but, dissenting in *Smith v. United States* (1977), called for a "principled re-examination" of the *Miller* standards (431 U.S. at 311).

Stevens was particularly bothered about the use of local community norms to determine what constitutes obscenity. This focus did nothing to make the definitional task any easier and in fact made it worse by adding the problem of defining the local community. Moreover, he argued, because sexually oriented material has a modicum of First Amendment protection, it should be governed by a national norm. He also objected to the vagueness of obscenity laws. In *Marks v. United States* (1977), he found the federal law against mailing obscene material "intolerably vague" (424 U.S. at 268) and chastised the Court for silently abandoning *Miller*'s specificity requirement. As he stated in *Ward v. Illinois* (1977), "One of the strongest arguments against regulating obscenity through criminal law is the inherent vagueness of the obscenity concept. [*Miller*] at least held out the promise of a principled effort to respond" to this argument (431 U.S. at 782).

Access to Information

Controversy developed during the Burger Court years about what degree of access, if any, the First Amendment accords the public—and, more particularly, the news media—to government proceedings and institutions. Stevens favored a broad right of access in appeals challenging the closing of criminal trials or pretrial hearings, although he did silently join the Court in *Gannett Co., Inc. v. DePasquale* (1979) in holding that a pretrial hearing could be closed when the defendant had waived his Sixth Amendment right to a public trial. The First Amendment access question in that case was ignored over the protest of four dissenters. In *Richmond Newspapers, Inc. v. Virginia* (1980), however, the Court held that the First Amendment implies a right of public access to judicial proceedings. Stevens, concurring, saw it as a "watershed case" because "never before has [the Court] squarely held that the acquisition of newsworthy matter is entitled to any constitutional protection whatsoever" (448 U.S. at 582).

The media's right to visit prisons (which, unlike courts, are not normally open to the public) and interview inmates was refused First Amendment protection by the Court in two 1974 cases, *Pell v. Procunier* and *Saxbe v. Washington Post Co.* The issue came to the Court again in *Houchins* (1978), and on a 4-3 vote, with no opinion for the Court, media access was again denied. For the dissenters (Brennan and Powell), Stevens argued that a denial of reasonable access violated the First Amendment. He asserted that confidence in the judicial system and in all governmental institutions depends upon an informed citizenry. "It is not sufficient, therefore, that the channels of communication be free of governmental restraints. Without some protection for the acquisition of information about the operation of public institutions such as prisons by the public at large, the process of self-governance contemplated by the Framers would be stripped of substance. For this reason information-gathering is entitled to some measure of constitutional protection" (438 U.S. at 32).

Freedom of Association

To Stevens, the First Amendment guarantees clearly imply the freedom to associate with others under minimal government constraint, especially when people associate for expression on public issues. Certainly political parties are protected, he held for the Court in *Anderson v. Celebreeze* (1983), and state governments cannot hamper smaller or developing parties by imposing unusually early filing deadlines on them or heightened requirements for their inclusion on the ballot. In another majority opinion, *NAACP v. Claiborne Hardware Co.* (1982), Stevens held that groups engaged in political protest are protected from tort liability when the protest spills over into violence, although those actually engaging in violence can be held liable.

Stevens concurred in *NLRB v. Retail Store Employees Union, Local 1001* (1980) in the Court's holding that, when association occurs primarily for nonpolitical reasons, more regulation can be tolerated. Stevens also stressed the converse right not to be compelled by law to associate, writing for a unanimous Court in *Chicago Teachers Union, Local No. 1, AFT, AFL-CIO v. Hudson* (1986).

Substantive Due Process

Stevens argued, especially off the Court, that the constitutional guarantees against deprivation of liberty without due process mean far more than "staying out of jail."[7] He also felt, however, that this is an area where judges need to tread cautiously, because the guidelines are few and the opportunities for unfettered judicial discretion many. "Wide-angle decision-making" here is inappropriate; judicial statements of substantive due process rights should be tailored to fit the case.[8]

Abortion

Although Stevens was not on the Court when *Roe v. Wade* (1973) was decided, he quickly made it clear that he accepted its holding with his concurrence in *Planned Parenthood of Central Missouri v. Danforth* (1976). Later votes and opinions by him more forcefully reflected a strong belief that the due process clauses guarantee a woman's right to an abortion. The best exposition is found in his concurring opinion in *Thornburgh v. College of Obstetricians and Gynecologists* (1986), in which he took detailed issue with Justice White's dissenting call for overruling *Roe*.

Nonetheless, Stevens was less inclined to strike down state laws regulating abortion than were Justices Brennan, Marshall, and Blackmun. Dissenting in part in *Danforth*, he argued that no constitutional infirmity was inherent in a law requiring parental consent before a minor could obtain an abortion. He drew an analogy to parental control of other constitutional rights of youths involving contracts, travel, and viewing adult films. He reiterated this position in *H. L. v. Matheson* (1981), concurring in the Court's decision to uphold a Utah law requiring parental notification before a minor could obtain an abortion (but not parental consent). Neither the fact that some daughters are mature or that parental notice might not always result in meaningful parent-child discussion diminishes the state's interest in "ensuring that a young woman receive . . . appropriate consultation" before making a decision about terminating her pregnancy (450 U.S. at 423). Likewise, Stevens was in the majority when the Court upheld, in *Maher v. Roe* (1977), a Connecticut law barring the use of state Medicaid funds to pay for therapeutic abortions. The Court reasoned that a state is not obligated to finance the exercise of a fundamental right when a citizen cannot afford it.

Stevens entered a vigorous protest in *Harris v. McRae* (1980), however, when the Court upheld the constitutionality of the highly controversial Hyde amendment, which prohibited the use of federal Medicaid funds for most nontherapeutic abortions. He saw the constitutional problem in *Harris* as a question of equal protection, not liberty. When an abortion is medically necessary and not an elective option, women who meet the law's criterion of indigency should not be denied access to Medicaid benefits "solely because they must exercise their constitutional right to have an abortion" (448 U.S. at 349). *Roe* should be "dispositive" in this case, and the Court was "shirking its duty to protect *Roe* by focusing on the state's interest in potential life" (351). He concluded, "Having decided to alleviate some of the hardships of poverty through provision of medical care, the Government must use neutral criteria in distributing the benefits. . . . [It may not] create exceptions for the sole purpose of furthering a government interest that is constitutionally subordinate to the individual interest that the entire program was designed to protect" (354).

Other Liberty and Privacy Issues

Other interesting substantive due process cases came to the Court during the Burger years. The claims were usually rejected with near unanimity, with Stevens often writing the opinion. Most significant perhaps was the *Whalen v. Roe* (1977) decision upholding a New York law requiring the registration of prescriptions for certain types of drugs. In response to the argument that the law was ineffective and a threat to privacy, Stevens used a legislative reasonableness test to analyze its validity. This law, he wrote, represented a "considered attempt" to meet the drug abuse problem; it was the product of "an orderly and rational legislative decision" (429 U.S. at 597). If it "results in the foolish expenditure of funds . . . the legislative process remains available to terminate the unwise experiment" (598).

Stevens used the same approach when he concurred in the more controversial *Carey* case but reached a different conclusion—that the legislature had acted irrationally. Preventing minors from obtaining contraceptives, he argued, would not stop them from engaging in sexual intercourse; more likely, it would simply increase their chances of acquiring venereal disease. The state was thus harming those it intended to help; he thought the law analogous to having a "state dramatize its disapproval of motorcycles by forbidding the use of helmets" (431 U.S. at 715).

In *Moore v. City of East Cleveland, Ohio* (1977) and *Bowers v. Hardwick* (1986), both decided on 5-4 votes, Stevens preferred to bypass the substantive due process question and approached the cases from another angle. The plurality in *Moore* held that an ordinance limiting the number of relatives allowed to live in a house deprives the owner of the liberty of associating with and caring for an extended family. Providing the fifth vote, Stevens saw the ordinance as a deprivation of property rather than liberty because it "cuts so deeply into a fundamental right normally associated with the ownership of residential property" and served no discernible purpose related to public health, safety, or morals (431 U.S. at 520).

Bowers, certainly the most controversial substantive due process case not involving abortion, sustained Georgia's sodomy law as it applied to homosexuals. Stevens did join Blackmun's dissent, which argued directly that consensual sodomy was protected by the due process clauses, but in his own dissent he used an equal protection approach, arguing that because the statute did not distinguish between homosexual and heterosexual sodomy, or between married and unmarried couples, it was inconsistent with precedents such as *Griswold v. Connecticut* (1965) and *Eisenstadt v. Baird* (1972), which protected sodomy between married persons. Equality means "that every free citizen has the same interest in 'liberty' that the members of the majority share. From the standpoint of the individual, the homosexual and the heterosexual have the same interest in deciding how he will live his own life. . . . State intrusion into the private conduct of either is equally burdensome" (478 U.S. at 218–19).

Equal Protection

Justice Stevens rejected the Court's use of two or three tiers of scrutiny to analyze equal protection claims. He took this position early when he concurred in *Craig v. Boren* (1976), the decision that gave birth to the "heightened scrutiny" standard. The best exposition of his philosophy is in his concurrence in *City of Cleburne v. Cleburne Living Center* (1985):

In every equal protection case, we have to ask certain basic questions. What class is harmed by the legislation, and has it been subjected to a "tradition of disfavor" by our laws? What is the public purpose that is being served by the law? What is the characteristic of the disadvantaged class that justifies the disparate treatment? In most cases the answer to these questions will tell us whether the statute has a "rational basis." The answers will result in virtually automatic invalidation of racial classifications and in the validation of most economic classifications, but they will provide differing results in cases involving classifications based on alienage, gender or illegitimacy. But that is not because we apply an "intermediate standard of review" in these cases; rather it is because the characteristics of these groups are sometimes relevant and sometimes irrelevant to a valid public purpose, or, more specifically, to the purpose that the challenged laws purportedly intended to serve. (473 U.S. at 453–54)

The key to relevancy, then, lies in examining legislative motives and rationality—and Stevens seemed more willing than his colleagues to engage in substantive equal protection decision making by realistically assessing them. While conceding in his dissent in *Fullilove v. Klutznick* (1980) that judges should not usually consider legislative motivation, he believed they had a special obligation to examine a law's legislative history in discrimination cases to see if the legislators had really desired the law's discriminatory result. He would have held the provision creating a ten-percent set-aside of contracts for minority businesses unconstitutional because Congress had adopted it in a "slapdash" manner under pressure from members of its Black Caucus (448 U.S. at 539).

Stereotyped distinctions embodied in law are also suspect in Stevens's view. In *Boren* he found it "difficult to believe" that barring the sale of beer to 18-to-20-year-old males, but not females, reduced drunken driving (429 U.S. at 213). The law was the product of "a stereotyped attitude about the relative maturity of . . . the two sexes at this age" (213 n. 5). Dissenting in *Michael M. v. Superior Court of Sonoma County* (1981), Stevens scorned the contention that a law punishing males but not females under 18 for engaging in consensual sexual intercourse reduced teenage pregnancies. "Local custom and belief—rather than statutory laws of venerable but doubtful ancestry—will determine the volume of sexual activity among unmarried teenagers. The empirical evidence cited by the plurality [one million teenage pregnancies in California in 1976] demonstrates the futility of the notion that a statutory prohibition will significantly affect the volume of that activity" (450 U.S. at 459). This statute rested on the unsupported stereotype that boys were always the instigators of teenage sexual encounters. Likewise, Stevens asserted in dissent in *Mathews v. Lucas* (1976), the presumption that fathers did not support their illegitimate children simply reflected habitual popular thinking, not reality. On occasion, however, Stevens did accept stereotypes. In *Caban v. Mohammed* (1979), a case in which, ironically, he was dissenting, he cited common understandings about how illegitimate infants have different relationships with their mothers than with their fathers to justify allowing adoptions without paternal consent.

Administrative convenience, and also public policy goals, if well thought out, may sometimes justify legislative distinctions, even unfair ones, according to Stevens's concurrence in *Personnel Administrator of Massachusetts v. Feeney* (1979). Stevens also believed that when the law gives advantages to a minority group, especially one not defined by birth characteristics such as race or gender, it might well be considered presumptively constitutional. As he noted in *Attorney General of New York v. Soto-Lopez* (1986), "In a democracy, a majority will seldom treat itself unfairly" (476 U.S. at 916).

Racial Discrimination Cases

Stevens was sympathetic (though not in knee-jerk fashion) to claims of racial discrimination, but he had a more mixed reaction to constitutional questions about affirmative action programs. Stevens also saw many cases involving the Fifteenth Amendment and the Voting Rights Act of 1965 as equal protection cases; they are included in this subsection. During his tenure on the Burger Court, in 67 racial discrimination cases, he voted for the claimant or program 43 times and against them 24 times, and he was in the majority in 53 (or 79 percent) of the 67 cases. Despite this plethora of opportunities, however, Stevens delivered only two opinions for the Court, both in minor cases. He wrote sixteen concurrences and seven dissents.

The constitutionality of affirmative action practices was far and away the most controversial equal protection issue during the later years of the Burger Court, arising in six major cases. Stevens did not participate in *United Steelworkers v. Weber* (1979) and avoided the main issue in *Firefighters Local No. 1784 v. Stotts* (1984). He split his votes evenly in the other four cases, pouring out his fiercest opposition in his *Fullilove* dissent. No previous federal law had ever made privileges contingent upon race, he said, and he warned against the danger of creating permanent classes of privileged citizens based upon birth characteristics. He even cited the constitutional prohibition against titles of nobility as a constitutional barrier and discussed the sad history of racial and communal strife in countries where such distinctions are allowed. He wondered why Hispanics were included in Congress's ten-percent set-aside legislation when they had never suffered slavery and were no more the victims of discrimination than other immigrant groups. In the short run our polity might benefit, he conceded, but the long-run consequences would be pernicious. Yet unlike Stewart and Rehnquist, the other dissenters in *Fullilove*, Stevens did not argue that race-conscious legislation was unconstitutional per se; instead he claimed that legislators could compensate for the effects of slavery or official discrimination, but that judges had a "special obligation to scrutinize" such laws for rationality (448 U.S. at 548). As noted above, Stevens found the ten-percent set-aside law irrational.

His position that not all race-conscious policies are unconstitutional was advanced in *Wygant v. Jackson Board of Education* (1986), in which, ironically, Stevens again was in dissent. Here he argued that the utility of minority teachers as role models outweighed the harm done to the white teachers who would not have been laid off in the absence of the contractual agreement favoring minority teachers when layoffs were necessary. *Wygant* differed from *Fullilove* because its collective bargaining agreement had been approved by all parties after much negotiation, while the ten-percent set-aside law had been adopted in ill-considered haste.

Stevens's view on Title VII of the 1964 Civil Rights Act, however, was that it never permits race-conscious policies, no matter how noninvidious. Its wording and legislative history make this clear, he said in *Regents of the University of California v. Bakke* (1978). Dissenting for Burger, Stewart, and Rehnquist, Stevens believed Powell's opinion announcing the judgment of the Court, which held that the equal protection clause did not foreclose race from being one of many factors considered in university admission policies, was totally unnecessary to decide the case because the university was subject to the 1964 act. Thus it was not free to adopt racial quotas even if the equal protection clause does not forbid them.

Stevens concurred in *Washington v. Davis* (1976), in which the Court held that the burden of proving discriminatory intent (as opposed to discriminatory effect) rested with the plaintiff in equal protection cases. He expressed reservation about the utility of intent as a criterion, stating that he thought "the most probative evidence of intent will be objective evidence of what actually happens" (426 U.S. at 253). In a later voting rights case, *Rogers v.*

Lodge (1982), he argued—in seeming contrast with his *Fullilove* dissent—that measuring intent was slippery, especially when the Court could not develop "an acceptable, judicially manageable standard" (458 U.S. at 638). The absence of an objective standard "lets federal judges pick and choose almost at will" which representation schemes violate the Constitution or the Voting Rights Act (652). Otherwise rational policies, he said, concurring in *City of Mobile, Alabama v. Bolden* (1980), should not be voided, even if the intent of some of the participants was discriminatory.[9]

Stevens was not comfortable with judicial expansion of various civil rights laws and tolerated it only in cases of retrospective interpretations where to do otherwise would be destabilizing, as was the case in *Runyon v. McCrary* (1976). His restraint in statutory interpretation can be seen in *Bakke* and especially in *United States v. City of Sheffield, Alabama* (1978). In *Sheffield* he admonished the majority for ignoring the language and intent of the compromise provisions of Section 5 of the 1965 Voting Rights Act, even though following them might not be consonant with the act's broad goal.

Gender Discrimination Cases

Stevens's Seventh Circuit record in support of gender equality was labeled "bad to fair" by one commentator.[10] Nonetheless, as a member of the high court, Stevens usually supported a policy of gender equality. In constitutional cases, Stevens was also disposed to nullify laws or policies distinguishing between the sexes. Here, too, he was in step with his colleagues; *Michael M.* and *Caban* were his only dissents in constitutional cases, one in each direction. In seventeen constitutional cases, he wrote three opinions for the Court and filed four concurring and two dissenting opinions. Many gender differentiation cases were close, and he provided the crucial fifth vote in six cases, four of which nullified discriminatory policies.

Stevens felt that defenses relying on statistical differences between the sexes were usually irrelevant and that those premised on natural gender differences were only relevant sometimes, as he claimed in the *Michael M.* case. For Stevens, the city's argument in *Los Angeles Department of Water and Power v. Manhart* (1978) was an example of one fraught with statistical irrelevance. Writing for a five-justice majority, Stevens held that public employee retirement programs could not structure contributions and payouts based on different actuarial tables for men and women any more than they could use such differences regarding whites and blacks. Likewise, in *Boren* he rejected the pertinency of data showing that more drunken driving incidents involved teenage males than teenage females. Stevens noted that 98 percent of teenage males were not involved in these incidents and should not be punished for the sins of the 2 percent.

Nor did Stevens allow natural differences to be disguised as irrelevant statistical differences. Dissenting in *General Electric Co. v. Gilbert* (1976), a case that involved the exclusion of pregnancy from disability benefits coverage, he derided Rehnquist's argument for the majority that the policy did not violate Title VII because it divided employees into two groups, "pregnant women and nonpregnant persons" (429 U.S. at 161 n. 5). The capacity to become pregnant immutably divided men from women, and to single this characteristic out for differential treatment was obviously discriminatory.

Stevens agreed that Title VII was adopted to benefit women as a class, not men, as he wrote for the Court in *Cannon v. University of Chicago* (1979). Nonetheless, he did not look kindly on laws giving women advantages. Concurring in *Goldfarb v. Califano* (1977), he rejected the contention that women who have lost a spouse need financial cushioning much more often than men who have — an argument that was offered to justify the automatic payment of Social Security survivors' benefits to widows versus payment to widowers only if they had been supported by their wives.[11] He felt that this provision mirrored prevailing stereotypes and that it would not be difficult for the government to make payments generally according to need if it considered need crucial to entitlement. He took a similar position concerning alimony payments in his concurrence in *Orr v. Orr* (1979).

Other Types of Discrimination

In accord with his *Cleburne* philosophy, Stevens's reaction to other groups' invocation of equal protection largely depended upon circumstances. While Stevens was not very tolerant of distinctions based upon birth characteristics, he was more receptive to distinctions — especially rewards — based upon a status acquired later, even an unchangeable one. For example, Stevens dissented when, in *Hooper v. Bernalillo County Assessor* (1985), the Court struck down civil service and tax assessment preferences for Vietnam veterans who were legal residents of the state during their service. In *Soto-Lopez* he argued, "A governmental decision to grant a special privilege to a minority group is less objectionable than a decision to impose a special burden on a minority group" (476 U.S. at 916).

Although his *Cleburne* philosophy predicted varied results in alienage cases, Stevens voted to apply equal protection in all seven alienage cases that occurred during his tenure. Six were won by the alien, four by a 5-4 vote. In his very first opinion for the Court, *Hampton v. Mow Sun Wong* (1976), Stevens struck down civil service regulations prohibiting aliens from holding most federal jobs. While Congress or the president might provide legitimate national security or foreign policy reasons for such a restriction, he said, the current regulations had been adopted without such reasons and seemed based largely on a desire to enhance citizens' employment opportunities at the expense of resident aliens.

As for other distinct groups, Stevens, in his Cleburne concurrence, rejected the contention that laws affecting the mentally retarded differentially were entitled to strict scrutiny. He noted that some such laws are not only rational but necessary. Nevertheless, he agreed that the use of a zoning ordinance to keep homes for the mentally retarded out of a particular neighborhood failed to meet even a minimal test of rationality. Writing on age discrimination, Stevens, in a concurring opinion in *EEOC v. Wyoming* (1983), suggested that the societal disadvantages of eliminating mandatory retirement ages probably exceeded the benefits, but nonetheless upheld the constitutionality of the elimination.

Criminal Justice

Although Stevens was in the majority in nearly three-fourths of the Court's criminal cases, he was seldom tapped to write its opinion. He did so only twenty-two times (7.9 percent of 277 opportunities). Only two cases, *Payton v. New York* (1980) and *United States v. Ross* (1982), are widely recognized; Stevens coauthored (with Stewart and Powell) the opinions announcing the judgment of the Court in the 1976 death penalty cases. A likely inference from the below-average assignment of opinions to him is that Stevens's doctrinal views about criminal justice did not accord very well with those of most of his brethren, especially Chief Justice Burger, who assigned the vast majority of opinions. Research indicates that in 5-4 civil liberties cases, the pivotal fifth justice is chosen more often than normal to write the opinion in order to keep that justice in the majority coalition.[12] Stevens was seldom the pivotal justice; he joined the majority in only thirty-one 5-4 criminal justice cases and gave the opinion in only three of them. He wrote 132 other opinions in criminal justice cases; 81 were dissents (out of a total of 100 dissenting votes), and the remaining 51 were concurrences.

Stevens was by no means always sympathetic to the defendant. He supported the prosecution in about 44 percent of criminal cases, a figure much higher than that of Brennan and Marshall, although lower than that of any other justice (Table 12.1). Ten of his 100 dissenting votes favored the government, and Stevens held some doctrinal positions favorable to the prosecution.

His support for the defendant increased significantly during the later part of his service on the Burger Court, going from a 51/49 percent split for the 1975–81 terms to a 62/38 percent split in the 1982–85 terms. Similarly, the number of his dissenting opinions doubled from five to ten per term. An explanation for this increase lies in the considerable decline in the Court's pro-defendant decisions (from 40.7 percent to 28.6 percent) that followed Justice O'Connor's arrival. With her addition to the Court, the conservatives, under the Rule of Four, were able to grant certiorari to more lower court pro-defendant decisions with an eye to reversing them. This may well have been the catalyst behind Stevens's public protest against the Rule of Four.[13] It was also reflected in Stevens's protest in *Florida v. Meyers* (1984) against the Court's increased use of summary disposition to reverse lower court decisions favoring the defendant. But nowhere were his accusations so blunt and his dissenting pen so caustic as when directed at what he saw as unjustified support for the prosecution by his colleagues. In *Garrett v. United States* (1985), Stevens charged them with being unwilling to vindicate the guarantee against double jeopardy "in order to avoid the risk that a retrial may result in freeing this petitioner after only 19 years of imprisonment" (471 U.S. at 807).

Stevens also charged that the Court majority manifested a lack of confidence in state judges' abilities. Its enthusiasm for upholding convictions led to gross instances of judicial activism as the Court ignored or reshaped trial courts' findings and unnecessarily reached out to decide constitutional issues, as Stevens argued, for example, in dissent in *Illinois v. Vitale* (1981). In *Meyers* he even suggested that the Court's prosecutorial bias governed its summary dispositions. He was particularly bothered about the Court's announcement in *Michigan v. Long* (1983) that, absent an explicit statement by a state appellate court that its decision overturning a criminal conviction rested entirely on state grounds, the Court considered itself free to rule on the case. Dissenting in *Delaware v. Van Arsdall*

(1986), he predicted that this "lack of respect for state courts ... will ... be a recurring source of friction" between the two judiciaries (475 U.S. at 691). Stevens argued, in fact, that the Court should deny certiorari to state cases overturning convictions, even when the overturn rested on federal grounds. Denial set no precedent, he reasoned, and the Court was free to decide differently later if a federal case came along. The Court's role is to protect constitutional rights, not to ensure that the convictions of seemingly guilty felons are sustained. In Stevens's view, the Court's primary duties in the criminal justice area are to protect the existing rights of the defendant and to hold law enforcement agents to the constraints of their office, as he put it in his dissent in *Dalia v. United States* (1979).

Fourth Amendment Rights

In general, Stevens favored a broader interpretation of the Fourth Amendment and its attendant exclusionary rule than did all his colleagues except Brennan and Marshall. In eighty cases he voted to uphold Fourth Amendment claims forty-six times, compared to twenty-four for the Court. Stevens's interpretive approach to the Fourth Amendment began with its text; the first or second footnote in virtually all of his search and seizure cases set out the words of the amendment. Many of his opinions then recounted the common law and constitutional development of the warrant requirement and the probable cause standard, a good example being his majority opinion in *Payton v. New York* (1980). But attention to the text cut both ways: if a search had been reasonable, warrantless or not, Stevens found no transgression against the Fourth Amendment. This approach is best seen in Stevens's opinions regarding "administrative searches" by fire marshals, health officials, and the like. Dissenting in *Marshall v. Barlow's, Inc.* (1978), he argued that warrants should not be necessary for searches of businesses by the Occupational Safety and Health Administration because such searches were inherently reasonable. To him the majority's ruling—if a business objects to such a search, a warrant will issue without any showing of probable cause—was a sham.

In the 1970s and 1980s, the most controversial Fourth Amendment issue both within and outside of the Court was the exclusionary rule prohibiting the introduction of illegally seized evidence at criminal trials. Only Brennan, Marshall, and Stevens actively supported its retention. Unlike his cohorts, however, Stevens accepted the majority's premise that the rule's primary rationale was to deter police wrongdoing rather than to preserve the rule of law and judicial integrity, as he explained concurring in *Dunaway v. New York* (1979). Like the rule's opponents, Stevens emphasized that society has a strong interest in efficient law enforcement, and he implied in *Dunaway*, and in his concurrence in *Massachusetts v. Sheppard* (1984), that evidence seized illegally should be admissible if its exclusion would not enhance deterrence. Unlike many of his fellow justices, who asserted that the exclusionary rule had little or no impact on police behavior, Stevens believed that it did. Dissenting in *Segura v. United States* (1984), he argued that, because of many factors, including the exclusionary rule, the police had outgrown the " 'Keystone Kop' era" and moved into an "era of professionalism" (468 U.S. at 838). Court decisions giving only "lip service" to the rule undermined this professionalism (840).

Like Brennan and Marshall, Stevens opposed the "good faith" exception to the rule announced in *United States v. Leon* (1984). He feared that when the police lacked probable cause, they would lose nothing by gambling that a magistrate would issue a warrant on an insufficient affidavit, thus reducing the likelihood that the rule would deter illegal searches. Concurring in *Nix v. Williams* (1984), Stevens approved the "inevitable discovery" exception to the rule as long as the burden of proving inevitability clearly rested on the prosecution.

For Stevens, the Fourth Amendment's main purpose is the protection of individual privacy against government intrusion. His essential belief, as he expressed it in *California v. Carney* (1985), was that privacy is an ascendant value that "must not be bullied aside by extravagant claims of necessity" (471 U.S. at 401). Infringements on legitimate expectations of privacy needed to be construed narrowly, and the greatest expectation of privacy is in the home. In *Payton*, Stevens held that a warrantless intrusion to arrest someone was just as invasive of the sanctity of the home as a warrantless search. In *Dalia* and elsewhere, he denounced the Court's approval of FBI agents' placing of electronic transmitting devices in homes or other private areas without a warrant. He also accorded a high degree of privacy to closed containers, packages, and envelopes, as he made evident in his dissent in *United States v. Karo* (1984). Nonetheless, he strongly believed in the automobile exception to the warrant requirement and wrote the Court's opinion in *United States v. Ross* (1982), its decision most restrictive of privacy in automobiles.

Self-Incrimination and Miranda Rights

Stevens generally construed the constitutional prohibition against compulsory self-incrimination expansively. In forty-one cases he supported the claimant thirty times, while the Court did so in only sixteen instances. Stevens deplored the Court's narrowing of *Miranda v. Arizona*'s (1966) application. Typical, perhaps, was his dissent in *Rhode Island v. Innis* (1980), in which he asserted that the conversation initiated by the police at issue in the case had obviously been designed to appeal to the suspect's conscience. The majority, in his opinion, gave *Miranda* a "stinted" application, a "new definition [which] will almost certainly exclude every statement that is not punctuated with a question mark from the concept of 'interrogation' " (446 U.S. at 312). He also protested the Court's refusal, in *Allen v. Illinois,* to apply the Fifth Amendment guarantee to civil proceedings to involuntarily commit a sexual psychopath to a mental institution. The crucial fact was that the commitment had followed criminal charges; the state should not be able to strip defendants of their rights by using the "civil" label.

By contrast, Stevens was sympathetic to the prosecution's right to use a defendant's silence following *Miranda* warnings for impeachment purposes. His position was that the Fifth Amendment prohibits only compelled self-incrimination. Concurring in *Jenkins v. Anderson* (1980), he argued that, when the defendant was under no compulsion either to speak or remain silent, the prohibition was irrelevant. Stevens also dissented when the Court, in *Doyle v. Ohio* (1976), held it error for the prosecutor to compare the defendant's silence following the *Miranda* warnings with his explanation given on the witness stand. It is the defendant's choice to take the stand, according to Stevens, and the post-*Miranda* warning silence gave "rise to an inference of guilt only because it belied the trial testimony" (426 U.S. at 28). Later, however, in *Wainwright v. Greenfield* (1986), Stevens accepted the *Doyle* holding.

Double Jeopardy

In thirty-four cases involving the double jeopardy clause, Stevens voted to support the claim in twenty-one, while a majority did so only in thirteen. His dissents vigorously protested what he perceived as encroachments on the guarantee: in *Garrett*, trial on multiple charges denouncing the same offense; in *Vitale*, trial on a lesser charge stemming from the same event after trial for the more serious offense; and in *Ohio v. Johnson* (1984), trial for a greater offense after pleading guilty to a lesser one. "What lies at the heart of the Double Jeopardy Clause," he said in *Garrett* "is the prohibition of multiple prosecutions for 'the same offense' " (471 U.S. at 807).

Perhaps the case with the most far-reaching implications was *United States v. DiFrancesco* (1980), in which the Court, in a 5-4 vote, upheld a provision of the Organized Crime Control Act allowing the government to appeal a less than maximum sentence for "dangerous special offenders." Stevens's dissent asserted that the double jeopardy clause applied to sentences as well as trials because a sentence was an integral part of a criminal trial. Once entered, a judge could not vacate it and impose a longer one. By the same logic, the government should not be able to appeal a sentence it considered unsatisfactory.

Death Penalty Cases

Stevens joined the Court just as it was considering *Gregg v. Georgia* (1976) and its companion cases. He found himself in the pivotal plurality (with Stewart and Powell) of a Court divided three ways. Because the plurality was able to gather requisite votes from each of the other blocs for parts of its opinion, this middle group established the Burger Court's basic constitutional policy: the death penalty did not constitute cruel and unusual punishment per se, but it could be applied only upon separate consideration of aggravating and mitigating circumstances.

Stevens was cautious about upholding death sentences, doing so in only six of twenty-nine cases, while the Court affirmed them fourteen times. As he reasoned in his dissent in *Spaziano v. Florida* (1984), because the death sentence was irrevocable and because its primary if not sole purpose was retribution, capital punishment differed from all other penalties in kind and not just degree. Stevens explained in *Gardner v. Florida* (1977): "From the point of view of the defendant, it is different in both its severity and finality. From the point of view of society, the action of the sovereign in taking the life of one of its citizens also differs dramatically from any other legitimate state action. It is of vital importance to the defendant and the community that any decision to impose the death sentence be, and appear to be, based on reason rather than caprice and emotion" (430 U.S. at 357–58). Thus the sentencing process must contain sufficient safeguards against the penalty's casual or emotional imposition and yet be flexible enough to be tailored to the circumstances.

For Stevens, both the judge and jury have crucial veto roles in the process, which he spelled out in *Beck v. Alabama* (1980). The jury is the voice of the community and therefore plays an important part in ensuring that capital punishment comports with the public's evolving standards of decency. It must have all feasible options including that of convicting for a lesser crime. But a jury's recommendation of death must be subject to more than a pro forma review by the trial and appellate judges if the sentence is to stand, an assertion he repeated in *Barclay v. Florida* (1983).

Miscellaneous Criminal Cases

Stevens was more likely to dissent in cases involving constitutional issues than in those involving statutory interpretation or federal criminal procedure. In 85 miscellaneous constitutional cases, he dissented thirty-four times, favoring the defendant all but two of those times. In nineteen cases, however, Stevens objected, as noted above, to the summary disposition of the case. He dissented in 11 of the Court's 32 statutory cases (two dissents favored the government), and in only 6 of the 53 procedural cases (one dissent favored the government).

Most notably, Stevens objected to the expansion of the "harmless error" rule. Dissenting in *United States v. Lane* (1986), he argued that "undertaking harmless error review is perhaps the least useful function this Court can perform" (474 U.S. at 476). When the Court upheld an Ohio trial judge's exclusion of the defendant's out-of-state attorney in *Leis v. Flynt* (1979), he dissented with considerable force, citing famous examples of the utility of such representation for locally unpopular clients. Another outspoken dissent occurred when the Court, in *Corbitt v. New Jersey* (1978), upheld a state law that imposed a mandatory maximum sentence on defendants who were convicted after pleading not guilty to murder, yet allowed the trial judge discretion in sentencing for the same crimes if defendants gave what amounted to a guilty plea. "A 'false' not guilty plea has no place in our jurisprudence," Stevens wrote (439 U.S. at 228). The argument that the statute is justified "by a valid state interest in conserving scarce prosecutorial resources is simply a restatement of the obvious purpose of the law to motivate defendants to plead guilty instead of exercising their expensive right to trial" (230).

Prisoners' Rights

In no other area of criminal justice did Stevens differentiate himself as much from the Burger Court majority as in prisoners' rights cases. He supported the prisoner in 16 of the 17 cases considered; the Court did so in only 5 cases—and in none after O'Connor's appointment. Throughout his tenure, Stevens took the lead in denouncing the majority's deferential stance. Dissenting in *Meachem v. Fano* (1976), he accused the Court of returning to the nineteenth-century doctrine that a prisoner is "a slave of the state." He disputed *Meachem*'s holding that convicts have no liberties other than those found in specific constitutional provisions or statutes, arguing instead that, as persons, they retain a "liberty interest" under the Fifth and Fourteenth Amendments to the extent this interest is not inconsistent with incarceration. He reiterated this theme in several dissents, protesting against the denial of promised or usual parole without a hearing or reason. Dissenting in *Connecticut Board of Pardons v. Dumschatt* (1981), Stevens asserted that, especially because prisoners have no other recourse, "the due process clause applies to each step [of the release process] and denies the state the power to act arbitrarily" (452 U.S. at 471).

Stevens's bitterest and most memorable dissent from the Court's swing back to the "hands off" approach came in *Hudson v. Palmer* (1984), in which he took the unusual step of reading his dissent orally from the bench. The majority ruled that prisoners lacked Fourth Amendment rights; no search within a prison was unreasonable; and any wrongful seizure of a prisoner's property could be remedied through state tort law. Stevens asserted strongly that prisoners have a possessory interest against unlawful destruction or confiscation of their property. The Court's stereotype that all prisoners were violent and incorrigible manifests a "nihilistic" view of the chances of rehabilitation. In closing he lamented, "By telling prisoners that no aspect of their individuality, from a photo of a child to a letter from a wife, is entitled to constitutional protection, the Court breaks with the ethical tradition that I had thought was enshrined in our jurisprudence forever" (468 U.S. at 558).

The constitutionality of harsh prison conditions—as well as the judiciary's role in remedying them—became a major judicial issue in the Burger Court era. After debate and various doctrines had percolated in the lower federal courts, the Supreme Court established the "intent to punish" standard for judicial intervention in *Bell v. Wolfish* (1979). But to the dissenting Stevens, the Court "seem[ed] to use" intent as meaning "the subjective intent of the prison administrators," an interpretation that would only encourage their "hypocrisy and unconscious self-deception" (441 U.S. at 585). "Under the test as the Court explains it today, prison guards could make regular use of dungeons, chains, and shackles, since such practices would make it possible to maintain security with a smaller number of guards" (587). In the same case, Stevens became almost apoplectic about the majority's willingness to allow pretrial detainees to be treated similarly to convicted inmates. He could not "believe the Court means what it seems to be saying"—that the presumption of innocence has no application to prisons (583 n. 11). In fact, in 1980 in *United States v. Bailey*, Stevens came close to upholding a prisoner's right to escape if justified by atrocious conditions within the prison.

Conclusion

John Paul Stevens came to the Court with a rather well-developed constitutional jurisprudence. It guided him through the Burger Court years without marked or significant change. He cited his Seventh Circuit opinions about as often during the 1985 term as he did during his first terms on the Court. Several of his major themes were advanced early in his Court years, for example, *Boren*, *Gregg*, and *American Mini Theaters*. He showed, of course, some growth and development, and during his tenure a few inconsistencies or shifts in doctrinal stance became apparent—the type of change that could be found in the record of any Supreme Court justice. But Stevens was not an Earl Warren or Harry Blackmun. To the extent that President Ford and Attorney General Levi were familiar with his approach to constitutional law, they had no cause for disappointment.

Stevens's constitutional jurisprudence cannot be summarized in any overarching interpretive approach or singular belief about the role of judges. His thoughts were too complex for these. I would argue that he decided cases in context, eschewing formalistic logic for common sense. But this does not tell us much; deciding cases in context can be an exercise in discretion, and one person's common sense is another's bad sense. In addition, some of Stevens's doctrinal positions were given to considerable discretion, for example, his continuum of protection approach to freedom of expression and his *Cleburne* analysis of equal protection.

Nonetheless, I doubt that Stevens's votes were given to very much discretion. In the course of writing this chapter over two years, I found I could predict his votes in upcoming Supreme Court cases quite well. Awareness of some of his overriding concerns made it possible to tell what he believed were the overriding factors in an upcoming case. These included the following: his seriousness about the *Ashwander* philosophy, his sense that important precedents should not be overruled except upon great reason, his belief that statutes should be interpreted as they read, his respect for the state judiciary, and his view on the Court's proper function in criminal appeals. When knowledge of his concerns was inadequate, knowledge of his substantive positions (such as his dislike of the overbreadth doctrine and his support for the automobile exception to the warrant requirement) usually served to forecast his position. Stevens's votes may not have been predictable or understandable from a highly ideological perspective, but he was hardly a wild card on the Court.

In fact, Stevens may well have been too rigid in his constitutional jurisprudence in terms of his influence both with his colleagues and on the policies advanced by the Court. Frequently he was in a position between Brennan and Marshall on one side and Burger, Rehnquist, and O'Connor on the other. Yet, as noted earlier, he wrote less than his fair share of major civil liberties opinions for the Court. Although his positions were often close to those of White, Blackmun, and Powell, he did not easily compromise with them or work well with them. He preferred, it seems, to advance his own uncompromised analyses in concurring or dissenting opinions to proposing ones that might have been diluted but would have carried the Court's imprimatur. This tendency of his was unfortunate because it added to the Burger Court's fractiousness— its appearance as more of a Hobbesian mini-world than a collegial policy-making body. It was also unfortunate because, at least in my judgment, Stevens's positions were often quite attractive. While separate opinions are an appeal to the future, when written in great number they lose their effect. Thus Justice John Paul Stevens might be characterized as the "Lone Ranger" of the Burger Court, championing principled constitutional interpretation and intelligent justice in a cloud of opinions, but, like the radio hero of the Old West, one whose effectiveness was limited by numbers and circumstance.

NOTES

My thanks go to Alvin Goldman of the University of Kentucky Law School for his comments on a draft of this chapter and to Lauren Bowen and Barbara Hettle, then political science graduate students at Kentucky, for research assistance.

1. The most comprehensive analysis of Stevens's jurisprudence to date is Robert Judd Sickels, *Justice John Paul Stevens and the Constitution: The Search for Balance* (University Park: Pennsylvania State University Press, 1989). I had completed this manuscript when Sickels's book was published. Analyses of Stevens's positions in given areas can be found in John P. Wagner, "Justice Stevens and the Emerging Law of Sex Discrimination," *Pepperdine Law Review* 9 (1981): 315–426 and Note, "Justice Stevens's Equal Protection Jurisprudence," *Harvard Law Review* 100 (1987): 1146–65.

2. See, for example, Bob Woodward and Scott Armstrong, *The Brethren: Inside the Supreme Court* (New York: Simon and Schuster, 1979), pp. 427ff.; Linda Greenhouse, "In the Matter of Labels, a Loner," *New York Times*, July 23, 1984, p. 8.

3. The aggregate data in Table 12.1 on Stevens's votes have been taken from the National Science Foundation's (NSF) Supreme Court Data Collection Project, Harold J. Spaeth, director. I have retained the project categorizations, except that I have included habeas corpus and prison condition cases in the larger criminal justice category. I appreciate Professor Spaeth's cooperation in sharing these data.

4. The comparison data are also taken from the NSF Project.

5. For Burger, see *Batson v. Kentucky* (1986); for Rehnquist, *Michael M. v. Superior Court of Sonoma County* (1981); for White, *Thornburgh v. American College of Obstetricians and Gynecologists* (1986); for O'Connor, *Oregon v. Elstad* (1985); for Powell, see *EEOC v. Wyoming* (1983); for Blackmun, see *Los Angeles Department of Water and Power v. Manhart* (1978); and for Marshall, see *United States v. Ross* (1982).

6. John Paul Stevens, "The Life Span of a Judge-Made Rule," *New York University Law Review* 58 (1983): 1–21.

7. Stevens, "The Third Branch of Liberty," *University of Miami Law Review* 41 (1986): 283.

8. Stevens, "Judicial Restraint," *San Diego Law Review* 22 (1985): 437–52.

9. Stevens believes that all apportionment and representational structure cases necessarily involve some skewing of group strength; it is unavoidable. The crucial question is to what degree are identifiable groups—including economic ones—injured. See his concurrence in *Bolden* and dissent in *Rogers*.

10. Wagner, "Justice Stevens and the Emerging Law of Sex Discrimination," p. 325.

11. In *Goldfarb* the Court said that working women are victims of discrimination, but in his concurrence Stevens held that the widowers were. Stevens argued in several other cases as well that men were the victims of discrimination.

12. David W. Rhode, "Policy Goals, Strategic Choices and Majority Opinion Assignment in the U.S. Supreme Court," *Midwest Journal of Political Science* 16 (1972): 652–82; and William P. McLauchlan, "Ideology and Conflict in Supreme Court Opinion Assignment, 1946–62," *Western Political Quarterly* 25 (1972): 16–27.

13. Stevens, "The Life Span of a Judge-Made Rule."

13

JUSTICE POTTER STEWART:
Decisional Patterns in Search
of Doctrinal Moorings

TINSLEY E. YARBROUGH

Introduction

Justice Potter Stewart served on the Supreme Court from 1958 to 1981, a period of twenty-three years that bridged the Warren and Burger Court eras. Like his colleagues Felix Frankfurter and John Harlan, Stewart had high regard for precedent, majoritarian institutions, and the role of the states in the federal system, as well as doubt whether most constitutional guarantees possess a clear, readily definable scope. Stewart did not permit his constitutional philosophy to lead him in pro-government directions, however, as frequently as did Frankfurter and Harlan. Instead, he developed a decidedly mixed voting record that enabled him, along with Justice Byron R. White, to become a classic "swing" justice during much of his judicial tenure.

Stewart's preference for narrowly drawn constitutional interpretations closely tied to the fact patterns of cases—and the mixed voting record this preference produced—undoubtedly enhanced his influence in close cases. Ironically, however, it has also diminished his standing as a judicial craftsman. Judicial opinions serve a critical role in the development of a meaningful body of constitutional law and theory. While one may applaud the sense of balance and attention to subtlety of a justice whose constructions of the Constitution are limited largely to the specific contexts within which cases are developed, such jurists generally have little impact on developing interpretations of the law and rarely achieve the stature of their counterparts who paint with a broader brush. The tentative nature of their pronouncements regarding the Constitution's meaning makes any assessment of their jurisprudence and impact, moreover, exceedingly difficult. Such is the case with Justice Stewart.

The Man and the Justice

Potter Stewart's roots were not unlikely ones for a future justice of the United States Supreme Court. He came from a wealthy and prominent Ohio Republican family. His paternal grandfather had been a distinguished Civil War soldier. His father, James Garfield Stewart, had been a member of the Cincinnati City Council from 1933 to 1947, mayor of the city from 1938 to 1947, and justice of the Ohio Supreme Court from 1947 until his death in 1959, as well as an unsuccessful candidate for the Ohio governorship in 1944. Although Potter's parents' marriage ended in divorce, Potter, his sister, and his brother all apparently had a pleasant childhood. After study at Cincinnati's University School and Hotchkiss, he graduated Phi Beta Kappa from Yale in 1937. Following a year at Cambridge on a Henry fellowship, he attended Yale Law School, made law review, and graduated cum laude in 1941.[1]

After law school, Stewart joined a Wall Street firm. Within a year, however, he entered the Navy and spent most of World War II on oil tankers in the Atlantic and Mediterranean—"floating around on a sea of 100-octane gas," he later remarked, "bored to death 99 percent of the time and scared to death 1 percent."[2] Any effect of his military experience on his later work is a matter of pure speculation, but Professor Jerold H. Israel, his 1959–61 law clerk, observed that Stewart's service as a general deck officer in the "dungaree" Navy put him in close contact with enlisted men from backgrounds quite different from his own. During his tour, moreover, he served as defense counsel in a number of summary court-martial proceedings.[3]

Following the war, Stewart returned briefly to New York, then joined a Cincinnati firm whose prominent clients included Procter and Gamble and whose senior partner had served as commerce secretary under President Truman. Like his father, Stewart quickly became interested in Cincinnati politics, winning election to the city council in 1949 and 1951 and serving one term as vice-mayor. A popular if reserved political figure, he might have made a successful career in electoral politics. In 1954, however, President Eisenhower appointed him to a seat on the Sixth Circuit. Just four

Justice Potter Stewart

years later, when Supreme Court Justice Harold H. Burton announced his retirement on October 6, 1958, Stewart was named the following day to a recess appointment replacing his fellow Ohioan on the Court.[4]

On the Sixth Circuit, Stewart began to acquire the reputation for succinct, lucid, closely reasoned opinions that he would enjoy during his Supreme Court tenure, and on the day of his appointment to the high court Bernard Segal of the American Bar Association's Committee on the Federal Judiciary remarked to reporters that Eisenhower had made an excellent choice.[5] Stewart's was the president's third recess appointment, however, and a number of senators found the practice increasingly irritating. In August, moreover, the Conference of State Chief Justices had adopted its controversial resolution charging the Supreme Court with tending "to adopt the role of policymaker without proper judicial restraint."[6] In addition, bills were pending in Congress that reflected hostility to some of the Court's decisions. These included *Brown v. Board of Education* (1954), outlawing segregated schools; decisions protecting the rights of Communists such as *Watkins v. United States* (1957); and decisions precluding state control of subversion against the national government such as *Pennsylvania v. Nelson* (1956), among other rulings. It was hardly surprising, then, that conservative southerners chose to make the Senate debate over Stewart's appointment a forum for attacks on the Supreme Court's civil rights and "pro-Communist" rulings, as well as on any strains of liberalism in the nominee's thinking and federal appellate court record.

In January, while Stewart served his first term on the Court, the administration submitted his nomination to the Senate. It was not until mid-April, however, that Mississippi Senator James Eastland's Committee on the Judiciary conducted hearings on the nomination. At the hearings, Eastland, John McClellan of Arkansas, and South Carolina's Olin Johnston first probed Stewart closely about *Brown*. Stewart replied, "I would not like you to vote for me on the assumption or the proposition that I am dedicated to the cause of overturning that decision, because I am not." When questioned about whether he would be a "creative judge" or "follow the law," he answered, "Certainly, if I can find precedents that are applicable, I'm happy. That makes it easy, unless it is shown that the whole basic reason for those precedents has disappeared." To the question whether "the Constitution has the same meaning as when it was adopted," he replied, "The genius of the framers was that they used words that can be made applicable to a changing and growing society." The committee voted twelve to three to confirm.[7]

On the Senate floor, a number of senators complained about the administration's resort to recess appointments. Several others spoke admiringly of the nominee. Eastland, McClellan, and Johnston, joined by southern colleagues, also continued their attacks, but on the floor, as in committee, the senators reserved their complaints largely for the Court rather than the nominee. On May 5, 1959, the Senate voted seventy to seventeen to confirm, with southerners casting every negative vote.[8]

Justice Stewart served on the Court until July 3, 1981. Although he found his work "all the fun of practicing law without the bother of clients," he asked that President Nixon withdraw his name as a possible replacement for Chief Justice Warren.[9] Largely because it is difficult to generalize about his jurisprudence and because of the moderate voting record Stewart developed on the Court, his work received little scholarly attention, and he pursued his career in relative obscurity. Even so, he proved to be a reasonably influential justice. His judicial and constitutional moderation enhanced his status as a pivotal justice and may have made it easier for him to promote negotiation and compromise on the Court. His temperament may also have contributed to his influence. The impression of one of Stewart's clerks that he was often instrumental in cooling tempers on the Warren Court probably accurately reflects Stewart's rapport with his colleagues.[10]

At the time of his appointment, of course, the Court was divided on civil liberties issues and had split into two fairly firm factions— the "liberal activists" Warren, Black, Douglas, and Brennan; and the "passivists" Frankfurter, Clark, Harlan, and Whittaker. In a survey of Justice Stewart's voting patterns during the 1958–61 terms, Professor Israel found that the justices divided five-to-four along activist-passivist lines in about forty-two civil liberties cases; and Stewart joined the activist group in only nine.[11] Several of the activist decisions, moreover, were bottomed on statutory rather than constitutional grounds.[12] After Arthur Goldberg replaced Justice Frankfurter in 1962, the activists assumed a fairly solid majority, and the influence of Stewart's civil liberties stance was substantially diminished for the balance of the Warren years.

With President Nixon's selection of Burger, Blackmun, Powell, and Rehnquist, Stewart's position, and especially White's, assumed renewed significance, with theirs the pivotal and restraintist vote in numerous cases. Throughout his career, however, Stewart was also keenly sympathetic to numerous free press, obscenity, religious liberty, and statutorily based civil liberties claims, among others—a true moderate in his voting patterns and jurisprudence. During Warren Burger's years as chief justice, for example, Stewart's average rate of support for civil liberties claims was 48 percent, while Rehnquist's and Burger's, in the years they served with Stewart, were 17 and 29 percent, respectively, and Brennan's and Marshall's were 80 and 81 percent.

For those familiar with his early life, political career, and Sixth Circuit record, Stewart's middle-ground Supreme Court stance was hardly unexpected. Though a Republican, at Yale he had been a vigorous supporter of President Roosevelt and the New Deal.[13] On the other hand, during a bitter city council race in 1953, he joined those demanding the resignation of a Cincinnati planning commissioner (and political opponent) who had once been associated with a Marxist study group—and of two other commissioners who had merely "known" of the Communist ties. The latter's silence, Stewart insisted, was "as inexcusable as it is incredible. . . . [T]he Republican Party," he added, "is made up of men and women who are loyal Americans."[14] Then, however, in his first Communist case on the Sixth Circuit, *NLRB v. Lannom Mfg. Co.* (1955), he dissented when a majority agreed that an affidavit in which a union official swore that he was not a Communist could be considered false since the official earlier had been convicted of filing a false affidavit to that effect (226 F.2d at 200). Moreover, in a concurrence registered in a Smith Act case, *Wellman v. United States* (1957), he agreed that defendants whose convictions had been vacated by the Supreme Court should be retried rather than set free, but he found unrewarding "the efforts to discern the germ of illegal advocacy in [the] handful of equivocal statements culled from the present record" (253 F.2d at 608).

Nor was Stewart's moderate approach to Sixth Circuit civil liberties issues confined to cases involving present and former Communists. When a district court approved a school board's plan to delay desegregation for several years pending construction of new buildings in *Clemons v. Board of Education* (1956), Stewart and Judge Florence Allen formed a majority reversing the lower court; unlike Judge Allen, however, Stewart favored delaying relief until the beginning of the following school year. Then there was *Henderson v. Bannan* (1958), a case brought by James Henderson. In 1942, Henderson (at that time a young black with an eleventh-grade education) pled guilty hours after his arrest for rape and was sentenced to life imprisonment for the rape of a white woman. Now he sought a new trial on due process grounds. Of the more than twenty judges who reviewed Henderson's case at one point or another, only Judge Stewart found a constitutional violation. Although Stewart, on the Sixth Circuit as well as the Supreme Court, was hardly a criminal procedure activist, the haste with which Henderson had been moved toward a guilty plea and life sentence convinced him that the defendant had been entitled to counsel. "The prompt and vigorous administration of the criminal law is to be commended and encouraged," he asserted. "But swift justice demands more than just swiftness" (256 F.2d at 390).[15]

Judicial and Constitutional Philosophy

Justice Stewart's moderate voting record is easily documented. More difficult is an understanding and assessment of his position regarding the proper approach of judges to constitutional interpretation.[16] When asked by reporters on the day of his appointment to describe his judicial philosophy, he replied, "I really don't know what it is. I'd like to be thought of as a lawyer."[17] During Senate Judiciary Committee hearings, however, he observed, "[F]or me there is only one possible way to judge cases and that is to judge each case on its own facts of record, under the law and the United States Constitution, conscientiously, independently, and with complete personal detachment."[18] After his retirement, Stewart indicated that he still held to that conception of the judicial function, though he agreed that many people found it "naive" and assumed that a judge "reaches the answer he wants to reach for his own political or policy reasons and then . . . makes up the rationalization for that result."[19] In various addresses during his career he condemned the notion that the Supreme Court was a "council of platonic guardians given the function of deciding our most difficult and emotional questions according to the Justices' own notions of what is good or wise or politic." He added, "*That* function is the function of the people's elected representatives, to be carried out by the executive branch of government. The Justices are charged with deciding according to the Constitution and the law. The Justices may and do consult history, economics, and other disciplines, but the text of the Constitution and the relevant judicial precedents dealing with that text are their primary tools."[20]

Stewart's language echoes ideas found in the opinions and off-the-bench writings of Justice Black, and in *Griswold v. Connecticut*

(1965) Stewart joined Black's staunchly literalist dissent (381 U.S. at 507) from the Court's conclusion that the Constitution includes a right of sexual privacy. Stewart also filed one of his own (at 527). Viewing his *Griswold* dissent in isolation, one might have expected Stewart to have registered another biting dissent in *Roe v. Wade* (1973). In *Roe*, however, he joined the majority decision, which based the abortion right on the due process guarantee. He now understood *Griswold*, he wrote in his *Roe* concurrence, as "one in a long line of" substantive due process cases, and he was willing to "accept it as such." Stewart quoted with approval passages from Justice Harlan's dissent in *Poe v. Ullman* (the 1961 case in which the Court had declined to rule on the merits of the contraception law at issue in the *Griswold* case) and from a Frankfurter opinion embracing an evolving, flexible conception of due process. He then expressed agreement with the proposition that "the 'liberty' protected by the Due Process Clause of the Fourteenth Amendment covers more than those freedoms explicitly named in the Bill of Rights" (410 U.S. at 168).

Two fundamental elements in Justice Stewart's jurisprudence help to reconcile the apparent inconsistencies in his *Griswold* and *Roe* positions. First, Stewart placed a high premium on adherence to precedent, and his stance in *Roe* can be viewed as simply his acceptance of the precedent established in *Griswold*. His regard for precedent was clearly evident in numerous fields of decision making, but especially so in the line of cases involving the constitutional status of administrative searches. During his first term, Stewart joined the majority in *Frank v. Maryland* (1959) in rejecting the claim that administrative searches were subject to Fourth/Fourteenth Amendment warrant standards, and he dissented when the Court overruled *Frank* in 1967 in *Camara v. Municipal Court*. Thereafter, however, he adhered to the Court's new position and resisted decisions expanding the scope of recognized exceptions to the warrant requirement for administrative searches, as he did, for example, in *Donovan v. Dewey* (1981). Moreover, although he dissented when the Court applied the Sixth Amendment jury trial guarantee to the states in *Duncan v. Louisiana* (1968), he later contended, in *Apodoca v. Oregon* (1972), that the Court should apply the right to state cases in precisely the same manner that it was applied in federal cases.

The fact that Stewart emphasized faithfulness to constitutional text and historical intent in *Griswold* and off-the-bench statements, while accepting substantive due process in *Roe*, reveals another important facet of his jurisprudence. Unlike Justice Black, who generally found clear commands in the Constitution's text and the history surrounding the adoption of its provisions, Justice Stewart rarely discovered such clarity. "[T]he Founding Fathers knew better than to pin down their descendants too closely. Enduring principles, rather than petty details, were what they sought to write down. Thus it is that the Constitution does not take the form of a litany of specifics. There are, therefore, very few cases where the constitutional answers are clear, all one way or all the other. Particularly difficult are the cases raising conflicts between the individual and governmental power."[21]

Stewart's belief that the framers intentionally couched many constitutional provisions in general, relatively open-ended language affected his decision making in a number of ways, contributing to his moderately restrained conception of judicial review, for example. For Stewart, the Constitution's general language was a call for judicial restraint, not an invitation to activism. In an admiring portrait of Justice Jackson, Stewart observed that his predecessor "saw in the heavy hand of a national policy-making court a threat to representative government."[22] In Stewart's view, the generalities of the Constitution were designed primarily to allow adaptation to changing conditions through representative institutions, not judicial policy-making.

His uncertainty about the framers' intent and his regard for representative institutions—and, no doubt, too, a desire to preserve for himself and the Court room for future modifications—normally meant that Stewart pursued an extremely cautious approach to constitutional issues. He crafted narrowly based opinions deciding—and holding—only what was necessary to resolve the dispute at issue. On occasion, as in *Duncan v. Louisiana*, he would join an opinion of a colleague that elaborately set forth its author's general interpretation of due process or some similarly indefinite provision. Rarely, however, did Stewart himself draft such opinions, and then only, as in *Roe*, by drawing heavily on the rhetoric of others.

Another element crucial to an understanding of Stewart's judicial philosophy was the significance he attached to the principles of federalism and the position of the states in the federal scheme. He concurred in the Court's decisions limiting federal district court intervention in pending state proceedings, for example, *Younger v. Harris* (1971); and, while he wrote or joined opinions employing the commerce clause to invalidate undue state interference with interstate commerce, such as *Pike v. Bruce Church, Inc.* (1970), he was not willing to leave the reach of congressional regulatory power purely to the political process. He joined, for example, the Court's remarkable holding in *National League of Cities v. Usery* (1976) that an otherwise valid congressional statute is unconstitutional if it interferes with "integral" state functions. He rejected, moreover, Congress's use of its enforcement powers under the Fourteenth Amendment to impose state voter qualifications in *Oregon v. Mitchell* (1970). In *Katzenbach v. Morgan* (1966), he joined Justice Harlan's dissent, rejecting the notion that Congress could outlaw English-language literacy tests despite the Court's earlier holding in *Lassiter v. Northampton County Board of Elections* (1959) that fairly administered tests did not offend the Constitution. Nor was Stewart willing to accept the notion, developed by the Court in *Perez v. United States* (1971), that a particular business is subject to federal control under the commerce clause merely on a finding that Congress had a rational basis for concluding that the class of business being regulated affected interstate commerce.

Justice Stewart's jurisprudence of moderation carried over, of course, to questions of standing, justiciability, and the scope of the state action concept. He wrote the Court's opinion in *Sierra Club v. Morton* (1972), for example, rejecting an expansive view of standing in environmental suits, and he joined other restrictive Burger Court standing rulings such as *Warth v. Seldin* (1975) and *Linda R. S. v. Richard D.* (1973). Yet he not only joined the Warren Court's relaxation of the bar to federal taxpayer suits in *Flast v. Cohen* (1968); he also contended there (392 U.S. at 114) and in *United States v. Richardson* (1974) that plaintiffs should be given standing to challenge a federal regulation as citizen-taxpayers whenever they allege that a governmental agency has failed to perform an affirmative constitutional duty (418 U.S. at 202). Moreover, while he rejected the "one person, one vote" doctrine in *Lucas v. Forty-Fourth General Assembly of State of Colorado* (1964), arguing that the equal protection guarantee prohibited only "irrational" apportionment schemes which defeated the principle of majority rule (377 U.S. at 744), he joined the Court's holding in *Baker v. Carr* (1962) that the issue was justiciable.[23] As Justice Powell pointed out in a *Richardson* concurrence, virtually all constitutional provisions can be construed as imposing an affirmative duty of one sort or another on government. Stewart's position in *Richardson* was thus a potentially significant threat to the Court's general opposition to citizen-taxpayer suits—and a position difficult to reconcile with the more restrictive conceptions of standing he joined in other cases. It is difficult to understand this position except as a further reflection of a moderate jurisprudence largely devoid of general principles, cutting across a variety of related contexts.

The same conclusion is necessary regarding Justice Stewart's approach to the "state action" issue. During his tenure, he concurred in a substantial number of decisions finding unconstitutional state action in the activities of ostensibly private entities, including *Peterson v. City of Greenville, S.C.* (1963) and *Gilmore v. City of Montgomery* (1974). He generally rejected such claims, however, when the issue was close—as it was in *Evans v. Newton* (1966), *Reitman v. Mulkey* (1967), and *Moose Lodge v. Irvis* (1972)—or when the potential reach of such a finding was great, as in *Jackson v. Metropolitan Edison Co.* (1974).

In a rare case in which Stewart endorsed an expansive view of state action, he did so only to limit the breadth of the Court's decision. In *United States v. Guest* (1966), the Court, per Stewart, construed 18 U.S.C. §241 to reach conspiracies to violate Fourteenth Amendment rights. In concurring opinions, six justices agreed that Congress had the power to punish private interference with these rights. Stewart, however, desiring to avoid a direct confrontation with the *Civil Rights Cases* (1883) holding that Congress can reach only state action under its Fourteenth Amendment enforcement powers, searched for some element of state action in the case—and found it in a count of the indictment charging the defendants with making false reports to the police that blacks had committed illegal acts.

Justice Stewart was occasionally willing, though, to give statutorily based rights an expansive reading. He authored the Court's opinions, for example, in *Jones v. Mayer* (1968) and *Runyon v. McCrary* (1976), broadly construing provisions of the Civil Rights Act of 1866 to reach private discrimination in housing and contract transactions, respectively, even though Justice Harlan in *Mayer,* and Justice White in *Runyon,* made convincing arguments that the law was intended to cover only governmental action. The power of Congress to repeal or modify judicial interpretations of its statutes through legislation obviously made Stewart less cautious in statutory cases than in those raising constitutional claims.

Incorporation

Very early in the incorporation revolution of the 1960s, Stewart also made it clear that he did not embrace either the total or the selective incorporation doctrine. He developed his opposition to incorporation most extensively in *Williams v. Florida* (1970), in which the Court upheld the constitutionality of a six-member jury. In his concurrence in *Williams*, and his dissent in *Baldwin v. New York* (1970) from the holding that any offense carrying more than six months' imprisonment requires a jury trial, Stewart condemned the "mechanistic 'incorporation' approach." In *Baldwin* he chided, "It is, at best, a theory that can lead the Court only to a Fourteenth Amendment dead end. And, at worst, the spell of the theory's logic compels the Court either to impose intolerable restrictions upon the constitutional sovereignty of the individual States in the administration of their own criminal law, or else intolerably to relax the explicit restrictions that the Framers actually did put upon the *Federal* Government in the administration of criminal justice" (399 U.S. at 143). If the Constitution forbids a particular state procedure, he contended, responding to the rhetoric of Justice Black, the "architect of the contemporary 'incorporation' approach," "it is because of the Fourteenth Amendment, and not because of either the specific words of the Bill of Rights or the history surrounding their adoption" (145).

Differences did exist, however, between Justice Stewart's approach to the incorporation issue and that of Justices Harlan, Frankfurter, and other anti-incorporationists. Once the Court had established that a particular Bill of Rights safeguard was binding on the states, Stewart, unlike his anti-incorporationist counterparts, apparently felt a commitment to accord the right equal meaning in federal and state cases. In the obscenity field, for example, Justice Harlan favored limiting federal control of erotica to "hard-core" pornography while recognizing considerably broader state authority over the distribution of erotic material. Stewart, on the other hand, regarded "hard-core" pornography as the only erotica subject to both national and state power—whatever his well-known difficulty in defining that term in *Jacobellis v. Ohio* (1964) (378 U.S. at 179) and *Ginzberg v. United States* (1966) (383 U.S. at 497).

Whether in opinions rejecting the incorporation thesis or in analyzing due process, Justice Stewart was also less likely than Harlan and Frankfurter to articulate the meaning of due process in broader language than that required to decide a particular case. In fact, he rarely attached any meaning to due process (or, for that matter, to most other constitutional provisions) not closely tied to specific fact patterns. Nevertheless, his concurrences in *Roe* and its companion case, *Doe v. Bolton* (1973), made it clear that he accepted substantive due process. His stance in post-*Roe* abortion cases and other cases with privacy contexts—(consistent with his position in *Eisenstadt v. Baird* (1972), a pre-*Roe* case)—raised no doubts about his continued adherence to the doctrine. When the Court rejected due process privacy claims, on the other hand, he followed the Court, helping to form the majority in *Harris v. McRae* (1980), for example, and *Doe v. Commonwealth's Attorney* (1976). While Stewart thus did not reject substantive due process completely (as Justice Black did) or subject regulations challenged on such grounds to an extremely lenient standard of scrutiny (as Rehnquist has), he was reluctant to give the concept the reach that Justices Brennan and Marshall have accorded it.

Procedural Due Process

Stewart's responses to procedural due process claims were equally mixed. In *Boddie v. Connecticut* (1971), he joined the Court's holding that due process forbids government to deny indigents access to divorce proceedings based on their inability to pay court costs. And he dissented when a majority refused to extend *Boddie* to bankruptcy filing fees in *United States v. Kras* (1973). In distinguishing *Boddie*, the *Kras* majority had emphasized the state's monopoly over the dissolution of marriage and concluded that access to courts was not the only conceivable relief available to bankrupts. For Stewart, however, a bankruptcy action was the only "effective means" of relief for the truly indigent. "The Court today holds that Congress may say that some of the poor are too poor even to go bankrupt. I cannot agree" (409 U.S. at 455, 457). He wrote or joined opinions, moreover, reversing criminal convictions on prejudicial publicity grounds, for example, *Sheppard v. Maxwell* (1966). But he was not willing to give as broad a construction to the due process rights of juveniles as the majority agreed to impose in cases such as *In re Gault* (1967) and *In re Winship* (1970). He also dissented in *Miranda v. Arizona* (1966) and joined later decisions limiting the reach of that controversial ruling, such as *Harris v. New York* (1971).

In cases involving the exclusionary rule, Stewart pursued a somewhat similar course. He adhered to *Mapp v. Ohio* (1961) and dissented when the Burger Court, in *United States v. Janis* (1976), refused to extend the exclusionary rule to federal civil proceedings conducted as an adjunct to criminal law enforcement (428 U.S. at 460). Furthermore, early in his tenure he authored the Court's opinion in *Elkins v. United States* (1960), rejecting the "silver platter" doctrine, under which evidence seized illegally by state officers could be turned over to federal prosecutors for use in federal trials. Stewart based *Elkins*, however, on the Court's supervisory power over the federal judiciary rather than on the Constitution, emphasizing that "any apparent limitation upon the process of discovering truth in a federal trial ought to be imposed only upon the basis of considerations which outweigh the general need for untrammeled disclosure of competent and relevant evidence in a court of justice" (364 U.S. at 216). It was not surprising, therefore, that he joined Burger Court decisions restricting the rule's reach and holding that it was merely a nonconstitutional, judicially created prophylactic, including *United States v. Calandra* (1974) and *Stone v. Powell* (1976).

Despite his stance regarding *Miranda* and the exclusionary rule, however, Stewart was less restrained than many of his colleagues in reviewing state, and especially federal, criminal proceedings. As his *Henderson* dissent on the Sixth Circuit indicated, for example, he attached great significance to the right to counsel. In a dissent registered for *Escobedo v. Illinois* (1964), he contended that the right did not attach until adversary proceedings had begun against a defendant, but beyond that point he gave the guarantee a broad reading. For example, he held for the Court in *Massiah v. United States* (1964) and *Brewer v. Williams* (1977) that the guarantee extended to police interrogations, and he joined the Court's decisions in *Argersinger v. Hamlin* (1972) and *Scott v. Illinois* (1979), which extended it to all cases involving a prison sentence of any length. He also limited the reach of warrantless searches in his opinion for the Court in *Chimel v. California* (1969) and extended the Fourth Amendment to police eavesdrop practices in *Katz v. United States* (1967).[24]

Although Stewart could not join Justices Brennan and Marshall in contending that the death penalty is inherently unconstitutional in *Furman v. Georgia* (1972), *Gregg v. Georgia* (1976), and *Coker v. Georgia* (1977), his position on the issue was probably closer to Brennan's and Marshall's than that of any of their contemporaries, with the probable exception of Justice Douglas. In *Furman*, Justice White joined Brennan, Marshall, Douglas, and Stewart in invalidating Georgia's death penalty statute, and he later spoke in *Coker* for a plurality that included Stewart in holding the death penalty disproportionate to the offense of rape. White parted with Stewart in *Woodson v. North Carolina* (1976), however. In *Woodson* White voted to uphold mandatory death sentences, while Stewart wrote for a plurality that rejected automatic schemes.

Equal Protection

Stewart's responses to equal protection claims were equally mixed. He had no patience with racial discrimination—whatever its victims' race, however benign its goals. In a rare departure from his usual narrowly crafted opinions, he asserted in a 1964 case, *McLaughlin v. Florida,* that he could conceive of no circumstance under which a person's race could be a legitimate basis for a governmental classification (379 U.S. at 198). He also joined Justice Stevens's opinion rejecting, on statutory grounds, the affirmative action program at issue in *Bakke,* and he apparently joined the Court in upholding the preferential employment program at issue in *Weber,* only because he agreed that it did not violate the 1964 Civil Rights Act.

But Congress was free to overrule *Weber* through clarifying legislation, and in *Fullilove v. Klutznick* (1980), Stewart left no doubt of his distaste for affirmative action. Condemning the preference for minority businesses at issue in *Fullilove,* he wrote: "Under our Constitution, the government may never act to the detriment of a person solely because of that person's race. . . . In short, racial discrimination is by definition invidious discrimination" (448 U.S. at 525). Nor, he added, was there any language in the equal protection clause singling "out some 'persons' for more 'equal' treatment than others" (526).

Intentional discrimination, however, was the limit of Justice Stewart's equal protection guarantee, whether the issue be school desegregation (*Milliken v. Bradley,* 1974, 418 U.S. at 753), government hiring practices (*Washington v. Davis,* 1976), restrictive zoning (*Arlington Heights v. Metropolitan Housing Development Corp.,* 1977), or at-large local elections (*Mobile v. Bolden,* 1980). Moreover, while Stewart joined the Court in subjecting to heightened scrutiny discriminatory regulations arguably affecting the implicit but long-recognized constitutional right to interstate travel (e.g., *Shapiro v. Thompson,* 1969, at 642; *Dunn v. Blumstein,* 1972), as well as those conditioning criminal punishment on ability to pay (*Williams v. Illinois,* 1970; *Tate v. Short,* 1971), he also wrote or joined opinions in which he generally objected to extensions of the "fundamental rights" branch of modern equal protection doctrine to voting (*Harper v. Virginia State Board of Elections,* 1966; *Kramer v. Union Free School District,* 1969), welfare benefits (*Dandridge v. Williams,* 1970), and educational expenditures (*San Antonio Independent School District v. Rodriguez,* 1973).

Although Stewart joined the Court's conclusion that alienage is a constitutionally suspect basis of classification in *Graham v. Richardson* (1971), he generally resisted Warren Court dicta that appeared to extend the "suspect categories" doctrine to wealth (e.g., *Harper v. Virginia State Board of Elections*, 1966) and illegitimacy (e.g., *Levy v. Louisiana*, 1968). In addition, he joined the Burger Court in rejecting age as a suspect class in *Massachusetts Board of Retirement v. Murgia* (1976). Similarly, he rejected the use of an intermediate standard of scrutiny for gender in *Craig v. Boren* (1976)—and, presumably, for any other "quasi-suspect" classification—preferring instead to apply a rationality standard (429 U.S. at 214), albeit one with more bite than Justice Rehnquist's. In the equal protection field, then, Stewart largely rejected the implications of Warren Court opinions that the equal protection clause embodies substantive rights not guaranteed elsewhere in the Constitution or extends special protection against classifications not based on race or such related factors as national origin or citizenship.

The First Amendment

While in college, Stewart initially was undecided whether to become a lawyer or a journalist. He headed Yale's student newspaper, and he also worked briefly as a reporter for the Cincinnati *Times-Star.* Henry Luce offered him a job with *Time* following college. Given this journalistic interest and background, it was not surprising that Stewart departed from his moderately conservative civil liberties stance most regularly in First Amendment cases.

He was the Court's most vigorous defender, in *Branzburg v. Hayes* (1972), of a testimonial privilege for newsmen (408 U.S. at 725) and in *Zurcher v. Stanford Daily* (1978), of the proposition that media facilities should normally be immune from third-party searches (436 U.S. at 570). Moreover, although he authored a number of opinions rejecting press claims of special access to government facilities not open to the general public, such as *Pell v. Procunier* (1974) and *Saxbe v. Washington Post Co.* (1974), he had long contended that the First Amendment's guarantee to freedom of "the press," as well as freedom of speech, gave special rights to professional journalists.[25] He believed that otherwise reasonable limitations on public access to government facilities, disputed in *Houchins v. KQED, Inc.* (1978), might be unacceptable as applied to reporters (438 U.S. at 16). Furthermore, although he spoke for the Court in rejecting press claims to a right of access to pretrial proceedings in *Gannett Co., Inc. v. DePasquale* (1979), he concurred in the Court's 1980 decision in *Richmond Newspapers, Inc. v. Virginia* (1980), which recognized the right of the press and public to be present at trial proceedings absent special circumstances justifying a closed trial (448 U.S. at 598), and had rejected, in *Estes v. Texas* (1965), any implication that due process imposes a per se ban on television coverage of trial proceedings (381 U.S. at 614). Moreover, Stewart joined the Court in *Chandler v. Florida* (1981) to uphold state rules allowing media coverage under controlled conditions (449 U.S. at 583), and he agreed with Justices Brennan and Marshall in *Nebraska Press Association v. Stuart* (1976) that a prior restraint on the press was an inherently impermissible method for enforcing the defendant's right to a fair trial (427 U.S. at 572).

For years, Justice Stewart conceded the government's power to punish distribution of "hard-core" pornography. In *Jacobellis v. Ohio* (1964), however, he confessed doubt whether he could ever "succeed in intelligibly" defining the term, then penned what is undoubtedly the best-known—and perhaps most intelligible—judicial pronouncement yet to appear regarding the nature of the obscene: "I know it when I see it, and the motion picture involved in this case is not that" (378 U.S. at 197).[26] Ultimately, he joined those justices who concluded that no obscenity standard could be established that would be both reasonably free of vagueness and sufficiently sensitive to First Amendment values. For them, forbidding exposure of erotic material to juveniles and unconsenting adults, as the Court held in *Paris Adult Theatre I v. Slaton* (1973), should be the limit of governmental power (413 U.S. at 70). He also joined the majority in *New York Times Co. v. Sullivan* (1964) in severely limiting the power of government to penalize libel against public officials and joined it again in *Curtis Publishing Co. v. Butts* (1967) when it established a public figures extension of *Sullivan*. Stewart also favored First Amendment protection for commercial speech in *Pittsburgh Press Co. v. Pittsburgh Commission on Human Relations* (1973), two years before the Court adopted such a stance.

For Justice Stewart, however, writing in *School District of Abington Township v. Schempp* (1963), religious liberty was the "central value" of the First and Fourteenth Amendments (374 U.S. at 312). Sensitive to free exercise claims, he joined the Court in *Sherbert v. Verner* (1963) in rejecting state power to deny unemployment benefits to a Seventh-Day Adventist unable to find employment not requiring Saturday work (374 U.S. at 413) and again, in *Thomas v. Review Board* (1981), which involved the same sort of violation, this time against a Jehovah's Witness who quit his job at a foundry after he was transferred to a department fabricating tank turrets. He dissented in *Braunfeld v. Brown* (1961) when the Court upheld Sunday closing legislation against the free exercise claims of Orthodox Jews, asserting: "Pennsylvania has passed a law which compels an Orthodox Jew to choose between his religious faith and his economic survival. That is a cruel choice. It is a choice which I think no State can constitutionally demand. For me this is not something that can be swept under the rug and forgotten in the interest of enforced Sunday togetherness" (366 U.S. at 616).

In the field of religious establishment, on the other hand, Stewart was deferential to government. He consistently supported the middle-ground positions of the majority or plurality in parochaid cases, such as *Meek v. Pittenger* (1975), and in most other establishment contexts. When the Court invalidated devotional exercises in the public schools in *Schempp* and *Engel v. Vitale* (1962), he registered lone but vehement dissents (374 U.S. at 308; 370 U.S. at 444). When, in 1980 in *Stone v. Graham*, the Court summarily extended *Engel* and *Schempp* to the posting of privately purchased copies of the Ten Commandments in public school classrooms, he contended in dissent that the state courts that had approved the scheme "applied wholly correct constitutional criteria" (449 U.S. at 43).

Stewart, the Court, and Sociopolitical Trends

At one point in their discussion of the Watergate Tapes episode, the authors of *The Brethren* offered their interpretation of what, in Stewart's mind, a chief justice should be, concluding: "But, most of all, the Chief Justice had to be a student of the nation's capital, able to see the politically inevitable, willing to weight the Court's destiny against other Washington institutions."[27] Like much in that fascinating but frustrating study of the Court's inner workings, the source for this passage is undocumented. It is thus uncertain whether it is drawn from Stewart's own words, the opinion of those around him, or sheer conjecture.

Whether or not Stewart believed that the Court's decisions should reflect political and social developments, his voting patterns were generally compatible with what could be considered the prevailing public mood. Especially in the latter years of the Warren era, when the Court's decisions expanding the reach of equal protection and the rights of suspects and defendants in criminal cases (as well as the egalitarian policies of the Johnson administration) were growing in public disfavor, he was a frequent dissenter, leading the justices in percentage of dissents during the 1966 term and falling behind only Black and Harlan in the 1968 term. When the Nixon appointments slowed the expansion of civil liberties, Stewart frequently helped to form the necessary majorities and at times authored the Court's rationale. Justice Powell's opinion for the majority in *San Antonio Independent School District v. Rodriguez* (1973) most fully developed Burger Court limitations on the fundamental rights branch of modern equal protection doctrine — restrictions dramatically curtailing the degree to which welfare and related social programs would be subjected to strict judicial scrutiny. But the *Rodriguez* Court's limitation of strict scrutiny to discriminatory regulations affecting rights expressed or implied in the Constitution can actually be traced to Justice Stewart's opinion for the Court in *Dandridge,* upholding a state-imposed family ceiling on AFDC benefits. His vote also helped to provide majorities curtailing the reach of the suspect-categories branch of equal protection philosophy in *Rodriguez,* limiting *Miranda* in *United States v. Mandujano* (1976), limiting the exclusionary rule in *Calandra,* upholding the death penalty for murder in *Gregg,* and expanding the scope of permissible warrantless searches in *United States v. Robinson* (1973) — decisions compatible with the growing national conservatism of the 1970s and 1980s.

Stewart's stance in a number of fields conflicted with the "pro-family" agenda of the radical right, however. Although he rejected any governmental obligation to fund abortions for indigent women, he did join *Roe.* He ultimately concluded that government should largely eliminate controls over the distribution of erotic material. His *Engel* and *Schempp* dissents, however, provided the New Right with the closest thing to authoritative judicial support for its school prayer position that it could muster, and Stewart's voting patterns were clearly of less concern to the radical right than those of Douglas, Brennan, or Marshall.

The Court largely avoided issues arising out of the Vietnam conflict; Stewart was one of five justices, however, who at one time or another — such as in *Mora v. McNamara* (1967) — favored hearing certain of the issues raised by challenges to the war. (The others were Douglas, Brennan, Marshall, and Harlan.) Like all his colleagues, moreover, he filed an opinion in the *Pentagon Papers Cases, New York Times Co. v. United States* (1971) and *United States v. Washington Post* (1971) (403 U.S. at 727). In his concurrence, Stewart conceded that Congress could and had enacted criminal statutes protecting confidential materials and that courts were responsible for hearing criminal prosecutions arising under these laws. He also agreed that if Congress ever chose to authorize civil proceedings to stop publication of classified materials, the courts would be obliged to hear cases under any of those regulations found to be constitutional. He emphasized, however, the primary obligation of the executive to assure the confidentiality of classified materials and concluded that the First Amendment allowed judicial intervention in the absence of statutory authorization only if publication would "surely result in direct, immediate, and irreparable damage to our Nation or its people" (730). No such conclusion, he asserted, could be drawn of the publications at issue.

Stewart's *New York Times* concurrence raised more questions than it resolved. While in prejudicial publicity cases, namely *Nebraska Press,* he rejected all prior restraints on the press (427 U.S. at 572), his response to the Nixon administration's attempts to enjoin publication of the Pentagon Papers made it clear that he would accept certain prior restraints in the national security field even in the absence of congressional authorization. What was left unclear was the extent to which he would defer to a president bolstered by a congressional statute. Presumably, he would have been extremely reluctant to substitute the judgment of the courts for that of both the executive and Congress. But he was never compelled to reach that question and, characteristically, never did.

In the Court's second great judicial confrontation with the Nixon administration, Stewart again demonstrated the limits of his deference to presidential authority. Apparently, Chief Justice Burger was little more than the nominal author of the Court's opinion in *United States v. Nixon* (1974), with Justice Stewart largely responsible for its treatment of the scope of executive privilege and its limits in the case. That portion of the opinion granted a large measure of discretion to the president: though not specifically provided for in the Constitution, presidential claims to executive privilege were presumptively valid, with the burden on challengers to demonstrate a compelling need to override the executive's claims in particular cases. Justice Stewart's draft version was much less deferential to presidential power than the chief justice's original draft. Stewart apparently led a move on the Court to strengthen the Court's response to each of President Nixon's claims.[28]

Major Contributions to Constitutional Law

Whatever the weight of Justice Stewart's votes and his influence on other justices in individual cases, his contributions to the development of constitutional law were of more limited significance. Yet he did write major opinions for the Court in cases involving the Fourth Amendment, abortion funding, and the death penalty, as well as in cases according a broad reach to congressional power under the Thirteenth Amendment. Perhaps more important, in both the Warren and Burger years he was often an insightful and articulate critic of the majority's position, drafting significant dissents regarding the scope of the establishment clause, the rights of juveniles, and the claims of newsmen to testimonial and search privileges.

Justice Stewart authored more of the Court's opinions in Fourth Amendment cases than any of his contemporaries. It was not until 1974, in fact, in *United States v. Edwards,* that he wrote his first dissenting opinion in a Fourth Amendment case.[29] Certain of his opinions barely survived his retirement. In *United States v. Ross* (1982), for example, the Court rejected the opacity standard Stewart had developed for evaluating warrantless searches of containers found in automobiles in cases such as *Arkansas v. Sanders* (1979) and *Robbins v. California* (1981). During Chief Justice Warren's tenure, however, he authored two extremely significant opinions giving the Fourth Amendment a broad reading. The second, *Chimel v. California* (1969), imposed strict limits on the scope of warrantless searches conducted incident to a valid arrest. Speaking for an eight-man majority in the first, *Katz v. United States* (1967), he overruled the *Olmstead* doctrine and subjected governmental eavesdropping to the Fourth Amendment's warrant requirements. In both cases, he concluded that warrantless searches are *"per se* unreasonable" except under very limited circumstances.

Despite his *Chimel* and *Katz* opinions, however, Justice Stewart's reading of the Fourth Amendment was hardly libertarian. We have already seen that he joined rulings limiting the reach of the exclusionary rule and objected to extending the Fourth Amendment's coverage to administrative searches. In *United States v. Robinson* (1973) and *Gustafson v. Florida* (1973), he also joined opinions extending *Chimel* to arrests for petty offenses—even though *Chimel* itself had at least suggested that justification for a search would turn to some degree on the nature of the arrest and the *Robinson-Gustafson* dissenters had argued convincingly that the majority was encouraging arrests for minor offenses as a convenient pretext for otherwise impermissible searches of suspicious persons. Stewart's important opinion for the Court in *Schneckloth v. Bustamonte* (1973), however, was perhaps most disconcerting to those favoring a broad construction of the Fourth Amendment. Speaking for a six-man *Schneckloth* majority, Stewart embraced a "totality of the circumstances" approach to consent searches and held that warrantless searches to which a suspect has "voluntarily" consented are constitutionally permissible even in the absence of evidence that the suspect was aware of the right not to consent.

Arguably, Stewart's approach to Fourth Amendment construction in *Schneckloth* differed markedly from that in *Chimel* and *Katz*. In the earlier cases, he had combined the amendment's two clauses, holding in effect that judgments regarding the reasonableness of a search or seizure required under the first were to be conditioned by the warrant requirements of the second. Only in that way, given the deference normally accorded government when standards of reasonableness are applied, could he logically have concluded that most warrantless searches are per se unreasonable. In *Schneckloth*, on the other hand, he determined the reasonableness of the search at issue without reference to the warrant clause and its possible impact on search and seizure judgments.

Another of Stewart's more significant constitutional opinions also appeared to conflict with his stance in an earlier case. Speaking for the Court in *Harris v. McRae* (1980), Stewart upheld the Hyde Amendment, which largely excluded abortions from federal Medicaid coverage. In defending the Court's position, he was obliged to distinguish *McRae* from earlier precedents that subjected to strict, and fatal, review laws that conditioned the receipt of government benefits on the forfeiture of a constitutional right. Under the Hyde Amendment, after all, pregnant women could receive assistance if they elected childbirth but not if they chose to exercise their constitutional right to abortion.

The most troubling precedent (discussed above) was *Sherbert v. Verner* (1963), in which Stewart had joined the Court in invalidating, on free exercise grounds, South Carolina's denial of unemployment compensation to a Seventh-Day Adventist unable to find employment not requiring Saturday work. In distinguishing *McRae* from *Sherbert* and other earlier cases, Stewart cited what he considered to be "the basic difference between direct state interference with a protected activity and state encouragement of an alternative activity" (448 U.S. at 315). In *Sherbert*, however, Justice Brennan had emphasized that even very indirect governmental burdens on constitutional liberties may trigger strict scrutiny: "For '[i]f the purpose or effect of a law is to impede the observance of one or all religions or is to discriminate invidiously between religions, that law is constitutionally invalid even though the burden may be characterized as being only indirect' " (374 U.S. at 42–43). Despite this language, Stewart went on to assert that a

> substantial constitutional question would arise if Congress had attempted to withhold all Medicaid benefits from an otherwise eligible candidate simply because that candidate had exercised her constitutionally protected freedom to terminate her pregnancy by abortion. This would be analogous to *Sherbert v. Verner*, . . . where this Court held that a State may not, consistent with the First and Fourteenth Amendments, withhold *all* unemployment compensation benefits from a claimant who would otherwise be eligible for such benefits but for the fact that she is unwilling to work one day per week on her Sabbath. But the Hyde Amendment . . . does not provide for such a broad disqualification from receipt of public benefits. (448 U.S. at 297 n. 19)

With due respect, however, this is not a meaningful distinction. Mrs. Sherbert's refusal to take Saturday work did disqualify her from all unemployment benefits, but not, presumably, from all other public benefits. Her position was thus analogous to that of the indigent woman excluded from one benefit (abortion funding), but not others, because of her choice of abortion over childbirth. In neither case, moreover, had the government actually forbidden a constitutionally protected activity.[30]

Stewart did attach a broad interpretation to a civil right in two cases involving congressional efforts to protect civil rights. His approach, however, enabled the Court largely to avoid overturning a precedent of long standing. My reference, of course, is to *Jones v. Mayer* (1968) and *Runyon v. McCrary* (1976), decisions upholding the power of Congress to reach private discrimination in housing and contract transactions via the long-neglected Thirteenth Amendment.

Stewart concluded for the *Mayer* and *Runyon* majorities that congressional power under the amendment reached all "badges" and "incidents" of slavery, as well as the institution itself, and that Congress had the power to determine the scope of these "badges" and "incidents," subject only to the condition that its judgments be rational ones. The cases, however, gave a broad reach only to congressional authority. " 'By its own unaided force and effect,' " Stewart wrote in *Mayer*, "the Thirteenth Amendment 'abolished slavery, and established universal freedom.' " He added, "Whether or not the Amendment *itself* did any more than that—a question not involved in this case—it is at least clear that the Enabling Clause of that Amendment empowered Congress to do much more" (392 U.S. at 439). The rulings, therefore, merely recognized an expanded congressional authority to forbid private discrimination against blacks—a power Congress could choose, or choose not, to exercise. They did not establish a cause of action against such discrimination based on the amendment alone; moreover, by basing congressional authority, over private racial discrimination, on the Thirteenth Amendment, Stewart avoided a confrontation with the holding of the *Civil Rights Cases* (1883) that congressional power to enforce the Fourteenth Amendment's equal protection guarantee reaches only state action. Viewed in this way, these important rulings appear compatible with Stewart's moderately conservative jurisprudence.

So also was the stance he assumed in death penalty litigation— the constitutional field in which he had perhaps the greatest impact on the Burger Court. Characteristically, he developed a checkered record in capital punishment cases. In *Witherspoon v. Illinois* (1968), he spoke for the Court in striking down a statute under which veniremen who expressed qualms about the death penalty were excluded from juries hearing capital cases. In two 1971 cases (*McGautha v. California* and *Crampton v. Ohio*), he joined a six-man majority in rejecting claims that due process is violated when a jury imposes the death penalty in the absence of legislative standards and separate hearings for determining guilt and punishment. Yet the following term, he joined the Court in *Furman v. Georgia* (1972) in invalidating just such a scheme. He agreed with Justices Brennan and Marshall that the death penalty differed "in kind" from all other forms of punishment—that it was "unique in its irrevocability," in "its rejection of rehabilitation of the convict as a basic purpose of criminal justice," and "in its absolute renunciation of all that is embodied in our concept of humanity" (408 U.S. at 306). Nevertheless, he found it unnecessary to decide whether such punishment violated the Eighth and Fourteenth Amendments. Instead, he emphasized the virtually unlimited discretion accorded juries and judges under the capital punishment provisions before the Court. The petitioners, he charged, were "among a capriciously selected random handful," and their death sentences "cruel and unusual in the same way that being struck by lightning is cruel and unusual." The Constitution simply did not permit "this unique penalty to be so wantonly and freakishly imposed" (309–10).

The importance of Justice Stewart's position regarding the death penalty became clear in 1976, when the Court reviewed capital punishment provisions enacted in *Furman*'s wake. In *Gregg v. Georgia* (1976), he announced the Court's judgment upholding Georgia's revised statute. Speaking for himself, Justice Stevens, and Justice Powell, who had dissented in *Furman,* Stewart rejected the claim that the death penalty was unconstitutional per se. Capital punishment, he observed, was not forbidden by the Constitution's language; moreover, execution of murderers enjoyed popular approval, served society's "legitimate" interest in retribution, and could reasonably be assumed to act as "a significant deterrent" for "many" murderers, though such an effect had not been empirically established (428 U.S. at 185–86). Nor, in Stewart's judgment, did the Georgia law allow the arbitrary and random imposition of the death sentence he had condemned in *Furman*: the trial and sentencing proceedings were separate; the sentencing authority was guided by standards taking into account aggravating and mitigating circumstances; and the sentences were subject to automatic review in the state supreme court.

For Stewart, however, mandatory death sentences were as arbitrary as those imposed in the complete discretion of judges and juries; and on the day *Gregg* was decided, he announced the Court's invalidating mandatory sentences in *Woodson v. North Carolina* (1976) and *Roberts v. Louisiana* (1976). He also believed that capital punishment should be limited to the gravest crimes; he joined Justice White's opinion in *Coker v. Georgia* (1977), for example, holding the death sentence for rape disproportionate to the gravity of the offense.

It is doubtful whether the procedural safeguards Stewart found controlling in *Gregg*—or similar devices—can truly eliminate the caprice that seems inevitable in all sentencing schemes, but especially critical when the punishment is execution. Indeed, the Court's conclusion in *Lockett v. Ohio* (1978) that a state cannot limit the sorts of mitigating circumstances that might save a defendant from execution—a ruling Stewart joined—would appear largely to have restored to sentencing authorities the unbridled discretion he found so reprehensible in *Furman*. Whatever the merits of the Court's middle-ground approach, however, Justice Stewart's imprint is obvious. In *Furman*, he and White were the pivotal justices; but White's position was closer to that of the *Furman* dissenters than was Stewart's, and White dissented from the Court's decisions invalidating mandatory sentences. Those latter rulings were by 5-4 votes. Justice Powell, a *Furman* dissenter, provided the fifth vote, but Stewart supplied the rationale and may well have influenced Powell's vote.

As noted earlier, however, Justice Stewart will perhaps best be remembered as a forceful and articulate critic of the Court in a number of constitutional fields. Especially important were his reactions to the Court's stance on press claims to testimonial and search privileges, the scope of rights required in juvenile proceedings, and devotional exercises in the public schools. The case *Branzburg v. Hayes* (1972) concerned the testimonial privilege, and *Zurcher v. Stanford Daily* (1978) concerned the search privilege.

In *Branzburg* the majority rejected the testimonial privilege at issue, and Justice White concluded for the Court that the public interest in the effective prosecution of crime outweighed any burden on the free flow of news from confidential sources that grand jury subpoenas of news reporters might impose. He also cited the difficulties in determining what persons are entitled to the testimonial privilege, the degree to which the press had flourished in the past without it, concerns that the conditional version of the privilege sought by the press would not eliminate the chilling effect claimed on confidential sources, and the impropriety of a judge's deciding what subpoenas—and thus what cases—warranted overriding a claim to the privilege. In upholding third-party searches of media offices for the majority in *Zurcher,* White voiced similar concerns and concluded that the warrant procedure mandated by the Fourth Amendment provided adequate protection for any First Amendment interests threatened by such searches.

Many of White's concerns were well taken. In a *Branzburg* dissent, however, Justice Stewart complained of "the Court's crabbed view of the First Amendment" (408 U.S. at 725) and accused the majority of inviting "state and federal authorities to undermine the historic independence of the press by attempting to annex the journalistic profession as an investigative arm of government" (725). His *Zurcher* dissent was equally biting.

But Stewart's attacks on the *Branzburg* and *Zurcher* majorities were more than mere rhetoric. In *Branzburg* he argued effectively that the Court had never before insisted on empirical evidence of a burden on First Amendment freedoms before triggering the "compelling interest" test under which news reporters wanted each claim to a privilege to be evaluated. Nor could he agree that the warrant procedure—with its emphasis on probable cause—was an appropriate forum for vindication of First Amendment rights threatened by third-party searches of media offices. In *Houchins v.*

KQED, Inc. (1978), he also provided an answer to the majority's concerns about whom to extend the privileges to and its rejection of the notion that journalists enjoy greater First Amendment rights than other persons. It is true that Stewart once contended that the professional press is entitled to special First Amendment rights.[31] But in his concurrence for *Houchins,* he agreed that journalists have no special per se right of access to government facilities not open to the public. Instead, he contended, the critical role of the press in our society means that the interests sufficient to justify restrictions on general public access to government facilities may not be adequate in particular cases to justify identical limitations on the press. This balancing approach would go far to alleviate the definitional problems that disturbed the Court in *Branzburg* and *Zurcher:* the privileges could be extended to all persons, but the interests of the working journalist would normally be accorded greater weight.[32]

Even better known than Stewart's above critiques, perhaps, is his opposition to the Court's extension of many procedural guarantees to juvenile proceedings. He did not oppose all of them, of course. In the case *In re Gault* (1967), he concluded that juveniles clearly were entitled to "timely notice" and "suppose[d]" that no "brutally coerced confession" could be used against a juvenile (387 U.S. at 80–81). He also joined the unanimous 1975 decision extending the double jeopardy guarantee to juveniles in *Breed v. Jones.* But he agreed with the Court, too, in *McKeiver v. Pennsylvania* (1971), that juveniles are not entitled to jury trials; he joined Chief Justice Burger's objections to the Court's extension of the "no reasonable doubt" standard of guilt to juvenile proceedings in *In re Winship* (1970); and he seemingly rejected, in *Gault,* the notion "that the testimonial privilege against self-incrimination is applicable in all" such cases (80), though concluding that most of the procedural claims in *Gault* were not properly before the Court.

Stewart feared that extending the procedural rights of adult defendants to juveniles might "invite a long step backwards into the nineteenth century. In that era," he warned in *Gault,* "there were no juvenile proceedings, and a child was tried in a conventional criminal court with all the trappings of a conventional criminal trial. So it was that a 12-year-old boy named James Guild was tried in New Jersey for killing Catharine Beakes. A jury found him guilty of murder, and he was sentenced to death by hanging. The sentence was executed. It was all very constitutional" (387 U.S. at 79–80). Gerald Gault was to be committed to a state industrial school from age fifteen to twenty-one for an offense that would have meted an adult a maximum fifty-dollar fine and two months' imprisonment. In view of the broad power of juvenile judges, the majority thought its ruling worth the risks Justice Stewart cited. Yet his dissent raised a real, if overdrawn, concern that remains valid today.

Finally, of course, his lone dissent from the Court's decisions invalidating devotional exercises in the public schools are of note. In 1981 in *Widmar v. Vincent*, the Burger Court obligated public colleges to open student forum facilities to religious groups. In *Lynch v. Donnelly* (1984), moreover, the Court upheld a city's inclusion of a nativity scene in its Christmas display. Chief Justice Burger's majority opinion in *Lynch* did not cite Stewart's *Engel* and *Schempp* dissents, and he was kinder to the "wall of separation" concept than Stewart had been. While Stewart, in *Schempp*, condemned the "wall of separation" as a "sterile metaphor which by its very nature may distort rather than illumine the problems involved in a particular case" (374 U.S. at 309), Burger called it a "useful figure of speech" in *Lynch*, though "not a wholly accurate description of the practical aspects of the relationship that in fact exists between church and state" (465 U.S. at 1359). Even so, Burger's opinion tracked much of Stewart's rhetoric and arguably provided a philosophical basis for a judicial overruling of *Engel* and *Schempp*. Accordingly, a precise understanding of the Stewart dissents is especially important.

In Stewart's judgment, the *Engel* and *Schempp* majorities gave the establishment clause an unduly "mechanistic" construction that ignored the nation's religious heritage, the numerous reflections of that heritage in its governmental institutions, and the inherent conflicts between dogmatic interpretations of the establishment clause and the First Amendment's commitment to religious liberty. For him, those parents preferring devotional exercises in the public schools, he said in *Schempp*, had "a substantial free exercise claim."

> For a contemporary state educational system so structures a child's life that if religious exercises are held to be an impermissible activity in schools, religion is placed at an artificial and state-created disadvantage. Viewed in this light, permission of such exercises for those who want them is necessary if the schools are truly to be neutral in the matter of religion. And a refusal to permit religious exercises thus is seen, not as the realization of state neutrality, but rather as the establishment of a religion of secularism, or at the least, as government support of the beliefs of those who think that

religious exercises should be conducted only in private. (374 U.S. at 309)

He insisted that devotional exercises should be "completely . . . free from any kind of official coercion [of] those who do not affirmatively want to participate" and found it "conceivable" that school boards might be unable to meet such a requirement. He contended, however, that courts should "not assume that school boards so lack the qualities of inventiveness and good will as to make impossible the achievement of that goal" (320). He also believed that programs incorporating desirable alternatives to participation could avoid the taint of official compulsion.

Given the vulnerability of youth to the pressures of peers and authorities, one well may doubt—as the *Engel* and *Schempp* majorities obviously did—whether a truly voluntary devotional program can ever be developed. For Stewart, however, the issue of coercion was the only legitimate First Amendment concern in a society traditionally permeated with church-state ties, and that issue should be resolved on a case-by-case basis.

Conclusion

A superficial review of Justice Stewart's Court career suggests that he lacked an internally consistent judicial and constitutional philosophy. His voting patterns and opinions were compatible, however, with his regard for state prerogatives and representative institutions, as well as his commitment to narrowly drawn decisions closely tied to specific fact patterns. His commitment to what Gayle Binion termed "non-anticipatory" decisions was consistent with his hope to be considered a "lawyer" justice who decided specific constitutional disputes without imposing an undue gloss on the Constitution's text.[33]

One can admire the humility of such a justice—or the cunning of a jurist bent on maximizing his flexibility in future cases. But while Stewart's emphasis on the narrow decision probably helped to maximize his influence during the early years of the Burger Court, it probably also contributed to his failure to achieve "greatness" as a justice.[34] In part, perhaps, because of his journalistic background, Stewart achieved a reputation for succinct, lucid opinions. His commitment to the justice-as-lawyer model, however, conflicted with what perhaps is the Court's most important role— the development of a body of constitutional law that serves as a guide not merely for resolving the comparatively few constitutional issues aired in the Court, but also for government officials and the people generally. For better or worse, the courts translate constitutional provisions into living law. With due respect, as Justice Owen Roberts noted in *Smith v. Allwright* (1944), the law reflected in the Supreme Court's opinions should be more enduring than "a restricted railroad ticket, good for this day and train only" (321 U.S. at 669).[35]

NOTES

1. For profiles of Stewart's early life and family background, see Henry J. Abraham, *Justices and Presidents* (New York: Oxford University Press, 1974), pp. 248–49; Jerold H. Israel, "Potter Stewart," in Leon Friedman and Fred L. Israel, eds., *The Justices of the United States Supreme Court: Their Lives and Major Opinions* (New York: Chelsea House, 1969), 4:2921–23; "Newsmaker: Mr. Justice Stewart," *Newsweek*, Oct. 20, 1958, p. 38; *New York Times*, Oct. 8, 1959, pp. 1, 26; Apr. 4, 1959, p. 19.

2. *New York Times*, Oct. 8, 1958, p. 26.

3. Israel, "Potter Stewart," p. 2923.

4. The Stewart family had long been associated with Ohio Republican Senator Robert A. Taft, and Potter Stewart had supported Taft's presidential aspirations in the late 1940s. In 1952 he had shifted his allegiance to the more politically moderate—and electorally promising—Eisenhower, but he maintained ties with Ohio's conservative Republican organization and Senator John Bricker. Bricker supported Stewart for seats on the Sixth Circuit and the Supreme Court. Abraham, *Justices and Presidents*, pp. 248–49. When Stewart was appointed to the Supreme Court, however, Justice Department officials indicated that the department had recommended Stewart independently of Bricker and that he had first been considered for an appointment in 1957. *New York Times*, Oct. 8, 1958, p. 1.

5. *New York Times*, Oct. 8, 1958, p. 1.

6. The text of the resolution is reprinted in "What 36 State Chief Justices Said about the Supreme Court," *U.S. News & World Report*, Oct. 3, 1958: 92–102.

7. *New York Times*, Apr. 10, 1959, pp. 1, 14; Apr. 21, 1959, p. 1. Apparently, the transcript of the committee hearings was never published.

8. *U.S. Congressional Record*, May 5, 1959, pp. 7452–72.

9. Bob Woodward and Scott Armstrong, *The Brethren: Inside the Supreme Court* (New York: Simon and Schuster, 1979), pp. 14, 16. Woodward and Armstrong attribute Stewart's decision largely to a personal family concern. Ibid., pp. 14–17.

10. *New York Times*, June 24, 1981, p. 23. The clerk was Steven M. Umin, who served Stewart during the Court's 1965 term. One clerkship applicant turned down by Stewart "felt easy and welcome in his presence." J. Harvie

Wilkinson III, *Serving Justice: A Supreme Court Clerk's View* (New York: Charterhouse, 1974), p. 7. Wilkinson served for Justice Powell.

11. Israel, "Potter Stewart," p. 2926.

12. For example, in *Dent v. United States* (1961) and *Russell v. United States* (1962), two cases reversing the congressional contempt convictions of witnesses who refused to answer questions during hearings of the House Committee on Un-American Activities, Justice Stewart's opinions for the Court were narrowly limited—based on the inadequacy of the indictment in one case and on the government's failure to prove a statutory element in the other.

13. Israel, "Potter Stewart," pp. 2922–23.

14. The incident is examined in Daniel M. Berman, "Mr. Justice Stewart: A Preliminary Appraisal," *University of Cincinnati Law Review* 28 (1959): 402–3.

15. The Supreme Court denied certiorari in the *Henderson* case. For an examination of Justice Stewart's Sixth Circuit record, see J. Francis Paschal, "Mr. Justice Stewart on the Court of Appeals," *Duke Law Journal* (1959): 325–40.

16. The most thorough analysis to date of Justice Stewart's judicial philosophy, developed in the context of his position in racial equality cases, is Gayle Binion, "Justice Potter Stewart on Racial Equality: What It Means to be a Moderate," *Hastings Constitutional Law Quarterly* 6 (1979): 853–908. See also Binion's "An Assessment of Potter Stewart," *The Center Magazine* 14 (Sept.–Oct. 1981): 2–5.

17. *New York Times*, Oct. 8, 1958, p. 1.

18. Potter Stewart, "Reflections on the Supreme Court [an interview]," *Litigation* 8 (1982): 8.

19. Ibid.

20. Potter Stewart, "Address to New Hampshire Bar Association," *New Hampshire Bar Journal* 18 (1977): 165.

21. Stewart, "Reflections on the Supreme Court," p. 165.

22. Potter Stewart, "Robert H. Jackson's Influence on Federal-State Relationships," *Record* 23 (1968): 27–28.

23. Stewart largely joined Justice Harlan's dissent in *Wesberry v. Sanders* (1964) rejecting the majority's conclusion that the provision in Article I, Section 1, for election of members of the House of Representatives "by the people" required congressional districts of substantially equal population (376 U.S. at 20).

24. For thorough treatments of Justice Stewart's Fourth Amendment jurisprudence, see Helaine M. Barnett, Janice Goldman, and Jeffrey B. Morris, "A Lawyer's Lawyer, a Judge's Judge: Justice Potter Stewart and the Fourth Amendment," *University of Cincinnati Law Review* 51 (1982): 509–44; Peter W. Lewis, "Justice Stewart and Fourth Amendment Probable Cause: 'Swing Voter' or Participant in a 'New Majority'?" *Loyola Law Review* 22 (1976): 713–42.

25. See, for example, Potter Stewart, "Or of the Press," *Hastings Law Journal* 26 (1975): 631.

26. Stewart grew to regret the statement and joked that it would probably be placed on his tombstone. He was better pleased with his assertion in the *Henderson* case that "swift justice demands more than just swiftness" (256 F.2d at 390). "Justice Stewart (Retired)," *New Yorker,* Oct. 18, 1981, p. 36.

27. Woodward and Armstrong, *The Brethren,* pp. 314–15.

28. Ibid., pp. 314–47.

29. Lewis, "Justice Stewart and Fourth Amendment Probable Cause," p. 714 n. 11.

30. For a general critique of the Court's abortion funding decisions, see Tinsley E. Yarbrough, "The Abortion-Funding Issue: A Study in Mixed Constitutional Cues," *North Carolina Law Review* 59 (1981): 611–27.

31. Stewart, "Or of the Press," p. 631.

32. For a critique of the Court's position in press privilege cases, see Tinsley E. Yarbrough, "Press Privilege Claims and Balancing Doctrine," *Alabama Law Review* 31 (1980): 523–46.

33. Binion, "An Assessment of Potter Stewart," p. 4.

34. In a 1970 survey of legal scholars, Stewart, along with fifty-four other justices, was ranked as "average." Abraham, *Justices and Presidents,* pp. 289–90.

35. For essentially the same sort of evaluation, see Binion, "An Assessment of Potter Stewart," pp. 1–5.

14

JUSTICE BYRON R. WHITE:
Good Friend to Polity and Solon

DANIEL C. KRAMER

Introduction

Justice Byron R. White was appointed a member of the Supreme Court in 1962. Though not the author of the majority opinion in any Burger Court case with which laypeople are likely to be familiar, he has written opinions and dissents that have had, or may have in the future, a significant impact on the behavior and rights of important American institutions and actors such as the broadcast media, high-level public officials, state legislatures, and administrative agencies (including the police). White was born in Fort Collins, Colorado, in 1917 and grew up in the small town of Wellington. His father was a branch manager for a lumber supply company. His family was not affluent, and White worked in sugar beet fields to eke out spending money. He was graduated first in his class from high school and received a scholarship to the University of Colorado in Boulder. There he made Phi Beta Kappa and was the University's star tailback.[1] During his college years he became impressed by the New Deal and switched his political allegiance from the Republicans to the Democrats, feeling that Roosevelt's party offered more forward-looking programs.[2]

White played professional football during the 1938–39 and 1940–41 seasons but found time during this period to attend Oxford University in England as a Rhodes Scholar and begin Yale Law School. At the end of his first year he became eligible for law review but opted to play for the Detroit Lions instead. While in England, he met John F. Kennedy at a diplomatic reception. The following summer, they saw one another in Munich when both were on vacation.[3] They met again during World War II.

White was a naval intelligence lieutenant in the South Pacific and won two Bronze Stars. After Kennedy's PT boat was destroyed, the future president returned to the Solomons, where White was stationed. White interviewed him about the sinking and wrote the official report on the matter.[4]

White completed Yale Law School in 1946 and was appointed law clerk to Chief Justice Fred Vinson for the 1946–47 term. During this year, he occasionally came across freshman Congressman John Kennedy and found that they always had something to talk about. In 1959, after White had returned to Denver and been practicing corporate law, the Kennedy forces came to Colorado seeking persons with ties to the Kennedys to help them in the upcoming presidential campaign. White was asked to organize the state, though he was not at the time a Kennedy intimate and had not been taking an active part in national politics.[5] White's hard work helped Kennedy obtain over half of Colorado's votes at the 1960 Democratic National Convention despite the fact that Lyndon Johnson thought the delegation was in his camp. After the convention, White left his private law practice to direct the nationwide volunteer effort known as Citizens for Kennedy and eventually, after Kennedy defeated Richard Nixon, was appointed deputy attorney general to serve under Robert Kennedy.[6] While in this post, he conducted investigations of potential judicial appointees, and, at risk to his physical safety, supervised the U.S. marshals and deputies sent to Alabama in 1961 to protect the Freedom Riders trying to end racial segregation on interstate buses and in southern bus terminals.[7]

White was named to the Supreme Court at the end of March 1962 to succeed Justice Charles Whittaker. President Kennedy thought for a full week about who should fill the vacancy and decided on White just a few hours before his choice was announced.[8] Initially Robert Kennedy had wanted U.S. Court of Appeals Justice William Hastie appointed, but this recommendation was shelved. Chief Justice Warren and Justice Douglas thought Hastie too conservative; Assistant Attorney General Nicholas Katzenbach felt that his appellate opinions were uninspired; and many in the White House felt that it would be politically unwise to choose a black.[9]

Eventually, the options boiled down to White—by then a good personal friend of the Kennedy brothers—and Professor Paul Freund of Harvard Law School, a noted legal scholar.[10] One reason White was chosen was the fact that, like the Kansan Whittaker, he

Justice Byron R. White

was from the West.[11] Also relevant was the fact that he received strong support from Robert Kennedy;[12] that Harvard Law School graduates Justices Frankfurter and Brennan were already on the Court;[13] and that the president knew White better than he did Freund.[14] Moreover, the president, Warren, and Douglas all preferred White's perceived moderate, pragmatic liberalism to Freund's more conservative philosophy.[15]

Reactions to White's appointment were generally favorable. As deputy attorney general, screening nominees for the federal judiciary, he had won the respect of the American Bar Association's Standing Committee on the Federal Judiciary. As a result, it endorsed him as "extremely well qualified."[16] Conservative Mississippi Senator James Eastland, head of the Senate Judiciary Committee, welcomed the nomination, as did Senate Minority Leader Everett Dirksen, Republican of Illinois.[17] Both the liberal *Washington Post*[18] and the conservative *Washington Star* were happy with the choice.[19] Though the *New York Times* would have preferred someone who was already a distinguished legal theorist,[20] White was shortly confirmed by a voice vote of the Senate.[21]

Major Opinions

Separation of Powers

An analysis of White's opinions shows, surprisingly, that he was arguably the member of the Burger Court most eager to preserve judicial and congressional limitations upon executive power. Witness, for example, his dissent in *Nixon v. Fitzgerald* (1982). This case involved a lawsuit brought by Ernest Fitzgerald, a Pentagon employee, against President Nixon and others. Fitzgerald had been fired during Nixon's administration, allegedly for bringing to the public's attention massive cost overruns in the building of the Lockheed C-5A transport plane. The majority held that a chief executive is absolutely immune from liability in civil suits for any action taken in his official capacity. White was one of four dissenters, and he lamented in his dissenting opinion, "Attaching absolute immunity to the Office of the President . . . places the President above the law. It is a reversion to the old notion that the King can do no wrong" (457 U.S. at 766).

The language here echoed his majority position in *Butz v. Economou* (1978). Arthur Economou was the head of a company registered with the Department of Agriculture as a commodity futures commission merchant. The department initiated an administrative proceeding to revoke the company's registration, averring that it had failed to meet certain prescribed financial requirements. While the administrative complaint was pending, Economou sued the secretary of agriculture and other department officials for damages, charging that the true reason for the proceedings against his business was his criticism of the staff and operations of the department's Commodity Exchange Authority. His suit asserted, therefore, that the attempt to cancel the registration violated his First Amendment rights.

The single defense raised by all the defendants was that, as government officials, they were absolutely immune from damages in civil actions, even assuming that they had knowingly and deliberately breached Economou's constitutional rights. White, for the Court, rejected this contention. "The extension of absolute immunity from damages liability to all federal executive officials would seriously erode the protection provided by basic constitutional guarantees" (438 U.S. at 505). Most of the defendants were, therefore, entitled merely to qualified immunity; this much is necessary to encourage them to vigorously enforce the laws for which they are responsible. White would accord absolute protection only to executive employees, such as administrative law judges, who carry out quasi-judicial functions. *Economou* was surely a major contribution to U.S. constitutional law. It should safeguard the liberties of us all by making the politically powerful wary of treading on them. One of White's ex-clerks believes that it was the justice's most noteworthy opinion.

In legislative-executive squabbles White also refused to automatically back up the executive. *INS v. Chadha* (1983) saw him the lone dissenter in a case that perhaps sounds the death knell for the legislative veto, a tool developed by Congress to prevent too much of its law-making power from being usurped by the executive. In *Chadha*, the Court overturned Sec. 244(c) (2) of the Immigration Act, which provided that either house of Congress could override a decision by the attorney general to suspend the deportation of an alien. White was distressed by language in the majority opinion that seemed to declare all legislative vetoes unconstitutional simply for being, in effect, laws: laws under the Constitution, must be passed by both houses and approved by the president. He felt that it was naive to assume that under the separation of powers doctrine the three branches are sealed off from each other; to place them in watertight compartments would make effective governing impossible. Moreover, the veto was a device for ensuring that the executive remained subject to Congress's will in implementing its statutes and has proven an "important if not indispensable political invention that allows the President and Congress to resolve major constitutional and policy differences" (462 U.S. at 972).

White was no more willing to give members of Congress absolute immunity from judicial consideration of any action that in some way related to their official duties than he was members of the executive, though he was willing to grant them a considerable degree of protection. Thus his opinion in *Gravel v. United States* (1972) declared that, while a senator and his aide could not be punished for introducing classified material (the Pentagon Papers) at a subcommittee hearing, they could be questioned by a grand jury for arranging to have them published by a commercial press. In *Doe v. McMillan* (1973), his majority opinion held that members of Congress, the committee staff, and the committee investigator were shielded from civil liability to the extent that they simply submitted a report to a congressional committee on conditions in the Washington, D.C., public schools that spoke unfavorably about specifically named children, thus infringing the childrens' right to privacy. The immunity also extended to voting for the publication of the report; however, those (including, according to a dictum, a member of Congress) who actually distributed the report to the public could be forced to pay damages.

Federalism

In conflicts between state and national authorities, White was more often than not on the side of the national government. Some of his ex-clerks referred to him in conversations with me as a "strong nationalist." He displayed a particularly jaundiced attitude toward state regulatory or tax legislation that threatened the free flow of interstate or foreign commerce. In *South-Central-Timber Development, Inc. v. Wunnicke* (1984), his part-plurality, part-majority opinion declared that an Alaska regulation providing that everyone who cuts timber from state lands must promise in advance to have it processed in Alaska was contrary to the commerce clause. Similarly, in *Bacchus Imports, Ltd. v. Dias* (1984), White, speaking for the Court, declared that the clause was violated by Hawaii's exemption of two local beverages, Okolehao brandy and pineapple wine, from its liquor tax. When White was faced with challenges to state regulation of business that did not discriminate against citizens of other states, he supported the relevant statutes. Thus in *Pittsburgh v. Alco Parking Corp.* (1974), White upheld, against due process clause objections, a city tax on private parking lots that threatened to make some of them unprofitable.

First Amendment

Freedom of Speech, Press, and Association. In a case involving a clash between the values embodied in the First Amendment and other goals, White was likely to opt for the latter. Nonetheless, on occasion he proved to be a defender of First Amendment rights.[22]

His pronouncements about freedom of speech and press suggest that he had misgivings about the press and other mass media as institutions. While aware of the necessity for an unfettered press, and although unwilling to let these misgivings always govern his votes at conference, he felt that in the United States the press's very real power could seriously harm private citizens; thus, it needed no special help from the Court.[23] In *Red Lion Broadcasting Co. v. FCC* (1969), a radio station had broadcast a bitter attack by a right-wing minister, Billy James Hargis, against liberal journalist Fred Cook. Relying on regulations of the Federal Communications Commission, Cook demanded free time to respond. The station claimed that the regulations violated its claimed First Amendment right to use its frequency as it saw fit and to bar whomever it wished from its studios. White's majority opinion denied that the First Amendment gives anyone a "right . . . to monopolize a radio frequency" (395 U.S. at 389). He proclaimed that the First Amendment is relevant to broadcasting, but more to protect the right of listeners to receive a variety of ideas than to safeguard station owners. Those who oppose deregulation of the airwaves still use these doctrines as the centerpiece of their argument.

In *Gertz v. Robert Welch, Inc.* (1974), the Court was faced with a libelous statement in a John Birch Society journal about a Chicago lawyer active in left-wing causes. The majority, and White in dissent, were in accord that Gertz was not a public figure within the meaning of *New York Times Co. v. Sullivan* (1964) and thus did not have to prove that the untruth about him was uttered maliciously. The majority did say, however, that even a private citizen such as Gertz could not recover in a suit against publishers or broadcasters without showing that the defendant was at fault through negligence or otherwise. This holding modified the traditional common law rule of libel that required no showing of fault for private citizens. White bitterly remarked that defamatory statements "serve no purpose whatsoever in furthering the public interest or the search for truth but, on the contrary, may frustrate that search and at the same time inflict great injury on the defenseless individual. The owners of the press and the stockholders of the communications enterprises can much better bear the burden" (418 U.S. at 392). White had joined the majority in *Sullivan*, but two decades later, in his concurring opinion in *Dun and Bradstreet v. Greenmoss Builders* (1985), he felt that the malice rule should not be applied in the case of functionaries seeking merely to clear their name rather than obtain damages. The majority held that a credit rating service had to pay libel damages to a firm it had erroneously reported as bankrupt.

In *Branzburg v. Hayes* (1972), White once again sided against the press, holding for the Court that the First Amendment gives newspaper reporters no privilege to refuse to disclose to a grand jury information about crimes they personally observed in the course of their newsgathering or the names of persons who gave them intelligence about criminal conduct by others. The media argued that if reporters had to make public the names of their tipsters, no one would be willing to be an informant, important sources about wrongdoing would be lost, and vital information would remain hidden from public view. White rebutted this argument by saying, first, that estimates about the possible loss of confidential sources were highly speculative. He then added that, even if it were true that some contacts would be deterred from talking, "we cannot accept the argument that the public interest in possible future news about crime from undisclosed, unverified sources must take precedence over the public interest in pursuing and prosecuting those crimes reported to the press by informants and in thus deterring the commission of such crimes in the future" (408 U.S. at 695).

In obscenity and related cases, White usually supported the punishment of those who made or sold sexually oriented works. In *United States v. Reidel* (1971), he declared that the government can constitutionally ban the distribution of pornography through the mails—even to willing recipients who state that they are adults. He formulated the opinion in *New York v. Ferber* (1982), holding that the state can punish individuals who employ children to engage in sexual activity even though the representation of that activity cannot be considered obscene under the guidelines of *Miller v. California* (1973). (The offending films in *Ferber* showed young boys masturbating.) But in *Schad v. Borough of Mt. Ephraim* (1981),

White spoke for the Court in declaring unconstitutional an ordinance that banned nonobscene nude dancing, indicating that this type of amusement was entitled to some First Amendment protection.

Persons involved in picketing, parading, and demonstrating received little sympathy from White. In *Clark v. Community for Creative Non-Violence* (1984), his opinion held that National Park Service regulations could constitutionally deny persons the right to camp overnight in District of Columbia parks even though the purpose of the camping was to protest widespread homelessness. White emphasized that these regulations were "content neutral"—that they applied to all demonstrations—and noted that the demonstrators had many other ways of communicating their ideas; besides, the ban on overnight camping helped keep the parks attractive.

The freedom of association that the Court finds implicit in the First Amendment also was no favorite of White. He dissented in *United States v. Robel* (1967), in which a Brennan effort for the Warren Court invalidated a section of the Subversive Activities Control Act of 1950 barring members of "Communist-action" organizations from working in defense plants. White protested that freedom of association is not mentioned in the Constitution but is just a "judicial construct"; moreover, it is subject to "significant regulation by the state" (389 U.S. at 282–83). This dim view of freedom of association led him to produce the majority opinion in *Civil Service Commission v. National Association of Letter Carriers* (1973), which sanctioned the Hatch Act's prohibiting federal civil servants from taking an active part in political campaigns. Continuing there to deny the absoluteness of the right to associate, White maintained that the Hatch Act's limitation was necessary to ensure that federal employees would enforce the laws impartially and that they would appear to be executing them in a nonpartisan spirit.

Establishment and Free Exercise of Religion

For White, the wall separating church and state was a leaky barrier. In every case involving public aid to religious schools, he voted to sustain the subsidy. He wrote the majority opinion for the Warren Court in *Board of Education v. Allen* (1966), upholding a New York measure requiring local public school boards to purchase secular textbooks for lending, free of charge, to private and parochial school pupils. He strongly emphasized that these loans would enable these schools to better perform their secular functions. *Allen* is a major decision not only because it permitted texts to be granted gratis to millions of students but also because it laid the groundwork for Burger Court decisions legitimating state assistance to schools maintained by religious institutions. An example is *Committee for Public Education v. Regan* (1980), in which White, writing for the Court, sanctioned a New York statute reimbursing parochial schools for the expenses of administering state-prepared examinations.

White was not overly hospitable to claims arising under the free exercise clause or under federal legislation recognizing freedom of religious belief. In *Welsh v. United States* (1970), he strongly attacked a plurality opinion written by Black regarding Section 6(j) of the Universal Military Training and Service Act granting conscientious objector status to men opposed to war by virtue of religious training and belief. Though the statute stated that essentially political, sociological, or philosophical views were not to be considered religious beliefs, Black asserted that they were to be deemed these if they were sincerely and deeply held. In *TWA v. Hardison* (1977), White's majority judgment declared that Title VII of the 1964 Civil Rights Act did not require a company to continue to employ someone who refused for religious reasons to work on Saturday if obtaining a substitute would cost the company overtime pay or force it to violate seniority rights under a collective bargaining agreement. And in *Heffron v. International Society for Krishna Consciousness* (1981), White, again speaking for the Court, claimed that a state had the right to prohibit a religious group from wandering around a state fairground soliciting funds or selling or distributing material as long as the regulations promulgated by fair officials provided that all such groups had the right to rent a booth for themselves on a first-come, first-served basis.

Civil Rights

Race. Until recent years, White usually took the side of blacks and other ethnic minority groups in discrimination cases. In *Milliken v. Bradley* (1974), he wrote a dissent contending that a federal court could order city-suburban busing of schoolchildren to achieve racial integration even though the outlying school districts had not been guilty of racial discrimination. In *Palmer v. Thompson* (1971), he spoke for the Court minority in vigorously protesting Jackson, Mississippi's closing all its swimming pools to avoid having to operate them on an integrated basis. And in *Columbus Board of Education v. Penick* (1979) and *Dayton Board of Education v. Brinkman*

II (1979), his decisions for the Court affirmed citywide school desegregation orders issued by lower federal courts.

In the waning years of the Burger Court, however, White was one of its stoutest opponents of affirmative action. His best-known decision on this matter was *Firefighters Local Union No. 1784 v. Stotts* (1984), a majority opinion declaring that a federal district court could not order the firing of whites before blacks with less seniority when a budget crisis forced the city of Memphis, Tennessee, to reduce the size of its fire department. The lower court had issued the order to protect a consent decree that had been issued on the basis of Title VII under which the city had agreed to hire and promote more blacks. On the basis of the language of Title VII, which protects bona fide seniority systems, White arguably had no other option than to reach the result he did. What stunned many who had previously thought him supportive of minority group aspirations was a dictum to the effect that Title VII does not permit the federal courts to order even businesses guilty of racial discrimination to hire a set quota of minority workers. These courts, according to him, may use their orders only to benefit those members of minority groups who have personally suffered from the employer's discriminatory practices.

Voting. White joined in the seminal "one person, one vote" decisions of *Wesberry v. Sanders* (1964) and *Reynolds v. Sims* (1964); but his subsequent path in the area of voting rights was a zigzag one. On the liberal side of the balance sheet, in *Phoenix v. Kolodziejski* (1970), White, speaking for the Court, declared that the equal protection clause was offended by a Phoenix, Arizona, rule that prevented persons not owning real estate from voting in referenda to approve city general obligation bond issues. And in *City of Mobile, Alabama v. Bolden* (1980), he disagreed with the Court's holding that it was neither unconstitutional nor a violation of the 1965 Voting Rights Act for Mobile to be governed by a three-member city commission elected at large, despite the fact that no black had ever sat on the commission.

In the fading days of the Warren Court, however, he dissented in *Kirkpatrick v. Preisler* (1969). The Court maintained in *Kirkpatrick* that a Missouri congressional districting plan violated Article I, Section 2, of the Constitution because the most populous district was 3.13 percent above the mathematical ideal while the least populous was 2.83 percent below it. He averred there that he "would not quibble with the legislative judgment if variations between districts were acceptably small" (394 U.S. at 553). *Davis v. Bandemer* (1986) saw White hold for the Court that issues of gerrymandering are justiciable and at the same time maintain for a plurality that partisan gerrymandering of district lines violates the Constitution only when it is so severe as to consistently degrade a political group's influence. *Bandemer* will allow legislatures to continue to draw district lines with an eye to partisan advantage and thus will exert a major influence upon the conduct of practical politics. Also of interest to those concerned with the mechanics of elections is *Whitcomb v. Chavis* (1971), a White majority decision declaring that Indiana statutes creating multimember state house and senate districts for Marion County were not in breach of the Fourteenth Amendment even though their effect was to make it less likely that black neighborhoods in Indianapolis would be represented by nonwhites. *White v. Regester* (1973), however, was a White opinion that invalidated a law providing for multimember state house districts in Dallas and San Antonio, Texas, because the act made it more difficult for blacks and Mexican-Americans to win elections in areas where almost none had ever been elected and thus invidiously minimized the voting strength of these communities.

Gender Discrimination. By and large White was a stout opponent of discrimination on account of sex. He wrote *Taylor v. Louisiana* (1975), insisting that Louisiana's exclusion of women from jury service (unless they had previously requested to be allowed to sit) was an abridgement of the Sixth Amendment's guarantee of an impartial jury. In the course of his opinion, he noted that the stereotypes of women as the weaker sex and as bound to the home were now outmoded. In *Kahn v. Shevin* (1974), he took issue with a decision written by Douglas granting widows but not widowers a five-hundred-dollar property tax exemption. In *Stanley v. Illinois* (1972), he was responsible for the opinion overturning an Illinois law that conclusively presumed unmarried fathers, but not unmarried mothers, unfit to have custody of their children. He was one of the dissenters in *Rostker v. Goldberg* (1981), claiming there that Congress could not constitutionally pass a draft law compelling only men to register. In *Grove City College v. Bell* (1984), however, he noted for the Court that Title IX of the Education Amendments of 1972 requires the cessation of gender discrimination only in the specific programs of a college that receive federal aid, as opposed to all activities of the institution.

Criminal Law

Death Penalty. In *Gregg v. Georgia* (1976), White was one of the several justices who concluded that capital punishment was not per se unconstitutional. *Roberts v. Louisiana* (1976), decided the same day, found Louisiana's mandatory capital punishment law invalid because it did not permit focusing on the particular circumstances of the offense and the offender: White dissented on the ground that the act had eliminated the unfettered jury discretion that several justices (including himself) had found obnoxious in *Furman v. Georgia* (1972). In *Pulley v. Harris* (1984), a White opinion, the Court proclaimed that the imposition of the death penalty was not automatically unconstitutional simply because in other courts of the same state persons who killed under similar circumstances were permitted to live.

White's backing of the death penalty was not unswerving. In *Coker v. Georgia* (1977), his plurality opinion labeled unconstitutional a Georgia law imposing the death penalty for rape. In *Enmund v. Florida* (1982), his majority opinion held that the defendant who drove the getaway car during a felony murder but did not pull the trigger or have any intent to kill could not constitutionally be sentenced to death. And in *Skipper v. South Carolina* (1986), he wrote the Court's opinion ruling that a convicted murderer has the right to present evidence of good behavior in jail to the jury considering whether to impose the death penalty.

Plea Bargaining, Miranda, and the Fifth Amendment. White was unreceptive to individuals who complained that they had been unconstitutionally convicted because of a violation of the self-incrimination clause of the Fifth Amendment. His dissent in *Miranda v. Arizona* (1966) was a bitter one. Thus White's majority opinion in *Edwards v. Arizona* (1981) was a real surprise. White held here that once criminal suspects have invoked the *Miranda* right to counsel, police cannot later begin questioning in the absence of their lawyer unless they have made overtures to them indicating that they want to talk.

Although plea bargaining raises the self-incrimination issue of whether the resulting confession is truly voluntary, the American criminal justice system would collapse without it. In a crucial set of cases White upheld the institution of plea bargaining through legitimating pleas made under dubious circumstances. In *McMann v. Richardson* (1970) he even upheld a guilty plea that the defendants apparently had made upon the advice of their counsel based on confessions that had been obtained from them earlier by police brutality (and thus were inadmissible at trial). For White, the confession resulting from a plea bargain was valid if it was "a voluntary and intelligent act of the defendant" (397 U.S. at 772). For a similar reason, he allowed the plea bargain to remain undisturbed in *Parker v. North Carolina* (1970) (guilty plea made because of counsel's misjudgment as to admissibility of a confession); *Brady v. United States* (1970) (plea arguably made to avoid death penalty under a statute later declared unconstitutional); and *North Carolina v. Alford* (1970) (defendant said, when pleading guilty to second degree murder, that he was really innocent, although substantial evidence showed he was guilty of first-degree murder, a capital offense).

The editors of the *Harvard Law Review* fervently stressed the importance of two of White's 1970 plea-bargaining decisions, but their appraisal applies to the entire quartet. "The decisions in *Brady* and *Parker* are crucial to the present administration of the criminal justice system. . . . Given the present amount of resources available to handle criminal trials, if approximately seventy percent of the dispositions and ninety percent of the convictions did not end in guilty pleas, the criminal justice system would shift from its present low gear to a halt. *Brady* and *Parker* so plainly accept the practice [of plea bargaining] as to stimulate a collective sigh of relief throughout the country from prosecutors and trials (*sic*) judges."[24]

Juries. White composed many of the Court's important post-1962 opinions in jury cases. Not infrequently, he was willing to let the states experiment in this area. Nevertheless, he was the justice responsible not only for *Taylor v. Louisiana* (1975) but also for the Warren Court's *Duncan v. Louisiana* (1968), in which the Sixth Amendment's jury trial provision was incorporated on the ground that it "is fundamental to the American scheme of justice" (391 U.S. at 149). He also expanded *Duncan* in cases such as *Baldwin v. New York* (1970), in which he held that defendants are entitled to a jury trial if they face a possible sentence of more than six months in jail, even though they are being tried for a misdemeanor. On the other hand, White wrote the decision in *Williams v. Florida* (1970), in which he maintained that a state could use six-person rather than twelve-person juries in criminal cases. Likewise, he penned *Johnson v. Louisiana* (1972) and *Apodaca v. Oregon* (1972), in which he held that it is permissible for the states to employ nonunanimous jury verdicts even in criminal cases.

Searches and Seizures. In some Fourth Amendment cases, White came out strongly for the defendant. In *Delaware v. Prouse* (1979) he proclaimed for the Court majority that random stops of cars on the highway for license and registration checks are illegal seizures because individuals are entitled to a reasonable expectation of privacy in their cars, and also because such checks would not significantly contribute to highway safety. He thus sustained the use of the exclusionary rule by the lower courts in this case to prevent the introduction of marijuana that had been taken by the police during a random automobile search. In *Florida v. Royer* (1983), his plurality opinion declared illegal the police confinement, for several minutes in an airport, of a person they merely suspected of transporting narcotics. Investigative detentions in the absence of probable cause "must be temporary and last no longer than is necessary to effectuate the purpose of the stop" (460 U.S. at 500).

In the usual Fourth Amendment case, however, the more conservative side of White came to the fore. He often stressed that the exclusionary rule requires the suppression of unreasonably seized evidence only. Certain types of warrantless seizures, especially those of moving cars upon probable cause and those of suspects incidental to a valid arrest, have for many years been deemed "reasonable" and thus permissible; accordingly, the evidence obtained from them can be introduced in court. White wrote quite a few opinions extending these two exceptions to the need for a search warrant, and he ultimately succeeded in this way in reducing the number of situations in which the exclusionary rule may be invoked. Thus the holding in *Chambers v. Maroney* (1970) averred that the warrantless search with probable cause of a moving vehicle could occur after the car had been taken to the police station. In *United States v. Edwards* (1974), White endorsed the view that a warrantless search of the defendant's clothing was incidental to his arrest, even though it took place ten hours after that event, because the defendant had been placed in his cell late at night. White argued that it was reasonable for the police to let him keep his clothes on while he slept, there being no substitute garb for him to wear.

In White's dissent in *Stone v. Powell* (1976), he contended that the exclusionary rule should not apply when the illegally obtained evidence "was seized by an officer acting in the good-faith belief that his conduct comported with existing law and having reasonable grounds for this belief" (428 U.S. at 538). A majority finally accepted this thesis in *United States v. Leon* (1984) and *Massachusetts v. Sheppard* (1984). In those cases, White held that evidence seized by the police under a warrant that they reasonably believed to be sound does not have to be rejected, even though in fact it was technically flawed. Suppressing evidence when the police have acted in objective good faith will in no way deter illegal behavior by them, which is the main purpose of the exclusionary rule. In *INS v. Lopez-Mendoza* (1984), the Court refused to apply the exclusionary rule at all in civil deportation proceedings. White, however, dissented, arguing that employing the rule (including *Leon*'s "objective good faith" exception) in these hearings would have a deterrent effect on U.S. immigration officers who wish to carry out illegal searches. In retrospect, *Leon* may prove to be one of White's prime legacies to American constitutional law. Paradoxically, by narrowing the exclusionary rule it may save it. The "objective good faith" exception will mean that the rule will less frequently require the freeing of criminals for what appear, to most lay persons, to be trivial reasons. Thus it might well relieve the pressure on the Court to jettison the rule.

Rights of Prisoners. It was a major White opinion, *Wolff v. McDonnell* (1974), that recognized more forcefully than had ever been done before that persons in jail have certain constitutionally guaranteed rights. "[T]hough his rights may be diminished by the needs and exigencies of the institutional environment, a prisoner is not wholly stripped of constitutional protections when he is imprisoned for crime. There is no iron curtain drawn between the Constitution and the prisons of the country" (418 U.S. at 555). White said in *Wolff* that a prisoner threatened with loss of good-time credits for early release has, under the due process clause, the right to a written notice of the violation that threatens his credits, a written statement of the evidence indicating that he has committed such a breach, and an administrative hearing, to be held at least twenty-four hours after receiving the notice, at which he must have an opportunity to rebut these charges. At this hearing the inmate should be allowed to call witnesses when this practice would not interfere with prison security. Also, if the inmate is illiterate or the case complex, the inmate has the right to consult a fellow prisoner or obtain assistance from the prison staff. After establishing these elaborate procedures in *Wolff*, however, White himself infrequently acceded to the claims of prisoners.

Administrative Due Process

Several of White's decisions constituted an important part of the administrative due process jurisprudence developed by the Court. Taken together, they can be considered a significant contribution to constitutional law. *Goss v. Lopez* (1975), one such case, arose when nine students were suspended for misconduct for up to ten days from various schools in Columbus, Ohio. None had had a hearing before being given their punishment, although all were offered the opportunity to confer with school officials after the penalty took effect. White's majority opinion found the suspensions invalid since students have a "property" interest in their entitlement to public education and a "liberty" interest in maintaining their reputations, and the due process clause bars the state from depriving one of property or liberty without some adherence to procedural fairness. Hence students must be given the chance, very soon after an alleged infraction has occurred and usually before removal from school, to assert their innocence or to furnish school authorities with their own version of the facts. This requirement necessitates, of course, telling students at the onset of an informal discussion of the incident what they are supposed to have done and the basis of the accusation.

Barry v. Barchi (1979) was another White opinion infused with the philosophy of the necessity for administrative due process. In *Barry* he held that though presuspension hearings were not required before a horse-racing trainer temporarily lost his license for allegedly drugging his animals, quick postsuspension proceedings were necessary. The ban imposed on the trainer was held invalid because the postsuspension proceeding could be delayed too long by the state. White's language in *Stanley v. Illinois*, mentioned earlier, further indicates his strong belief that persons whom civil servants threaten with the loss or reduction of important interests must be given fair play. In *Stanley* White had held that a state could not, without a hearing in the individual case, assume that an unmarried father was an unfit parent when it made no such conclusive presumption for an unmarried mother. He emphasized there that "The Constitution recognizes higher values than speed and efficiency. Indeed, one might fairly say of the Bill of Rights in general, and the Due Process Clause in particular, that they were designed to protect the fragile values of a vulnerable citizenry from the overbearing concern for efficiency and efficacy which may characterize praiseworthy government officials no less, and perhaps more, than mediocre ones" (405 U.S. at 656).

Abortion and the Right to Privacy

White was a staunch opponent of the Court's efforts invalidating or constricting anti-abortion legislation. He wrote a brief yet fervent dissent in *Roe v. Wade* (1973) accusing the majority of valuing "the convenience of the pregnant mother more than the continued existence of the life or potential life that she carries. Whether or not I might agree with that marshaling of values . . . I find no constitutional warrant for imposing such an order of priorities on the people and legislatures of the states" (410 U.S. at 222). He also dissented on all other occasions when the majority nullified anti-abortion laws.

In some cases White was skeptical of the state's right to regulate sexual relationships. For example, he concurred in *Carey v. Population Services International* (1977), in which the Court struck down a New York act barring the advertisement of contraceptives and their sale to persons under sixteen years of age. He joined with the majority on the advertising issue and concurred regarding the problem of distribution to minors because he did not think that the prohibition on sale would do much to stop promiscuous sex among the young. In *Bowers v. Hardwick* (1986), however, he asserted that homosexuals could be prosecuted for sodomy even though they made love in the privacy of a home.

White's Position and Influence on the Burger Court

White's position on the Burger Court was somewhat different from his position on the Warren Court. Although many scholars feel he was a member of a conservative bloc during the Warren era, the best view is that he was a moderate liberal from the 1963–64 term through the 1968–69 term. For these six sessions taken as a whole, he voted more often with Brennan (80%) and Warren (77%) than with any other colleague. The justices he joined least during this period were the strong liberal Douglas and the moderate conservative Harlan.[25]

During the first four terms of the Burger Court (1969–72), however, White was often, but certainly not always, aligned with its relatively conservative Nixon appointees. He voted with Blackmun 74% of the time, Powell 74%, Burger 70%, and Rehnquist

71%. The statistic for his old Warren Court friend Brennan was down to 67%. Once again, he disagreed with Douglas more often than with anyone else.[26] It was in these years that he played the role of "swing man," the results of cases depending on whether he joined the Nixon justices or the rest of the Court.[27] Most frequently he swung to the "Four."[28]

During the beginning of the five-year period running from the 1973 through the 1977 terms, when it still made sense to call the Nixon Four a cohesive group, White continued to ally himself with them more often than not and thus to show himself a moderate conservative. The Four voted together in 75% of all the cases decided on the merits during the 1973–74 term; and in those cases White agreed with them 85% of the time.[29] During the 1974–75 term the Four voted together in 69% of the cases; White joined them in 91% of these.[30] In the five-year period from 1978 through 1982 he cemented his alliances with the conservatives, cooperating most often with Burger, Powell, O'Connor, and Rehnquist. Brennan is seventh on the list and Marshall last.[31] In fact, for the last years of the Burger Court, as Table 1.8 clearly shows, he, the chief justice, Powell, Rehnquist, and O'Connor (with occasional help from Blackmun) made up the Court's conservative bloc. The *Economist*'s comment in July, 1984, that White had by then completed his "move into the right-wing camp" is basically correct[32] — though the question of where to locate him on the political spectrum is not as simple as that.

White will never go down in history as a "great dissenter." Table 1.7 shows that, for the seven justices who were on the Burger Court continually during the terms spanning 1971 through 1985, the total number of his dissents was far less than the figures for Brennan, Marshall, and Rehnquist and about equal to those for Powell and Blackmun. The fact that he was rarely in the minority on the Burger Court is hardly surprising, given his highly competitive personality and the fact that he was first its swing man and later a member of a conservative quintet that won with reasonable frequency when the Court was closely divided.[33]

White's position and influence on the Burger Court are in many respects not revealed by the above quantitative data. His former clerks to whom I spoke said that his views were sought after by his associates and respected by them. At conference he joyfully and seriously debated the issues and the others listened closely, partly because his frame of mind usually was not a rigid, dogmatic one and partly because they recognized his mental acumen.[34] "Several justices over the years have privately referred to White in conference as 'tough' and as 'a fighter' who shapes their thinking by the force of his intellect and his rigorous preparation and analysis of cases."[35] His colleagues also paid attention to him because he treated their assertions with respect (though he was not unwilling to point out the weaknesses in their positions)[36] and because he was, on occasion, willing to take into account their feelings. As an example of this last point, White wrote a plurality opinion in *United States v. Thirty Seven Photographs* (1971), stating that customs agents could seize obscene materials imported for private use, that distinguished, rather than overruled, *Stanley v. Georgia* (1969). *Stanley* was a Marshall opinion holding that the possession of obscene materials in the privacy of one's home cannot be constitutionally punished. A former clerk of White told me that *Thirty-Seven Photographs* did not overturn *Stanley* because White did not want to offend Marshall.

The former clerks of justices other than White whom I interviewed provided additional information about his relationships with his Burger Court colleagues. He was not a "coalition builder"; that is, he rarely actively lobbied his colleagues to obtain a majority for a result he wished the Court to reach. Nonetheless, when it became clear to him that he would have to modify the language of his draft to win over a "fifth" justice, he did so. For example, he inserted some of the phrases in *Enmund v. Florida* to convince Brennan to join in his opinion (and thus make it a majority opinion) rather than simply to concur. Moreover, he was not reluctant to ask the justices for changes in the wording of their circulated drafts. On the other hand, his colleagues courted his support less than one would expect given his centrist, swing position. At least two reasons explain why: first, because his views on a few issues, such as abortion and parochial aid, had soon become fixed it was useless to lobby him on these matters; second, it was known that once he had made up his mind about a case he rarely changed it.

White's Judicial Philosophy and the Political Context

What were Justice White's general views on law, the courts, and the government, and when did he develop these perspectives? Most of his former clerks to whom I spoke are convinced that his tendency to side with the state in criminal justice cases came to some extent from his having grown up in a small town where there was little crime and police abuse—a background that might lead one to believe that the decision to violate the law is more a product of free will rather than of poverty and racism and that the police are, on the whole, likely to behave well. Two former clerks maintained that his stint at the Justice Department, where some of the cases he worked on involved organized crime, strengthened his belief that law enforcement officials must not be hobbled by an overwhelming number of procedural restraints. Moreover, some of his former clerks think that his experience as deputy attorney general supervising the protection of the freedom riders made him sympathetic to the claims of ethnic and racial minorities, especially blacks, for equal treatment. Blackmun agrees.[37]

His stance in favor of state aid to parochial schools sprang to a considerable extent from his theory that in a democracy courts ought normally to be unwilling to interfere with the work of legislators, who are, after all, the representatives of the people.[38] In White's eyes, disputes over religion, just like disagreements about other social matters, should be resolved through the legislative process of accommodation and compromise.[39] To a considerable degree his siding with the state in criminal law cases also came from his philosophy that legislation is the business of Congress, statehouses, and city halls—not of the courts.

Faith in legislative and popular supremacy partially explains other of his conservative decisions. A belief that the courts must interpret the law in accordance with the will of Congress implies, of course, that it must not ignore unambiguous congressional language. For example, the Civil Rights Act of 1964 makes it clear that it cannot be used to disturb bona fide seniority systems—probably one reason why he overturned, in *Stotts,* the district court order commanding that senior whites be discharged before more recently hired blacks.

To say that White championed legislative supremacy is to say that he was very suspicious of the concept of "substantive due process." He denounced this doctrine for the majority in the gay rights case of *Bowers v. Hardwick* and also in dissent in *Moore v. City of East Cleveland, Ohio* (1977), in which the Court overturned a zoning ordinance that had the effect of prohibiting a grandparent from residing with two grandsons who were cousins rather than brothers. In this dissent, as one of White's former clerks pointed out to me, he referred to *Roe v. Wade* as a substantive due process case. In fact, one of his major objections to the abortion decision was that it was an example of judicial refusal to accord the legislative resolution of a problem the proper quantum of deference.

This creed of legislative supremacy, with its corollary that the courts cannot be the major agent of social change, was another attitude he embraced before he became a supreme court justice. At the Senate Judiciary Committee hearings on his nomination, he declared, "I think it is clear under the Constitution that legislative power is not vested in the Supreme Court. It is vested in the Congress; and I feel the major institution for changing the laws in this country is the Congress of the United States."[40] In an article written in the mid-1960s he asserted that "I think it is only fair to say that . . . the major load for the further development of the law has come to rest on the legislative and executive branches of our federal, state, and local governments. Change is too rampant and too demanding, too complex and massive, for either wise or efficient handling in the courts."[41]

Yet another aspect of White's judicial philosophy antedated his accession to the Court: the view, mentioned by his former clerks, that government tends to act for the good of society as a whole; that, in essence, it is a mechanism for helping people. He passed his adolescence and early manhood under the shadow of the Great Depression, and he saw the government, in the shape of the New Deal, take the lead in fighting this hydra. Moreover, he studied at a state college that had been set up with assistance from the federal government. His Department of Justice stay, which he enjoyed thoroughly, further convinced him that government is basically a beneficent force. Even when he was a corporate lawyer in Denver, he remained a staunch New Deal Democrat. In those "apolitical" years, he was a Democratic precinct captain for a brief time and often helped the campaigns of prominent Colorado Democrats.[42] And the heart of the New Deal Democratic philosophy is that state action is a superb tool for aiding the individual and promoting the general welfare. According to Table 1.10, White's average pro-economic liberalism score for the 1969 through the 1985 terms was 61.4% compared with 50.3% for the Court as a whole.

Conclusions

White's just-noted positive perception of the polity (like his belief in legislative supremacy) had obvious connections with his usual support of the police and with his acceptance of legislation that was antiabortion, antiobscenity, anticommunist, or pro–state parochial aid. His votes in cases involving these issues and others did place him on the unqualifiedly conservative side of the Burger

Court during its last years—and kept him from being one of that Court's avid defenders of civil liberties like Brennan, Douglas, and Marshall (see Table 1.8). Paradoxically, as was also true for Felix Frankfurter, his votes were, to a significant extent, based on a liberal philosophy (that of popular supremacy and the likely wholesomeness of governmental action). In such areas as criminal justice, speech and press, and sexual relationships, the people and the state are likely to lean to the restrictive side. Thus in these areas a judge who believes in waltzing to the tune of demos, solon, and polis is likely to produce decisions that also veer in that direction.[43]

An evaluation of White must begin by referring to his great intelligence and his considerable influence with his colleagues. A few ideas he expressed make sense but have not yet caught the imagination of a majority of the justices. For example, his *Roe v. Wade* dissenting contention that the majority opinion values the convenience of the pregnant mother over the life or potential life of the fetus and his point that nothing in the Constitution requires the states to accept this prioritizing was not grappled with by the majority opinion in *Roe* and is glossed over by *Roe*'s defenders. Why, White perceptively asked here, when the state opts for one admittedly important value over another, ought its sense of the relative importance of the two be disturbed? No matter what the answer, no one yet has adequately addressed this question.

Of course, White fashioned some weak arguments. Cases involving Marxists inspired some of White's worst opinions. For example, his dissent in *United States v. Robel* (1967) misrepresented the tired, dispirited, infiltrated U.S. Communist Party as a conspiracy controlled by the Soviet Union that was boring its way into important American institutions. In another area, his contention in *Bowers v. Hardwick* (1986) that granting constitutional protection to private homosexual acts implies similar safeguards for the non-victimless crime of adultery simply does not hold water. And the case taken as a whole manifests far too great a willingness to accede to irrational majoritarian preferences.

Though I personally give White a high rating as a Supreme Court justice, it is improbable that scholarly opinion in general will deem him one of the greatest Supreme Court justices of all time. Though he could produce sparkling sentences (reconsider the excerpts furnished here from his *Roe* dissent and his majority opinions in *Wolff* and *Stanley*), more often than not he employed pedestrian language in his prose (sometimes hastily written) rather than broad, well-crafted, inspiring statements of principle.[44] Moreover, the former clerks to whom I spoke unanimously agreed that (with the exception of the abortion and parochial aid arenas) he adopted a quintessentially lawyer-like approach and was more concerned with the facts of each case than with the political, sociological, and philosophical credos that could be invoked to resolve it. (The 1979 citywide school desegregation cases from Columbus and Dayton are good illustrations of this approach.) When White's penchant for the particular is added to his often colorless, undoctrinaire writing style and to his hatred of publicizing himself through media interviews, it is understandable why little has been written about his jurisprudence. This neglect is a shame, and I hope that this chapter begins to remedy it.

NOTES

I was very fortunate to have been granted interviews with seven of White's former law clerks and five former clerks of other justices. I promised them that I would not reveal their names. The reader will see from a glance at this chapter how incredibly helpful they were, and I want to take this opportunity to thank them collectively for taking time from their busy schedules to let me speak with them.

1. Fred L. Israel, "Byron R. White," in Leon Friedman and Fred L. Israel, eds., *The Justices of the U.S. Supreme Court, 1789–1969: Their Lives and Major Opinions* (New York: Chelsea House, 1969), 4:2951–53.

2. *Time*, Apr. 6, 1962, p. 16.

3. Israel, "Byron R. White," pp. 2953–54.

4. Ibid., pp. 2953–54; *Christian Science Monitor*, March 31, 1962, p. 13, and Apr. 2, 1962, p. 10.

5. Israel, "Byron R. White," p. 2954.

6. Ibid.; Penn Kimball, *Bobby Kennedy and the New Politics* (Englewood Cliffs, N.J.: Prentice-Hall, 1968), p. 112.

7. Israel, "Byron R. White," p. 2955; William R. Manchester, *The Glory and the Dream: A Narrative History of America* (Boston: Little, Brown, 1973), pp. 941–43.

8. Arthur M. Schlesinger, Jr., *A Thousand Days: John F. Kennedy in the White House* (Boston: Houghton Mifflin, 1965), p. 698; *Washington Post*, Apr. 1, 1962, p. A1.

9. Schlesinger, *Robert Kennedy and His Times* (Boston: Houghton Mifflin, 1978), pp. 392–93.

10. Kenneth O'Donnell and David F. Powers, *Johnny, We Hardly Knew Ye: Memories of John Fitzgerald Kennedy* (Boston: Little, Brown, 1972), p. 280; *Washington Post*, Apr. 1, 1962, p. A1.

11. *Washington Post*, Apr. 1, 1962, p. A1.

12. Ibid.

13. Schlesinger, *Robert Kennedy and His Times,* p. 393.

14. *New York Times,* Apr. 2, 1962, p. 17.

15. Schlesinger, *Robert Kennedy and His Times,* p. 393; *Newsweek,* Apr. 9, 1962, p. 33; *Wall Street Journal,* Apr. 2, 1962, p. 4.

16. *Washington Star,* Mar. 31, 1962, pp. 1, 3.

17. *Washington Post,* Mar. 31, 1962, p. 1.

18. Ibid., Apr. 1, 1962, p. E4.

19. *Washington Star,* Apr. 1, 1962, p. B4.

20. *New York Times,* Apr. 1, 1962, Sec. 4, p. 10.

21. *Washington Star,* Apr. 12, 1962, p. A5.

22. For an excellent summary of White's decisions dealing with press freedom, see Michael J. Armstrong, "A Barometer of Freedom of the Press: The Opinions of Mr. Justice White," *Pepperdine Law Review* 8 (1980): 157.

23. Ibid., pp. 174–75, 178.

24. "The Supreme Court, 1969 Term," *Harvard Law Review* 84 (1970): 32, 150.

25. These statistics are calculated from "The Supreme Court, 1967 Term: The Statistics," *Harvard Law Review* 82 (1968): 301, 311; "The Supreme Court, 1972 Term: The Statistics," *Harvard Law Review* 87 (1973): 303, 312.

26. All these statistics are calculated from "The Supreme Court, 1972 Term," p. 313. The data concerning Blackmun are for the 1970–72 terms only; for Powell, the 1971–72 terms; for Burger, the 1969–72 terms; and for Rehnquist, the 1971–72 terms.

27. See, for example, Robert Zelnick, "Whizzer White and the Fearsome Foursome," *Washington Monthly* 4 (Dec. 1972): 46, 48.

28. See Leonard W. Levy, *Against the Law: The Nixon Court and Criminal Justice* (New York: Harper and Row, 1974), pp. 432–33.

29. Warren Weaver, Jr., "Four Nixon Judges on High Court Vote in Bloc that Could Become Majority," *New York Times,* July 1, 1974, p. 10.

30. Weaver, "Four Nixon Judges Dominate Decisions," *New York Times,* July 3, 1975, p. 19.

31. Calculated from "The Supreme Court, 1982 Term: The Statistics," *Harvard Law Review* 97 (1983): 295, 305.

32. *Economist,* July 14, 1984, p. 21.

33. For example, out of a total of thirty-two 5-4 decisions during the 1982–83 term, the White, Rehnquist, O'Connor, Powell, and Burger grouping formed the majority in twelve cases. "The Supreme Court, 1982 Term," p. 298.

34. On this matter of White's considerable brilliance, John P. Mackenzie's "Editorial Notebook," *New York Times,* June 17, 1986, p. A26, referred to both White and Stevens as "heavyweights" even though they disagreed strongly about *Roe v. Wade.* Four of the five former clerks of justices other than White whom I interviewed agreed that White (and Stevens) probably had the sharpest minds on the Burger Court.

35. Al Kamen, "Justice White: Twenty-Five Years of Defying Labels," *Washington Post*, Apr. 16, 1987, p. 1.

36. Bob Woodward and Scott Armstrong, *The Brethren: Inside the Supreme Court* (New York: Simon and Schuster, 1979), p. 185.

37. *New York Times*, Mar. 8, 1986, p. 7.

38. See the article by White's former law clerk Lance Liebman, "Swing Man on the Supreme Court," *New York Times Magazine*, Oct. 8, 1972, pp. 16, 94.

39. Ibid., p. 95.

40. U.S. Congress, Senate Committee on the Judiciary, *Nomination of Byron R. White* (Washington, D.C.: U.S. Government Printing Office, 1962), p. 23.

41. Byron R. White, "The United States Supreme Court—1966–1967," *Natural Resources Lawyer* 1 (1968): 24, 31.

42. *Rocky Mountain News* (Denver), Mar. 31, 1962, p. 5.

43. If I may be a bit speculative here, I think there is a residual individualism in White left over from his days growing up in the relatively unsettled West of the 1920s and 1930s. It may be this surviving individualism that led him to pen opinions such as *Delaware v. Prouse* and *Butz v. Economou.*

44. See Liebman, "Swing Man on the Supreme Court," p. 17. Another journalist said that "White's sometimes slapdash opinions do not display his formidable mind to best advantage." Stuart Taylor, Jr., "Rehnquist's Court: Tuning Out the White House," *New York Times Magazine*, Sept. 11, 1988, pp. 38, 98.

15

THE BURGER COURT AND BEYOND

CHARLES M. LAMB
AND STEPHEN C. HALPERN

The Burger Court era was a period in which New Deal Democratic liberalism wilted and Republican conservatism blossomed. A Republican sat in the White House for all but four years of that era, and Republican presidents made six consecutive appointments to the Supreme Court. The Burger Court was the product of those appointments. Those appointments, in turn, may have established conditions that will foster dramatic constitutional changes in the years ahead under Chief Justice Rehnquist.

The Burger Court and Its Members

Richard Nixon and Ronald Reagan, the two most prominent national political figures of the Burger period, stressed similar themes about the Supreme Court. Both emphasized the need for justices who were "strict constructionists" or advocates of judicial restraint who would "interpret" rather than "make" law. Nixon and Reagan both embraced the view that liberal justices had often acted as "super-legislators" who imposed their own personal political and social views on the American public under the guise of constitutional interpretation.[1] The Nixon-Reagan message was clear: path-breaking, liberal social policy innovations by the Supreme Court must end, and they would use their control over judicial nominations to achieve that goal. Given this presidential rhetoric, conservatives thought that the Burger Court would provide a much needed, long overdue antidote to the Warren Court's liberal activism.[2] In many ways they were disappointed.

The Burger Court did not meet conservatives' expectations for at least two reasons. First, the Nixon, Ford, and Reagan appointees did not reverse the jurisprudential cornerstones of the Warren Court. As the contributors to this book demonstrate, the most important Warren Court doctrines survived. What Alpheus Thomas Mason wrote in 1974 was still true twelve years later when Warren Burger retired: "The three major pillars of the Warren Court's constitutional edifice—Race Relations, Reapportionment, and Rules of Criminal Procedure—though somewhat eroded, are still virtually intact."[3] Fundamental changes in American constitutional law wrought by conservative judicial activism simply did not materialize during Burger's tenure as chief justice. Conservatives were upset that the Burger Court failed to deliver a "constitutional counterrevolution"—a conservative version of Warren Court activism.

Second, although the Burger Court significantly chipped away at Warren Court precedents in such constitutional areas as criminal procedure[4] and obscenity,[5] it strengthened or extended some Warren Court doctrines[6] and evinced its own brand of liberal activism, in other areas in which the Warren Court had done little or nothing—most notably in abortion, gender discrimination, busing, and affirmative action.[7] Addressing a new agenda of social controversies that emerged in the 1970s and 1980s, many Burger Court decisions fit quite nicely into the Warren Court mold. That is why, more than a decade after the beginning of the Burger era, the Court remained a sore spot for Reagan. He lamented its policies on abortion, school desegregation, school prayer, and affirmative action, much as Nixon had decried Warren Court policies on criminal procedure. Notwithstanding the criticisms by Republican presidents and the corrective measures they tried to take through their nominations to the Court, at the end of the Nixon-Reagan era, American constitutional jurisprudence did not reflect the values and preferences of conservatives on social agenda issues. Rather, the record was mixed.

The Burger Court was much less likely than its predecessor to decide in favor of civil liberties claims.[8] Yet, with some exceptions, as in criminal procedure, the Burger Court consolidated and occasionally extended the Warren Court "revolution." As Richard Funston wrote in 1987, the Warren and Burger Courts produced many results that "tended to vary in degree rather than in kind."[9] Although unmistakable differences appeared between the two Courts, at times they were subtle. Perhaps this explains why the scholarly criticism of the "Imperial Judiciary" emerged not during the heyday of the Warren Court era but rather during the Burger years, often taking aim directly at the Burger Court.[10] A few illustrations underscore the continuities between the Warren and Burger Courts.

Consider the law of racial discrimination. The Burger Court, although announcing a mixture of decisions in this area, remained largely wedded to the liberal constitutional policies from the Warren years. In some ways the racial discrimination cases of the Warren Court era had been easy to decide: they had involved blatant, if not brutal discrimination, and the intent to discriminate had been explicit.[11] The problems and remedies became more complex, and the answers less morally compelling, once the issues moved beyond de jure discrimination. The Burger Court was forced to wrestle with the more sophisticated forms of racial discrimination surrounding de facto school segregation, institutional racism, and most explosively, affirmative action. For the most part, it rejected cross-district busing and rigid affirmative action quotas, and its record demonstrated little sympathy for fair housing principles. Yet in the areas of school desegregation and affirmative action, the Burger Court supported the general direction and philosophical thrust of the Warren Court. It was often sympathetic to the claims of minority plaintiffs and at times expanded the constitutional protections they enjoyed.[12] In relation to affirmative action, a controversial issue that did not emerge until the 1970s, the Burger Court's record was especially noteworthy and consistent with the Warren Court's orientation. Important favorable decisions were advanced in *Regents of the University of California v. Bakke* (1978), *United Steelworkers v. Weber* (1979), and *Fullilove v. Klutznick* (1980). Constitutional rights had historically been judicially recognized on the basis of an individual's right; in these affirmative action decisions, however, the Burger Court advanced a conception of constitutional rights premised on racial and ethnic identities.

While the civil rights revolution for racial minorities emerged in the 1950s and 1960s, the women's rights movement did not arise as a national issue until the Burger era. On gender discrimination the Burger Court evolved an important and decidedly liberal body of law. Those policy initiatives were consistent with the spirit of Warren Court reforms, extending greater constitutional protection to a politically weak and historically mistreated group. Although the Burger Court might be faulted for failing to make gender a suspect classification or for not going far enough in terms of specific reforms, it laid a foundation in American constitutional jurisprudence that addressed traditional forms of gender discrimination and stereotyping in such cases as *Frontiero v. Richardson* (1973), *Craig v. Boren* (1976), and *Roberts v. United States Jaycees* (1984). Its legacy in this area reflects a sympathy for the social and economic policies central to the women's movement of the 1970s and 1980s. Indeed, both conservatives and liberals alike would probably agree that there is no more extreme example of liberal judicial activism in modern times than the Burger Court's decision in *Roe v. Wade* (1973). The Burger Court also provided greater constitutional protections for aliens and illegitimates.

During the Burger era, America experienced a revival of religious fundamentalism. Powerful religious figures led a vocal and well-financed movement seeking to play a leading role in the nation's political life. That movement decried certain "immoralities" that had allegedly come to pervade national life. The religious right believed that Supreme Court decisions on criminal defendants' rights, obscenity, school prayer, and abortion had eroded the nation's proper moral sensibilities. Motivated by these concerns, these critics allied themselves with the resurgent conservative wing of the Republican party and especially with the presidency of Ronald Reagan. But although the wall of separation that the Court wrote of in *Everson v. Board of Education* (1947) was under attack, again the record of the Burger Court shows a response that was not decidedly conservative. The Court banned various forms of public financial support to sectarian elementary and secondary schools,[13] and in *Wallace v. Jaffree* (1985) it declared unconstitutional a state statute authorizing public schools to have one minute of silence for meditation or voluntary prayer. Hence, despite the prominence of fundamentalist religious interests during the Burger era, the Court's policies on school prayer and other controversial establishment clause issues did not take a pronounced and swift turn to the right. Although the Court's policies on these issues were not as liberal as its policies on gender discrimination, they remained in large measure an anathema to fundamentalist religious leaders when Warren Burger resigned the chief justiceship.

All in all, it is difficult to label the Burger Court because of its mixed behavior regarding various issues. Still, several generalizations seem warranted. The Warren Court's liberalism in some areas of constitutional law was moderated by the Burger Court, but it was not expunged and replaced by an overarching conservative constitutional jurisprudence. While the Burger Court did decide a much smaller percentage of cases in favor of civil liberties claims, particularly in the 1980s, and did whittle away at Warren

Court reforms in some areas, it did not reverse the landmark civil liberties decisions for which the Warren Court is best known. Sometimes the Burger Court assumed a middle ground, serving up something to everyone (depending on the issue and the case). At other times it broke new liberal ground.

True, the Burger Court did not extend the rationale of some Warren Court decisions, as when it refused to declare education a fundamental right or wealth a suspect class in *San Antonio School District v. Rodriguez* (1973). Nonetheless, even in *Rodriguez*, as Gerald Gunther has observed, the Burger Court "generally adhered to [the] well-established strands of the Warren Court's fundamental interests — 'new' equal protection," only "refus[ing] to expand that analysis into new spheres."[14] Both liberals and conservatives had occasion to criticize Burger Court decisions. While conservatives were often disappointed, liberals were largely relieved. Their deepest fears were seldom realized.

As the chapters in this volume suggest, one way to understand the Burger Court is to analyze the personnel changes on the Court and the evolution of the judicial philosophies of particular justices. The Court's two liberal holdovers, Justices Brennan and Marshall, though aging and occasionally in bad health, still held their seats through the end of the fourth term of the Rehnquist Court. During the Burger years, they remained predictably liberal. As Stanley H. Friedelbaum points out, Brennan, the most senior associate justice until his retirement in July 1990, often played a key role as intellectual leader and spokesman for liberal causes and as an influential and powerful voice within the Court.

Chief Justice Burger and Justices Rehnquist and O'Connor constituted the core of the conservative bloc.[15] Rehnquist, in particular, was the kind of justice that conservatives hoped would eventually control the Court. Possessing a first-rate intellect, he wrote with elegance, was committed to conservative goals, and was willing to use constitutional interpretation to further those goals. He voted less frequently for civil liberties claims than any other justice, typically opposing them over 80 percent of the time (see Table 1.9). Even before ascending to the center seat, Rehnquist had become the unquestioned leader of the Court's conservatives. His analytical and writing skills and warm personal manner enabled him to become an influential member of the Burger Court, even if frequently in dissent. Given Reagan's values and objectives, Rehnquist was an excellent choice to succeed Burger.

Burger's record was somewhat more complicated. Although he

Members of the United States Supreme Court from September 1981 through September 1986. *Seated, from left to right:* Justice Thurgood Marshall, Justice William J. Brennan, Jr., Chief Justice Warren E. Burger, Justice Byron R. White, and Justice Harry A. Blackmun. *Standing, from left to right:* Justice John Paul Stevens, Justice Lewis F. Powell, Jr., Justice William H. Rehnquist, and Justice Sandra Day O'Connor.

voted against civil liberties claims more regularly than any other justice save Rehnquist (Table 1.9), he was sometimes unpredictable. He authored such landmark liberal decisions as *Swann v. Charlotte-Mecklenburg Board of Education* (1971), *United States v. Nixon* (1974), and *Fullilove v. Klutznick* (1980). Although the chief justice was consistently conservative on criminal procedure issues and most First Amendment issues, some of his freedom of press and civil rights opinions were more moderate or even liberal. Burger's occasional unpredictability may be partly explained by his desire to control opinion assignments and by the absence of an overarching constitutional philosophy guiding his decision making.

Nor was Justice Powell a doctrinaire, ideologically committed political conservative. As Jacob W. Landynski's chapter emphasizes, Powell was often the Court's balance wheel. Powell, a conservative somewhat in the tradition of Harlan, the justice he most admired and sought to emulate, played a crucial role in several leading liberal decisions of the Burger Court. He voted with the majority in *Roe v. Wade* and provided the pivotal fifth vote in such cases as *Apodaca v. Oregon* (1972) and *Bakke.*

If conservatives were sometimes disappointed by Burger and Powell, they experienced even greater frustration with Justice Blackmun. After several years on the Court, Blackmun seemed to undergo a metamorphosis. By the 1977 term he was no longer a mainstay of the Court's most conservative bloc. Rather, he evidenced a strong independent streak as his voting behavior became surprisingly liberal and he increasingly aligned with Brennan, Marshall, and Stevens.[16] His opinion for the Court in *Roe*, of course, advanced a cause associated with the most liberal elements of the Democratic party and was in keeping with the most extreme examples of Warren Court activism. Indeed, for sheer constitutional policy innovation, *Roe* may have surpassed any decision of the Warren Court, including *Brown v. Board of Education* (1954), *Baker v. Carr* (1962), and *Miranda v. Arizona* (1966).[17] Little wonder that conservatives were occasionally angered by Nixon's second appointee.

Justice Stevens's record was no more reassuring to conservatives. Typically a loner on the Burger Court, he was something of a maverick. His trenchant analysis and sharp pen were often directed critically at some of the Court's more conservative pronouncements, as in *National League of Cities v. Usery* (1976), *Rhode Island v. Innis* (1980), and *Hudson v. Palmer* (1984). Writing more opinions than most of his colleagues and at times advancing unorthodox and independent analyses, Stevens could not be counted on to align with the conservative bloc. In fact, over time Stevens exhibited a greater tendency to vote for civil liberties claims (Table 1.9).

The independence and moderation of Stevens and Blackmun, the predictable liberalism of Brennan and Marshall, and the occasional penchant of Powell and White to assume middle-ground positions to the left of Burger and Rehnquist—all combined to help frustrate the conservatives' hopes of controlling the Court during the Burger years. Five votes for the conservative side in crucial matters frequently remained impossible to muster, even though only two justices were Democratic appointees. As the years passed, it became increasingly clear that the constitutional cornerstones laid during the Warren years would weather the age of Nixon and Reagan surprisingly intact. Ironically, perhaps the political attacks on the Court by Nixon and Reagan stiffened the resolve of Brennan, Marshall, and some moderate justices to resist a rightward movement.[18]

The Burger Court's Place in Supreme Court Development

At various times during the 1970s and 1980s, some scholars suggested that the Burger Court was ushering in an era of contemporary judicial conservatism. In 1974, for example, Glendon Schubert observed: "The era of modern liberalism [on the Supreme Court] had come to an abrupt end, and in its place the prospects seemed inescapable for the predominance of a strongly conservative mood in both the Supreme Court and the rest of the federal judiciary, at least throughout the seventies and probably beyond that."[19] In retrospect, such conclusions were premature.

From the vantage point of 1990, if one looks for a consistent overarching theme to the politics and jurisprudence of the Burger Court, none is easily and indisputably identifiable. Although the Court was conservative in some areas, in others it was not. Even in areas in which it was conservative, it was not always consistently so through the years. Did the Court exhibit strong conservative tendencies? Certainly. Did it bring modern liberalism on the Court to an abrupt halt? By no means.

During this period the Court, like the political system itself, was in flux, lacking the sense of direction and purpose that animated the Warren years.[20] Nixon, Ford, and Reagan failed to put in place a lasting, significant network of conservative programs in domestic and foreign affairs, in large part because control of Congress eluded them. During the Burger years, notwithstanding Republican presidential successes, no national governing coalition emerged capable of imposing a coherent, enduring set of conservative programs. Nor did the Burger Court fill that vacuum with consistent and significant conservative policy initiatives of its own. In comparison to the Warren years, during the Burger period the Court often seemed to recede in prominence and visibility, fading into the background of American politics.[21] Neither consistently activist nor passive, neither stridently conservative nor liberal, the Burger Court had a chameleon-like quality. It is not readily categorizable by conventional labels. Its place and legacy in the Court's history is not easy to evaluate.

Where does the Burger Court fit in the overall history of the United States Supreme Court? One cannot answer that question without stepping back and reviewing, if only briefly, the larger historical context and jurisprudential tradition that frame the issue. Robert G. McCloskey, perhaps the greatest political historian of the Court, analyzed the Court's development in terms of eras encompassing several decades during which dominant jurisprudential and political themes emerged.[22] McCloskey argued that the history of the Court—and perhaps, one might add, of the nation— may be understood in terms of three great epochs. The first dealt with what he called "the struggle to promote the principle of national union."[23] During that era the Supreme Court confirmed and legitimated the broad powers of the federal government under the leadership of John Marshall, and the nation fought a civil war to resolve the federal government's authority over the states.[24]

The second constitutional epoch, triggered by the industrial developments following the Civil War, dominated American political life and constitutional law from roughly 1885 to 1935 and turned on what McCloskey called "business-government relationships."[25] The key questions before the Court during this era dealt with the constitutional powers of Congress and of the state legislatures to regulate property. That struggle turned on the kinds of government regulation of business that the Court said the Constitution permitted. It pitted powerful business interests against political movements seeking to diminish business's power. Business interests tried to shield themselves from the reach of those movements by winning constitutional victories protecting property rights. Ultimately, the Court relented and conceded that the Constitution permitted extensive public regulation of what were previously thought of as constitutionally protected property rights.

The third epoch that McCloskey identified was characterized by the modern Court's espousal of civil rights.[26] During this era a dramatic shift occurred in American constitutional jurisprudence from the scrupulous protection of property rights to a newfound constitutional vigilance in protecting civil rights. McCloskey described the rationale for this transition and transformation in this way: "Economic rights ought to be subject to such governmental control as the community desires; civil rights ought to be cherished and constitutionally protected. Sustained by those two simple verities, the judges' special universe seemed orderly and predictable."[27]

For our purposes, it is essential to appreciate the origins and character of this civil rights–civil liberties orientation, for this orientation has been the hallmark of the modern Court, and the Burger Court's legacy can best be defined by understanding how it fits into that tradition. Precisely when the civil liberties era began is difficult to pinpoint, save to say that its beginnings predated the Warren Court by decades. As far back as the 1920s, crucial gains were made in protecting civil rights and liberties. For example, a 1925 Minnesota law permitted punishing an individual for publishing any "malicious, scandalous and defamatory" newspaper article, and recognized truth as a defense only if the motives were good and the ends justifiable. The Supreme Court, in its first great anti-censorship decision, invalidated that law in *Near v. Minnesota* (1931). Earlier, in *Gitlow v. New York* (1925), the Court assumed that the liberty protected by the Fourteenth Amendment included free speech and, implicitly, other protections of the First Amendment. That position eventually resulted in a revolution over the next few decades in which the Court recognized that the liberty protected by the Fourteenth Amendment embraced the rights set forth in the federal Bill of Rights.[28]

Strong indications of the Court's civil rights–civil liberties orientation were evident in the 1930s. In *Grosjean v. American Press Co.* (1936), the Court struck down a law enacted under Huey Long's leadership in Louisiana that had imposed a tax on newspapers critical of Long. The following year, in *DeJonge v. Oregon* (1937), the Court invalidated a criminal syndicalism law that made attending a communist meeting a crime. *Herndon v. Lowry* (1937) dealt with the arrest of a black organizer, working for the Communist party, who possessed literature advocating equal rights for

blacks, as well as unemployment insurance and other social welfare
rights. The Court found that possession of such literature was
wholly insufficient to prove incitement to riot. Rounding out a trio
of memorable decisions in 1937, Justice Cardozo declared in *Palko
v. Connecticut* that First Amendment liberties are on "a different
plane of social and moral values" and that freedom of thought
and speech are "the matrix, the indispensable condition, of nearly
every other form of freedom. . . . [N]either liberty nor justice would
exist if they were sacrificed" (302 U.S. at 326–27). A year later
Justice Stone expanded on that theme and planted the doctrinal
seeds for the Court's civil liberties orientation for the next half
century when, in *United States v. Carolene Products Co.* (1938), he
advanced a rationale for the "preferred freedoms."

During the 1940s, dramatic confrontations in the flag salute case
and the Japanese relocation cases sharpened the Court's focus on
civil liberties issues and the visibility of those issues.[29] Additionally,
in *Skinner v. Oklahoma* (1942), Justice Douglas advanced the notion
of "strict scrutiny." He maintained that when "invidious discrim-
inations" are made against groups or types of individuals and affect
basic civil rights, strict scrutiny of the allegedly discriminatory
classification may be warranted. Two years later in *Korematsu v.
United States* (1944), the Court, through Justice Black, held that
"all legal restrictions which curtail the civil rights of a single racial
group are immediately suspect" (323 U.S. at 216).

The philosophical seeds for an individual rights orientation, sown
during the Hughes, Stone, and Vinson Courts, flowered during
the Warren era as the Court trumpeted its power in defense of
civil liberties—even if much of the public, many states, and the
Court's sister branches remained unsupportive or downright re-
sistant. The result, in McCloskey's words, was "government by
judiciary."[30] Yet it was not so much the unrestrained policy-making
of the Warren Court that set it apart; it was the consistently liberal
political bent of its policies. Historically, business interests and other
conservative political forces had dominated the legal system and
the Court sitting atop that system. That domination was to change.
The Warren Court played a historically anomalous role: it championed society's underdogs—racial minorities, political dissenters,
and criminal defendants. During the Burger era, as we have argued, conservatives were unable to recapture the Court fully and
return it to its traditionally conservative fold.

Hence, Americans have come to look to courts in the last half
century increasingly as institutions especially committed to and

concerned about individual rights. At the same time the nation has become more and more controlled by big government—at the national, state, and local levels—and by big private organizations, especially corporations. In modern America, vast and complex public and private organizations have come to have an enormous hold on the nation's people and their lives. By mid-century William Whyte could declare the age of the "organization man" because large-scale organizations so pervasively affected critical daily life experiences.[31] Large organizations employ, train, and socialize the work force. They produce, market, and distribute a bewildering array of consumer goods and provide the myriad health, social, and personal services that Americans have come to rely on and expect. They control the financial nerve centers on which national economic strength is founded. They educate the young and care for the ever-growing numbers of the aged. Nineteenth-century America celebrated independence and individualism—in the farmer, frontiersman, and entrepreneur; twentieth-century America celebrates large organizations and is dominated by them.

Although our lives have doubtlessly been enhanced by the accomplishments of large-scale public and private organizations, as individuals we have lost something. Each of us is increasingly "processed," be it for a driver's license, an airline ticket, or privileges at the local public library. And each of us has adjusted to and accepted the kind of nameless, faceless processing that is part of the modern condition. Meanwhile our individual importance and sense of individuality has inevitably been diminished. In subtle and not so subtle ways, individuality has been eroded by the impersonal, bureaucratic modern management techniques and processes that contemporary complex organizations—public and private—use to function and serve us. Big government and big business are of inestimable service, yet their very mode and method of operation all too often dominate and demean us. The modern state and modern mass society threaten individualism, individuality, and personal autonomy as never before. Given these realities, the modern Court's focus on individual rights and liberties is understandable and beneficial.

In its classic form, litigation is the antithesis of anonymous bureaucratic processing. It offers a highly individualized process that turns on the application of general rules to specific factual situations. It is labor-intensive and time-consuming for both the litigants and the state. Constitutional liberties, especially procedural due process, contribute to the slowness, expense, and labor-intensiveness of the legal process. Yet such protections as procedural due process, substantive due process rights involving privacy or the family, and most other constitutional liberties throw a protective shell around the individual—a shell that the individual needs more than ever in the modern state.[32]

Because it has dominated American constitutional jurisprudence since the 1930s, the Supreme Court's civil rights–civil liberties focus is what contemporary legal scholars know best, and what most of them personally prefer as its proper constitutional orientation. Indeed, Jesse Choper, among others, has suggested that the paramount function of judicial review is to resolve disputes between the individual and the government.[33] However appealing this view, it is an outlook decidedly influenced—one might say distorted—by the prevailing orientation and performance of the Supreme Court over the past half century. Before that time the Court was not noted for its protection of civil liberties.[34]

Yet it is a mistake to equate what contemporary commentators have known, studied, and often embraced with what will necessarily continue and always be. The civil rights–civil liberties era of the modern Court will not endure forever. The Court's role is not fixed—it evolves. The Court is an organic institution linked inextricably to the society that produces the controversies it adjudicates. Woodrow Wilson observed that the proper relationship between the national and state governments "cannot . . . be settled by the opinion of any one generation, because it is a question of growth, and every successive stage of our political and economic development gives it a new aspect, makes it a new question."[35] So it is with the role of the Supreme Court. The ablest constitutional scholars have recognized, as did McCloskey, that historical context and social milieu set the parameters for the Court. The genius of the system is that each new generation, facing its peculiar problems, must determine anew how to realize the goals and to protect the values of the constitutional order.[36]

Given what has been said thus far, how does the Burger Court fit into the larger history of the Court and nation? Can we reconcile our understanding of the Burger Court with the theories of constitutional epochs that McCloskey advanced? Although it may be too early to answer that question with confidence, we may begin that analysis by emphasizing two seemingly contradictory interpretations of the Burger era. First, while the Burger Court reacted negatively to some liberal doctrines, it ultimately accepted the need to protect individual rights. Indeed, in such areas as equal protection for women, personal autonomy in terms of abortion, and capital punishment, it "went far beyond its predecessor."[37] Yet the Burger Court's perhaps surprising failure to undo major liberal initiatives of the Warren Court may be only part of its legacy, for the Burger Court was Janus-faced. Historically situated at the end of an unparalleled era of constitutional reform that had emphasized the protection of civil liberties, the Burger Court did halt the momentum of liberal constitutional standards in some areas by chipping away at Warren Court precedent.[38]

Second, therefore, the Burger Court may have laid the foundation for, and provided a bridge to, a new era in the Supreme Court's history. In light of McCloskey's notion of historical epochs during which fundamental constitutional themes emerge, dominate for several decades, and then are replaced by the new policy emphases, in time the Burger Court may come to be viewed as a transitional Court that moved the nation to the precipice of a new constitutional period.[39] The Burger Court may be seen in the future as a bridge spanning the Warren Court's liberalism and concern for individual rights, on the one hand, and the Rehnquist Court's conservatism on the other. That conservatism may come to be characterized by a diminished solicitude for individual rights and a heightened concern for new emerging constitutional issues not yet readily apparent to Court members and observers alike.

Nixon and Reagan and their political allies sought to promote and speed this transition. Those controlling nominations to the Court and to the lower federal judiciary during the Nixon-Reagan years deliberately intended to use that power to steer the courts away from a liberal focus on individual rights. The unusually combative confirmation battle over Robert Bork in 1987 reflected the high stakes that both liberals and conservatives perceived to be at issue and the critical juncture at which some thought the Court was poised. Certainly, many perceived that Bork's appointment might hasten the movement to a Court dominated by a conservative majority and animated by a new agenda. While the nomination of Justice Kennedy caused much less political uproar, Kennedy's appointment—along with that of Justice Scalia—may prove to be critical to the policies articulated by the Rehnquist Court. Some observers expect a steady flow of conservative decisions from Rehnquist, Scalia, O'Connor, and Kennedy, with White frequently joining them. These observers further anticipate that the Reagan nominees will often vote together as a conservative bloc, as Blackmun publicly complained they were doing in 1988.[40]

The differences between Chief Justice Burger and his successor may be significant as well in moving the Court toward a new constitutional era. Rehnquist possesses greater leadership potential because of his greater analytical skills, coherent judicial philosophy, lucid writing style, and warm personable manner. Beyond that, he has a more conservative majority to lead. Referring to the Supreme Court from 1969 through 1986 as the "Burger Court" is little more than a convenient and perhaps arbitrary label for identifying a chunk of history; that may be less true of the Rehnquist Court. Chief Justice Rehnquist may have the skills and allies necessary to move the Court into a new constitutional era.

The Early Rehnquist Court

After the first two terms of the Rehnquist Court, it was too early to know whether the civil liberties orientation of the Warren and Burger Courts, and indeed of the last half century, would be substantially revised or give way to a new agenda dominated by different constitutional priorities.[41] Through the 1987 term, the Rehnquist Court was responsible for a mixture of conservative and liberal decisions.[42] Voting data collected by Lawrence Baum surprisingly indicated an increase in the percentage of decisions favoring civil liberties claims during the early Rehnquist Court when compared to the late Burger Court (46.0 percent for the 1986 and 1987 terms compared to 37.2 percent for the combined 1981– 85 terms of the Burger Court). Yet, as Baum noted, this might well be "a temporary phenomenon."[43]

In fact, during the October 1988 term, the Rehnquist Court provided some disturbing indications of substantial change in key areas of civil rights–civil liberties jurisprudence as Reagan's four appointees were often joined by Justice White and occasionally another Court member in major cases. While still announcing a mix of liberal and conservative decisions, and although repeatedly fragmented, the Rehnquist Court clearly became a serious concern for civil libertarians and proponents of civil rights.[44] During the spring and summer of 1989, the Court made more than a small move to the right as it handed down some of the most conservative civil rights decisions in the modern era.[45] The alarms sounded by these cases were not muffled by the Court's pro–civil rights decisions the following term (*Metro Broadcasting v. FCC*, 1990; *Missouri v. Jenkins*, 1990).

On the thorny issue of affirmative action, the Rehnquist Court handed down two notable opinions in 1989. Its decision in *City of Richmond v. J. A. Croson Co.* cast doubt on the constitutionality of many government hiring and contract programs aiding racial minorities. The Court invalidated a Richmond, Virginia, plan, which was comparable to others in various states and localities, that channeled 30 percent of the money spent on city construction contracts to minority-owned businesses. Despite the fact that 50 percent of Richmond's population was black but less than 1 percent of the city's prime construction contracts went to minority businesses, Justice O'Connor's opinion for the Court held that no compelling governmental interest had been established to justify the set-aside plan because the plan was not narrowly designed to remedy the effects of past discrimination specifically against minority contractors in Richmond. Apparently Richmond, in seeking to compensate for some instances of past discrimination, had chosen the 30-percent figure arbitrarily, as there was no evidence in the record demonstrating the actual extent to which minority contractors had been discriminated against. In the words of O'Connor, "it is almost impossible to assess whether the Richmond Plan is narrowly tailored to remedy prior discrimination since it is not linked to identified discrimination in any way" (109 S.Ct. 728). Marshall, Brennan, and Blackmun dissented, asserting that "today's decision marks a deliberate and giant step backward in this Court's affirmative action jurisprudence" (109 S.Ct. at 740).

Five months later, affirmative action proponents were dealt another blow in *Martin v. Wilks* (1989). The dispute in that case had originated in the early 1970s when the NAACP chapter in Birmingham, Alabama, supported by the Justice Department, sued the city alleging racial discrimination in the hiring and promotion of firefighters in violation of Title VII of the 1964 Civil Rights Act. After several years the parties entered into a consent decree, approved by the federal district court, that included affirmative action goals for hiring and promoting black firefighters. A group of white firefighters then sued the city months after the consent decree was approved, claiming that the decree illegally discriminated against them. During the Reagan administration, the Justice Department reversed its position and supported the challenge to the decree. Chief Justice Rehnquist, writing for the 5-4 majority in *Wilks*, argued that the consent decree could bind only the parties to the litigation and that, consequently, a group not a party to the litigation, like the white firefighters, could challenge the consent decree in a subsequent and separate action. Reflecting arguments suggested by Stevens's dissent, which was joined by Brennan, Marshall, and Blackmun, some civil rights and employers' groups insisted that *Wilks* would wreak havoc with affirmative action plans entered into and approved pursuant to a decree. The fear was that such decrees might be indefinitely subject to subsequent attack by individuals or groups not a party to the original suit.

Had the Court consistently continued along the path of *Croson* and *Wilks,* the affirmative action movement would have been severely weakened. In *Metro Broadcasting v. FCC* (1990), however, a majority surprisingly upheld two federal affirmative action programs mandated by Congress. These programs did not compensate for past or present discrimination but instead gave a preference to minorities to purchase radio and television stations in danger of losing their licenses. Even though only a small percentage of the broadcast industry was owned by minorities and the effect of these programs was slight, the Reagan and Bush administrations insisted that they were unconstitutional.

Justice Brennan—joined by Marshall, Blackmun, Stevens, and White—concluded that the programs did not violate the Fifth Amendment's equal protection component. For the majority, the key to the case, as in *Fullilove,* was that Congress had specifically mandated the minority-preference programs in order to increase the diversity of viewpoints in the media, which was an important governmental objective, and the programs were substantially related to accomplishing that goal. Brennan wrote, "We hold that benign race-conscious measures mandated by Congress—even if those measures are not 'remedial' in the sense of being designed to compensate victims of past governmental or societal discrimination—are constitutionally permissible" (110 S.Ct. 3008–9). In dissent, Justice O'Connor accused the majority of repudiating the view that the right to equal protection extends to all citizens equally, and Justice Kennedy argued that the Constitution does not permit racial discrimination for such a "trivial" interest as broadcast diversity (3045).

Other recent decisions by the Rehnquist Court turned on the interpretation of Title VII. *Lorance v. AT&T Technologies, Inc.,* handed down the same day as *Wilks,* involved claims by women workers that a new seniority system at an AT&T plant had the purpose and effect of excluding women from certain jobs traditionally filled by men. In a 5-3 decision, Justice Scalia declared that the time period within which to challenge a new seniority system alleged to be discriminatory begins to run immediately on adoption of the system, not from the time the system actually worked harm on an employee. Joined by Rehnquist, Kennedy, White, and Stevens, Scalia ruled as he did even though an employee could not reasonably expect to be demoted or otherwise injured at the time the system was adopted. Marshall, Brennan, and Blackmun dissented, emphasizing that the majority's interpretation of Title VII was "glaringly at odds" with its purposes and was "compelled neither by the text of the statute nor our precedents interpreting it" (109 S.Ct. 2270).

In *Griggs v. Duke Power Co.* (1971), one of the Burger Court's leading employment discrimination decisions, the justices unanimously agreed that Title VII prohibits employment practices that have racially discriminatory effects (as well as those intended to discriminate). According to Chief Justice Burger's opinion in *Griggs,* when an employer's employment practice "operate[s] to 'freeze' the status quo of prior discriminatory employment practices," the employer has the burden of proving that the practice in question serves a valid business purpose (401 U.S. at 430–31). The Rehnquist Court seemed to relieve employers of that burden in *Wards Cove Packing Company, Inc. v. Atonio* (1989). Justice White, writing for a five-member majority, instead of following *Griggs,* imposed a demanding burden on plaintiffs to prove that the employer's practice had no business-related purpose. Employers could avoid liability by showing the practice had a "reasonable" business purpose. White's opinion evoked bitter dissents from Stevens and Blackmun, joined by Brennan and Marshall. "Turning a blind eye to the meaning and purpose of Title VII," Stevens wrote, "the majority's opinion perfunctorily rejects a long-standing rule of law and underestimates the probative value of evidence of a racially stratified work force. I cannot join this latest sojourn into judicial activism" (109 S.Ct. at 2127–28). Blackmun was equally angered: "One wonders whether the majority still believes that race discrimination—or, more accurately, race discrimination against nonwhites—is a problem in our society, or even remembers that it ever was" (2136).

Another area of civil rights change involved a 1988 development that could have dramatically affected the right of racial minorities to sue private parties for discrimination. Earlier, in another leading case, *Runyon v. McCrary* (1976), the Burger Court had held by a 7-2 vote that 42 U.S.C. Section 1981 (a crucial provision of federal civil rights law derived from the 1866 Civil Rights Act) prohibited private, commercially operated nonsectarian schools from denying admission to students because they were African-Americans. Only Rehnquist and White had dissented. The Burger Court's holding in *Runyon* turned on a broad reading of the 1866 Act and was consistent with the Warren Court's energetic support of civil rights. Subsequently the holding was applied to cases concerning racial discrimination in private commercial transactions, thereby giving victims of job discrimination, for example, broader protection and more effective remedies than those available under modern statutes like the Civil Rights Act of 1964. Eventually *Runyon* came under fire during the Rehnquist Court.

In *Patterson v. McLean Credit Union* (1988), the Rehnquist Court voted five to four for a rehearing to consider whether an employee who alleged job harassment because of her race could sue under Section 1981. The five-person majority included Rehnquist, White, O'Connor, Scalia, and Kennedy. *Patterson* was especially noteworthy because the issue of whether *Runyon* should be reconsidered was never raised during Court proceedings—not by the defendant, not by the solicitor general, not by any member of the Court at oral argument. A slim Court majority "reached" for the question by requesting a rehearing on an issue not raised by the parties. The Rehnquist Court's behavior suggested the possibility of a reversal of a major liberal civil rights precedent—the kind of reversal never seen during the entire Burger era.

Subsequently, an outpouring of political support to uphold *Runyon* came as forty-seven state attorneys general, over one hundred public interest and civil rights groups, and a bipartisan group of more than half the members of Congress joined briefs urging the Court to stand behind the 1976 decision.[46] In light of clear, recent precedent and the impressive coalition put together to protect it, only a very bold Court would have overruled *Runyon*. Thus, in June 1989 the Rehnquist Court announced its decision in *Patterson*. Justice Kennedy, writing for the Court's 5-4 majority, explained that the principle of stare decisis compelled the justices to reaffirm *Runyon*, but the majority's conservative nature was evident in its holding that Section 1981 could not be relied on to combat racial harassment because that had not been the law's intention. Joined by Rehnquist, White, O'Connor, and Scalia, Kennedy argued that Section 1981 applied to contractual rights, not an employer's racially discriminatory harassment after hiring an individual.[47] Brennan responded in dissent: "What the Court declines to snatch away with one hand, it takes with the other" (109 S.Ct. 2379). Although the majority's ruling was not as limiting as the Reagan administration had hoped, conservatives could embrace the decision as another victory.

The Rehnquist Court took its most dramatic and long-awaited step of the 1988 term in *Webster v. Reproductive Health Services* (1989), reviewing Missouri's appeal of a lower federal court ruling that had declared the state's anti-abortion statute unconstitutional. The law, drafted by abortion foes in the Missouri state legislature, prohibited public employees from performing or assisting in an abortion unless essential to save the life of a pregnant woman and also made it illegal to use public buildings to perform abortions. The Missouri law also required that physicians carry out tests to determine the fetus's viability if the woman seeking its abortion was at least twenty weeks pregnant. Although not expressly over-ruling *Roe v. Wade*, the Rehnquist Court, by a 5-4 vote, upheld the constitutionality of each of these provisions.

Chief Justice Rehnquist, writing for a majority consisting of Justices White, Kennedy, O'Connor, and Scalia, made two major points clear in *Webster*. First, states were now free to legislate new restrictions on a woman's right to abortion. How far the states could go was indicated in part by the Missouri provisions upheld by the Court in *Webster*, but at least three additional cases accepted for the October 1989 term were to clarify the issue further.[48] Second, the *Webster* majority abandoned the trimester concept enunciated in *Roe*. Justice Blackmun's opinion for the Court in *Roe* had created the legal concept of three trimesters of pregnancy. In the first trimester the abortion decision was left totally in the hands of a woman and her physician; in the second trimester the state was allowed to regulate abortion procedures in the interest of maternal health; and in the third trimester the state's "compelling interest" became so strong (because the fetus was viable) that it could prohibit an abortion (unless necessary to protect the woman's health or life) (410 U.S. at 163–64). However, in the *Webster* retreat, Rehnquist enunciated his strong opposition to this trimester concept. "We think that the doubt cast upon the Missouri statute by these cases is not so much a flaw in the statute as it is a reflection of the fact that the rigid trimester analysis of the course of a pregnancy [under *Roe* has made] constitutional law in this area a virtual Procrustean bed" (109 S.Ct. 3056). O'Connor's concurring opinion acknowledged problems with this trimester approach as well, while Scalia's concurrence would have overruled *Roe* completely.

In a bitter dissent, Blackmun acknowledged the threat to *Roe*.

"For today," he wrote, "the women of this Nation still retain the liberty to control their destinies. But the signs are evident and very ominous, and a chill wind blows" (109 S.Ct. 3079). Blackmun expressed fears, shared by many, that *Webster* would lead to many more back-alley abortions, particularly for poor and minority women. Conservatives had won yet another victory during 1989 even though the Court had not reversed *Roe,* as the Reagan and Bush administrations had urged. The stage was set for even greater national division over the question of abortion. State legislatures would increasingly feel the pressure of pro-choice and pro-life forces as the Supreme Court failed to find a politically acceptable solution to this most contested issue.

In *Hodgson v. Minnesota* (1990) and *Ohio v. Akron Center for Reproductive Health* (1990), the Court addressed state statutes requiring parental notification in the case of pregnant, unmarried women under the age of eighteen who decided to have an abortion. In *Hodgson* a 5-4 majority held that a statute containing a two-parent provision, with no judicial alternative, would be unconstitutional, but a more conservative 5-4 majority upheld the Minnesota law because it provided a pregnant minor with the option of a judicial hearing to show her maturity or to demonstrate that the notification of both parents would conflict with her own best interests. In *Akron Center for Reproductive Health,* by a 5–4 vote the Court upheld the Ohio statute since it only required the minor to notify one parent of her abortion decision or else obtain a judge's permission prior to the abortion.

The Court announced two other decisions in the spring of 1989, both authored by Kennedy, which upheld mandatory drug- or alcohol-testing programs for federal employees. In *National Treasury Employees Union v. Von Raab* (1989), an employee's union challenged a U.S. Customs Service drug-testing program that required the analysis of urine samples of workers seeking promotions to drug-law enforcement jobs or jobs requiring employees to carry firearms or deal with classified materials. In *Skinner v. Railway Labor Executives' Association* (1989), employees of the Federal Railroad Administration challenged agency regulations requiring blood and urine tests of workers involved in certain train accidents. The Rehnquist Court held in these cases that government's compelling interest to protect the public health and welfare outweighed employees' privacy rights, and that the drug-testing programs did not violate the Fourth Amendment's prohibition against unreasonable searches and seizures—even though no reasonable suspicion existed that the particular employees tested were using drugs or alcohol on the job. Rehnquist, O'Connor, White, and Blackmun joined Kennedy in both cases; Scalia and Stevens dissented in *Von Raab* but joined the majority in *Skinner.* These rulings struck a balance against the civil liberties claims of public employees and in favor of what the Court majority viewed as the rights of society writ large. How these decisions—the first by the Court on mandatory drug testing—will affect random testing of public employees or mandatory testing in the private sector is still unclear.[49]

It is clear, however, that the Rehnquist Court is inclined to be hard-nosed on most criminal procedure issues. Prior to the drug-testing cases, for example, it had ruled in *Murray v. United States* (1988) that evidence obtained during an illegal search is admissible in court if the police later secure an independent search warrant and "rediscover" the incriminating evidence. Nor, said the Court in *California v. Greenwood* (1988), does a reasonable expectation of privacy attach to the contents of garbage bags left outside a residence for collection; the police may search them. More recently, in *Michigan v. Sitz* (1990), the Court upheld the constitutionality of sobriety checkpoints. In a similar vein, the Court declared that confessions are involuntary only if coerced by governmental officials (*Colorado v. Connelly,* 1986); that the destruction of evidence that may have proven a defendant's innocence is unconstitutional only if the defendant can prove that the police acted in bad faith (*Arizona v. Youngblood,* 1988); and that without giving any *Miranda* warnings, an undercover police officer may constitutionally pose as a prison inmate and elicit a confession from another inmate (*Eastern Airlines v. Floyd,* 1990). As for capital punishment, in 1987 the Court upheld a racially discriminatory capital sentencing system (*McCleskey v. Kemp*) and ruled that a major participant in a felony may be executed if he or she demonstrated a reckless indifference to life—even if the defendant did not kill, attempt to kill, or intend to kill (*Tison v. Arizona*). In 1989 the Court said that the Eighth Amendment does not prohibit the execution of a mentally retarded person (*Penry v. Lynaugh*) or a person as young as sixteen at the time a crime was committed (*Stanford v. Kentucky*).

These examples of Rehnquist Court activity will not bring an abrupt end to the individual-rights era of the modern Supreme Court; however, they may symbolize and presage things to come. They are initial and disturbing stirrings to some—telltale signs— signaling what may be in the offing. They suggest that some of the building blocks of the liberal civil-rights jurisprudence of the

Warren and Burger eras may be in jeopardy and that the Rehnquist Court may be unsympathetic to emerging civil liberties issues such as drug testing. They also may contribute to a less sympathetic climate of opinion for individual liberties, which in turn may legitimate and encourage greater public, scholarly, and legal debate about the validity of the Court's past civil rights–civil liberties policies.

Is America now moving toward the end of one of those great constitutional epochs analyzed by McCloskey? After four terms of the Rehnquist Court, the convergence of a series of events and conditions may suggest that the nation may be approaching a historical watershed. The appointment of an astute, forceful, and ideological chief justice who has regularly opposed the civil-liberties orientation of the Court, the emergence of an ostensibly cohesive conservative bloc on the Court, and some initial soundings from the Court itself all point in that direction. Beyond the addition of Justice David H. Souter in 1990 to fill Brennan's seat, more conservative additions to the Court could come during the Bush administration, and the political climate may be reasonably ripe for change. During the 1970s and 1980s a conservative tide swept America, leaving many citizens less sympathetic to the protection of individual and minority rights. In the 1988 presidential campaign the American Civil Liberties Union became an epithet, and the traditional liberal rationale in defense of individual rights seemed to enjoy little mass support. These public sentiments overwhelmed Michael Dukakis, the "card-carrying" ACLU member, who, in opposing George Bush, became associated with liberal positions on abortion, mandatory flag salute, obscenity, and criminal defendants' rights. The public's near-hysteria in the late 1980s over the need to crack down on drugs could foster further insensitivity to personal liberties. All of these events and others, when viewed together, suggest that the times may be right for an end to liberalism's dominant hold on American constitutional law. And as Sheldon Goldman has concluded, because of Reagan's Supreme Court and lower federal court appointments, "Reagan will be seen as having had the greatest influence on the shape of the American judiciary and law since Franklin Roosevelt."[50]

Did the Burger Court essentially secure the Warren Court's liberal reforms in civil rights and liberties, or did it pave the way to a new conservative era in Supreme Court history? Paradoxically, it may have done both, and the transition to a new epoch could occur in at least two different ways. First, the Rehnquist Court, like the Roosevelt Court, could reject in large measure the civil rights–civil liberties jurisprudence of the preceding era. By overturning *Roe v. Wade* and significantly revising Court doctrine on racial discrimination and affirmative action, for example, the Rehnquist Court could undermine some of the cornerstone policies of the prior epoch and remake them in a conservative mold. Another possible scenario is that the Court, as it moves from one constitutional era to the next, may not necessarily need to repudiate the central constitutional contributions of the earlier era. During the pro-business period from the 1880s through the mid-1930s, for example, the Court did not reject the fundamental jurisprudential elements of the Marshall era that legitimated broad national power. Similarly, the Rehnquist Court, in inaugurating a new constitutional era, need not repudiate or even modify the major doctrines advanced in the civil-liberties era. The Rehnquist Court could accept the building blocks of the past fifty years and go on to establish its own contributions in emerging areas of constitutional law that reflect the dominant issues and concerns of America in the 1990s and beyond.

Consider McCloskey's characterization of the transition after the Civil War to a constitutional jurisprudence focusing on the business-government relationship: "The Court had finally adjusted itself and the Constitution to the altered conditions of the postwar order. Old problems like slavery had been forgotten. The question of Negro rights, and with it the question of civil rights in general, had been relegated to a minor and almost negligible place among the Court's concerns. The once preponderant issue of federalism was now subordinated to the government-business preoccupation: the formerly ruling value of nationalism was replaced by a judicial ideal called economic freedom. *The process of redefining the Court's role, a process impelled by the transfiguration of the nation itself, was not complete to be sure. But the enabling conditions had been met*" (emphasis added).[51] Emphasizing that the nation was at a critical juncture in its development, McCloskey pointed to essential "enabling conditions" that facilitated the emergence of a new dominating constitutional theme.

During the 1990s, will the nation have transfigured itself again? Will the enabling conditions be in place so that the Rehnquist Court may begin the process of redefining the Court's role? In a key passage McCloskey notes that the themes of each of the Court's great epochs were "less a matter of deliberate choice than of predictable response to the wave of history."[52] Is a wave of history discernible in contemporary America that will somehow control the future role and policies of the Court?

Of course, only time will provide definitive answers to these questions. It is important to note, however, that in the three previous constitutional epochs that McCloskey identified, transcending political events appeared that either caused or made possible the restructuring of the Court's orientation. For the Marshall Court that event was the very founding of the nation and the ratification of the Constitution. For the government-business era, the end of the Civil War and the ensuing drive toward industrialization created the conditions that led to the constitutional themes of that period. For the modern civil rights–civil liberties period, the New Deal and World War II appear to have been transfiguring events that shaped and prompted the Court's reorientation. For the future, key questions include the following: Must the nation experience an event of transcending historical power and importance for a reorientation of the Court to occur? If the nation experiences no critical election, yet the presidency and new Supreme Court appointments continue to be controlled by the Republican party, under what circumstances might these political conditions permit a reorientation by the Court? Under what conditions, if any, may the Court, of its own volition and power, prompt and pull the nation into a new era?

Perhaps the nation will experience circumstances, both outside and within the Court, that will sweep it to the beginning of a new constitutional epoch as America approaches the millennium. Our greatest hope is that the Court, riding the next wave of history and dominated by a new conservative majority, will not abandon vital elements of the Supreme Court's civil rights–civil liberties era. Our greatest faith is that the American people and their other political institutions will not permit the Court to succeed should it make a wholehearted attempt.

NOTES

1. See, for example, *Public Papers of the Presidents of the United States: Richard M. Nixon* (Washington, D.C.: U.S. Government Printing Office, 1971), p. 396; Bernard Weinraub, "Reagan Says He'll Use Vacancies to Discourage Judicial Activism," *New York Times,* Oct. 22, 1985, p. 1. See generally Willliam Lasser, *The Limits of Judicial Power: The Supreme Court in American Politics* (Chapel Hill: University of North Carolina Press, 1988), chap. 5.

2. This chapter refers to the concepts of liberalism, conservatism, activism,

and restraint as typically defined in the political science literature on the courts. For liberalism and conservatism, see Sheldon Goldman and Thomas P. Jahnige, *The Federal Courts as a Political System*, 3d ed. (New York: Harper and Row, 1985), chap. 5, esp. pp. 137–46. For activism and restraint, see Stephen C. Halpern and Charles M. Lamb, eds., *Supreme Court Activism and Restraint* (Lexington, Mass.: Lexington Books, 1982), esp. chaps. 1–2.

3. Alpheus Thomas Mason, "The Burger Court in Historical Perspective," *Political Science Quarterly* 89 (1974): 35. Similar conclusions were reached in subsequent years by other students of the Court. See, for example, Vincent Blasi, ed., *The Burger Court: The Counter-Revolution That Wasn't* (New Haven, Conn.: Yale University Press, 1983); Bernard Schwartz, *The Ascent of Pragmatism: The Burger Court in Action* (Reading, Mass.: Addison-Wesley, 1990).

4. The Burger Court was responsible for a number of retreats on *Miranda*, search and seizure, and the right to counsel such as *Harris v. New York* (1971), *Kirby v. Illinois* (1972), *Oregon v. Hass* (1975), *Wainwright v. Sykes* (1977), *Zurcher v. Stanford Daily* (1978), *Rhode Island v. Innis* (1980), *New York v. Quarles* (1984), *United States v. Leon* (1984), *Moran v. Burbine* (1986), and *California v. Ciraolo* (1986).

5. The Burger Court often drew back from the Warren Court's direction in obscenity cases. See, for example, *United States v. Reidel* (1971), *United States v. Thirty-Seven Photographs* (1971), *Miller v. California* (1973), *Paris Adult Theater I v. Slayton* (1973), *Hamling v. United States* (1974), *Young v. American Mini Theatres, Inc.* (1976), and *Ward v. Illinois* (1977).

6. See, for example, *Alexander v. Holmes County Board of Education* (1969), *Eisenstadt v. Baird* (1972), *Argersinger v. Hamlin* (1972), *Wisconsin v. Yoder* (1972), *White v. Weiser* (1973), *Wooley v. Maynard* (1977), *Richmond Newspapers, Inc. v. Virginia* (1980), *Estelle v. Smith* (1981), and *Ake v. Oklahoma* (1985).

7. See, for example, *Roe v. Wade* (1973), *Thornburgh v. American College of Obstetricians and Gynecologists* (1986), *Frontiero v. Richardson* (1973), *Craig v. Boren* (1976), *Swann v. Charlotte-Mecklenburg Board of Education* (1971), *Keyes v. School District No. 1, Denver* (1973), *United Steelworkers v. Weber* (1979), and *Fullilove v. Klutznick* (1980).

8. Leading examples include *United States v. Harris* (1971), *Miller v. California* (1973), *Milliken v. Bradley* (1974), *Gregg v. Georgia* (1976), *Washington v. Davis* (1976), *Rhode Island v. Innis* (1980), *Hudson v. Palmer* (1984), *United States v. Leon* (1984), *Firefighters Local Union No. 1784 v. Stotts* (1984), and *Bowers v. Hardwick* (1986).

9. Richard Funston, "The Burger Court and Era," in Robert J. Janosik, ed., *Encyclopedia of the American Judicial System* (New York: Charles Scribner's Sons, 1987), 1: 190.

10. One example is Raoul Berger, *Government by Judiciary: The Transformation of the Fourteenth Amendment* (Cambridge, Mass.: Harvard University Press, 1977).

11. These cases include *Brown v. Board of Education* (1954), *Cooper v. Aaron* (1958), *Reitman v. Mulkey* (1967), and *Jones v. Alfred H. Mayer Co.* (1968).

12. Notable cases in this vein are *Swann, Keyes, Lau v. Nichols* (1974), and *Runyon v. McCrary* (1976).

13. See, for example, *Lemon v. Kurtzman* (1971), *Committee for Public Education v. Nyquist* (1973), *Meek v. Pittenger* (1975), *Aguilar v. Felton* (1985), *Grand Rapids School District v. Ball* (1985). Aside from the question of assistance to parochial schools, the Burger Court upheld the principle of separation of church and state in various other contexts such as *Stone v. Graham* (1980) and *Larkin v. Grendel's Den, Inc.* (1982). Overall, though, its record on the establishment clause was mixed, as demonstrated by *Tilton v. Richardson* (1971), *Roemer v. Maryland Board of Public Works* (1976), *Committee for Public Education and Religious Liberty v. Regan* (1980), *Marsh v. Chambers* (1983), and *Lynch v. Donnelly* (1984).

14. Gerald Gunther, *Constitutional Law*, 11th ed. (Mineola, N.Y.: Foundation Press, 1985), p. 788.

15. See Sheldon Goldman, *Constitutional Law: Cases and Essays* (New York: Harper and Row, 1987), pp. 158–62; Jeffrey A. Segal and Albert D. Cover, "Ideological Values and the Votes of U.S. Supreme Court Justices," *American Political Science Review* 83 (1989): 557, 560–62.

16. On the average, Blackmun voted for civil liberties claims in roughly 35 percent of the civil liberties cases during the 1970–76 terms (Table 1.9). For the 1977–85 terms, that figure rose to nearly 50 percent. Yet Blackmun's overall record was erratic as he shifted away from the Burger-Rehnquist bloc in 1977 and 1978, shifted back to it in 1979 and 1980, and then moved to a moderate bloc with Stevens in 1981 (Table 1.8). In the 1982 and 1985 terms, he voted with the liberal Brennan-Marshall-Stevens bloc, but in the 1983 and 1984 terms he rejoined the conservatives.

17. See Bradley C. Canon, "A Framework for the Analysis of Judicial Activism," in Halpern and Lamb, eds., *Supreme Court Activism and Restraint*, p. 407.

18. Justice Brennan, for example, engaged Attorney General Edwin Meese in an unusually direct and public confrontation on the proper method of constitutional analysis. Meese championed original intent and Brennan rejected historicism as narrow-minded. See Sheldon Goldman and Austin Sarat, eds., *American Court Systems: Readings in Judicial Process and Behavior*, 2d ed. (New York: Longman, 1989), pp. 584–92; Chap. 4 above, pp. 120-21.

19. Glendon Schubert, *Judicial Policy Making*, rev. ed. (Glenview, Ill.: Scott, Foresman, 1974), p. 198. Schubert was by no means alone in reaching this type of conclusion.

20. See Blasi, "The Rootless Activism of the Burger Court," in Blasi, ed., *The Burger Court;* Albert W. Alschuler, "Failed Pragmatism: Reflections on the Burger Court," *Harvard Law Review* 100 (1987): 1436–56.

21. The Burger Court's seeming tendency to fade from national political prominence during these years is suggested by an analysis of the newspaper coverage of the Court from 1970 through 1986. If one examines Supreme Court coverage during these years by the *New York Times*, for example, the number of news articles, op-ed pieces, letters to the editor, editorials, and

edited texts of opinions that appeared decreased markedly after the early 1970s.

22. Robert G. McCloskey, *The American Supreme Court* (Chicago: University of Chicago Press, 1960).

23. Ibid., p. 79.

24. Legal historian Lawrence M. Friedman sees the Civil War as a transcending event that transformed the nation and the Court, laying the foundation for the next great constitutional epoch. See Lawrence M. Friedman, *American Law: An Introduction* (New York: Norton, 1984), p. 186.

25. McCloskey, *The American Supreme Court*, p. 134.

26. Ibid., p. 226. It is noteworthy that Archibald Cox organized the first three sections of his most recent book on the Court along the lines of the historical epochs outlined by McCloskey. See Archibald Cox, *The Court and the Constitution* (Boston: Houghton Mifflin, 1987).

27. Robert G. McCloskey, *The Modern Supreme Court* (Cambridge, Mass.: Harvard University Press, 1972), p. 3.

28. See Richard C. Cortner, *The Supreme Court and the Second Bill of Rights* (Madison: University of Wisconsin Press, 1981).

29. See, for example, *West Virginia State Board of Education v. Barnette* (1943); *Korematsu v. United States* (1944).

30. McCloskey, *The Modern Supreme Court*, p. 10.

31. William H. Whyte, Jr., *The Organization Man* (New York: Simon and Schuster, 1956).

32. See, for example, Michael J. Perry, *The Constitution, the Courts, and Human Rights* (New Haven, Conn.: Yale University Press, 1982), p. 165.

33. Jesse H. Choper, *Judicial Review and the National Political Process* (Chicago: University of Chicago Press, 1980), pp. 60–64. The contemporary Court is also analyzed largely in terms of its function in protecting individual rights in John Hart Ely, *Democracy and Distrust: A Theory of Judicial Review* (Cambridge, Mass.: Harvard University Press, 1982) and Perry, *The Constitution, the Courts, and Human Rights.*

34. See, for example, Benjamin F. Wright, *The Growth of American Constitutional Law* (New York: Henry Holt, 1942), pp. 252–53.

35. Woodrow Wilson, *Constitutional Government in the United States* (New York: Columbia University Press, 1911), p. 173.

36. Melvin I. Urofsky, *The March of Liberty: A Constitutional History of the United States* (New York: Knopf, 1988), p. 969.

37. Ibid., p. 936.

38. See notes 4 and 5 above.

39. See G. Edward White, *The American Judicial Tradition: Profiles of Leading American Judges,* expanded edition (New York: Oxford University Press, 1988), chap. 16.

40. "Blackmun Has Sharp Opinions of Colleagues," *New York Times,* July 18, 1988, p. A-7.

41. See David M. O'Brien, "The Supreme Court: From Warren to Burger to Rehnquist," *PS* 20 (1987): 15–20.

42. See "The Supreme Court, 1986 Term," *Harvard Law Review* 101 (1987): 119–361; "The Supreme Court, 1987 Term," *Harvard Law Review* 102 (1988): 143–358.

43. Lawrence Baum, *The Supreme Court*, 3d ed. (Washington, D.C.: Congressional Quarterly, 1989), p. 147.

44. For prominent 1989 decisions favoring civil liberties claims, see, for example, *Texas v. Johnson* (flag desecration) and *Sable Communications of California, Inc. v. FCC* (dial-a-porn). For pro-civil liberties decisions in 1990, see *Cruzan v. Missouri* ("right to die"), *Missouri v. Jenkins* (taxes to desegregate public schools), *Rutan v. Republican Party of Illinois* (public employment and the First Amendment), *United States v. Eichman* and *United States v. Haggerty* (flag burning).

45. See Erwin Chemerinsky, "Foreword: The Vanishing Constitution," *Harvard Law Review* 103 (1989): 43–104.

46. Linda Greenhouse, "Court Upholds Use of Rights Law But Limits How It Can Be Applied," *New York Times*, June 16, 1989, p. A-12.

47. The Court also narrowly construed Section 1981 in *Jett v. Dallas Independent School District* (1989), holding five to four that it could not be relied on in damage suits against state or local governments for racial discrimination.

48. The three new cases accepted included *Turnock v. Ragsdale, Ohio v. Akron Center for Reproductive Health,* and *Hodgson v. Minnesota.*

49. In a third case, *Consolidated Rail Corporation v. Railway Labor Executives' Association* (1989), the Court ruled seven to two that railroads were not required by federal labor law to bargain with an employee union before mandating a drug-testing program.

50. Sheldon Goldman, "Reagan's Judicial Legacy: Completing the Puzzle and Summing Up," *Judicature* 72 (1989): 330.

51. McCloskey, *The American Supreme Court*, pp. 134–35.

52. Ibid., p. 226.

SELECT BIBLIOGRAPHY

BURGER COURT

Books

Blasi, Vincent, ed. *The Burger Court: The Counter-Revolution That Wasn't.* New Haven, Conn.: Yale University Press, 1983.

Cox, Archibald. *Freedom of Expression.* Cambridge, Mass.: Harvard University Press, 1980.

Friedman, Leon, ed. *The Justices of the United States Supreme Court: Their Lives and Major Opinions.* Vol. 5. New York: Chelsea House, 1978.

Funston, Richard. *Constitutional Counter-Revolution? The Warren Court and the Burger Court: Judicial Policy-Making in Modern America.* New York: Schenkman, 1977.

Galub, Arthur L. *The Burger Court, 1968–1984.* New York: Associated Faculty Press, 1986.

Levy, Leonard W. *Against the Law: The Nixon Court and Criminal Justice.* New York: Harper and Row, 1974.

Mason, Alpheus Thomas. *The Supreme Court from Taft to Burger.* 3d ed., rev. Baton Rouge: Louisiana State University Press, 1979.

Schwartz, Bernard. *The Ascent of Pragmatism: The Burger Court in Action.* Reading, Mass.: Addison-Wesley, 1990.

_____. *The Unpublished Opinions of the Burger Court.* New York: Oxford University Press, 1988.

Schwartz, Herman, ed. *The Burger Years: Rights and Wrongs in the Supreme Court, 1969–1986.* New York: Viking, 1987.

Thomas, William R. *The Burger Court and Civil Liberties.* Rev. ed. Brunswick, Ohio: King's Court Communications, 1979.

Wasby, Stephen L. *Continuity and Change: From the Warren Court to the Burger Court.* Pacific Palisades, Calif.: Goodyear, 1976.

Wilkinson, J. Harvie, III. *From Brown to Bakke: The Supreme Court and School Integration, 1954–1978.* New York: Oxford University Press, 1979.

Witt, Elder. *A Different Justice: Reagan and the Supreme Court.* Washington, D.C.: Congressional Quarterly Press, 1986.

Woodward, Bob, and Scott Armstrong. *The Brethren: Inside the Supreme Court.* New York: Simon and Schuster, 1979.

Articles

Alschuler, Albert W. " 'Close Enough for Government Work': The Exclusionary Rule after *Leon.*" *Supreme Court Review* 1984: 309–58.

———. "Failed Pragmatism: Reflections on the Burger Court." *Harvard Law Review* 100 (1987): 1436–56.

Baum, Lawrence. "Explaining the Burger Court's Support for Civil Liberties." *PS* 20 (1987): 21–28.

Chase, Edward. "The Burger Court, the Individual and the Criminal Process: Directions and Misdirections." *New York University Law Review* 52 (1977): 518–97.

Dorsen, Norman. "The United States Supreme Court: Trends and Prospects." *Harvard Civil Rights–Civil Liberties Law Review* 21 (1986): 1–26.

Ducat, Craig R., and Robert L. Dudley. "Dimensions Underlying Economic Policy-Making in the Early and Late Burger Courts." *Journal of Politics* 49 (1987): 521–39.

Dudley, Robert L., and Craig R. Ducat. "The Burger Court and Economic Liberalism." *Western Political Quarterly* 39 (1986): 236–49.

Eagleton, Thomas E. "Rights without Remedies: The Burger Court in Full Bloom." *Washington University Law Quarterly* 63 (1985): 365–76.

Emerson, Thomas I. "First Amendment Doctrine and the Burger Court." *California Law Review* 68 (1980): 422–81.

Funston, Richard. "The Burger Court and Era." In Robert J. Janosik, ed., *Encyclopedia of the American Judicial System,* 1: 174–95. New York: Charles Scribner's Sons, 1987.

———. "The Double Standard of Constitutional Protection in the Era of the Welfare State." *Political Science Quarterly* 90 (1975): 261–87.

Ginsburg, Ruth Bader. "Gender in the Supreme Court: The 1973 and 1974 Terms." *Supreme Court Review* 1975: 1–24.

Gunther, Gerald. "Foreword: In Search of Evolving Doctrine on a Changing Court: A Model for a Newer Equal Protection." *Harvard Law Review* 86 (1972): 1–48.

Heck, Edward V. "Changing Voting Patterns in the Warren and Burger Courts." In *Judicial Conflict and Consensus: Behavioral Studies of American Appellate Courts,* edited by Sheldon Goldman and Charles M. Lamb, pp. 68–86. Lexington: University Press of Kentucky, 1986.

———. "Civil Liberties Voting Patterns in the Burger Court, 1975–1978." *Western Political Quarterly* 34 (1981): 193–202.

———, and Albert C. Ringelstein. "The Burger Court and the Primacy of Political Expression." *Western Political Quarterly* 40 (1987): 413–25.

Hodder-Williams, Richard. "Is There a Burger Court?" *British Journal of Political Science* 9 (1979): 173–200.

Howard, A. E. Dick. "State Courts and Constitutional Rights in the Day of the Burger Court." *Virginia Law Review* 62 (1976): 873–944.

Kurland, Phillip B. "1970 Term: Notes on the Emergence of the Burger Court." *Supreme Court Review* 1971: 265–322.

———. "1971 Term: The Year of the Stewart-White Court." *Supreme Court Review* 1972: 181–329.

Lamb, Charles M., and Mitchell S. Lustig. "The Burger Court, Exclusionary Zoning, and the Activist-Restraint Debate." *University of Pittsburgh Law Review* 40 (1979): 169–226.

Mason, Alpheus Thomas. "The Burger Court in Historical Perspective." *Political Science Quarterly* 89 (1974): 27–45.

———. "Whence and Whither the Burger Court? Judicial Self-Restraint: A Beguiling Myth." *Review of Politics* 41 (1979): 3–37.

McFeeley, Neil D. "A Change of Direction: Habeas Corpus from Warren to Burger." *Western Political Quarterly* 32 (1979): 172–88.

Mendelson, Wallace. "From Warren to Burger: The Rise and Decline of Substantive Equal Protection." *American Political Science Review* 66 (1972): 1226–33.

O'Brien, David M. "The Supreme Court: From Warren to Burger to Rehnquist." *PS* 20 (1987): 12–20.

Rathjen, Gregory J., and Harold J. Spaeth. "Access to the Federal Courts: An Analysis of Burger Court Policy-Making." *American Journal of Political Science* 23 (1979): 360–82.

Saltzburg, Stephen A. "Foreword: The Flow and Ebb of Constitutional Criminal Procedure in the Warren and Burger Courts." *Georgetown Law Journal* 69 (1980): 151–209.

Segal, Jeffrey A. "Supreme Court Justices as Human Decision Makers: An Individual-Level Analysis of the Search and Seizure Cases." *Journal of Politics* 48 (1986): 938–55.

———, and Albert D. Cover. "Ideological Values and the Votes of U.S. Supreme Court Justices." *American Political Science Review* 83 (1989): 557–65.

Seidman, Louis Michael. "Factual Guilt and the Burger Court: An Examination of Continuity and Change in Criminal Procedure." *Columbia Law Review* 80 (1980): 436–503.

Shapiro, Martin. "The Supreme Court from Early Burger to Early Rehnquist." In *The New American Political System*, edited by Anthony King, pp. 47–85. Washington, D.C.: American Enterprise Institute, 1990.

Slotnick, Elliot E. "Who Speaks for the Court? Majority Opinion Assignment from Taft to Burger." *American Journal of Political Science* 23 (1979): 60–77.

Spaeth, Harold J. "Burger Court Review of State Court Civil Liberties Decisions." *Judicature* 68 (1985): 285–91.

———. "Distributive Justice: Majority Opinion Assignments in the Burger Court." *Judicature* 67 (1983–84): 299–304.

Spaeth, Harold J., and Michael F. Altfeld, "Influence Relationships within the Supreme Court: A Comparison of the Warren and Burger Courts." *Western Political Quarterly* 38 (1985): 70–83.

Spaeth, Harold J., and Stuart H. Teger. "Activism and Restraint: A Cloak for the Justices' Policy Preferences." In *Supreme Court Activism and Restraint,* edited by Stephen C. Halpern and Charles M. Lamb, pp. 277–301. Lexington, Mass.: Lexington Books, 1982.

Steamer, Robert J. "Contemporary Supreme Court Directions in Civil Liberties." *Political Science Quarterly* 92 (1977): 425–42.

Taggart, William A., and Matthew R. DeZee. "A Note on Substantive Access Doctrines in the U.S. Supreme Court: A Comparative Analysis of the Warren and Burger Courts." *Western Political Quarterly* 38 (1985): 84–93.

BLACK, HUGO L.

Ball, Howard. *The Vision and the Dream of Justice Hugo L. Black: An Examination of a Judicial Philosophy.* University: University of Alabama Press, 1975.

Black, Hugo L. *A Constitutional Faith.* New York: Knopf, 1968.

———. "The Bill of Rights." *New York University Law Review* 35 (1960): 865–81.

Dunne, Gerald T. *Hugo Black and the Judicial Revolution.* New York: Simon and Schuster, 1977.

Hamilton, Virginia Van derVeer. *Hugo Black: The Alabama Years.* University: University of Alabama Press, 1982.

Magee, James J. *Mr. Justice Black: Absolutist on the Court.* Charlottesville: University Press of Virginia, 1979.

Mendelson, Wallace. *Justices Black and Frankfurter: Conflict on the Court.* 2d ed. Chicago: University of Chicago Press, 1966.

Ulmer, S. Sidney. "The Longitudinal Behavior of Hugo Lafayette Black: Parabolic Support for Civil Liberties, 1937–1971." *Florida State University Law Review* 1 (1973): 131–53.

Williams, Charlotte. *Hugo L. Black: A Study in the Judicial Process.* Baltimore: Johns Hopkins University Press, 1950.

Yarbrough, Tinsley E. *Mr. Justice Black and His Critics.* Durham, N.C.: Duke University Press, 1988.

BLACKMUN, HARRY A.

Blackmun, Harry A. "Thoughts about Ethics." *Emory Law Journal* 24 (1975): 3–20.

Jenkins, John A. "A Candid Talk with Justice Blackmun." *New York Times Magazine,* Feb. 20, 1983, pp. 20–26, 57–66.

Kobylka, Joseph F. "Justice Harry A. Blackmun and Federalism: A Subtle Movement with Potentially Greater Ramifications." *Creighton Law Review* 19 (1985-86): 9-49.

Note. "The Changing Social Vision of Justice Blackmun." *Harvard Law Review* 96 (1983): 717–36.

Pollet, Michael. "Harry A. Blackmun." In *The Justices of the United States*

Supreme Court: Their Lives and Major Opinions, vol. 5, edited by Leon Friedman, pp. 3–60. New York: Chelsea House, 1978.

Schlesinger, Steven R., and Janet Nesse. "Justice Harry Blackmun and Empirical Jurisprudence." *American University Law Review* 29 (1980): 405–37.

United States. Senate. Committee on the Judiciary. *Nomination of Harry A. Blackmun, Hearings.* 91st Cong., 2d sess. Washington, D.C.: U.S. Government Printing Office, 1970.

Wasby, Stephen L. "Justice Harry A. Blackmun in the Burger Court." *Hamline Law Review* 11 (1988): 183–245.

BRENNAN, WILLIAM J., JR.

Brennan, William J., Jr. "Constitutional Adjudication." *Notre Dame Lawyer* 40 (1965): 559–69.

———. "Constitutional Adjudication and the Death Penalty: A View from the Court." *Harvard Law Review* 100 (1986): 313–31.

———. "The National Court of Appeals: Another Dissent." *University of Chicago Law Review* 40 (1973): 473–85.

———. "State Constitutions and the Protection of Individual Rights." *Harvard Law Review* 90 (1977): 489–504.

Comment. "A Tribute to Justice William Brennan." *Harvard Civil Rights–Civil Liberties Law Review* 15 (1980): 279–308.

Dorman, Charles W. "Justice Brennan: The Individual and Labor Law." *Chicago-Kent Law Review* 58 (1982): 1003–52.

Friedman, Stephen J. *William J. Brennan, Jr.: An Affair with Freedom.* New York: Atheneum, 1967.

Gazell, James A. "Justice Brennan's Reflections on Judicial Modernization." *Rutgers-Camden Law Journal* 10 (1978): 1–23.

Heck, Edward V. "Justice Brennan and the Heyday of Warren Court Liberalism." *Santa Clara Law Review* 20 (1980): 841–87.

———. "The Socialization of a Freshman Justice: The Early Years of Justice Brennan." *Pacific Law Journal* 10 (1979): 707–28.

BURGER, WARREN E.

Braswell, Mark K., and John M. Scheb II. "Conservative Pragmatism versus Liberal Principles: Warren E. Burger on the Suppression of Evidence, 1956–86." *Creighton Law Review* 20 (1987): 789–831.

Chesler, Robert Douglas. "Imagery of Community, Ideology of Authority: The Moral Reasoning of Chief Justice Burger." *Harvard Civil Rights–Civil Liberties Law Review* 18 (1983): 457–82.

Duscha, Julius. "Chief Justice Burger Asks: If It Doesn't Make Good Sense, How Can It Make Good Law?" *New York Times Magazine,* Oct. 5, 1969, pp. 30–31, 140–52.

Gazell, James A. "Chief Justice Burger's Quest for Judicial Administrative Efficiency." *Detroit College of Law Review* 1977: 455–97.

Kobylka, Joseph F. "Leadership on the Supreme Court of the United States: Chief Justice Burger and the Establishment Clause." *Western Political Quarterly* 42 (1989): 545–68.

Lamb, Charles M. "The Making of a Chief Justice: Warren Burger on Criminal Procedure, 1956–1969," *Cornell Law Review* 60 (1975): 743–88.

———. "A Microlevel Analysis of Appeals Court Conflict: Warren Burger and His Colleagues on the D.C. Circuit." In *Judicial Conflict and Consensus: Behavioral Studies of American Appellate Courts*, edited by Sheldon Goldman and Charles M. Lamb, pp. 179–96. Lexington: University Press of Kentucky, 1986.

———. "Warren Burger and the Insanity Defense—Judicial Philosophy and Voting Behavior on a U.S. Court of Appeals." *American University Law Review* 24 (1974): 91–128.

Landever, Arthur R. "Chief Justice Burger and Extra-case Activism." *Journal of Public Law* 20 (1971): 523–41.

Norman, Andrew E. "Warren E. Burger." In *The Justices of the United States Supreme Court, 1789–1978*, vol. 5, edited by Leon Friedman, pp. 461–94. New York: Chelsea House, 1978.

Rehnquist, William H., "A Tribute to Chief Justice Warren E. Burger." *Harvard Law Review* 100 (1987): 969–71.

Tamm, Edward A., and Paul C. Reardon. "Warren E. Burger and the Administration of Justice." *Brigham Young University Law Review* 1981: 447–521.

DOUGLAS, WILLIAM O.

Brenner, Saul, and Theodore Arrington. "William O. Douglas: Consistent Civil Libertarian or Parabolic Supporter?" *Journal of Politics* 45 (1983): 490–96.

Comment. "Toward a Constitutional Theory of Individuality: The Privacy Opinions of Justice Douglas." *Yale Law Journal* 87 (1978): 1579–1600.

Countryman, Vern, ed. *The Judicial Record of Justice William O. Douglas.* Cambridge, Mass.: Harvard University Press, 1974.

———. "Justice Douglas and the Freedom of Expression." *University of Illinois Law Forum* 1978: 301–27.

Douglas, William O. *An Almanac of Liberty.* Garden City, N.Y.: Doubleday, 1954; reprint, Westport, Conn.: Greenwood Press, 1973.

———. *The Court Years, 1939–1975: The Autobiography of William O. Douglas.* New York: Random House, 1980.

———. *Go East, Young Man: The Early Years. The Autobiography of William O. Douglas.* New York: Dell, 1974.

Mendelson, Wallace. "Mr. Justice Douglas and Government by the Judiciary." *Journal of Politics* 38 (1976): 918–37.

Simon, James F. *Independent Journey: The Life of William O. Douglas.* New York: Harper and Row, 1980.

Ulmer, S. Sidney. "Parabolic Support of Civil Liberty Claims: The Case of William O. Douglas." *Journal of Politics* 41 (1979): 634–39.

HARLAN, JOHN MARSHALL

Bourguignon, Henry J. "Second Mr. Justice Harlan: His Principles of Judicial Decision Making." *Supreme Court Review* 1979: 251–328.
Dane, Stephen M. " 'Ordered Liberty' and Self-Restraint: The Judicial Philosophy of the Second Justice Harlan." *University of Cincinnati Law Review* 51 (1982): 545–73.
Dorsen, Norman. "Mr. Justice Black and Mr. Justice Harlan." *New York University Law Review* 46 (1971): 649–52.
Friedman, Edward L., Jr. "Mr. Justice Harlan," *Notre Dame Lawyer* 30 (1955): 349–59.
Leedes, Gary C. "Revival of Interest in Justice Harlan's Flexible Due Process Balancing Approach." *San Diego Law Review* 19 (1982): 737–71.
Maddocks, Lewis I. "Two Justices Harlan on Civil Rights and Liberties: A Study in Judicial Contrasts." *Kentucky Law Journal* 68 (1979–80): 301–43.
Shapiro, David L., ed. *The Evolution of a Judicial Philosophy: Selected Opinions and Papers of Justice John M. Harlan.* Cambridge, Mass.: Harvard University Press, 1969.
Symposium. "Mr. Justice John Marshall Harlan." *Harvard Law Review* 85 (1971): 369–91.
Wilkinson, J. Harvie, III. "Justice John M. Harlan and the Values of Federalism." *Virginia Law Review* 57 (1971): 1185–1221.
Wright, Charles Alan. "Order and Predictability in Law: A Tribute to John M. Harlan." *Journal of Public Law* 20 (1971): 365–70.

MARSHALL, THURGOOD

Bland, Randall W. *Private Pressure on Public Law: The Legal Career of Justice Thurgood Marshall.* Port Washington, N.Y.: Kennikat Press, 1973.
Fenderson, Lewis H. *Thurgood Marshall: Fighter for Justice.* New York: McGraw-Hill, 1969.
Hayes, William K. "Thurgood Marshall: Rampart Against Racism." *Black Law Journal* 2 (1972): 240–47.
Marshall, Thurgood. "The Continuing Challenge of the Fourteenth Amendment." *Georgia Law Review* 3 (1968): 1–10.
———. "Group Action in the Pursuit of Justice." *New York University Law Review* 44 (1969): 661–72.
Ripple, Kenneth F. "Thurgood Marshall and the Forgotten Legacy of *Brown v. Board of Education.*" *Notre Dame Lawyer* 55 (1980): 471–84.
Special Issue. "Dedication and Justice Marshall." *Texas Southern University Law Review* 4 (1977): 175–308.

"Tribute to Justice Thurgood Marshall." *Maryland Law Review* 40 (1981): 389–434.

O'CONNOR, SANDRA DAY

Comment. "Justice Sandra Day O'Connor: Token or Triumph from a Feminist Perspective." *Golden Gate University Law Review* 15 (1985): 493–525.

Cordray, Richard A., and James T. Vradelis. "The Emerging Jurisprudence of Justice Sandra Day O'Connor." *University of Chicago Law Review* 52 (1985): 389–459.

Cook, Beverly B. "Women as Supreme Court Candidates: From Florence Allen to Sandra O'Connor." *Judicature* 65 (1981–82): 314–26.

O'Connor, Sandra Day. "Our Judicial Federalism." *Case Western Reserve Law Review* 35 (1984–85): 1–12.

———. "Trends in the Relationship between the Federal and State Courts from the Perspective of a State Court Judge." *William and Mary Law Review* 22 (1981): 801–19.

Riggs, Robert E. "Justice O'Connor: A First Term Appraisal." *Brigham Young University Law Review* 1983: 1–46.

Scheb, John M., II, and Lee W. Ailshie. "Justice Sandra Day O'Connor and the 'Freshman Effect.' " *Judicature* 69 (1985): 9–12.

Schenker, Carl R., Jr. " 'Reading' Justice Sandra Day O'Connor." *Catholic University Law Review* 31 (1982): 487–503.

United States Senate. Committee on the Judiciary. *Hearings on the Nomination of Sandra Day O'Connor.* 97th Cong., 1st sess. Washington, D.C.: U.S. Government Printing Office, 1981.

POWELL, LEWIS F., JR.

BeVier, Lillian R. "Justice Powell and the First Amendment's 'Societal Function': A Preliminary Analysis." *Virginia Law Review* 68 (1982): 177–201.

Blasecki, Janet L. "Justice Lewis F. Powell: Swing Voter or Staunch Conservative?" *Journal of Politics* 52 (1990): 530-47.

Gunther, Gerald. "In Search of Judicial Quality on a Changing Court: The Case of Justice Powell." *Stanford Law Review* 24 (1972): 1001–35.

Howard, A. E. Dick. "Mr. Justice Powell and the Emerging Nixon Majority." *Michigan Law Review* 70 (1972): 445–68.

Maltz, Earl M. "Portrait of a Man in the Middle—Mr. Justice Powell, Equal Protection and the Pure Classification Problem." *Ohio State Law Journal* 40 (1979): 941–64.

Powell, Lewis F., Jr. "Duty to Serve the Common Good." *Catholic Lawyer* 24 (1979): 295–300.

———. "Myths and Misconceptions about the Supreme Court." *New York State Bar Journal* 48 (1976): 6–10.

"Symposium in Honor of Justice Lewis F. Powell, Jr." *Virginia Law Review* 68 (1982): 161–332.

Wilkinson, J. Harvie, III. *Serving Justice: A Supreme Court Clerk's View.* New York: Charterhouse, 1974.

———. "Honorable Lewis F. Powell, Jr.: Five Years on the Supreme Court." *University of Richmond Law Review* 11 (1977): 259–67.

Yackle, Larry W. "Thoughts on Rodriguez: Mr. Justice Powell and the Demise of Equal Protection Analysis in the Supreme Court?" *University of Richmond Law Review* 9 (1975): 181–247.

REHNQUIST, WILLIAM H.

Davis, Sue. "Federalism and Property Rights: An Examination of Justice Rehnquist's Legal Positivism." *Western Political Quarterly* 39 (1986): 250–64.

———. "Justice Rehnquist's Equal Protection Clause: An Interim Analysis." *Nebraska Law Review* 63 (1984): 288–313.

———. *Justice Rehnquist and the Constitution.* Princeton, N.J.: Princeton University Press, 1989.

Denvir, John. "Justice Rehnquist and Constitutional Interpretation." *Hastings Law Journal* 34 (1983): 1011–53.

Maveety, Nancy. "The Populist of the Adversary System: The Jurisprudence of Justice Rehnquist." *Journal of Contemporary Law* 13 (1987): 221–47.

Powell, Jeff. "The Compleat Jeffersonian: Justice Rehnquist and Federalism." *Yale Law Journal* 91 (1982): 1317–70.

Rehnquist, William H. "All Discord, Harmony Not Understood: The Performance of the Supreme Court of the United States." *Arizona Law Review* 22 (1980): 973–86.

———. "Chief Justices I Never Knew." *Hastings Constitutional Law Quarterly* 3 (1976): 637–55.

———. "Is an Expanded Right of Privacy Consistent with Fair and Effective Law Enforcement?" *University of Kansas Law Review* 23 (1974): 1–22.

———. "The Notion of a Living Constitution." *Texas Law Review* 54 (1976): 693–706.

———. "Political Battles for Judicial Independence." *Washington Law Review* 50 (1975): 835–51.

———. *The Supreme Court: How It Was, How It Is.* New York: Morrow, 1987.

Rydell, John R., II. "Mr. Justice Rehnquist and Judicial Self-Restraint." *Hastings Law Journal* 26 (1975): 875–915.

Shapiro, David L. "Mr. Justice Rehnquist: A Preliminary View." *Harvard Law Review* 90 (1976): 293–357.

STEVENS, JOHN PAUL

Ball, Branch Y., and Thomas M. Uhlman. "Justice John Paul Stevens: An Initial Assessment." *Brigham Young University Law Review* 1978: 567–91.

Beytagh, Francis X., Jr. "Mr. Justice Stevens and the Burger Court's Uncertain Trumpet." *Notre Dame Lawyer* 51 (1976): 946–55.

Comment. "The Emerging Constitutional Jurisprudence of Justice Stevens." *University of Chicago Law Review* 46 (1978): 155–235.

Comment. "Interpenetration of Narrow Construction and Policy: Mr. Justice Stevens' Circuit Opinions." *San Diego Law Review* 13 (1976): 899–930.

Comment. "Mr. Justice Stevens: An Examination of a Judicial Philosophy." *St. Louis University Law Journal* 23 (1979): 126–62.

Note, "Justice Stevens's Equal Protection Jurisprudence." *Harvard Law Review* 100 (1987): 1146–65.

Sickels, Robert Judd. *Justice John Paul Stevens and the Constitution: The Search for Balance.* University Park: Pennsylvania State University Press, 1989.

Special Project. "Justice Stevens: The First Three Terms." *Vanderbilt Law Review* 32 (1979): 671–754.

Special Project. "The One Hundred and First Justice: An Analysis of the Opinions of Justice John Paul Stevens, Sitting as Judge on the Seventh Circuit Court of Appeals." *Vanderbilt Law Review* 29 (1976): 125–209.

Stevens, John Paul. "The Life Span of a Judge-Made Rule." *New York University Law Review* 58 (1983): 1–21.

———. "Reflections on the Removal of Sitting Judges." *Stetson Law Review* 13 (1984): 215–20.

STEWART, POTTER

Barnett, Helaine M., Janice Goldman, and Jeffrey B. Morris. "A Lawyer's Lawyer, a Judge's Judge: Justice Potter Stewart and the Fourth Amendment." *University of Cincinnati Law Review* 51 (1982): 509–44.

Berman, Daniel M. "Mr. Justice Stewart: A Preliminary Appraisal." *University of Cincinnati Law Review* 28 (1959): 401–21.

Binion, Gayle. "Justice Potter Stewart on Racial Equality: What It Means to Be a Moderate." *Hastings Constitutional Law Quarterly* 6 (1979): 853–908.

Friedman, Leon. "Potter Stewart." In *The Justices of the United States Supreme Court: Their Lives and Major Opinions,* vol. 5, edited by Leon Friedman, pp. 291–341. New York: Chelsea House, 1978.

Lewis, Peter W. "Justice Stewart and Fourth Amendment Probable Cause: 'Swing Voter' or Participant in a 'New Majority'?" *Loyola Law Review* 22 (1976): 713–42.

Palmer, Larry I. "Two Perspectives on Structuring Discretion: Justices Stewart and White on the Death Penalty." *Journal of Criminal Law and Criminology* 70 (1979): 194–213.

Paschal, J. Francis. "Mr. Justice Stewart on the Court of Appeals." *Duke Law Journal* (1959): 325–40.

Smith, Rodney K. "Justice Potter Stewart: A Contemporary Jurist's View of Religious Liberty." *North Dakota Law Review* 59 (1983): 183–210.

Stewart, Potter. "Or of the Press." *Hastings Law Journal* 26 (1975): 631–37.

———. "The Road to *Mapp v. Ohio* and Beyond: The Origins, Development and Future of the Exclusionary Rule in Search-and-Seizure Cases." *Columbia Law Review* 83 (1983): 1365–1404.

WHITE, BYRON R.

Armstrong, Michael J. "A Barometer of Freedom of the Press: The Opinions of Mr. Justice White." *Pepperdine Law Review* 8 (1980): 157–87.

Friedman, Leon. "Byron R. White." In *The Justices of the United States Supreme Court: Their Lives and Major Opinions*, edited by Leon Friedman. 5: 345–82. New York, Chelsea House, 1978.

Leibman, Lance. "Swing Man on the Supreme Court." *New York Times Magazine*, Oct. 8, 1972, pp. 16–17, 94–100.

Palmer, Larry I. "Two Perspectives on Structuring Discretion: Justices Stewart and White on the Death Penalty." *Journal of Criminal Law and Criminology* 70 (1979): 194–213.

White, Byron R. "State of the Law: The Bar's Responsibility." *Gonzaga Law Review* 17 (1982): 849–67.

Zelnick, Robert. "Whizzer White and the Fearsome Foursome." *Washington Monthly* 4 (Dec. 1972): 46–54.

NOTES ON CONTRIBUTORS

CHARLES M. LAMB is Associate Professor of Political Science at the State University of New York at Buffalo and, presently, Visiting Associate Professor at the Robert M. La Follette Institute of Public Affairs, University of Wisconsin–Madison. He received his Ph.D. in political science from the University of Alabama, and he served on the staffs of George Washington University from 1973 to 1975 and the U.S. Commission on Civil Rights from 1975 to 1977. He is coeditor of *Supreme Court Activism and Restraint* (1982) with Stephen C. Halpern, of *Implementation of Civil Rights Policy* (1984) with Charles S. Bullock III, and of *Judicial Conflict and Consensus: Behavioral Studies of American Appellate Courts* (1986) with Sheldon Goldman. Currently he is writing a book on fair housing in America and then plans to complete a judicial biography of Chief Justice Burger.

STEPHEN C. HALPERN, Associate Professor of Political Science at the State University of New York at Buffalo, received his Ph.D. in political science from The Johns Hopkins University and the J.D. from the State University of New York at Buffalo. He has been a Fellow at the Institute in Behavioral Science and Law, associate editor of the *Law and Society Review,* and a Fulbright Scholar at the University of Utrecht, the Netherlands. He is the author of *Police Association and Department Leaders* (1974), editor of *The Future of Our Liberties: Perspectives on the Bill of Rights* (1982), and coeditor, with Charles M. Lamb, of *Supreme Court Activism and Restraint* (1982). At present he is completing a book on school desegregation and consulting with the law firm of Moot & Sprague in Buffalo.

HOWARD BALL, Dean of the College of Arts and Sciences and Professor of Political Science at the University of Vermont, received his Ph.D. from Rutgers University. His teaching and research interests

475

are in the fields of judicial process and constitutional law, and he has been a prolific author of articles and books in these areas. His most recent publications are *Of Power and Right: Justices Hugo L. Black and William O. Douglas and America's Tumultuous Years* (Oxford University Press, 1991), coauthored with Phillip J. Cooper, and *Behind the Velvet Curtains: The Supreme Court and the Watergate Litigation* (Praeger, 1990).

STEPHEN L. WASBY, Professor of Political Science at the State University of New York at Albany, received his Ph.D. in political science at the University of Oregon. His research has focused on the federal courts, with particular attention to the impact of court rulings, the U.S. Court of Appeals for the Ninth Circuit, and civil rights litigation by interest groups. He is the author of *The Supreme Court in the Federal Judicial System* (3rd ed., 1988).

STANLEY H. FRIEDELBAUM, Professor of Political Science and Director of the Burns Center for State Constitutional Studies at Rutgers University, received his Ph.D. from Columbia University. He is the author of *Contemporary Constitutional Law* (Houghton Mifflin, 1972) and editor of *Human Rights in the States* (Greenwood, 1988). He has also written numerous articles on judicial deference and state constitutional law that have appeared in such journals as *The Supreme Court Review, University of Chicago Law Review, Publius, Emory Law Journal,* and *Dickinson Law Review.* Currently he is the founder and editor of the Burns Center's quarterly review, *State Constitutional Commentaries and Notes.*

PHILLIP J. COOPER, Professor of Political Science, Public Administration, and Policy in the Rockefeller College of Public Affairs and Policy of the State University of New York at Albany, received his Ph.D. in political science from Syracuse University. He is the author of works on law and public policy and public law and public administration. With Howard Ball, he is the author of *Of Power and Right: Justices Hugo L. Black and William O. Douglas and America's Tumultuous Years* (Oxford University Press, 1991).

WALLACE MENDELSON is Professor of Government at the University of Texas at Austin. He has an LL.B. from Harvard (1936) and a Ph.D. from the University of Wisconsin (1940). His extra-academic work includes some four years of military service during World War II; a year with Mr. Justice Frankfurter (1953–54); editor of the 1961 Report of the United States Civil Rights Commission;

assistant to the Attorney General of the United States (1973); and at various times consultant to the National Endowment for the Humanities; regional representative, United States Civil Rights Commission; and regional representative, National Labor Relations Board. He has been president of the Southern Political Science Association and a member of the executive council of the American Political Science Association. He is author of several books and scores of articles on public law problems.

WILLIAM J. DANIELS, Dean, College of Liberal Arts, and Professor of Political Science at Rochester Institute of Technology, received his Ph.D. in political science at the University of Iowa. He has served as an Alfred E. Smith Fellow in New York State government, Fulbright Lecturer in Japan, and a Judicial Fellow at the United States Supreme Court. His research and publications involve state government, jurisprudence, constitutional law, racial justice, and the U.S. Supreme Court.

BEVERLY B. COOK, Professor Emeritus at the University of Wisconsin at Milwaukee, received her Ph.D. in political science from Claremont Graduate School. Her current research interests are in the opinion assignment practices of the U.S. Supreme Court, the identification of significant cases, and the reexamination of the conventional behavioral model for explaining justices' voting choices. Her numerous works on the cultural and personal determinants of judicial decision making and on the changing status of women judges include articles in such journals as the *American Journal of Political Science, U.S. Supreme Court Historical Society Yearbook, Cincinnati Law Review, Washington University Law Quarterly,* and *International Political Science Review,* as well as chapters in *Political Women* (1984), *The Quest for Social Justice* (1983), *The Study of Criminal Courts* (1979), *Women in the Judicial Process* (1987), and *Women, the Courts, and Equality* (1987).

JACOB W. LANDYNSKI received his Ph.D. from The Johns Hopkins University and is Professor of Political Science in the graduate faculty of the New School for Social Research. His books include *Search and Seizure and the Supreme Court: A Study in Constitutional Interpretation* (1966), and he was a contributor to the *Encyclopedia of the American Constitution* (1987). He is currently engaged in a study of the first Justice John Marshall Harlan.

SUE DAVIS is Associate Professor of Political Science at the University of Delaware. Her book, *Justice Rehnquist and the Constitution*, in which she explored the justice's judicial philosophy, was published by Princeton University Press in 1989. She is currently working on a study of the women judges on the U.S. Courts of Appeals.

BRADLEY C. CANON is Professor of Political Science at the University of Kentucky. He received his Ph.D. from the University of Wisconsin–Madison. His major research interests have focused on policy-making by state appellate courts, systems of selecting appellate judges, the implementation of the exclusionary rule in search and seizure, and the impact of U.S. Supreme Court decisions on society. He is coauthor, with Charles Johnson, of *Judicial Policies: Implementation and Impact* (1984).

TINSLEY E. YARBROUGH, Professor of Political Science at East Carolina University, received his Ph.D. from the University of Alabama. His works in the fields of jurisprudence and judicial biography include numerous journal articles and the following books: *Mr. Justice Black and His Critics* (1988), *A Passion for Justice: J. Waties Waring and Civil Rights* (1987), *The Reagan Administration and Human Rights* (1985), *Judge Frank Johnson and Human Rights in Alabama* (1981), and the forthcoming *Judge's Judge: The Second Justice Harlan and the Judicial Revolution*. His biography of Judge Johnson received a Silver Gavel Award from the American Bar Association in 1982, and *Choice* named his biography of Judge Waring one of the outstanding books of 1988.

DANIEL C. KRAMER is Professor of Political Science at the College of Staten Island, CUNY. He has written on a wide variety of topics in the areas of constitutional law and civil liberties. He is the author of three books: *Participatory Democracy: Developing Ideals of the Political Left* (1972), *Comparative Civil Rights and Liberties* (1982), and *State Capital and Private Enterprise: The Case of the UK National Enterprise Board* (1988).

Case Index

Abington School District v. Schempp, 374 U.S. 203 (1963), 16, 391, 392, 393, 402–3

Adamson v. California, 332 U.S. 46 (1947), 43, 47–48, 61, 211

Adderley v. Florida, 385 U.S. 39 (1966), 190

Adickes v. S. H. Kress & Co., 398 U.S. 144 (1970), 200, 210

Aguilar v. Felton, 473 U.S. 402 (1985), 127, 161, 259, 459

Ake v. Oklahoma, 470 U.S. 68 (1985), 458

Albemarle Paper Co. v. Moody, 422 U.S. 405 (1975), 161

Alexander v. "Americans United," Inc., 416 U.S. 752 (1974), 75, 97

Alexander v. Holmes County Board of Education, 396 U.S. 19 (1969), 50, 458

Allen v. Illinois, 478 U.S. 364 (1986), 346, 368

Allen v. McCurry, 449 U.S. 90 (1980), 77

Allen v. Wright, 468 U.S. 737 (1984), 269, 270

Allis-Chalmers Corp. v. Lueck, 471 U.S. 202 (1985), 98

Almeida-Sanchez v. United States, 413 U.S. 266 (1973), 281

Amalgamated Food Employees Union v. Logan Valley Plaza, Inc., 391 U.S. 308 (1968), 190

Ambach v. Norwick, 441 U.S. 68 (1979), 86, 299

American Farm Lines v. Black Ball Freight, 397 U.S. 532 (1970), 190

American Textile Manufacturers Institute v. Donovan, 452 U.S. 490 (1981), 321

American Tobacco Co. v. Patterson, 456 U.S. 63 (1982), 268

Anderson v. Celebreeze, 460 U.S. 780 (1983), 355

Andresen v. Maryland, 427 U.S. 463 (1976), 91

Apodaca v. Oregon, 406 U.S. 404 (1972), 191, 208, 282–83, 284, 382, 420–21, 439

Arcara v. Cloud Books, Inc., 478 U.S. 697 (1986), 82

Argersinger v. Hamlin, 407 U.S. 25 (1972), 22, 187, 283, 284, 388, 458

Arizona v. Rumsley, 467 U.S. 203 (1984), 257

Arizona v. Youngblood, 109 S.Ct. 333 (1988), 454

Arizona Governing Committee v. Norris, 463 U.S. 1073 (1983), 267

Arkansas v. Sanders, 442 U.S. 753 (1979), 92, 395

Arlington Heights v. Metropolitan Housing Development Corp., 429 U.S. 252 (1977), 389

Armco v. Hardesty, 467 U.S. 638 (1984), 303

Arnett v. Kennedy, 416 U.S. 134 (1974), 75, 302

Asarco Inc. v. Idaho State Tax Commission, 458 U.S. 307 (1982), 274

Ashe v. Swenson, 397 U.S. 436 (1970), 55, 56–57, 62

Ashwander v. Tennessee Valley Authority, 297 U.S. 288 (1936), 348, 373

Association of Data Processing Service Organizations, Inc. v. Camp, 397 U.S. 150 (1970), 190

Astrup v. INS, 402 U.S. 509 (1971), 55

Atascadero State Hospital v. Scanlon, 473 U.S. 234 (1985), 77, 323, 349

Attorney General of New York v. Soto-Lopez, 476 U.S. 898 (1986), 360, 363

Bacchus Imports, Ltd. v. Dias, 468 U.S. 263 (1984), 412

Baird v. State Bar of Arizona, 401 U.S. 1 (1971), 62, 82

Baker v. Carr, 369 U.S. 186 (1962), 16, 104, 108, 202, 204, 205, 210, 384, 439

Baker v. McCollan, 443 U.S. 137 (1979), 323

Baldwin v. Alabama, 472 U.S. 372 (1985), 99

Baldwin v. Fish and Game Commission of Montana, 436 U.S. 371 (1978), 81

Baldwin v. New York, 399 U.S. 66 (1970), 62, 386, 420

Ballew v. Georgia, 435 U.S. 223 (1978), 63, 94

Baltimore Gas & Electric Co. v. Natural Resources Defense Council, 462 U.S. 87 (1983), 260

Barclay v. Florida, 463 U.S. 939 (1983), 95, 370

Barefoot v. Estelle, 463 U.S. 880 (1983), 95

Barker v. Wingo, 407 U.S. 514 (1972), 284

Barlow v. Collins, 397 U.S. 159 (1970), 190

Barrett v. United States, 423 U.S. 212 (1976), 99

Barry v. Barchi, 443 U.S. 55 (1979), 423

Bates v. State Bar of Arizona, 433 U.S. 350 (1977), 83, 328

Batson v. Kentucky, 476 U.S. 79 (1986), 325-26, 374

Beal v. Doe, 432 U.S. 438 (1977), 88

Beck v. Alabama, 447 U.S. 625 (1980), 370

Beckwith v. United States, 425 U.S. 341 (1976), 162

Bell v. Wolfish, 441 U.S. 520 (1979), 331, 371-72

Bellotti v. Baird, 428 U.S. 132 (1976), 99

Bellotti v. Baird, 443 U.S. 622 (1979), 291

Bender v. Williamsport Area School District, 475 U.S. 534 (1986), 313

Berger v. New York, 388 U.S. 41 (1967), 45, 191

Berkemer v. McCarty, 468 U.S. 420 (1984), 348

Bethel School District No. 403 v. Fraser, 106 S.Ct. 3159 (1986), 144

Betts v. Brady, 316 U.S. 455 (1942), 283

Bigelow v. Virginia, 421 U.S. 809 (1975), 23, 81, 83, 328, 330

Bishop v. Wood, 426 U.S. 341 (1976), 75

Bivens v. Six Unknown Named Agents of the Federal Bureau of Narcotics, 403 U.S. 388 (1971), 58, 90-91, 153

Blackledge v. Allison, 431 U.S. 63 (1977), 301

Block v. Community Nutrition Institute, 467 U.S. 340 (1984), 260

Block v. North Dakota, 461 U.S. 273 (1983), 252

Block v. Rutherford, 468 U.S. 576 (1984), 97

Board of Curators of the University of Missouri v. Horowitz, 435 U.S. 78 (1978), 97, 218

Board of Education v. Allen, 392 U.S. 236 (1968), 191, 415

Board of Education of Hendrick Hudson Central School Dist. v. Rowley, 458 U.S. 176 (1982), 85

Board of Education, Island Trees Union Free School Dist. No. 26 v. Pico, 457 U.S. 853 (1982), 82, 111-12, 288, 331

Board of Education of Rodgers v. McCluskey, 458 U.S. 966 (1982), 346, 348

Board of Regents v. Roth, 408 U.S. 564 (1972), 177

Bob Jones University v. United States, 461 U.S. 574 (1983), 149

Boddie v. Connecticut, 401 U.S. 371 (1971), 58, 191, 205-6, 387

Bolger v. Youngs Drug Products Corp., 463 U.S. 60 (1983), 353

Booth v. Maryland, 483 U.S. 1056 (1987), 286

Bordenkircher v. Hayes, 434 U.S. 357 (1978), 90, 284

Bowers v. Hardwick, 478 U.S. 186 (1986), 24, 67, 84, 150–51, 264, 313, 358, 424, 427, 429

Bowsher v. Merck & Co., Inc., 460 U.S. 824 (1983), 74

Bowsher v. Synar, 478 U.S. 714 (1986), 24, 74, 134, 320, 350

Boyd v. United States, 116 U.S. 616 (1886), 91

Boys Markets, Inc. v. Retail Clerks Union Local 770, 398 U.S. 235 (1970), 52–53, 58

Braden v. 30th Judicial Circuit Court of Kentucky, 410 U.S. 484 (1973), 98

Bradwell v. Illinois, 16 Wallace 131 (1973), 266

Brady v. Maryland, 373 U.S. 83 (1963), 89

Brady v. United States, 397 U.S. 742 (1970), 420

Brandenburg v. Ohio, 395 U.S. 444 (1969), 190

Branti v. Finkel, 445 U.S. 507 (1980), 287

Branzburg v. Hayes, 408 U.S. 665 (1972), 178, 390, 400, 401, 414

Braunfeld v. Brown, 366 U.S. 599 (1961), 392

Breed v. Jones, 421 U.S. 519 (1975), 401

Breen v. Selective Service Local Board No. 16, 396 U.S. 460 (1970), 62

Brewer v. Williams, 430 U.S. 387 (1977), 162, 388

Briscoe v. LaHue, 460 U.S. 325 (1983), 77

Broadrick v. Oklahoma, 413 U.S. 601 (1973), 178, 191

Brown v. Allen, 344 U.S. 443 (1953), 253

Brown v. Board of Education of Topeka (Brown I), 347 U.S. 483 (1954), 36, 105, 147, 148, 214, 224, 294, 318, 378, 439, 458

Brown v. Board of Education of Topeka (Brown II), 349 U.S. 294 (1955), 199, 294

Brown v. Hotel & Restaurant Employees & Bartenders International Union Local 54, 468 U.S. 491 (1984), 252

Brown v. Illinois, 422 U.S. 590 (1975), 91

Brown v. Texas, 443 U.S. 47 (1979), 161

Brown v. Thompson, 462 U.S. 835 (1983), 125, 300

Buckley v. Valeo, 424 U.S. 1 (1976), 320, 329, 330

Buffalo Forge Company, Inc. v. Steelworkers, 428 U.S. 397 (1976), 232

Bullington v. Missouri, 451 U.S. 430 (1981), 95

Butz, v. Economou, 438 U.S. 478 (1978), 320, 410–11, 432

Caban v. Mohammed, 441 U.S. 380 (1979), 298, 360, 362

Cabell v. Chavez-Salido, 454 U.S. 432 (1982), 86

Caldwell v. Mississippi, 472 U.S. 320 (1985), 233, 258

Califano v. Westcott, 442 U.S. 682 (1979), 84

California v. Carney, 471 U.S. 386 (1985), 161, 348, 367

California v. Ciraolo, 476 U.S. 207 (1986), 161, 281, 458

California v. Greenwood, 108 S.Ct. 1625 (1988), 454

California v. LaRue, 409 U.S. 109 (1972), 329

California v. Ramos, 463 U.S. 992 (1983), 95, 232, 258

Camara v. Municipal Court, 387 U.S. 523 (1967), 382

Cannon v. University of Chicago, 441 U.S. 677 (1979), 363

Cantor v. Detroit Edison Co., 428 U.S. 579 (1976), 80

Cardwell v. Lewis, 417 U.S. 583 (1974), 99

Carey v. Population Services International, 431 U.S. 678 (1977), 328, 352, 357, 424

Carter v. Kentucky, 450 U.S. 288 (1981), 58, 323

Castaneda v. Partida, 430 U.S. 482 (1977), 63, 94

CBS, Inc. v. Democratic National Committee, 412 U.S. 94 (1973), 190, 191

Central Hudson Gas and Electric Corp. v. Public Service Commission of New York, 447 U.S. 557 (1980), 98, 328, 352–53

Chambers v. Florida, 309 U.S. 227 (1940), 36

Chambers v. Maroney, 399 U.S. 42 (1970), 421

Chandler v. Florida, 449 U.S. 560 (1981), 155, 391

Chaplinsky v. New Hampshire, 315 U.S. 568 (1942), 288

Chicago Teachers Union, Local No. 1, AFT, AFL-CIO v. Hudson, 475 U.S. 292 (1986), 356

Chimel v. California, 395 U.S. 752 (1969), 388, 395, 396

Citizens to Preserve Overton Park v. Volpe, 401 U.S. 402 (1971), 61

City of Akron v. Akron Center for Reproductive Health, Inc., 462 U.S. 416 (1983), 264, 291, 308

City of Cleburne, Texas v. Cleburne Living Center, 473 U.S. 432 (1985), 358–59, 363, 364, 372

City of Los Angeles v. Taxpayers for Vincent, 466 U.S. 289 (1984), 352

City of Los Angeles, Dept. of Water and Power v. Manhart, 435 U.S. 702 (1978), 85, 267, 362, 374

City of Mobile, Alabama v. Bolden, 446 U.S. 55 (1980), 226, 362, 374, 389, 417

City of Newport v. Fact Concerts, Inc., 453 U.S. 247 (1981), 77

City of Richmond v. J. A. Croson Co., 109 S.Ct. 706 (1989), 448, 449

Civil Rights Cases, 109 U.S. 3 (1983), 174, 385, 398

Civil Service Commission v. National Association of Letter Carriers, 413 U.S. 548 (1973), 191, 415

Clark v. Community for Creative Non-Violence, 468 U.S. 288 (1984), 230–31

Clay v. United States, 403 U.S. 698 (1971), 415

Cleavinger v. Saxner, 469 U.S. 1206 (1985), 90

Clemons v. Board of Education, 228 F.2d 853 (6th Cir. 1956), 380

Cleveland Board of Education v. LaFleur, 414 U.S. 632 (1974), 161

Codispoti v. Pennsylvania, 418 U.S. 506 (1974), 99

Cohen v. California, 403 U.S. 15 (1971), 55, 81, 196, 199

Coker v. Georgia, 433 U.S. 584 (1977), 156, 312, 388, 399, 419

Colautti v. Franklin, 439 U.S. 379 (1979), 99

Colegrove v. Green, 328 U.S. 549 (1946), 204, 210

Coleman v. Alabama, 399 U.S. 1 (1970), 55–56, 58, 62, 155

Colonial Pipeline Co. v. Traigle, 421 U.S. 100 (1975), 80

Colonnade Catering Corp. v. United States, 397 U.S. 72 (1970), 62

Colorado v. Connelly, 107 S.Ct. 515 (1986), 454

Columbia Broadcasting System, Inc. v. Democratic National Committee, 412 U.S. 94 (1973), 191

Columbus Board of Education v. Penick, 443 U.S. 449 (1979), 296, 326, 416, 430

Commissioner of Internal Revenue v. Shapiro, 424 U.S. 614 (1976), 75

Committee for Public Education and Religious Liberty v. Nyquist, 413 U.S. 756 (1973), 313, 459

Committee for Public Education and Religious Liberty v. Regan, 444 U.S. 646 (1980), 84, 313, 350–51, 416, 459

Commodity Futures Trading Commission v. Schor, 478 U.S. 833 (1986), 261

Commonwealth Edison Co. v. Montana, 453 U.S. 609 (1981), 98

Communist Party of Indiana v. Whitcomb, 414 U.S. 441 (1974), 342

Complete Auto Transit, Inc. v. Brady, 430 U.S. 274 (1977), 80

Connecticut v. Teal, 457 U.S. 440 (1982), 268

Connecticut Board of Pardons v. Dumschat, 452 U.S. 458 (1981), 371

Connick v. Myers, 461 U.S. 138 (1983), 111

Connolly v. Pension Ben. Guar. Corp., 475 U.S. 211 (1986), 261

Connor v. Finch, 431 U.S. 407 (1977), 299

Consolidated Edison Co. of New York v. Public Service Commission of New York, 447 U.S. 530 (1980), 98, 313

Consolidated Rail Corporation v. Railway Labor Executives Association, 109 S.Ct. 2477 (1989), 461

Container Corp. v. Franchise Tax Board, 463 U.S. 159 (1983), 303–4

Coolidge v. New Hampshire, 403 U.S. 443 (1971), 45, 55, 57–58, 62

Cooper v. Aaron, 358 U.S. 1 (1958), 458

Corbitt v. New Jersey, 439 U.S. 212 (1978), 370

Cornelius v. NAACP Legal Defense and Educational Fund, Inc., 473 U.S. 788 (1985), 262

Couch v. United States, 409 U.S. 322 (1973), 187

Counselman v. Hitchcock, 142 U.S. 547 (1892), 283

Cox v. Louisiana, 379 U.S. 559 (1965), 44

Craig v. Boren, 429 U.S. 190 (1976), 23, 266, 298, 328, 358, 359, 362, 372, 390, 436, 458

Crampton v. Ohio, 402 U.S. 183 (1971), 398

Crane v. Kentucky, 476 U.S. 683 (1986), 256

Crawford v. Board of Education of City of Los Angeles, 458 U.S. 527 (1982), 86, 269

Cruzan v. Missouri, 110 S.Ct. 2841 (1990), 461

Curtis Pub. Co. v. Butts, 388 U.S. 130 (1967), 289, 391

Dalia v. United States, 441 U.S. 238 (1979), 366, 367

Dames & Moore v. Regan, 453 U.S. 654 (1981), 301, 320

Dandridge v. Williams, 397 U.S. 471 (1970), 62, 191, 202, 206, 226, 227, 389, 393

Darden v. Wainwright, 477 U.S. 168 (1986), 90

Davidson v. Cannon, 474 U.S. 344 (1986), 90

Davis v. Bandemer, 478 U.S. 109 (1986), 204, 210, 300, 417–18

Day-Brite Lighting Co. v. Missouri, 342 U.S. 421 (1952), 190

Dayton Board of Education v. Brinkman (Dayton II), 443 U.S. 526 (1979), 326, 416, 430

DeFunis v. Odegaard, 416 U.S. 312 (1974), 184

DeJonge v. Oregon, 299 U.S. 353 (1937), 442

Delaware v. Prouse, 440 U.S. 648 (1979), 421, 432

Delaware v. Van Arsdall, 475 U.S. 673 (1986), 365–66

DelCostello v. International Brotherhood of Teamsters, 462 U.S. 151 (1983), 274

Dennis v. United States, 341 U.S. 494 (1951), 190

Dent v. United States, 367 U.S. 456 (1961), 405

Department of Revenue of State of Washington v. Association of Washington Stevedoring Companies, 435 U.S. 734 (1978), 98, 304

Doe v. Bolton, 410 U.S. 179 (1973), 98, 150, 186, 386

Doe v. Commonwealth's Attorney, 425 U.S. 901 (1976), 387

Doe v. McMillan, 412 U.S. 306 (1973), 137, 412

Donovan v. Dewey, 452 U.S. 594 (1981), 382

Douglas v. California, 372 U.S. 353 (1963), 206

Dow Chemical Co. v. United States, 476 U.S. 227 (1986), 161

Doyle v. Ohio, 427 U.S. 610 (1976), 368

Dun & Bradstreet, Inc. v. Greenmoss Builders, Inc., 472 U.S. 749 (1985), 113, 414

Dunaway v. New York, 442 U.S. 200 (1979), 367

Duncan v. Louisiana, 391 U.S. 145 (1968), 382, 383, 420
Dunn v. Blumstein, 405 U.S. 330 (1972), 161, 389
Dutton v. Evans, 400 U.S. 74 (1970), 219–20
Dyson v. Stein, 401 U.S. 200 (1971), 179

Eakin v. Raub, 12 Sergeant & Rawle 330 (Pa., 1825), 126
Eastern Airlines v. Floyd, 110 S.Ct. 2585 (1990), 454
Eastland v. United States Servicemen's Fund, 421 U.S. 491 (1975), 138–39
Edelman v. Jordan, 415 U.S. 651 (1974), 323
Edwards v. Aguillard, 107 S.Ct. 2573 (1987), 290
Edwards v. Arizona, 451 U.S. 477 (1981), 419
EEOC v. Wyoming, 460 U.S. 226 (1983), 118–19, 250, 305, 348–49, 364, 374
Ehlert v. United States, 402 U.S. 99 (1971), 190
Eisen v. Carlisle & Jacquelin, 417 U.S. 156 (1974), 190
Eisenstadt v. Baird, 405 U.S. 438 (1972), 150, 185, 358, 387
Elkins v. United States, 364 U.S. 206 (1960), 387–88
Ellis v. Dyson, 421 U.S. 426 (1975), 77
Elrod v. Burns, 427 U.S. 347 (1976), 287–88
Energy Reserves Group, Inc. v. Kansas Power & Light Co., 459 U.S. 400 (1983), 126
Engel v. Vitale, 370 U.S. 421 (1962), 16, 392, 393, 402, 403
Engle v. Isaac, 456 U.S. 107 (1982), 254, 255
Enmund v. Florida, 458 U.S. 782 (1982), 125, 258, 419, 426
Environmental Protection Agency v. Mink, 410 U.S. 73 (1973), 190
Erznoznik v. Jacksonville, 422 U.S. 205 (1975), 312
Escobedo v. Illinois, 378 U.S. 478 (1964), 388
Estelle v. Smith, 451 U.S. 454 (1981), 154, 156, 458

Estep v. United States, 327 U.S. 114 (1946), 190
Estes v. Dallas NAACP, 444 U.S. 437 (1980), 295–96
Estes v. Texas, 381 U.S. 532 (1965), 391
Evans v. Abney, 396 U.S. 435 (1970), 50–51, 62, 191
Evans v. Newton, 382 U.S. 296 (1966), 385
Everson v. Board of Education, 330 U.S. 1 (1947), 180, 436
Examining Board of Engineers, Architects and Surveyors v. Flores de Otero, 426 U.S. 572 (1976), 85–86
Exxon Corp. v. Eagerton, 462 U.S. 176 (1983), 126
Exxon Corp. v. Governor of Maryland, 437 U.S. 117 (1978), 80

Fare v. Michael C., 442 U.S. 707 (1979), 93
Faretta v. California, 422 U.S. 806 (1975), 93
FCC v. League of Women Voters of California, 468 U.S. 364 (1984), 351
FCC v. Pacifica Foundation, 438 U.S. 726 (1978), 353
Federal Bureau of Investigation v. Abramson, 456 U.S. 615 (1982), 264
Federal Energy Regulatory Commission v. Mississippi, 456 U.S. 742 (1982), 70, 78, 242, 251, 305
Federal Power Commission v. Natural Gas Pipeline Co., 315 U.S. 575 (1942), 211
Fein v. Selective Service System, 405 U.S. 365 (1972), 190
Firefighters Local Union No. 1784 v. Stotts, 467 U.S. 561 (1984), 24, 87, 270–71, 327, 348, 360, 417, 427, 458
First National Bank of Boston v. Bellotti, 435 U.S. 765 (1978), 144, 313, 329, 330
Flast v. Cohen, 392 U.S. 83 (1968), 175, 384
Flood v. Kuhn, 407 U.S. 258 (1972), 74
Florida v. Meyers, 466 U.S. 380 (1984), 365
Florida v. Royer, 460 U.S. 491 (1983), 99, 421
Florida Department of State v. Treasure

Salvors, Inc., 458 U.S. 670 (1982), 349

Flower v. United States, 407 U.S. 197 (1972), 331

Foley v. Connelie, 435 U.S. 291 (1978), 86

Ford Motor Co. v. EEOC, 458 U.S. 219 (1982), 268

Francis v. Henderson, 425 U.S. 536 (1976), 323

Frank v. Maryland, 359 U.S. 360 (1959), 382

Franks v. Bowman Transportation Co., 424 U.S. 747 (1976), 161

Franks v. Delaware, 438 U.S. 154 (1978), 91

Freedman v. Maryland, 380 U.S. 51 (1965), 210

Friedman v. Rogers, 440 U.S. 1 (1979), 98

Frontiero v. Richardson, 411 U.S. 677 (1973), 22, 161, 191, 266, 267, 298, 436, 458

Fry v. United States, 421 U.S. 542 (1975), 322, 337

Fullilove v. Klutznick, 448 U.S. 448 (1980), 149, 297, 346, 359, 360–61, 362, 389, 435, 439, 449, 458

Furman v. Georgia, 408 U.S. 238 (1972), 22, 74, 94, 114, 156, 187–88, 222–24, 237, 284–85, 286, 332, 388, 398, 399, 419

Furnco Construction Corp. v. Waters, 438 U.S. 567 (1978), 217–18

F. W. Woolworth Co. v. Taxation and Revenue Department of State of New Mexico, 458 U.S. 354 (1982), 274

Gaffney v. Cummings, 412 U.S. 735 (1973), 210

Gannett Co., Inc. v. DePasquale, 443 U.S. 368 (1979), 144, 354–55, 390

Garcia v. San Antonio Metropolitan Transit Authority, 469 U.S. 528 (1985), 23, 76, 78–79, 119, 250, 251, 305, 349

Gardner v. Florida, 430 U.S. 349 (1977), 369

Garner v. Louisiana, 368 U.S. 157 (1961), 196, 197, 199, 200

Garrett v. United States, 471 U.S. 773 (1985), 365, 368, 369

Geders v. United States, 425 U.S. 80 (1976), 162

General Building Contractors Association v. Pennsylvania, 458 U.S. 375 (1982), 271

General Electric Co. v. Gilbert, 429 U.S. 125 (1976), 363

Georgia v. United States, 411 U.S. 526 (1973), 313

Gertz v. Robert Welch, Inc., 418 U.S. 323 (1974), 113, 289, 413

Gideon v. Wainwright, 372 U.S. 335 (1963), 16, 196, 208, 283

Gilette v. United States, 401 U.S. 437 (1971), 169–70

Gilligan v. Morgan, 413 U.S. 1 (1973), 73

Gilmore v. City of Montgomery, 417 U.S. 556 (1974), 86, 385

Ginzburg v. Goldwater, 396 U.S. 1049 (1970), 62, 196

Ginzburg v. United States, 383 U.S. 463 (1966), 196, 386

Gitlow v. New York, 268 U.S. 652 (1925), 442

Glass v. Louisiana, 471 U.S. 1080 (1985), 126

GM Leasing Corporation v. United States, 429 U.S. 338 (1977), 99

Goesaert v. Cleary, 335 U.S. 464 (1948), 266

Goldberg v. Kelly, 397 U.S. 254 (1970), 62, 126, 191, 192, 301–2

Golden State Transit Corp. v. City of Los Angeles, 475 U.S. 608 (1986), 98

Goldfarb v. Califano, 430 U.S. 199 (1977), 363, 374

Goldman v. Weinberger, 475 U.S. 503 (1986), 83, 264

Gooding v. Wilson, 405 U.S. 518 (1972), 81

Goodwin v. United States, 446 U.S. 986 (1980), 89–90

Gosa v. Mayden, 413 U.S. 665 (1973), 92

Goss v. Lopez, 419 U.S. 565 (1975), 302–3, 423

Graham v. Richardson, 403 U.S. 365 (1971), 85, 191, 299, 390

Grand Rapids School District v. Ball, 473
U.S. 373 (1985), 127, 259, 459
Gravel v. United States, 408 U.S. 606
(1972), 137, 172, 174–75, 412
Green v. County Board of Education of New
Kent County, Va., 391 U.S. 430 (1968),
295, 326
Greene v. Lindsey, 456 U.S. 444 (1982),
260
Gregg v. Georgia, 428 U.S. 153 (1976),
23, 125, 156, 222–24, 285–86, 309,
369, 372, 388, 393, 399, 419, 458
Griffin v. Illinois, 351 U.S. 12 (1956),
206
Griggs v. Duke Power Co., 401 U.S. 424
(1971), 149, 450
Griswold v. Connecticut, 381 U.S. 479
(1965), 16, 45, 53, 184, 185, 196,
208, 211, 290, 291, 358, 381–82
Grosjean v. American Press Co., 297 U.S.
233 (1936), 263, 442
Grove City College v. Bell, 465 U.S. 555
(1984), 84, 269, 313, 418
Gustafson v. Florida, 414 U.S. 260
(1973), 395
Gutknecht v. United States, 396 U.S. 295
(1970), 170

Haig v. Agee, 453 U.S. 280 (1981), 74,
139
Hamling v. United States, 418 U.S. 87
(1974), 191, 458
Hampton v. Mow Sun Wong, 426 U.S. 88
(1976), 364
Harlow v. Fitzgerald, 457 U.S. 800
(1982), 320
Harper v. Virginia State Board of Elections,
383 U.S. 663 (1966), 46, 389, 390
Harper & Row Publishers, Inc. v. Nation
Enterprises, 471 U.S. 539 (1985), 260
Harris v. McRae, 448 U.S. 297 (1980),
88, 357, 387, 396
Harris v. New York, 401 U.S. 222 (1971),
21, 154, 161, 237, 387, 458
Hawaii Housing Authority v. Midkiff, 467
U.S. 229 (1984), 260
Healy v. James, 408 U.S. 169 (1972),
331, 342
Heart of Atlanta Motel v. United States,
379 U.S. 241 (1964), 16, 126, 174

Heath v. Alabama, 474 U.S. 82 (1985),
257
Heffron v. International Society for Krishna
Consciousness, 452 U.S. 640 (1981),
416
Henderson v. Bannan, 256 F.2d 363 (6th
Cir. 1958), 380–81, 388
Hensley v. Municipal Court, 411 U.S. 345
(1973), 98
Herndon v. Lowry, 301 U.S. 242 (1937),
442
Hicks v. Miranda, 422 U.S. 332 (1975),
323
Hills v. Gautreaux, 425 U.S. 284 (1976),
233
Hishon v. King & Spalding, 467 U.S. 69
(1984), 267
Hisquierdo v. Hisquierdo, 439 U.S. 572
(1979), 98
H. L. v. Matheson, 450 U.S. 398 (1981),
356
Hobby v. United States, 468 U.S. 339
(1984), 267
Hodel v. Virginia Surface Mining and
Reclamation Association, 452 U.S. 264
(1981), 322
Hodgson v. Minnestoa, 110 S.Ct. 2926
(1980), 453, 461
Holloway v. Arkansas, 435 U.S. 475
(1978), 162
Hooper v. Bernalillo County Assessor, 472
U.S. 612 (1985), 363
Houchins v. KQED, Inc., 438 U.S. 1
(1978), 144, 335, 346, 390, 400–401
Hoyt v. Minnesota, 399 U.S. 524 (1970),
64
Hudnut v. American Booksellers Association,
475 U.S. 1132 (1986), 263
Hudson v. Palmer, 468 U.S. 517 (1984),
24, 161, 261, 346, 371, 439, 458
Huffman v. Pursue, Ltd., 420 U.S. 592
(1975), 323
Hunt v. McNair, 413 U.S. 734 (1973),
275
Hunter v. Underwood, 471 U.S. 222
(1985), 325
Hutchinson v. Proxmire, 443 U.S. 111
(1979), 137
Hutto v. Finney, 437 U.S. 678 (1978),
324, 349

Hynes v. Mayor of Oradell, 425 U.S. 610 (1976), 161

Illinois v. Allen, 397 U.S. 337 (1970), 51–52
Illinois v. Gates, 462 U.S. 213 (1983), 324
Illinois v. Vitale, 447 U.S. 410 (1981), 365, 368
Industrial Union Dept., AFL-CIO v. American Petroleum Institute, 448 U.S. 607 (1980), 321
Ingraham v. Wright, 430 U.S. 651 (1977), 287
In re Gault, 387 U.S. 1 (1967), 387, 401–2
In re Griffiths, 413 U.S. 717 (1973), 299
In re Primus, 436 U.S. 412 (1978), 330
In re Stolar, 401 U.S. 23 (1971), 62, 82
In re Winship, 397 U.S. 358 (1970), 51, 58, 155, 207, 208, 387, 401
INS v. Chadha, 462 U.S. 919 (1983), 24, 134–35, 136, 341, 411–12
INS v. Lopez-Mendoza, 468 U.S. 1032 (1984), 422

Jackson v. Indiana, 406 U.S. 715 (1972), 85
Jackson v. Metropolitan Edison Co., 419 U.S. 345 (1974), 385
Jacksonville Bulk Terminals v. International Longshoreman's Association, 457 U.S. 702 (1982), 232
Jacobellis v. Ohio, 378 U.S. 184 (1964), 386, 391
James v. Valtierra, 402 U.S. 137 (1971), 52, 237
Japan Line, Ltd. v. County of Los Angeles, 441 U.S. 434 (1979), 80
Jefferson v. Hackney, 406 U.S. 535 (1972), 227
Jefferson County Pharmaceutical Association, Inc. v. Abbott Laboratories, 460 U.S. 150 (1983), 274
Jenkins v. Anderson, 447 U.S. 231 (1980), 368
Jenkins v. Georgia, 418 U.S. 153 (1974), 342
Jett v. Dallas Independent School District, 109 S.Ct. 2702 (1989), 461

Johnson v. Louisiana, 406 U.S. 356 (1972), 73, 191, 282, 420–21
Johnson v. State of New Jersey, 384 U.S. 719 (1966), 209
Johnson v. Transportation Agency, 94 L.Ed. 2d 615 (1987), 107, 313
Jones v. Alfred H. Mayer Co., 392 U.S. 409 (1968), 385, 397–98, 458
Jones v. Barnes, 463 U.S. 745 (1983), 162
Jones v. Board of Education, 397 U.S. 31 (1970), 191
Jones v. North Carolina Prisoners Union, 433 U.S. 119 (1977), 331
Jones v. Wolf, 443 U.S. 595 (1979), 313
Jurek v. Texas, 428 U.S. 262 (1976), 125

Kahn v. Shevin, 416 U.S. 351 (1974), 84, 184, 418
Kaplan v. California, 413 U.S. 115 (1973), 191
Karcher v. Daggett, 462 U.S. 725 (1983), 108–9, 299–300
Karr v. Schmidt, 401 U.S. 1201 (1971), 62
Kassel v. Consolidated Freightways Corp., 450 U.S. 662 (1981), 303, 322
Kastigar v. United States, 406 U.S. 441 (1972), 283, 284, 312
Katz v. United States, 389 U.S. 347 (1967), 45, 191, 388, 395, 396
Katzenbach v. McClung, 379 U.S. 294 (1964), 126, 174
Katzenbach v. Morgan, 384 U.S. 641 (1966), 384
Keyes v. School District No. 1, Denver, 413 U.S. 189 (1973), 22, 148, 183, 294–95, 326, 458, 459
Keyishian v. Board of Regents, 385 U.S. 589 (1967), 111, 125
Kingsley Books v. Brown, 354 U.S. 436 (1957), 210
Kirby v. Illinois, 406 U.S. 682 (1972), 237, 458
Kirkpatrick v. Preisler, 394 U.S. 526 (1969), 417
Kleindienst v. Mandel, 408 U.S. 753 (1972), 74, 178
Korematsu v. United States, 323 U.S. 214 (1944), 42, 189, 443, 460

Kramer v. Union Free School District, 395 U.S. 621 (1969), 389

Labine v. Vincent, 401 U.S. 532 (1971), 62

Laird v. Tatum, 408 U.S. 1 (1972), 142, 172

Larkin v. Grendel's Den, Inc., 459 U.S. 116 (1982), 147, 459

Lassiter v. Department of Social Services of Durham County, North Carolina, 452 U.S. 18 (1981), 67, 93

Lassiter v. Northampton County Board of Elections, 360 U.S. 45 (1959), 384

Lau v. Nichols, 414 U.S. 563 (1974), 459

Law Students Civil Rights Research Council v. Wadmond, 401 U.S. 154 (1971), 62

Lehman v. Lycoming County Children's Services Agency, 458 U.S. 502 (1982), 98

Lehr v. Robertson, 463 U.S. 248 (1983), 268

Leis v. Flynt, 439 U.S. 438 (1979), 370

Lemon v. Kurtzman, 403 U.S. 602 (1971), 21, 146, 147, 181, 191, 258, 290, 459

Levitt v. Committee for Public Education and Religious Liberty, 413 U.S. 472 (1973), 161

Levy v. Louisiana, 391 U.S. 68 (1968), 191, 390

Lewis v. BT Investment Managers, 447 U.S. 27 (1980), 80

Lewis v. City of New Orleans, 408 U.S. 913 (1972), 161, 288

Lewis v. Martin, 397 U.S. 552 (1970), 62

Linda R. S. v. Richard D., 410 U.S. 614 (1973), 384

Lindsey v. Normet, 405 U.S. 56 (1972), 192

Lloyd Corporation v. Tanner, 407 U.S. 551 (1972), 177, 289, 329

Local Number 93, International Association of Firefighters, AFL-CIO CLC v. City of Cleveland, 478 U.S. 501 (1986), 270, 271, 327

Local 28 of the Sheet Metal Workers' International Association v. EEOC, 478 U.S. 421 (1986), 270, 271, 327

Lockett v. Ohio, 438 U.S. 586 (1978), 94, 156, 399

Logan v. Zimmerman Brush Co., 455 U.S. 422 (1982), 87

Lo-Ji Sales, Inc. v. New York, 442 U.S. 319 (1979), 161

Lorance v. AT&T Technologies, Inc., 109 S.Ct. 2261 (1989), 449–50

Lucas v. Forty-Fourth General Assembly of State of Colorado, 377 U.S. 713 (1964), 205, 384

Ludwig v. Massachusetts, 427 U.S. 618 (1976), 99

Lynch v. Donnelly, 465 U.S. 668 (1984), 24, 83, 147, 258, 264, 402, 459

Lyng v. Payne, 476 U.S. 926 (1986), 260

Maher v. Roe, 432 U.S. 464 (1977), 291, 356–57

Maine v. Taylor, 477 U.S. 131 (1986), 80

Maine v. Thiboutot, 488 U.S. 1 (1980), 307

Mancusi v. Stubbs, 408 U.S. 204 (1972), 219, 220

Manson v. Brathwaite, 432 U.S. 98 (1977), 99

Mapp v. Ohio, 367 U.S. 643 (1961), 16, 45, 57, 91, 191, 337, 387

Marbury v. Madison, 1 Cranch 137 (1803), 126

Marchetti v. United States, 390 U.S. 39 (1968), 196

Marcus v. Search Warrant, 367 U.S. 717 (1961), 210

Marks v. United States, 430 U.S. 188 (1977), 354

Marrese v. American Academy of Orthopedic Surgeons, 470 U.S. 373 (1985), 274

Marsh v. Chambers, 463 U.S. 783 (1983), 147, 459

Marshall v. Barlow's, Inc., 436 U.S. 307 (1978), 366

Martin v. Ohio, 445 U.S. 953 (1982), 284

Martin v. Wilks, 109 S.Ct. 2180 (1989), 448, 449

Maryland v. Macon, 472 U.S. 463 (1985), 263

Massachusetts v. Laird, 400 U.S. 886 (1970), 190

Massachusetts v. Sheppard, 468 U.S. 981 (1984), 367, 422

Massachusetts Board of Retirement v. Murgia, 427 U.S. 307 (1976), 390

Massiah v. United States, 377 U.S. 201 (1964), 93, 388

Mathews v. Eldridge, 424 U.S. 319 (1976), 302

Mathews v. Lucas, 427 U.S. 495 (1976), 85, 360

Mayberry v. Pennsylvania, 400 U.S. 455 (1971), 62

McCarty v. McCarty, 453 U.S. 210 (1981), 97, 98

McClesky v. Kemp, 482 U.S. 920 (1987), 286, 454

McCollum v. Board of Education, 333 U.S. 203 (1948), 313

McElroy v. United States, 455 U.S. 642 (1982), 253

McGautha v. California, 402 U.S. 183 (1971), 398

McKart v. United States, 395 U.S. 185 (1969), 190

McKeiver v. Pennsylvania, 403 U.S. 528 (1971), 94, 187, 401

McLaughlin v. Florida, 379 U.S. 184 (1964), 389

McMann v. Richardson, 397 U.S. 759 (1970), 419–20

Meachem v. Fano, 427 U.S. 215 (1976), 371

Meek v. Pittenger, 421 U.S. 349 (1975), 392, 459

Memoirs v. Massachusetts, 383 U.S. 413 (1966), 125

Memphis Light, Gas and Water Division v. Craft, 436 U.S. 1 (1978), 302

Meritor Savings Bank v. Vinson, 477 U.S. 57 (1986), 218, 268

Metro Broadcasting v. FCC, 110 S.Ct. 2997 (1990), 447, 449

Metromedia, Inc. v. City of San Diego, 453 U.S. 490 (1981), 352

Metropolitan Life Ins. Co. v. Ward, 470 U.S. 869 (1985), 252

Meyer v. Nebraska, 262 U.S. 390 (1923), 184

Miami Herald Publishing Co. v. Tornillo, 418 U.S. 241 (1974), 144, 342

Michael M. v. Superior Court of Sonoma County, 450 U.S. 464 (1981), 24, 266, 328, 359, 362, 374

Michigan v. DeFillippo, 443 U.S. 31 (1979), 153–54

Michigan v. Long, 463 U.S. 1032 (1983), 76, 254–55, 365

Michigan v. Mosley, 423 U.S. 96 (1975), 116

Michigan v. Sitz, 110 S.Ct. 2481 (1990), 454

Migra v. Warren City School Dist. Bd. of Educ., 465 U.S. 75 (1984), 77

Miller v. California, 413 U.S. 15 (1973), 22, 125, 145, 179, 191, 354, 414, 458

Miller v. Fenton, 474 U.S. 104 (1985), 255

Milliken v. Bradley (Milliken I), 418 U.S. 717 (1974), 23, 149, 183, 233, 237, 389, 416, 458

Mills v. Electric Auto-Lite Co., 396 U.S. 375 (1970), 58

Minneapolis Star & Tribune Co. v. Minnesota Commissioner of Revenue, 460 U.S. 575 (1983), 263, 265

Minnesota State Board for Community Colleges v. Knight, 465 U.S. 271 (1984), 262

Miranda v. Arizona, 384 U.S. 436 (1966), 16, 91, 93, 115, 116, 132, 154, 208, 209, 211, 219, 221, 233, 255, 337, 338, 368, 387, 388, 393, 419, 439, 454

Mississippi University for Women v. Hogan, 458 U.S. 718 (1982), 85, 265–66, 267, 298

Missouri v. Jenkins, 110 S.Ct. 1651 (1990), 447, 461

Mitchell v. United States, 386 U.S. 972 (1967), 190

Mohasco Corp. v. Silver, 447 U.S. 807 (1980), 87

Monell v. New York City Department of Social Services, 436 U.S. 658 (1978), 308

Monroe v. Pape, 365 U.S. 167 (1961), 308

Moore v. City of East Cleveland, Ohio, 431 U.S. 494 (1977), 292, 358, 427

Moorman Co. v. Bair, 437 U.S. 267 (1978), 303

Moose Lodge No. 107 v. Irvis, 407 U.S. 163 (1972), 191, 200–201, 325, 385

Mora v. McNamara, 389 U.S. 934 (1967), 190, 393

Moran v. Burbine, 475 U.S. 412 (1986), 255, 256, 458

Morris v. Slappy, 461 U.S. 1 (1983), 162

Morse v. Boswell, 393 U.S. 1052 (1969), 190

Morton v. Mancari, 417 U.S. 535 (1974), 87

Murray v. Carrier, 477 U.S. 478 (1986), 256

Murray v. United States, 108 S.Ct. 2529 (1988), 454

NAACP v. Alabama, 357 U.S. 449 (1958), 196

NAACP v. Claiborne Hardware Co., 458 U.S. 886 (1982), 355

National Cable Television Association, Inc. v. United States, 415 U.S. 336 (1974), 190

National League of Cities v. Usery, 426 U.S. 833 (1976), 23, 76, 78–79, 117–19, 250, 251, 305, 322, 348–49, 384, 439

National R.R. Passenger Corp. v. National Assn. of R.R. Passengers, 414 U.S. 453 (1974), 190

National Treasury Employees Union v. Von Raab, 109 S.Ct. 1384 (1989), 453, 454

Near v. Minnesota, 283 U.S. 697 (1931), 442

Nebraska Press Association v. Stuart, 423 U.S. 1327 (1975), 82

Nebraska Press Association v. Stuart, 427 U.S. 539 (1976), 144, 342, 351, 391, 394

Nelson v. O'Neil, 402 U.S. 622 (1971), 219, 220

Nevada v. Hall, 440 U.S. 410 (1979), 336

New Jersey v. Portash, 440 U.S. 450 (1979), 126

New Jersey v. T. L. O., 469 U.S. 325 (1985), 99

New Motor Vehicle Board of California v. Orrin W. Fox Co., 439 U.S. 96 (1978), 97

Newport News Shipbuilding and Dry Dock Co. v. EEOC, 462 U.S. 669 (1983), 268

New York v. Class, 475 U.S. 106 (1986), 255

New York v. Ferber, 458 U.S. 747 (1982), 263, 353–54, 414

New York v. Quarles, 467 U.S. 649 (1984), 255, 324, 458

New York v. United States, 342 U.S. 882 (1951), 190

New York Times Co. v. Sullivan, 376 U.S. 254 (1964), 16, 113, 179, 289, 391, 413

New York Times Co. v. United States, 403 U.S. 713 (1971), 22, 43–44, 53–55, 62, 82, 139, 144, 171, 197–99, 200, 393

Nix v. Williams, 467 U.S. 431 (1984), 24, 154, 255, 367

Nixon v. Administrator of General Services, 433 U.S. 425 (1977), 320

Nixon v. Fitzgerald, 457 U.S. 731 (1982), 73, 139, 237, 320, 410

NLRB v. Catholic Bishop of Chicago, 440 U.S. 490 (1979), 161

NLRB v. Lannom Mfg. Co., 226 F.2d 194 (6th Cir. 1955), 380

NLRB v. Retail Store Employees Union, Local 1001, 447 U.S. 607 (1980), 355

North v. Russell, 427 U.S. 328 (1976), 162

North Carolina v. Alford, 400 U.S. 25 (1970), 420

Northeast Bancorp, Inc. v. Board of Governors of Federal Reserve System, 472 U.S. 159 (1985), 252–53

North Haven Board of Education v. Bell, 456 U.S. 512 (1982), 84, 268

Nyquist v. Mauclet, 432 U.S. 1 (1977), 98, 299

O'Bannon v. Town Court Nursing Center, 447 U.S. 773 (1980), 75

Ocala Star-Banner Co. v. Damron, 401 U.S. 295 (1971), 62

Ohio v. Akron Center for Reproductive

Health, 110 S.Ct. 2972 (1990), 453, 461

Ohio v. Johnson, 467 U.S. 493 (1984), 368

Oliver v. United States, 446 U.S. 170 (1984), 281

Olmstead v. United States, 277 U.S. 438 (1928), 185, 395

On Lee v. United States, 343 U.S. 747 (1952), 191

Oregon v. Elstad, 470 U.S. 298 (1985), 221, 255, 374

Oregon v. Hass, 420 U.S. 714 (1975), 76, 233–34, 458

Oregon v. Kennedy, 456 U.S. 667 (1982), 126

Oregon v. Mitchell, 400 U.S. 112 (1970), 161, 384

Organization for a Better Austin v. Keefe, 402 U.S. 415 (1971), 161

Orr v. Orr, 440 U.S. 268 (1979), 85

Ortwein v. Schwab, 410 U.S. 656 (1973), 192

O'Shea v. Littleton, 414 U.S. 488 (1974), 190

Pacific Gas and Electric Co. v. Public Utilities Commission of California, 475 U.S. 1 (1986), 313

Pacific Gas & Electric Co. v. State Energy Resources Conservation and Development Commission, 461 U.S. 190 (1983), 98

Palko v. Connecticut, 302 U.S. 319 (1937), 207, 208, 443

Palmer v. Thompson, 403 U.S. 217 (1971), 50–51, 86, 191, 416

Papachristou v. City of Jacksonville, 405 U.S. 156 (1972), 192

Papish v. Board of Curators of University of Missouri, 410 U.S. 667 (1973), 331

Paris Adult Theatre I v. Slaton, 413 U.S. 49 (1973), 110, 125, 145, 191, 391, 458

Parisi v. Davidson, 405 U.S. 34 (1972), 190

Parker v. Levy, 417 U.S. 733 (1974), 81, 171, 190, 331

Parker v. North Carolina, 397 U.S. 790 (1970), 420

Parratt v. Taylor, 451 U.S. 527 (1981), 90, 218–19, 323

Patriot Co. v. Roy, 401 U.S. 265 (1971), 62

Pattern Makers' League of North America v. NLRB, 473 U.S. 95 (1985), 76

Patterson v. McLean Credit Union, 109 S.Ct. 2363 (1989), 451

Patton v. Young, 467 U.S. 1025 (1984), 348

Paul v. Davis, 424 U.S. 693 (1976), 323

Payton v. New York, 445 U.S. 573 (1980), 23, 91, 364, 366, 367

Pell v. Procunier, 417 U.S. 817 (1974), 191, 355, 390

Pennhurst v. Halderman, 451 U.S. 1 (1981), 323

Pennhurst State School and Hospital v. Halderman, 465 U.S. 89 (1984), 313–14, 349

Pennsylvania v. Nelson, 350 U.S. 497 (1956), 378

Penry v. Lynaugh, 109 S.Ct. 2934 (1989), 454

Perez v. Campbell, 402 U.S. 637 (1971), 79

Perez v. United States, 402 U.S. 146 (1971), 384

Perry Education Association v. Perry Local Educators' Association, 460 U.S. 37 (1983), 112–13, 262

Personnel Administrator of Massachusetts v. Feeney, 442 U.S. 256 (1979), 360

Peterson v. City of Greenville, S.C., 373 U.S. 244 (1963), 385

Philadelphia v. New Jersey, 437 U.S. 617 (1978), 321–22

Philadelphia Newspapers, Inc. v. Hepps, 475 U.S. 767 (1986), 263, 264

Phoenix v. Kolodziejski, 399 U.S. 204 (1970), 417

Pickering v. Board of Education, 391 U.S. 563 (1968), 111

Pierce v. Society of Sisters, 268 U.S. 510 (1925), 184

Pike v. Bruce Church, Inc., 397 U.S. 137 (1970), 384

Pinkus v. United States, 436 U.S. 293 (1978), 342

Pittsburgh v. Alco Parking Corp., 417 U.S. 369 (1974), 412–13

Pittsburgh Press Co. v. Pittsburgh

Commission on Human Relations, 413 U.S. 376 (1973), 191, 391

Planned Parenthood Association of Kansas City, Missouri, Inc. v. Ashcroft, 462 U.S. 476 (1983), 98, 99

Planned Parenthood of Central Missouri v. Danforth, 428 U.S. 52 (1976), 99, 150, 356

Plessy v. Ferguson, 163 U.S. 537 (1896), 200, 217, 318

Plyler v. Doe, 457 U.S. 202 (1982), 85, 293–94

Poe v. Ullman, 367 U.S. 497 (1961), 196, 382

Polk County v. Dodson, 454 U.S. 312 (1981), 77, 97

Posadas de Puerto Rico Associates v. Tourism Co. of Puerto Rico, 478 U.S. 328 (1986), 351, 352

Powell v. Alabama, 287 U.S. 45 (1932), 208

Powell v. McCormack, 395 U.S. 486 (1969), 174

Proffitt v. Florida, 428 U.S. 242 (1976), 125

Pruneyard Shopping Center v. Robins, 447 U.S. 74 (1980), 329, 334

Pulley v. Harris, 465 U.S. 37 (1984), 125, 419

Pulliam v. Allen, 466 U.S. 522 (1984), 87

Quantity of Copies of Books v. Kansas, 378 U.S. 205 (1964), 210

Rakas v. Illinois, 439 U.S. 128 (1978), 324

Rawlings v. Kentucky, 448 U.S. 98 (1980), 324

Red Lion Broadcasting Co. v. FCC, 395 U.S. 367 (1969), 413

Reed v. Reed, 404 U.S. 71 (1971), 22, 150, 266

Reeves, Inc. v. State, 447 U.S. 429 (1980), 81, 97, 304

Regan v. Wald, 468 U.S. 222 (1984), 74, 139, 237, 320

Regents of the University of California v. Bakke, 438 U.S. 265 (1978), 23, 87, 97, 184, 225, 292, 296–97, 326, 361, 362, 389, 435, 439

Reitman v. Mulkey, 387 U.S. 369 (1967), 385, 458

Relford v. Commandant, 401 U.S. 355 (1971), 97

Reynolds v. Sims, 377 U.S. 533 (1964), 16, 202–5, 300–301, 417

Rhode Island v. Innis, 446 U.S. 291 (1980), 368, 439, 458

Rhodes v. Chapman, 452 U.S. 337 (1981), 97

Richardson v. Perales, 402 U.S. 389 (1971), 75, 191, 192

Richmond Newspapers, Inc. v. Virginia, 448 U.S. 555 (1980), 144, 324, 355, 391, 458

Ridgway v. Ridgway, 454 U.S. 46 (1981), 98

Rizzo v. Goode, 423 U.S. 362 (1976), 77, 323

Robbins v. California, 453 U.S. 420 (1981), 395

Roberts v. Louisiana, 431 U.S. 633 (1977), 94, 125, 399

Roberts v. Louisiana, 428 U.S. 325 (1976), 419

Roberts v. United States Jaycees, 468 U.S. 609 (1984), 109–10, 267, 436

Robinson v. Cahill, 62 N.J. 473 (1973), 105

Robinson v. California, 370 U.S. 660 (1962), 125

Roe v. Wade, 410 U.S. 113 (1973), 22, 70, 71, 73, 88, 98, 150, 185, 186, 243, 264–65, 271, 290–91, 308, 309, 323, 324, 333, 337, 356–57, 382, 383, 386, 387, 393, 424, 427, 429, 431, 436, 439, 452–53, 456, 458

Roemer v. Maryland Board of Public Works, 426 U.S. 736 (1976), 275, 459

Rogers v. Lodge, 458 U.S. 613 (1982), 361–62, 374

Rosado v. Wyman, 397 U.S. 397 (1970), 62, 192

Rose v. Lundy, 455 U.S. 509 (1982), 253

Rose v. Mitchell, 443 U.S. 545 (1979), 94, 98, 307

Rosenblatt v. Baer, 383 U.S. 75 (1966), 191

Rosenbloom v. Metromedia, Inc., 403 U.S. 29 (1971), 62, 125

Rosenfeld v. New Jersey, 408 U.S. 901 (1972), 288

Rostker v.Goldberg, 453 U.S. 57 (1981), 23, 266, 418

Roth v. United States, 354 U.S. 476 (1957), 110

Roudebush v. Hartke, 405 U.S. 15 (1972), 174

Rowland v. Mad River Local School District, 470 U.S. 1009 (1985), 111

Royster Guano Co. v. Virginia, 253 U.S. 412 (1920), 341

Rummel v. Estelle, 445 U.S. 263 (1980), 286–87

Runyon v. McCrary, 427 U.S. 160 (1976), 362, 385, 397, 450–51, 459

Russell v. United States, 369 U.S. 749 (1962), 405

Rutan v. Republican Party of Illinois, 110 S.Ct. 2729 (1990), 461

Sable Communications of California, Inc. v. FCC, 109 S.Ct. 2829 (1989), 461

Samuels v. Mackell, 401 U.S. 66 (1971), 177

San Antonio Independent School District v. Rodriguez, 411 U.S. 1 (1973), 225–27, 292–93, 309, 389, 393, 437

Santosky v. Kramer, 455 U.S. 745 (1982), 67

Saxbe v. Washington Post Co., 417 U.S. 843 (1974), 191, 287, 355, 390

Schad v. Borough of Mt. Ephraim, 452 U.S. 61 (1981), 414

Schall v. Martin, 467 U.S. 253 (1984), 255

Schenck v. United States, 249 U.S. 47 (1919), 177, 353

Schick v. Reed, 419 U.S. 256 (1974), 139

Schlesinger v. Reservists Committee to Stop the War, 418 U.S. 208 (1974), 142, 190

Schmerber v. California, 384 U.S. 757 (1966), 209

Schneckloth v. Bustamonte, 412 U.S. 218 (1973), 281–82, 284, 395–96

Scott v. Illinois, 440 U.S. 367 (1979), 93, 388

SEC v. Medical Committee for Human Rights, 404 U.S. 403 (1972), 190

Secretary of Interior v. California, 464 U.S. 312 (1984), 261

Segura v. United States, 468 U.S. 796 (1984), 367

Shapiro v. Thompson, 394 U.S. 618 (1969), 202, 389

Shaw v. Delta Air Lines, Inc., 463 U.S. 85 (1983), 79

Shea v. Louisiana, 470 U.S. 51 (1985), 92

Sheppard v. Maxwell, 384 U.S. 333 (1966), 387

Sherbert v. Verner, 374 U.S. 398 (1963), 391, 396–97

Sierra Club v. Morton, 405 U.S. 727 (1972), 68, 73, 190, 384

Silkwood v. Kerr-McGee Corp., 464 U.S. 238 (1984), 79, 304

Singleton v. Wulff, 428 U.S. 106 (1976), 73, 161

Skinner v. Oklahoma, 316 U.S. 535 (1942), 185, 443

Skinner v. Railway Labor Executives' Association, 109 S.Ct. 1402 (1989), 453, 454

Skipper v. South Carolina, 476 U.S. 1 (1986), 419

Slaughter House Cases, 16 Wallace 36 (1873), 210

Sloan v. Lemon, 43 U.S. 825 (1973), 313

Smith v. Allwright, 321 U.S. 649 (1944), 404

Smith v. Goguen, 415 U.S. 566 (1974), 81, 161

Smith v. Maryland, 442 U.S. 735 (1979), 99

Smith v. Murray, 477 U.S. 527 (1986), 256

Smith v. Organization of Foster Families, 431 U.S. 816 (1977), 128

Smith v. United States, 431 U.S. 291 (1977), 354

Snepp v. United States, 444 U.S. 507 (1980), 351–52

Sniadach v. Family Finance Corp., 395 U.S. 337 (1969), 191, 192

Solem v. Helm, 463 U.S. 277 (1983), 286–87

SONY Corp. of America v. Universal City Studios, 464 U.S. 417 (1984), 97

South Carolina v. Katzenbach, 383 U.S. 301 (1966), 16

South Carolina v. Regan, 465 U.S. 367 (1983), 349

South-Central-Timber Development, Inc. v. Wunnicke, 467 U.S. 82 (1984), 412

South Dakota v. Neville, 459 U.S. 553 (1983), 254

South Dakota v. Opperman, 428 U.S. 364 (1976), 161

Southeastern Promotions, Ltd. v. Conrad, 420 U.S. 546 (1975), 82, 330

Southern Burlington County NAACP v. Township of Mt. Laurel, 67 N.J. 151, 336 A.2d 713 (1975), 105, 125

Southland Corp. v. Keating, 465 U.S. 1 (1984), 251

Spaziano v. Florida, 468 U.S. 447 (1984), 99, 369

Spector Motor Service v. O'Connor, 340 U.S. 602 (1951), 80

Spence v. Washington, 418 U.S. 405 (1974), 161

Spinelli v. United States, 393 U.S. 410 (1969), 151

Stanford v. Kentucky, 109 S.Ct. 2969 (1989), 454

Stanley v. Georgia, 394 U.S. 557 (1969), 179, 426, 429

Stanley v. Illinois, 405 U.S. 645 (1972), 418, 423–24

Stanton v. Stanton, 421 U.S. 7 (1975), 84

Steffel v. Thompson, 415 U.S. 452 (1974), 342

Stone v. Graham, 449 U.S. 39 (1980), 392, 459

Stone v. Powell, 428 U.S. 465 (1976), 153, 253, 282, 388, 421

Strickland v. Washington, 466 U.S. 668 (1984), 256

Sugarman v. Dougall, 413 U.S. 634 (1973), 85

Sumner v. Mata, 449 U.S. 539 (1981), 323

Swann v. Charlotte-Mecklenburg Board of Education, 402 U.S. 1 (1971), 21, 49–50, 148, 199, 294, 439, 458, 459

Tate v. Short, 401 U.S. 395 (1971), 389

Taylor v. Louisiana, 419 U.S. 522 (1975), 420

Terry v. Ohio, 392 U.S. 1 (1968), 191, 281

Texas v. Johnson, 109 S.Ct. 2533 (1989), 461

Thomas v. Review Board, 450 U.S. 707 (1981), 391

Thomas v. Union Carbide Agr. Products Co., 473 U.S. 568 (1985), 261

Thornburgh v. American College of Obstetricians and Gynecologists, 476 U.S. 747 (1986), 89, 99, 150, 265, 356, 374, 458

Thornton, Estate of v. Caldor, 472 U.S. 703 (1985), 259–60

Tibbs v. Florida, 457 U.S. 31 (1982), 257

Tillman v. Wheaton-Haven Recreation Ass'n, Inc., 410 U.S. 431 (1973), 86

Tilton v. Richardson, 403 U.S. 672 (1971), 146, 181, 275, 459

Time v. Hill, 385 U.S. 374 (1967), 191

Time, Inc. v. Pape, 401 U.S. 279 (1971), 62

Tison v. Arizona, 107 S.Ct. 1676 (1987), 454

Toll v. Moreno, 458 U.S. 1 (1982), 69–70, 98

Toussie v. United States, 397 U.S. 112 (1970), 62

Tower v. Glover, 467 U.S. 914 (1984), 253

Train v. City of New York, 420 U.S. 35 (1975), 261

Trop v. Dulles, 356 U.S. 86 (1958), 125

Turner v. United States, 396 U.S. 398 (1970), 62

Turnock v. Ragsdale, 110 S.Ct. 532 (1990), 461

TWA v. Hardison, 432 U.S. 63 (1977), 416

Twitchell v. Pennsylvania, 7 Wall. 321 (1869), 210

United Building and Construction Trades Council of Camden County and Vicinity v. Mayor and Council of City of Camden, 465 U.S. 208 (1984), 98

United Jewish Organizations of Williamsburgh, Inc. v. Carey, 430 U.S. 144 (1977), 161

United Public Workers v. Mitchell, 330 U.S. 75 (1947), 191

United States v. Ash, 413 U.S. 300 (1973), 99

United States v. Bailey, 444 U.S. 394 (1980), 67, 90, 372

United States v. Bass, 404 U.S. 336 (1971), 99

United States v. Brewster, 408 U.S. 501 (1972), 136–37

United States v. Brignoni-Ponce, 422 U.S. 873 (1975), 281

United States v. Butler, 297 U.S. 1 (1936), 208, 211

United States v. Calandra, 414 U.S. 338 (1974), 312, 388, 393

United States v. Carolene Products Co., 304 U.S. 144 (1938), 313, 443

United States v. Chadwick, 433 U.S. 1 (1977), 92, 161, 162

United States v. City of Sheffield, Alabama, 435 U.S. 110 (1978), 362

United States v. Cortez, 449 U.S. 411 (1981), 161

United States v. DiFrancesco, 449 U.S. 117 (1980), 369

United States v. Edwards, 415 U.S. 800 (1974), 395, 421

United States v. Eichman, 110 S.Ct. 2404 (1990), 461

United States v. $8,850, 461 U.S. 555 (1983), 261

United States v. Enmons, 410 U.S. 396 (1973), 89, 97

United States v. 50 Acres of Land, 469 U.S. 24 (1984), 261

United States v. Frady, 456 U.S. 152 (1982), 254

United States v. Fuller, 409 U.S. 488 (1973), 301

United States v. Grace, 461 U.S. 171 (1983), 352

United States v. Grayson, 438 U.S. 41 (1978), 162

United States v. Guest, 383 U.S. 745 (1966), 385

United States v. Haggerty, 110 S.Ct. 2404 (1990), 461

United States v. Harris, 404 U.S. 1232 (1971), 151, 458

United States v. Helstoski, 442 U.S. 477 (1979), 137–38

United States v. Henry, 447 U.S. 264 (1980), 93, 156, 162

United States v. Janis, 428 U.S. 433 (1976), 90, 387

United States v. Johnson, 457 U.S. 537 (1982), 92

United States v. Jorn, 400 U.S. 470 (1971), 68

United States v. Karo, 468 U.S. 705 (1984), 367

United States v. Kras, 409 U.S. 434 (1973), 67, 191

United States v. Lane, 474 U.S. 438 (1986), 370

United States v. Leon, 468 U.S. 897 (1984), 24, 90, 221–22, 237, 282, 325, 367, 422, 458

United States v. MacDonald, 456 U.S. 1 (1982), 162, 230

United States v. Mandujano, 425 U.S. 564 (1976), 162, 393

United States v. Midwest Video, 406 U.S. 649 (1972), 190

United States v. Miller, 425 U.S. 435 (1976), 116, 126

United States v. Nixon, 418 U.S. 683 (1974), 22, 139–42, 172, 237, 320, 394, 439

United States v. Orito, 413 U.S. 139 (1973), 145, 191

United States v. Ortiz, 422 U.S. 891 (1975), 152

United States v. Pink, 315 U.S. 203 (1942), 189

United States v. Place, 462 U.S. 696 (1983), 99

United States v. Reidel, 402 U.S. 351 (1971), 62, 414, 458

United States v. Richardson, 418 U.S. 166 (1974), 142, 190, 307, 308–9, 384

United States v. Robel, 389 U.S. 258 (1967), 415, 429

United States v. Robinson, 414 U.S. 218 (1973), 393, 395

United States v. Ross, 456 U.S. 798 (1982), 92, 220–21, 364, 367, 374, 395

United States v. Salvucci, 448 U.S. 83 (1980), 324

United States v. Seeger, 380 U.S. 163 (1965), 190

United States v. Sharpe, 470 U.S. 675 (1985), 161

United States v. Students Challenging Regulatory Agency Procedures (SCRAP), 412 U.S. 669 (1973), 161

United States v. Thirty-Seven Photographs, 402 U.S. 363 (1971), 62, 426, 458

United States v. 12,200-Ft. Reels of Super 8MM. Film, 413 U.S. 123 (1973), 191

United States v. United States District Court, 407 U.S. 297 (1972), 171–72, 280–81, 284

United States v. Vuitch, 402 U.S. 62 (1971), 185

United States v. Washington, 431 U.S. 181 (1977), 162

United States v. Washington Post, 403 U.S. 713 (1971), 197, 200, 393

United States v. Weller, 401 U.S. 254 (1971), 190

United States v. White, 401 U.S. 745 (1971), 62, 186–87

United States v. Wunderlich, 342 U.S. 98 (1951), 190

United States v. Young, 470 U.S 1 (1985), 162

United States Railroad Retirement Board v. Fritz, 449 U.S. 166 (1980), 126

United States Trust Co. of New York v. New Jersey, 431 U.S. 1 (1977), 119

United Steelworkers v. Weber, 443 U.S. 193 (1979), 23, 106–7, 161, 327, 360, 389, 435, 458

Vale v. Louisiana, 399 U.S. 30 (1970), 62

Village of Belle Terre v. Boraas, 416 U.S. 1 (1974), 186

Virginia State Board of Pharmacy v. Virginia Citizens Consumer Council, Inc., 425 U.S. 748 (1976), 83, 191, 328

Wainwright v. Greenfield, 474 U.S. 284 (1986), 368

Wainwright v. Sykes, 433 U.S. 72 (1977), 323, 458

Wallace v. Jaffree, 472 U.S. 38 (1985), 24, 161, 258, 259, 351, 436

Walter v. United States, 447 U.S. 649 (1980), 99

Walters v. National Association of Radiation Survivors, 473 U.S. 305 (1985), 346

Walz v. Tax Commission of City of New York, 397 U.S. 664 (1970), 146, 180

Ward v. Illinois, 431 U.S. 767 (1977), 354, 458

Wards Cove Packing Company, Inc. v. Atonio, 109 S.Ct. 2115 (1989), 450

Warth v. Seldin, 422 U.S. 490 (1975), 175–76, 190, 306–7, 384

Washington, v. Chrisman, 455 U.S. 1 (1982), 161

Washington v. Davis, 426 U.S. 229 (1976), 23, 361, 389

Washington v. Seattle School District No. 1, 458 U.S. 457 (1982), 86, 269

Watkins v. United States, 354 U.S. 178 (1957), 378

Weber v. Aetna Casualty & Surety Co., 406 U.S. 164 (1972), 87

Webster v. Reproductive Health Services, 109 S.Ct. 3040 (1989), 452–53

Weinberger v. Hynson, Wescott & Dunning, 412 U.S. 609 (1973), 190

Wellmann v. United States, 253 F.2d 601 (6th Cir. 1957), 380

Welsh v. United States, 398 U.S. 333 (1970), 62, 190, 416

Wesberry v. Sanders, 376 U.S. 1 (1964), 417

West Coast Hotel v. Parrish, 300 U.S. 379 (1937), 202

West Virginia State Board of Education v. Barnette, 319 U.S. 624 (1943), 460

Westinghouse Electric Corp. v. Tully, 466 U.S. 388 (1984), 80

Whalen v. Roe, 429 U.S. 589 (1977), 357

Wheeler v. Barrera, 417 U.S. 402 (1974), 79

Wheeler v. Montgomery, 397 U.S. 280 (1970), 62

Whitcomb v. Chavis, 403 U.S. 124 (1971), 202–4, 210, 418

White v. Massachusetts Council of Construction Employers, 460 U.S. 204 (1983), 98, 322

White v. Regester, 412 U.S. 755 (1973), 418

White v. Weiser, 412 U.S. 783 (1973), 299, 458

Wickard v. Filburn, 317 U.S. 111 (1942), 126

Widmar v. Vincent, 454 U.S. 263 (1981), 402

Williams v. Florida, 399 U.S. 78 (1970), 94, 207, 208, 386

Williams v. Illinois, 399 U.S. 235 (1970), 389

Williams v. United States, 401 U.S. 646 (1971), 62, 161

Williamson v. Lee Optical Co., 348 U.S. 483 (1955), 190

Wilson v. Garcia, 471 U.S. 261 (1985), 274

Wisconsin v. Constantineau, 400 U.S. 433 (1971), 62, 181–82

Wisconsin v. Yoder, 406 U.S. 205 (1972), 146, 181, 458

Wisconsin Department of Industry, Labor and Human Relations v. Gould, Inc., 475 U.S. 282 (1986), 98

Witherspoon v. Illinois, 391 U.S. 510 (1968), 398

Witters v. Washington Dept. of Services for the Blind, 474 U.S. 481 (1986), 258–59

Wolf v. Colorado, 338 U.S. 25 (1949), 45

Wolff v. McDonnell, 418 U.S. 539 (1974), 422–23, 429

Wolman v. Walter, 433 U.S. 229 (1977), 84, 313, 350–51

Wood v. Strickland, 420 U.S. 308 (1975), 161

Woodson v. North Carolina, 428 U.S. 280 (1976), 125, 388, 399

Wooley v. Maynard, 430 U.S. 705 (1977), 458

Wright v. Florida, 474 U.S. 1094 (1986), 89

Wygant v. Jackson Board of Education, 476 U.S. 267 (1986), 270, 297–98, 361

Wyman v. James, 400 U.S. 309 (1971), 64, 91, 192, 228–30

Wyman v. Rothstein, 398 U.S. 275 (1970), 62

Young v. American Mini Theatres, Inc., 427 U.S. 50 (1976), 82, 313, 353, 372, 458

Young v. Community Nutrition Institute, 476 U.S. 974 (1986), 260–61

Youngberg v. Romero, 457 U.S. 307 (1982), 85

Younger v. Harris, 401 U.S. 37 (1971), 77, 383

Youngstown Sheet & Tube Co. v. Sawyer, 343 U.S. 579 (1952), 168, 319, 320

Zorach v. Clauson, 343 U.S. 306 (1952), 180

Zuber v. Allen, 396 U.S. 168 (1969), 62

Zurcher v. Stanford Daily, 436 U.S. 547 (1978), 390, 400, 401, 458

General Index

Abortion
—consent: Burger, 150; Powell, 291; Stevens, 356
—funding: Blackmun, 88; Burger, 143; Stevens, 356; Stewart, 393, 395, 396, 397
—parental notification: Rehnquist Court, 453
—right to: Blackmun, 87, 88, 439, 452, 453; Burger, 150; Douglas 185, 186; O'Connor, 264–65, 452; Powell, 290, 291; R. Reagan, 11, 453; Rehnquist, 452; Stevens, 356–57; Stewart, 382; White, 424, 427, 429, 451
Abraham, Henry J., 318
Access to courts: Blackmun, 73; Burger, 142, 143; O'Connor, 253–55; Rehnquist, 339
Administrative law
—deference to bureaucracy: Blackmun, 74, 75; Douglas, 172, 73; Marshall, 228–31; O'Connor, 261, 262; White, 411, 423
—deference to institutional authority: Blackmun, 73, 74; Brennan, 117, 228, 229; Burger, 134, 158; Marshall, 228, 229; O'Connor, 260, 261; Rehnquist, 228, 229; White, 428, 429
—deference to law enforcement: Blackmun, 89; Burger, 151; O'Connor, 253, 255, 271; Rehnquist, 316, 324, 338; Stevens, 364, 365; White, 419, 421, 422
—deference to military authority: O'Connor, 264

—deference to prison administrators: Blackmun, 90
Affirmative action: Blackmun, 87; Brennan, 106–8, 448, 449; Burger, 149, 150; Burger Court, 435; Marshall, 225, 448; O'Connor, 270, 271, 448, 449; Powell, 296–98, 361; Rehnquist, 326–27, 448; Rehnquist Court, 447–49; Stevens, 360–61, 449; Stewart, 389
Age discrimination: Brennan, 118, 119; Powell, 305; Stevens, 364
Aliens
—education: Blackmun, 85; Powell, 293, 294
—employment: Blackmun, 85, 86; Stevens, 364
—search and seizure: Burger, 152
—welfare: Blackmun, 85
American Bar Association, 120, 240, 316; Brennan, 102; Burger, 132; Powell, 277; Stewart, 378; White, 410
Amish, 146, 181
Article I. *See* Congressional power; Legislative apportionment
Article II. *See* Presidential power
Article III. *See* Judicial power

Balanced Budget and Emergency Deficit Act of 1985, 24, 134, 320, 350
Bankruptcy, 67, 79
Baum, Lawrence, 447
Bazelon, David L., 130
Bill of Rights. *See* Eighth Amendment;

Eleventh Amendment; Fifteenth
Amendment; Fifth Amendment; First
Amendment; Fourteenth
Amendment; Fourth Amendment;
Sixth Amendment; Tenth
Amendment; Thirteenth
Amendment; Twenty-first
Amendment
Binion, Gayle, 403
Birth control: Black, 381, 382; Douglas,
184, 185, 208; Rehnquist, 328;
Stevens, 357; Stewart, 382; White,
424
Black, Hugo L.: appointment, 35, 36;
background, 35, 36; confirmation,
35; dissent behavior, 26, 29; and
F. D. Roosevelt, 35, 36; judicial
philosophy, 39–41, 44, 46, 47, 53,
59, 60; opinion writing, 26, 49;
personality traits, 36, 38–39, 100,
117; political views, 36, 39, 40, 41;
resignation, 8, 35, 167; voting
patterns, 29, 31, 32, 33, 34, 49;
writing style, 38
—and other justices, 38, 39; Burger,
39, 40, 48, 49, 50, 51, 53, 55;
Douglas, 38, 46, 166, 167, 176, 177,
179, 180, 181, 188; Harlan, 43, 49,
51, 56, 57; Stewart, 381, 382, 383,
386, 393
—opinions on: birth control, 381, 382;
congressional power, 40, 41, 42, 52;
criminal procedure, 55–58;
desegregation, 49, 50; due process,
44, 55; equal protection clause, 44–
46; establishment clause, 290, 350,
351; exclusionary rule, 57, 58;
freedom of expression, 42, 53;
freedom of the press, 42, 43, 53, 54,
55; incorporation, 43, 44, 47–48;
judicial power, 41, 46–48, 59; privacy,
45, 48; right to counsel, 57; search
and seizure, 57–58
Blackmun, Harry A.: appointment, 6, 8,
63, 64, 68; background, 63, 64, 66;
confirmation, 64, 68; dissent
behavior, 26, 29, 71; and D. D.
Eisenhower, 102, 132; and interviews,
67; judicial philosophy, 64, 71, 72,
73, 95, 96, 315; and medicine and

doctors, 63, 64, 75, 88, 95; and
E. Meese, 120–22; "Minnesota
Twins," 68, 70, 72; opinion writing,
26, 64, 66, 67, 70; personality traits,
66; political views, 71, 246, 248; and
R. Nixon, 64, 68, 71, 76; voting
interagreement, 31, 32; voting
patterns, 29, 31, 32, 33, 34, 68–69,
89, 246, 248, 439; work habits, 66,
68, 70; writing style, 66
—and other justices: Brennan,69, 70,
86, 87, 350; Burger, 63, 64, 68, 69,
70, 71, 133; Marshall, 217, 235;
O'Connor, 69, 70, 84, 265, 268;
Rehnquist, 68, 69, 228, 229
—opinions on: abortion, 87, 88, 439,
452, 453; administrative law, 74, 75,
76, 95, 96; capital punishment, 94–
95; commerce, 74, 76, 80, 81;
congressional power, 74, 76, 79;
criminal procedure, 89–95;
federalism, 76–79; freedom of
speech, 81, 82; judicial power, 73, 74,
76, 80; legislative power, 73, 74;
obscenity, 64, 82; presidential power,
74, 95, 96; privacy, 88, 92; racial
discrimination, 86, 87, 450; search
and seizure, 90–93; separation of
church and state, 83, 350; sex
discrimination, 84, 268; trial by jury,
94
Blasi, Vincent, 309
Bork, Robert H., 15, 132, 446
Brandeis, Louis D., 164, 184, 185, 201,
348
Brennan, William J.: appointment, 102;
background, 101, 102, 104, 116, 117;
confirmation, 102; dissent behavior,
26, 29; economic and social views,
116, 117; judicial philosophy, 105,
107, 117, 120, 121, 122, 123, 124;
opinion writing, 26, 105, 106, 107,
108; personality traits, 100, 120, 124;
philosophy and ideology, 105, 122,
123, 124; political views, 102, 104,
116, 117, 246, 248, 249; voting
interagreement, 31, 32; voting
patterns, 29, 31, 32, 33, 34, 246, 248
—and other justices: Blackmun, 69, 70,
86, 87, 350; Douglas, 117, 122, 123,

169, 185, 188; Marshall, 216, 217, 228, 229, 235, 437; Stevens, 121, 344, 345, 346, 350, 351, 352, 356, 365, 366, 373; A. T. Vanderbilt, 102, 104, 105; White, 109, 424, 425, 426, 429
—opinions on: affirmative action, 106–8, 448, 449; capital punishment, 113–15; censorship, 111, 112; congressional power, 118–19; federalism, 115–19, 123, 246; freedom of expression, 110–13; freedom of speech, 110–11; libel, 113; obscenity, 110; poverty, 116, 123, 307; regulation of interstate commerce, 117, 118, 119; self-incrimination, 116, 209; sex discrimination, 109, 110
Brisbin, Richard A., Jr., 228
Brownell, Herbert, Jr., 102, 129
Buckner, Emory, 193
Bureaucracy, deference to. *See* Administrative law
Burger Court: activism, 434, 441; conservatism, 31–34, 116, 132, 157, 234, 248, 437, 439, 440, 441; data, 25–34; formation, 6, 8; historical context, 10, 11; leading decisions, 21–24; legacy, 433–37, 439–41, 445, 446; liberalism, 31–34, 434–36, 441; opinion writing, 26–28; overview, 440–47; voting interagreement, 31–32; voting patterns, 29–34, 229, 246–49, 310, 344, 345; and the Warren Court, 9, 10, 114, 122, 157, 253, 338, 433–37, 442, 443, 446, 455
Burger, Warren E.: appointment, 6, 10, 130, 132, 157; assignment of opinions, 70, 71, 134, 140, 148, 240, 250, 271, 439; background, 129, 130, 147, 157, 162; conservatism, 31, 32, 33, 34, 132, 133, 143, 144, 147, 151, 158, 159; dissent behavior, 26, 29, 154, 155; and D. D. Eisenhower, 129, 130, 157; judicial philosophy, 134, 139, 142, 143, 147, 151, 157, 159; leadership, 134, 148, 157, 159, 315; and R. M. Nixon, 6, 8, 129, 130, 132, 139, 140, 141, 142, 157, 159, 315; opinion writing, 26, 132, 133,

157, 158, 159; political views, 129, 133, 143, 147, 151, 157, 246, 248, 249; voting interagreement, 31, 32, 133; voting patterns, 29, 31, 32, 33, 34, 133, 143, 159, 246, 248; work habits, 130, 132, 157; writing style, 157, 158, 159
—and other justices: Black, 39, 40, 48, 49, 50, 51, 53, 55; Blackmun, 64, 68, 71, 133; O'Connor, 133, 240, 248, 249, 250, 271, 272; Rehnquist, 112, 133, 159, 315, 437, 447; Stevens, 344, 345, 346, 351, 364, 373
—opinions on: abortion, 150; affirmative action, 149, 150; capital punishment, 156; congressional immunity, 135–39; congressional power, 134–39; desegregation, 147–49; equal employment opportunity, 149, 150, 450; exclusionary rule, 153–54; freedom of expression, 143–45; freedom of the press, 144, 145; legislative veto, 134, 135; obscenity, 143, 145, 146; presidential power, 139–42; search and seizure, 151–54; separation of church and state, 146, 147, 158, 351; separation of powers, 134–35, 139, 140, 141, 142; speech or debate clause, 135–39
Burton, Harold H., 378
Bush, George, 6, 445
Busing: Black, 49, 50; Burger, 147, 148, 149; O'Connor, 245; Powell, 294, 295; White, 416

Cahn, Edmund N., 175
Capital punishment: Blackmun, 94–95; Brennan, 113–15; Burger, 156; Douglas, 187, 188; Marshall, 222–24; O'Connor, 257, 258; Powell, 284–86; Rehnquist, 324, 332; Stevens, 369, 370; Stewart, 388; White, 419. *See also* Cruel and unusual punishment
Cardozo, Benjamin, N., 311, 443
Carswell, G. Harrold, 8, 64, 278, 316
Carter, Jimmy, 4, 5, 8, 320
Choper, Jesse H., 445
CIA, 142, 280, 352
Citizens' travel abroad: Burger, 139; Rehnquist, 320

Civil rights. *See* Affirmative action; Age
    discrimination; Aliens; Busing;
    Desegregation; Equal employment
    opportunity; Equal protection clause;
    Fair housing; Sex discrimination;
    Voting rights
Civil Rights Act of 1866: Blackmun,
    77, 78; Harlan, 385; Kennedy, 451;
    Stewart, 385; White, 385
Civil Rights Act of 1964, 2, 79, 87,
    105, 106, 108, 117, 149, 150, 174,
    217, 218, 268, 269, 271, 326, 327,
    361, 389, 416, 417, 448, 449, 450
Civil Rights Act of 1968, 2
Civil Rights Attorneys Fees Act of
    1976, 87
Clark, Tom C., 38, 212, 379
Clear and present danger test, 176
Cleveland, Grover S., 10
Commerce clause: Blackmun, 74, 76,
    80; Brennan, 117, 118, 119; Powell,
    303, 304, 305; Rehnquist, 321, 322;
    Stewart, 383, 384; White, 412
Committee to Re-Elect the President,
    140
Communism, 3, 378, 380, 415, 429,
    442
Conference of State Chief Justices, 378
Confession, voluntariness of. *See* Self-
    incrimination, right against
Confrontation, right of. *See* Fair trial
Congressional immunity: Burger, 135–
    39; White, 412
Congressional power: Black, 40, 41, 42,
    52; Blackmun, 74, 76, 79; Brennan,
    118, 119; Burger, 134–39; Douglas,
    168, 173, 174, 175; O'Connor, 251;
    Rehnquist, 320, 321, 322, 323, 332,
    339; Stevens, 348, 349, 350; Stewart,
    383, 384; White, 411, 412, 427
Conscientious objectors: Black, 416;
    Douglas, 169, 170; White, 416
Conscription: Black, 55; Douglas, 168,
    169; White, 418. *See also*
    Conscientious objectors
Constitution. *See* Congressional power;
    Eighth Amendment; Eleventh
    Amendment; Fifteenth Amendment;
    Fifth Amendment; First Amendment;
    Fourteenth Amendment; Fourth

Amendment; Judicial power;
    Presidential power; Sixth
    Amendment; Tenth Amendment;
    Thirteenth Amendment; Twenty-first
    Amendment
Constitutional counterrevolution, 8, 9–
    10, 434
Constitutional eras, 441–43, 445, 455–
    57
Contract clause: Blackmun, 119;
    Brennan, 119, 124
Counsel, right to: Black, 57; Brennan,
    116; Burger, 154, 155; Douglas, 187;
    O'Connor, 256; Rehnquist, 338;
    Stewart, 381, 388
—effective assistance of counsel:
    Burger, 154, 155; O'Connor, 256
—exclusionary rule: Burger, 154
—indigents: Blackmun, 93: Rehnquist,
    338
—plea bargaining: Blackmun, 89, 90;
    White, 419, 420
—preliminary hearings: Black, 55, 56;
    Burger, 155; Stewart, 388
—self-incrimination: Burger, 155
—self-representation: Blackmun, 93
Cox, Archibald, 140
Crime Commission, 277
Criminal procedure: Black, 55–58;
    Blackmun, 89–95; Brennan, 113–15;
    Burger, 130, 132, 151–56; Burger
    Court, 219, 434; Douglas, 186–88;
    Harlan, 196, 207, 208; Marshall,
    219–24; O'Connor, 253–58; Powell,
    280–87; Rehnquist, 315, 316, 324,
    325, 331, 332, 337, 338, 339;
    Rehnquist Court, 453–55; Stevens,
    364–72; Stewart, 381, 382, 384, 386,
    387, 388, 393, 395, 396, 398, 399,
    401, 402; Warren Court, 3, 11, 130,
    219, 434, 446; White, 419–23. *See
    also* Capital punishment; Counsel,
    right to; Fair trial; Search and
    seizure; Self-incrimination, right
    against
Cruel and unusual punishment:
    Blackmun, 94, 95; Brennan, 113–15;
    Burger, 156; Douglas, 187, 188;
    Marshall, 222–24; O'Connor, 257,
    258; Powell, 284–87; Rehnquist, 324,

332; Stevens, 369, 370; Stewart, 388, 398, 399; White, 419. *See also* Capital punishment

Death penalty. *See* Capital punishment; Cruel and unusual punishment
Declaration of Independence: Black, 43
Democratic National Committee, 140
Democratic party, 1, 2, 3, 4, 5, 6, 10, 11, 12, 130, 204, 300, 433; agenda of, 2, 3, 240, 261–71
Department of Justice, 130, 240, 316, 427, 428, 448
Desegregation: Black, 49, 50; Blackmun, 86, 87; Burger, 147–49; Burger Court, 147, 148, 294, 435; Harlan, 199, 200; Marshall, 214, 215, 225, 233; Powell, 277, 294–96; Rehnquist, 326; Stewart, 389; White, 416. *See also* Busing; Equal protection clause; Fair housing; Segregation, racial
Dewey, Thomas E., 129
Dirksen, Everett, 410
Disabled persons' rights, 85
Dorsen, Norman, 72
Double jeopardy: O'Connor, 257; Stevens, 365, 368, 369; Stewart, 410
Douglas, William O.: appointment, 164, 166; background, 163, 164, 166, 167; call for impeachment, 167; dissent behavior, 26, 29, 167, 168, 169, 188; family, 163, 164, 167; health, 163, 167; and L. B. Johnson, 166, 168; judicial philosophy, 164, 168, 171, 173, 174, 176, 184, 186, 188; and R. M. Nixon, 171, 172; opinion writing, 26; political views, 163, 164, 166, 167, 173, 188; and F. D. Roosevelt, 164, 166; and H. Truman, 166, 168; voting patterns, 29, 31, 32, 33, 34
—and other justices: Black, 38, 46, 166, 167, 176, 177, 179, 180, 181, 188; L. Brandeis, 164, 184, 185; Brennan, 117, 122, 123, 169, 185, 188
—opinions on: abortion, 185, 186; affirmative action, 184; capital punishment, 187, 188; conscientious

objectors, 169–70; criminal procedure, 186–88; First Amendment, 176–81; Fourth Amendment, 181–84; legislative apportionment, 202, 203, 204; legislative power, 173–75; presidential power, 168–72; privacy, 184–86; search and seizure, 186, 187; segregation, 182, 183; separation of church and state, 180, 181; standing, 175, 176; Vietnam cases, 168–71
Draft. *See* Conscription
Driscoll, Alfred E., 102
Drug testing, 453–54
Due process: Black, 44, 55; Burger, 155; Douglas, 181, 182, 186; Harlan, 206; Marshall, 218; O'Connor, 256; Powell, 284, 290, 292, 301, 302, 303; Rehnquist, 323, 338; Stevens, 356–58, 371; Stewart, 382, 383, 386, 387–88; White, 423, 424. *See also* Counsel, right to; Fifth Amendment; Fourteenth Amendment; Sixth Amendment
Dukakis, Michael S., 3, 6, 455

Eastland, James O., 138, 378, 379, 410
Eighth Amendment. *See* Capital punishment; Cruel and unusual punishment
Eisenhower, Dwight D., 1, 2, 3, 5, 9; and Blackmun, 64; and Brennan, 102, 132; and Burger, 129, 130, 157; and Harlan, 193; and Stewart, 376, 378
Electronic eavesdropping. *See* Search and seizure
Eleventh Amendment: Blackmun, 77; O'Connor, 252; Rehnquist, 323, 336; Stevens, 349
Entrapment. *See* Fair trial
Environmental issues: Burger, 143; O'Connor, 261; Powell, 304; Stewart, 384
Equal educational opportunity. *See* Desegregation
Equal employment opportunity: Blackmun, 67, 79, 87; Burger, 149, 150; Burger Court, 149, 450; Marshall, 217, 218; O'Connor, 267,

268, 269, 270, 271; Rehnquist, 327, 328; Rehnquist Court, 449–51; Stevens, 360, 361; White, 416, 417. *See also* Affirmative action

Equal protection clause: Black, 44–46; Blackmun, 84–85; Brennan, 107, 108, 117, 123; Burger, 148; Douglas, 181, 182, 183, 184, 185; Harlan, 201–6; Marshall, 224–26; O'Connor, 245, 252, 266, 270; Powell, 296–300; Rehnquist, 325, 326; Stevens, 358–64; Stewart, 389, 390; White, 416, 417, 418. *See also* Fourteenth Amendment

Equal Rights Amendment, 105, 239; O'Connor, 245

Establishment clause: Black, 290, 350, 351; Blackmun, 83, 350; Brennan, 350; Burger, 146, 147, 158, 351; Douglas, 180, 181; Marshall, 350; O'Connor, 258–60; Powell, 289, 290; Rehnquist, 339; Stevens, 350–51; Stewart, 391, 392, 395, 402, 403; White, 415, 416. *See also* Separation of church and state

Exclusionary rule: Black, 57, 58; Burger, 153–54; Rehnquist, 316; Stewart, 393, 395; White, 421, 422

Executive power. *See* Presidential power

Executive privilege: Burger, 139, 140, 141, 142, 394; Rehnquist, 320; Stewart, 394

Exhaustion of remedies: O'Connor, 253, 254

Fair housing: Brennan, 307; Douglas, 175, 176; Powell, 306, 307; Stewart, 397, 398

Fair Labor Standards Act of 1938, 118

Fair trial: Burger Court, 219; Brennan, 391; Burger, 155, 156; Marshall, 391; Powell, 282–84; Rehnquist, 324; Stevens, 370; Stewart, 391. *See also* Counsel, right to; Sixth Amendment

—confrontation, right of: Burger Court, 219; Marshall, 220

—due process: Powell, 284

—harmless error doctrine: Blackmun, 66

—juveniles: Burger, 155

—plea bargaining: Powell, 284

—speedy trial, right to: Burger Court, 230; Marshall, 230; Powell, 284

Fairman, Charles, 207

FBI, 264, 367

Federal Communications Commission, 413

Federal Election Commission, 320

Federalism: Blackmun, 64, 76–79, 95, 246; Brennan, 115–19, 123, 246; Burger, 246; Marshall, 246; O'Connor, 238, 242, 246, 247, 249, 250–53, 265, 271, 272; Powell, 246, 303–6; Rehnquist, 246, 321–23, 334, 338, 339; Stevens, 246, 344, 348–50; Stewart, 383, 384; White, 246, 412, 413

Fifteenth Amendment: Douglas, 174, 203; Marshall, 226

Fifth Amendment: Black, 44; Blackmun, 89, 91, 92, 93; Burger, 154, 155; Douglas, 168, 169; O'Connor, 254, 256; Powell, 283; Stevens, 368, 371. *See also* Double jeopardy; Due process; Self-incrimination, right against

First Amendment: Black, 43–44, 53, 54; Blackmun, 74, 81, 246; Brennan, 110–13, 246; Burger, 143–47, 246; Douglas, 170, 171, 177–81, 185; Marshall, 231, 246; O'Connor, 246, 248, 249, 258, 259, 260, 262, 263, 264; Powell, 246, 280, 287–90; Rehnquist, 246, 328–31, 335, 336; Stevens, 246, 350–56; Stewart, 390–92, 400, 401; White, 246, 414, 415. *See also* Freedom of association; Freedom of religion; Freedom of speech; Freedom of the press; Separation of church and state

Ford, Gerald R., 4, 8, 167, 343, 372, 433, 440

Fortas, Abe, 6, 8, 64, 167; and Black, 38; and Brennan, 209; and self-incrimination, 209; and E. Warren, 209

Fourteenth Amendment: Black, 44–46; Blackmun, 84, 85, 86, 87; Brennan, 108; Burger, 148, 149; Douglas, 174, 181–84, 201; Harlan, 199, 200, 205,

206, 207, 208; Marshall, 224, 225, 226; Powell, 294–96; Rehnquist, 323–28, 334, 335, 338; Stevens, 358–64; Stewart, 416, 423, 424. *See also* Due process; Equal protection clause; Privileges and immunities clause

Fourth Amendment: Black, 44, 45; Blackmun, 77, 89, 90–92; Burger, 151–53; Douglas, 186, 187; Marshall, 230; Powell, 280–82; Rehnquist, 324, 325; Stevens, 366–67; Stewart, 393; White, 421, 422. *See also* Search and seizure

Frank, Jerome N., 216

Frankfurter, Felix, 43, 45, 60, 134, 158, 320, 370
—and Constitution: civil liberties, 370; civil rights, 370; due process, 282, 308, 382, 386; executive privilege, 320; Fourteenth Amendment, 205; incorporation, 282, 386; judicial restraint, 308; presidential power, 320
—and other justices, 222; Black, 39, 45, 47, 60, 320; Douglas, 166; Harlan, 204, 205, 370, 382; Powell, 277, 282, 308, 311; Stewart, 375, 382, 386
—opinions on: legislative apportionment, 204, 205

Freedom of association: Black, 53; Brennan, 109, 110; Douglas, 178, 183, 186; Harlan, 196; Stevens, 355, 356; White, 415

Freedom of expression: Black, 42, 53; Brennan, 110–13; Douglas, 177, 178; Harlan, 196–99; Rehnquist, 328–31; Stevens, 351–56

Freedom of Information Act of 1956 Douglas, 173

Freedom of the press: Black, 42, 43, 53, 54, 55; Burger, 144, 145; Douglas, 178, 179; Harlan, 197, 198; O'Connor, 263, 264; Powell, 288; Stevens, 354, 355; Stewart, 390, 391, 401, 402; White, 413, 414

Freedom of religion: Black, 42, 43; Burger, 146; Douglas, 180; O'Connor, 264; Powell, 290;

Rehnquist, 339; Stevens, 350–51; Stewart, 391, 392; White, 416

Freedom Riders, 408

Freedom of speech: Blackmun, 81–82; Brennan, 110–11; Burger, 143, 144; Douglas, 176, 177, 178; Harlan, 196; O'Connor, 262, 263; Powell, 287–89; Rehnquist, 328, 329, 330, 331; Stevens, 351–52; White 413, 414, 415
—commercial speech: Blackmun, 83; Douglas, 179; Powell, 288, 289; Rehnquist, 328, 329; Stevens, 352, 353
—internal security: Blackmun, 82
—prior restraint: Blackmun, 82
—public employees: Brennan, 111; Marshall, 111; White, 111
—speech plus: Black, 44; Douglas, 177; Harlan, 196, 200; Marshall, 231

Freund, Paul, 194, 198, 408, 410

Fuller, Melville W., 130

Funston, Richard Y., 219, 221, 434

Gallup Poll, 224

Goldberg, Arthur J., 167, 379

Goldman, Sheldon, 455

Goldwater, Barry M., 2, 4, 5, 6, 318

Gunther, Gerald, 311, 437

Habeas corpus: Blackmun, 76, 94; Powell, 307; Rehnquist, 316, 323

Hand, Learned, 216, 311

Harlan, John Marshall: appointment, 193; background, 193, 194; dissent behavior, 26, 29, 196; family, 193; judicial philosophy, 194, 209, 278; opinion writing, 27, 194; resignation, 8, 316; voting interagreement, 31; voting patterns, 29, 31, 33, 34
—and other justices: Black, 43, 49, 51, 56, 57, 198; F. Frankfurter, 204, 205, 282; Powell, 208, 277, 278, 282, 308, 311; Stewart, 375, 382, 385, 386, 393; Warren, 193, 194, 196, 208, 209
—opinions on: criminal procedure, 196, 207, 208; desegregation, 199, 200; due process, 206; equal protection, 201–7; freedom of

expression, 196–99; freedom of the press, 197, 198; incorporation, 207–8; legislative apportionment, 202, 203, 204, 205; presidential power, 197, 198; privacy, 196; self-incrimination, 196, 209; state action, 199–201
Hastie, William H., 213, 408
Hatch Act: Douglas, 178; White, 415
Haynsworth, Clement F., 8, 64, 278, 316
Herbert, F. Edward, 170, 171
Holmes, Oliver Wendell, 41, 134, 196, 201, 277, 280, 311, 353
Homosexuals: Blackmun, 84, 358; Burger, 150, 151; Stevens, 358; White, 424, 427, 429
Hoover, Herbert C., 5
Housing, racial discrimination in: Blackmun, 86; Stewart, 397. See also Fair housing
Houston, Charles Hamilton, 214
Howard, A. E. Dick, 319
Hughes, Charles E., 443
Humphrey, Hubert H., 3, 8, 277
Hyde Amendment of 1976: Blackmun, 88; Stevens, 357; Stewart, 396

Immigration and Nationality Act, 135, 411
Incorporation, 282, 386; Black, 43, 44, 47, 48; Douglas, 181; Harlan, 207–8; Powell, 282; Rehnquist, 323, 324, 329, 337, 338, 339; Stewart, 385–87; Warren Court, 282
Indian cases: Blackmun, 71, 87
Indian Claims Commission, 87
INS: Brennan, 229; Burger, 135; Marshall, 228, 229; Rehnquist, 224
Institutional authority, deference to. See Administrative law
Interstate commerce. See Commerce clause
IRS: Blackmun, 73; Brennan, 229; Burger, 149, 154; Douglas, 187; O'Connor, 269
Israel, Jerold H., 376, 379

Jackson, Robert H., 166; and Rehnquist, 217, 318, 319, 340; and Stewart, 383

Jaworski, Leon, 140
Jews, Hasidic, 151
John Birch Society, 413
Johnson, Lyndon B., 2, 3, 5, 209, 408; and Douglas, 166, 188; and Marshall, 216; and Powell, 277
Johnson, Mordacai, 213
Johnston, Olin, 378, 379
Judicial biography, 12, 15, 16
Judicial power: Black, 41, 46–48, 59; Blackmun, 73, 74, 76, 80; Brennan, 120, 121, 122; Burger, 138, 139, 142; Douglas, 168, 175, 176; Rehnquist, 322, 323. See also Justiciability; Standing
Jury trial. See Trial by jury
Justiciability: Blackmun, 73; Douglas, 174; Stewart, 384; White, 418
Juvenile proceedings: Black, 51; Stewart, 400, 401, 402. See also Due process; Fair trial; Self-incrimination, right against; Trial by jury

Kahn, Ronald, 226, 227
Kaiser Aluminum, 326, 327
Katzenbach, Nicholas deB., 408
Kennedy, Anthony M., 9, 133, 446, 449, 450, 451, 452; and drug testing, 453, 454; and R. Reagan, 9, 133
Kennedy, Edward M., 68
Kennedy, John F., 2, 216, 407, 408
Kennedy, Robert F., 3, 408, 410
King, Martin Luther, Jr., 3
Ku Klux Klan: Black, 35, 36

Labor issues: Blackmun, 79; Brennan, 112, 113; O'Connor, 252; Stewart, 380
Landynski, Jacob W., 439
Legislative apportionment: Brennan, 104, 108, 109; Burger, 151; Douglas, 202, 203, 204; Harlan, 202, 203, 204, 205; Powell, 299–301; Stewart, 384; White, 417, 418
Legislative apportionment: Brennan, 104, 108, 109; Burger, 151; Douglas, 202, 203, 204; Harlan, 202, 203, 204, 205; Powell, 299–301; Stewart, 384; White, 417, 418
Legislative immunity. See Congressional immunity

Legislative veto, 134, 135; White, 411, 412

Levi, Edward H., 343, 372

Libel. *See* First Amendment; Freedom of speech; Freedom of the press

McCarthy Era, 120, 130

McCarthy, Joseph R., 100, 102

McClellan, John L., 378, 379

McCloskey, Robert G., 441, 442, 443, 445, 446, 455, 456, 457

McGovern, George S., 3, 4, 5, 8

Marshall, John, 130, 441, 456, 457

Marshall, Thurgood: appointment, 216; background, 212–16; confirmation, 216; dissent behavior, 27, 29, 216, 217, 219, 220, 221, 232–33, 235; family, 212, 213; and L. B. Johnson, 216; judicial philosophy, 217, 234, 235; and J. F. Kennedy, 216; NAACP, 214, 216, 235; opinion writing, 27, 235, 236; political views, 246, 248; voting interagreement, 31, 32, 217; voting patterns, 29, 31, 32, 33, 34, 228, 229, 246, 248

—and other justices: Blackmun, 217, 235; Brennan, 216, 217, 228, 229, 235, 437; C. Houston, 214; Rehnquist, 217, 218, 219, 228, 229; White, 426, 429

—opinions on: affirmative action, 225, 448; bureaucracy, 228–31; capital punishment, 222–24; criminal procedure, 219–24; due process, 218; employment discrimination, 450; executive power, 228; racial discrimination, 214, 216, 217, 218, 224–28, 233, 234, 235; search and seizure, 220, 221; self-incrimination, 220, 221; separation of church and state, 350; voting rights, 226; welfare issues, 227, 228, 229, 246

Mason, Alpheus Thomas, 310, 434

Medicaid, 291, 396

Medina, Harold R., 216

Meese, Edwin H., III, 120, 121, 122; and Brennan, 120, 121, 122; and judicial activism, 120

Mikva, Abner J., 124

Minton, Sherman, 38, 102

Mitchell, Clarence M., Jr., 213

Mondale, Walter F., 3, 6

Murphy, Frank, 38, 166

NAACP, 214, 216, 235

NAACP Legal Defense and Education Fund, 214

National Advisory Committee on Legal Services to the Poor, 277

National Park Service, 230

National security: Burger, 138, 142; Douglas, 171, 172; Harlan, 198

New Deal, 2, 12, 39, 120, 166, 246, 260, 308, 380, 407, 428, 433, 457

New Jersey Supreme Court: Brennan, 101, 102, 104, 115

New York Bar Association, 194

New York Crime Commission, 193, 194

New York Department of Social Services, 229

Nixon, Richard M., 3, 4, 5, 9, 50, 54, 68, 69, 76, 129, 163, 209, 247, 394, 408, 410; and Blackmun, 6, 8, 64, 68, 69, 71, 76, 439; and Burger, 6, 8, 129, 130, 132, 139, 140, 141, 151, 157, 159, 315; and Burger Court, 6, 8, 277, 278, 315, 337, 433, 434; and criminal procedure, 3, 11, 130, 132, 143, 151, 157, 324, 434; and Douglas, 171, 172; and Powell, 8, 277, 278; and Rehnquist, 8, 217, 278, 315, 337; and Stewart, 379; and strict construction, 3, 130, 157, 278, 315, 339, 340, 433; and Warren Court, 3, 130, 167, 337, 440; and Watergate, 4, 5, 139–40

Nixon administration, 394

Norris-LaGuardia Act of 1932, 52, 232

Nuclear Regulatory Commission, 79, 304

Obscenity: Blackmun, 64, 82; Brennan, 110; Burger, 143, 145, 146; Douglas, 179; Powell, 288; Stevens, 353–54; Stewart, 386, 391; White, 414, 426. *See also* First Amendment

Occupational Safety and Health Act of 1970, 321, 366

O'Connor, Sandra Day: appointment, 9, 238, 239, 240, 242, 243; background,

8, 238, 239, 244, 245; dissent behavior, 27, 30; family, 238, 239, 243; judicial philosophy, 242, 243, 245, 246, 247, 248, 249, 271, 272; leadership, 272; opinion writing, 27, 240, 250, 271; political views, 245, 246, 247, 248, 249; and R. Reagan, 9, 239, 240, 242, 243, 244, 246, 248, 271, 272; voting interagreement, 32; voting patterns, 30, 32, 33, 34
—and other justices: Blackmun, 69, 70, 84, 265, 268; Burger, 133, 240, 248, 249, 250, 271, 272; Powell, 250, 251, 309; Rehnquist, 238, 243, 247, 248, 249, 250, 255, 256, 259, 261, 263, 265, 272; Stevens, 248, 249
—opinions on: abortion, 264–65, 452; affirmative action, 270, 271, 448, 449; capital punishment, 257, 258; deference to institutional authority, 260, 261; double jeopardy, 257; federalism, 238, 242, 246, 247, 249, 250–53, 265, 271, 272; freedom of the press, 263, 264; freedom of religion, 264; freedom of speech, 262, 263; right to counsel, 256; self-incrimination, 254, 255, 256; separation of church and state, 258–60; sex discrimination, 265, 266, 267, 268
Ohio Supreme Court, 376
Omnibus Crime Control Act of 1968, 171, 280
Opinion assignments, 70, 71, 134, 140, 148, 240, 250, 271, 439
Orfield, Gary, 319
Organized Crime Control Act of 1970, 369
Overbreadth doctrine: Brennan, 352; Marshall, 352; Stevens, 352, 373. See also First Amendment

Parental rights: Blackmun, 67, 93; due process, 93; White, 418, 423
Passports. See Presidential power
Pentagon Papers, 197, 198; Black, 43, 53, 54, 55, 198; Blackmun, 82; Brennan, 198; Burger, 139, 144; Douglas, 171; Harlan, 198, 199; Marshall, 198; Stewart, 393, 394

Perry, Michael J., 222
Plea bargaining. See Counsel, right to
Police power (state): Rehnquist, 334
Political parties: control of Congress, 2–6, 9–12, 441
Political question doctrine: Burger Court, 174; Douglas, 174; Warren Court, 174
Pornography. See Obscenity
Poverty: Blackmun, 67, 93; Brennan, 116, 123, 307; Burger, 157; Douglas, 181, 186, 187; Harlan, 205, 206, 207; Marshall, 225; Powell, 283, 285, 291, 292, 293, 306; Stevens, 357; Stewart, 387, 397. See also Welfare issues
Powell, Adam Clayton, 174
Powell, Lewis F.: appointment, 8, 276, 277, 278; background, 276, 277; confirmation, 277; dissent behavior, 27, 29, 310; family, 276; judicial philosophy, 308, 309, 310, 311, 439; leadership, 310, 311; and R. M. Nixon, 8, 277, 278; opinion writing, 27; political views, 246, 248, 277, 278, 309; retirement, 9, 133; voting interagreement, 31, 32; voting patterns, 10, 30, 31, 32, 33, 34, 289, 310, 439
—and other justices, 444, 451, 468, 469, 472, 474; Harlan, 208, 277, 278, 282, 308, 311, 439; O'Connor, 250, 251, 309; Rehnquist, 278, 315; Stevens, 285, 361; Stewart, 285, 384
—opinions on: abortion, 290, 291; affirmative action, 296–98, 361; alienage, 299; commerce clause, 303, 304, 305; cruel and unusual punishment, 284–87; desegregation, 277, 294–96; establishment clause, 289, 290; federalism, 303–6; freedom of the press, 288; freedom of speech, 287–89; habeas corpus, 306, 307; legislative apportionment, 299–301; right to counsel, 283; search and seizure, 280–82; sex discrimination, 298; standing, 306, 307
Presidential power: Burger, 139–42; Douglas, 168–73; Marshall, 228, 229;

Rehnquist, 319, 320, 332, 337, 339;
Stewart, 394; White, 410, 411, 412
—executive privilege: Burger, 139,
140, 141, 142, 394; Rehnquist, 320;
Stewart, 394
—foreign affairs: Blackmun, 74, 82;
Burger, 139; Douglas, 171; Harlan,
197; Stewart, 393, 394
—passports, 74, 139
—public concern about, 136
Press, the. *See* Freedom of the press
Prison conditions: Blackmun, 67, 90;
Marshall, 219; Rehnquist, 331;
Stevens, 371, 372; White, 422
Privacy, right of, 184; Black, 45, 48;
Blackmun, 88, 92; Burger, 152;
Douglas, 184–86; Harlan, 196;
Powell, 281, 291; Rehnquist, 324,
333; Stevens, 347, 367; Stewart, 382,
387, 395; White, 412, 421, 427, 429
Privileges and immunities clause, 76, 81
Probable cause. *See* Search and seizure
Property rights: Powell, 301;
Rehnquist, 329, 334, 335, 336;
Stevens, 358
Proxmire, E. William, 137
Public schools. *See* Schools

Quotas. *See* Affirmative action

Racial discrimination. *See* Affirmative
action; Desegregation; Equal
employment opportunity; Equal
protection clause
Rational basis test, 117, 225, 328
Reagan administration, 5, 6, 239, 319,
351; and abortion, 453; and civil
rights, 449, 451, 452; and judicial
activism, 120, 121; and quotas, 448,
449, 451, 452
Reagan, Ronald W., 5, 6, 10, 132, 156,
329, 440; and abortion, 11, 243, 434;
and affirmative action, 11, 434; and
R. Bork, 446; and citizens' travel
abroad, 139, 320; and A. Kennedy, 8,
133, 446; and O'Connor, 8, 239, 240,
242, 245, 248, 258, 271, 272, 446;
and Rehnquist, 9, 133, 437; and
religious issues, 11, 244, 434, 436;
and A. Scalia, 8, 133, 446; and

school desegregation, 11, 434; and
Supreme Court appointments, 8, 243,
446, 447, 455
Reed, Stanley, F., 38, 47
Rehnquist Court: abortion, 452, 453;
affirmative action, 447–49;
conservatism, 443, 446, 447–57;
criminal procedure, 454; drug
testing, 453–54
Rehnquist, William H.: appointment, 8,
133, 315, 316, 317, 319, 455;
background, 316, 318; confirmation,
316; dissent behavior, 27, 30, 318;
judicial philosophy, 332–38;
leadership, 437, 447; and R. M.
Nixon, 8, 217, 278, 315, 316, 337;
opinion writing, 27, 318; personality
traits, 318, 319; political views, 246,
248, 249, 315, 318; voting
interagreement, 31, 32; voting
patterns, 30, 31, 32, 33, 34, 228,
229, 437
—and other justices, 479; Blackmun,
68, 69, 228, 229; Burger, 112, 133,
159, 315, 437, 447; R. Jackson, 217,
318, 319, 340; Marshall, 217, 218,
219, 228, 229; O'Connor, 238, 243,
247, 248, 249, 250, 255, 256, 259,
261, 263, 265, 272; Powell, 278, 315;
R. Reagan, 133; Stevens, 345, 348,
351, 353, 361, 363, 373; Stewart,
379, 387, 390; White, 259, 424, 425
—opinions on: abortion, 452;
affirmative action, 326–27, 448;
capital punishment, 324, 332;
commerce clause, 321, 322;
congressional power, 320, 321, 322;
criminal procedure, 315, 316, 324,
325, 331, 332, 337, 338, 339;
desegregation, 326; federalism, 246,
321–23, 334, 338, 339; First
Amendment, 328–31; Fourteenth
Amendment, 323–28; freedom of
religion, 339; freedom of speech,
328, 329, 330, 331; judicial power,
322, 323; presidential power, 319,
320, 332, 337, 339; racial
discrimination, 325, 327, 451; search
and seizure, 324, 325, 454;
separation of church and state, 339;

sex discrimination, 327, 328; voting rights, 325
Religion. *See* First Amendment; Freedom of religion; Separation of church and state
Religious issues. *See* Establishment clause; Freedom of religion; Separation of church and state
Republican party, 2, 3, 4, 5, 6, 10, 11, 12, 234, 238, 239, 243, 300, 318, 407, 433, 434, 436, 441, 457; agenda of, 3, 4, 240, 243–44, 250–61, 271
Right-to-life movement: Blackmun, 88
Right to vote. *See* Voting rights
Rights of the accused. *See* Capital punishment; Counsel, right to; Double jeopardy; Fair trial; Search and seizure; Self-incrimination, right against
Roberts, Owen J., 208
Rohde, David W., 245, 246
Roosevelt, Franklin D., 2, 35, 36, 39, 47, 455; Brennan, 116; Douglas, 164, 166; and Stewart, 380
Rosenberg case: Douglas, 166
Rule of four: Stevens, 347, 365
Rule of lenity, 89
Rutledge, Wiley B., 166, 180; and Black, 38; and Stevens, 343

St. Paul Council on Human Relations, 147
Scalia, Antonin, 9, 107, 133, 446; and abortion, 452; and affirmative action, 107, 449, 450; and drug testing, 454
School desegregation. *See* Busing; Desegregation
Schorr, Daniel, 67
Schubert, Glendon, 249, 440
Schwartz, Bernard, 310
Search and seizure: Black, 57–58; Blackmun, 90–93; Burger, 151–54; Burger Court, 151; Marshall, 220, 221; Powell, 280–82; Rehnquist, 324, 325, 454; Rehnquist Court, 453, 454; Stevens, 366–67; Stewart, 393; White, 421, 422, 454. *See also* Fourth Amendment
—aliens: Burger, 152
—drug testing: Kennedy, 453, 454

—electronic eavesdropping: Douglas, 186; Powell, 280; Rehnquist, 316; Stewart, 395
—exclusionary rule: Black, 57, 58; Blackmun, 77; Burger, 153, 154; Marshall, 221, 222; Powell, 281, 282; Stevens, 366, 367; White, 421, 422
—warrantless search and seizure: Black, 57; Blackmun, 92; Burger, 152; Douglas, 171, 172; Marshall, 220; Powell, 280, 281; Steens, 366, 367; Stewart, 395, 396; White, 421, 422
Securities and Exchange Act of 1934, 58
Securities and Exchange Commission, 164
Segal, Bernard, 378
Segregation, racial: Black, 50; Brennan, 270; Burger, 149; Douglas, 182, 183; Marshall, 214, 234; O'Connor, 270; Powell, 294, 295; White, 408. *See also* Busing; Desegregation; Equal protection clause; Fair housing
Self-incrimination, right against: Brennan, 116, 209; Burger, 154; Douglas, 187; Harlan, 196, 209; Marshall, 220, 221; O'Connor, 254, 255, 256; Rehnquist, 339; Stevens, 368; Stewart, 401; White, 419, 420
—confession, voluntariness of: Marshall, 220, 221
—exclusionary rule: O'Connor, 255
—grand juries: Burger, 154
—juvenile proceedings: Stewart, 401
—right to counsel: Burger, 154; White, 419, 420
—transactional immunity: Powell, 283
Separation of church and state: Black, 350, 351; Blackmun, 83, 350; Burger, 146, 147, 158, 351; Burger Court, 436; Douglas, 180, 181; O'Connor, 258–60; Powell, 289, 290; Rehnquist, 339; Stevens, 350–51; Stewart, 402, 403; White, 391, 392, 395, 402, 403. *See also* Establishment clause
Separation of powers: Blackmun, 73–76; Burger, 134–35, 139, 140, 141, 142; Douglas, 168, 172; Harlan, 198; Marshall, 198; O'Connor, 261, 270;

Rehnquist, 319–21; Stevens, 349, 350; White, 410–12

Sex Discrimination: Blackmun, 84, 268; Brennan, 109, 110; Burger, 150; Burger Court, 435, 436; O'Connor, 265, 266, 267, 268; Powell, 298; Rehnquist, 327, 328; Stevens, 358–60; White, 418, 450. *See also* Women's issues

Sherman Antitrust Act of 1890: Blackmun, 80

Sixth Amendment: Black, 44, 55; Blackmun, 89; Burger, 155; Douglas, 187; Harlan, 208; O'Connor, 256; Rehnquist, 324; Stevens, 354; Stewart, 382; White, 420

Slander. *See* First Amendment; Freedom of speech

Smith Act of 1940, 380

Social security, 302

Solzhenitsyn, Alexander I., 311

Souter, David H., 21, 455

Spaeth, Harold J., 245, 246, 249

Speech or debate clause: Burger, 135–39, 158; Douglas, 174

Speedy trial, right to. *See* Fair trial

Standing: Burger, 142; Douglas, 175, 176; O'Connor, 269; Powell, 306, 307; Rehnquist, 324; Stevens, 348; Stewart, 384

Stassen, Harold E., 129

State action doctrine: Brennan, 200; Douglas, 183, 200; Harlan, 199–201; Marshall, 200; Stewart, 384, 385; Warren Court, 200

Stevens, John Paul: appointment, 8, 343; background, 343; dissent behavior, 28, 30, 346, 348, 365; and G. Ford, 343, 372; judicial philosophy, 345, 348, 372, 373; and E. Meese, 121; opinion writing, 28, 344–45, 346, 439; personality traits, 345–46; political views, 246, 248, 343; and Supreme Court case load, 347; voting interagreement, 31, 32; voting patterns, 30, 31, 32, 33, 34, 344, 345, 346, 350, 364, 365, 370, 371; writing style, 346, 347, 365, 439
—and other justices, 527, 528, 529, 530, 531, 532, 536, 553, 571;

Brennan, 121, 344–45, 350, 351, 352, 356, 365, 366, 373; Burger, 344, 345, 351, 364, 373; O'Connor, 248, 249; Powell, 285, 361; Rehnquist, 345, 347, 351, 353, 361, 373; White, 346, 356, 373, 450
—opinions on: abortion, 356–57; affirmative action, 360–61, 449; capital punishment, 369, 370; commercial speech, 352–53; criminal procedure, 364–72; double jeopardy, 365, 368, 369; equal protection clause, 358–64; establishment clause, 350–51; federalism, 348–49; freedom of expression, 351–56; obscenity, 353–54; prisons, 370–72; privacy, 356–58; racial discrimination, 360–62, 450; search and seizure, 366–67; self-incrimination, 368; separation of powers, 349, 350; sex discrimination, 358–60, 362–63

Stewart, Potter: appointment, 378; background, 376, 378, 380; confirmation, 378, 379; dissent behavior, 28, 30, 392, 393; and D. D. Eisenhower, 376, 378; family, 376; judicial philosophy, 375, 381–85, 403, 404; and R. M. Nixon, 379; opinion writing, 28, 378, 383, 403; personality traits, 379; political views, 380; resignation, 8; voting interagreement, 31, 32; voting patterns, 30, 31, 32, 33, 34, 35, 392, 393, 403; writing style, 378, 403
—and other justices, 583, 607; Black, 381, 382, 383, 386, 393; Burger, 394; Harlan, 375, 382, 385, 386, 393; Powell, 285, 384; Rehnquist, 379, 387, 390; White, 375, 379, 385, 388, 399
—opinions on: abortion, 382; affirmative action, 389; capital punishment, 388, 389, 399; commerce clause, 383, 384; equal protection, 389–90; federalism, 383, 384; freedom of the press, 391, 392, 401, 402; incorporation, 385–87; obscenity, 391; presidential power, 393, 394; procedural due process, 387–88; right to counsel, 381, 388;

search and seizure, 393; separation of
church and state, 391, 392, 395, 402,
403
Stone, Harlan Fiske, 280, 443
Strict construction, 3, 130, 157, 278,
315, 339, 340, 433
Strict scrutiny text, 225
Supreme Court. *See* Burger Court;
Rehnquist Court; Warren Court
Surface Mining Control and
Reclamation Act of 1977, 85

Taft, Robert A., 2, 3, 129
Taney, Roger B., 130
Tenth Amendment: Blackmun, 78, 79;
Brennan, 117, 119, 124; Burger, 251;
O'Connor, 250, 251, 252, 257;
Powell, 251, 306; Rehnquist, 336;
Stevens, 348
Thirteenth Amendment: Stewart, 395,
398
Trade embargoes: Rehnquist, 320
Travel. *See* Citizens' travel abroad
Trial by jury: Blackmun, 94; Burger,
155; Douglas, 187; Stewart, 382;
White, 420, 421
— grand juries and minorities:
Blackmun, 94
— juvenile proceedings: Blackmun, 94;
Stewart, 401
— misdemeanors: White, 420
— nonunanimous verdict: White, 420
— size of jury: Blackmun, 94; Stewart,
386
— unaminous verdict: Harlan, 207;
Stewart, 382
Tribe, Laurence H., 76
Truman, Harry S., 66, 376; and
Douglas, 166, 168
Twenty-first Amendment: Rehnquist,
329

Unanimous verdict. *See* Trial by jury
Universal Military Training and Service
Act of 1948, 416

Vanderbilt, Arthur T., 101, 102
Vietnam War, 2, 3, 4, 5, 49, 53, 130,
138, 143, 166, 168, 169, 170, 194,
199, 363; Brennan, 393; Douglas,

166, 167, 168, 169, 170, 171, 393;
Harlan, 393; Marshall, 393; Powell,
278; Stewart, 393
Vinson, Fred, 408, 443
Voting rights: Burger, 151; Harlan,
384; Marshall, 226; Powell, 292, 293;
Rehnquist, 318, 325; Stevens, 361,
362; Stewart, 384, 389; White, 417,
418
Voting Rights Act of 1965, 151, 361

Wallace, George C., 4
Warren Court, 2, 3, 11, 122, 134, 145,
147, 149, 151, 157, 193, 255, 276;
and Black, 100; and Brennan, 100,
104; and Burger, 130; and the
Burger Court, 9, 10, 114, 122, 157,
253, 338, 433–37, 442, 443, 446,
455; and Harlan, 196, 206; and
Marshall, 224, 234; and R. M. Nixon,
3, 130, 167, 337, 440; and O'Connor,
253; and Powell, 307; and Stewart,
379, 384, 390, 395; and White, 424
Warren, Earl, 9, 132, 159, 209, 379,
408; and Black, 38, 39, 379; and
Brennan, 379; and Burger, 132; and
civil liberties, 379; and civil rights,
379; and desegregation, 199; and
Douglas, 379; and D. D. Eisenhower,
132, 193; family of, 193; and Harlan,
194, 199, 202; and judicial activism,
194; leadership of, 132, 193, 194;
political views of, 193; and poverty,
193; retirement of, 6; and Stewart,
379; and the Supreme Court, 100,
132, 194; and White, 410
Wasby, Stephen L., 217
Watergate, 4, 140, 168; Burger, 140;
Douglas, 168; Rehnquist, 140, 320,
337
Wechsler, Herbert, 305, 306
Welfare issues: Blackmun, 75, 91, 246;
Brennan, 117, 246; Burger, 246;
Marshall, 227, 228, 229, 246;
O'Connor, 246; Powell, 246, 302;
Rehnquist, 246; Stevens, 246;
Stewart, 389, 393; White, 246
White, Byron R.: appointment, 407,
408, 410; background, 407, 408, 410,
428; confirmation, 410, 428; dissent

behavior, 28, 30, 425; family, 407;
judicial philosophy, 426–28; J. F.
Kennedy, 407, 408; and R. F.
Kennedy, 408, 410; opinion writing,
28, 407, 429, 430; personality traits,
425, 426, 429; political views, 246,
248, 407, 408, 428, 429; voting
interagreement, 31, 32, 424, 425;
voting patterns, 30, 31, 32, 33, 34,
424, 425; writing style, 429
—and other justices, 661, 662, 663,
664, 676; Brennan, 109, 424, 425,
426, 429; Marshall, 426, 429;
Rehnquist, 259, 424, 425; Stevens,
345, 356, 373, 450; Stewart, 375,
379, 385, 388, 399
—opinions on: abortion, 424, 427, 429,
451; congressional power, 411, 412;
criminal procedure, 419–23; due
process, 423, 424; exclusionary rule,
421, 422; federalism, 412, 413;
freedom of the press, 413, 414;
freedom of speech, 413, 414, 415;
legislative apportionment, 417, 418;
legislative veto, 411, 412; plea
bargaining, 419, 420; presidential
power, 410, 411; prisoners, 422, 423;
racial discrimination, 416, 417, 451;
search and seizure, 421, 422, 454;
self-incrimination, 419, 420;
separation of church and state, 415,
416; separation of powers, 410–12;
sex discrimination, 418, 450; trial by
jury, 420, 421; voting rights, 417,
418
Whittaker, Charles E., 379, 408
Whyte, William H., 444
Women's issues: Blackmun, 67, 84, 85,
87, 88, 89; Brennan, 105, 107, 109;
Burger, 150; Marshall, 218;
O'Connor, 238, 239, 244, 245, 248,
262, 265, 266, 267, 268, 269, 271;
Powell, 298; Rehnquist, 327, 328,
338. *See also* Sex discrimination
Workers compensation: Blackmun, 67